SOCIAL INSURANCE
AND
ECONOMIC SECURITY

The Prentice-Hall Series in Risk, Insurance and Security
Kenneth Black, Jr. and H. Wayne Snider, Series Editors

Denenberg, Eilers, Melone, & Zelton	*Risk and Insurance*
Huebner & Black	*Life Insurance*
Huebner, Black, & Cline	*Property and Liability Insurance*
Marshall & Zubay	*The Debit System of Marketing Life and Health Insurance*
Pfeffer & Klock	*Perspectives on Insurance*
Rejda	*Social Insurance and Economic Security*
Riegel, Miller, & Williams	*Insurance Principles and Practice*
Rodda	*Property and Liability Insurance*
Rodda	*Marine Insurance*
Rosenbloom	*A Case Study in Risk Management*
Russell & Black	*Human Behavior and Life Insurance*
Russell & Black	*Human Behavior in Business*
Stephenson & Wiggins	*Estates and Trusts*

SOCIAL INSURANCE
AND
ECONOMIC SECURITY

George E. Rejda, *Ph.D., C.L.U.*

Professor of Economics
University of Nebraska-Lincoln

PRENTICE-HALL, INC., *Englewood Cliffs, New Jersey*

Library of Congress Cataloging in Publication Data

Rejda, George E.   (date)
   Social insurance and economic security.

   Includes index.
   1. Social Security—United States.   2. Economic
Security—United States.   I. Title.
HD7125.R37 1976   368.4′00973   75-19166
ISBN   0-13-815779-0

© 1976 by PRENTICE-HALL, INC.
Englewood Cliffs, New Jersey

Printed in the United States of America

10 9 8 7 6 5 4 3 2 1

Prentice-Hall International, Inc., *London*
Prentice-Hall of Australia, Pty. Ltd., *Sydney*
Prentice-Hall of Canada, Ltd., *Toronto*
Prentice-Hall of India Private Limited, *New Delhi*
Prentice-Hall of Japan, Inc., *Tokyo*
Prentice-Hall of Southeast Asia (Pte.) Ltd., *Singapore*

To Lu

Contents

Preface

This textbook is designed for a one-semester undergraduate course in social insurance at the junior or senior level. Much of the subject matter has evolved out of my social insurance course at the University of Nebraska.

Social insurance is a difficult and complex area to study and master. Having taught the subject for several years, I am well aware of the problems that many students encounter in trying to understand its complex principles and programs. Nor am I unsympathetic to the needs of a typical professor who must often struggle with voluminous amounts of economic-security materials, most of which are difficult to teach. Thus, I am writing for both students and professors: I have attempted to write a book out of which students can learn and professors can teach.

The text emphasizes social insurance as a primary technique for meeting and alleviating the problems of economic insecurity. Although some attention is devoted to other economic-security programs, primarily public assistance, the central thrust of the book is devoted to social insurance principles, programs, and issues. Each major cause of economic insecurity is examined, and the appropriate social insurance program is then analyzed. In particular, an entire chapter is devoted to the problem of premature death, since recent research studies clearly indicate that economic insecurity can occur months or even years before a terminally ill family head actually dies. In addition, the timely and important problem of health care in the United States is analyzed in some depth. The various solutions to the health-care crisis are examined, with heavy emphasis on a new system of national health insurance to correct the numerous defects now found in the health-services delivery system. Other important causes of economic insecurity are also analyzed, including old age, unemployment, occupational safety and health, and poverty. Existing and proposed new social insurance programs are examined as techniques for meeting these problems. Also, the important and controversial issues surrounding the OASDHI program, workmen's compensation, unemployment insurance, and public assistance are treated in some detail.

Finally, I continually stress basic social insurance principles and concepts in the text. My experience in teaching social insurance has indicated to me that many students have considerable difficulty in comprehending the basic principles; in addition, many fail to understand clearly the fundamental differences between private and social insurance. I am firmly convinced that much of the nonsense and errors that appear in newspapers, magazines, and other news media concerning the OASDHI program is due to a lack of knowledge of basic social insurance principles; and even much of the professional literature on social insurance is defective in this regard, since the basic principles are not presented clearly and unequivocally to the reader. I have attempted to correct this problem by devoting an entire chapter to basic social insurance principles.

I would like to acknowledge the assistance of several people who helped me complete the text. First, special thanks go to my colleague, Dr. Wallace C. Peterson, chairman of the Economics Department at the University of Nebraska. Professor Peterson provided constant encouragement over the years by urging me to finish this book and adjusted my teaching load downward so that time was available. Also, I gratefully acknowledge the help of Senator Carl T. Curtis and Representative Charles Thone for their prompt assistance in sending me numerous government documents. Government documents are a rich and fertile source of new ideas, and both Senator Curtis and Representative Thone were extremely gracious in honoring my persistent and repeated requests over the years for hundreds of these. Without their assistance, this book could not have been written. In addition, I have a deep sense of gratitude to Robert J. Myers, former Chief Actuary of the Social Security Administration, and now Professor of Actuarial Science at Temple University. My thinking and ideas concerning social insurance programs have been greatly stimulated over the years by his many professional publications. I am also indebted to Dr. Wilbur J. Cohen, former Secretary of Health, Education and Welfare, Dr. Herbert S. Denenberg, Insurance Commissioner for the Commonwealth of Pennsylvania, Dr. Charles E. Hughes, CLU, CPCU, the American College of Life Underwriters, Dr. H. Wayne Snider, chairman, Department of Insurance and Risk, Temple University, and Dr. Maurice E. McDonald, Georgia State University, for their critical and valuable reviews of an earlier draft of this manuscript. The views expressed in this book, of course, do not necessarily represent the viewpoints of the persons whose help I am gratefully acknowledging.

Finally, as tradition demands, any errors or omissions in this text are due solely to the author.

George E. Rejda
University of Nebraska-Lincoln

SOCIAL INSURANCE
AND
ECONOMIC SECURITY

chapter 1

Economic Security and Insecurity

Man has continually sought security, and protection against those forces that have threatened his security. In prehistoric times, he was concerned with physical protection against the brute forces of nature. As civilization progressed, man's quest for security has become more sophisticated, involving numerous social, political, international, and economic techniques.

Security has many faces and dimensions. Since life is full of uncertainty and surrounded by complex threatening forces, the concept of security can be analyzed from several disciplines, including philosophy, sociology, psychiatry, political science, and economics.[1] A complete analysis of security, however, is a burdensome if not impossible task. Thus, the concept must be narrowed. In this text, primary emphasis will be devoted to economic security, with specific emphasis on social insurance as a technique for combating insecurity.

In this chapter, we shall treat the following fundamental concepts: (1) nature of economic security, (2) nature of economic insecurity, (3) causes of economic insecurity, (4) meaning of social security and social insurance, and (5) methods for attacking economic insecurity.

NATURE OF ECONOMIC SECURITY

A human being's *total welfare* is the sum of a large number of different elements. Although the concept of total welfare cannot be broken up in the sense that one can attribute parts of the whole to the various elements from which that welfare is obtained, it is clear that a large part of our total welfare is

[1]For a discussion of security from several disciplines, see E.J. Faulkner, ed., *Man's Quest for Security, A Symposium* (Lincoln: University of Nebraska Press, 1966).

derived from things obtainable with money.[2] Economic security, which is part of our total welfare, can be defined as *a state of mind or sense of well-being whereby an individual is relatively certain he can satisfy his basic needs and wants, both present and future.* The term "basic needs and wants" refers to a person's desire for food, clothing, housing, medical care, and other necessities. When he is relatively certain he can satisfy both his present and future needs and wants for all these necessities, then he may experience a sense of well-being. This sense of well-being, which results from the satisfaction of human needs and wants, is dependent on the use of economic goods and services. An individual must have access to goods and services to attain economic security. It is obvious, therefore, that in a highly industrialized economy, economic security is closely related to income maintenance. The more income a person has—whether from money wages, public or private transfer payments, or the ownership of property—the greater is the level of economic security that is possible for him.

In analyzing the preceding concept of economic security, several points are worth noting. First, we saw that the receipt of income is a key factor in attaining economic security. The income, however, must be *continuous.* A person must have some reasonable expectation that his income will continue into the future so that his future needs and wants will be satisfied. If his income is lost or significantly reduced, his economic security is threatened.

Second, *real income* must be emphasized. Real income refers to the goods and services that can be purchased with money income. If real income increases, an improvement in economic security is possible. For example, if consumer prices increase 20 percent and money income increases 30 percent, real income is increased and greater economic security is possible. But if both money income and prices increase at the same rate, real income is unchanged, and economic security is not enhanced.

Third, for most people, economic security also requires the receipt of income that is *above the poverty or subsistence level* of living. Poverty can be defined as an insufficiency of material goods and services, whereby the basic needs of individuals or families exceed their means to satisfy them. Poverty can be crudely measured by the various poverty thresholds established by the Social Security Administration and the Bureau of the Census. In 1973, the poverty-income threshold for a four-member nonfarm family was $4,540. Based on this measure, the Bureau of the Census has estimated that about 23 million Americans, or 11 percent of the total population, were living in poverty.[3] In contrast, the median family income during the same period was $12,050, an amount substantially above the poverty threshold. Thus, millions of Americans currently are not economically secure, because their incomes are below poverty levels.

Finally, economic security is *relative to the standard of living enjoyed by others.* As that standard of living changes over time, the concept of economic

[2]S.G. Sturmey, *Income and Economic Welfare* (London: Longmans, Green, 1959), p. 2.

[3]Standards of poverty thresholds were established by the Social Security Administration in 1964. They provide a range of income cutoffs, which are adjusted for family size, number of children under age 18, sex of the family head, and farm-nonfarm residence. In addition, the various thresholds are adjusted for increases in the cost of living. See U.S. Bureau of the Census, *Current Population Reports,* Series P-60, No. 98, "Characteristics of the Low-Income Population: 1973," (Washington, D.C.: U.S. Government Printing Office, 1975).

security must also change. The nation's social mores, cultural background, educational level, and stage of economic development also influence the concept of economic security. As these factors change over time, the expectations of consumers and families will also change, in turn resulting in a changing concept of economic security.

NATURE OF ECONOMIC INSECURITY

Economic insecurity is the opposite of economic security; that is, the sense of well-being or state of mind that results from being relatively able to satisfy both present and future needs and wants is lacking. Instead, there is considerable worry, fear, anxiety, and psychological discomfort.

Economic insecurity can be caused by a person's losing his income, or being forced to assume excessive or additional expenses, or earning an insufficient income. Finally, economic insecurity may be experienced if there is uncertainty regarding the continuation of future income. Thus economic insecurity consists of one or more of the following: (1) loss of income, (2) additional expenses, (3) insufficient income, and (4) uncertainty of income.[4]

Loss of Income

Regardless of whether the income loss is relative or absolute, economic insecurity is present when the worker's income is lost. In such a case, unless he has sufficient financial assets, past savings, or other sources of replacement income, he cannot satisfy his basic needs and wants. Moreover, the continuous consumption of goods and services substantially above the poverty line may be difficult because of the income loss.

A knotty problem arises at this point. Is a man economically insecure when he loses his job but has $10,000 in a savings account on which to draw? The answer is yes. He is insecure because of the loss of his job, even though he has $10,000 that can be used to substitute for the lost income. In this case, the past savings can be used to alleviate the undesirable financial consequences attributable to the termination of employment.[5]

Additional Expenses

Economic insecurity can also result from additional expenses. For example, a person may be injured and unable to work. In addition to the income loss, he may incur additional expenses because of substantial hospital, medical, and surgical bills. Or a breadwinner may have a member of his family sustain a serious accident or illness that requires a substantial sum of money. Unless the worker has adequate past savings, health insurance, or other sources

---

[4]John G. Turnbull, C. Arthur Williams, Jr., and Earl F. Cheit, *Economic and Social Security,* 4th ed. (New York: Ronald Press, 1973), pp. 3-4.

[5]John G. Turnbull, *The Changing Faces of Economic Insecurity* (Minneapolis: The University of Minnesota Press, 1966), p. 4.

of funds on which to draw, economic insecurity is aggravated because of the additional expenses.

Insufficient Income

Economic insecurity is also present if a person is employed but earns an insufficient income; that is, if his total income during the year is less than the amount needed to satisfy his basic wants and needs. The worker may be employed full-time throughout the entire year, but economic insecurity is still the result if the level of his income does not permit him to satisfy his basic necessities.

As noted earlier, millions of Americans are economically insecure because of poverty. The viewpoint that people are poor because they cannot find employment, or because they have some mental or physical defect that makes employment difficult, is not entirely correct, because many of the poor are steadily employed, working regularly throughout the entire year, but their incomes are insufficient to provide for their basic needs and wants.

In 1973 about 27 percent of all poor male family heads worked the entire year at a full-time job, which indicates that earnings alone are not always sufficient to bring these families above the poverty level. During the same period, about 44 percent of the poor female family heads worked some time.[6] The incomes they received, however, were insufficient for satisfying their basic needs and wants, and economic insecurity was present to a considerable degree.

Uncertainty of Income

Economic insecurity may also be present if the worker, although employed, is uncertain of the future continuation of his present income. For example, a highly paid space engineer may become fearful and apprehensive because his firm did not receive an expected government contract. In such a case, he experiences a form of economic insecurity because of the uncertainty of his future income.

In the highly industrialized American economy, a chronic fear of unemployment may create considerable anxiety for the worker, because, although the economy provides the worker with a relatively high standard of living, it also threatens his feeling of economic security. The worker sells his labor in the marketplace and depends on the receipt of money wages. The basic feeling of security may be destroyed if he believes that his services will not be demanded in the future, or that his wages will be significantly reduced in the future; in such cases, economic insecurity is present because of the uncertainty of future income.

Some scholars have argued that economic insecurity should not be measured by the total amount of income that a worker receives, by the irregularity of such income, but rather by the degree of uncertainty surrounding his future income.[7] According to this view, the worker with a low standard of living

[6]U.S. Bureau of the Census, "Characteristics of the Low-Income Population: 1973," p. 6.

[7]See Domenico Gagliardo, *American Social Insurance,* rev. ed. (New York: Harper & Row, 1955), pp. 8-9.

who is relatively certain of realizing that standard should enjoy greater economic security than the worker with a higher standard of living who is uncertain whether he can maintain that standard. For example, a bricklayer who earns $5 an hour at a full-time job throughout the entire year should enjoy greater economic security than the bricklayer who earns $6 an hour but is unemployed during the winter months.

The preceding analysis must be carefully qualified. The relative certainty of future income by itself does not contribute to economic security if the income one actually receives is insufficient to satisfy his basic needs and wants. A person may be relatively certain that his present income will continue into the future, but he may not experience economic security if his income is insufficient for satisfying his basic needs and wants. For example, assume that an aged person with no other source of income receives an old-age retirement benefit of $150 monthly from a public pension. Although he is relatively certain that the pension will continue as long as he lives, economic security is impossible because the income is insufficient. In short, it is not merely the relative certainty of future income that makes a person economically secure, since the income may be insufficient; it is the continuous receipt of an adequate income that enables him to enjoy economic security.

CAUSES OF ECONOMIC INSECURITY

Numerous elements cause economic insecurity. The major causes include (1) premature death of the family head, (2) old age, (3) injury and disease, (4) unemployment, (5) substandard wage, (6) price-level changes, (7) natural disasters, and (8) personal factors.[8]

Premature Death of the Family Head

Premature death of the family head can be defined as his death with unfulfilled financial obligations—such as dependents to support, a mortgage to be paid, or children to educate. Premature death causes economic insecurity because of the loss of income to the dependents. If the family lacks additional sources of income or has insufficient financial assets to replace the lost income, financial hardship may result. In addition, the family may also incur sizable additional expenses because of burial costs, estate and death taxes, expenses of last illness, and funds to pay off outstanding installment debts. Finally, a large unpaid mortgage may still be outstanding, and funds may be needed to educate the children.

If the wife dies prematurely, the family may also experience economic insecurity. Additional expenses may be incurred because of the need of a housekeeper or baby-sitter. If the wife works, the family's share of her future earnings is also lost forever.

---

[8]Clair Wilcox, *Toward Social Welfare* (Homewood, Ill.: Richard D. Irwin, 1969), pp. 40-47; and Turnbull, Williams, and Cheit, *Economic and Social Security,* pp. 3-4.

Finally, premature death can create economic insecurity only if the deceased has dependents and has died with unsatisfied financial obligations. Thus, the death of a child aged 7 is not regarded as being premature in the economic sense.

Old Age

Old age is another cause of economic insecurity. Because of social custom, age 65 is considered to be the normal or customary retirement age in the United States. Most workers must retire on or before that age, and as a result, they lose their work earnings. Unless older workers have accumulated sufficient financial assets on which to draw or have access to other sources of income, such as a public or private pension, they will be confronted with the problem of economic insecurity.

Injury and Disease

A disabled worker may be economically insecure because of the reduction, interruption, or termination of his income-earning capacity; and in addition to the income loss, he may also incur sizable medical expenses. An unexpected disabling illness that results in catastrophic medical expenses can drain the family's financial resources. Unless the worker has adequate health insurance or has access to other sources of income to meet these expenditures, considerable economic insecurity is present.

Unemployment

Unemployment can result from a deficiency in aggregate demand, technological and structural changes in the economy, seasonal factors, or frictions in the labor market.[9] Regardless of the cause, economic insecurity results in at least four ways: First, unemployment causes the worker to lose his income. Unless he has replacement income from other sources (such as unemployment insurance) or past savings on which to draw, he will be economically insecure. Second, because of economic reasons, the worker may work only part-time. Since his work earnings are reduced, his income may be inadequate to maintain himself and his family. Third, unemployment causes economic insecurity because of the uncertainty of income. Because of seasonal elements, the worker may be unemployed for a certain period each year. A construction worker, for example, may experience some anxiety as the layoff season approaches because of uncertainty regarding his future income. Finally, some groups experience considerable difficulty in finding new jobs. These groups include older workers, disadvantaged members of minority groups, ex-convicts, and the hard-core unemployed. Also older workers, beyond age 45 or 50, may have an extended duration of unemployment, and the hard-care unemployed may be out of work for months or even years. Economic insecurity is present to a considerable degree for workers within these categories.

[9]See Chapter 14.

Substandard Wage

A substandard wage means a wage that is below some specified minimum necessary for the worker to support himself and his family. A careful distinction must be made between a substandard wage and insufficient income. A substandard wage refers to a *wage rate* so low that the worker cannot adequately support himself and his family if he is paid at that rate for any extended period. The federal minimum wage of $2.10 per hour for 1975 is an example of a substandard wage. If a worker with several dependents is paid only the federal minimum wage for any extended period, he and his family will be living in poverty. On the other hand, insufficient income means that the *absolute* amount of income received during some time period is inadequate in terms of the worker's basic needs and wants. The substandard wage is the cause, and insufficient income is the result. If the worker is paid a substandard wage for any extended period, he may find himself living in chronic poverty.

It should be pointed out that insufficient income may be attributable to causes other than a substandard wage—for example, seasonal unemployment, poor health, or mental or physical defects that render a person incapable of employment. In all cases, the insufficient income leads to economic insecurity.

A case in point can illustrate the distinction between a substandard wage and insufficient income. Assume that a dishwasher with three dependents works full-time in a restaurant and earns the federal minimum wage during the entire year. His annual income is $4,368, which is below the poverty line for a four-member nonfarm family. If he has no other income, he may find it extremely difficult to support himself and his family. The low minimum wage ($2.10) is the causal factor leading to insufficient income, which in turn gives rise to economic insecurity.

On the other hand, the wage rate may be adequate, but the worker still has an insufficient income because of other factors. For example, assume that a factory worker with three dependents earns $4.20 per hour and works 40 hours per week. If, because of a severe recession, he loses his job after working 26 weeks, his total annual income is also $4,368 the same income received by the dishwasher. In both cases, economic insecurity is present because of insufficient income. The insufficient income of the dishwasher is attributable to a substandard wage, whereas with the factory worker, it is due to cyclical unemployment.

Price-Level Changes

As we stated earlier, if consumer prices increase at a faster rate than money income, real income declines and economic security is threatened. The United States has been plagued by severe inflation in recent years. Between 1967 and October 1974 alone, the Consumer Price Index rose 56 percent.[10] Such a rapid increase in prices tends to hurt the aged, whose money incomes are relatively fixed. In addition, the working poor are also severely hurt by inflation, at least in the short run, because the money wages they receive increase less rapidly than consumer prices. In particular, food costs may rise substantially,

[10]*Social Security Bulletin,* Vol. 38, No. 1 (January 1975), 72, Table M-31.

and the working poor are then confronted with the unpleasant dilemma of spending relatively more of their limited incomes on food simply to survive. Considerable economic insecurity is the result.

Natural Disasters

Floods, hurricanes, tornadoes, earthquakes, forest and grass fires, and other violent natural disasters can result in a loss of billions of dollars in property damage, as well as thousands of deaths. More than 600 tornadoes annually strike various parts of the United States, each causing an average $75 million in property damage and from 25 to several hundred lost lives. Hurricane Agnes in 1972, the worst storm in the history of the United States, caused more than 120 deaths and property losses of about $2 billion. The San Fernando Valley earthquake in 1971 caused more than $550 million in property-damage losses. Severe floods in the United States annually cost about $1 billion in property damage and an average of 80 lives lost.[11]

Natural disasters cause economic insecurity because of the considerable loss of human lives and a resultant loss of income to the striken families. In addition, many property-damage losses are either uninsured or underinsured, causing substantial additional expenses. Although insurance by the federal government is available for certain natural-disaster perils—such as federal flood insurance under the National Flood Insurance Act of 1968—relatively few consumers take advantage of this protection.[12]

Personal Factors

In some cases, people are primarily responsible for their own economic insecurity. Some are poorly motivated, lack drive and ambition, and have little desire to improve themselves economically. Others are spendthrifts and are indifferent to a personal savings program of investments and private life insurance. Still others are apathetic to education and its importance in improving their economic status. Finally, some people lack the foresight and wisdom to provide for potential risks that could cause economic insecurity.

Personal factors are especially important in certain major social problems that cause economic insecurity to individuals and families. Physical and psychological addiction to hard drugs, excessive use of alcohol, and widespread divorce all contribute to economic insecurity.

There are an estimated 10 million alcoholics in the United States, most of them unaware of their true condition. At least half are under age 30. Alcoholism

[11]General Adjustment Bureau, Inc., *Nature's Destructive Forces* (New York: General Adjustment Bureau, Inc., 1972), pp. 8, 14, and 42.

[12]For an excellent discussion of the various techniques available for meeting the losses from natural disasters, see Howard Kunreuther, "Disaster Insurance: A Tool for Hazard Mitigation," *The Journal of Risk and Insurance*, Vol. XLI, No. 2 (June 1974), 287-303. See also Kunreuther, *Recovery from Natural Disasters: Insurance or Federal Aid?* (Washington, D.C.: American Enterprise Institute for Public Policy Research, 1973).

is considered by the American Medical Association to be a medical rather than a moral problem and is now recognized as an important national disease. Physical and psychological addiction to alcohol often results in poor health, the inability to hold a job, family frictions, and disintegration of family life. The additional expenses of supporting an expensive alcoholic habit and the loss of income to the family because of alcoholism can result in considerable economic insecurity.

Alcohol is also an important factor in divorce. More than one out of three American marriages end up in the divorce courts, and for teen-age marriages, the divorce rate is even higher. Excessive use of alcohol is an important element in many of these divorces. Divorce can cause economic insecurity because the father may be required to make alimony or child-support payments, and if he remarries, the cost of supporting two households can be staggering. His income may be insufficient in view of his needs. Also, the mother's income may be inadequate if the husband refuses to make the required payments. Legal measures are often ineffective in forcing a divorced father to contribute to the financial support of his family.

Thus, is it clear that alcoholism and divorce significantly contribute to the economic insecurity experienced by many households in the United States.

MEANING OF SOCIAL SECURITY

Social-security programs are part of the overall economic-security programs in the United States, but are narrower in scope. There is no universal agreement on the meaning of social security; nevertheless, fairly widespread agreement exists regarding the chief characteristics of the programs. First, social-security programs are established by government statute. Second, the programs generally provide individuals with cash payments that replace at least part of the income loss from old age, invalidism and death, sickness and maternity, unemployment, and occupational injuries. Family allowances and statutory programs that provide medical care (other than public health services) are also considered social-security programs. Finally, social-security programs can be distinguished by the major approaches used to provide cash payments and services. These approaches include (1) social insurance, (2) social assistance, and (3) public service. [13]

Social Insurance

General Characteristics. Social insurance is a part of social security. Social insurance programs are not financed primarily out of the general revenues of government, but are financed entirely or in large part by special contributions from employers, employees, or both. These contributions are usually ear-

[13]U.S. Department of Health, Education and Welfare, Social Security Administration, Office of Research and Statistics, *Social Security Programs throughout the World, 1971,* Research Report No. 40 (Washington, D.C.: U.S. Government Printing Office, 1971), pp. IX-X. See also *Social Security Programs throughout the World, 1973,* pp. vii-xii.

marked for special funds that are kept separate from ordinary government accounts; the benefits, in turn, are paid from these funds. In addition, the right to receive benefits is ordinarily either derived from or linked to the recipient's past contributions or coverage under the program, and the benefits and contributions generally vary among the beneficiaries, according to their prior earnings. Most social insurance programs are compulsory; certain categories of workers and employers are required by law to pay contributions and participate in the programs. Finally, qualifying conditions and benefit rights are usually prescribed exactly in the statutes, leaving little room for administrative discretion in the award of benefits.

One example of social insurance in the United States is the Old-Age, Survivors, Disability, and Health Insurance Program, commonly known as OASDHI. It should be noted that OASDHI is often referred to as "Social Security" in the United States. This is not entirely correct. OASDHI is one of the many forms of social insurance; social insurance, in turn, is part of the overall social-security system.

Definition of Social Insurance. Because of conceptual and practical difficulties, the task of defining social insurance is a complicated if not impossible task. Moreover, after defining it, there is still the problem of determining those programs that can be called social insurance and excluding those that fall outside the definition. After careful study and discussion, the Committee on Social Insurance Terminology of the American Risk and Insurance Association has defined social insurance as follows:

> A device for the pooling of risks by their transfer to an organization, usually governmental, that is required by law to provide pecuniary or service benefits to or on behalf of covered persons upon the occurrence of certain predesignated losses under all of the following conditions:
>
> 1. Coverage is compulsory by law in virtually all instances.
> 2. Except during a transition period following its introduction, eligibility for benefits is derived, in fact or in effect, from contributions having been made to the program by or in respect of the claimant or the person as to whom the claimant is a dependent; there is no requirement that the individual demonstrate inadequate financial resources, although a dependency status may need to be established.
> 3. The method for determining the benefits is prescribed by law.
> 4. The benefits for any individual are not usually directly related to contributions made by or in respect of him but instead usually redistribute income so as to favor certain groups such as those with low former wages or a large number of dependents.
> 5. There is a definite plan for financing the benefits that is designed to be adequate in terms of long-range considerations.
> 6. The cost is borne primarily by contributions which are usually made by covered persons, their employers, or both.
> 7. The plan is administered or at least supervised by the government.
> 8. The plan is not established by the government solely for its present or former employees.[14]

[14]*Bulletin of the Commission on Insurance Terminology of the American Risk and Insurance Association,* Vol. 1, No. 2 (May 1965), and Vol. 2, No. 2 (July 1966).

This definition indicates clearly that, although social insurance is similar to private insurance in several respects, it does possess some unique characteristics normally not found in private insurance. Failure to recognize these similarities and differences has led to much error and confusion regarding the desirability of economic-security programs. The unique characteristics of social insurance will be analyzed in Chapter 2.

The Committee on Social Insurance Terminology considers the following programs to be social insurance because they fall under the definition above:

1. Old-Age Survivors, Disability, and Health Insurance
2. Unemployment Insurance
3. Workmen's Compensation
4. Compulsory Temporary Disability Insurance
5. Railroad Retirement System
6. Railroad Unemployment and Temporary Disability Insurance

The following programs are *not* social insurance, because they do not satisfy that definition:

1. *Civil Service Retirement System.* This is not social insurance because the plan was established by the government solely for its own employees.

2. *National Service Life Insurance.* This program is not compulsory; in addition, it was established by the government solely for its present or former employees.

3. *Federal Crop Insurance.* The program is not compulsory.

4. *Public Assistance.* The individual must demonstrate that he has inadequate financial resources; the method of determining the benefits is not usually prescribed by statute; and finally, the cost is not borne directly by employers and their employees.

5. *Veterans' Benefits.* The plan is financed entirely out of general revenues; it was established by the government solely for its former employees; and some benefits require that the applicant's income be below a specified level.

Social Assistance

Social assistance is another approach to social security. Social assistance programs—often referred to in different countries as public assistance, national assistance, old-age assistance, unemployment assistance, social pensions, and so on—provide cash payments and other benefits to individuals. These programs have several common features. The benefits are usually confined to low-income or poor recipients; the benefits are normally granted only after an investigation of the recipient's financial resources and needs; the benefit amount is commonly adjusted to his financial resources and needs; and the benefits are usually financed entirely out of the general revenues of government.

In the United States, public assistance, or "welfare," is used to provide cash income and other benefits to poor people who are not covered under social insurance programs. Public assistance is also used to supplement social insurance benefits that may be inadequate for people whose other financial resources are small or nonexistent, or for those with special needs. Public-assistance programs will be treated in greater detail in Chapters 17 and 18.

Public Service

Public service is another approach to social-security programs in many countries. The public-service approach involves government cash payments or services to each person in the country who falls within a specifically defined category. These payments include an old-age pension to each citizen above a certain age, a survivorship pension to every widow and orphan, a maternity grant to each woman bearing a child, and a family allowance to each family with a specified number of children. Medical services under a national health insurance plan are also considered to be a public-service approach. The cash payments or services are generally financed out of government general revenues. Benefits are paid to each person within a specific category and are not limited only to those covered under social insurance or to poor people meeting a needs test.

THE ATTACK ON ECONOMIC INSECURITY

A wide variety of public and private techniques are used in the United States to attack economic insecurity. Some aim at preventing economic insecurity by reducing or eliminating a cause of it. Other approaches are designed to alleviate the undesirable financial consequences after a loss occurs. Some techniques entail highly formalized public or private insurance programs, while other measures are very informal.[15]

Private Economic-Security Programs

The individual and his family can be protected against economic insecurity through the purchase of individual life, health, property, and liability insurance. Savings can be accumulated to meet the financial impact of economic insecurity. Fraternal-society benefits may be available; property may be sold or used as collateral for loans; assistance may be available from friends, relatives, or private welfare agencies; earnings of other family members may be at hand; free treatment at hospitals may be obtained by the poor. Finally, the person may be able to improve his job skills, thus enhancing his future income.

The worker and his family are also protected against economic insecurity through various group insurance programs of private firms. The employer may provide a private pension. Group life, health, and disability-income benefits may be available. The firm may have a program for a guaranteed annual wage,

---

[15]For a discussion of the various approaches for attaining economic security, see U.S. Department of Health, Education and Welfare, Social Security Administration, *Social Security Programs in the United States* (Washington, D.C.: U.S. Government Printing Office, 1973), Chap. 1.

severance pay, supplementary unemployment benefits, and employee profit-sharing plans. Finally, the firm may utilize employment-stabilization techniques to maintain and stabilize its employment.

Public Economic-Security Programs

In the public sector, government combats economic insecurity in several ways. First, social insurance and public assistance are used to alleviate the economic insecurity resulting from the social perils described earlier. Second, through the use of full-employment policies designed to counter cyclical unemployment, the government attempts to deal with a major source of economic insecurity. Monetary and fiscal policies are also used to promote economic growth and maintain full employment. Finally, the government may attack economic insecurity through specific legislation designed to deal with an important social problem. For example, the Fair Labor Standards Act attempts to deal with the problem of substandard wages, through minimum-wage provisions; the Employment Act of 1946 commits the federal government to a policy of reasonable full employment; the Economic Opportunity Act of 1964 and the Manpower Development and Training Act are designed to attack the problems of poverty and underutilization of manpower resources; Medicare benefits under OASDHI are designed to meet the economic problem of high medical expenses for the aged; and the new Supplementary Security Income program under the 1972 OASDHI amendments is designed to provide cash payments to the needy aged, blind, and disabled.

Table 1-1, although it is not exhaustive, presents a list of selected programs and techniques used in the United States to combat economic insecurity. Since it is impossible in a basic textbook to analyze in great depth all such programs, our primary attention will be devoted to the various social insurance programs in the United States as a basic technique for achieving economic security.

AREAS OF AGREEMENT IN
ECONOMIC SECURITY PROGRAMS

Considerable discussion and heated controversy often arise concerning the enactment or expansion of economic-security programs. A person's attitude toward existing programs and proposed legislation may be biased because of economic, political, philosophical, and religious beliefs. In order to think objectively about economic-security issues, let us delineate those areas where some agreement generally exists regarding them. These areas of general agreement can be stated as principles.[16]

---

[16]Herbert S. Denenberg et al., *Risk and Insurance* (Englewood Cliffs, N.J.: Prentice Hall, 1964), pp. 517-18.

TABLE 1-1 Selected Programs and Techniques Used in the United States to Combat the Problem of Economic Insecurity

---

I. Private Programs and Techniques

Individual	Employer

A. Private insurance:
  1. Life insurance and annuities
  2. Health insurance (including disability-income payments)
  3. Property and liability insurance
B. Private savings
C. Fraternal-society benefits
D. Property for sale or use as loan collateral
E. Assistance from children, relatives, and private welfare agencies
F. Earnings of other family members
G. Charity programs at hospitals
H. Improvement in job skills
	A. Private pensions (including widow pensions)
	B. Group insurance:
	  1. Life
	  2. Health (including disability income and paid sick leave)
	C. Guaranteed annual wage
	D. Severance pay
	E. Supplementary unemployment benefits
	F. Employment-stabilization techniques
	G. Employee profit-sharing plans

II. Public Programs and Techniques

A. Social insurance:
  1. Old-Age, Survivors, Disability, and Health Insurance
  2. Unemployment insurance
  3. Workmen's compensation
  4. Compulsory temporary-disability insurance
  5. Railroad Retirement System
  6. Railroad Unemployment Insurance Act

B. Public assistance:
  1. Supplemental Security Income for the Aged, Blind, and Disabled
  2. Aid to Families with Dependent Children
  3. Medicaid
  4. General Assistance

C. Selected economic welfare legislation:
  1. Fair Labor Standards Act
  2. Employment Act of 1946
  3. Area Redevelopment Act
  4. Manpower Development and Training Act
  5. Economic Opportunity Act of 1964
  6. National Health Services Corps
  7. National Flood Insurance Act

D. Government policies:
  1. Stimulation of economic growth
  2. Monetary policy to stabilize output and employment
  3. Fiscal policy to stabilize output and employment
  4. Government regulation

E. Other programs:
  1. Veterans' benefits
  2. Civil Service Retirement System
  3. Services for children
  4. Food stamps
  5. Housing programs
  6. Mental-health programs
  7. Vocational rehabilitation
  8. Crime compensation plans

Principle of Subsidiarity

One fundamental problem in economic-security programs is to determine the extent of government and individual responsibility. That is, society must decide whether a given social problem should be solved by government or by the individual. The principle of subsidiarity provides a guide to the problem. This principle states that a higher government unit should not perform the tasks that can be effectively performed by a lower unit. This means that in the area of economic security, government should perform only those tasks that cannot be performed efficiently by the people themselves. Moreover, if government intervention *is* necessary, it should be done first at the local level, then the state level, and finally at the federal level. The principle of subsidiarity promotes the desirable qualities of personal initiative, freedom, and self-reliance in solving social problems. Excessive reliance on the federal government can discourage flexibility and innovation at the local level.

Principle of Sovereignty of Demand

Critics of economic-security programs often deplore the movement of the federal government into economic-security areas. However, in a democratic society, government actions usually reflect the will of the people. The principle of sovereignty of demand illustrates this idea; it is stated as follows: A democratic government does essentially what the citizens want it to do. In effect, this principle is an application of the majority rule, and holds that, in the long run, the desires of the citizenry will be reflected in the passage of legislation reflecting their wishes. If certain economic-security programs are desired, the citizenry will tend to vote for political representatives who will support these programs.

Principles of Loss Prevention and Rehabilitation

It is generally agreed that activities that minimize losses or reduce loss severity, such as rehabilitation of disabled workers, are highly desirable in economic-security programs.

Society benefits in several ways through loss prevention and rehabilitation activities. First, they increase the gross national product. If a worker is disabled and unemployed, the goods and services he could have produced had he worked are lost forever. In addition, if a potential economic loss is prevented or its severity reduced, the economic burden of risk on society is reduced. Finally, rehabilitation of the disabled by surgery, physical restoration, occupational training, physiotherapy, and job placement is also necessary in a viable economic-security program. The family's income can still continue, and economic security is thereby enhanced.

Principle of Diversity

The principle of diversity states that no single approach should be used to solve the economic-security problems in the United States. Various approaches and techniques are employed that supplement and complement each other. For example, a federal-state program of unemployment insurance is designed to help meet the financial problems of the unemployed. But unemployment itself may be reduced by expansionary monetary and fiscal policies of the federal government. And federal legislation such as the Manpower Development and Training Act also reduces unemployment and poverty through the establishment of job-training programs, which provide people with skills the modern economy demands.

The point is that numerous approaches are used to attack economic insecurity, and it is generally agreed that the advantages of diverse programs generally outweigh the disadvantages. On the other hand, excessive economic-security programs can result in substantial costs, overlapping programs, administrative inefficiencies, and considerable waste.

SUGGESTIONS FOR ADDITIONAL READING

Carlson, Valdemar, *Economic Security in the United States,* Chap. 1. New York: McGraw-Hill, 1962.

Denenberg, Herbert S., et al., *Risk and Insurance,* Chaps. 33-34. Englewood Cliffs, N.J.: Prentice-Hall, 1964.

Gregg, Davis W., "Economic Security: Patterns and Philosophies," in Davis W. Gregg and Vane B. Lucas, eds., *Life and Health Insurance Handbook,* 3rd ed., pp. 3-18. Homewood, Ill.: Richard D. Irwin, 1973.

Turnbull, John G., *The Changing Faces of Economic Insecurity.* Minneapolis: University of Minnesota Press, 1966.

_____, C. Arthur Williams, Jr., and Earl F. Cheit, *Economic and Social Security,* 4th ed., Chap. 1. New York: Ronald Press, 1973.

U.S. Department of Health, Education and Welfare, Social Security Administration, Office of Research and Statistics, *Social Security Programs in the United States.* Washington, D.C.: U.S. Government Printing Office, 1973.

_____, *Social Security Programs throughout the World, 1973,* Research Report No. 44. Washington, D.C.: U.S. Government Printing Office, 1974.

Wilcox, Clair, *Toward Social Welfare,* Chap. 3. Homewood, Ill.: Richard D. Irwin, 1969.

chapter 2

Basic Principles
of Social Insurance

A multitude of errors in thinking surround our social insurance programs. This confusion is due largely to a misunderstanding of the principles, nature, and objectives of social insurance. Comparisons with private insurance are often improperly made. It is important, therefore, to analyze the basic principles and characteristics of social insurance programs so that these programs can be viewed in their proper perspective.

In this chapter, we shall consider the following fundamental concepts: (1) basic principles and characteristics of the OASDHI program, (2) desirability of a voluntary OASDHI program, (3) whether the OASDHI program can properly be called insurance, (4) comparison of social insurance with private insurance, (5) comparison of social insurance with public assistance, and (6) economic objectives of social insurance.

BASIC PRINCIPLES AND CHARACTERISTICS
OF OASDHI

The well-known OASDHI program is perhaps the most important public income-maintenance program in providing economic security to individuals and families. For the sake of convenience, the basic principles and characteristics of social insurance may be illustrated by analyzing the OASDHI program. However, these principles and characteristics can also be applied to other social insurance programs.[1]

---

[1]For an extensive discussion of social insurance principles and characteristics, see John G. Turnbull, C. Arthur Williams, Jr., and Earl F. Cheit, *Economic and Social Security*, 4th ed. (New York: Ronald Press, 1973), pp. 10-17; and Robert J. Myers, "Social Security Benefits for Retirement, Disability, and Survivorship," in Davis W. Greg and Vane B. Lucas, eds., *Life and Health Insurance Handbook*, 3rd ed. (Homewood, Ill.: Richard D. Irwin, 1973), pp. 751-67. See also Ray M. Peterson, "Misconceptions and Missing Perceptions of Our Social Security System (Actuarial Anesthesia)," *Transactions of Society of Actuaries*, No. 1 (March 1960), 812-51.

Compulsory Program

With few exceptions, coverage under the OASDHI program is compulsory. This principle has been consistently followed since the passage of the original Social Security Act in 1935. A compulsory program makes it easier to protect the population against certain social risks, including premature death of the family head, old age, long-term disability, and medical expenses for the aged. By a compulsory program, a basic floor of income protection to the masses can be more easily achieved, and both healthy and unhealthy people can be covered. A social insurance program covering only unhealthy lives on a massive scale would be extremely costly and would be difficult to implement. Finally, the OASDHI program is a large social insurance system because of its compulsory nature, and a large system has an advantage over smaller systems. Since fewer random and accidental fluctuations in experience are likely to occur, the necessity of providing margins in contingency reserves is reduced.[2]

Minimum Floor of Income

The OASDHI program provides only a minimum floor of income protection against the various risks covered. Traditional philosophy in the United States says that the individual is primarily responsible for his own economic security, and if government assistance is necessary, only a minimum benefit should be paid. People are expected to supplement government economic-security programs with their own personal programs of savings, investments, and insurance.

The concept of a minimum floor of income is difficult to define precisely, and much disagreement exists concerning the minimum and maximum benefits that should be paid. Generally speaking, there are three views regarding the minimum floor.[3] First, one extreme view is that the minimum should be so low as to be virtually nonexistent. Second, the other extreme says that it should be high enough to provide a comfortable standard of living by itself, with no consideration given to other economic-security programs provided by private or group methods (private insurance, group insurance, private pensions). Third, a middle view is that the minimum income should, in combination with other income and financial assets, be sufficient to maintain a reasonable standard of living for the vast majority of people. Any residual group whose basic needs are then still unmet would be provided for by supplementary public assistance.

Social Adequacy Rather Than Individual Equity

The OASDHI program emphasizes the payment of benefits based on social adequacy rather than individual equity.[4] *Social adequacy* means that the

---

[2]Robert J. Myers, *Social Insurance and Allied Government Programs* (Homewood, Ill.: Richard D. Irwin, 1965), p. 7.

[3]*Ibid.*, p. 25.

[4]The classic paper in the professional literature on the social-adequacy principle is Reinard A. Hohaus, "Equity, Adequacy, and Related Factors in Old-Age Security," in William Haber and Wilbur J. Cohen, eds., *Social Security: Programs, Problems, and Policies* (Homewood, Ill.: Richard D. Irwin, 1960), pp. 61-63. See also Myers, *Social Insurance,* p. 6.

benefits paid provide a certain standard of living to all contributors. *Individual equity* means that contributors receive benefits directly related to their contributions; in technical terms, the actuarial value of the benefits is closely related to the actuarial value of the contributions. The OASDHI program provides benefits on a basis falling between complete social adequacy and complete individual equity, with the emphasis on the former.

The social-adequacy principle results in the payment of OASDHI benefits that are heavily weighted in favor of certain groups, such as the lower-income groups, people with large families, and those who were near retirement when first covered by the OASDHI program. The actuarial value of the benefits received by these groups exceeds the actuarial value of their contributions; this means that they receive relatively larger benefits compared to their contributions than other groups. For example, based on January 1975 benefits and ignoring the cost-of-living adjustment, a low-income worker with no dependents who retires at age 65 with an average monthly wage of $165 would receive a monthly retirement benefit of $157.20, or about 95 percent of his average monthly wage. In contrast, if another worker in the same category also retires at age 65 but has an average monthly wage of $500, he would receive a monthly retirement benefit of $299.40, or about 60 percent of his average wage. Thus, the low-income worker receives relatively larger benefits.

The purpose of the social-adequacy principle is to provide a minimum floor of income to all groups. If certain groups received OASDHI benefits actuarially equal to the value of their contributions (individual-equity principle), the benefits paid would be so small for some groups (for instance, lower-income groups) that the objective of providing a minimum floor of income to everyone would not be achieved.

Whereas the OASDHI program and other social insurance programs emphasize social adequacy, private insurance stresses the individual-equity principle. Losses are pooled, and people with roughly the same loss-producing characteristics are grouped into the same class and pay roughly equal premiums. Private insurance is voluntary and must be built on equity between different classes of insureds. It is considered inequitable to have one relatively homogeneous group of insureds pay part of the loss costs for another group whose loss-producing characteristics are substantially different. Furthermore, once people in the first category became aware they could save money by being treated as independent, financially self-contained units, they would tend to drop their insurance.

However, the OASDHI program and other social insurance programs are different in character and have different functions. Since social insurance programs are generally compulsory, they are aimed at providing society with some protection against major social risks. The benefit structure is designed to provide society with a minimum floor of income so that people do not become wards of society. It is only after this objective is achieved that any remaining funds can be considered available for providing additional benefits based on individual equity.

In addition, private insurance is aimed at the individual's needs and ability to pay for protection against a large number of risks, whereas social insurance is molded to society's needs for a minimum floor of income protection against a more limited number of recognized social risks. Private insurance would collapse if it stressed social adequacy over individual equity, but social insurance must do so if the objective of providing a minimum income to all is to be achieved. This does not mean that individual-equity considerations are completely discarded in social insurance, but that social adequacy is considered more essential.

Methods of Providing Socially Adequate Benefits. Several methods are used to provide socially adequate OASDHI benefits.[5] First, as stated earlier, the benefit formula is heavily skewed in favor of the lower-income groups. The benefit rate applied to the lower portion of wages is higher than the rate applied to the higher portion. This allows the lower-income groups to receive proportionately larger benefits compared to their contributions than do the upper-income groups.

Second, the OASDHI program has a statutory minimum benefit. Regardless of how low the earnings of the eligible worker are, he can never receive less than the minimum benefit established by law. As of January 1975, the lowest minimum monthly retirement benefit at age 65 is $93.80.

Third, when dependents' benefits are paid, the recipient with a large family receives relatively larger OASDHI benefits than does the one with no dependents. In addition, dependents' benefits are also paid under workmen's compensation insurance programs in some states.

Fourth, social adequacy is emphasized by favoring the initial older workers, those near retirement when first covered by the OASDHI program. In establishing a social insurance plan, a problem often arises regarding the adequacy of benefits for people near retirement. If the individual-equity principle were closely followed, it would be difficult to provide socially adequate benefits. For example, in testimony before the Committee on Ways and Means prior to enactment of the original Social Security Act, Dr. Edwin Witte estimated that, if earned annuties only were paid, a worker with monthly wages of $100 would receive a monthly benefit of 48 cents after five years of contributions, under the tax schedule in the bill introduced in Congress; after ten years, his benefit would be $1.55, and after 15 years, it would be $3.35.[6]

This situation is not unique to social insurance. When private pension plans are initially established, the benefits for an older worker, near retirement, may be inadequate if they are based only on his future service with the company. A future-service benefit is that portion of a participant's retirement benefit that relates to his period of credited service after the effective date of the plan. So future service alone will not provide adequate benefits to a worker who is near retirement when the plan is first installed. Thus, most private pension plans also recognize past service. A past-service benefit is that portion of a participant's retirement benefit that relates to his period of credited service *before* the effective date of the plan. Since the older worker often receives credit for past service, the actuarial value of his benefits may exceed the actuarial value of his contributions. Also, private-pension benefits may be increased for those already retired. This again reflects an application of the social-adequacy principle in private

[5]Margaret S. Gordon, *The Economics of Welfare Policies* (New York and London: Columbia University Press, 1963), p. 56.

[6]See Merrill G. Murray, "Social Insurance Perspectives: Background Philosophy and Early Program Developments," *The Journal of Insurance,* Vol. XXX, No. 2 (June 1963), 195.

pensions, since the retired participants generally do not pay for the higher benefits.

Redistribution-of-Income Effect.   Emphasis on the social-adequacy principle in the OASDHI program results in a redistribution of income. As stated earlier, certain groups receive benefits that actuarially exceed the value of their contributions. In effect, these groups (lower-income groups, people with large families, and older workers initially covered) are undercharged for their benefits, and other groups (such as younger workers) are overcharged. This redistributes income, by taking away income from one group and giving it to another. Some view the redistribution of income under the OASDHI program and other social insurance programs as a form of "wealth sharing" and think it indicates the movement toward socialism in the United States. The redistribution-of-income effect under the OASDHI program is an important economic issue that will be analyzed later in Chapter 19.

Benefits Loosely Related to Earnings

OASDHI benefits are loosely related to earnings within minimum and maximum amounts. This means that some relationship exists between individual equity and social adequacy; and in general, the higher the worker's average covered earnings, the greater will be his benefits. The relationship between higher average earnings and higher benefits is loose and disproportionate, but it does exist.

The payment of higher benefits because of higher earnings can be defended in several ways.[7] First, the free-enterprise system stresses economic rewards to the individual based upon his personal talents and initiative, and this principle is reflected in the OASDHI program. A worker who earns a higher income because of his personal efforts is rewarded with larger OASDHI benefits.

Second, relating benefits to earnings implies their relation to different standards of living and to diverse economic conditions and price levels in various parts of the country. Generally speaking, the worker's earnings establish his individual standard of living and his income level at retirement. If flat benefits were paid to everyone, the amount paid to some workers could equal or exceed their preretirement earnings, whereas the same amount paid to those who had worked at higher income levels would not provide them with meaningful economic security.

Finally, some argue that relating benefits to earnings is desirable because the OASDHI benefits are a form of "deferred wage," and the benefit payments are merely an extension of the wage contract. From the employer's viewpoint, OASDHI contributions are costs involved in obtaining labor; these contributions can be looked upon as deferred wages to be received by workers in the future. From the employee's viewpoint, his OASDHI contributions amount to income earned but withheld, to be received in the future when he retires or becomes unemployed because of disability. Thus, according to this view, it is

[7]Eveline M. Burns, *Social Security and Public Policy* (New York: McGraw-Hill, 1956), pp. 38-41.

logical to award the worker higher OASDHI benefits because of higher earnings.

The preceding theory is faulty because it would impede the attainment of economic security for the lower-income groups. Strict adherence to the principle of relating benefits to earnings would mean that the benefits received by the lower-paid worker, being only a percentage of his already low wages, would be inadequate to provide even a modest existence. Carried to its logical conclusion, an OASDHI program based upon the deferred-wage theory would imply a restricted program, limited to workers whose earnings were high enough so that the benefits (some fraction of high earnings) would meet the worker's demand for security. Society would still have the problem, however, of providing economic security to the lower-paid workers.[8]

Right to Benefits with No Needs Test

OASDHI benefits are paid as a matter of right, without the demonstration of need. Although need is clearly recognized in the program,[9] a needs or means test is never required. A needs test is used in public assistance, where an applicant must demonstrate that his income and financial assets are insufficient to maintain himself or his family. In OASDHI, however, the recipient has a right to the benefits with no such demonstration, assuming that he fulfills the eligibility requirements.

The concept of the "right to benefits" has created some confusion, and numerous views prevail regarding the meaning of this term. These views may be classified as meaning (1) contractual right, (2) earned right, and (3) statutory right.

Contractual Right. The right to OASDHI benefits is clearly not a contractual right, because no formal contract exists between the insureds and the government. In the Nestor case, the Supreme Court held that the right to OASDHI retirement benefits was not comparable to that of the holder of an annuity contract, whose right to benefits was based on his contractual premium payments.[10] A contractual right can be modified only by agreement between two parties, so the right to OASDHI benefits is not contractual, since Congress can alter, amend, and repeal the benefits without the insured's consent.

Earned Right. Another view is that the right to OASDHI benefits is an earned right, because the recipient has contributed to and has paid for the benefits throughout his lifetime, and/or someone has contributed on his behalf. This view of an earned right is misleading for several reasons. First, the payment of OASDHI taxes by itself does not give the person an unequivocal right to benefits, since other eligibility conditions must be fulfilled.

Second, many who are eligible for benefits have contributed little or nothing to the program. One example would be the 1.98 million people aged 65

[8]Burns, *Social Security,* p. 40.

[9]For example, a retired person with dependents has a greater need for income than the one with no dependents. Thus, higher benefits are paid to retired workers with dependents.

[10]*Flemming v. Nestor,* 363 U.S. 603 (1960).

or over who were never covered under OASDHI or the Railroad Retirement System but were blanketed in for health insurance benefits under the 1965 amendments.

Finally, the groups that are favored in order to provide socially adequate benefits have not strictly "earned" the right to benefits, because the actuarial value of their benefits substantially exceeds the actuarial value of their contributions.

Statutory Right.   This is probably the correct view regarding the right to OASDHI benefits.[11] A statutory right can be enforced in the courts; and individuals can and do sue to enforce their rights to benefits. This is a powerful right, because specific benefits established by statute must be paid to an eligible recipient, and cannot be withheld or reduced because of administrative discretion.

It should be pointed out, however, that Congress can alter, amend, or repeal any provision of the Social Security Act if public policy so demands. In the Nestor case, the Supreme Court ruled that, although there were substantial property rights involved in the benefits, Congress could modify the benefits in any reasonable way, but that there was protection under the Constitution against arbitrary change on the part of Congress. This means that any modification of benefits by Congress, even in a downward direction, would be constitutional as long as there were sound reasons for it.

Some social insurance scholars argue that the statutory right to benefits under the OASDHI program is stronger than the contractual right under private insurance. They state that Congress is a responsible legislative body and would never take action jeopardizing the rights of millions of people who have accumulated wage credits.[12] And, indeed, Congress has generally moved in the direction of liberalizing OASDHI benefits over time rather than restricting them.

Benefits Based on Presumed Need

OASDHI benefits are also based upon presumed need.[13] The law establishes certain categories of covered risks, and benefits are paid when losses occur. For example, retirement benefits are never automatically paid upon the attainment of a minimum retirement age, such as 62, but only upon retirement. In this case, the gainfully employed worker is presumed not to need the benefits, since he has not lost his earned income. However, the retired worker, who has lost his work earnings, is presumed to need the benefits.

Failure to recognize that benefits are based on presumed need has led to error in thinking. For example, critics of the OASDHI earnings test[14] argue that the right to receive benefits is fictitious, since the benefits are not automati-

---

[11]Arthur J. Altmeyer, *The Formative Years of Social Security* (Madison: University of Wisconsin Press, 1966), pp. 227-28.

[12]*Ibid.,* p. 228.

[13]Myers, "Social Security Benefits," p. 763.

[14]See Chapter 5 for an explanation of the retirement or earnings test.

cally paid upon attainment of the normal retirement age of 65, despite years of compulsory contributions. Although a statutory right to benefits exists, this right is contingent upon fulfillment of certain conditions set down in the law. Since the benefits are based on presumed need, they are not paid if the worker is gainfully employed and his work earnings exceed some maximum limit as defined in the law.

Self-Supporting Contributory Principle

Another important principle of the OASDHI program, adopted by Congress in 1950 and still followed today, is that the program should be financially self-supporting, from the tax contributions of employers, employees, and the self-employed, and interest on the trust-fund investments. General-revenue appropriations are normally not used to pay benefits and administrative expenses, except for transitional benefits for certain closed groups.[15]

The contributory-financing principle is justified on several grounds. First, because employers, employees, and the self-employed contribute to the program, they are made aware of the relationship between the benefits received and the contributions paid, and the fact that increased benefits will generally require increased tax contributions. For example, just as few people relate the taxes on gasoline and tires to the federal program for highway improvement, it is doubtful that the covered worker would relate the taxes paid to the benefits received if the OASDHI contributions were based on something other than earnings (such as a sales tax). However, workers *are* aware that part of their earnings are deducted for OASDHI benefits, and that higher benefits will require higher tax contributions.

Second, the contributory principle also encourages a more responsible attitude on the part of the covered worker. He knows that his benefits and those of his family are made possible by OASDHI contributions, and this knowledge gives him a greater personal interest in the soundness of the program.

Third, the contributory principle also encourages a more responsible attitude on the part of elected representatives. Any social insurance program can be changed by legislative action; such legislative action in a democracy ultimately depends upon the voters. If the voters are contributors, as well as the ultimate decision makers regarding the program, a more responsible attitude will be taken by their elected representatives with regard to the program.

Finally, most gainfully employed workers contribute to the OASDHI program; this has an important psychological appeal, which results in widespread acceptance of OASDHI.[16] The protected groups feel greater psychological security in the coverage provided, and at the same time, the program is less susceptible to unsound changes because of political pressure groups.

---

[15]Myers, "Social Security Benefits," pp. 764-65.

[16]A discussion of the advantages of the contributory principle and other principles followed in the OASDHI program can be found in Charles I. Schottland, *The Social Security Program in the United States,* 2nd ed. (New York: Appleton-Century-Crofts, 1970).

No Full Funding

In the OASDHI program, the trust funds are built up from the accumulated excess of income over outgo, but the program itself is not fully funded.[17] It does not have legal reserves similar to those required of a private life insurer. In permanent individual life insurance, the company must carry a legal-reserve liability item on its balance sheet, representing the difference between the present value of future benefits promised under the policies in force and the present value of future premiums. The company could terminate the sale of new policies at any time, and if its actuarial assumptions are correct, the future premiums plus the legal reserves, improved by compound interest, would be sufficient to pay all future claims. Permanent life insurance contracts must be fully funded to protect the rights of policyholders.

The OASDHI trust funds are not as large as the legal reserves of private life insurers. Full funding is considered unnecessary because the program is expected to operate indefinitely and will not terminate in the predictable future. Also, since the OASDHI program is compulsory, new entrants will always enter the program and make contributions to support it. Finally, from an economic viewpoint, full funding may be undesirable.[18]

The lack of full funding does not mean that the OASDHI program is financially unsound. Assuming that it operates indefinitely, with new entrants constantly coming into the program, the current amounts in the trust funds, improved by compound interest, plus future tax contributions, are expected to be sufficient to pay all future benefits and administrative expenses.

Benefits Prescribed by Law

In the OASDHI program and other social insurance programs, the benefits are prescribed by law, with the administration or supervision of the plan performed by government. In all social insurance programs, the benefits or benefit formulas are established by statute, as are the eligibility requirements. Although the OASDHI program is administered by the federal government, the level of administration in other social insurance programs may be state or local.

Plan Not Established Solely for Government Employees

Social insurance can be distinguished from other government insurance programs. A social insurance program is established by the government not solely for its own employees, but for the solution of a social problem requiring government intervention. A plan established only for government employees is not social insurance because the government is acting like any other employer in

---

[17]See Chapter 7 for an explanation of the nature and operations of the various OASDHI trust funds.

[18]Turnbull, Williams, and Cheit, *Economic and Social Security,* pp. 88 and 114-15. Also the economic effects of a fully funded program are treated in greater detail in Chapter 7 of the present volume.

providing fringe benefits to employees. For example, if General Motors establishes a group life insurance plan for its employees, the plan is not social insurance. Likewise, a group life insurance plan only for federal employees—as is Federal Employees Group Life Insurance—is not social insurance.

SHOULD THE OASDHI PROGRAM BE MADE VOLUNTARY?

The fact that the OASDHI program is generally compulsory makes the program repugnant to many people who believe that they are coerced into participating. The right to live one's life in freedom, as long as the rights of others are not impaired, is a well-established American principle. The compulsory nature of the OASDHI program appears to violate this principle.

Proposals for a voluntary OASDHI program are not new. In the report prepared by the Committee on Economic Security to President Roosevelt prior to the enactment of the Social Security Act in 1935, a voluntary system of old-age annuities was proposed.[19] The government would sell deferred life annuities to individuals, similar to those issued by private companies, on a cost basis. In consideration for the premiums paid at specified ages, the government would guarantee a definite income to the purchaser of the annuity, starting at age 65 and continuing throughout his lifetime.

The proposal for voluntary annuities was not included in the original Social Security Act. It was dropped because it appeared to compete with private insurers, and because the experience of foreign nations indicated the ineffectiveness of voluntary methods in meeting the economic problem of old age.[20]

Arguments for a Voluntary OASDHI Program

Powerful arguments are advanced for a voluntary program. The most important emphasize the following: (1) expansion of economic freedom, (2) greater flexibility with private insurance, (3) restriction of government, and (4) equity to younger workers.

Expansion of Economic Freedom. The problems of economic freedom and the role of the federal government in providing economic security are delicate and sensitive issues. Bitter arguments have been advanced concerning the restriction of economic freedom by a compulsory government program. One argument is that economic freedom is diminished by a compulsory program because the number of the individual's decisions is reduced. A person with a given amount of income has a certain number of decisions available to him regarding the spending of his income. The fact that OASDHI contributions (taxes) are involuntarily taken away from him reduces the number of decisions he may make regarding the disposition of his income, thereby reducing his economic freedom. Under a voluntary program, however, he himself decides

[19]U.S. Committee on Economic Security, *Social Security in America* (Washington, D.C.: U.S. Government Printing Office, 1937), p. 214.

[20]Wilbur J. Cohen, *Retirement Policies under Social Security* (Berkeley: University of California Press, 1957), p. 4.

whether to participate. Since the number of his decisions is increased, economic freedom is enhanced.

It is difficult to determine precisely whether a compulsory program reduces economic freedom. Generally speaking, the meaning of economic freedom depends upon individual value judgments regarding politics, philosophy, economics, religion, and the role of the federal government in providing economic security. In the last analysis, each person must decide for himself whether a compulsory OASDHI program reduces his economic freedom. However, certain guidelines are helpful in analyzing the problem.

First, given the present institutional framework and value judgments that prevail in the United States, a truly voluntary OASDHI program is theoretically difficult, if not impossible. A truly voluntary program would have to allow the individual three major choices: (1) to participate in the present OASDHI program, (2) to purchase an annuity from a private insurer, or (3) not to participate in any program, either public or private. All three options must be present to have a truly voluntary program.

Some take the position that people should be required either to participate in the OASDHI program or to purchase annuities from private insurers.[21] In this case, they would be given two choices. A compulsory program would still exist, however, because people would still be compelled to purchase either a government or a private annuity. A truly voluntary program would allow a third choice: that of not participating in any program, public or private.

Of course, some people might not purchase any annuities and thus not provide for their own economic security. But "true freedom" implies that people should be free to make their own mistakes, and if they should willingly decide against participation in any program, they should then suffer the consequences of that decision. This would mean that society should not assist them in any way, and for all practical purposes, the imprudent would starve. But this is the nub of the problem. A philosophy has developed in the United States that people should not be allowed to starve—regardless of how imprudent and undeserving of aid they might be. This implies that public assistance should be made available to the imprudent, and that society, through general taxation, should assume that burden.

For the most part, society would prefer that the imprudent should provide for their own economic security (at least in part) through compulsory participation in the OASDHI program, or else through the purchase of private annuities. Since the decision of not participating in any program would be absent, the number of individual decisions would be reduced from three to two; thus, a truly voluntary program would be conceptually difficult to attain.

Second, if economic freedom is reduced for those who make the compul-

---

[21]For example, Milton Friedman argues that government should not be given a monopoly in the sale of annuities, but should compete actively with private insurers. A person would not be compelled to buy an annuity from the government, but would be given the option to buy one from a private company. If he purchased privately, he would include a copy of his premium receipts with his income tax return to show that he had provided for his own security. See Milton Friedman, *Capitalism and Freedom* (Chicago: University of Chicago Press, 1962), p. 186. See also Wilbur J. Cohen and Milton Friedman, *Social Security: Universal or Selective?* Rational Debate Series (Washington, D.C.: American Enterprise Institute for Public Policy Research, 1972).

sory contributions, it is expanded for those who receive these contributions as benefit payments. The people receiving them will have an increase in their income, thereby increasing the number of personal decisions they have on how to spend their income. Thus, there is a net gain in economic freedom—the increase in freedom for the recipients of benefits exceeds the loss of freedom because of the involuntary contributions.

Finally, the loss in freedom may be small when the worker is earning an income, because the contributions paid are relatively small compared to his income and are paid in installments throughout his working lifetime. But when the worker retires and receives his benefits, economic freedom and security may be substantially increased. The retired worker receives the benefits when his need for them is greatest, because his earned income has terminated or has been reduced. The marginal-utility principle is relevant here. The marginal utility of small increments of income paid by the worker in the form of taxes is *less* than the marginal utility of the larger amounts of income received in the form of benefits when he retires and his income terminates. In this sense, economic freedom is increased rather than reduced.[22]

Greater Flexibility with Private Insurance. Another argument for a voluntary program is that private insurance provides greater flexibility. This argument has considerable merit. Private insurance permits an insured to select diverse types of benefits in terms of his individual needs, dependents, ability to pay, and financial goals. Additional insurance may be added or dropped as needed. The OASDHI program, however, is relatively inflexible. The insured is not given a choice of benefits or benefit amounts, since these are prescribed by law, and he cannot select coverages to conform to his individual needs, objectives, and financial goals.

Restriction of Government. Another argument is that a voluntary program may curb the encroachment of government into the private sector, and thereby foster the free enterprise system. The OASDHI program is viewed as a threat to the survival of private insurance, and this threat is reduced by a voluntary program.

This argument indicates confusion concerning the role of government and private insurers in providing economic security. The OASDHI program and private insurance should complement rather than compete with each other. First, OASDHI and other social insurance programs are designed to meet certain risks that cannot be privately insured. For example, the risks of unemployment and premature death of an uninsurable family head cannot be privately insured, but can be publicly insured under a compulsory social insurance program.

Second, the OASDHI program generally provides only a minimum floor of income protection; the worker is encouraged to increase his protection through a private program of individual insurance. A compulsory OASDHI program can never replace a private program of insurance, investments, and savings. Both OASDHI and private insurance are necessary for economic security.

Finally, some OASDHI objectives are inappropriate to or incompatible

---

[22]John G. Turnbull, *The Changing Faces of Economic Insecurity* (Minneapolis: University of Minnesota Press, 1966), p. 140.

with private insurance. For example, strict application of the social-adequacy principle in the payment of benefits (rather than individual equity) would be clearly out of place for private insurance. On the other hand, the OASDHI program must of necessity emphasize the social-adequacy principle. Since the character and objectives of OASDHI and private insurance are different, both are necessary for economic security.

Equity to Younger Workers. A final argument for a voluntary system is that the present OASDHI program is unfair to younger workers, since new OASDHI entrants will receive benefits that are actuarially less than the actuarial value of the combined employer-employee tax contributions, and new workers entering the program in the future will be cheated. Thus, it is argued, in a voluntary plan, the younger workers could purchase the equivalent protection from private insurers more cheaply, and the benefits paid would be based on greater individual equity, with a closer actuarial relationship between benefits and contributions.

The argument that the OASDHI program cheats younger workers and is a "bad buy" is an important issue that merits careful analysis. It will be treated in greater detail in Chapter 6, when the controversial problems and issues surrounding the OASDHI program are analyzed.

Arguments against a Voluntary OASDHI Program

The major arguments against a voluntary OASDHI program are more numerous and perhaps more convincing that the arguments for it. The major arguments against a voluntary program are as follows: (1) greater probability of adverse selection, (2) more difficulty in achieving minimum economic security, (3) financial disruption of the present program, (4) inability of lower-income groups to purchase private insurance, and (5) higher administrative costs to the economy.

Greater Probability of Adverse Selection. Adverse selection is any process whereby the exercise of choice by insureds leads to higher-than-average loss levels. Without adequate controls, the people who obtain insurance tend to be those who need it most—those with a greater probability of loss than the average.

A voluntary system could increase adverse selection for several reasons: first, because of the inequitable rating structure that now exists in the OASDHI program. As indicated earlier, OASDHI benefits are largely paid on the basis of social adequacy rather than individual equity. In private insurance, individual-equity considerations require that each insured must be charged a rate that closely reflects the probability of occurrence and the probable severity of loss to which he is exposed. This is not true in social insurance, where an inequity in the rating structure arises out of the social desirability of providing a minimum floor of income to groups most in need of the protection. The result is that some groups are overcharged, while other groups are undercharged. If the program became voluntary, the overcharged groups might withdraw and provide for their own economic security by insuring with private insurers, where individual-equity considerations prevail. Since it is the more desirable insureds that would withdraw because of the rate inequity (primarily younger, healthy workers), the contributions collected from the remainder (less desirable risks) might be insufficient to pay socially adequate benefits to those most in need of the protection. Thus, it might become necessary to increase contribution rates to pay adequate benefits. But the contribution-rate increase could easily cause others to withdraw from the program. This process would continue until the only people covered by the OASDHI program were the worst risks, with the final contribution rate quite high. On the other hand, if contribution rates were not increased, it would be difficult to provide socially adequate benefits. It is only by having a compulsory OASDHI program that an inequitable rate structure can be maintained for any extended period, in order to provide socially adequate benefits. [23]

Second, adverse selection might increase if, because of underwriting standards, private insurers could offer the insurance at lower premiums to potential insureds. People in poor health, in extra-hazardous occupations, or with poor moral character might be unable to purchase private insurance, or be able to obtain it only by the payment of higher premiums. Thus, company underwriting procedures would eliminate some who were in a position to have an immediate loss, and by their elimination, private insurers would be enabled to offer protection at a lower cost. From a loss viewpoint, private companies might insure only the more desirable individuals, and only the less desirable would be left for the OASDHI program to insure. Since the program would then consist of a relatively larger number of less desirable or substandard insureds, higher loss levels would result. It would be inconceivable for OASDHI to apply private-insurer underwriting standards, since this would defeat the basic objective of providing a minimum floor of income protection to all. A compulsory program avoids the problem of underwriting and covers both desirable and undesirable insureds, with a reduction in adverse selection as a result.

Third, adverse selection might result from a voluntary program because the firms and individuals most likely to participate would be those who stood to gain disproportionately large benefits relative to their contributions. Thus, those firms that employ large numbers of workers who are near retirement, or have large families, or are in poor health, might be more inclined to participate. Furthermore, some firms are small and employ only a few workers. The smaller the firm, the greater is the probability that the distribution of employees by sex, age, and family dependents will differ from the universe distribution underlying the employee population as a whole; this increases the probability of adverse selection. Also, the young and healthy might feel no need to participate; this increases further the probability of adverse selection, since the more desirable workers would not be covered.

Fourth, a compulsory program reduces the problem of overinsurance. The problems of overinsurance and profiting from insurance are well known in the private insurance industry, since people can buy whatever amount of coverage they can afford and qualify for. But in a compulsory program with the benefits fixed by law, those who are in a position to have a loss cannot select additional amounts of insurance. Because of competition from private insurers, however, a voluntary program might force the OASDHI program to offer additional benefits. Once this occurred, the probability of adverse selection might increase;

[23]See O.D. Dickerson, *Health Insurance,* 3rd ed. (Homewood, Ill.: Richard D. Irwin, 1968), pp. 468-69, for a discussion of an inequitable rating structure and adverse selection.

without some type of underwriting controls, people in poor health, near retirement, or with large families might select additional coverages.

Finally, the history of voluntary social insurance indicates that those most in need of protection seldom participate. The people who do are usually those who expect a large return for their contributions and have the necessary funds to pay for the protection. There is no justification in offering insurance protection at "bargain" rates to a select group, consisting primarily of people who recognize the bargain and are financially able to take advantage of it, and in requiring the covered group as a whole to bear the cost of the difference between what the select group pays and what it receives.[24]

More Difficulty in Achieving Minimum Economic Security. A voluntary program may make it more difficult for society to achieve a minimum level of economic security. First, some people might neither participate in the OASDHI program nor purchase private insurance, thereby exposing themselves to possible economic insecurity. A compulsory OASDHI program currently covers most of the population and provides some protection against the risks of premature death, old age, disability, and high medical expenses for the aged. A voluntary program could dilute this wide base of protection.

Second, some people who purchase private insurance benefits in lieu of participation in the OASDHI program might decide later to cancel their policies or let them lapse. This problem does not arise in a compulsory program, since, with few exceptions, they must participate.

Third, some argue that the OASDHI program should not cover the wealthy because they do not need the benefits. In this case, they say, the principle of subsidiarity is violated by compelling the wealthy to participate when they can provide for their own economic security; the government should not do those things that individuals can do for themselves.

Although the subsidiarity principle is clearly violated by requiring the wealthy to participate, coverage can be justified on both theoretical and practical grounds. If the premise is accepted that society should provide some economic security to everyone, the rich would have to show that they can provide for their own economic security. In effect, they would have the burden of demonstrating that their income and assets are sufficiently large to justify exclusion from the OASDHI program. In this case, a *negative means test* would be introduced into the program. But it would be wrong in principle to require a needs test in social insurance, regardless of the form of the test, and the principle of not requiring a needs test in the OASDHI program would be violated.

Moreover, technical problems may make it administratively difficult to determine the level of income and assets necessary for persons to be considered "wealthy" and therefore eligible for exclusion under OASDHI. The technical problem of administration is one reason why the wealthy aged were covered under the Medicare program. Furthermore, the wealthy always face the risk of losing their wealth at some future date because of conditions over which they have no control. Many rich people saved and provided for their retirement needs in the 1920s, only to see their financial assets decline sharply or become worthless as a result of the Great Depression of the 1930s. A compulsory OASDHI

---

[24]"Nature and Functions of Old-Age and Survivors Insurance," in William Haber and Wilbur J. Cohen, eds., *Readings in Social Security* (Englewood Cliffs, N.J.: Prentice-Hall, 1948), pp. 258-59.

program assures the wealthy of at least a minimum base of economic security if financial misfortune should occur.

Finally, if the wealthy can elect out, other groups may demand the same right, thereby weakening the entire program. Except for constitutional or administrative reasons that justify voluntary participation, minimum economic security can be achieved with greater certainty by a compulsory program.

Financial Disruption of the Present Program. The OASDHI program could be exposed to serious financial disruption by a voluntary scheme. As stated earlier, a truly voluntary program would allow currently covered workers the right of withdrawal. Many people have contributed to the OASDHI program for years, and refunds would have to be made. Since the trust funds are not fully funded, they are insufficient for providing refunds to all who might desire to withdraw. Congress would then be forced to increase taxes to raise the additional sums for refunds; if Congress were unwilling to do this, the possibility exists (although slight) that the present OASDHI program could default on its obligations. On the other hand, if the OASDHI program were still compulsory for those currently covered, but made voluntary for new entrants who ordinarily would be covered, a truly voluntary program would not exist.

In any event, a severe financial disruption could take place if the OASDHI program were made voluntary.

Inability of Lower-Income Groups to Purchase Private Insurance. Another argument against a voluntary plan is that the lower-income groups might be unable to afford private insurance (assuming that they preferred private coverage to OASDHI) because of insufficient incomes. On the other hand, a compulsory OASDHI program provides certain advantages to the lower-income groups. As we have seen, the benefit formula is heavily weighted in their favor. In addition, some low-income workers may be uninsurable or substandard by private standards. Thus, private insurance may be unavailable to them, or may be obtainable only by the payment of higher premiums, which they may be unable to afford. Protection is available to these people, however, under a compulsory OASDHI program.

Higher Administrative Expenses. A final argument against a voluntary program is that administrative expenses to the economy would be increased. Administrative expenses under the compulsory OASDHI program are relatively low; they account for about 2 percent of total benefit costs, minimizing the administrative costs of providing a base of protection to the masses. No policies are issued; premium notices are unnecessary; commissions to agents are not paid; medical examinations are unnecessary; employers collect the contributions and remit them to the government; and record keeping is facilitated by computers.

Emphasis on low administrative costs as an argument for a compulsory program, however, is misleading. The costs of any insurance program are determined by the benefits paid and the administrative expenses. If the relative benefit costs of social insurance are the same as that of private individual or group insurance, any difference in total cost is due to different administrative expenses—and these represent only a small fraction of the total benefit costs. Thus, from the viewpoint of total cost, any advantage that a social insurance program possesses is small, and arises primarily because of its size. The major reason for a compulsory OASDHI program is not lower administrative costs, but the fact that it can provide socially adequate benefits more efficiently to an entire population.[25]

IS THE OASDHI PROGRAM INSURANCE?

Disagreements concerning the meaning of *insurance* have formed the basis of serious debate among economists, insurance scholars, legal technicians, and private insurance practitioners. The controversy becomes even more intense when the OASDHI program is analyzed as a form of insurance. One position, generally presented by economists, is that the OASDHI program should not be considered insurance, on the grounds that it is compulsory, contracts are not issued, the actuarial relationship between benefits and contributions is imprecise, a redistribution of income is heavily stressed, certain groups are heavily subsidized, and the compulsory tax contributions are not the same as private insurance premiums.[26] Instead, these economists view OASDHI as a massive government income-maintenance program for promoting national economic security through the imposition of compulsory payroll taxes.

This viewpoint is misleading and incorrect. Its proponents generally ignore the important insurance elements of pooling, fortuitous losses, risk transfer, and indemnification.[27] It is true, however, that the OASDHI program differs from private insurance in several respects. The OASDHI program can be correctly viewed as a form of social insurance, which contains both (1) private insurance elements, and (2) a strong welfare element.

Private Insurance Elements

Insurance can be defined in a way that includes or excludes the OASDHI program, depending on the definition adopted. After careful study, the Commission on Insurance Terminology of the American Risk and Insurance Association has defined insurance as follows:

> Pooling of risks of fortuitous losses by transfer of such risks to insurers who agree to indemnify insureds for such losses, to provide other pecuniary benefits on their occurrence, or to render services connected with the risks.[28]

[25]Myers, *Social Insurance,* p. 7.

[26]For example, see the position taken, concerning the OASDHI program as a form of insurance, by John A. Brittain, *The Payroll Tax for Social Security* (Washington, D.C.: The Brookings Institution, 1972), pp. 6-13.

[27]For an excellent discussion of the OASDHI program as a legitimate form of insurance, see Robert J. Myers, "Is Social Security Really Insurance?" *The Journal of the American Society of Chartered Life Underwriters,* Vol. XXVIII, No. 3 (July 1974), 32-35.

[28]*Bulletin of the Commission on Insurance Terminology of the American Risk and Insurance Association,* Vol. 1, No. 4 (October 1965), 1.

Although this definition may be unacceptable to some insurance scholars, it forms a suitable basis for determining whether OASDHI is a true form of insurance. Several critical elements in the definition are worthy of discussion. They are (1) pooling, (2) fortuitous losses, (3) risk transfer, and (4) indemnification.

Pooling. Private insurance utilizes the pooling technique for meeting risk. Pooling, or combination, is a technique whereby a large number of homogeneous exposure units are combined or grouped so that the Law of Large Numbers can operate to provide a substantially accurate prediction of future losses. In addition, pooling involves the spreading of losses over the entire group. The losses of individuals exposed to certain risks are pooled or averaged, and average loss is substituted for actual loss. Thus, pooling implies the prediction of future losses with some accuracy and the spreading of these losses over the group.

Because of complex sociological, economic, and demographic variables, the social insurance actuary has a more difficult task of predicting future losses than has the private insurance actuary. The Law of Large Numbers is of little practical value in predicting future long-run OASDHI experience because of the difficulty of computing the standard deviations of the many variables on which the cost estimates are based. Although OASDHI experience can be predicted rather closely for the short-term future, cost estimates and anticipated future losses may prove to be quite different because of the large compounding effects of variations in the many factors involved.

It is questionable, however, whether application of the Law of Large Numbers is necessary for a true insurance program. In an exhaustive analysis of the meaning of insurance, Prof. Irving Pfeffer argues that no line of insurance is able to meet the complete set of tests implied by the Law of Large Numbers, because the universe of insurance experience is constantly changing with respect to the economic and social environment, so past loss experience may not have the same relevance with respect to future loss experience. For some insurance lines, the requirements for applying the Law of Large Numbers can generally be fulfilled, but for other lines, few requisites can be met. Thus, Professor Pfeffer argues that application of the Law of Large Numbers is a *sufficient* condition for insurance, but not a *necessary* condition.[29] To the extent, however, that future short-run OASDHI experience can be closely estimated by application of the Law of Large Numbers, the OASDHI program can legitimately be called insurance.

Although the Law of Large Numbers is difficult to apply to long-run future OASDHI experience, nevertheless the pooling device involves the spreading of losses over the entire covered group. For example, the loss of earned income because of mandatory retirement can be viewed as a loss attributable to a social risk. If OASDHI retirement benefits are payable, a person can recoup part of the income loss. In effect, the loss experienced by a retired person is spread over and paid for by the group that has not yet suffered any loss—those not yet retired and still making OASDHI contributions. Thus, the OASDHI program utilizes the pooling technique.

[29]Irving Pfeffer, *Insurance and Economic Theory* (Homewood, Ill.: Richard D. Irwin, 1956), p. 43.

Some insurance scholars take the position that pooling is unnecessary for a true insurance scheme.[30] However, pooling or combination of risks, when it does exist, constitutes a legitimate insurance scheme, even though it is not a necessary condition for insurance. Since the pooling technique can be applied to the OASDHI program, the program can be called a true form of insurance.

Fortuitous Loss. Private insurance also involves the pooling of fortuitous losses. Fortuitous losses are unforeseen and unexpected, and ideally, they should be accidental and outside the insured's control. Most OASDHI losses are fortuitous and outside the individual's control. For example, the family may experience economic insecurity because of the family head's premature death, or the worker may be exposed to financial hardship because of permanent disability. These losses are largely fortuitous and unforeseen. Thus, both private insurance and the OASDHI program treat fortuitous losses.

Risk Transfer. Risk transfer is another technique for handling risk. In private insurance, a pure risk is transferred to the insurer, which is in a stronger financial position to pay losses than the individual is. Risk transfer also takes place in the OASDHI program. The risks associated with premature death, old age, disability, or high medical expenses for the aged are shifted, at least partly, from the individual to the OASDHI program. If the position is taken that only transfer of a pure risk is necessary to constitute insurance, then the OASDHI program fulfills this requirement.

Indemnification. Private insurance indemnifies the insured for losses. Indemnification means compensation to the victim of a loss, in whole or in part, by payment, repair, or replacement. The OASDHI program also involves indemnification for losses. Survivorship benefits restore, at least partly, the family's share of the deceased family head's income; retirement benefits restore part of the income loss from mandatory retirement; disability benefits indemnify people for accidental injuries or serious diseases; high medical expenses for the aged are also paid under the Medicare portion of the OASDHI program. Thus, both private and social insurance indemnify insureds for losses.

Welfare Element

The welfare element in the OASDHI program can be defined as that part of the benefits paid that have little or no relationship to the covered worker's earnings and the payroll-tax contributions paid on these earnings. It can be viewed primarily as unearned benefits; that is, the benefits received by certain groups, such as the aged, have little or no actuarial relationship to the value of their OASDHI tax contributions. These unearned benefits account for at least one-third of the benefit costs of the OASDHI program.[31]

The welfare element in the OASDHI program is derived from the principle of social adequacy, whereby certain groups receive benefits exceeding the

[30]*Ibid.,* p. 185.

[31]*Reports of the 1971 Advisory Council on Social Security,* H.D. No. 92-80, Committee on Ways and Means, 92nd Cong., 1st sess., 1971 (Washington, D.C.: U.S. Government Printing Office, 1971), p. 75.

actuarial value of their contributions.[32] The relation between the benefits received and the average monthly earnings on which the tax contributions are paid is loose and tenuous. As stated earlier, the social-adequacy principle is reflected in the benefit formula whereby the benefits are heavily weighted or skewed in favor of the lower-income groups. In addition, the minimum benefit also reflects the social-adequacy principle. The relation between the minimum benefit and average monthly earnings is largely nonexistent, with the exception that earnings must be low and the worker must have a record of some covered employment. In contrast, the insurance element can be defined as that portion of the benefits paid that have some actuarial relationship (in the private sense) to the covered person's average earnings and the payroll-tax contributions paid on these earnings. The relation between the benefits received and the contributions paid, of course, is not as close as that found in private insurance. Nevertheless, some relation exists.

In summary, the OASDHI program appears to meet the definition of insurance adopted by the Commission on Insurance Terminology and can be considered a form of insurance. Two critical elements normally found in any insurance program—pooling and risk transfer—are present in the OASDHI program. From this viewpoint, the OASDHI program is insurance. But it should not be viewed as pure insurance, since a strong welfare element is also embodied in the benefit structure.

SOCIAL INSURANCE COMPARED WITH PRIVATE INSURANCE

Much confusion between social and private insurance arises from the application of private insurance performance standards to social insurance. Social and private insurance are quite different in character and content, and identical performance standards should not be used to judge them. Also, they do not have identical goals; therefore, they cannot be compared by the same standard of success.

As an example of the error of *noncomparable performance standards,* a Honda motor bike and a Rolls Royce automobile are both machines; but if the same efficiency test, such as gasoline mileage, is used to evaluate them, the motor bike would be judged a superior machine—a dubious conclusion at best. The error of noncomparable performance standards has been committed. Likewise, one cannot compare the standards of social insurance and private insurance. True, they are similar, since both are forms of insurance. But social insurance differs from private insurance in many respects.[33]

[32]For a complete discussion of this concept, see George A. Bishop, "Issues in Future Financing of Social Security," in *Old Age Income Assurance, A Compendium of Papers on Problems and Policy Issues in the Public and Private Pension System, Part II: Public Programs,* Subcommittee on Fiscal Policy of the Joint Economic Committee, 90th Cong., 1st sess. (Washington, D.C.: U.S. Government Printing Office, 1967), pp. 51-63. See also George E. Rejda and Richard J. Shepler, "The Impact of Zero Population Growth on the OASDHI Program," *The Journal of Risk and Insurance,* Vol. XL, No. 3 (September 1973), 323-24.

[33]The major similarities and differences between private insurance and social insurance can be found in Peterson, "Misconceptions," pp. 812-51; Myers, *Social Insurance,* pp. 8-10; and Turnbull, Williams, and Cheit, *Economic and Social Security,* pp. 11-17. See also C.A. Kulp, "Social and Private Insurance—Contrasts and Similarities," in H. Wayne Snider, ed., *Readings in Property and Casualty Insurance* (Homewood, Ill.: Richard D. Irwin, 1959), pp. 27-35. The following discussion is based on these sources.

Applying private insurance standards to social insurance is also inappropriate because the *fallacy of composition* may nullify such comparisons. What is true for private insurance may be incorrect when applied to social insurance. For example, private insurance stresses individual equity, whereas social insurance must emphasize the social-adequacy principle. The fallacy of composition is committed if one contends that, because private insurance stresses individual equity, social insurance must also stress individual equity rather than social adequacy in the payment of benefits.

Similarities

First, as noted earlier, both social and private insurance are based on risk transfer and the widespread pooling of definite risks. Second, both provide for specific and complete descriptions of all conditions relating to coverage, benefits, and financing. Third, both require precise mathematical calculations of benefit eligibility and amounts. Fourth, both require contributions and the payment of premiums sufficient to meet the estimated costs of the programs. Fifth, both provide predetermined benefits not based upon demonstrated need. Finally, both benefit society as a whole in providing economic security.

Differences

The major differences between social and private insurance may be listed as follows:

Social Insurance	Private Insurance
1. Compulsory	Voluntary
2. Minimum floor of income protection	Larger amounts available, depending on individual desires and ability to pay
3. Emphasis on social adequacy (welfare element)	Emphasis on individual equity (insurance element)
4. Benefits prescribed by law that can be changed (statutory right)	Benefits established by legal contract (contractual right)
5. Government monopoly	Competition
6. Costs difficult to predict	Costs more readily predictable
7. Full funding not needed because of compulsory contributions from new entrants and because program is assumed to last indefinitely	Must operate on fully funded basis without reliance on new entrants' contributions
8. No underwriting	Individual or group underwriting
9. Widespread differences of opinion regarding objectives and results	Opinions generally more uniform regarding objectives and results
10. Investments generally in obligations of federal government	Investments mainly in private channels
11. Taxing power readily available to combat erosion by inflation	Greater vulnerability to inflation

The first three items in this comparison are self-explanatory and have been covered. In the fourth, we see that social insurance benefits are prescribed by laws that can be changed; a statutory right to benefits exists. However, private insurance benefits are established by a legal contract enforceable in the courts; a contractual right to benefits exists. In social insurance, a contract is unnecessary. The terms are established by law and by interpretative regulations, and emphasis is placed on administrative regulation to carry out the intent of the law. This is considered a virtue and not a defect, because it is difficult to provide precise answers in the statutes for every conceivable set of circumstances; the rigidities of tight legal documents that are necessary in private insurance are out of place in social insurance.[34] Moreover, since social insurance is generally compulsory and can be amended by legislation, precise legal language is unnecessary and unwise. On the other hand, private insurance is competitive, and people cannot be coerced into purchasing the coverage; thus, the contractual terms must be stated clearly in the contract when it is first written. Finally, the virtues of a legally enforceable contract in private insurance may be overemphasized in providing economic security. Even though a contract exists, the protection may be inadequate, unsound, unreliable, or excessively costly. Some private insurance contracts are cancellable, the terms can be altered, or premiums can be increased (there are cancellable contracts, optionally renewable contracts, and guaranteed renewable contracts). In the last analysis, the economic security provided by a private contract depends upon the continued existence and financial strength of the insurer. If the company becomes bankrupt, the economic security provided by the legal contract may be lost.

Also, government usually has a monopoly in social insurance, whereas competition from other insurers prevails in private insurance. A monopolistic government carrier may be sound public policy. Since the programs are normally compulsory, competitive selling costs can be eliminated or reduced by a monopoly carrier; moreover, the public may consider it undesirable for profit to accrue to private insurers because of a compulsory program made possible by government.[35] Finally, it is possible that a more liberal interpretation of the law and adjudication of claims can be made with a monopolistic carrier.

Another difference is that prediction of costs in social insurance is more difficult and less precise than in private insurance. The social insurance actuary is required to make rate and reserve calculations for risks whose insurability may be questionable (for instance, unemployment). Moreover, he must work with economic, demographic, and sociological variables, such as births, deaths, marriages, remarriage, employment, unemployment, disability, retirement, average wage levels, benefit levels, interest rates, and numerous additional factors that make prediction of costs difficult.

In addition, social insurance programs may not be fully funded, whereas private insurance and private pension plans stress fully funded programs. And underwriting selection procedures are not generally employed in social insur-

[34] Kulp, "Social and Private Insurance," p. 32.

[35] Workmen's compensation insurance is an exception to government monopoly in social insurance. Although most state workmen's compensation laws are compulsory, the benefits are generally underwritten by private insurers. Thus, profits could accrue to private insurers.

ance, whereas they are applied to individuals or groups in private insurance. Underwriting is inappropriate in social insurance because the objective is to provide a base of economic protection for all; this means that most of the population should be covered. In private insurance, however, underwriting is necessary because the objective is to insure *profitable* risks.

Another difference is that in social insurance, serious disagreement may exist concerning the method of financing, benefit levels, eligibility requirements, periods to be covered, the role of government, and numerous other factors. Opinions and objectives regarding private insurance programs are more uniform.

Also, the investments of the various social insurance trust funds are confined to the obligations of the federal government. In private insurance, investments in private securities are emphasized. (In some foreign countries, however, social insurance investments may be made in private securities.)

Finally, the government's taxing powers can more readily overcome the impact of inflation on social insurance programs. During inflationary periods, social insurance benefits may be increased, thereby providing the recipient some relief against higher prices. In private insurance, the benefits may be fixed and therefore more vulnerable to inflation.

SOCIAL INSURANCE COMPARED WITH PUBLIC ASSISTANCE

Although clear-cut differences between social insurance and public assistance are difficult to define precisely, certain dissimilarities appear.[36] They are in the following areas: (1) prediction of eligibility requirements and benefit amounts, (2) demonstration of need, (3) method of financing, (4) level of administration, (5) number of participants, and (6) stigma attached to benefits.

Prediction of Eligibility Requirements and Benefit Amounts

Benefit amounts are generally predictable in social insurance; they are more difficult to predict in public assistance. In social insurance, the law precisely defines the eligibility requirements and benefit amounts; if the amount is not defined precisely, the law contains a formula that enables the worker to compute the size of his benefit. In public assistance, the law seldom spells out precisely the benefit amount. The recipient's benefit is determined by the program administrator's judgment of his need relative to his income and assets, and the concept of need, when related to income and assets, is seldom precisely defined in the law. Moreover, among the various states, there is variation in the concept of need, the amount of income and assets allowed a recipient, and the prevailing standard of living and financial resources; and a poor community or one insensitive to the poor may take a restricted view concerning the benefit to

[36]Turnbull, Williams, and Cheit, *Economic and Social Security,* pp. 10-11.

be paid. For these reasons, a worker seldom considers the availability of public assistance in his financial plans.

Demonstration of Need

Social insurance programs never require a needs test; public assistance always involves a needs test. A person must demonstrate that his income and financial assets are insufficient to maintain himself or his family, and the public-assistance benefit is based on the extent of his *demonstrated need,* in contrast to the *presumed need* on which social insurance is based.[37] Also, social insurance is based on *average need,* whereas public assistance is based on *individual need.* Because of this fact, public assistance may be necessary to supplement social insurance to provide for emergencies and special needs.

Method of Financing

Social insurance benefits are normally financed out of specifically earmarked taxes. However, public-assistance benefits are usually financed out of the general revenues of government, and these are usually derived from a more progressive tax system than the one used to finance social insurance.

Also, in public assistance, the benefit recipient does not make specific contributions to the program before he is eligible for benefits, and there is no relation between the benefits received and the contributions made, since the funds are normally derived from general revenues.

Level of Administration

Public assistance is generally administered by state and local government, whereas social insurance may be administered by the federal government.[38] Because discretion by administrative officials or agencies is necessary in determining need and benefit amount in public assistance, its administration at the state and local level is desirable. However, because the amount of discretion in social insurance is slight and uniformity among the states is highly desirable, some social insurance programs are administered only by the federal government.

Number of Participants

All those participating in social insurance programs are the insureds; only a small percentage of the participants will actually be beneficiaries at any given time. However, the direct participants in public-assistance programs are only the people who receive benefits. Thus, more people are involved in social insurance than in public assistance.

---

[37]For an extensive discussion of demonstrated need, see Burns, *Social Security,* pp. 19-26.

[38]State workmen's compensation and unemployment insurance programs are exceptions.

Stigma to Receipt of Benefits

No stigma is attached to the receipt of social insurance benefits, since recipients have a statutory right to them, without showing need, if the eligibility requirements are met. Many eligible people, however, fail to apply for public assistance because of the needs test, which they consider repugnant and degrading, believing that a stigma is attached to the receipt of public-assistance benefits. Since no stigma is attached to social insurance benefits, relatively few eligible participants refuse to make a claim.

ECONOMIC OBJECTIVES OF SOCIAL INSURANCE

From an economic viewpoint, social insurance programs have several important objectives: to (1) provide basic economic security to the population, (2) prevent poverty, (3) provide stability to the economy, and (4) preserve important values.

Provide Basic Economic Security to the Population

The primary objective of social insurance is to afford basic economic security to most people against the long-range risks of premature death, old age, sickness and disability, and unemployment. As indicated in Chapter 1, these events cause economic insecurity because of the loss of income and additional expenses. Social insurance programs should provide a layer or a base of income protection to the population. In this context, basic economic security means that the social insurance benefit, along with other sources of income and other financial assets, should be sufficiently high to provide a minimum standard of living to most of the population.

Prevent Poverty

By their operations, social insurance programs prevent a considerable amount of poverty. For example, although this is not the sole aim of the OASDHI program, it does tend to prevent a relatively large number of aged persons from falling into poverty. In 1969, the incomes of nearly 4.8 million persons aged 65 and over fell below the poverty line. However, between 1969 and 1974, Congress increased monthly OASDHI benefits several times. This had the powerful effect of reducing substantially the number of aged people who were counted poor. The March 1974 Current Population Survey indicated that about 3.4 million of the aged were counted poor, a sharp reduction in aged poverty of about 29 percent.[39]

---

[39]U.S. Bureau of the Census, *Current Population Reports,* Series P-60, No. 98, "Characteristics of the Low-Income Population: 1973," (Washington, D.C.: U.S. Government Printing Office, 1975), Table H, p. 9.

Although the OASDHI program tends to prevent poverty among the aged, it has serious limitations as an efficient antipoverty tool. These limitations will be discussed more fully in Chapter 6.

Provide Stability to the Economy

Another objective of social insurance is to enhance and contribute to the nation's economic stability. This means that the programs should influence consumption, saving, and investment in a desirable way and should tend to move in a desirable countercyclical direction against the business cycle. For example, unemployment insurance benefits are sensitive to business downswings and tend to pump funds into the economy during periods of unemployment, thereby bolstering and maintaining personal income and consumption. In addition, the methods of financing of the programs should contribute to economic stability.

Although economic-stability considerations are important in social insurance, they must never overshadow and override its primary objective: providing basic economic security to the individual and his family against widespread social risks confronting them. Economists generally tend to evaluate the various programs in terms of their macroeconomic impact on the economy, and view this primary objective as secondary.

Preserve Important Values

A final objective of social insurance is to promote and not stifle the desirable qualities of personal incentives, initiative, and thrift. Many social insurance programs embody the concept that a person's economic security should arise out of his own work, and they relate the worker's right to benefits, the benefit amount, and the benefits received by his family to his earnings. Thus, basing eligibility on a demonstration of work and paying variable benefits related to the worker's wage appear to fit in well with our system of economic incentives. Moreover, social insurance benefits are paid regardless of income received from savings, private pensions, and financial investments. Thrift is thereby promoted, since the worker is encouraged to augment his basic layer of protection by a personal program of savings, investments, and private insurance.

The social insurance technique is an important device in providing economic security. Need is prevented as a result of the work and contributions of the worker and the contributions of his employer. This approach fits in well with our generally accepted system of economic values and personal incentives. Because social insurance is geared to a conservative value system, it has the stability that comes from widespread appeal and acceptance.[40]

---

[40]Robert M. Ball, "Some Reflections on Selected Issues in Social Security," in *Old-Age Income Assurance, A Compendium of Papers on Problems and Policy Issues in the Public and Private Pension System, Part I: General Policy Guidelines,* Subcommittee on Fiscal Policy of the Joint Economic Committee, 90th Cong., 1st sess., (Washington, D.C.: U.S. Government Printing Office, 1967), pp. 49-51.

SUGGESTIONS FOR ADDITIONAL READING

Bowen, William G., Frederick H. Harbison, Richard A. Lester, and Herman M. Somers, eds., *The Princeton Symposium on the American System of Social Insurance: Its Philosophy, Impact, and Future Development.* New York: McGraw-Hill, 1968.

Brown, J. Douglas, *An American Philosophy of Social Security: Evaluation and Issues.* Princeton, N.J.: Princeton University Press, 1972.

Burns, Eveline M., *Social Security and Public Policy.* New York: McGraw-Hill, 1956.

Cohen, Wilbur J., and Milton Friedman, *Social Security: Universal or Selective?* Washington, D.C.: American Enterprise Institute for Public Policy Research, 1972.

Haber, William, and Wilbur J. Cohen, eds., *Social Security: Programs, Problems, and Policies.* Homewood, Ill.: Richard D. Irwin, 1960.

Myers, Robert J., "Is Social Security Really Insurance?" *The Journal of the American Society of Chartered Life Underwriters,* Vol. XXVIII, No. 3 (July 1974).

Pechman, Joseph, Henry J. Aaron, and Michael K. Taussig, *Social Security: Perspectives for Reform.* Washington, D.C.: The Brookings Institution, 1968.

Peterson, Ray M., "Misconceptions and Missing Perceptions of Our Social Security System (Actuarial Anesthesia)," *Transactions of Society of Actuaries,* No. 1 (March 1960).

Richardson, J. Henry, *Economic and Financial Aspects of Social Security: An International Survey.* Toronto: University of Toronto Press, 1960.

Schottland, Charles I., *The Social Security Program in the United States,* 2nd ed. New York: Appleton-Century-Crofts, 1970.

Turnbull, John G., C. Arthur Williams, Jr., and Earl F. Cheit, *Economic and Social Security,* 4th ed. New York: Ronald Press, 1973.

Witte, Edwin E., "The Objectives of Social Security," in Robert J. Lampman, ed., *Social Security Perspectives.* Madison: University of Wisconsin Press, 1962.

chapter 3

The Problem of
Premature Death

Death is a distasteful idea to most Americans. Although everyone must die, the subject of death is seldom discussed between husband and wife, at social affairs, or with friends. Medical schools seldom devote adequate attention to the psychology of death in the training of their students. Physicians are often extremely reluctant to talk openly about death with their terminally ill patients, and hospital nurses generally avoid discussing the subject with such a patient even though he may be segregated from the other patients and knows he is dying. Life insurance agents, even though it is the central fact of their business, avoid discussing death when calling on their clients. Even some ministers are ill-equipped to provide meaningful advice to a bereaved family. And little or no attention is given to the feelings and attitudes of patients who are aware they are terminally ill.

Research on the economic impact of premature death has generally focused on the family's financial situation after the death has occurred. Yet, long before the terminally ill patient actually dies, the family may be experiencing a serious decline in its standard of living, severe financial hardship, disruption of normal family living, emotional problems, and considerable economic insecurity. Any analysis of premature death must consider the economic and psychological impact on the family *before* that death, if it is expected.

More than 9 million American women are widows, most of them older women. Because of premature death of the family head, they must often adjust their consumption level and standard of living downward, and the period of financial readjustment is often painful. Most family heads die with outstanding financial obligations and debts, leaving insufficient amounts of life insurance to reduce or prevent this financial readjustment. The widow may be forced to work to supplement the family's income, and this can create additional problems.

Efforts to work full-time, especially when she has preschool children, often result in a severe drain on her time, energy, and nervous system. In addition, her intense emotional grief may compound her economic insecurity.

Some families are forced into poverty because of premature death of the family head; the family's income from all sources is reduced to below the poverty threshold. Finally, premature death deprives the children of the counsel and guidance of one or both parents during the critical formative years when parental influence on the children's habits, character, education, and intelligence is enormous.

In this chapter, we shall examine the following important areas: (1) nature of premature death, (2) psychology of death, (3) economic impact of premature death on the family both before and after death, and (4) techniques for meeting the problem of premature death.

ECONOMIC PROBLEM OF PREMATURE DEATH

Meaning of Premature Death

Premature death of the family head can be defined as death with unfulfilled financial obligations,[1] such as a wife and family to support, children to educate, or a mortgage to be paid. In this sense, the death is considered premature if it occurs between the ages of 14 and 65. A person younger than 14 is less likely to be employed full-time, to be married, or to have dependents; and since retirement at age 65 is customary, employment opportunities after that age are limited, and the family head is less likely to have children depending on him for financial support.

Premature death causes economic insecurity to the family in at least four ways: First, the human-life value is lost to the family; the family's share of the deceased's future income is lost forever. Second, additional expenses may be incurred because of burial costs, expenses of last illness, probate costs, estate and inheritance taxes, and the forced liquidation of assets. Third, the family may be uncertain regarding the continuation and amount of future income. Finally, the family may be confronted with the additional problem of insufficient income. It should be noted, however, that economic insecurity from insufficient income, uncertainty of income, and additional expenses may occur months and years before the family head dies. This important point will be developed more fully later in the chapter.

Loss of Human-Life Value

The loss of the human-life value by premature death can be enormous, especially if death occurs at a relatively young age. The human-life value is defined as the capitalized value of a worker's net future earnings. It represents

[1]John G. Turnbull, *The Changing Faces of Economic Insecurity* (Minneapolis: University of Minnesota Press, 1966), p. 13.

the family's share of the deceased's future income, which is lost forever by premature death.[2]

The human-life value can be estimated by four steps:

1. Estimate the family head's expected annual earnings net after taxes.
2. Estimate his annual expenses for personal maintenance.
3. Estimate his working-life expectancy.
4. Select an appropriate discount rate.

Then multiply 1 minus 2 by the present value of $1 annually for the period determined in 3 at the rate of discount selected in 4. For example, assume that a family head aged 35 earns $16,000 annually, and expects his income to remain at this level in the future. Personal income taxes are estimated to be $2,000; his personal-maintenance expenses are estimated to be $4,000; he has a working-life expectancy of 28.6 years (average number of years that he can expect to be both alive and working); and a 5 percent discount rate is selected. The present value of $1 annually for 28.6 years, payable in twelve equal monthly installments, is $15.38. Thus, his human-life value is ($14,000 — $4,000) x $15.38, or $153,800. This sum represents the family's share of his future income based on his working-life expectancy, which is lost forever by premature death. The preceding illustration clearly indicates that the loss of human-life value is monumental.

Causes of Death

Some major causes of death in the United States are heart disease, cancer, motor vehicle and other accidents, pneumonia and influenza, and suicide and homicide. The percentage distribution of these causes can be broken down as follows:[3]

Heart disease	51%
Cancer	20
Other diseases	17
Motor vehicle and other accidents	7
Pneumonia and influenza	3
Suicide and homicide	2

More than a million Americans die annually from heart disease, and more than 340,000 cancer deaths occur each year. In addition, more than 55,000 persons die annually from motor vehicle accidents, with half the deaths involving motorists or pedestrians under the influence of alcohol.

Suicide, also one of the top ten causes of death in the United States, is a

[2]For an extensive discussion of this concept, see Kenneth Black, Jr., "Human Life Values," in Davis W. Gregg and Vane B. Lucas, eds., *Life and Health Insurance Handbook*, 3rd ed. (Homewood, Ill.: Richard D. Irwin, 1973), pp. 17-26.

[3]Institute of Life Insurance, *Life Insurance Fact Book, 1974* (New York: Institute of Life Insurance, 1974), p. 92.

leading cause of death at the younger ages. Although suicide officially accounts for about 1 percent of all deaths, the actual suicide rate may be twice the reported figures.[4] Suicide data based on cause-of-death certification may be grossly understated because of reluctance to admit the suicidal intent of friends and relatives and the difficulty in recognizing suicide under certain circumstances.[5] For example, many automobile deaths involving only the driver are reported as accidents, when suicide is the actual cause of death.

Chances of Dying Prematurely

The chances of dying prematurely have declined over time because of breakthroughs in medical science, improvements in public health and sanitation, and increased economic growth and development. However, those chances are generally higher than is commonly believed, especially at the younger ages. Based on total-population death rates, the chances at various selected ages of dying before age 65 are as follows:[6]

Age 20	299 out of 1,000
Age 30	286 out of 1,000
Age 40	267 out of 1,000
Age 50	219 out of 1,000
Age 60	104 out of 1,000

THE PSYCHOLOGY OF DEATH

Until recently, there was little meaningful research on the psychology of death and the attitudes of dying patients. Research data were scarce and difficult to obtain. Physicians were often defensive in talking about death and refused to permit their terminally ill patients to be interviewed, in order to protect them. Family members, relatives, and nurses normally avoided discussing death with a terminally ill patient, in order to avoid upsetting him.

In a pathbreaking study based on interviews with dying patients, Dr. Elisabeth Kubler-Ross has provided valuable information concerning the attitudes and emotions of dying patients and the psychology of death. A person who has a terminal illness, Dr. Kubler-Ross finds, generally reacts by progressing through five distinct stages: (1) denial, (2) anger, (3) bargaining, (4) depression, and (5) acceptance.[7]

---

[4]U.S. Department of Health, Education and Welfare, Public Health Service, *Suicide in the United States: 1950-1964*, National Center for Health Statistics, Series 20, No. 5 (Washington, D.C.: U.S. Government Printing Office, 1967), p. 1.

[5]*Ibid.*

[6]*Life Insurance Fact Book, 1974*, pp. 108-9. The mortality data are based on total-population death rates in the United States, 1959-61.

[7]Elisabeth Kubler-Ross, *On Death and Dying* (New York: Macmillan, 1969), pp. 38-137. The following discussion is based on this material.

Denial Stage

As a temporary stage of shock, from which he gradually recovers, denial is the first reaction of a person who is made aware of his terminal illness. It is a stage of disbelief. The patient simply cannot believe he has a severe illness, such as leukemia, Hodgkin's disease, terminal cancer, or malignant brain tumor. He denies the existence of the problem, and that he must eventually die of it.

Anger Stage

Anger is the second stage in a terminal illness. After the patient is unable to maintain the denial stage any longer, he reacts with strong feelings of anger, rage, and resentment. An attitude of "Why must this happen to me?" is common. The terminally ill patient is often angry at physicians, nurses, and the hospital. He may complain bitterly about the competence of physicians, the tests they prescribe, and the quality of medical care they provide. Nurses are often a special target of his anger. Family and staff members may often react with anger of their own, which only fuels the patient's hostile behavior.

Bargaining Stage

The anger stage is often followed by a stage in which the terminally ill patient, willing to do anything to stay alive a little longer, hopes to be thus rewarded for exceptionally good behavior. For example, an opera star with cancer may wish to stay alive just long enough to give one more performance; a mother wants to remain alive until her son's wedding. Often, patients try to make bargains with God to gain additional time.

Depression Stage

Depression is the fourth stage in a terminal illness. Aside from the knowledge of his impending death, the patient may be deeply depressed because of extensive hospitalization, unsuccessful surgery, and physical pain. The piling up of catastrophic medical expenses from an extended illness can also cause immense grief to a dying patient. He may be forced to sell his house or be unable to send his children through college because of the high medical costs that are being incurred, for which private health insurance benefits may be inadequate. In addition, the dying patient may be further depressed because he cannot work, and the family may have inadequate income on which to live. The mother may be forced to work to support the family, thereby depriving the children of the attention they need. When these financial burdens are added to the emotional burden, the terminally ill patient is often deeply depressed.

Acceptance Stage

Acceptance is the final stage in a terminal illness. The patient accepts the fact that he must die. It is not necessarily a feeling of serenity or happiness, but merely an acknowledgment that death is near. The patient may be in a weakened condition, may sleep often, and may wish to be left alone. He may no longer be interested in visitors and is often uncommunicative. The presence of close family members or friends is often reassuring to the dying patient.

ECONOMIC IMPACT OF PREMATURE DEATH ON THE FAMILY

Any analysis of premature death must consider the economic impact on the family both *before* the terminally ill family head dies and *after* death occurs. The Kubler-Ross study provides valuable information concerning the emotional problems and grief of the family members during the periods before and after death. In addition, the Life Underwriter Training Council and Life Insurance Agency Management Association made a study of widows of men who died before age 65 in four metropolitan cities; the study provides extremely valuable data on the family's standard of living and financial adjustments both before and after the family head dies.[8]

Impact before Death Occurs

An impending premature death in the family often involves a serious disruption of family life, an extended duration of illness, reduced-employment status, decline in family income, and substantial medical expenses. In addition, most wives are inadequately prepared for widowhood.

Disruption of Family Household. When the husband is terminally ill, the family's normal living patterns are often seriously disrupted. The wife must perform many tasks formerly performed by her husband; family meals are irregular; if the family's income is inadequate, the wife may be forced to work, further disrupting the normal household schedule. In addition, the wife may have intense negative feelings of guilt, resentment, anger, and loneliness. Finally, there is often a serious lack of communication between the wife and her terminally ill husband.[9]

Duration of Illness or Disability. Premature death often strikes suddenly, without warning. *The Widows Study* indicated that death was instantaneous for about one-third of the husbands. In the majority of cases, however, the husbands were ill or disabled for longer periods before death occurred. More than one-half lingered on for at least one month before they died; more than one-fourth were sick or disabled for at least a year before they died. An extended duration of illness or disability often results in substantial medical bills and a serious decline in the family's income.

[8]Life Underwriter Training Council and Life Insurance Agency Management Association, *The Widows Study,* Vol. 1, *The Onset of Widowhood* (Hartford, Conn.: Life Underwriter Training Council and Life Insurance Agency Management Association, 1970). See also *The Widows Study,* Vol. 2, *Adjustment to Widowhood: The First Two Years* (Hartford, 1971). The following discussion is based on these sources. It should be noted that the dollar amounts reported refer to the 1966-68 period; today, the results could be quite different.

[9]Kubler-Ross, *On Death and Dying,* pp. 157-60.

Reduced-Employment Status.   A serious impairment can severely reduce the husband's employment opportunities. *The Widows Study* revealed that only 69 percent of the husbands were employed at the time of death. The husband's employment status was inversely related to the duration of illness or disability. Ninety percent of the husbands who died within one week after the onset of their terminal illness or disability were employed; but only 34 percent of those who were ill or disabled for two years or more were employed at the time of their death.

Finally, some wives may enter the labor force to compensate for the reduction in family income. There is reason to believe that, as the duration of terminal illness or disability increases, the proportion of families with a working wife also tends to increase.

Decline in Family Income.   An extended duration of terminal illness or disability often results in a decline in family income, or if family income does not decline, it may increase less rapidly because of the impairment. Opportunities for promotion and advancement in position may be limited; the number of hours of work may be reduced; the husband may be forced to shift to a less demanding but lower-paying job; there may be a complete loss of income to the family if the husband is unable to work; there may also be a loss of substantial group insurance benefits to the survivors. Finally, as the duration of terminal illness or disability increases, some families may fall below the poverty level of income, and thereby experience great economic insecurity.

The Widows Study also indicated that family incomes during the year prior to the husband's death tended to be lower than those of an age-equivalent segment of the total population.[10] This can be illustrated by the following income distribution, which compares the proportion of families at various income levels in the year before the death with a comparable age-equivalent segment of the population.[11]

Family Income before Death		
Income	*The Widows Study*	*Estimated U.S. Age-Equivalent*
$ 15,000 or more	9%	19%
$ 10,000 - $ 14,999	22	29
$ 5,000 - $ 9,999	48	40
Under $ 5,000	20	12

As we see, only 31 percent of the widows reported family incomes exceeding $10,000 at the time their husbands died, compared with an expected 48 percent for an age-equivalent segment of the population; and 20 percent of the widows reported family incomes below $5,000, compared with an expected 12 percent for comparable age-equivalent families. These relatively lower incomes can be

[10]An age-equivalent segment of the total population is, in this case, one in which the characteristics of individuals or families in the total population are adjusted to match the age distribution of males who die between ages 25 and 64.

[11]*The Widows Study.* Vol. 1, p. 19, Table 8.

accounted for, at least partly, by the income reductions that occurred during the husband's final year. In addition, the widows were asked to compare the family's income before and after death, and to account for any differences. It is important to note that overall, 21 percent of the widows reported a decline in income directly related to the husband's illness or disability. Thus, the longer the duration of terminal illness or disability, the greater the likelihood that the family's income will be relatively lower than for comparable age-equivalent families in the population.

If the family's income is insufficient in terms of their needs, this can result in a poverty level of living. The adequacy of the family's income can be compared with the budget standards developed by the Bureau of Labor Statistics of the U.S. Department of Labor. Three budgets are developed: higher standard, moderate standard, and lower standard. If the family's income falls below the lower standard, the family can be considered to be living in poverty. The incidence of poverty tends to increase as the duration of terminal illness or disability increases. The following table indicates the proportion of families that have attained different standards of living according to the duration of the husband's terminal illness or disability:[12]

Standard of Living by Duration of
Terminal Illness or Disability

Standard of Living	1 day	1 month but under 6 months	2 years or more	Total
Higher standard	39%	31%	18%	28%
Moderate standard	25	26	21	24
Lower standard	20	24	21	23
Below lower standard	16	19	40	25

One-fourth of the widows were living in poverty before their husband's death. As the duration of terminal illness increased, however, the proportion of families living in poverty also tended to increase. Forty percent of the widows whose husbands were terminally ill or disabled for two years or more before death were living in poverty. Thus, it is clear that, for some families, economic insecurity from insufficient income can occur long before the husband actually dies.

Finally, many families with terminally ill or disabled husbands have insufficient financial assets before the death. About one in three widows had no financial assets before the husband's death, and one-half had financial assets of less than $1,000. Financial assets included liquid assets, stocks, mutual funds, net value of real estate excluding the home, and miscellaneous savings and investment. A prolonged terminal illness, which results in substantial medical expenses, can severely deplete the family's liquid savings. Also, an extended disability can result in both an income reduction and failure to realize a growth in income, which makes it more difficult for the family to accumulate future addi-

---

[12]*Ibid.*, p. 21, Table 11.

tional savings and financial assets. Thus, for many families, a cushion of liquid
assets is disturbingly absent before death.

Substantial Medical Expenses.   An extended duration of terminal illness
or disability can result in substantial medical expenses to the family. When the
duration of impariment was six months to two years, about one-fourth of the
widows reported medical expenses exceeding $5,000.

Medical costs, however, were unevenly distributed among the widows. For
those families in which the husbands had incurred medical expenses, average
expenses were $2,800, of which health insurance paid an average of only 60
percent. However, only two-thirds of the families with medical expenses
reported receiving health insurance payments; for this group, health insurance
paid 77 percent of the total expenses.

Inadequate Preparation for Widowhood.   The Widows Study indicated
that about seven out of ten husbands died without a will; and fewer than one in
five widows had discussed with their husbands the need for life insurance protection and the disposition of the policy proceeds if death should occur. Only
one in four indicated that the husband's needs for life insurance had been pro-
grammed. In addition, over half the widows had little or no knowledge of
OASDHI survivorship benefits. Finally, in those families where the husband
handled the family funds, almost two-thirds of the widows reported difficulty in
money management. Thus, these data clearly indicate most wives are inadequately prepared to become widows.

In summary, for many families, economic insecurity from premature
death does not occur suddenly but may begin months and years before the
husband finally dies. In the professional literature on economic insecurity, the
risks of premature death, substantial medical costs, and unemployment are
generally analyzed separately. It must be recognized, however, that all three
risks may be simultaneously present in the premature-death problem. *The
Widows Study* clearly indicates this point. All the women had lost their husbands; almost four in ten families had medical expenses exceeding $1,000; and
in three out of ten families, the husband lost his job before dying. In short, any
attack on premature death must also consider protection against the other risks
that simultaneously accompany the problem.

Impact after Death Occurs

After the husband finally dies, the widow is often confronted with problems of loneliness and grief, payment of final expenses, inadequate life insurance proceeds, and a decline in her former standard of living. In addition, many
widows must work to augment the family's income. On the positive side, in
some cases the family's financial-asset position may be substantially improved
after the death.

Loneliness and Grief.   After her husband's death, the widow often experiences intense emotional suffering. About four out of ten widows reporting
indicated that loneliness was their most serious problem in widowhood. Most

felt a deep sense of loss and lack of companionship after the death of their husbands. A painful period of psychological readjustment was necessary. During this readjustment period, many widows felt bitter, angry, and numb. In addition, the children may experience considerable guilt feelings and remorse after a parent dies.[13]

Finally, many widows have serious problems in raising their children without fathers, especially when the children are below high school age, and particularly in the case of boys. One out of five widows indicated problems in raising children in the absence of their father.

Payment of Final Expenses. In addition to loss of the husband's income, a widow has the burden of funeral expenses, medical bills, estate taxes, administration expenses, installment loans, and other expenses that must be paid. The average widow reported $3,900 in final expenses. Life and health insurance paid about two-thirds. The remainder was paid by savings, estate assets, and other miscellaneous sources.

The amount of final expenses is closely related to the duration of illness or disability and to the family's income. The longer the duration of illness, the greater will be the medical expenses incurred. And the higher the family's income, the greater the final expenses will be, because of higher estate administration costs, estate taxes, and installment loans.

Inadequate Life Insurance. Most terminally ill husbands have inadequate life insurance protection. Average life insurance benefits received by widows of insured husbands amounted to $9,900, and about half received less than $5,000. And life insurance proceeds are often quickly depleted; one in four widows indicated that the proceeds were exhausted shortly after the death.

In addition, relatively few widows—only 8 percent of those reporting—received income payments under the various settlement options. It is apparent that life insurance agents are not advising widows concerning the various income options open to them. More than eight out of every ten widows said no one had advised them regarding this choice when the claim was paid. This is disturbing, since monthly payments under the various income options could have provided some economic security to these families. The loss of income from premature death could have been offset, at least partly, by the greater use of life insurance settlement options.

Finally, most deceased husbands made no provision for paying off the mortgage with life insurance. Fewer than one out of eight families with mortgages made such provisions.

Decline in Standard of Living. Many families experience a sharp decline in income and living standards after the husband's death. It is again important to stress that the income decline can occur long before the actual death, especially if the duration of disability is prolonged.

The following table illustrates the distribution of family incomes both before and after death:[14]

[13]Kubler-Ross, *On Death and Dying,* pp. 179-88.

[14]*The Widows Study,* Vol. 2, pp. 16-17.

Distribution of Family Income in the Predeath and Postdeath Periods

	Under $3,000	$3,000-$4,999	$5,000-$6,999	$7,000-$9,999	$10,000-$14,999	$15,000 or more
Predeath, normal year	5%	10%	20%	29%	25%	11%
Postdeath period	23%	27%	24%	18%	6%	2%

As the data indicate, there is a pronounced downward shift in income after the husband's death. The median income for the families during the year of death was $8,420. Two years later, the median income had declined to $4,910, or by about 42 percent.

It is also valuable to compare the family's standard of living before and after the husband's death. Two criteria can be used to evaluate the adequacy of the family's income: (1) the widow's perception of changes in her standard of living, and (2) comparison of the family's income with the bench-mark budgets developed by the Bureau of Labor Statistics (BLS).

With respect to the first criterion, half the widows said that their standard of living was lower after the husband's death. One out of five indicated that the reduction was substantial.

With respect to the second criterion, the widow's income can be compared with the various BLS budgets to determine the standard of living actually attained. The following data indicate the proportion of families with different standards of living before and after the husband's death.[15]

Duration of Husband's Terminal Illness

BLS-Defined Standard	Less than 6 months		6 months or more		All families	
	Predeath	Postdeath	Predeath	Postdeath	Predeath	Postdeath
Higher standard	35%	23%	17%	23%	28%	23%
Adequate standard	26	19	22	19	24	19
Lower standard	22	26	24	26	23	26
Below lower standard	17	32	37	32	25	32
	100%	100%	100%	100%	100%	100%

Before death, 52 percent of all families had incomes equal to or greater than the modest but adequate budget. After death, the proportion of families meeting this standard declined to 42 percent. Before death, one in four families was living in poverty; after death, about one in three lived in poverty.

One effect of the lower standard of living is the pervasive concern about money. Many families were forced to cut all unnecessary spending and were afraid of going into debt. Cutbacks in food, clothing, and recreation were commonly reported. Plans for college education of the children were altered in many families.

Finally, changes in the standard of living before and after death were rela-

[15]*Ibid.*, p. 23, Table 3.

tively small for those families in which husbands were terminally ill for six months or more. When the illness was prolonged, death actually produced a small net improvement in their standard of living based on BLS budgets. This reflects the point stressed earlier: *The long-term illness or disability resulted in a modification of living standards long before the husband's death. After his death, many families experienced little or no further reduction in their standard of living.*

Increase in Working Wives. After the husband's death occurs, many widows are forced to work to supplement the family's income. During the year before the husband died, 47 percent of the widows in the study worked. After his death, the proportion of working wives increased to 56 percent, a net change of 9 percentage points. But this figure understates the impact of death on the widow's need to work, since many wives enter the labor market long before their husbands actually die, especially when the duration of terminal illness or disability is prolonged. Because family income may decline long before death in a prolonged terminal illness, many wives must go to work before the death occurs.

Improved Financial-Asset Position. On the positive side, many families significantly improved their financial-asset position after the husband's death. In the predeath period, fewer than seven out of ten families had some financial assets. In the postdeath period, about eight out of ten families had some assets in reserve two years after the husbands passed away. This is not surprising. After their husbands died, most widows received lump-sum cash settlements from life insurance, survivor benefits under other programs, gifts, and receipts from the sale of household possessions and business interests. Median assets before death were only $1,000, compared to median cash benefits received of $6,050 after the husbands died. The bulk of the cash came from life insurance. Finally, the greater the widow's financial-asset position after death, the more likely she would be to state that she had maintained her former standard of living.

In summary, the three most serious problems of widowhood are (1) loneliness, (2) financial problems, and (3) raising the children without their father. The preceding data clearly indicate that premature death causes great economic insecurity.

MEETING THE PROBLEM OF PREMATURE DEATH

Numerous public and private income-maintenance programs and other techniques are used to meet the problem of premature death. These approaches include the following: (1) loss prevention, (2) employment earnings, (3) OASDHI benefits, (4) private life insurance and private-pension benefits, (5) investment income, (6) veterans' benefits, (7) relatives, friends, and charities, and (8) public assistance and other miscellaneous sources of income.

Loss Prevention

Loss prevention is the ideal technique for meeting the risk of premature death. Both private and public loss-prevention activities can reduce this probability. Traditional private loss-prevention methods include health education, medical research, accident prevention, and individual medical examinations. *Predictive medicine* is a new and exciting approach for reducing the incidence of high-risk diseases, such as heart attacks, cancer, diabetes, and strokes. The physician seeks clues indicating that an otherwise healthy person will later contract a high-risk disease. For example, a blood serum test can reveal the future possibility of emphysema, which might be prevented by not smoking. Other tests, such as multiphasic screening, are designed to detect symptoms in an otherwise healthy person that indicate the high probability of his dying from a certain disease. Preventive measures can then be prescribed. Predictive medicine offers great potential for reducing premature death in the future.[16]

Public loss-prevention activities can also reduce the probability of premature death. These activities include public health and sanitation measures, reduction of air and water pollution, control of communicable diseases, regulation of food and drugs, highway and occupational safety programs, early detection of childhood diseases, and many other techniques.

Employment Earnings

The widow's employment earnings are another important factor in attacking economic insecurity from premature death. *The Widows Study* indicated that earnings from work were the largest single source of income to the surviving dependents. A widow who can work after her husband's death is more likely to maintain or improve her previous standard of living. In many cases, the widow has no choice but to work if the survivorship benefits from the OASDHI program, private pensions, and other income-maintenance programs are insufficient for meeting the family's needs. And working has the additional advantage of helping her overcome her loneliness and grief.

Numerous obstacles, however, must be overcome if the widow wishes to work. First, she may have young preschool children who require her presence in the home. If she attempts to work by placing her children in a day-care center or by hiring a baby-sitter, additional expenses are incurred, reducing the family's income.

Second, even if free child-care centers are available, especially in the case of low-income mothers, that availability will not result in a vast inflow of mothers into the labor force. The reasons are that many low-income mothers outside the labor force are not interested in working; the wages paid may be insufficient to attract them from the home; the wage-subsidy effect of day-care provisions is often low; and public-assistance laws under the Aid to Families with Dependent Children program may discourage entry into the labor force. Finally, the additional role of a working mother, when added to the normal mother's role, may prove too great a strain for many women. For these reasons, adequate day-care centers may not produce the desired labor-force response.[17]

---

[16]James Carberry, "Early Warnings: Physicians Can Detect Clues That Indicate Chance of an Illness," *Wall Street Journal*, November 8, 1972, p. 1.

[17]See Jack Ditmore and W.R. Prosser, *A Study of Day Care's Effect on the Labor Force Participation of Low-Income Mothers*, Evaluation Division, Office of Planning, Research and Evaluation, Office of Economic Opportunity, June 1973.

Third, even if the children are in school or day-care centers and the widow can work, she may lack employable skills, or her present work skills may be obsolete. Many employed widows work in low-paying occupations, such as service, sales, and household work, where few skills are required and part-time work often predominates. Also, if the widow is an older woman, she may experience some discrimination by employers because of her age. Everything else equal, the younger applicant is likely to receive preference for the job over the older widow.

Fourth, the OASDHI earnings test can reduce or terminate the widow's survivorship benefits. Unless substantial modification is made in the test, emphasis on increased employment earnings may be self-defeating, because the widow's monthly benefits may be reduced.

Finally, many widows prefer to stay home to raise their children during the critical formative years. The decision of whether to work and improve the family's financial position or to remain at home to care for the children is often a hard choice.

OASDHI Benefits

OASDHI survivorship benefits are extremely important in reducing economic insecurity from premature death. Next to employment earnings, they are the second most important source of income to widows and orphans. The benefits include both monthly income payments to widows with dependent children, and a nominal funeral benefit.

The Widows Study indicated that more than nine out of ten widows received some OASDHI survivorship benefits. Most widows receiving monthly income benefits said that the benefits were of great help in maintaining their standard of living and preventing financial hardship. Without the benefits, they would be deeply in debt, would have experienced financial hardship, would have to work to increase their income, and would have to give up their homes or apartments.

Although the OASDHI program provides an important layer of income protection, the economic position of some widows is still precarious. Not all widows receive monthly income payments. *The Widows Study* revealed that most widows received a modest funeral benefit, but four out of ten did not receive any monthly cash payments. Many widows are ineligible for monthly OASDHI benefits because they are under age 60 and have no children under age 18 in their care. Or they may work and earn an income in excess of the earnings-test limitation, resulting in a reduction or termination of their monthly benefits. Also, some younger widows may remarry, thereby losing their benefits. Finally, a small number of widows fail to apply for benefits, or the deceased husband had insufficient work experience to qualify for benefits.

The problem of an older widow without children is difficult. Since OASDHI monthly cash benefits may not be available, if other income sources are inadequate, the older widow must find a job. Employment opportunities may be limited because of her age, because she lacks highly paid skills, or because of an ineffective job search. An older widow with limited employment opportunities may find it extremely difficult to attain meaningful economic security. One suggestion that has been made is to provide a readjustment or transition benefit for a few months or years after the husband's death. Another solution is the payment of a widow's pension under a private pension plan.

Private Life Insurance

Both individual and group life insurance benefits are excellent techniques for attacking the problem of premature death. Private individual life insurance, however, is not being used to the maximum extent possible. *The Widows Study* clearly indicates that most husbands die underinsured, with only a small fraction of their human-life values insured. Many family heads fail to recognize that, as their family needs change over time, the amount of life insurance coverage should also change, since it often becomes inadequate because of rapid increases in inflation, upgrading of aspirations, increases in productivity and real wages, and substantial improvements in the nation's standard of living. Failure to upgrade the amount of life insurance is especially prevalent with older husbands who purchased their insurance many years prior to their death. *The Widows Study* also indicated that agents should attempt to sell more life insurance to the over-40 market, which undoubtedly contains a large proportion of family heads who need significantly larger amounts of life insurance than they currently own. More aggressive selling to this market could do much to reduce future economic insecurity from premature death.

In addition, most family heads are not utilizing the income settlement options. After death occurs, the family requires continuous and adequate replacement income, which can be partly provided by greater use of these options. Yet, as we saw, most widows did not receive any monthly income payments under the various settlement options.

Although individual life insurance can significantly reduce economic insecurity from premature death, certain limitations must be recognized. Life insurance may not be available if the family head is uninsurable; the lower-income groups, most in need of protection, lack the ability to pay for large amounts of insurance; the insured often receives poor advice from his agent concerning the type of insurance to purchase. In many cases, substantial amounts of term insurance can be justified for younger family heads, whose need for protection is great but whose income is limited. Some husbands are persuaded to purchase the more expensive types of insurance, such as a 20-payment life or endowment policy, and are substantially underinsured as a result. In addition, many family heads have inadequate knowledge of life insurance and believe they have no need for additional coverage. Finally, agents often give inadequate service and advice to their clients, regarding not only settlement options, but also the programming, disposition, and investment of policy proceeds.

Group life insurance also offers great potential in reducing economic insecurity from premature death. Most employers provide some group life insurance benefits to their workers. Group insurance has the advantages of low-cost protection, mass coverage, and the availability of insurance even if the worker is substandard or uninsurable. The coverage is normally available with no evidence of insurability required if the employee applies before or during his eligibility period.

Present group life insurance, however, has two major disadvantages that limit its effectiveness in attacking economic insecurity from premature death. First, the amount of group life insurance on an employee's life is relatively low. The average certificate is about $8,000, which is generally inadequate for most families.[18] Second, and more important, as in the case of individual insurance, most widows do not receive group insurance proceeds in the form of monthly income. The widow needs both continuous and adequate monthly replacement income after her husband's death to maintain her previous standard of living, but although group life insurance settlement options are generally available, they are seldom used. *The Widows Study* indicated that only 2 percent of the widows entitled to group life insurance benefits received the proceeds under an income option.

There is a great need for group life insurance benefits to be paid as monthly income to the survivors for an extended period. Moreover, the monthly income should be related to the worker's salary and family needs. In this respect, Survivor Income Benefit Insurance (SIBI) offers tremendous potential in reducing economic insecurity from premature death. SIBI benefits are paid only if a qualified survivor exists, such as an unmarried wife. In addition, there is no lump-sum payment. The benefits, which are related to the worker's earnings, are paid in equal monthly installments. The monthly payments are generally a maximum of 40 percent of the worker's monthly earnings and are paid to the wife until she remarries, dies, or attains age 62. If children's benefits are included, they are paid until the youngest unmarried child attains age 19 or until there is no living unmarried child.[19] SIBI benefits, along with monthly OASDHI survivorship benefits, practically guarantee that the family can maintain its former standard of living after the worker's death.

Private-Pension Death Benefits

Most private pensions provide some benefits if death occurs prior to retirement. About one out of three widows surveyed in *The Widows Study* said they had received benefits from a retirement plan after their husbands died.

Several preretirement death benefits are available, depending on the type of plan.[20] In a contributory plan, the employee's contributions are refunded to the widow. In a fully insured individual plan, such as a retirement-income contract, a death benefit is paid equal to $1,000 for each $10 of monthly income, or the reserve if greater. Group permanent pension plans also provide death benefits. Also, in many group pension contracts or trust-fund plans, death benefits may be available from group term life insurance, commonly one or two times the employee's annual earnings.

[18]*Life Insurance Fact Book, 1974,* p. 26.

[19]William G. Williams, "Group Life Insurance," in Gregg and Lucas, eds., *Life and Health Insurance Handbook,* pp. 384-85.

[20]Joseph J. Melone and Everett T. Allen, Jr., *Pension Planning,* rev. ed. (Homewood, Ill.: Richard D. Irwin, 1972), pp. 50-52.

In addition, a widow's pension may be available in some plans, providing monthly income to the widow of an employee who dies after meeting certain requirements. Although interest in a widow's pension is increasing, most plans do not provide this benefit; certain social considerations associated with it may restrict its growth. There is the problem of whether benefits should be paid to the widow if she was married to the deceased worker for less than a certain minimum number of years. Also, some plans pay benefits only if the widow remains unmarried, so there arises the problem of determining whether the widow is still eligible for benefits.

Finally, death benefits may also be available to the widow from a profit-sharing or deferred-compensation plan.

Private-pension death benefits are generally inadequate for attacking economic insecurity from premature death in a meaningful way. Although most private pension plans provide some death benefits, these often consist of relatively small lump sums rather than adequate monthly survivorship benefits providing continuous monthly income to the widows and children. Many thoughtful scholars have called attention to this big gap in private pensions. Professor Merton C. Bernstein has proposed the widespread addition of significant survivorship benefits to private pensions. Although this would require larger pension contributions, the additional cost does not appear to be unmanageable.[21] Finally, private pension plans do not cover the entire labor force; slightly more than half the workers are covered. Thus, pension survivorship benefits are not available to widows whose husbands are ineligible or are not participating in a private plan.

Investment Income

Interest, investment, and rental income can also be used to supplement the family's income after the husband's death. As *The Widows Study* indicated, relatively few widows had accumulated substantial financial assets prior to the death, and investment income was only a small fraction of the total income received. During the postdeath period, however, widows at all income levels received higher amounts of investment income than when their husbands were alive. Before his death, about 5 percent of total annual family income ($450) was received by all families in the form of interest, investment, and rental income. After the death, investment income from these sources more than doubled, to about 17 percent of total family income ($910).[22]

How can this paradox be explained? The increased interest and investment income generally resulted from the life insurance proceeds that accounted for most of the lump-sum assets the widows received following their husbands' deaths. That portion of the proceeds not needed for final expenses was saved or invested to provide additional income.

The preceding discussion indicates that the widow's need to maintain substantial cash reserves for everyday purposes may be greater than is commonly realized. Like most normal families, widows need cash reserves for large non-

[21]Merton C. Bernstein, *The Future of Private Pensions* (New York: Free Press, 1964), p. 183.

[22]*The Widows Study,* Vol. 2, p. 24, Table 4.

recurring expenditures—for instance, a wedding, a new roof, or college costs. Funds are also needed for the widow's retirement. In a family where the husband is present, a substantial expenditure can be made out of accumulated reserves, which can then be rebuilt for future needs. This is generally not true for a widow. Once she makes a substantial nonrecurring expenditure, she may have little future opportunity to rebuild her cash reserves to their level at the onset of widowhood. As she depletes her cash reserves, her economic security is also being eroded. Her realization that cash reserves may not be replenished explains why some widows have a strong desire to keep the life insurance proceeds intact and not use them for supplemental income.[23]

Veterans' Benefits

The widows of deceased veterans may also be eligible for certain benefits, including up to $250 for funeral expenses and a continuing pension if they meet certain conditions. One out of three widows reported receiving some veterans' benefits after their husbands' death.[24] The various programs for veterans will be analyzed in Chapter 20.

Relatives and Friends

Relatives and friends can also help meet the problem of premature death. Gifts of money are the most common type of assistance given; about one in four widows received money from relatives and friends after their husbands' death. This sort of financial assistance, however, is generally ineffective as a long-run solution to economic insecurity from premature death. The amount is usually small, amounting to less than $500 in most cases.[25] More important, the widow needs adequate and continuing income to attain meaningful economic security, and few friends or relatives are financially able to provide continuous financial assistance to a bereaved family. Temporary assistance, however, in the form of gifts and loans can be especially valuable until other income is received, from the OASDHI program or from other sources. It often takes three months or more before OASDHI survivorship benefits are received, and temporary financial aid from relatives and friends can be extremely helpful during this period.

Private Charities

Private charities—churches, labor unions, fraternal organizations, and charitable institutions such as the Salvation Army—may also provide temporary financial assistance to widows. The effectiveness, however, of private charities in reducing economic insecurity from premature death is limited. As in the case of relatives and friends, the amount of aid that private charities can provide is

[23]*Ibid.*, p. 7.

[24]*The Widows Study*, Vol. 1, p. 55.

[25]*Ibid.*, p. 56.

limited. Few of them are financially able to provide continuous income payments to a large number of widows. In addition, some widows with children who
need financial help find it repugnant to appeal to private charities for it. Most
widows would not consider charity an acceptable solution to their need for continuous and adequate income.

Public Assistance

Public-assistance benefits may also be available to some widows and their
children; however, these benefits are relatively unimportant in meeting the
problem of premature death. *The Widows Study* revealed that only 3 percent of
the widows received welfare assistance after their husbands' death.[26]

Increased dependence on public assistance is an ineffective solution to the
problem of premature death. Many widows are reluctant to apply for public
assistance because of the stigma attached to the benefits. Also, the needs test
and stringent eligibility requirements may disqualify some widows who apply for
benefits; they are simply not poor enough to qualify for aid. Finally, if aid is
received, the income is generally insufficient for meeting the full needs of the
widow and her chilren; unfulfilled need makes if difficult to attain economic
security, because a reasonable standard of living is not being attained.

Other Sources of Income

The family may also be eligible to receive monthly income payments from
other public income-maintenance programs, including civil service death
benefits, railroad retirement death benefits, and workmen's compensation if the
death is related to the job.

In addition, the widow may receive funds from the sale of her husband's
business interest or from the sale of certain household possessions no longer
needed. For example, after the husband's death, boats, shop tools, hobby
equipment, and sporting equipment may not be needed. About one-fourth of
the widows surveyed in *The Widows Study* received funds from the sale of goods
and possessions.[27]

[26]*Ibid.*, p. 57.
[27]*Ibid.*, p. 56.

SUGGESTIONS FOR ADDITIONAL READING

Black, Kenneth, Jr., "Human Life Values," in Davis W. Gregg and Vane
B. Lucas, eds., *Life and Health Insurance Handbook,* 3rd ed.
Homewood, Ill.: Richard D. Irwin, 1973.

Caine, Lynn, *Widow.* New York: Morrow, 1974.

Kubler-Ross, Elisabeth, *On Death and Dying.* New York: Macmillan,
1969.

Life Underwriter Training Council and Life Insurance Agency Management Association, *The Widows Study*. Vol. 1, *The Onset of Widowhood*. Hartford, Conn.: Life Underwriter Training Council and Life Insurance Agency Management Association, 1970.

_____, *The Widows Study*. Vol. 2, *Adjustment to Widowhood: The First Two Years*. Hartford, Conn.: Life Underwriter Training Council and Life Insurance Agency Management Association, 1971.

Palmore, Erdman, Gertrude L. Stanley, and Robert H. Cormier, *Widows with Children under Social Security, Research Report No. 24*, Social Security Administration, Office of Research and Statistics. Washington, D.C.: U.S. Government Printing Office, 1966.

Schoenberg, Bernard, and Robert A. Senescu, "The Patient's Reaction to Fatal Illness," in Bernard Schoenberg, Arthur C. Carr, David Peretz, and Austin H. Kutscher, *Loss and Grief: Psychological Management in Medical Practice*. New York and London: Columbia University Press, 1970.

chapter 4

The Problem of Old Age

The United States is a relatively young nation, but a large proportion of the total population—more than 20 million persons, or nearly 10 percent—is aged 65 and over. Millions of retired people are exposed to considerable economic insecurity in their old age. Many older workers lose their incomes because of compulsory retirement. Other workers are forced into early retirement because of technological change and automation, plant shutdowns, or poor health. As a result, they are spending a relatively larger proportion of their adult lives in retirement, and the incomes they receive may be insufficient for providing them with a reasonable standard of living. Millions of elderly citizens live in poverty, many of them residing in rural and urban slums, often socially isolated from the rest of the community; and the problem of poverty among aged widows is particularly acute. Furthermore, many of the aged have serious financial problems because of poor health and spiraling medical expenses, high property taxes, inadequate low-cost housing, inflation, inadequate transportation, and exploitation. Finally, many older workers experience great difficulty in finding jobs because of arbitrary and unjust age discrimination.

In this chapter, we shall analyze each of the preceding problems in greater detail. In particular, we shall consider the following major areas: (1) nature of the old-age problem, (2) employment problems of older workers, and (3) techniques for attacking the economic problem of old age.

NATURE OF THE PROBLEM

The economic problems of old age are largely the loss of income because of compulsory retirement, a lengthening period of retirement, insufficient income, erosion of real income, and additional expenses, including medical expenses and property taxes. We shall deal more specifically with these problems under the heads of (1) compulsory retirement, (2) longer retirement period, (3) insufficient income during retirement, (4) poor health, (5) heavy property taxes, (6) inflation, and (7) other financial problems.

Compulsory Retirement

Compulsory retirement is an important part of the old-age problem. More than half the men who apply for full OASDHI benefits at age 65 have been forced to do so because of compulsory retirement, as a result of which they lose their earned incomes. Unless they have adequate replacement income from the OASDHI program, private pensions, or other sources, they will be exposed to considerable economic insecurity in their old age.

Age 65 is the customary retirement age in the United States, stemming from the passage of the Social Security Act of 1935, which permitted retirement benefits to be paid at that age. Because of the severe depression and abnormal unemployment of the 1930s, older workers were encouraged to retire at 65 to expand opportunities for employment and promotion of younger workers; and this reasoning still prevails today. In addition, compulsory retirement is used by employers as a device to retire older workers in a dignified fashion. Since a uniform retirement policy applies to all, the firms are relieved of the problem of permitting certain older workers to continue working while asking others to retire.

Longer Retirement Period

The retired aged are spending a relatively larger proportion of their adult lives in retirement. Because of a shorter period of productive earnings, the average worker may not save enough during his working years to maintain a reasonable standard of living during the longer retirement period.

The evidence clearly indicates that the length of the retirement period is increasing, while the working period is declining. The following table shows, for selected years, the remaining life expectancy for a man aged 65, the number of years he can expect still to work, and the remaining years he can expect to be retired:[1]

	1940	1960	1968
Remaining life expectancy	12.2	12.8	12.8
Expectation of work life	6.8	6.3	5.5
Expectation of retirement	5.4	6.5	7.3
Percent of remaining lifetime spent in retirement	44%	51%	57%

[1]U.S. Department of Labor, Bureau of Labor Statistics, *The Employment Problems of Older Workers,* Bulletin 1721 (Washington, D.C.: U.S. Government Printing Office, 1971), p. 4, Table A. Prepared for the White House Conference on Aging, November 29, 1971.

As we see, an average male, aged 65 in 1940, could expect to live for 12.2 more years. He could expect to spend 5.4 years, or 44 percent of his remaining years, in retirement. By 1968, an average male aged 65 could expect to live 12.8 years, and to spend 7.3 years, or 57 percent of his remaining years, in retirement. Thus, the expectation of retirement has increased, while the expectation of work life has declined.

The relatively longer retirement period and shorter working period can be explained by a slight increase in life expectancy at the older ages, a longer period of formal education, and the trend toward early retirement.

Increase in Life Expectancy. Although most of the increase in life expectancy has occurred at the younger ages, there has been a slight increase as well at the older ages. The life expectancy of a white male 65-year-old, for example, increased from 12.2 years in 1940 to 13.1 years in 1972.

Longer Period of Formal Education. A highly industrialized economy requires a skilled labor force, which necessitates a longer period of formal education; and a longer period of formal education necessarily delays entry into the labor force, thereby reducing the period of productive earnings. The need for a more highly educated labor force and the growth of child-labor legislation have both increased the average age of entry into the labor force. The higher entry age reduces the proportion of an average worker's lifetime that can be considered economically productive, thereby increasing the proportion that can be considered economically nonproductive. Thus, in a highly industrialized economy, the average person spends a relatively shorter period preparing economically for a relatively longer retirement period.

Trend toward Early Retirement. There is also a distinct trend toward early retirement, which also reduces the period of productive earnings and increases the length of the retirement period. More than half the men who are eligible for OASDHI retirement benefits apply before age 65. Since the benefits are actuarially reduced for early retirement, many retired workers fail to receive an adequate retirement income.

A Social Security Administration study on early retirement revealed the various reasons why men retire before age 65.[2] More than half the men indicated that they did not want to retire and would have preferred working. For those workers who retired at 65, 52 percent of the wage and salary workers were victims of compulsory retirement. Poor health was the reason for retirement for 21 percent of the beneficiaries. Among the men retiring at ages 62 through 64, 54 percent indicated that failing health was the reason.

Other reasons for early retirement include automation and technological change, discontinued jobs, layoffs, plant closings, job discrimination based on age, labor-union pressures to expand employment, and the desire for leisure. Finally, the availability of early-retirement benefits under the OASDHI program and private pension plans encourages some older workers to retire early. Studies indicate a strong relationship between the expected retirement

[2]Virginia Reno, "Why Men Stop Working at or before Age 65: Findings from the Survey of New Beneficiaries," *Social Security Bulletin,* Vol. 34, No. 6 (June 1971), 3-17. See also Karen Schwab, "Early Labor-Force Withdrawal of Men: Participants and Nonparticipants Aged 58-63," *Social Security Bulletin,* Vol. 37, No. 8 (August 1974), 24-38.

income and the willingness to retire. Those workers who can look forward to substantial private-pension benefits are more likely to retire early.[3]

Impact of Early Retirement.   The trend toward early retirement and a subsequent increase in the retirement period compound the problem of economic insecurity in old age. First, whether compulsory or voluntary, early retirement makes it more difficult for the worker to provide an adequate income for himself and his family during retirement. Early retirement may reduce the amount of accumulated savings, since the period of productive earnings is shortened, with the result that the worker may be unable to save a sufficient amount to provide for income during the longer retirement period.

For example, assume that a white male worker works W years and lives in retirement for R years. If interest is ignored and the worker desires to maintain the same standard of living after retirement as he had before, he must save R/W of his earnings. If the worker enters the labor force at age 20 and retires at age 70, and assuming a retirement period of ten years, he must save 10/50, or 20 percent, of his preretirement income to maintain the same standard of living after retirement as he had before. On the other hand, if he retires early, at age 60, he can expect to live about 16 years in retirement, so to maintain his average consumption, he must save 16/40 of his preretirement earnings, or 40 percent, disregarding interest.[4] Although higher average real income during the working years may increase, the increase may be insufficient to offset the increase in the average length of retirement and the shrinkage in the working lifetime of an individual.

If workers are encouraged or forced to retire early, their private and public pension benefits are also reduced, and their retirement income may be seriously inadequate for maintaining a reasonable standard of living. Workers who retire early are more likely to be those with low educational levels, low earnings, and poor work histories, which result in a relatively low pension income. Also, early retirement actuarially reduces both OASDHI and private-pension retirement benefits. About half the men who claim OASDHI retirement benefits receive reduced amounts.[5]

Finally, because of the relative reduction in the labor force from early retirement, there is a loss of real gross national product to the economy; and the real burden of supporting an increasing proportion of nonproductive retired aged falls heavily on the active workers.

[3]Don M. Bechter, "The Retirement Decision: Social Pressures and Economic Trends," *Monthly Review,* November 1972, p. 22. See also Richard Barfield and James Morgan, *Early Retirement: The Decision and the Experience* (Ann Arbor, Mich.: Institute for Social Research, 1969); and Richard Barfield, *The Automobile Worker and Retirement: A Second Look* (Ann Arbor, Mich.: Institute for Social Research, 1970).

[4]For a discussion of this concept, see Joseph J. Spengler, "Some Economic and Related Determinants Affecting the Older Worker's Occupational Role," in Ida Harper Simpson and John C. McKinney, eds. *Social Aspects of Aging* (Durham, N.C.: Duke University Press, 1966), pp. 32-33.

[5]Julian Abbott, "Covered Employment and the Age Men Claim Retirement Benefits," *Social Security Bulletin,* Vol. 37, No. 4 (April 1974), 3.

Insufficient Income

The aged as a group have a serious problem of insufficient income. In many cases, the incomes actually received are insufficient for providing them with a reasonable standard of living.

Size of Income. The money incomes of aged families and individuals in the United States fall substantially below the income level attained by the total population. The following table compares the median money incomes of families and unrelated individuals aged 65 and over with the median family incomes of all families and unrelated individuals in the United States. The data are based on the March 1974 Current Population Survey conducted by the Bureau of the Census.[6]

Median family income for all families	$12,051
Median family income for family heads, age 65 or over	$ 6,426
Median income all unrelated individuals	$ 4,134
Median income all unrelated individuals, age 65 and over	$ 2,725

As the table shows, the median family income where the family head was 65 was only about 53 percent of the income level for all families; and for unrelated aged persons, the median income was only about 66 percent of the income level for all unrelated individuals. Thus, it is clear that the aged as a group have substantially lower incomes than the general population, which can result in serious economic insecurity for them.

Sources of Income. It is important to analyze the sources of income to the aged, to determine their relative contributions. The following distribution indicates the percentage of all aged units receiving income from certain sources and the percentage of total income received from each source.[7]

Source	Percent of Aged Units Receiving Income from Specified Source	Percent of Total Income Received from Each Source
OASDHI	86%	34%
Earnings	27	29
Income from assets	50	15
Private group pensions	12	5
Public assistance	12	4
Other public pensions	10	7
Veterans' benefits	3	3
Contributions from relatives and friends not in household	3	1
Other sources	3	3

---

[6]U.S. Bureau of the Census, *Current Population Reports,* Series P-60, No. 93, "Money Income in 1973 of Families and Persons in the United States (Advance Report)" (Washington, D.C.: U.S. Government Printing Office, July 1974), p. 9, Table 6.

[7]Lenore E. Bixby, "Income of People Aged 65 and Older: Overview from 1968 Survey of the Aged," *Social Security Bulletin,* Vol. 33, No. 4 (April 1970), 10-11, Tables 2 and 3.

Total Assets. A complete analysis of the financial situation of the aged must also consider the total assets that they own. Although work earnings may terminate or be reduced at retirement, accumulated financial assets can be used to offset the loss of income. They can provide a cushion during retirement for emergencies and can also be used to supplement any retirement income.

The Social Security Administration has provided valuable information on the asset position of older workers on the threshold of retirement.[8] It is especially important, for two reasons, to determine the amount of assets owned by workers between 62 and 63 who are near retirement. First, as stated earlier, about half the men retiring apply for OASDHI retirement benefits before age 65, and the financial assets that they own can be used to help meet their postretirement income needs. Second, unlike the assets accumulated by younger persons, the assets of the aged during retirement are not easily replaced once they are spent.

As a generalization, the asset situation of workers aged 62 and 63 is bleak. Most workers in this age category have relatively modest asset holdings, which consist primarily of the equity in their homes. The median value of the total assets for married men, including equity in the home, was only $17,500. When home equity is excluded, however, the median total asset value sharply declined, to $6,068.[9] The situation is even worse for unmarried men and women—the single, widowed, or divorced. When the equity in the home is excluded, the median value of total financial assets for unmarried men between 62 and 63 is only $787. The corresponding amount for unmarried women in the same age category is only $833.[10]

Thus, men and women approaching retirement obviously cannot rely entirely on their accumulated assets to help meet their income needs during retirement. Although the married men are financially better off, their total asset position, excluding equity in the home, is still far from satisfactory.

There are several reasons for the unsatisfactory total-asset position of older workers. First, there is some evidence that many workers are unaware of their future retirement needs and may undersave for their old age.[11] In addition, many older workers near retirement have inadequate financial assets because they have earned insufficient incomes during their working lifetime and have therefore been unable to save substantial amounts for their old age. Finally, inflation, high income taxes, poor health or personal misfortune, and the influence of advertising also help explain the relatively low asset position of many older workers.

Poverty among the Aged. The March 1974 Current Population Survey by

---

[8]Sally R. Sherman, "Assets on the Threshold of Retirement," *Social Security Bulletin,* Vol. 36, No. 8 (August 1973), 3-17. See also Schwab, "Early Labor-Force Withdrawal," pp. 34-35.

[9]Sherman, "Assets," p. 9, Table 8, p. 13, Table 14.

[10]*Ibid.,* p. 13, Table 14.

[11]Joseph A. Pechman, Henry J. Aaron, and Michael Taussig, "The Objectives of Social Security," *Old Age Income Insurance, Part III: A Compendium of Papers on Problems and Policy Issues in the Public and Private Pension System,* Subcommittee on Fiscal Policy of the Joint Economic Committee, 90th Cong., 1st sess., 1967 (Washington, D.C.: U.S. Government Printing Office, 1967), p. 10.

the Bureau of the Census revealed that about 23 million Americans, or about 11 percent of the population, were living in poverty. The incidence of poverty, however, is considerably higher for the aged, especially those who are members of minority groups. The following table illustrates the extent of poverty among the aged for selected categories of aged persons: [12]

Percent of total population poor	11.1%
Percent of aged 65 and over poor	16.3%
White males age 65 and over poor	10.4%
Black males age 65 and over poor	32.4%
White females age 65 and over poor	17.2%
Black females age 65 and over poor	40.5%

Thus, many of the aged, especially elderly black citizens, are exposed to considerable economic insecurity.

A serious problem of poverty among aged widows must also be recognized. More than half the 12 million women aged 65 and over in 1972 were widows. Of this number, about three out of ten were counted as poor based on the poverty thresholds established for low-income families. The incidence of poverty was even higher for minority groups; about 48 percent of the black widows 65 or over were living in poverty.[13]

The aged-widow problem can be explained by two factors. First, a female age 20 will, on the average, tend to outlive her husband of the same age by about seven years. And since most women marry men who are several years older, the husbands are far more likely to die first. Second, since most husbands own inadequate amounts of life insurance, and survivorship benefits from other sources may be inadequate, many elderly widows experience great economic insecurity because of poverty during their old age.

Poor Health

The aged as a group are in relatively poorer health than is the general population. Older people see physicians more frequently, are more likely to become disabled, and have more frequent and longer hospital stays. Most aged persons—at least 86 percent—also have some chronic disease, impairment, or condition that results in an additional drain on their limited incomes. As indicated earlier, several million aged live in poverty. Despite the Medicare program, the poverty-stricken aged may have difficulty paying for the medical care they require. And because of insufficient incomes, the aged poor are often unable to maintain minimum nutritional standards, perhaps causing loss of memory, disordered thought, and senility.[14]

[12] U.S. Bureau of the Census, *Current Population Reports,* Series P-60, No. 94, "Characteristics of the Low-Income Population: 1973 (Advance Report)" (Washington, D.C.: U.S. Government Printing Office, July 1974), pp. 6-7, Table 3.

[13] U.S. Bureau of the Census, *Current Population Reports,* Series P-60, No. 91, "Characteristics of the Low-Income Population, 1972" (Washington, D.C.: U.S. Government Printing Office, 1973), pp. 78-79, Table 16.

[14] U.S. Congress, Senate, Subcommittee on Aging, *Research in Aging, 1972,* Hearings before the Subcommittee on Aging of the Committee on Labor and Public Welfare, 92nd Cong., 2d sess., on S.887, S.1925, and S.2934, 1972, p. 134.

Finally, many aged people require long-term custodial care in nursing homes, and the financial burden for this type of care is staggering. The cost of long-term care in a skilled nursing home often exceeds $800 a month, and the Medicare program and most private health insurance plans do not cover this care. The result is that the limited assets of some disabled elderly patients in nursing homes are quickly depleted. The aged must then seek financial assistance from their children or apply for welfare benefits under the Medicaid program. Neither solution is likely to be satisfactory for an aged person.

Heavy Property-Tax Burden

In many communities, property taxes have doubled or even tripled during the past ten years. Although a large proportion of aged homeowners have their homes paid for by retirement, the property taxes they must pay can be a crushing financial burden. The result is that some aged homeowners on limited incomes must give up their homes or liquidate some financial assets to pay these taxes. In many cases, the low-income aged are unable to locate suitable alternate housing at rents they can afford to pay.

The property-tax burden falls heavily on those aged persons with limited incomes. A study of low-income aged households in Wisconsin with annual incomes of less than $1,000 indicated that the aged homeowners paid 30 percent of their total family incomes for property taxes.[15] The ability of low-income homeowners to keep their homes under such conditions is most precarious.

In addition, many retired aged, especially the low-income and poverty-stricken aged, do not own their homes but must rent. The higher property taxes are merely shifted from the landlords to the tenants in the form of higher rents. Although aged homeowners may receive personal income tax relief because of property-tax deductions, aged renters cannot take advantage of this deduction even though they are paying the property taxes in the form of higher rents.

Inflation

A rapid increase in consumer prices can also cause considerable financial hardship to the aged. The costs of food, housing, clothing, medical care, and other consumer items have substantially increased over time. Food costs in particular have soared in recent years: Between 1967 and October 1974 alone, they increased about 66 percent, according to the Consumer Price Index. And food costs tend to absorb a relatively larger proportion of an aged person's income than that of the general population. Because of more limited income, the aged spend about 27 percent of their income on food, compared to about 16 percent for the total population. The result, as we have said, can be inadequate diets and serious nutrition problems for the aged because they cannot afford the proper food, thus increasing their economic insecurity, especially for those living in poverty.

[15]U.S. Congress, Senate, Special Committee on Aging, *Economics of Aging: Toward a Full Share in Abundance,* Report by the Special Subcommittee on Aging, 91st Cong., 2d sess., 1970 (Washington, D.C.: U.S. Government Printing Office, 1970), pp. 25-57.

In addition, medical expenses have increased sharply over time. Between 1967 and October 1974, medical-care costs increased about 56 percent, based on the Consumer Price Index. Although the aged have considerable protection against catastrophic medical expenses under the Medicare program, certain important expenditures are excluded. Medicare covers less than half the total medical expenses incurred by the aged. In particular, prescription drugs outside of hospitals, eyeglasses and hearing aids, and false teeth—items necessary for their health and well-being—are not covered, and they can cause a serious dent in the budget of a low-income household. Finally, long-term custodial care in nursing homes is also excluded. Thus, rapid inflation in medical costs can also erode the economic-security position of the aged.

Other Financial Problems

The aged are subject to other financial problems that add to their economic insecurity. Low-cost housing at affordable rents is generally in short supply. Lack of adequate transportation is another problem; many aged persons cannot afford automobiles, and public transportation, especially to shopping centers where prices are often lower, may be unavailable. And the aged are often exploited by unscrupulous entrepreneurs who promote land sales or home repairs, and by deceptive health insurance advertising.

EMPLOYMENT PROBLEMS OF OLDER WORKERS

The economic problems of old age cannot be separated from the employment problems of older workers. The economic insecurity experienced by some aged people can be traced directly to the employment problems they experienced prior to their retirement. Thus, many older workers carry into old age the economic-insecurity problems, including the loss of income and insufficient income, that they were experiencing for years prior to their actual retirement.

Although age 65 is thought to mark the beginning of old age, the employment problems of workers over 45 must also be considered. This age usually marks the beginning of an increase in withdrawals from the labor force, a decline in weekly and annual earnings, a lengthening of the duration of unemployment, and an increase in part-time work and part-time workers. These factors tend to increase in importance for subsequently older age groups. The employment problems of older workers can be summarized as follows:

1. *Declining Labor-Force Participation Rates.* The labor-force participation rates for older men decline with age, while the labor-force participation of older women continues to increase. By ages 55-59, 11 out of 100 men have dropped out of the labor force, and by ages 60-64, 28 out of 100 men have dropped out of the labor force. The decline in labor-force participation is due to sickness and disability, retirement, temporary withdrawals, family responsibilities, and personal reasons.

2. *Longer Duration of Unemployment.* Although older workers have lower un-

employment rates, the duration of unemployment is considerably longer. Older workers have seniority rights and are less likely to leave their jobs voluntarily, which accounts for the lower unemployment rates. If they become unemployed, however, the duration of unemployment is considerably longer than for younger men. In 1970, the average duration for unemployment for older men age 45 and over was about double that of younger men under age 25.

3. *Lower Earnings.* The incomes of older workers age 45 and over are generally lower than for workers aged 35-44. The difference between the incomes of older and younger workers tends to widen as the workers grow older.

4. *Decline in Full-Time Work.* The proportion of men working full-time the entire year tends to decline for older workers in each age group after ages 35-44. However, the proportion of older workers who work part-time has increased over time. In particular, the proportion of older workers aged 65 and over who voluntarily work part-time has tended to increase over time. Only a small proportion of older workers is involuntarily employed part-time because of slack business conditions: A larger proportion of older workers works part-time because of poor health, partial disability, or personal reasons.

5. *Job Discrimination.* Many older workers experience job discrimination. Over one-half million workers aged 45 and over in 1969 experienced job discrimination. Other unemployed older workers may experience age discrimination in their job search. Job discrimination takes the form of illegal advertising, refusal to hire older workers because of the physical requirements of the job, a policy of promotion from within, wage demands of older workers, an increase in pension and group insurance costs, and lack of skills and education. However, studies by the Bureau of Labor Statistics show that the job performance and productivity of older workers are as good as that of younger workers. Older workers have less absenteeism, lower accident rates, and high production rates, and, based on other indices, are reliable, productive, and useful workers.

6. *Inadequate Pension-Plan Coverage.* A majority of older workers near retirement are either not covered for private-pension benefits or may not have worked a sufficient number of years to qualify for coverage. Substantial numbers of workers in the trade, services, and construction industries are not covered for private pensions. In addition, only a small fraction of retired older women are presently collecting pension benefits.

7. *Less Mobility.* Older workers are less mobile than younger workers. Older workers are less likely to move voluntarily from one job, residence, or occupation to another. The unwillingness to relocate geographically to another area often makes it difficult for them to find new jobs. They often prefer to remain in a relatively high unemployment area rather than relocate because of homes, families, friends, and attachment to the area.

8. *Less Education.* Older workers are not as well educated as younger workers, which restricts their employment opportunities and helps account for their relatively lower earnings. Older workers with lower educational attainment levels are more likely to withdraw from the labor force; older unskilled and less-educated workers are also more likely to experience higher unemployment rates; finally, education is important for jobs in the various professions. A smaller proportion of workers aged 45 and over is employed in professional and highly skilled jobs than for the younger workers.[16]

[16]U.S. Department of Labor, *Employment Problems of Older Workers,* pp. 1-2.

ATTACKING THE ECONOMIC PROBLEM OF OLD AGE

Numerous private and public techniques are currently used to meet the economic problem of old age. We shall consider the most important approaches under the following heads: (1) continued employment, (2) OASDHI benefits, (3) private pensions, (4) Supplemental Security Income, and (5) other techniques.

Continued Employment

Although a national policy of compulsory retirement at age 65 may have been justified during the Great Depression of the 1930s, such a policy may be inappropriate today. Studies indicate that many older workers have a definite need for additional income and wish to continue working, at least on a part-time or intermittent basis. A study of compulsory retirement by the Social Security Administration indicated that only two out of five workers wanted to retire at age 65; the others would have preferred working.[17] It is worthwhile, therefore, to examine some employment policies that can be applied as alternatives to compulsory retirement for older workers.

Flexible Retirement Age. Some firms maintain a policy of flexible retirement age, by which older workers who are physically able and willing can continue to work beyond age 65.

A policy of compulsory retirement, with no consideration of the older workers's desires, often deprives society of the skills, education, and mature judgment of these older workers. It would appear that the time of retirement should be based more on the nature of employment than on chronological age. Three employment categories should be considered in this regard: Early retirement and compulsory retirement are more easily justified for heavy and automated industries; service and clerical work would seem to permit retirement at a later age; and professional employment appears to permit the longest span of employment and the latest retirement.

A flexible retirement age benefits both older workers and employers. The workers do not lose their incomes from compulsory retirement, making it easier to attain greater economic security in their old age. And they also maintain from their jobs a status and psychological satisfaction that can be destroyed by compulsory retirement. Employers also benefit, since the skills, talents, experience, and judgment of valuable workers can still be utilized. Also, private-pension costs may be reduced by delayed retirement; an initial net savings for a pension plan may be as high as 9 percent for each year of employment beyond the normal retirement age.[18]

Part-Time Employment. Part-time employment beyond age 65 is another technique for meeting the economic problem of old age. Part-time employment opportunities have increased over time, permitting many older people to work and supplement their limited retirement incomes. Poor health or

[17]Reno, "Why Men Stop Working," p. 14.

[18]Merton C. Bernstein, *The Future of Private Pensions* (New York: Free Press, 1964), p. 233.

the desire for leisure may make full-time work relatively unattractive to older workers; however, many of them can work part-time—although not, perhaps, in jobs involving strenuous physical obligations that they cannot meet—and can make a valuable contribution to the sustaining and strengthening of our economic system. The income from part-time employment often means the difference between a poverty level and a relatively higher standard of living.

Gradual Retirement. Gradual retirement is another approach to the economic problem of old age. Under this concept, employment is not abruptly terminated by retirement; instead, partial employment and partial retirement are combined so that older workers can obtain the advantages of both continued employment and retirement.

Numerous approaches to gradual retirement are possible. First, the older worker can be given an extended leave in the last year, or longer time off each year for a period of three to five years prior to his retirement. Or the employee may be allowed to work beyond age 65, but only with a progressively reduced schedule and commensurately reduced pay. Or the worker may be permitted to transfer to less-demanding work or to part-time employment; many firms can accommodate older workers in this manner without a formal designation of the work load as gradual retirement.

Finally, for professional workers and executives, gradual retirement may take the form of rehiring them after retirement on a temporary basis, to perform specific jobs for which their talents quality them. The older employees benefits, since he can accept work on terms that suit him. And management also benefits, since the younger workers can be promoted, yet the employer can retain the services and skills of valuable employees; in addition, management can provide employment only for those workers considered valuable.

Retraining Older Workers. Retraining older workers is another technique for expanding their employment opportunities. Many states and communities sponsor adult vocational-training programs that are designed to retrain older workers who are unemployed because of automation and technological change, plant closings, or age discrimination. The Manpower Development and Training Act also provides various programs for retraining workers who have obsolete skills. And the U.S. Employment Service provides job counseling, job development, and selective placement of older workers. The retraining programs are designed to equip older workers with the knowledge and skills that the modern economy demands.

The suggestion has been made that older workers could be retrained for the various service, technical, and semiprofessional jobs that serve the needs of older people themselves. These occupations include employment in nursing homes and old-age homes, recreational and counseling programs, and housing projects for the aged—ideal part-time employment opportunities for retired workers who wish to supplement their retirement incomes. The potential is great for expanding job opportunities in the service occupations and for training older people to fill jobs in nursing homes, home care, homemaker services, and various other areas that lack an adequate supply of trained workers.

Retirement-Planning Programs. To help prepare a worker for eventual retirement, about half of U.S. firms provide some form of preretirement training program or advice to retiring workers.[19] The programs provide useful information to workers about to retire, usually covering such topics as financial planning for retirement, money management, physical aspects of aging, mental health in later years, increasing retirement income, housing and nutrition problems, living arrangements in later life, and the use of leisure time.

Postretirement adjustment is often closely related to preretirement training. Older workers are seldom aware of the extensive changes that will occur after retirement. The decision to retire may present a considerable amount of uncertainty, and the necessary adjustments to retirement are more easily made if these uncertainties are removed. Counseling by trained experts in gerontology can often make the difference between successful and unsuccessful retirement. In this regard, however, the personnel conducting the preretirement programs are often not trained in gerontology and the specifics of aging. They are usually personnel men who are assigned preretirement training programs as part of their normal duties. The result is that some preretirement training courses are not as effective as they might be.[20]

OASDHI BENEFITS

Both OASDHI retirement and Medicare benefits are extremely important in promoting economic security for the aged. The retirement benefits reduce the problem of the loss of income from compulsory retirement, while the Medicare program helps meet the problem of additional expenses in old age because of high medical costs.

Retirement Benefits. Social Security retirement benefits are the most important single source of income to the aged. About half the aged couples and about two-thirds of the retired single workers receive more than 50 percent of their retirement income from the OASDHI program; and OASDHI retirement benefits are just about the *only* source of income (over 90 percent of total income) for about one in three single retired workers and about one in seven retired couples.[21]

Recent OASDHI benefit increases have had a substantial impact in reducing poverty among the aged. In 1969, about 4.8 million aged people lived in poverty. By 1973, the number of aged poor had declined to about 3.4 million, a decrease of about 29 percent. Much of this reduction is due to the substantial OASDHI benefit increases between 1969 and 1973.[22]

But despite these increases, the retirement benefits are still inadequate for many who must rely almost exclusively on the OASDHI program as their major source of income. In particular, the monthly benefits paid to aged widows are generally inadequate in terms of their needs. In 1973, the average benefits paid

[19]U.S. Congress, Senate, Subcommittee on Aging, *Older Americans Act Amendments of 1972,* Hearings before the Subcommittee on Aging of the Committee on Labor and Public Welfare, 92d Cong., 2d sess., on S.3181, S.3076, and S.3391, 1972, p. 327.

[20]*Ibid.*

[21]U.S. Congress, Senate, Special Committee on Aging, *Future Directions in Social Security,* Hearings before the Special Committee on Aging, 93d Cong., 1st sess., 1973, Part 1, p. 83.

[22]*Ibid.,* pp. 82-83.

to widows amounted to $1,872 annually, or about $225 below the 1973 projected poverty standard for people aged 65 or over.[23]

Also, the OASDHI retirement benefits are generally inadequate for many aged couples when measured against the intermediate budget standard of the Bureau of Labor Statistics. Income adequacy during old age was one of the highest-priority items at the 1972 White House Conference on Aging. One strong recommendation was that the minimum standard of income for an aged couple should be equal to the BLS intermediate budget standard. In 1972, that standard for an elderly couple was $5,000, and *about three out of five retired couples did not meet this standard.* The average OASDHI benefits paid to retired couples in 1972 was $3,252, or only about 65 percent of the BLS intermediate budget standard.[24] Thus, for many aged couples, economic insecurity will continue to be a major problem because of insufficient income.

Medicare Benefits. As a result of the 1965 amendments, most aged Americans have health insurance protection under the Medicare program, which relieves them and their children of a major portion of the financial burden of poor health in their old age. But since older persons under age 65 are generally ineligible for these benefits, and since many older workers retire early, the problem of medical expenses for those within the early-retirement category can be especially acute. The Medicare program will be analyzed later, in Chapter 10, when the economic problem of poor health among the aged is discussed in greater detail.

Private Pensions

Private pensions are extremely important for meeting the problem of economic insecurity in old age, especially for those workers with average or above-average earnings, by supplementing OASDHI retirement benefits. Private pension plans also have an important macroeconomic impact on the economy. The pension contributions are an important source of private savings; they affect economic growth; and pension-fund investments have an enormous influence on the financial markets and concentration of economic power. Finally, private pensions have an impact on the redistribution of income, labor mobility, early retirement, and the employment opportunities for older persons.

The private-pension field is big business that affects the lives of millions of both active and retired workers. More than 33 million workers are currently covered under 150,000 private pension plans with accumulated assets in excess of $150 billion. By 1980, more than 42 million workers are expected to participate, and pension-plan assets will skyrocket to over $250 billion.

Although private pensions provide an important layer of economic security to the aged, only a small proportion of the retired aged receive benefits from them. A Social Security Administration study revealed that only 32 percent of the married men and 19 percent of the nonmarried men who were entitled to OASDHI retirement benefits reported also receiving benefits from a private

[23]*Ibid.*, p. 83.

[24]*Ibid.*, p. 84.

pension.[25] The receipt of a second pension, however, often made the difference between living in poverty and a higher standard of living.

Although private pensions have great potential in reducing economic insecurity among the aged, certain problems and issues must be resolved. The most important center around incomplete coverage, inadequate vesting, adequacy of funding, termination insurance, and the portability of pension credits.

Incomplete Coverage. Although private-pension coverage has expanded rapidly over time, the coverage is still incomplete. Only about half the labor force is covered by private pensions. In particular, employees working in small firms, in agriculture, and in the trade and service industries are inadequately covered. Many female employees are also inadequately covered; although the labor-force participation rate for women has increased, and about one-third of the labor force now consists of women, most retired women are not receiving private-pension benefits. Since many women are in and out of the labor force several times during their working careers because of responsibilities to family and children, they may not be employed long enough to become eligible to participate in a plan. And even if they are participating, they may not meet the vesting provisions; thus, when they terminate their employment prior to retirement, they may forfeit their accrued pension benefits. Also, many women work only part-time and are excluded from coverage. Finally, many women are employed by firms in the trade and service industries, where the pension coverage is incomplete.

Inadequate Vesting. Pension plans often have stringent vesting provisions that prevent many terminating employees from receiving retirement benefits under them. Vesting is the nonforfeitable right to pension benefits attributable to the employer's contributions even though the employee terminates his employment prior to retirement. Most plans require the covered employee to meet either an age or a service requirement, or both, before the benefits vest. If the employee terminates his service with the firm prior to vesting, he loses the pension benefits accrued on his behalf. Thus, a worker who changes jobs several times during his career could end up at retirement with no private-pension benefits, since the vesting provisions in the plans are never met. A study by the Subcommittee on Labor concluded that, as a result of harsh vesting provisions, only about one person in ten will collect pension benefits under his employer's plan.[26] Although this estimate is undoubtedly too low because of the failure to consider a mature distribution and small sample size, it underscores the fact that many workers now covered by private pensions may never receive benefits under the plans.

Several arguments are advanced for more liberal vesting provisions in

[25]U.S. Department of Health, Education and Welfare, Social Security Administration, Office of Research and Statistics, *Income of Newly Entitled Beneficiaries,* Report No. 10 (June 1973), p. 20, Table 1.

[26]U.S. Congress, Senate, Subcommittee on Labor, *Preliminary Report of the Private Welfare and Pension Plan Study, 1971* (Pursuant to S. Res. 35, Section 4), Subcommittee on Labor and Public Welfare, 92d Cong., 1st sess., 1971 (Washington, D.C.: U.S. Government Printing Office, 1971).

private pensions.[27] First, as a matter of equity and fair treatment, the covered worker should have his future pension benefits protected against forfeiture after a reasonable period of service. Second, more liberal vesting also provides certain advantages to the employer, such as removing a source of employee discontent from the operation of the plan. Third, it encourages greater labor mobility, which is desirable from a macroeconomic viewpoint. Finally, it makes pension benefits more secure, which strengthens and protects the nation's entire system of retirement plans.

On the other hand, critics offer powerful counterarguments against liberalized vesting. They state that it increases pension costs, making it more difficult to incorporate other desirable features into the plan, such as higher retirement benefits, survivorship benefits for widows, and disability benefits. The additional costs of mandatory vesting provisions, however, are relatively modest. Under present plans, the cost of vesting ranges from 1.8 percent to 11.9 percent of payroll. Depending on the type of vesting, more liberal provisions would increase the costs, as a percent of payroll, from nothing in some plans to a maximum of 1.4 percent in others.[28]

In addition, it is argued, equity may be achieved by less-liberal vesting provisions by making it possible to pay higher benefits to long-service employees who remain with the firm until retirement rather than smaller vested benefits to terminating employees. Also, compulsory vesting may restrict the right of management and labor to determine how pension resources should be allocated, and may restrict the growth of private pensions.

Adequacy of Funding. Most private pension plans are adequately funded. A study by the Pension Research Council of almost 4,000 private plans indicated a high degree of funding for most plans. For all plans combined, there was about one dollar of assets for each dollar of accrued benefits. More than half the plans, irrespective of duration, were fully funded. More than nine out of ten were fully funded after fifteen or more years of effective funding.[29]

Termination Insurance. When a company relocates, shuts down, or merges with another firm, termination insurance can protect the pension rights of workers who would otherwise lose their benefits if the plan should terminate. The closing of the Studebaker plant in 1964, whereby about two-thirds of all Studebaker employees lost part or all of their expected pension benefits, is cited to support the need for termination insurance.[30]

[27]President's Committee on Corporate Pension Funds and Other Private Retirement and Welfare Programs, *Public Policy and Private Pension Programs: A Report to the President on Private Employee Retirement Plans* (Washington, D.C.: U.S. Government Printing Office, 1965), pp. 39-41.

[28]U.S. Congress, Senate, Subcommittee on Labor, *Study of the Cost of Mandatory Vesting Provisions Proposed for Private Pension Plans,* Subcommittee on Labor and Public Welfare, 93d Cong., 1st sess., 1973 (Washington, D.C.: U.S. Government Printing Office, 1973), p. 3.

[29]See Frank L. Griffin and Charles L. Trowbridge, *Status of Funding under Private Pension Plans,* Pension Research Council (Homewood, Ill.: Richard D. Irwin, 1969).

[30]U.S. Congress, Senate, Subcommittee on Labor, *Private Welfare and Pension Plan Study-Report of Hearings on Pension Plans* (Pursuant to S. Res. 235, Section 4), Subcommittee on Labor of the Committee on Labor and Public Welfare, 92d Cong., 2d sess., 1972 (Washington, D.C.: U.S. Government Printing Office, 1972), p. 2.

However, the number of pension-plan terminations and the number of workers who are affected are relatively small at the present time. One study, covering 4,259 pension-plan terminations between 1955 and 1965, indicated that the ratio of terminated plans to continued plans remained constant at about 1 percent. Only about one-tenth of 1 percent of the workers exposed to loss were affected by the terminations. A more recent study, of 683 pension-plan terminations during the first seven months of 1972, showed that only about 22,700 pension participants were affected, or less than 1 percent of all covered workers.[31] Thus, overall, the evidence indicates a high level of stability and protection inherent in private pensions. However, for those workers who may be adversely affected if the plan should terminate with insufficient assets for paying off all employees with vested benefits, termination insurance is highly desirable, since it would pay all or part of the promised benefits.

Portability. Portability means the ability of an employee to transfer his vested pension benefit credits to another plan if he changes jobs. At retirement, he would then convert all his pension credits into a final retirement benefit that would reflect all previous employment.

Most private pension plans are not portable. The major exceptions are multiemployer pension plans that permit pension credits to be transferred when the worker changes jobs within the industry.

A suggested system of national portable pensions would require a central clearinghouse through which the earned pension credits would be channeled. The federal government would administer and regulate the plan so that it could function properly. Participating employees would be required to transfer the vested pension credits from one employer to another through a central fund.

However, the concept of a central clearinghouse to hold the pension funds has been criticized in several respects: First, difficult technical problems would be encountered in placing an exact value on the pension rights accumulated by employees under present plans. Second, because of labor mobility and the size of pension funds, the central agency would hold huge sums, a situation that could result in investment problems and a concentration of economic power. Third, if the central agency were a federal agency, there is the possibility of government intervention into the private-pension system, whereby the federal government could sell annuities in competition with private companies. Finally a central clearinghouse might be unnecessary, since the pension plan through which the employee has acquired vested rights during his working career could make payment to him at retirement. If vesting provisions were liberalized, the need for portable pensions would thereby be reduced.

Pension-Reform Legislation

After seven years of debate, Congress passed the historical Employee Retirement Income Security Act of 1974.[32] The act is an important piece of pen-

---

[31]U.S. Congress, Senate, Committee on Labor and Public Welfare, *Retirement Income Security for Employees Act of 1973, S. 4,* Committee on Labor and Public Welfare, 93d Cong., 1st sess., 1973 (Washington, D.C.: U.S. Government Printing Office, 1973), p. 209.

[32]A detailed discussion of this legislation can be found in Alfred M. Skolnik, "Pension Reform Legislation of 1974," *Social Security Bulletin,* Vol. 37, No. 12 (December 1974), 35-42.

sion-reform legislation that aims at correcting each of the pension defects discussed earlier. For the first time in the United States, most private pension plans must fulfill certain federal minimum standards. Although firms are not required to establish a pension plan, most existing and new plans must meet these standards. The act is designed to protect the pension rights of covered workers and provides for liberalized eligibility and vesting provisions, minimum funding requirements, voluntary portability, and fiduciary standards. In addition, the self-employed are permitted to deduct larger amounts for their pension contributions, and private-pension coverage is extended to employees in firms with no pension plans.

Eligibility Standards. Prior to enactment of the new law, a firm could require an employee to be at least 30 years old and have a maximum of five years' service before he could participate in a pension plan. The new law relaxes this requirement. In general, all employees must be eligible to participate in the plan if they are at least 25 years old and have worked for the firm for one year. However, if the plan provides for 100 percent full vesting, the employee could be required to be at least 25 and have three years of service before he is eligible to participate.

The liberalized eligibility standard will enable more employees, especially younger ones, to participate in private pension plans.

Liberalized Vesting. The act also provides for more liberal vesting provisions. The employer must select one of the following three vesting standards:

1. *Full Vesting.* The participant must be 100 percent vested after 10 years of service, with no vesting prior to that time.

2. *Graded Vesting.* The participant must be at least 25 percent vested after 5 years, 50 percent after 10 years, and fully vested after 15 years.

3. *Rule of 45.* The participant with at least 5 years of service must be 50 percent vested when his age plus years of service total 45, with an additional 10 percent vesting each year until full vesting is provided.

These liberalized vesting provisions will enable greater numbers of terminating employees to receive at least part of the accrued pension benefits they have earned even though they are no longer employed by the firm at retirement. Prior to passage of the law, about 13 percent of the private pension plans did not provide for any vesting.

Minimum Funding Requirements. The law establishes minimum funding standards, which require firms to make sufficient pension contributions so that the promised benefits can be paid. The normal costs of a pension plan must be currently funded; these are the annual costs that are associated with a given year of operation. Most private pension plans, however, also provide for past-service credits, which are given for service prior to the inception of the plan. The new law requires plans in existence as of January 1, 1974, and multiemployer plans to amortize the past-service costs over a maximum period of forty years. Newly established pension plans must amortize the past-service costs over a maximum period of thirty years.

The objective of this provision is to force private pension plans to acquire a fully funded status more quickly. Prior to passage of the act, federal law did not require a pension plan to be fully funded. But without the mandatory funding of past-service credits, some pension plans may not be financially strong enough to meet the pension obligations promised to the employees. Without adequate funding, the promise of pension benefits to the active workers is empty and illusory. The new law will ensure that most existing and new pension plans will at least meet minimum funding standards, thereby strengthening and protecting the workers' pension rights.

Termination Insurance. The act also provides for termination insurance, which pays pension benefits to covered workers if the firm goes bankrupt or runs short of funds. The maximum benefits are limited to $750 monthly, or 100 percent of the average monthly compensation received during the worker's highest-paid five consecutive years of service, whichever is less. The $750 limit will be adjusted in the future according to changes in the OASDHI contribution and benefit base.

The new law establishes within the Department of Labor a Pension Benefit Guaranty Corporation, which pays pension claims when the terminating plan's assets are insufficient for discharging all claims. During the first year of operation, single-employer pension plans must pay a premium of $1 per participant to finance the termination insurance, and multiemployer plans must pay 50 cents for each covered worker. In subsequent years, termination insurance will be financed by contributions from employers based on a complex formula that considers both unfunded vested benefits and total insured benefits.

Voluntary Portability. The new law does not require mandatory portability, which allows terminating employees to transfer their pension credits to another job. Instead, a voluntary-portability system is established whereby terminating employees can transfer their vested pension benefits to a tax-free individual retirement account (IRA). If the new employer consents, the worker can then transfer the pension funds in his individual account to the pension plan of the new employer.

Fiduciary and Disclosure Standards. The 1974 act establishes fiduciary and disclosure standards that are designed to promote competent investment management and provide the workers with more adequate information about the plans. Fiduciaries must invest the pension contributions in accordance with the "prudent man" rule, must diversify the pension assets to avoid large losses, and must act in a manner beneficial to only the plan participants and their beneficiaries. Certain transactions by the plan trustee are prohibited, including "kickbacks" from the plan and selling of plan assets without adequate consideration.

Self-Employed and Individual Accounts. The self-employed were previously limited to a maximum annual tax deduction of $2,500 if they contributed to a qualified self-employed pension plan. Under the new law, they can contribute to a pension plan, and claim a maximum annual deduction of 15 percent of net earnings, or $7,500, whichever is less.

The new law also expands pension coverage to an estimated 25 million workers who are not covered by any tax-qualified, government, or annuity pension plan. The worker can contribute to an individual retirement account on a voluntary basis. The maximum tax deduction he can claim is 15 percent of annual earnings, or $1,500, whichever is less. The pension contributions can be invested in a wide variety of investment vehicles, including special government bonds and mutual funds. The sponsoring institution holds the funds, and the investment earnings are tax-free until the benefits are actually disbursed.

Evaluation. The new legislation has both positive and negative features. On the positive side, the act strengthens the individual worker's pension rights and economic security through more stringent funding requirements and liberalized vesting provisions. In particular, the mandatory-vesting provisions will enable about 13 million workers who formerly had no vested rights under existing plans to acquire a vested status more easily. And most employers will be confronted with only a modest cost increase of less than 5 percent to implement the new legislation.

On the negative side, the new legislation should not be viewed as a panacea to pension reform. First, no worker is guaranteed a private pension. The law does not force any employer to establish such a plan, but merely imposes minimum standards on existing and new pension plans.

Second, the worker who frequently changes jobs may retire with no pension benefits from any plan. Under the ten-year vesting standard, one option available to the firm, a worker with 9½ years of service who terminated his employment would receive no benefits under the plan.

Termination insurance may also present certain problems. The plan guarantees a maximum monthly benefit of only $750. Workers with vested benefits in excess of $750 may receive no additional benefits if the pension plan terminates and is inadequately funded. Also, the risk involved in a recession or depression is great, since pension benefits would be insured only against the risk that the pension plan would fail, and the employer may have to discontinue contributions before the pension liabilities are fully funded. Finally, technical problems of determining the occurrence and the amount of the loss must also be overcome.

Supplemental Security Income

The aged may also be eligible for monthly income benefits under the new Supplemental Security Income (SSI) program for the aged, blind, and disabled. The SSI program, which became effective in January 1974, replaces the former state-federal public-assistance programs of Old-Age Assistance, Aid to the Blind, and Aid to the Permanently and Totally Disabled.

The SSI program guarantees a minimum monthly income of $146 to an eligible individual with no other source of income, and $219 to a married couple. To qualify for benefits, the aged applicant must be 65 or over and meet a needs test. The financial resources are limited to $1,500 for an individual and $2,250 for a married couple, excluding the reasonable value of a home, automobile, personal possessions, and life insurance. "Reasonable value" currently means that the market value of a home cannot exceed $25,000 ($35,000 in Hawaii and Alaska), and of an automobile, $1,200. In addition, if the face value of life insurance of SSI beneficiaries exceeds $1,500, the cash value must be counted as a resource.[33]

In calculating the SSI benefits from the federal government, on a quarterly basis, the first $60 of any earned or unearned income is excluded; in addition, $195 of earned income plus one-half the remainder is also excluded in determining benefits. Since most aged persons receive income from other sources, such as OASDHI retirement benefits, the effect of these provisions is to guarantee a minimum monthly income of at least $166 to most individuals and $239 to most married couples.

The SSI program adds a new dimension of economic security to the aged. For the first time, they are guaranteed a minimum monthly income by the federal government. About 3.4 million aged people are currently receiving benefits under the new program. The benefits are paid entirely by the federal government, but the states are free to supplement the monthly payments if they wish.

The SSI program is part of the overall system of public assistance in the United States. Public assistance and the controversial issues surrounding welfare programs will be analyzed in greater detail in Chapters 17 and 18.

Other Approaches

Other approaches for attacking the economic problem of old age include laws prohibiting age descrimination, tax relief, the Older Americans Act, and other government programs.

Legislation Prohibiting Age Discrimination.   Both the federal government and the states have enacted laws prohibiting age discrinimation in employment.[34] The federal Age Discrimination Act of 1967 prohibits employers, employment agencies, and labor unions from discriminating against older workers because of age; and 31 states also have laws forbidding age discrimination.

The federal law applies to firms with 20 or more employees, to employment agencies serving covered employers, and to labor unions with 20 or more members. Employers are forbidden to:

1. Discriminate against an older worker with respect to compensation or conditions of employment.

2. Reduce wage rates of other employees to make them equal to the wages paid to workers between ages 40 and 65.

3. Use advertising that favors workers under age 40 or over age 65.

4. Refuse to hire or discharge any individual because of his age.

5. Classify older workers in such a way as to deprive them of employment opportunities or otherwise adversely affect their status based on their age.

[33]James C. Callison, "Early Experience under the Supplemental Security Income Program," *Social Security Bulletin,* Vol. 37, No. 6 (June 1974), 6-7.

[34]An excellent discussion of these laws can be found in Irving Kovarsky and Joel Kovarsky, "Economic, Medical and Legal Aspects of the Age Discrimination Laws in Employment," *Vanderbilt Law Review,* Vol. 27, No. 5 (October 1974), 839-924.

Despite the existence of these laws, however, more than a half-million workers reported age discrimination on the job in 1969. Common violations included illegal advertising, refusal to hire, refusal to promote, and discharges because of age. Stronger law enforcement by both the federal and state governments can undoubtedly do much to reduce future age discrimination in employment.

Tax Relief. Various tax-relief programs may benefit some senior citizens. Under the personal income tax, the aged receive favorable tax treatment, such as a double exemption, retirement-income credit, minimum standard deduction, deductions for medical expenses, and favorable capital-gains treatment when a home is sold. Also, many states provide for state property-tax relief or a homestead exemption. The tax relief may be in the form of a reduction in the assessed value of the home or a tax credit or tax rebate, usually on the income tax return.

However, the importance of favorable tax treatment to the aged is grossly overstated. The various tax savings are relatively meaningless to many low-income aged, since their incomes are not sufficiently high to itemize deductions. Most tax savings accrue to those middle- and upper-income aged who can take advantage of the favorable tax treatment by itemizing their deductions, and less than half the aged do so.[35] Also, most low-income renters cannot take advantage of property-tax deductions even though the rents they pay reflect the property taxes paid. In short, the basic problem of the aged is insufficient income; tax savings are of doubtful value to the low-income aged with inadequate incomes.

Older Americans Act. The Older Americans Act of 1965 is also designed to meet the economic problem of old age. The act created the Administration on Aging in the Department of Health, Education and Welfare. The Administration on Aging is a central focal point in the federal government on matters vital to the economic security of older people, including income maintenance, health, job opportunities, housing, and opportunities for the aged to make a meaningful contribution to the life of a community.

The specific objectives of the Older Americans Act are as follows:

1. An adequate income in retirement, in accordance with the American standard of living.

2. The best possible physical and mental health that science can make available and without regard to economic status.

3. Suitable housing, independently selected, designed, and located with reference to special needs and available at costs older citizens can afford.

4. Full restorative services for those who require institutional care.

5. Opportunity for employment with no discriminatory personnel practices because of age.

6. Retirement in health, honor, and dignity, after years of contribution to the economy.

7. Pursuit of meaningful activity within the widest range of civic, cultural, and recreational opportunities.

[35]U.S. Congress, *Economics of Aging,* p. 26.

8. Efficient community services, which provide social assistance in a coordinated manner and which are readily available when needed.

9. Immediate benefit from proven research knowledge, which can sustain and improve health and happiness.

10. Freedom, independence, and the free exercise of individual initiative in planning and managing their own lives.[36]

To implement these objectives, the act now provides grants for state and area programs, training and research in aging, multipurpose senior centers, volunteer programs for older Americans (such as senior health aides), nutritional programs for the elderly, and a community-service employment program to provide part-time work for low-income people aged 55 and over who are poor employment prospects.

If the objectives of the Older Americans Act are achieved, the economic security of the aged will be significantly improved. Two goals, however, must be emphasized. First, the retired aged who are unable to work must receive an adequate retirement income. Second, employment opportunities without age discrimination must be provided for those aged workers who are physically able and willing to work.

Other Government Programs.   Retirement benefits are also paid under other government programs, including the Railroad Retirement Act, Civil Service Retirement System, retirement plans of state and local governments, and programs for veterans. These ancillary government programs will be analyzed in Chapter 20.

SUGGESTIONS FOR ADDITIONAL READING

Abbott, Julian, "Covered Employment and the Age Men Claim Retirement Benefits," *Social Security Bulletin,* Vol. 37, No. 4 (April 1974).

Brennan, Michael, Philip Taft, and Mark Schupack, *The Economics of Age.* New York: Norton, 1967.

Brinker, Paul A., *Economic Insecurity and Social Security,* Chap. 2. New York: Appleton-Century-Crofts, 1968.

Callison, James C., "Early Experience under the Supplemental Security Income Program," *Social Security Bulletin,* Vol. 37, No. 6 (June 1974).

Committee on Finance, *First Panel Discussion on Private Pension Plan Reform: Which Federal Enforcement Agency; Self-Employed and Voluntary Employee Plans,* Committee on Finance, 93d Cong., 1st sess., 1973. Washington, D.C.: U.S. Government Printing Office, 1973.

[36]U.S. Congress, Senate, Subcommittee on Aging, *Older Americans Comprehensive Service Amendments of 1973, Exploration of 1973 Amendments and Selected Background Material,* Subcommittee on Aging of the Committee on Labor and Public Welfare, 93d Cong., 1st sess., 1973 (Washington, D.C.: U.S. Government Printing Office, 1973), pp. 227-28.

_____, *Second Panel Discussion on Private Pension Plan Reform: Vesting and Funding Provisions, Termination Insurance, Portability, and Fiduciary Standards,* Committee on Finance, 93d Cong., 1st sess., 1973. Washington D.C.: U.S. Government Printing Office, 1973.

Kovarsky, Irving and Joel Kovarsky, "Economic, Medical, and Legal Aspects of the Age Discrimination Laws in Employment," *Vanderbilt Law Review,* Vol. 27, No. 5 (October 1974).

President's Committee on Corporate Pension Funds and Other Private Retirement and Welfare Programs, *Public Policy and Private Pension Programs: A Report to the President on Private Employee Retirement Plans.* Washington, D.C.: U.S. Government Printing Office, 1965.

Schwab, Karen, "Early Labor-Force Withdrawal of Men: Participants and Nonparticipants Aged 58-63," *Social Security Bulletin,* Vol. 37, No. 8 (August 1974).

Simpson, Ida Harper, and John C. McKinney, eds., *Social Aspects of Aging.* Durham, N.C.: Duke University Press, 1966.

Skolnik, Alfred, " Pension Reform Legislation of 1974," *Social Security Bulletin,* Vol. 37, No. 12 (December 1974).

Special Committee on Aging, *Economics of Aging: Toward a Full Share in Abundance,* Report by the Special Committee on Aging, 91st Cong., 2d sess., 1970. Washington, D.C.: U.S. Government Printing Office, 1970.

Subcommittee on Private Pension Plans, *Private Pension Plan Reform.* Hearings before the Subcommittee on Private Pension Plans, Committee on Finance, 93d Cong., 1st sess., 1973. Washington, D.C.: U.S. Government Printing Office, 1973.

Turnbull, John G., C. Arthur Williams, Jr., and Earl F. Cheit, *Economic and Social Security,* 4th ed., Chap. 2. New York: Ronald Press, 1973.

U.S. Department of Health, Education and Welfare, Social Security Administration, Office of Research and Statistics, *Resources of People 65 or Over.* Washington, D.C.: U.S. Government Printing Office, 1971.

U.S. Department of Labor, Bureau of Labor Statistics, *The Employment Problems of Older Workers,* Bulletin 1721. Washington, D.C.: U.S. Government Printing Office, 1971.

White House Conference on Aging, *1971 White House Conference on Aging, A Report to the Delegates from the Conference Sections and Special Concerns Sessions.* Washington, D.C.: U.S. Government Printing Office, 1971.

chapter 5

Old-Age, Survivors, Disability, and Health Insurance

The Old-Age, Survivors, Disability, and Health Insurance (OASDHI) program is the most important public program in the United States for attacking economic insecurity from premature death and old age. It also provides valuable protection against the loss of earnings from disability and high medical expenses for the aged. The OASDHI program is a massive income-maintenance program that provides an important layer of income protection to most individuals and families. More than nine out of ten workers are currently covered for OASDHI benefits, about one out of seven people are currently receiving monthly benefits, and about 22 million of the aged have coverage for their medical expenses under the Medicare program.

In this chapter, we shall be primarily concerned with the current provisions of the OASDHI program. In particular, we shall consider the following: (1) development of the Social Security Act, (2) coverage, (3) determination of insured status, (4) amounts and types of benefits, (5) loss of benefits, and (6) financing and administration.

DEVELOPMENT OF THE SOCIAL SECURITY ACT

Changing Structure of the Economy

The present OASDHI program had its genesis in the Social Security Act of 1935.[1] The enactment of the act was partly the result of the changing social and economic conditions in the United States prior to 1935.

---

[1]The history of the development of the Social Security Act of 1935 can be found in Committee on Economic Security, *Social Security in America: The Factual Background of the Social Security Act as Summarized from Staff Reports to the Committee on Economic Security* (Washington, D.C.:

Before 1870, the United States was predominantly an agricultural economy, which made it possible for many individuals to become financially self-sufficient and provide for their own economic security. A rapidly growing population, an abundance of natural resources, and an open frontier offered economic opportunities to workers and their families. The shift from a predominantly rural to a highly industrialized economy, however, created new risks for the workers. They became dependent on money wages and the sale of their services in the labor markets, and any event that interrupted their incomes, such as old age, unemployment, occupational injuries, or disease, could lead to destitution and poverty. Workers were no longer self-sufficient, but had to depend on a viable economy for jobs and their economic security.

During the early development of the United States, many cities and towns provided some assistance to poor individuals and families, although the aid, often consisting of the poor-relief system and almhouses, was in many cases grudgingly given. As the economy continued to expand, many states enacted laws that provided some financial assistance to widows and orphans. In the 1920s, a few states also provided financial help to the poor, under old age assistance and programs for aid to the blind. Also, after 1900, both the federal government and the states began to enact workmen's compensation legislation. By 1929, most states had passed laws covering occupational injuries to workers. Finally, retirement programs for teachers, policemen, firemen, and military personnel were also established.

The enactment of social insurance programs in the United States, however, lagged behind those in foreign nations. Although Germany established an old-age pension program in 1889 and Great Britain did so in 1909, the United States did not enact such a national program until 1935. The lagging development can be explained by the great American stress on rugged self-individualism, by the unconstitutionality of some early social insurance laws, by the relatively high wages paid before the depression of the 1930s, and by the lack of strong support by some labor unions.

The Great Depression

The Great Depression of the 1930s underscored the need for massive federal action to meet the problem of economic insecurity from old age, unemployment, premature death, and disability. Widespread unemployment, hunger, poverty, and wasted human resources highlighted the need for corrective federal legislation to reduce the economic distress from the severe depression.

The Townsend Plan, proposed in 1934, also focused attention on this need. Under the plan, each citizen aged 60 or over would receive a monthly pension of $200, which had to be spent within thirty days, and the recipient could not engage in any employment. A 2 percent transaction tax was proposed

U.S. Government Printing Office, 1937). See also U.S. Department of Health, Education and Welfare, Social Security Administration, Social Security Programs in the United States (Washington, D.C.: U.S. Government Printing Office, 1973), pp. 1-54; and U.S. Department of Health, Education and Welfare, Social Security Administration, Office of the Actuary, History of the Provisions of Old-Age, Survivors, Disability, and Health Insurance, 1935-72 (February 1937).

to finance the plan. The Townsend Plan was never realized, however, primarily because of the financing problem, concerns about the incidence of the tax, possible inflationary effects, and the fact that $200 was such a relatively high benefit compared to prevailing wage levels.[2]

Enactment of the Social Security Act

President Franklin D. Roosevelt created the Committee on Economic Security in 1934 to study the problem of economic insecurity and make suggestions for legislation. The committee's report, submitted in 1935, culminated in the passage of the historical Social Security Act on August 14, 1935. The original act provided for a compulsory federal program of old-age benefits for workers in industry and commerce, a federal-state program of unemployment insurance, and federal grants-in-aid to the states for old-age assistance, aid to the blind, and aid to dependent children. In addition, the act established federal grants to the states for maternal and child health services, services for crippled children, public health services, and vocational rehabilitation.

The old-age benefits provided for in the original act were only retirement benefits at age 65 for most workers in industry and commerce. Since then, the program has been changed and liberalized several times. In 1939, survivorship benefits were added. In the 1950s, coverage was broadened to include most self-employed persons, household and farm employees, members of the armed services, clergymen, and most state and local government employees; today, most of the labor force is covered for benefits. In 1954, disability insurance was added, to cover the loss of earnings from total disability. In 1965, the Medicare program was enacted, to provide hospital and medical insurance for the aged. Since July 1, 1973, Medicare is available also to people under 65 who are entitled to disability-income checks for two or more years, and to those with a serious kidney disease requiring dialysis treatment or a kidney transplant.

Congress has been extremely generous to OASDHI beneficiaries in recent years. Monthly benefits were increased approximately 13 percent and 15 percent in 1967 and 1969, respectively, and 10 percent in 1971. The 1972 amendments provided for a 20 percent increase in benefits and also increased the maximum taxable earnings base to $10,800 in 1973 and $12,000 in 1974.[3] The 1972 amendments also added an automatic cost of living provision whereby benefits would be increased based on significant changes in the Consumer Price Index (CPI). If the cost of living increased 3 percent or more between specified base periods, the benefits would be automatically increased by the same amount the following January unless Congress had already acted to increase benefits. The first automatic increase could not occur before January 1975.

In 1973, the program was again changed. The July 9, 1973 amendments provided for a 5.9 percent increase in benefits and changed the taxable earnings base in 1974 from $12,000 to $12,600. The increase in benefits was to become

[2]For a historical discussion of the Townsend Plan, see Arthur J. Altmeyer, *The Formative Years of Social Security* (Madison: University of Wisconsin Press, 1966), pp. 9-11, 105-6, 242-43.

[3]U.S. Department of Health, Education and Welfare, Social Security Administration, *History of the Provisions of Old-Age, Survivors, Disability, and Health Insurance 1935-72* (February 1973), p. 3.

effective in June 1974 and would be reflected in the July 1974 checks. The scheduled increase of 5.9 percent was based on the increase in the CPI from June 1972 to June 1973. The benefit increase was considered only temporary and was to be replaced by an automatic increase in benefits in January 1975 based on the increase in the CPI from the third quarter of 1972 to the second quarter of 1974.

Because of the rapid increase in prices and erosion of benefits, however, the July 9, 1973 amendments never became fully operational. Congress again changed the law in late 1973. The December 31, 1973 amendments modified the earlier July 9, 1973 amendments that provided for a 5.9 percent benefit increase and an increase in the taxable earnings base to $12,600 in 1974. Monthly benefits were increased 11 percent in two steps to compensate for the sharp rise in the cost of living. The first step was a 7 percent benefit increase, effective March 1974. The remaining 4 percent became effective in June 1974. The December 31, 1973 amendments also increased the maximum taxable earnings base to $13,200 in 1974 (rather than $12,600). Also, the law provided that the first possible automatic increase in benefits would become effective in June 1975 (rather than January 1975) based on the increase in the CPI from the second quarter of 1974 to the first quarter of 1975.

Because of the continuing rapid increase in prices, the maximum taxable earnings base was increased automatically to $14,100 in 1975. Benefits were also increased 8 percent in June 1975 according to the automatic provisions.

COVERED OCCUPATIONS

The OASDHI program is a compulsory program that covers most gainfully employed workers.[4] Most occupations are covered, but in certain occupations, the employee or employer must elect the coverage, or coverage is provided only after certain conditions are met. The major occupations that require the election of coverage or fulfillment of certain conditions include the following:

1. *Self-Employment.* Self-employed people are covered on a compulsory basis if their net annual earnings are $400 or more. This includes self-employed professionals, such as physicians, dentists, and attorneys.

2. *Farm Operator.* Self-employed farmers are covered if their net annual earnings are at least $400. There is an alternate reporting system based on gross income for low-income farmers.

3. *Farm Worker.* A farm worker is covered if he earns $150 or more in cash wages from any employer during the year, or if he works for an employer on twenty or more days during the year for cash wages based on time rather than piecework.

4. *Household Workers.* Household workers are covered if they receive cash wages of $50 or more in a calendar quarter from any employer.

[4]A current description of the OASDHI program can be found in Commerce Clearing House, Inc., *1974 Social Security and Medicare Explained—Including Medicaid* (Chicago: Commerce Clearing House, Inc., 1974). See also Social Security Administration, *Your Social Security,* DHEW Publication No. (SSA) 75-10035 (November 1974). The basic characteristics of the OASDHI program can be found in Social Security Administration, *Social Security Programs in the United States.* Answers to specific questions can be found in The National Underwriter Company, *Social Security Manual, Including January 1974 Amendments* (Cincinnati, O.: The National Underwriter Company, 1974).

5. *Employees Receiving Tips.* Employees receiving cash tips of $20 or more in a month from one employer are also covered. The employer reports the tips, but does not match the Social Security tax contributions on the tips.

6. *Employees of Nonprofit Organizations.* Employees of nonprofit organizations, such as religious, charitable, or educational organizations, are covered if the organization waives its exemption from the payment of Social Security tax contributions, and the employees elect coverage. The coverage is voluntary when the organization first elects coverage. Thereafter, coverage is compulsory for new employees.

7. *Employees of State and Local Governments.* State and local government employees can be covered by a voluntary agreement between the state and the federal government.

8. *Ministers.* Ministers are automatically covered unless they elect out because of conscience or religious principles. Those electing out must file an exemption form. Once filed, the form cannot be withdrawn. Although clergymen may be working as employees, they report their income and pay tax contributions as if they were self-employed.

9. *Federal Employment.* Most federal government employees not covered by their own retirement system are covered by the OASDHI program.

10. *Family Employment.* A parent employed in a son's or daughter's business or trade is covered. But domestic work performed by a parent in the household of a son or daughter is not covered unless certain conditions are fulfilled, and a son or daughter under age 21 who is employed in a parent's business is not covered. Also, there is no coverage if a wife works for her husband, or the husband works for his wife.

11. *Foreign Employment.* United States citizens employed by American firms in foreign countries or on American vessels or aircraft are also covered. American citizens working abroad for a foreign subsidiary of a United States corporation are covered if the parent firm makes arrangements with the Secretary of the Treasury for the payment of OASDHI tax contributions.

12. *Military Service.* People on active duty in the military uniformed services after 1956 are also covered by the OASDHI program. Wage credits of $160 monthly are granted for military service from September 16, 1940, through 1956. An additional wage credit of $100 is granted for each month of active military service after 1956.

13. *Railroad Employment.* Railroad workers have their own retirement system under the Railroad Retirement Act. Those with ten or more years of service generally receive benefits paid by the Railroad Retirement Board. However, for those workers with less than ten years of service who retire or become disabled, railroad employment earnings are also considered in determining their retirement or disability benefits under the Social Security law. A railroad worker with at least ten years of service may also have worked in covered employment under the OASDHI program and may be eligible for both Railroad Retirement and OASDHI benefits. However, the survivors of a deceased worker can receive benefits from only one system, even though the worker may have been covered under both during his lifetime. Regardless of the program that pays benefits, both railroad and OASDHI earnings are combined to determine survivorship benefits.

14. *Excluded Occupations.* Except in a few states, policemen and firemen with their own retirement systems are excluded. Federal government employees covered

under the Civil Service Retirement System are also excluded. The U.S. president and vice-president, members of Congress, and other special classes are not covered. Farm work performed by foreign workers temporarily admitted into the United States is also excluded. Finally, foreign-exchange visitors who are temporarily admitted into the United States to study, teach, conduct research, and perform similar activities are not covered if the work is necessary to carry out the purpose for which they were admitted.

DETERMINATION OF INSURED STATUS

Before a worker can receive OASDHI benefits for himself or his family, he must have credit for a certain amount of work in covered employment. The worker receives one quarter of coverage if he earns $50 or more in covered employment during a calendar quarter. If he works the entire year, he receives four quarters of coverage. A self-employed person receives four quarters of coverage if his annual net income from self-employment is $400 or more.

The worker must attain an insured status to become eligible for the various benefits. There are three types of insured status: (1) fully insured, (2) currently insured, and (3) disability insured. Retirement benefits require a fully insured status; survivorship benefits require either a fully insured or currently insured; and disability benefits require a disability-insured status.

Fully Insured

A person is fully insured if he meets one of the following tests: (1) He has 40 quarters of coverage in covered employment, or (2) he has one quarter of coverage for each year after 1950 (or after age 21 if later) up to the year he dies, becomes disabled, or attains age 62. A minimum of six quarters is required under the second test. The quarters of coverage can be counted any time they are earned. For example, if Len Walle works during high school, college, or later, he is fully insured after acquiring 40 quarters of coverage, or ten years of work. He retains this status even though he may never work again in covered employment. A fully insured status can also be attained under the second test. For example, if George May retires in 1976 at age 62, he is fully insured if he has 25 quarters of coverage.

Currently Insured

A person is currently insured if he has at least six quarters of coverage out of the last 13 quarters, including the quarter in which he dies, reaches age 62, or retires. Most workers can easily attain a currently insured status.

Disability Insured

A worker is insured for disability benefits if he attains a fully insured status and has 20 quarters of coverage out of the last 40 quarters, including the quarter in which he becomes disabled. A smaller number of quarters is required if the disabled worker is under age 31. In addition, a special exception applies to the blind in determining a disability-insured status, since they are exempt from the requirement of recent attachment to covered work.[5]

BENEFIT AMOUNTS

Average Monthly Wage

All monthly income benefits are based on the worker's primary insurance amount (PIA). The primary insurance amount, in turn, is derived from the worker's average monthly wage (AMW). The benefits can be based on average monthly earnings beginning with 1951 (or 1937 if higher benefits result). A certain number of low years of earnings can be eliminated in computing the AMW. The AMW can be determined by the following steps:

1. Count the number of years after 1950 (or after age 21, if later) up to the year the worker dies, becomes disabled, or attains age 62, whichever is appropriate.

2. Subtract 5 from the number of years determined in the first step. This has the effect of eliminating some years with little or no earnings. Also, years during which the worker is partly or wholly disabled can be eliminated. At least two years must be included in the base for disability or survivorship benefits.

3. Count the worker's earnings for all years after 1950 up to the year that he retires. Include earnings in the year of death or year the disability began. Do not count more than the following amounts:

1951-54	$ 3,600
1955-58	4,200
1959-65	4,800
1966-67	6,600
1968-71	7,800
1972	9,000
1973	10,800
1974	13,200
1975	14,100*

*Subject to an automatic adjustment for 1976 and later if benefits are automatically increased.

4. Select the highest years of earnings equal to the number of years determined in Step 2. Add the earnings and then divide by the appropriate number of months to compute the AMW.

[5]See Chapter 10.

For example, ignoring the effect of the automatic cost-of-living adjustment (discussed later), assume that Joe Oziah reaches age 62 in 1975 and then retires in 1978. There are 24 years between 1951 and 1975, the year Joe attains age 62. Five years can be dropped. In determining Joe's AMW, the highest 19 years of earnings must be selected (1975-1951, less 5). Assume that Joe has earned the maximum amount each year that is subject to OASDHI taxes. In this case the highest 19 years are 1959-77. Thus, Joe's AMW is $672 ($153,300 ÷ 228). The AMW is then used to determine the worker's primary insurance amount. In this case, Joe's primary insurance amount is $373.60.[6]

Primary Insurance Amount

The primary insurance amount is the monthly benefit paid to a retired or disabled worker and is based on his average monthly wage. All additional benefits are expressed as a percentage of the primary insurance amount.

A complex formula is used to determine the primary insurance amount. Based on the benefit table effective June 1974, the current formula is as follows:

119.89 percent of the first $110 of AMW
+
43.61 percent of the next $290 of AMW
+
40.75 percent of the next $150 of AMW
+
47.90 percent of the next $100 of AMW
+
26.64 percent of the next $100 of AMW
+
22.20 percent of the next $250 of AMW
+
20.00 percent of the next $100 of AMW,
subject to a minimum primary insurance
amount of $93.80 for AMWs of $76 or less.[7]

The formula above weighs the benefits heavily in favor of the low-income groups. This is necessary to provide socially adequate benefits to people with low earnings. In addition, the formula also reflects the principle of relating the OASDHI benefits to the worker's earnings. As the worker's average monthly wage increases, the primary insurance amount also increases, but not proportionally to the increase in earnings.

Table 5-1 illustrates the benefit amounts for selected categories of retirement and survivorship beneficiaries.

[6]For other examples, see National Underwriter Company, *Social Security Manual,* pp. 70-86.

[7]Albert Rettig and Orlo R. Nichols, Social Security Administration, Office of the Actuary, *Actuarial Note Number 83, Changes in Social Security Benefits under Public Law 93-233* (March 1974), p. 2.

Automatic Cost-of-Living Adjustment

As a result of the 1972 amendments, the monthly OASDHI cash payments are now inflation-proof. As prices rise, an automatic cost-of-living adjustment based on the Consumer Price Index (CPI) will be applied to each factor in the benefit formula, in order to protect the real purchasing power of the benefits. The original cost-of-living provision was modified by the December 31, 1973, amendments.

The benefits will automatically increase whenever the CPI over the measuring period increases by at least 3 percent. In accordance with the revised law, the first possible benefit increase, effective June 1975, was based on the increase in the cost of living from the second quarter of 1974 through the first quarter of 1975. (The CPI for a calendar quarter is based on the average of three monthly CPIs). In future years, automatic benefit increases will be effective in the month of June, and in general, they will be based on the cost of living from the first quarter of one year to the first quarter of the next year.

This measuring period will be modified if Congress should legislate a benefit increase. In such a case, the measuring period would be from the quarter in which the legislated increase becomes effective to the applicable first quarter. However, the automatic adjustment will not apply if Congress has enacted a general benefit increase in the preceding year, or if an *ad hoc* benefit increase should become effective.[8]

Finally, if an automatic adjustment occurs, the taxable wage base and earnings test (discussed later) are also to be automatically adjusted.

Special Minimum Benefit

The 1972 amendments also established a special minimum retirement benefit for workers who have been covered under the OASDHI program for at least 20 years. This benefit was later modified by the December 31, 1973 amendments.

The special minimum benefit amount depends on the number of years of coverage. (After 1950, a year of coverage is defined as a year in which the worker has earnings equal to at least 25 percent of the OASDHI taxable wage base.) Based on current law, the special minimum benefit is $9 per month for each year of coverage above ten years and up to 30 years, with a maximum monthly benefit of $180. Thus, a worker aged 65, with 25 years of coverage, would receive a minimum monthly benefit of $135, and one with 30 years of coverage would receive $180. The purpose of the special minimum benefit is to enable some low-income workers with a long history of coverage to receive higher retire-

[8]*Ibid.*, p. 16.

TABLE 5-1 Examples of Monthly OASDHI Cash Benefits

Disabled or Retired Worker

Average Monthly Wage	Worker Aged 65	Worker and Spouse Aged 65 or over	Worker and Spouse Aged 62	Worker, Wife, and One Child
$ 76 or less	$ 93.80	$140.70	$129.00	$140.80
250	194.10	291.20	267.00	296.90
350	236.80	355.20	325.60	411.60
450	278.20	417.30	382.60	519.40
550	320.20	480.30	440.30	579.80
650	367.50	551.30	505.40	643.10
750	393.50	590.30	541.10	688.70
900	426.80	640.20	586.90	747.00
1,100	469.00	703.50	644.90	820.80

Survivorship Benefits

Average Monthly Wage	Widow Aged 65	Widow Aged 60	Mother and One Child	Mother and Two Children	Maximum Family Budget
$ 76 or less	$ 93.80	$ 74.90	$140.80	$141.00	$140.80
250	194.10	138.80	291.20	297.00	296.80
350	236.80	169.40	355.20	411.60	411.50
450	278.20	199.00	417.40	519.60	519.40
550	320.20	229.00	480.40	579.90	579.80
650	367.50	262.80	551.40	643.20	643.10
750	393.50	281.40	590.40	688.80	688.70
900	426.80	305.20	640.20	747.00	747.00
1,100	469.00	335.40	703.60	820.80	820.80

Note: The benefits reflect the level of benefits as of January, 1975 and are subject to the automatic cost-of-living provision. Maximum benefit amounts, however, will not be paid until later years. This is because maximum earnings covered by the OASDHI program were lower in previous years, and those years with a lower taxable wage base must be included with the higher limits of recent years, and determining the worker's average monthly wage. However, up to 5 years of low earnings or no earnings can be excluded in determining the average monthly wage.

Source: Social Security Administration.

ment benefits. At the end of December 1973, only 200,000 persons, or less than 1 percent of all beneficiaries, were receiving special minimum benefits.[9]

Delayed-Retirement Credit

The 1972 amendments also established a special retirement credit for workers who do not receive OASDHI benefits before age 65 and continue to work beyond that age. The primary benefit is increased 1 percent for each year of delay beyond age 65 and before age 72. The special credit applies only to people who have worked after 1970, and only to the worker's benefits, not to those of survivors or dependents.

TYPES OF BENEFITS

OASDHI benefits can be classified into four major categories: (1) retirement benefits, (2) survivorship benefits, (3) disability benefits, and (4) Medicare benefits. We shall analyze only retirement and survivorship benefits in this chapter. Disability benefits and the Medicare program will be treated in Chapter 10, when the role of social insurance programs in meeting the health-care problem in the United States will be examined.

Retirement Benefits

Retirement benefits provide an important layer of income protection to a retired worker and his family. Without these benefits, economic insecurity among the aged would be substantially increased.

The Retired Worker. A retired worker receives a monthly income benefit equal to his primary insurance amount if he meets certain requirements. He must be fully insured; he must be aged 65 to receive full benefits; and he must not earn an income in excess of the maximum permitted by the earnings test. The worker can retire earlier, as early as age 62, and receive actuarially reduced benefits: The benefits payable at age 65 are reduced by 5/9 of 1 percent for each month he is under 65. Thus, a worker retiring at 62 receives 80 percent of his full primary insurance amount. If a person retires early and works after early retirement and has benefits withheld, the benefits are automatically recomputed at age 65 to in recognition of the earnings.

Unmarried Children under 18. Unmarried children under age 18, or 22 if in school, are eligible for benefits based on the retired worker's earnings. If the child reaches 22 after the semester or quarter begins, the benefits are paid to the end of the term. The retired worker must be supporting the children or have some obligation to do so when the application for benefits is made. Each un-

---

[9]Barbara A. Lingg, Social Security Administration, Division of OASDHI Statistics, *Research and Statistics Note 17; The Effects of the Special Minimum Primary Insurance Amount and the Delayed Retirement Credit: Initial Findings* (June 21, 1974), p. 2.

married child receives a maximum benefit equal to 50 percent of the worker's primary insurance amount until age 18, or until 22 if in school.

Finally, grandchildren are eligible for benefits based on a grandparent's earnings if they are supported by and are living with the grandparent. The children's parents must have died or must be totally disabled.

Unmarried Disabled Children. Unmarried disabled children aged 18 or over, if they were severely disabled before age 22 and continue to be disabled, are also eligible for benefits based on the retired worker's earnings. The benefit is 50 percent of the primary insurance amount.

Wife of Retired Worker. The wife of a retired worker can also receive retirement benefits. If she is aged 65, she receives a full benefit equal to 50 percent of her husband's primary insurance amount. If the husband is receiving reduced benefits because of early retirement, the wife's benefit is computed on the amount the husband would have received had he actually retired at 65, not on a percentage of her husband's reduced benefit.

The wife can elect reduced benefits at age 62, but her benefit is reduced 25/36 of 1 percent for each month under age 65. Thus, if she retires at 62, she receives a benefit equal to 75 percent of what she would have had if she had waited until age 65 (75 percent of 50 percent of the husband's primary insurance amount).

A divorced wife is also eligible for benefits under certain conditions. She must have been married to the insured for at least 20 years, must be at least 62, and must not have remarried.

Finally, the wife who has worked may be eligible for benefits based on her own earnings as well as those of her husband. However, she does not receive two benefits, but only the higher of the two.

Wife with Children under 18. A wife under age 62 is entitled to a monthly benefit if she is caring for an eligible child under 18 (or a child of any age who was totally disabled before age 22) who is receiving a benefit based upon the retired worker's earnings. The benefit is equal to 50 percent of the primary insurance amount. The mother's benefit terminates when the youngest child reaches age 18 (unless the mother is caring for a disabled child over 18 who became disabled before age 22).

Dependent Husband. A dependent husband of a retired woman worker is also eligible for benefits under certain conditions. He must be at least 62, the wife must be fully insured, and she must contribute at least half his support. If the dependent husband is 65 or over, he receives 50 percent of his wife's primary insurance amount. If he desires, he can receive reduced benefits earlier, at age 62.

Maximum Family Benefit. The maximum family benefit is based on a complex formula that weights the benefits heavily in favor of low-income families. Based on current law, the maximum family benefit ranges from $140.80, on an average monthly wage of $76 or less, to $820.80, based on an average monthly wage of $1,100. These amounts are all subject to the automatic-adjustment provision described earlier.

Special Transitional Benefits. Special transitional benefits can be paid to certain people aged 72 and over who have an insufficient number of quarters of coverage to be fully insured under the law. A monthly benefit of $64.40 can be paid to an individual, and a couple can receive $96.60. These amounts are also subject to the automatic-adjustment provision. The purpose of the special benefit is to provide some income to older people who did not acquire a fully insured status during their working years. The special benefit is suspended if the person is receiving Supplemental Security Income benefits. In addition, the amount paid is reduced by any other government pension the person may be receiving. These special payments are financed out of the general revenues of the federal government, not out of the OASDHI trust funds.

Survivorship Benefits

OASDHI survivorship benefits provide considerable protection against economic insecurity because of premature death. These benefits compare favorably with private insurance equivalents. A young worker with two dependents, who has average monthly earnings of $600, has insurance protection with a present value of about $90,000. Moreover, the benefits are inflation-proof because of the automatic-adjustment provision.[10]

Unmarried Children under 18. An unmarried child under 18, or 22 if a full-time student, is eligible for benefits based on the deceased parent's earnings. The deceased parent must be either fully or currently insured. The benefit for each child is 75 percent of the deceased's primary insurance amount. The income continues until the child reaches age 18, or 22 if in school. Finally, grandchildren may be eligible for benefits based on a grandparent's earnings, if the requirements described earlier for retirement benefits are met.

Unmarried Disabled Children. An unmarried child aged 18 or over is also eligible for survivorship benefits is he becomes severely disabled before age 22 and continues to be disabled. The benefit is 75 percent of the primary insurance amount. The deceased parent must be either fully or currently insured.

Widow of the Deceased. A widow (or dependent widower) aged 60 or older is also eligible for survivorship benefits. The deceased must be fully insured. The widow receives a full benefit equal to 100 percent of the primary insurance amount if she waits until age 65. She can receive reduced benefits as early as age 60, but the benefits are reduced by 19/40 of 1 percent for each month under 65. Thus, a widow aged 60 would receive only 71.5 percent of the primary insurance amount. A divorced wife of a deceased worker may also be eligible for survivorship benefits under certain conditions.

Widow with Children under 18. A widow is entitled to a monthly benefit

---

[10]U.S. Congress, Senate, Special Committee on Aging, *Future Directions in Social Security,* Hearings before the Special Committee on Aging, United States Senate, 93d Cong., 1st sess., 1973, Part 1, p. 19.

if she is caring for an eligible child under age 18 (or disabled) who is receiving a benefit based on the deceased worker's earnings. The deceased must be either fully or currently insured. The benefit is 75 percent of the primary insurance amount, which is paid until the youngest child reaches age 18. If the widow is under 60 and remarries, or has earned income exceeding the maximum permitted by the earnings test, she will lose all or some of her monthly benefits. The children's benefits, however, will still continue. Finally, a divorced wife with children in her care under age 18 at the time of the deceased's death is also eligible for survivorship benefits under certain conditions.

Disabled Widow. A disabled widow (or dependent widower) aged 50 or older is also eligible for survivorship benefits under certain conditions. The widow must have become disabled within seven years after her husband's death, or within seven years after she stops receiving benefits as a mother caring for the deceased's children. In addition, she must be unable to engage in any substantial gainful activity, which is a more severe test of disability than that applied to other disabled beneficiaries. She can receive survivorship benefits as early as age 50, but the benefits are reduced for each month under age 65. The following reductions apply:

Ages 60 through 64	19/40 of 1 percent for each month under age 65
Ages 50 through 59	43/240 of 1 percent for each month under age 60

Thus, if she claims the benefits at age 60, she receives 71.5 percent of the primary insurance amount; at age 50 she receives 50 percent.

Dependent Parents. Parents at least age 62 are eligible for survivorship benefits if they are dependent on the deceased's earnings for at least half their support. The deceased worker must be fully insured. The benefit is 75 percent of the primary insurance amount if both parents are receiving benefits, and 82.5 percent if only one parent is receiving them.

Lump-Sum Death Benefit. A lump-sum death benefit is also payable, equal to three times the primary insurance amount, with a maximum amount of $255. The worker must be either fully or currently insured. The death benefit is paid to the surviving spouse or the person responsible for the burial expenses.

LOSS OF BENEFITS

OASDHI benfits may terminate under certain conditions. Also, if a beneficiary has work earnings in excess of a specified maximum, he may lose all or part of his benefits.

General Situations

A mother loses her benefits when she is no longer caring for a child under age 18 or no longer caring for a disabled child. A child loses his benefits when he reaches age 18, or 22 if in school, with the exception that benefits can continue if he becomes disabled before age 22. Death or recovery from disability also causes the benefits to terminate. In addition, the benefits are suspended if the person is deported because of conviction for a crime, or because of conviction of certain crimes committed against the United States, such as treason or espionage. Finally, the benefits paid to a child, an aged parent, a widow receiving mother's benefits, a widower, a divorced wife, or a disabled widow generally terminate when the beneficiary marries a person who is not receiving dependents' or survivorship benefits. One exception is a widow who remarries after age 60 or a widower after age 62.

Earnings Test

The earnings test (retirement test) can also result in a loss of benefits. If the person who is receiving benefits has excess earnings, he will lose some or all of his benefits. The purpose of the test is to restrict the payment of benefits only to those who have lost their earned income, and also to hold down the cost of the program. Based on the provisions in effect in 1975, the following test was applied to annual earnings:

> $0 - $2,520:   No loss of benefits
> Over $2,520:   Loss of $1 of benefits
>   for each $2 of earnings

Thus, a worker could earn up to $2,520 annually without losing any benefits for the year. If his earnings exceeded $2,520, however, he would lose $1 of benefits for each $2 of earnings in excess of $2,520. For example, if George May, 66, earned $400 monthly after retiring, he would lose $1,140 in benefits for the year.

The amount of earned income exempted from the retirement test will be automatically increased in the future as wage levels increase. Under the revised law, the monthly exempt amount for 1975 is determined by multiplying $200 (amount exempt in 1974) by the ratio of the average taxable wage for the first quarter of 1974 to such average wage for the first quarter of 1973, and cannot be less than the exempt amount for 1974. The product is rounded off to the nearest multiple of $10. The annual exempt amount will always be twelve times the monthly exempt amount.

After 1975, automatic adjustments in the exempt amount can be effective only for the calendar year following the effective date of an automatic benefit increase. The exempt amount will be based on the ratio of the average first-quarter wage in the year of an automatic benefit increase to the average first-quarter wage in the year before the year in which the exempt amount was most recently increased.[11] This provision will ensure that automatic increases in exempt amounts will be proportional to all increases in wage levels.

Finally, the earnings test applies only to survivorship and retirement benefits. Special rules apply to disability-income benefits.[12]

The earnings test has three major exceptions. First, a person aged 72 or older can earn any amount and still receive full benefits. This exception violates sound logic and good economics. In effect, the law encourages a worker of 72 or older to reenter the labor force, since he is not penalized by working. However, if he is under 72, the test discourages him from working, since he is penalized if he earns more than the maximums allowed. Thus, the law encourages him to work when he is perhaps least able to work because of old age, senility, and poor health, but discourages employment at a younger age when he can work if his health permits.

Second, income from savings, investments, insurance, pensions, or royalties is not subject to the earnings test, so a person could have an unlimited amount of income from these sources and still receive full benefits. The purpose of this exception is to encourage private savings and investments to supplement the OASDHI benefits. If the benefits were reduced or terminated because of investment income or private insurance, individual savings and thrift would be discouraged.

Finally, regardless of total earnings for the year, full benefits are paid for any month during which the worker neither earns wages of more than $210 nor performs substantial services in self-employment. The purpose of the third exception is to pay full retirement benefits, starting with the first month of retirement, to the worker who retires in the middle or near the end of the year. Otherwise, he would lose some or all of his benefits if he retired after earning the maximum allowed under the test.

The earnings test is a highly controversial issue that will be analyzed in greater detail in Chapter 6.

FINANCING

The OASDHI program is financed by a payroll tax paid by employees, employers, and the self-employed, plus a relatively small amount of interest income on trust-fund investments. Except for a few special situations, the general revenues of the federal government are not used to finance the program.[13]

---

[11]Rettig and Nichols, *Actuarial Note Number 83*, p. 16.

[12]See Chapter 10.

[13]General revenues of the federal government are used to pay the costs of noncontributory wage credits for military service, payments to noninsured persons aged 72 and over, the federal government's matching share of Supplementary Medical Insurance premiums, and the costs of covering certain uninsured persons under the Hospital Insurance portion of the Medicare Program. General revenues are also used to pay the interest on the OASDHI trust funds.

Payroll Tax

The covered worker pays a payroll tax on his earnings up to a specified maximum limit, and the amount is matched by an identical contribution from the employer. The self-employed contribute at a slightly lower rate than the combined rate paid by employers and employees.

In 1975, the worker paid a tax contribution rate of 5.85 percent on a maximum taxable earnings base of $14,100. This amount was matched by an identical contribution from the employer. The self-employed paid 7.90 percent on the same earnings base. The contribution rate is scheduled to increase in the future, and the maximum-earnings base will also be adjusted if the benefits are increased according to the automatic cost-of-living provisions. Table 5-2 illustrates the present contribution-rate schedule for the OASDI, and HI portions of the total OASDHI program.

As stated earlier, the taxable earnings base will be adjusted as average wages and benefit levels increase. The earnings base for 1975 is determined by multiplying $13,200 (1974 base) by the ratio of the average taxable wage of all covered workers for the first quarter of 1974 to such average wage for the first quarter of 1973. The product is rounded to the nearest multiple of $300 and cannot be less than the base in 1974.

After 1975, automatic adjustments in the earnings base can be effective only for the calendar year that follows the effective date of an automatic benefit increase. The automatic adjustment in the earnings base will be based on the ratio of the average first-quarter wage in the year of an automatic benefit increase to the average first-quarter wage in the year before the year in which the earnings base was most recently increased.[14]

Trust Funds

The tax contributions are deposited into four federal trust funds. The contributions for retirement, survivors, and disability benefits are deposited into the Old-Age and Survivors and Disability Insurance Trust Funds. The contributions for financing the health insurance portion are deposited into the Hospital Insurance Trust Fund. The monthly premiums to finance the medical insurance portion are deposited, along with the federal government's matching contributions, into the Supplemental Medical Insurance Trust Fund. All sums needed for the various benefits and administrative expenses are paid out of the trust funds. The excess contributions not needed for current benefits and administrative expenses are invested in interest-bearing federal government securities.

This brief discussion is only a highlight of some important financing provisions. However, there are numerous controversial problems and issues associated with the financing of the OASDHI program, including whether the program is actuarially sound and whether the financing should be changed to

[14]Rettig and Nichols, *Actuarial Note Number 83*, p. 16.

TABLE 5-2   OASDHI Contribution Rates

Year	OASDI	HI	Total
	Employer and Employee Each		
1974-77	4.95%	0.90%	5.85%
1978-80	4.95	1.10	6.05
1981-85	4.95	1.35	6.30
1986-2010	4.95	1.50	6.45
2011 and thereafter	5.95	1.50	7.45
	Self-Employed		
1974-77	7.0%	0.90%	7.90%
1978-80	7.0	1.10	8.10
1981-85	7.0	1.35	8.35
1986-2010	7.0	1.50	8.50
2011 and thereafter	7.0	1.50	8.50

Source: Social Security Administration.

include general-revenue financing. These important issues will be discussed in Chapter 7, when the financing provisions of OASDHI and the trust funds are analyzed in greater detail.

ADMINISTRATION

The federal government administers the OASDHI program. The Social Security Administration, which is a part of the Department of Health, Education and Welfare, has about 1,300 regional and district offices located in various parts of the country. The offices provide local residents with information and assist them in filing claims.

Each covered worker receives a Social Security card and a number that is used to record his earnings. The Social Security number is also used for income tax purposes. The earnings record is filed by the Social Security Administration at its central office in Baltimore, Maryland. The worker needs only one card during his lifetime, and duplicate cards are issued if the original is lost. The insured person is encouraged to check periodically on his earnings to make sure they are correctly reported. If the worker believes a decision on a claim or earnings record is incorrect, he can ask the Social Security Administration to reconsider the decision. If he is still dissatisfied, he can request a hearing before the Bureau of Hearings and Appeals and a review by the Appeals Council. The final step is to appeal to the federal courts. Thus, the covered worker has many avenues open to him to protect his rights.

SUGGESTIONS FOR ADDITIONAL READING

Altmeyer, Arthur J., *The Formative Years of Social Security.* Madison: University of Wisconsin Press, 1966.

Brown, J. Douglas, *The Genesis of Social Security in America.* Princeton, N.J.: Princeton University, Industrial Relations Section, 1969.

Commerce Clearing House, Inc., *1974 Social Security and Medicare Explained—Including Medicaid.* Chicago: Commerce Clearing House, Inc., 1974.

Committee on Economic Security, *Social Security in America: The Factual Background of the Social Security Act as Summarized from Staff Reports to the Committee on Economic Security.* Washington, D.C.: U.S. Government Printing Office, 1937.

Myers, Robert J., *Social Insurance and Allied Government Programs.* Homewood, Ill.: Richard D. Irwin, 1965.

_____, "Social Security Benefits for Retirement, Disability, and Survivorship," in Davis W. Gregg and Vane B. Lucas, eds., *Life and Health Insurance Handbook,* 3rd ed. Homewood, Ill.: Richard D. Irwin, 1973.

The National Underwriter Company, *Social Security Manual, Including January 1974 Amendments.* Cincinnati, O.: The National Underwriter Company, 1974.

Rettig, Albert, and Orlo R. Nichols, Social Security Administration, Office of the Actuary, *Actuarial Note Number 83, Changes in Social Security Benefits under Public Law 93-233,* March 1974.

_____, Social Security Administration, Office of the Actuary, *Actuarial Note Number 87, Some Aspects of the Dynamic Projections of Benefits under the 1973 Social Security Amendments (P.L. 93-233),* April 1974.

Schottland, Charles I., *The Social Security Program in the United States,* 2nd ed. New York: Appleton-Century-Crofts, 1970.

Social Security Administration, "Social Security Act Amendments, End of 1973," *Social Security Bulletin,* Vol. 37, No. 4 (April 1974), 35-40.

Turnbull, John G., C. Arthur Williams, Jr., and Earl F. Cheit, *Economic and Social Security,* 4th ed., Chap. 4. New York: Ronald Press, 1973.

U.S. Department of Health, Education and Welfare, Social Security Administration, *Social Security Programs in the United States.* Washington, D.C.: U.S. Government Printing Office, 1973.

Witte, Edwin E., *The Development of the Social Security Act: A Memorandum on the History of the Committee on Economic Security and Drafting and Legislative History of the Social Security Act.* Madison: University of Wisconsin Press, 1962.

_____, *Your Social Security*, DHEW Publication No. (SSA) 75-10035 (November 1974).

chapter 6

Problems and Issues
in the OASDHI Program

A great many problems and issues are associated with the OASDHI program, some of them very controversial, and there are few clear-cut answers. In this chapter, we shall examine some of these important issues—in particular, the following: (1) coverage, (2) benefits, (3) treatment of women, (4) retirement test, (5) early retirement, (6) the OASDHI program as an antipoverty tool, and (7) the treatment of younger workers under the OASDHI program.

COVERAGE

The OASDHI program is a nearly universal system, covering 91 percent of those aged 65 and over at the present time. Four percent of the aged are covered under other federal retirement systems, and only 5 percent are ineligible for retirement benefits under any federal system.[1] Thus, one important objective of social insurance—providing a layer of income protection to the masses—has been largely achieved for the old-age risk. However, certain problem areas still remain.

Civil Service

One important problem that remains to be solved is the lack of coordination between the Civil Service Retirement System and the OASDHI program. This lack of coordination often leads to inequities and gaps in protection for

---

[1]U.S. Congress, Senate, Special Committee on Aging, *Future Directions in Social Security,* Hearings before the Special Committee on Aging, 93d Cong., 1st sess., 1973, Part 1, p. 18.

those whose lifetime employment is divided between civil-service jobs and jobs covered by the OASDHI program. More than half a million workers annually either enter or leave federal civil-service employment. The result is that some terminating employees are inadequately protected under both systems.

If a worker terminates his federal employment prior to retirement, he has no disability or survivorship protection under the Civil Service Retirement System, so many workers are not covered for these benefits under any system for substantial periods. Fewer than one in twelve of those workers who terminate their federal employment receives retirement benefits based on his years of federal service.

Of those workers who remain in federal employment long enough to qualify for civil service retirement benefits, a high proportion have also worked in occupations covered by the OASDHI program. More than half of the civil service retirement beneficiaries age 65 and over receive OASDHI retirement benefits. In contrast, about one-fourth of the aged civil service retirement beneficiaries have some quarters of coverage under the OASDHI program, but since they are not fully insured, they cannot receive OASDHI retirement benefits. This problem will become more critical in the future. Since the number of required quarters of coverage will eventually increase to 40, the number of civil-service retirement beneficiaries who receive no credit for their OASDHI contributions will also increase. Thus, it could be possible for a worker to pay OASDHI contributions for 9¾ years and yet not qualify for OASDHI retirement benefits.

In view of the inequities and gaps in protection, the Advisory Council on Social Security recommends that the earnings credits under OASDHI and civil service should be combined for those workers who retire, die, or become disabled but are not entitled to benefits under either system alone. In this way, the retiree could receive benefits under one or the other system, according to his combined earnings under both systems.[2]

Farm Workers

Another important coverage problem applies to farm workers, especially migrants. Under the present law, farm workers are covered only if they earn at least $150 in cash wages from any employer in the year or work 20 or more days on a time basis. They receive one quarter of coverage for each $100 of cash wages paid to them during the year. If the farm worker is a member of a migrant labor crew, the crew leader, rather than the farmer, is ordinarily considered the employer.

The present law prevents many migrant farm workers from receiving OASDHI credits for all or part of their work. Also, although they are required to by law, many crew leaders fail to report the covered earnings of the migrant workers, thus contributing to the inadequate protection now provided to them.

---

[2]*Reports of the 1971 Advisory Council on Social Security,* H.D. 92-80, Committee on Ways and Means, 92d Cong., 1st sess., 1971 (Washington, D.C.: U.S. Government Printing Office, 1971), pp. 36-38.

Migrant farm workers are generally low-income, poverty-stricken people, who are rarely covered under private pensions but must rely almost exclusively on OASDHI benefits for their protection.

The Advisory Council on Social Security recommends repealing the provision under which a crew leader is considered the employer for members of his crew. Instead, a farmer who has a large farm payroll would be considered the employer and would report all the cash wages paid to the workers. Thus, coverage and reported wages would improve, thereby reducing the economic insecurity of migrant workers. [3]

BENEFITS

In regard to the retirement and survivorship benefits paid under the OASDHI program, some of the important issues are the adequacy of benefits, the size of the minimum benefit, and the level of death benefits.

Adequacy of Benefits

The adequacy of OASDHI benefits is a highly controversial issue. We noted in Chapter 2 that the OASDHI program is meant to provide only a minimum floor of income. However, there is considerable disagreement concerning the meaning of a "minimum floor of income" and few clear-cut answers exist regarding the proper benefit level. Some people take the position that the benefits now paid represent a serious departure from the concept of a minimum floor of income; others argue that the minimum-floor objective is no longer applicable in view of the changing structure of the economy and changing labor-force characteristics.

Congress has been extremely generous to OASDHI recipients within the past ten years. Monthly benefits were increased across the board by 7 percent in 1965, 13 percent in 1967, 15 percent in 1969, 10 percent in 1971, 20 percent in 1972, and 5.9 percent during the first half of 1973. The 5.9 percent increase was to have become effective in June 1974, but it was replaced by an even higher increase of 11 percent, as a result of the December 31, 1973 amendments. The 11 percent increase was to be implemented in two stages. A 7 percent increase became effective in March 1974, and the remaining 4 percent increase became effective in June 1974. Finally, because of an increase in the cost of living, benefits were increased 8 percent in June 1975 according to the automatic provisions.

The benefit increases overall have exceeded the increase in the Consumer Price Index, significantly improving the real incomes of the aged. Between 1970 and 1975, average payments per OASDHI beneficiary have increased 22 percent in *constant prices,* that is, after adjusting for the 38 percent rise in consumer prices.[4] But whether the benefits are considered adequate today depends on the

[3]*Ibid.,* pp. 38-39.

[4]*The Budget of the United States Fiscal Year 1976* (Washington, D.C.: U.S. Government Printing Office, 1975), p. 8.

standard of measurement that is selected. The following section presents some major viewpoints concerning the adequacy of OASDHI retirement benefits.

Full Replacement of Earnings. One extreme view is that the OASDHI benefits should replace completely the loss of earnings from retirement, disability, or premature death, so that the standard of living is not reduced. This argument is often used to justify the payment of relatively high benefits to low-income workers who must rely almost entirely on OASDHI benefits for their financial support, having little supplemental income from dividends, interest, rents, or private pensions.

Although the argument may be defensible for low-income workers, it is clearly wrong in principle to apply the full-replacement standard to the middle- and upper-income groups. It would mean that the middle-income aged and other beneficiaries would receive OASDHI benefits in amounts sufficient to be their sole source of income. This position obviously ignores other, supplemental sources of income from private pensions, savings, and investments. Under the concept of the full replacement of earnings, private savings—other than small amounts—and private pensions are considered unnecessary for the majority of the population. Most social insurance scholars, however, believe that the OASDHI benefits should not be a complete substitute for private pensions and individual savings, but should be considered adequate if *both together* provide a reasonable standard of living.

A recent study by the Social Security Administration indicates the extent to which OASDHI retirement benefits will replace the loss of income from retirement in future years. Table 6-1 illustrates the replacement ratios for a low-income male worker, median-income male worker, and maximum-income (for OASDHI tax purposes) male worker. The replacement ratio is the ratio of the primary insurance amount (PIA) at award to the monthly taxable earnings in the year just prior to retirement.

The full-replacement standard will generally be met for low-income aged couples but not for low-income retired single workers; the percentage of replace-

TABLE 6-1 Replacement Ratios for Male Low-Income Worker, Median-Income Worker, and Maximum-Income Worker, 1974-80

			Low-Income Worker			
Year of Attainment of Age 65	*Computation Period*	*Taxable Earnings in Year*	*AMW*	*PIA at Award*	*Replacement Ratio*	*Replacement Ratio, Man and Wife Aged 65*
1974	18	$ 3,200	$ 169	$ 157.20	.630	.945
1975	19	3,360	174	162.80	.611	.917
1976	19	3,528	183	172.20	.615	.923
1977	19	3,704	192	181.80	.618	.927
1978	19	3,889	201	191.70	.621	.932
1979	20	4,084	207	200.20	.618	.927
1980	21	4,288	214	210.80	.619	.929

Median-Income Worker

Year of Attainment of Age 65	Computation Period	Taxable Earnings in Year	AMW	PIA at Award	Replacement Ratio	Replacement Ratio, Man and Wife Aged 65
1974	18	$ 7,681	$ 407	$ 261.30	.436	.654
1975	19	8,065	419	272.90	.426	.639
1976	19	8,468	439	289.40	.431	.647
1977	19	8,892	460	308.20	.437	.656
1978	19	9,336	484	328.30	.443	.665
1979	20	9,803	499	344.80	.443	.665
1980	21	10,293	514	361.80	.443	.665

Maximum-Income Worker

Year of Attainment of Age 65	Computation Period	Taxable Earnings in Year	AMW	PIA at Award	Replacement Ratio	Replacement Ratio, Man and Wife Aged 65
1974	18	$ 13,200	$ 511	$ 304.90	.339	.509
1975	19	13,800	542	323.50	.294	.441
1976	19	14,400	584	353.40	.307	.461
1977	19	15,000	628	387.80	.323	.485
1978	19	15,900	676	419.20	.335	.503
1979	20	16,800	708	441.00	.333	.500
1980	21	17,700	741	465.20	.332	.498

Note: Earnings are assumed to increase 5 percent annually, and the CPI 3 percent. The low-income male worker is assumed to earn $3,200 annually in 1974; the median-income earner, $7,681; and the maximum-taxable earner, $13,200. An automatic increase in benefits and the taxable wage base are assumed to occur annually. The male worker is also assumed to retire in June. The Replacement Ratio represents the ratio of the PIA at award to monthly taxable earnings in the year just prior to retirement.

Source: Albert Rettig and Orlo R. Nichols, Social Security Administration, Office of the Actuary, *Actuarial Note Number 87, Some Aspects of the Dynamic Benefits under the 1973 Social Security Amendments* (P.L. 923-233), April 1974, Tables 1, 2, and 3.

ment is greater for couples at all income levels than for single people. However, for median- and maximum-income workers, both single and married, the full replacement standard will not be met. This suggests, therefore, that private pension plans will continue to play an important role in the future in filling this gap.

Comparison with BLS Intermediate Budget. Another viewpoint is that the OASDHI retirement benefits should be at least high enough to meet the intermediate budget standard of the Bureau of Labor Statistics. This budget provides a modest but adequate standard of living for aged persons living in retirement in an urban area. The Bureau of Labor Statistics has estimated that in autumn 1973, a single person aged 65 or over needed an annual income of $2,730 to meet the intermediate budget standard, while a married couple needed $4,980.[5] However, between autumn 1973 and May 1974, the Consumer

[5]Jean Brackett, "Urban Family Budgets Updated to Autumn, 1973," *Monthly Labor Review,* Vol. 97, No. 8 (August 1974), 57-62.

Price Index rose by 6.6 percent. If these earlier budgets are adjusted upward by the increase in the CPI, a single aged person living in an urban area would need an annual income of about $2,910 to meet the intermediate budget standard in May 1974, and a married couple would need $5,309. These required budget amounts can then be compared with the OASDHI benefits level after the full 11 percent increase became effective in June 1974.

TABLE 6-2 Comparison of Maximum and Average OASDHI Retirement Benefits with an Estimated BLS Intermediate Budget Standard

	OASDHI Retirement Benefits	Estimated BLS Budget for Single Aged Person	Dollar Difference	Percent of BLS Standard Met by OASDHI Benefits
		Male Retired Worker		
Maximum benefits	$ 3,659	$ 2,910	$ + 749	126%
Average benefits	2,232	2,910	− 678	77%
		Married Retired Couple		
Maximum benefits	$ 5,488	$ 5,309	$ + 179	103%
Average benefits	3,720	5,309	− 1,589	70%

Note: The estimated BLS intermediate budget standard is for May 1974 and is computed by adjusting upward the autumn 1973 intermediate budget by the increase in the cost of living. The CPI increased 6.6 percent between autumn 1973 and May 1974. The average OASDHI retirement benefits are estimates based on the June 1974 benefit table after the full 11 percent benefit increase became effective. The maximum retirement benefit for a male worker who attains age 65 in 1974 is $304.90.

Source: Computed from "Social Security Act Amendments, End of 1973," *Social Security Bulletin,* Vol. 37, No. 4 (April 1974), 35, Table 1; and Jean Brackett, "Urban Family Budgets Updated to Autumn, 1973," *Monthly Labor Review,* Vol. 97, No. 8 (August 1974), 58 (Table 2) and 62.

Table 6-2 indicates the extent to which average and maximum OASDHI retirement benefits in June 1974 met the estimated BLS intermediate budget standard for an aged single individual and a retired married couple. Although the *maximum* OASDHI benefits more than met that standard, *average* retirement benefits met only 77 percent of the amount needed for a single male worker and only 70 percent of the amount for a couple. Thus, for the aged who must rely exclusively on OASDHI benefits for their retirement income, a satisfactory standard of living based on the intermediate budget is not being achieved.

Benefits Equal to Poverty Threshold. The minimum floor of income can also be defined in terms of the poverty threshold. The Social Security Administration poverty indexes are used as measuring rods, and the OASDHI benefits are considered inadequate if they fall below the poverty thresholds. The poverty index is a harsh standard, since it indicates only a subsistence level of living. Those individuals and families falling below the poverty line experience considerable economic insecurity since a minimum standard of living is not being attained.

TABLE 6-3 Comparison of OASDHI Retirement Benefits with the Poverty Thresholds for Retired Workers, Retired Couples, and Aged Widows, 1972

	1972 Annual OASDHI Retirement Benefits	Poverty Threshold, Single Person Aged 65 or Older	Poverty Threshold, Couple with a Head Aged 65 or Older	Dollar Difference: 1972 OASDHI Benefits to Applicable Poverty Threshold	Percent of Poverty Threshold Met by OASDHI Benefits
Maximum benefits, retired workers	$ 3,108	$ 1,980	---------	$ + 1,128	157%
Maximum benefits, retired couples	4,668	---------	$ 2,520	+ 2,148	185
Average benefits, retired workers	1,944	1,980	---------	−36	98
Average benefits, retired couples	3,252	---------	2,520	+ 732	129
Average benefits, widows	1,656	1,980	---------	−324	84
Minimum benefits, retired workers	1,014	1,980	---------	−966	51
Minimum benefits, retired couples	1,522	---------	2,520	−998	60

Source: U.S. Congress, Senate, Special Committee on Aging, *Future Directions in Social Security*, Hearings before the Special Committee on Aging, 93d Cong., 1st sess., 1973, Part 1, p. 83.

Table 6-3 compares the OASDHI retirement benefits with the poverty thresholds in 1972 for retired workers, retired couples, and aged widows. The *maximum* benefits paid to both retired workers and retired couples exceed the poverty thresholds by a considerable margin; and the *average* benefits paid to retired workers are generally equal to the poverty threshold, while the average benefits to retired couples substantially exceed it. However, the *average* benefits paid to widows and the *minimum* benefits paid to both retired workers and couples fall substantially below the poverty line. Thus, OASDHI retirement benefits generally equal or exceed the poverty thresholds for most groups, with the exception of aged widows and those receiving only minimum benefits.

Benefits Equal to 50 Percent of Earnings. Another viewpoint is that the OASDHI retirement benefits are adequate if they replace at least 50 percent of the preretirement earnings for the worker (with a lower ratio for the highly paid and a higher ratio for low-income workers), thus allowing for supplemental sources of income from private pensions, investment income, and savings to supplement the OASDHI benefits.

This standard will generally be fulfilled in the future for many workers. Based on the June 1974 benefit table and assuming an automatic increase in benefits, most retired married couples at all income levels will have at least 50 percent of the preretirement earnings restored by OASDHI benefits. The standard will also be met for *low-income* retired individual workers aged 65 and over. However, for the *median-* and *maximum*-income retired worker 65 or over, the 50 percent replacement standard will not be met,[6] although this gap can be adequately closed by private pensions. And in the case of many workers who retire early with actuarially reduced benefits, the 50 percent replacement standard will not be attained.

OASDHI Benefits and Public Assistance. It is also suggested that the OASDHI benefits are adequate if most beneficiaries are not forced to apply for supplemental public-assistance benefits. Public-assistance benefits are based on individual need, and all income sources must be considered in determining that need. Thus, if most OASDHI beneficiaries are forced to apply for public assistance, the overall level of benefits would seem to be inadequate.

In 1973, only 56 people per 1,000 population aged 65 and over were receiving both OASDHI and Old-Age Assistance benefits;[7] thus, the OASDHI benefits appear to be sufficiently high to keep most aged persons off the welfare rolls.

In summary, with the possible exception of aged widows and those individuals and couples receiving only minimum benefits, the overall benefit levels appear adequate. The benefits paid to the low-income groups will replace all or most of their preretirement earnings, thereby providing them a more adequate standard of living in their old age. The benefits are generally equal to or above the poverty threshold for most retired workers and couples. However, based on the BLS intermediate budget standard, the benefits are still inadequate for

[6]See Table 6-1.

[7]*Social Security Bulletin,* Vol. 37, No. 6 (June 1974), 57, Table Q-4.

many aged persons. Finally, it must be noted that the OASDHI program is now inflation-proof; thus, the real incomes of the beneficiaries will be protected in the future.

Size of Minimum Benefit

The June 1974 benefit table provides a minimum monthly benefit of $93.80 (subject to the automatic-adjustment provisions) for individual retired workers aged 65 and over. In addition, a special minimum monthly benefit of $180 can be paid to covered workers with 30 years of coverage.

The size of the minimum benefit is an important issue for several reasons. First, a minimum benefit is necessary for socially adequate benefits and for a minimum standard of living. Few, however, would claim that the minimum benefits paid in the past were socially adequate, or even provided a minimum standard of living. Second, the minimum benefit should be large enough so that the recipients are not required to seek additional income from public-assistance programs; otherwise, the OASDHI program would fail to achieve one of its major objectives, that of keeping the beneficiaries off the welfare rolls. Finally, a substantial increase in the minimum benefit can do much to reduce poverty among the aged. The poverty threshold for a retired worker in 1973 was about $2,100.[8] If all aged OASDHI beneficiaries at that time had been guaranteed the special minimum benefit of $170 monthly (highest payable in 1973), or $2,040 annually, absolute poverty among the aged would have been largely eliminated.

Some people who are receiving minimum benefits have been covered under the OASDHI program for only a relatively short period. These groups include former employees of the federal and state governments who retired early under an existing public retirement plan and then reentered the labor force later to acquire a fully insured status under the OASDHI program. A fully insured status is often easily acquired. For example, a male worker retiring in 1976 needs only 25 quarters of coverage to be fully insured. Some groups receiving only minimum benefits have paid into the system only a short period, and because of the weighted benefit formula, the actuarial value of their benefits substantially exceeds the actuarial values of their contributions.

But aside from those who have been covered for only a relatively short period, minimum-benefit recipients are likely to be low-income people with very little outside income. The lower the benefit, the less likely that the beneficiary will have other income or financial resources. These people must depend almost entirely on their OASDHI benefits as their source of income, but the minimum benefits are often so low that a reasonable standard of living is impossible. As a result, many of the aged who receive only minimum benefits must also apply for public-assistance benefits, thus contravening a basic principle of the OASDHI program.[9] A more adequate minimum benefit would help these groups.

Although a strong argument can be made for paying higher minimum

[8]Special Committee on Aging, *Future Directions in Social Security,* p. 83.

[9]See Lenore A. Epstein, "Workers Entitled to Minimum Retirement Benefits under OASDHI," *Social Security Bulletin,* Vol. 30, No. 3 (March 1967), 3-13.

benefits to low-income beneficiaries, two major problems must be clearly recognized. First, the well-established social insurance principle of relating the benefits paid to average monthly wages is severely violated by such a policy. If the minimum benefit were substantially increased to provide a minimum floor of income to the poverty-stricken, then that principle must be abandoned.

Second, and perhaps more important, the welfare element embodied in the OASDHI program would be substantially increased. The relationship between the benefits received and the average monthly wages on which the tax contributions are paid would become more tenuous, and the benefits paid would be largely unearned. Since the welfare element would be expanding relative to the insurance element, the present system of financing the OASDHI program by payroll taxes could then be seriously questioned.[10]

Lump-Sum Death Benefit

Although the maximum death benefit of $255 has not been changed since the 1952 amendments, funeral costs have increased greatly over time. And, since most family heads have inadequate private life insurance, a strong case can be made for increasing the death benefit. The Advisory Council on Social Security Recommends the elimination of the $255 maximum and suggests making the death benefit three times the primary insurance amount, with a maximum payment equal to the highest monthly benefit for a family. [11]

TREATMENT OF MARRIED WOMEN

Married women often complain bitterly about the sex discrimination in the OASDHI program. One problem involves the payment of OASDHI retirement benefits to a working wife. Under the law, a working wife receives a retirement benefit based on either her own earnings or those of her husband, but not both; and the benefit based on her husband's earnings is generally larger than the one based on her own. She may have lower covered earnings because of irregular employment, discrimination in pay based on sex, or employment in low-paying occupations. Thus, a working wife often receives a retirement benefit that is no larger than the one received by a nonworking wife, and she may feel that her contributions into the OASDHI program are wasted. This view, of course, is incorrect, since the wife receives valuable survivorship and disability insurance protection while she is working.

Another problem is that a working couple may receive lower total OASDHI retirement benefits than another couple with the same earned income, but in which the husband is the only worker. For example, assume that Jim is an accountant who retires at age 65 with average annual covered earnings of $12,000. Jim's nonworking wife is also 65. Bob and Mary, however, both having worked full-time in a factory, retire at age 65 with identical average covered

[10]See Chapters 7 and 19.

[11]*Reports of the 1971 Advisory Council,* p. 5.

earnings of $6,000 each. Based on the June 1974 benefit table, and ignoring the automatic-adjustment provisions, Jim and his nonworking wife would receive a total monthly retirement benefit of $673.50. However, even though Bob and Mary together have the same average annual earnings as Jim, they would receive only $598.80 monthly ($299.40 each), or $74.70 less than Jim. One proposal for correcting this inequity would be to combine the annual earnings of a man and wife up to the maximum-earnings base, with 50 percent added as the wife's benefit. Each would then receive half of the higher retirement benefit that would result from combining their earnings.[12]

RETIREMENT TEST

The retirement test is one of the most controversial issues in the OASDHI program, and many erroneous views exist regarding its nature and purpose. Numerous groups, including Congress, the Social Security Administration, labor unions, and consumer organizations, have debated, often bitterly and heatedly, the arguments for and against the test. Although several bills have been introduced to abolish it, Congress has chosen to move toward liberalization of the test rather than its abolishment. And although proponents of the earnings test with to retain it, they are not necessarily opposed to its liberalization.[13]

Arguments in Support of the Retirement Test

Insurance against the Loss of Earned Income.   One argument for retention of the test is that the OASDHI program insures against the loss of earned income; if work earnings are not lost, the benefits should not be paid, and the retirement test is necessary to implement this purpose.

One risk insured against is the loss of earned income because of *retirement* at a specified age, and not merely the *attainment* of a certain age. That is, the OASDHI program is a retirement program and not merely an annuity program. If the benefits were automatically paid at age 65 to a worker with substantial work earnings, he could be receiving benefits even though he has not lost his earned income, and the event being insured against has not occurred. The retirement test is necessary as an objective measure for determining whether a loss of earned income has occurred from retirement.

Benefits Based on Presumed Need.   Since the OASDHI retirement

[12]Lenore E. Bixby, "Women and Social Security in the United States," *Social Security Bulletin,* Vol. 35, No. 9 (September 1972), 9-10.

[13]For an excellent discussion of the OASDHI retirement test, see Nelson H. Cruikshank, National Council of Senior Citizens, "The Retirement Test in Social Security," in U.S. Congress, Senate, Special Committee on Aging, *Economics of Aging: Toward a Full Share in Abundance,* Hearings before the Special Committee on Aging, 91st Cong., 2d sess., 1970, Part 11, pp. 1945-52. See also Robert J. Myers, "The Past and Future of Old-Age, Survivors, and Disability Insurance," in William G. Bowen, Frederick H. Harbison, Richard A. Lester, and Herman M. Somers, eds., *The Princeton Symposium on the American System of Social Insurance: Its Philosophy, Impact, and Future Development* (New York: McGraw-Hill, 1968), pp. 88-89.

benefits are based on presumed need, they are never paid automatically at a certain age, but only if certain eligibility requirements are fulfilled. If the worker earns an income in excess of the maximums allowed under the law, he is presumed not to have retired and thus not to have suffered a loss of his earned income, and so the benefits are withheld. However, if he actually retires and loses his earned income, it is presumed that he needs the retirement benefits to replace it, and the benefits are paid. Here again, the retirement test is an objective measure to determine whether he has retired and thereby suffered a loss of earned income.

Increase in Costs. Elimination of the retirement test would substantially increase the costs of the OASDHI program. If the benefits were automatically paid at age 65, the combined employee-employer tax rate would increase by about .70 percent, or an additional $4 billion. Since the additional benefits would go to workers who are now ineligible for them, mostly because of excessive employment earnings, relatively few retired aged would benefit from the higher expenditures. It is estimated that less than 8 percent of the beneficiaries aged 65 and over would receive benefits from the higher expenditures.[14] Elimination of the test could actually harm the aged, since the cost of the change would mean that fewer funds would be available for program improvements. Thus, instead of additional amounts to workers who might not need them because they have substantial work earnings, the funds could be used more effectively to pay higher benefits to people who are retired or unable to work.

Few Persons Affected. Another argument for retention of the test is that relatively few beneficiaries are affected. In June 1974, about 30 million persons were in a current-payment status. During this same period, only about 1 million beneficiaries had their benefits withheld because of excessive earnings.[15] Thus, it is argued, since relatively few persons are affected by the test, it should be retained.

Of course, this argument can be used equally well in favor of abolishment of the test. If relatively few persons are affected by the test, why not abolish it? The answer once again is that the program normally insures against the loss of earned income, and if work earnings are not lost, the benefits should not be paid; and that the costs of the program would be substantially increased by eliminating the test.

Expansion of Employment Opportunities. Finally, it is argued that the retirement test keeps older workers out of the labor force and expands employment opportunities for younger workers. This argument is a carryover from the retirement provisions of the original Social Security Act, which reflected the lack of employment opportunities for younger workers during the 1930s, and may not be relevant during periods of full employment when labor is relatively scarce. However, during periods of high unemployment, employment of the aged may be less important than the loss of job opportunities for younger workers, and arguments for rationing jobs in favor of the young have more validity.

[14]*Reports of the 1971 Advisory Council,* p. 24.

[15]*Social Security Bulletin,* Vol. 37, No. 12 (December 1974), 87, Table Q-13.

Arguments against the Retirement Test

Inadequate OASDHI Benefits.   It is argued that the retirement test should be abolished because the OASDHI benefits are inadequate, and the aged should be allowed to work to supplement them. This argument loses much of its force when the recent legislative history of benefit increases is considered. Between 1969 and October 1974 alone, average monthly retirement benefits increased by 87 percent. The average monthly benefit paid to a retired worker increased from $100 to $187, and to a retired worker and wife from $152 to $283. Also, as indicated earlier, the average benefits currently paid are at least equal to the poverty line for most retired workers and couples. Undoubtedly, some retired aged may feel feel that their retirement benefits are inadequate and may wish to supplement their incomes. The earnings test in 1975 permitted an additional $2,520 to be earned with no loss of benefits, and the benefits were reduced by only $1 for each $2 of earnings over $2,520. Rather than abolishing the test, a better solution is to raise the maximum-earnings limit. Congress has periodically done so, and the limit will increase automatically in the future as average wages increase.

Reduces Work Incentives.   Another argument is that the retirement test reduces work incentives, with a loss of gross national product as a result. Critics of the test say that, although the OASDHI program is based on work, since the benefits have some relation to earnings, and the work ethic permeates the entire program, the retirement test violates the work-ethic concept by discouraging older people from working because of the possible loss or reduction of benefits from application of the test.

Before we examine the extent to which the retirement test can dampen work incentives, three general observations are relevant. First, anything that limits the earnings of a worker will undoubtedly act as a deterrent to work for some people. The real issue is whether the magnitude of the reduction in work effort is sizable or minor. Second, if the older worker has the choice of either working or not, he will usually find he has higher total income and is better off financially by working full-time despite the retirement test. Third, for those workers with earnings substantially below or well above the maximum limit permitted by the test, there is no dampening of work incentives. The retirement test has relevance primarily for those workers whose earned incomes are approaching the maximum limit permitted by the test.

The empirical studies of the impact of the retirement test on work incentives are generally inconclusive. However, there does appear to be some dampening of work incentive for those with earnings approaching the maximum-earnings level permitted by the test. On the other hand, the number of workers affected appears to be relatively small, and the deterrent to work somewhat limited. One earlier study of 1967 beneficiaries indicated that, of the 17 million persons eligible for OASDHI cash benefits, less than 200,000 were holding their earnings down because of the retirement test in effect at that time.[16]

---

[16]U.S. Congress, House, Committee on Ways and Means, *President's Proposals for Revision in the Social Security System,* Hearings before the Committee on Ways and Means, 90th Cong., 1st sess., on H.R. 5710, 1967, Part 1, p. 319. See also U.S. Department of Health, Education and Welfare, Social Security Administration, Office of Research and Statistics, *The Effects of the 1966 Retirement Test Changes on the Earnings of Workers Aged 65-72,* Note No. 1 (January 30, 1970).

(The first $1,500 was exempt; between $1,501 and $2,700, there was a loss of $1 for each $2 of earnings; over $2,700, there was a loss of $1 in benefits for each $1 of earnings.)

A later study of the impact of the 1965 amendments on work incentives indicated that raising the maximum-earnings limit may encourage greater work efforts, but, once again, the effect may not be great. More than 10 percent of the workers who were receiving retirement benefits increased their earnings from about $1,200 in 1965 to about $1,500 in 1966 and 1967 as a result of changes in the earnings test. This indicates that many retired workers who receive benefits will control their work efforts by earning the maximum permitted without losing any of their benefits.[17]

As a generalization, it is safe to conclude that the retirement test has dampened work incentives for some, but that the overall impact appears to be relatively slight. And the maximum-earnings limits have been periodically raised over the years. Under the retirement test in effect before the 1972 amendments, the first $1,680 of earnings were exempt from the test; over $1,680 and under $2,880, there was a loss of $1 of benefits for each $2 of earnings; on amounts over $2,880, there was a loss of $1 in benefits for each $1 of earnings. In effect, this last bracket constituted a marginal tax rate of 100 percent on all earnings above $2,880. The 1972 amendments eliminated this income bracket. The first $2,100 of earnings was made exempt from the test, and there was only a loss of $1 in benefits for each $2 of earnings in any amount over $2,100. (The 1973 amendments increased the limit to $2,400, effective 1974. The automatic provisions increased the exempt amount to $2,520 in 1975.) The marginal tax rate on earnings above the maximum was effectively lowered to 50 percent. Thus, work disincentives should be reduced in the future by the new retirement test.

Exemption of Unearned Income. Another argument against the retirement test is that it unfairly discriminates against wage earners in favor of those who receive unearned income, which is exempt from the earnings test. Full retirement benefits are paid to people who receive any amount of unearned income from private pensions, insurance, savings, and investments, but the benefits are reduced or terminated entirely for those who *earn* more than $2,520 per year.

This argument is erroneous in several respects. First, if the retirement test were applied to unearned income, it would be in effect a needs test, since those receiving substantial amounts of unearned income would be considered as not needing the benefits. And the OASDHI program does not require a needs test.

Second, application of the test to unearned income would run contrary to one basic purpose of the OASDHI program—providing a *floor of protection,* on which additional economic security can be built through private pensions, insurance, individual savings, and other forms of nonearned income.

Finally, application of the test to unearned income would seriously hinder the growth of private pensions and other forms of private savings.

[17]Wayne Vroman, *Older Worker Earnings and the 1965 Social Security Amendments,* U.S. Department of Health, Education and Welfare, Social Security Administration, Office of Research and Statistics, Research Report No. 38 (Washington, D.C.: U.S. Government Printing Office, 1971), p. 43.

Another, closely related argument is that a beneficiary under age 72 not only loses part or all of his benefits if his earnings exceed the allowable maximum, but he is penalized further by having to pay OASDHI taxes on his earnings. It is doubtful, however, whether this argument is valid for a worker earning more than $2,520 per year, because he is considered not yet retired; thus, the withholding of $1 of benefits for each $2 of his earnings over $2,520 is justified. He should be treated like any other worker and should pay OASDHI taxes on his earnings up to the taxable maximum.

Earned Right to Benefits.   Some critics think the retirement test should be eliminated and the benefits automatically paid at age 65 because the worker has purchased and paid for his benefits and so has earned the right to them at that age. This argument is fallacious on several grounds. First, currently retired workers have paid only a small fraction of the true actuarial costs of their OASDHI benefits, so they have not strictly earned the right to them. Second, the benefits are paid on the basis of a statutory right to them, not on the basis of an earned right. Finally, although a younger worker, who contributes for his entire working lifetime, has a more defensible claim to benefits on the basis of an earned right, it does not follow that he should receive them automatically at 65 because he has earned them. The benefits are never paid automatically, even after a lifetime of contributions. Certain eligibility requirements must be fulfilled, including that of retirement.

Causes the Event Insured Against.   The retirement test is sometimes said to cause the very event against which the OASDHI program insures—the loss of earned income—since some people who would otherwise continue working will withdraw from the labor force because of the possible reduction or termination of their benefits. However, although some may retire for fear of losing their benefits, the number involved, as indicated earlier, is relatively small. Thus, the test does not cause a massive withdrawal from the labor force and the widespread loss of earned income.

EARLY RETIREMENT

Early retirement with permanently reduced actuarial benefits is another important issue. Under the present law, workers and their spouses can elect permanently reduced actuarial benefits as early as age 62. The worker's benefit at 62 is reduced 20 percent, and the wife's or dependent husband's benefit is reduced 25 percent at the same age. Widows without children can receive reduced benefits at age 60, and disabled widows at age 50. The actuarial reduction and lower benefits are designed to compensate for the longer payout period.

Actuarially Reduced Benefits

A large proportion of older workers retire early on reduced benefits. Of the people currently being paid benefits, more than half the men, and about two-thirds of the women, are receiving permanently reduced benefits. Many male workers retire early because of poor health, automation and technological change that eliminate jobs, labor-union pressures for early retirement, inability of older workers to find employment, and the desire for leisure. Many female workers are secondary wage earners who withdraw from the labor force years prior to the normal retirement age, and thus also claim early-retirement benefits.

Reduced benefits in early retirement can cause two major problems. First, if the benefits are inadequate, some OASDHI recipients must apply for supplemental public-assistance benefits. In June 1974, the average monthly retirement benefit without reduction for early retirement was about $208, but with the reduction it was $168, or $40 less.[18] The longer the retirement period, the greater is the likelihood that a retired worker will exhaust his accumulated assets, and the more dependent he becomes on his OASDHI retirement benefits. The reduced benefits could result in an increasing number of retired persons who require public assistance. Even though, as the OASDHI program has gradually expanded in coverage and benefits, public assistance as a source of old-age income has declined in importance, this desirable trend could be slowed or even reversed in the future if large numbers of OASDHI recipients of reduced benefits are forced to apply for welfare.

Second, the actuarially reduced benefits are generally inadequate for providing even a poverty standard of living. The average early retirement benefit in June 1974 amounted to about $2,018 annually, which was below the estimated poverty threshold of $2,200 for a retired individual aged 65 or over. This is inconsistent with the objective of the OASDHI program of providing a minimum floor of income for all. Thus, some critics of the OASDHI program propose a reduction in the age at which full benefits are paid.

Arguments for Lowering the Retirement Age

Labor unions and other proponents of a lower normal retirement age present several arguments to bolster their position. First, it is argued that a lower retirement age might reduce the unemployment problems of younger workers. Second, early retirement at full benefits would help some older workers who are unable to maintain the production pace of younger workers. Third, older workers who have chronic health problems, which are not severe enough to qualify for OASDHI disability benefits but are serious enough to restrict their ability to work, would also be helped by a lower retirement age. Fourth, because automation and technological change displace many workers, they should receive full benefits at a lower age. Finally, it is argued that many private pension plans have lowered their normal retirement age to 62 or below (and in some plans, to 55), and the OASDHI program should do likewise.

Arguments against Lowering the Retirement Age

On the other hand, opponents of the lower normal retirement age argue that the costs of the program would be substantially increased. One estimate is

[18]*Social Security Bulletin,* Vol. 37, No. 12 (December 1974), 82, Table Q-5.

that lowering the normal retirement age from 65 to 62, with average benefits and total production held constant, would increase the cost by about 30 percent for each active worker.[19]

In addition, reducing the minimum retirement age and encouraging early retirement may increase poverty among the aged. Since a larger proportion of the worker's lifetime would be spent in retirement, he might be unable, during his shorter period of productive earnings, to save sufficient sums or accumulate adequate private-pension benefits to provide a reasonable standard of living during the relatively longer retirement period.

Finally, it is argued that lowering the retirement age to 62, or even 60, will result in greater pressures to provide higher private-pension benefits to the aged to supplement their OASDHI benefits. Since the private-pension benefits would then be paid earlier than age 65, private-pension costs would be substantially increased.

OASDHI AS AN ANTIPOVERTY PROGRAM

Another important issue is the extent to which OASDHI should be used as an antipoverty program. The OASDHI program in its operations keeps a large number of people out of poverty, especially the aged. About 24.5 million people were counted poor in 1972; 12.2 million others were kept out of poverty by the OASDHI program. Thus, the poverty rolls would have been about 50 percent higher if OASDHI benefits had not been paid. The program is especially effective in reducing poverty among the aged. Between 1969 and 1973, the proportion of aged persons living in poverty declined almost 35 percent,[20] a reduction due primarily to the substantial benefit increases during that period.

Those who support the use of the OASDHI program as an antipoverty tool say that the poor can be better served by the same institutions that provide economic security to the masses than by a separate program, so the OASDHI program should be modified to help the poor as much as possible. Although this proposal has a desirable objective, there are conceptual and practical problems in implementing it. The OASDHI program has serious limitations as an antipoverty tool.[21] An analysis of these limitations suggests that the OASDHI program alone cannot achieve the goal of improved income maintenance for all the poor.

Limitations in Redistributing Income

The OASDHI program is limited in its ability to redistribute income downward to the poor. In the first place, it is designed primarily for the aged,

[19]Joseph A. Pechman, Henry J. Aaron, and Michael K. Taussig, *Social Security: Perspectives for Reform* (Washington, D.C.: The Brookings Institution, 1968), p. 134.

[20]Special Committee on Aging, *Future Directions in Social Security,* pp. 83-86.

[21]See George E. Rejda, "Social Security and the Paradox of the Welfare State," *The Journal of Risk and Insurance,* Vol. XXXVII, No. 1 (March 1970), 17-39.

but the majority of the poor—about 85 percent in 1973—are under age 65.[22] Thus, any OASDHI benefit increase specifically aimed at reducing poverty tends to benefit primarily the aged poor.

Second, the OASDHI program is a costly and inefficient technique for reducing poverty, since most OASDHI benefits go to people who are *not* poor. The OASDHI program replaces the earned incomes of people at all income levels. Thus, any benefit increase designed to reduce poverty would necessitate increased payments to the nonpoor beneficiaries as well. For example, an earlier study by the U.S. Department of Health, Education and Welfare indicated that the nonpoor received about two-thirds of the OASDHI payments in 1965.[23]

Third, the OASDHI program is limited in redistributing income because relatively large amounts must be spent to close a relatively small fraction of the poverty gap—the aggregate dollar amount by which the incomes of the poor fall short of the poverty level. If the poor had received an additional $12 billion in 1973, absolute poverty would have been completely eliminated for that year. However, a research study by Raymond Munts indicates that large OASDHI benefit increases are necessary to reduce the poverty gap of the aged poor, but the same benefit increases have only a relatively modest impact on the poverty gap of the nonaged poor.[24]

Finally, the poor may receive relatively fewer benefits than do the upper-income groups, despite the weighted benefit formula. Prof. Milton Friedman states that the poor start working at an earlier age and therefore must pay OASDHI taxes for a longer period; the poor also have a shorter life expectancy and thus receive benefits for a shorter period; and the fact that OASDHI payments are not taxable benefits the wealthy more than the poor.[25]

Increase in the Welfare Element

Changing the OASDHI program into an antipoverty program would also introduce a far stronger element of welfare and charity into the system. In Chapter 2, we noted that the OASDHI program contains both welfare and insurance elements. The welfare element is that part of the benefits paid largely on the basis of social adequacy, whereby certain groups receive benefits that ex-

[22] U.S. Bureau of the Census, *Current Population Reports,* P-60, No. 98, "Characteristics of the Low-Income Population: 1973," (Washington, D.C.: U.S. Government Printing Office, 1975), Table A, p. 1.

[23] U.S. Department of Health, Education and Welfare, Office of the Assistant Secretary for Program Coordination, *Income and Benefit Programs,* October 1966, p. 13.

[24] See Raymond Munts, "Minimum Income as a Retirement Policy Objective," *Old Age Income Assurance, Part II: The Aged Population and Retirement Income Programs,* A Compendium of Papers on Problems and Policy Issues in the Public and Private Pension System, Subcommittee on Fiscal Policy of the Joint Economic Committee, 90th Cong., 1st sess., 1967 (Washington, D.C.: U.S. Government Printing Office, 1967), p. 299, Table III; and p. 301, Table V.

[25] Wilbur J. Cohen and Milton Friedman, *Social Security: Universal or Selective?,* Rational Debate Seminars (Washington, D.C.: American Enterprise Institute for Public Policy Research, 1972), p. 35.

ceed the actuarial value of their contributions. The insurance element is that part of the benefits paid that can be related to average covered earnings.

Many social insurance scholars consider it desirable to have some reasonable relationship between the benefit amounts and average monthly earnings. As average earnings increase, OASDHI benefits should also increase, although not necessarily proportionately. If certain groups, however, receive benefits that have little or no relationship to their average earnings and the tax contributions paid on these earnings, a substantial welfare element is introduced into the program. But this is precisely the dilemma of molding the OASDHI program into an antipoverty device.

The poor would be helped by a greater weighting in the benefit formula and by a sharp increase in the minimum benefit. But this would violate the well-established principle of relating, however loosely, the benefits paid to average monthly earnings and would increase the welfare element in the program. On the other hand, if the insurance element were emphasized (as by greater emphasis on the individual-equity principle and a closer actuarial relationship between benefits received and contributions paid), then the effectiveness of the OASDHI program as an antipoverty tool would be seriously weakened.

Present System of Financing Unsuitable

The present financing system, based as it is on the self-supporting contributory principle, would clearly be unsound if the OASDHI program were to be changed into an antipoverty program. First, the substantial benefit increases to reduce poverty would necessitate weighting the benefit formula even more heavily in favor of the lower-income groups, and the minimum OASDHI benefit paid to these groups would also have to be substantially increased. But the relation between the benefits received and average covered earnings (that is, the insurance element) would be weakened further by this approach, since the lower-income groups would receive benefits that have little or no relation to their average covered earnings. Thus, the welfare element of the OASDHI program would be increased. Under the present financing system, these increased welfare costs would fall heavily on the covered employees, employers, and self-employed who are now making tax contributions under the program.

But because the costs of public welfare and charity are social costs that should be shared equitably by all segments of society, this would mean that general-revenue financing should be used, at least in part, to finance the OASDHI program. The increased welfare costs of the program would then be spread over a more appropriate social base, rather than falling heavily on those now contributing. General revenues could be used to finance the welfare component, and the present system of employee-employer contributions to finance the insurance element.[26]

Second, if society must pay the higher welfare costs associated with the OASDHI program, the present financing system is questionable because it does

[26]See Chapter 7.

not consider, to any great extent, ability to pay. General-revenue financing is superior for financing welfare costs because most general revenues are raised through the progressive income tax, which is based on the ability to pay. People with high incomes pay relatively higher taxes that flow into the general fund. If part of the general fund were used to finance the welfare component of the OASDHI program, the welfare burden would be spread more equitably over all of society.[27] However, reliance on general revenues would represent a radical change in the financing principles now followed and would change completely the present character of the OASDHI program.

Third, the higher OASDHI taxes needed to finance substantial benefit increases would fall heavily on the working poor, who are least able to pay. Moreover, if the covered employers shifted their portion of the tax, either forward to the general public through higher prices or backward to the workers through lower wage increases, the working poor would again bear an additional burden. If general revenues, however, were used to finance higher benefits to reduce poverty, the burden would not be as heavy on the working poor and those with incomes near the poverty line.

Finally, the needed benefit increases for making a sizable dent in the poverty threshold might be restricted by the difficulty of increasing employee-employer contribution rates to finance these benefits. Higher payroll taxes would intensify the regressive character of the present OASDHI tax [28] and would fall heavily on certain workers—in particular, the working poor, middle-income families with only two wage earners, and younger workers entering the work force for the first time. Based on the 1975 contribution schedule, the combined employer-employee tax is 11.7 percent on a taxable earnings base of $14,100, or $1649.70. There may be some maximum practical upper limit on OASDHI taxes, beyond which the taxpayers may rebel. Thus general-revenue financing, rather than higher OASDHI taxes, should be used to finance the needed benefit improvements to reduce poverty.

Helps Least Those Who Need Benefits

Because of its categorical nature, the present OASDHI program is unsuited to be an antipoverty tool because it helps least those poor persons and families most in need of benefits. Some poor individuals and families fall between the categories and are excluded. Eligibility for OASDHI benefits is generally confined to the aged, disabled, and survivors of insured workers. Many of the poor, however, are none of these. The result is that only a fraction of the total poor are eligible to receive OASDHI benefits at any one time.

Working Poor. The working poor generally receive few cash benefits under the OASDHI program. Other than in survivorship and disability-income benefits, the OASDHI program does not generally place cash in the hands of

[27]Otto Eckstein, "Financing the System of Social Insurance," in Bowen et al., eds., *The Princeton Symposium,* p. 56.

[28]*Ibid.,* pp. 55-57.

the working poor. For example, about 2.6 million families headed by males were counted poor in 1973. This group contained large numbers of the working poor, but only about 31 percent reported receiving OASDHI benefits.[29] Thus, the majority of the working poor do not receive cash payments under the OASDHI program. Indeed, it does just the opposite. Cash is taken away from the working poor by requiring them to pay OASDHI tax contributions on their covered earnings.

Families Headed by Women. Data suggest that the OASDHI program does not significantly help poor families headed by women. The incidence of poverty for this group is worsening, yet relatively few poor families in this category receive OASDHI benefits. For example, about 2.2 million families headed by females were counted poor in 1973. Of this number, only about 19 percent received OASDHI benefits.[30]

Wage-Related Character of the Program

OASDHI is also limited in reducing poverty because of its wage-related character. The benefits are loosely related to earnings, but many poor people simply do not earn sufficiently high wages to enable them to receive higher OASDHI benefits. Although the ratio of OASDHI benefits to earnings is higher for the lower-income groups than for high-income groups, the benefit is still only a fraction of previous earnings. But this is the nub of the problem. If the worker's earnings are below the poverty line, any resulting OASDHI benefit is also below the line, and poverty is still present. Even worse off, of course, are families or household units with no present or past income earners, because of the wage-related character of the OASDHI program.

Declining Poverty Trend

If poverty continues to decline because of sustained economic growth, it will be more difficult for the OASDHI program to reach the remaining hard-core poor. As poverty declines, an increasing fraction of the remaining poor reside in households whose economic status is least affected by improvement in the OASDHI program. This includes the hard-core unemployed poor under age 65, the educationally disadvantaged with a limited attachment to the labor force, and the poor households headed by working women under 65. In order to cope with these groups, special training programs are needed, including job-training programs, educational programs for the disadvantaged, and new alternative income-maintenance techniques, such as reformed public-assistance programs, a negative income tax, or a universal demogrant plan (see Chapter 18).

---

[29]"Characteristics of the Low-Income Population: 1973," *Current Population Reports,* Table 42, p. 129.

[30]*Ibid.,* Table 42, p. 130.

Not Solely an Antipoverty Tool

Finally, the OASDHI program must not be viewed solely as an antipoverty tool. Although it tends to prevent poverty among the aged, it is also important in providing a base of economic security to the vast majority of middle-class Americans who are neither rich nor poor, but rely heavily on the OASDHI program for part of their economic security. Viewing OASDHI solely as a poverty program, or changing it drastically to reflect predominantly the income-maintenance needs of the poor, would overlook this large group whose needs and desires must also be considered.

IS THE YOUNGER WORKER TREATED FAIRLY UNDER THE OASDHI PROGRAM?

One of the most controversial and complex issues in the OASDHI program is whether a young worker receives his money's worth in terms of the contributions paid and the benefits received. It is argued that the OASDHI program is a "bad buy" for the younger worker, since the actuarial value of the *combined* employer-employee tax contributions made by and for him will exceed the actuarial value of the benefits he will receive. Thus, some critics say, the younger worker is "cheated," and they argue that he should be allowed to purchase his protection from private insurers, from whom superior benefits could be obtained. Let us examine the argument that the OASDHI program is inequitable to younger workers.

Illustrative Studies

Several researchers and organizations have attempted to measure and compare the actuarial values of the OASDHI protection and the OASDHI tax contributions, in order to determine whether the younger worker receives his money's worth under the program.[31] Most of the studies have concentrated on only the retirement portion of the OASDHI program. In addition, most studies assume that the *employer's portion* of the total combined OASDHI tax should be made completely available for the individual worker; that is, both the employer's portion and the employee's portion should be used to provide benefits for the individual employee. This is a key point, which we shall examine later. Let us first examine a study by the Social Security Administration that measures

---

[31]In addition to those cited below, see Shirley Scheibla, "Anti-Social Security: The System Is Inflationary and Loaded with Inequities," *Barron's*, January 21, 1974, pp. 3 and 16-18; Elizabeth Deran, "Some Economic Effects of High Taxes for Social Insurance," *Old Age Income Assurance, Part III: Public Programs,* A Compendium of Papers on Problems and Policy Issues in the Public and Private System, Subcommittee on Fiscal Policy of the Joint Economic Committee, 90th Cong., 1st sess., 1967 (Washington, D.C.: U.S. Government Printing Office, 1967), pp. 181-201; and John A. Brittain, *The Payroll Tax for Social Security* (Washington, D.C.: The Brookings Institution, 1972), Chap. VI.

Table 6-4   Value of Employee Contributions as Percentage of
Value of Total Benefits for Illustrative Maximum-Earnings Case

Year of Retirement	Value of Contributions		Value of Benefits		Ratio, Value of Contributions to Value of Benefits	
	Without Interest	*With 3% Interest*	*Without Interest*	*With 3% Interest*	*Without Interest*	*With 3% Interest*
			Single Male			
1962	$ 1,434	$ 1,885	$ 18,768	$ 14,764	7.6%	12.8%
1965	1,932	2,580	19,074	15,005	10.1	17.2
1970	2,946	4,080	19,227	15,125	15.3	27.0
1980	5,166	8,066	19,380	15,246	26.7	52.9
1990	7,146	12,399	19,533	15,366	36.6	80.7
2000	8,937	17,407	19,686	15,487	45.4	112.4
2010	9,894	20,543	19,686	15,487	50.3	132.6
			Married Male			
1962	$ 1,434	$ 1,885	$ 32,331	$ 24,906	4.4%	7.6%
1965	1,932	2,580	32,862	25,316	5.9	10.2
1970	2,946	4,080	33,128	25,520	8.9	16.0
1980	5,166	8,066	33,393	25,725	15.5	31.4
1990	7,146	12,399	33,653	25,925	21.2	47.8
2000	8,937	17,407	33,919	26,130	26.3	66.6
2010	9,894	20,543	33,919	26,130	29.2	78.6
			Single Female			
1962	$ 1,434	$ 1,885	$ 22,395	$ 17,182	6.4%	11.0%
1965	1,932	2,580	23,115	17,735	8.4	14.5
1970	2,946	4,080	23,115	17,735	12.7	23.0
1980	5,166	8,066	23,115	17,735	22.3	45.5
1990	7,146	12,399	23,115	17,735	30.9	69.9
2000	8,937	17,407	23,115	17,735	38.7	98.2
2010	9,894	20,543	23,115	17,735	42.8	115.8

Basic Assumptions:

[1]Worker is alive at age 65 and retires at that time (attaining age 65 at the beginning of the year).

[2]Worker is employed (as an employee) at maximum covered earnings in all years after 1937, or after attaining age 20, if later.

[3]Married worker has a wife the same age as he is.

[4]Mortality basis: U.S. Life Table for White Persons, 1949-51.

[5]Disability and survivorship benefits are not reflected in the data.

[6]The data do not reflect the 1965 amendments to the Social Security Act.

Source: Robert J. Myers and Bertram Oppal, *Actuarial Note Number 20, Studies on the Relationship of Contributions to Benefits in Old-Age Benefit Awards,* U.S. Department of Health, Education and Welfare, Social Security Administration, Division of the Actuary (June 1965).

the value of only the *employee's* tax contributions relative to the benefits he will receive.

Social Security Administration Study.   Table 6-4 illustrates the actuarial relationship between the employee contributions to the OASDHI program and the retirement benefits for different classifications of people attaining age 65 in different years from 1962 to 2010, based on the schedule in effect in early 1965. If a 3 percent interest rate is assumed, the value of the contributions of a single male who retired in 1962 is only $1,885, but the value of his benefits is given as $14,764; the ratio of the value of his contributions to that of his benefits is approximately 13 percent. For a married male who retired in 1962, the value of contributions to benefits was approximately 8 percent. Thus, even at 1965 levels, today's retired workers have paid only a small fraction of the true actuarial cost of their benefits.

On the other hand, the actuarial relationship between contributions and benefits is much closer for younger workers who will retire in the future. For example, based on the law in effect before the 1965 amendments, the actuarial value of the contributions of a single male who retires in 2010 would be $20,543, but the value of his anticipated benefits would be only $15,487—with the ratio of the value of contributions to the value of benefits approximately 133 percent. Thus, some younger unmarried workers who would retire in the future would not receive benefits exceeding the value of their own contributions.

Peterson Study. In an analysis of the OASDHI program prior to the 1958 amendments (then called OASDI), Ray M. Peterson, a private insurance actuary, estimated that current members and their employers, as a class, paid only about 42 percent of the value of their benefits, whereas new entrants and their employers would pay 169 percent of the value of their benefits.[32] It should be noted that the Peterson study assumed that the total *combined* employer-employee tax contributions should be made available for benefits for the individual employee.

Campbell and Campbell Study. Prof. Colin D. Campbell and Rosemary G. Campbell also prepared a study comparing the value of OASDHI retirement benefits with the contributions made.[33] The study was based on the law in effect in 1967 and does not reflect the 1967 amendments to the Social Security Act. It compared the cost-benefit ratios for persons of different ages under the OASDHI program and was also based on the assumption of *combined* employer-employee taxes in determining the value of the benefits. Table 6-5 summarizes the results of the study. A cost-benefit ratio of less than 100 indicates that the OASDHI program is a "good buy," but a ratio exceeding 100 indicates a "bad buy." The authors conclude that, if the workers paid the maximum taxes and continued to do so until retirement, the breakeven point under the law, before the 1967 amendments, was 39 years of age. That is, the workers over that age enjoyed a gain, but those under it would lose. In addition, the cost-benefit ratio was relatively high for a single person who was starting employment in 1967 at age 22 (248 percent). The authors concluded that the OASDHI program was an attractive bargain for those currently retired.

[32]Ray M. Peterson, "Misconceptions and Missing Perspectives of Our Social Security System (Actuarial Anesthesia)," *Transactions of the Society of Actuaries,* Vol. XI, No. 31 (November 1959), 812-51.

[33]Colin D. Campbell and Rosemary G. Campbell, "Cost-Benefit Ratios under the Federal Old-Age Insurance Program," in *Old Age Income Assurance, Part III: Public Programs,* pp. 72-108.

TABLE 6-5 Cost-Benefit Ratios for Persons of Different Ages Scheduled under the Current Federal Old-Age Insurance Program

Age and Starting Date	Retirement Date	Average Annual Wage	Total Value of OASDI Taxes[a]	Total Value of Taxes for Old-Age Insurance Alone[b]	Annual Pension	Value of Pension for 14 Years[c]	Cost-Benefit Ratio (col. 5 divided by col. 7) (percent)
(1)	(2)	(3)	(4)	(5)	(6)	(7)	(8)
Married man:							
30 in 1937	1972	Maximum base	$ 11,000	$ 8,800	$ 2,636	$ 28,688	31
22 in 1937	1980	Maximum base	20,873	16,698	2,776	30,212	55
22 in 1945	1988	Maximum base	32,002	25,602	2,848	30,995	83
22 in 1949	1992	Maximum base	38,932	31,145	2,871	31,246	100
22 in 1955	1998	Maximum base	50,108	40,087	2,963	32,247	124
22 in 1967	2010	$6,600 or more	68,076	54,461	3,024	32,911	165
22 in 1967	2010	$4,950	51,057	40,846	2,496	27,164	150
22 in 1967	2010	$3,300	34,038	27,230	1,927	20,977	130
Married man with working wife: 22 in 1967.	2010	$6,600 or more each	136,152	108,922	4,032	43,881	248
Single Person: 22 in 1967	2010	$6,600 or more	68,076	54,461	2,016	21,941	248
Self-employed, married man: 22 in 1967.	2010	$6,600 or more	49,608	39,686	3,024	32,911	121

[a]Compounded at E-bond rates of interest until 1963 and 4 percent thereafter.

[b]80 percent of column 4.

[c]Discounted at 4 percent interest.

Source: Colin D. Campbell and Rosemary G. Campbell, "Cost-Benefit Ratios under the Federal Old-Age Insurance Program," *Old Age Income Assurance, Part III: Public Programs,* A Compendium of Papers on Problems and Policy Issues in the Public and Private Pension System, Subcommittee on Fiscal Policy of the Joint Economic Committee, 90th Cong., 1st sess., 1967 (Washington D.C.: U.S. Government Printing Office 1967), p. 77, Table 3.

Criticisms of the "Bad Buy" Argument

The allegation that the younger worker is "cheated" under the OASDHI program because the actuarial value of the total tax contributions paid exceeds that of the benefits can be criticized on several grounds; for instance: (1) imputation of the employer's contribution to a specific individual; (2) assumption of fixed benefits; (3) failure to make adjustments for other benefits; (4) doubtful assumptions used; and (5) noncomparable forms of insurance.

Imputation of the Employer's Contribution to a Specific Individual. Almost all empirical studies attempting to show that the OASDHI program is a "bad buy" for younger workers use contribution figures that include the employer's portion of the tax; that is, the value of the *entire combined* employer-employee contribution is measured against the value of the retired employee's benefit. This is a clearly unreasonable assumption.

The employer's portion of the total contribution is often interpreted incorrectly in one of two ways: either as a private insurance premium that is segregated solely for the employer's own employees, or as a general tax rather than a social insurance contribution. A more correct interpretation of the employer contribution is somewhere between these two extremes. The employer tax is neither a private insurance premium (and thus available for a specific employee) nor a tax for general government purposes. It can be considered a social insurance premium (or benefit tax) for all covered employees. More specifically, *the employer's contribution is considered to be pooled for the general benefit of all covered persons and is not earmarked for the benefit of any specific person.*[34]

This condition is necessary to achieve the objectives of a social insurance program. When such a program is first started, some people are already near retirement. In order to achieve the purposes for which the social insurance program was begun and to provide socially adequate benefits, full benefits must be paid to these people when they retire, even though the actuarial value of the protection provided them exceeds the actuarial value of the contributions made by them or on their behalf. However, someone must pay for these "windfall" benefits. And their cost can be viewed largely as paid by the *pooled employers' contributions.*[35]

Based on a broad group basis and taking into account mortality rates, disability rates, family-status probabilities, retirement and marriage probabilities, and similar factors, it is estimated that the average new entrant now pays 80 to 85 percent of his future benefit protection under the OASDHI program;[36] the employer's contribution pays only about 15 to 20 percent of it. The remainder of the employer's contribution is used largely to pay the benefits of those who retired during the early years of the OASDHI program and also of the lower-

---

[34]For an extensive discussion of this concept, see Robert J. Myers, Memorandum, "Analysis of Whether the Young Worker Receives His Money's Worth under Social Security," in Committee on Ways and Means, *President's Proposals,* pp. 331-32. See also "The Value of Social Security Protection in Relation to the Value of Social Security Contribution," in the same volume, pp. 330-31.

[35]*Ibid.,* p. 332.

[36]*Ibid.*

income groups who are unable to pay the full actuarial cost of their protection. Thus, the employer's contribution should not be viewed as being made completely available for the individual employee on whose behalf the contribution is made, since the employer's contribution is pooled for the general benefits of all covered persons.

This use of the employer's contribution under the OASDHI program is not unique. In a contributory private pension plan, the employer's contribution is used in similar situations. For instance, workers who are close to retirement age when they are first covered receive past-service credits so that their retirement benefits can be more adequate, and they can retire in a socially acceptable manner. Thus, these workers also receive windfall benefits for which someone must pay. And once again, the employer's contribution is partly used for this purpose. Also, if the private pension plan is liberalized with increased benefits, part of the employer's contribution pays for the greater value of the past-service credits.[37]

Robert Myers, former chief actuary of the Social Security Administration, claims that the assumption is completely valid that the employer's contribution belongs to the system as a whole and not to any specific employee. Although the burden of the employer's contribution is ultimately borne by the workers in the form of lower wages or of higher prices that they must pay for goods and services, he says, it does not fall on the wage earners in exact proportion to the earnings on which the tax is paid. The incidence of the tax depends on many complex factors. Therefore, he concludes, the employer's tax should not be viewed as a matching contribution that is credited to each employee on the basis of the tax the employee pays.[38] Based on the preceding viewpoint, the younger worker is not cheated in terms of the total combined employer-employee contribution, since he is not entitled to the benefits based on the entire employer's contribution.

This argument however, is challenged by many researchers. Prof. Colin Campbell says the employer's contribution must be included as part of the cost of the worker's old-age pension, since many tax economists believe that a payroll tax paid by employers is quickly shifted to the employees in the form of lower wages. The employer's portion of the combined OASDHI tax increases the firm's labor costs and reduces the demand for labor. As this effect spreads over all firms, the level of money wages falls (or increases less than it otherwise would). Campbell concludes that, in effect, the wage earner pays not only his part of the total tax but the employer's portion as well. Thus, the tax payments of the employer should be included in the cost of the worker's OASDHI pension.[39]

This criticism of the Myers position is further buttressed by the argument presented by Dr. John Brittain.[40] Brittain says that, even if the employer's contribution is used for the system as a whole as Myers contends, it does not follow

[37]*Ibid.*, p. 330.

[38]*Ibid.*, pp. 330-31.

[39]Statement of Prof. Colin D. Campbell in *President's Proposals for Revision in the Social Security System,* Part 3, p. 1389.

[40]John A. Brittain, in *Old Age Income Assurance, Part III: Public Programs,* pp. 112-14.

that the OASDHI tax burdens no one. Concerned with the cost of the tax to the individual worker and not to the system as a whole, Brittain argues that although Myers accepts the idea that the employer tax is borne in large part by the employees as a group, he ignores it in evaluating the tax paid by individuals. In other words, if the employer tax is paid by the employees as a group, it must also be paid by them as individuals, and it is better, says Brittain, to make an imperfect imputation (allocation of the employer's tax to individuals) that is roughly right than one that is precisely wrong. Thus, he would also include the employer's contribution in determining the cost of the worker's OASDHI retirement benefits.

Finally, those who think that most or all of the employer's contributions should be assigned to a specific individual base their argument on grounds of greater individual equity in the OASDHI program. However, if such a proposal were carried out, it would be extremely difficult to pay benefits based on the social-adequacy principle without some general-revenue contributions. For example, the weighted benefit formula and the minimum OASDHI benefit significantly favor the lower-income groups, which receive benefits that substantially exceed the actuarial value of their contributions. And part of the employer's contribution can be viewed as being used to cover this deficit. True, this results in a potentially lower benefit for a younger worker than he would receive if the entire employer-employee contribution had been earmarked for him; but this is justified because the OASDHI program is social insurance. If most or all of the employer's contribution were used to provide greater individual benefits for a specific worker (individual equity), it would be difficult to pay socially adequate benefits to the lower-income groups, who are unable to pay the full actuarial cost of their protection, and they would then receive relatively smaller OASDHI benefits based on their smaller contributions. Thus, the program would not achieve the basic objective of providing a minimum floor of income protection to all.

It should be noted, however, that if general-revenue financing were introduced into the OASDHI program, it would be possible to allocate more (or all) of the employer's contribution to the benefits of a specific individual to attain greater individual equity. General revenues would then be used to provide socially adequate benefits to those groups who are unable to pay the full actuarial cost of their benefits.

Assumption of Fixed Benefits. Another criticism of the "bad buy" argument is that many of the studies assume fixed OASDHI benefits, and fail to allow for increases in the future because of economic growth, rising incomes, and population increases.[41] However, Prof. Paul Samuelson argues that everyone can draw more in benefits from the OASDHI program than he pays in contributions; that is, each generation that retires can expect to receive more from the system than it paid in. This is called the *social insurance paradox,*[42] and it is possible because the gross national product can be expected to increase in the future. In a growing economy, there are relatively more youths than older

---

[41]The research by John Brittain is an exception to this statement.

[42]See Paul A. Samuelson, "On Social Security," *Newsweek* (February 13, 1967), p. 88. See also Samuelson, "Keeping the Score," *Newsweek* (May 1, 1967), p. 80.

people, and with real income increasing at a rate of 3 percent, the taxes paid into the system in any one period, out of which benefits are paid, are greater than the taxes paid historically by the generation now retired. Stated differently, this means that if prices, real income, and population growth continue to increase at a compound rate of interest in the future, each new retired group can be paid OASDHI benefits far exceeding the benefits that a private insurer could provide. Samuelson concludes that the future youth will be cheated only in the remote political event that the more numerous young people of tomorrow are allowed to opt out of the system. The 22-year-old youth in 1976 will not retire on 1976 OASDHI benefits in 2019, and hence he will not be cheated. It can be realistically assumed that there will be future changes in the law and higher future benefits. Thus, younger workers who contribute for 40 or 45 years to the OASDHI program will receive benefits considerably higher than the benefits indicated in the studies showing that the program is a bad buy.

Lack of Adjustments for Other Benefits.   In the studies showing that the OASDHI program is a bad buy for the younger worker, adjustments for other OASDHI benefits are often lacking. In many cases, the size of the retirement benefit is compared with the size of an annuity that could be purchased from a private insurer with the equivalent taxes. This is an improper comparison, since the tax contributions also pay for Medicare, survivorship, and disability-income benefits.

The contribution for hospital insurance (HI) should be eliminated in comparing the OASDHI retirement benefit with a private annuity because the HI benefits are normally not considered in the analysis; the contribution for disability income (DI) should also be eliminated, since the covered worker has already received the protection before retirement; and an adjustment for survivorship benefits under the program should also be made because the insured has coverage for a certain amount of survivorship benefits before he reaches retirement age. (Robert Myers estimates that about 20 percent of the OASDI tax contributions represent the value of the survivorship benefits that the dependents would receive if the worker died prior to age 65.)[43] Failure to make these adjustments for disability-income and survivorship benefits can result in serious bias.

Another often ignored factor is that the OASDHI benefits are tax-free, a matter of considerable value to the upper-income recipient. For example, assume that a retired person is in the 50 percent federal income tax bracket because of substantial investment income. If he receives a $5,000 OASDHI benefit, it is worth twice as much, or $10,000. So adjustment must also be made for the tax-free status of the OASDHI benefits.

Doubtful Assumptions.   Another criticism of the various studies that compare the OASDHI program with private insurance is that these studies are often based on doubtful assumptions. In particular, the implicit assumption may be made that, if the total combined OASDHI tax contributions were instead given to the worker, he could obtain superior income protection from a private insurer. It is improbable that, in the absence of a compulsory OASDHI program, an employer would make available to the individual worker an

[43]Myers, "Analysis," p. 331.

amount equal to the employer's contribution, which the worker can then add to his own contributions. The employer's contribution could be used instead to increase the firm's profit margin, or to reduce prices, or both. It could also be used to provide other fringe benefits for the workers. Then, too, some employers might be more willing to contribute to the OASDHI program than to grant a wage increase equal to the employer's tax, because they believe that such a policy could save them charitable obligations later on or that the OASDHI program is worthy of support.

Second, the studies that compare the OASDHI program with private insurance may also be based on the implicit assumption that if the employees were given the equivalent of the combined OASDHI tax contributions, they would buy private annuities from private companies. There is no reason to believe that all employees would do this, even if given the opportunity—and especially in the case of the lower-income groups, who would probably spend the equivalent of the combined taxes for their present consumption needs rather than for their future retirement.

Finally, the studies are usually based on the assumption that the workers now covered under the OASDHI program can obtain equal protection from private insurers. This viewpoint is incorrect because private insurers have underwriting standards that are designed to weed out the undesirable risks because of occupation, age, health, and similar factors. So even if the entire combined OASDHI contribution were made available to the workers to purchase private individual insurance, some workers would be unacceptable to private insurers and would have to obtain their protection from the OASDHI program, which would then experience serious adverse selection.

There is room for both private insurance and the OASDHI program in the economic-security plans for most people. An error creeps in when it is assumed that only private insurance, or only OASDHI, should be used as the major tool for economic security. Actually, both forms of insurance are necessary, to augment and supplement each other in a highly desirable manner.

Noncomparable Types of Insurance. Critics also complain that many of the studies of the OASDHI program versus private insurance are comparing two noncomparable forms of insurance; they are not based on a true comparison between the value of the OASDHI protection and that of the protection available from private life insurers or private pension plans. After all, no private plans carry protection identical to the package of benefits provided under the OASDHI program. It must be kept in mind that the OASDHI program provides retirement, survivorship, disability, and Medicare benefits; and private insurance plans do not provide all these coverages in one package. Indeed, even if they did, they would have to charge rates that covered administration, marketing, payment of commissions, and similar expenses. Thus, to buy from a private insurer something comparable to the OASDHI program, even if it were available, would cost more than the values indicated in many of the studies.[44]

---

[44]Myers, "Analysis," p. 332.

Evaluation of the "Bad Buy" Issue

Based on the realistic assumption that the employer's contribution belongs to the system as a whole and is not earmarked for a specific individual, the evidence indicates that the *average new entrant* receives his money's worth in terms of *his own* contributions. Myers's conclusion that the average new entrant pays for about 80 to 85 percent of his future protection under the OASDHI program is based on a broad group of people in all salary ranges and takes into account the future probabilities of getting married and having children. In the case of a group of new entrants with *maximum covered earnings* during their lifetime, rather than average earnings, the value of the benefit protection is about equal to the value of the employee contributions. For example, based on the law in effect in 1967 (excluding the 1967 amendments) and eliminating the OASDHI tax attributable to disability-income, survivorship, and hospital insurance benefits, a male worker aged 22, with maximum annual earnings until age 65, would pay total contributions with a value of $26,412 and receive retirement benefits with a value of $32,853. The ratio of contributions to benefits would be 80 percent. Thus, in terms of his own contributions, the younger worker receives his money's worth under the OASDHI program.[45]

So the workers who pay maximum tax rates based on maximum taxable earnings will receive their money's worth. However, workers who pay for shorter periods or earn less than the maximum-earnings base will receive *more* than their money's worth. And furthermore, all the foregoing conclusions are based on the unrealistic assumption that Congress will never liberalize OASDHI benefits in the future.

SUGGESTIONS FOR ADDITIONAL READING

Advisory Council on Social Security, *Reports of the 1971 Advisory Council on Social Security,* H.D. No. 92-80, Committee on Ways and Means. Washington, D.C.: U.S. Government Printing Office, 1971.

Brittain, John A., *The Payroll Tax for Social Security.* Washington, D.C.: The Brookings Institution, 1972.

Brown, J. Douglas, *An American Philosophy of Social Security: Evolution and Issues.* Princeton, N.J.: Princeton University Press, 1972.

Cohen, Wilbur, J., *Social Security Is Safe, Sound, and Working.* Mimeo, unpublished, University of Michigan, August 28, 1974.

_____, and Milton Friedman, *Social Security: Universal or Selective?* Rational Debate Seminars. Washington, D.C.: American Enterprise Institute for Public Policy Research, 1972.

Mead, William B., "The Squeeze Ahead for Social Security," *Money,* Vol. 3, No. 10 (October 1974), 32-35.

Myers, Robert J., "Analysis of Whether the Young Worker Receives His Money's Worth under Social Security," in *President's Proposals for*

[45]*Ibid.*

Revision in the Social Security System, Hearings before the Committee on Ways and Means on H.R. 5710, 90th Cong., 1st sess., 1967, Part 1, pp. 331-41. Washington, D.C.: U.S. Government Printing Office, 1967.

_____, "The Past and Future of Old-Age, Survivors, and Disability Insurance," in *The Princeton Symposium on the American System of Social Insurance: Its Philosophy, Impact, and Future Development,* eds. William G. Bowen, Frederick H. Harbison, Richard A. Lester, and Herman M. Somers, pp. 77-105. New York: McGraw-Hill, 1968.

Pechman, Joseph A., Henry J. Aaron, and Michael K. Taussig, *Social Security: Perspectives for Reform.* Washington, D.C.: The Brookings Institution, 1968.

Rejda, George E., "Social Security and the Paradox of the Welfare State," *The Journal of Risk and Insurance,* Vol. XXXVII, No. 1 (March 1970), 17-39.

Scheibla, Shirley, "Anti-Social Security: The System Is Inflationary and Loaded with Inequities," *Barron's,* January 21, 1974.

Schultz, James et al., *Providing Adequate Retirement Income.* Hanover, N.H.: University Press of New England, 1975.

Social Security Administration, "The Value of Social Security Protection in Relation to the Value of Social Security Contribution," in *President's Proposals for Revision in the Social Security System,* Hearings before the Committee on Ways and Means on H.R. 5710, 90th Cong., 1st sess., 1967, Part 1, pp. 330-31.

Social Security: A Sound and Durable Institution of Great Value, White Paper by Elliot L. Richardson, John W. Gardner, Wilbur J. Cohen, Arthur Fleming, Robert Finch, Robert M. Ball, William L. Mitchell, and Charles I. Schottland, February 1975.

Special Committee on Aging, *Future Directions in Social Security,* Hearings before the Special Committee on Aging, 93d Cong., 1st sess., 1973, Parts 1-3. Washington, D.C.: U.S. Government Printing Office, 1973.

Turnbull, John G., C. Arthur Williams, Jr., and Earl F. Cheit, *Economic and Social Security,* 4th ed., Chap. 4. New York: Ronald Press, 1973.

chapter 7

Financing the
OASDHI Program

The OASDHI program is the major economic-security program for most Americans, and it must be soundly financed to deliver the promised benefits. The present financing system has been subjected to severe criticism. Critics argue that the OASDHI program is actuarially unsound and is on the brink of financial bankruptcy. Economists state that the OASDHI payroll tax is regressive, falling more heavily on the lower-income groups, who are least able to pay. Less critical observers claim that a change in financing is needed to provide for substantial benefit increases, for greater individual equity, and for the growing welfare element embodied in the program. In addition, the present financing system requires the active workers to support the nonproductive retired aged; and, since the future age distribution of the population, as we move in the direction of zero population growth (ZPG), will result in a larger proportion of aged in the economy, the financial burden of supporting the retired aged will fall more heavily on the smaller proportion of active workers. These financing problems and issues bear serious consideration and analysis.

In Chapter 5, we examined briefly the financing of the OASDHI program. In this chapter, we shall analyze its financing principles and operations in greater detail. In particular, we shall consider the following areas: (1) financing principles, (2) nature, purposes, and investments of the trust funds, (3) actuarial soundness of the OASDHI program, (4) the impact of zero population growth on the program's financing, (5) the desirability of general-revenue financing, and (6) future financing of the OASDHI program.

FINANCING PRINCIPLES

The financing principles that are followed in the financing of OASDHI benefits include the following:(1) current-cost financing, (2) self-supporting program, (3) actuarially sound program, (4) weighted benefit formula, and (5) some individual-equity considerations.[1]

Current-Cost Financing

To finance any social insurance program, two basic approaches and numerous variations between them are possible.[2] One approach is a pay-as-you-go financing plan, in which the government raises funds through taxation as they are needed to pay the benefits and expenses currently due under the program. The element of prepayment is not present, and a reserve fund is not accumulated. The second approach is full-reserve financing, which emphasizes a fully funded program and can be viewed as a prepayment system of financing. All benefits are paid for or financed during the years prior to their receipt. Under this approach, the dollar sum of all payments into the fund, added to the investment income from the fund's assets, is sufficient to pay all guaranteed or promised benefits. At any given time, the promised benefits are limited to that amount.

The OASDHI program is neither a completely unfunded program nor one financed on the basis of full-reserve financing and full funding. Instead, it employs *current-cost financing,* which is basically a pay-as-you-go system, plus the maintenance of contingency trust funds equal to approximately one year's outlay. Trust funds equal to one year's expenditures are considered adequate for contingency-reserve purposes when there are temporary excesses of outgo over income because of relatively high benefit costs or low tax yields during a particular period. The tax contributions and investment earnings on the trust-fund assets are sufficient for meeting the current expenditures for benefits and administrative costs. Under current-cost financing, the contribution rates are established at a level that will permit meeting the current costs of the program and enabling the trust funds to grow over time until they eventually equal 100 percent of the ensuing year's outgo.

Arguments against Larger Trust Funds. Changes in the financing of the program in 1972 have resulted in almost a completely pay-as-you-go program with relatively small trust funds. Prior to 1972, the funding philosophy was based on trust funds that were considerably larger than contingency funds, but

---

[1]The basic actuarial principles and considerations underlying the financing of the OASDHI program can be found in Social Security Administration, Office of the Actuary, *Actuarial Cost Estimates for the Old-Age, Survivors, Disability, and Hospital Insurance System as Modified by the Social Security Provisions of Public Law 92-336* (September 1972); and Robert J. Myers, *The Financial Principle of Self-Support in the Old-Age and Survivors Insurance System,* U.S. Department of Health, Education and Welfare, Social Security Administration, Division of the Actuary, Actuarial Study No. 40 (April, 1955). See also Myers, *Social Insurance and Allied Government Programs* (Homewood, Ill.: Richard D. Irwin, 1965), Chaps. 3 and 5.

[2]Ray M. Peterson, "The Coming Din of Inequity," in U.S. Congress, House, Committee on Ways and Means, *President's Proposals for Revision in the Social Security System,* Hearings before the Committee on Ways and Means, 90th Cong., 1st sess., on H.R. 5710, 1967, Part 2, pp. 633-34.

considerably smaller than in a fully funded program. Let us see why larger trust funds are considered unnecessary.[3]

First, the OASDHI program is compulsory and is expected to operate indefinitely; so there will always be a flow of new entrants to make contributions toward the payment of benefits, and the amounts in the trust funds plus future tax contributions are expected to be sufficient to pay all future benefits and administrative expenses. In contrast, private insurers must emphasize full funding, since private insurance is voluntary, and a company cannot assume that it will operate indefinitely with a continuous inflow of new policyholders to help pay benefits.

Second, large trust funds are unnecessary because the federal government has taxing powers that can be used if additional revenues are needed. If the contribution rates are insufficient for supporting present or future benefits, Congress can increase the rates or the taxable payroll base to finance the necessary benefits.

Third, larger trust funds might lead to an unjustified liberalization of benefits, if such a move were pressed for by political representatives, labor union leaders, and others.

Finally, larger trust funds would require significantly higher tax rates, which would constitute a "fiscal drag" on the economy and could result in deflation.

Arguments for Larger Trust Funds. Although few social insurance scholars desire a fully funded OASDHI program, several arguments are made for increasing the level of funding and stressing larger trust funds in the future. First, it is said that larger trust funds, resulting in more nearly adequate reserves, would better protect the rights of future recipients by providing a greater guarantee that their benefits would be paid. Also, if larger trust funds were established, the present generation would be less dependent on the future generation and their elected representatives for benefits.

A second point is that larger trust funds would reduce the financial burden passed on to future generations. The present generation is currently financing most of the benefits paid to those now retired; and the benefits that will ultimately be paid to members of the present generation when *they* retire will be financed by the future generation. If larger trust funds were established, a greater amount of compound interest could be earned on these funds, thereby reducing the financial burden to be assumed by future workers.

Finally, it is argued that having larger trust funds would reflect more accurately the true costs of the OASDHI program. The real test of Social Security financing will occur sometime in the future, when the tax burden increases and windfall benefits disappear. In particular, some critics are disturbed that the actuarial value of the total combined tax contributions of the average new worker and his employer will exceed the actuarial value of his benefits. If the younger workers become aware of this fact, and as the payroll-tax burden in-

[3]See John G. Turnbull, C. Arthur Williams, Jr., and Earl F. Cheit, *Economic and Social Security* (New York: Ronald Press, 1973), pp. 112-18. See also *Reports of the 1971 Advisory Council on Social Security,* H.D. No. 92-80, Committee on Ways and Means, 92d Cong., 1st sess., 1971 (Washington, D.C.: U.S. Government Printing Office, 1971), pp. 58-74. This report has an extensive discussion of the financing of the OASDHI program.

creases, some workers may rebel. Through exercise of their voting power, they could repeal the institutionalized compact between the generations whereby the younger active workers are subsidizing the nonproductive aged with the expectation of similar support from the future active workers during their own retirement.[4] It is feared that the younger workers may wish to suspend or reduce benefits, or may press for higher benefits with no tax increases. These dangers might be reduced if greater emphasis were placed on larger trust funds as a more accurate measure of the true cost of the program, especially the cost impact on the younger workers.

Self-Supporting Program

In the 1950 amendments to the Social Security Act, Congress stated that the OASDHI program should be completely self-supporting from the contributions of covered individuals and employers, and therefore repealed the provision that permitted appropriations to the system from the general revenues of the Treasury. Since 1950, Congress has consistently reaffirmed this principle in all subsequent legislation. The principle of self-support means that the OASDHI program is supported by the payroll-tax contributions of covered employees, employers, and the self-employed, plus investment income on trust-fund assets, and that general-revenue appropriations will not be needed in the long run to pay the benefits and administrative expenses under the program.

General revenues *are* typically used to pay (1) the cost of Hospital Insurance (HI) benefits to aged persons who were blanketed in under Medicare, (2) the federal government's share of the costs of Supplementary Medical Insurance (SMI), (3) the costs of the special payments made to certain uninsured persons aged 72 and over, and (4) the wage credits granted to people in the active military service. General revenues are also used to pay interest on the trust-fund assets. However, with these exceptions, the program is self-supporting.

Actuarially Sound Program

Congress has consistently indicated that, in addition to being self-supporting, the OASDHI program should be actuarially sound. This is important because it is the major economic-security program for most Americans, and if it fails to provide the promised benefits, economic security would be jeopardized for many.

The term "actuarial soundness" has different meanings, and whether the OASDHI program is actuarially sound depends on the definition that is adopted. We shall analyze this important issue later in the chapter.

Weighted Benefit Formula

Another important financing principle is that the benefit formula is heavily weighted in favor of the lower-income groups, resulting in a benefit that

---

[4]Wilbur J. Cohen and Milton Friedman, *Social Security: Universal or Selective?* (Washington, D.C.: American Enterprise Institute for Public Policy Research, 1972), pp. 37-38.

replaces a relatively larger proportion of their average earnings than it does of the upper-income groups. In addition, the minimum OASDHI benefit also favors the lower-income groups, since the actuarial value of the minimum benefit is substantially greater than the actuarial value of the contributions paid by the low-income recipient.

Some Individual Equity

Although the OASDHI program pays benefits largely on the basis of the social-adequacy principle, there is some consideration of individual equity in the contribution schedule. This means that the tax paid by younger workers entering the program must not be so high that it could purchase more protection from private insurers. This principle has been reaffirmed many times by social insurance students, although it was never set forth any of the congressional committee reports underlying the 1950 and subsequent amendments.

THE OASDHI TRUST FUNDS

Nature of Trust Funds

The OASDHI program is financed through four separate trust funds. The Federal Old-Age and Survivors Insurance Trust Fund was established in 1940, the Federal Disability Insurance Trust Fund in 1956, and the Federal Hospital Insurance Trust Fund and Federal Supplementary Medical Insurance Trust Fund in 1965.[5]

The major sources of receipts to the OASI, DI, and HI trust funds are the following: (1) amounts appropriated to them on the basis of contributions paid by covered employers, employees, and the self-employed, and (2) amounts deposited in them representing the tax contributions paid by workers employed by state and local government and by such employers with respect to work covered by the program. The major sources of receipts to the SMI trust fund are (1) premiums paid by eligible persons participating in the program, and (2) contributions by the federal government representing its matching share of SMI premiums. The funds not needed for current benefits and administrative costs are invested in the securities of the federal government, interest from which helps meet the cost of the program.

The trust funds are managed by a board of trustees consisting of the secretaries of the Departments of the Treasury, Labor, and Health, Education and Welfare. The board of trustees has the responsibility of holding all trust funds.

---

[5]The current operations of the various trust funds can be found in *1974 Annual Report of the Board of Trustees of the Federal Old-Age and Survivors Insurance and Disability Insurance Trust Funds,* H.D. No. 93-313, Committee on Ways and Means, 93d Cong., 2d sess., 1974 (Washington, D.C.: U.S. Government Printing Office, 1974); *1974 Annual Report of the Board of Trustees of the Federal Hospital Insurance Trust Fund* (Washington, D.C.: U.S. Government Printing Office, 1974); and *1974 Annual Report of the Board of Trustees of the Federal Supplementary Medical Insurance Trust Fund* (Washington, D.C.: U.S. Government Printing Office, 1974). The following discussion is based on these reports.

It is required to report annually to Congress the operations and status of the trust funds during the preceding fiscal year, and must also report to Congress if the amounts in any of the trust funds become unduly low. Finally, the board must review the general policies followed in managing the trust funds and make recommendations for necessary changes in policy.

Purposes of Trust Funds

The trust funds serve three useful purposes.[6] First, they provide interest earnings, which help to reduce the program's cost. It is estimated that interest earnings on the trust funds will defray between 5 and 10 percent of the benefit costs in the long run. Second, the trust funds are available as contingency reserves to help meet any deficiency in contribution income during periods of economic recessions or other periods when that income declines. And third, the trust funds help to establish greater public confidence in the OASDHI program.

Investments of Trust Funds

Any excess funds not needed currently to pay benefits and administrative costs are invested (1) in interest-bearing obligations of the federal government, (2) in obligations guaranteed as to principal and interest by the United States, or (3) in certain federally sponsored agency obligations. The trust funds can invest either in the public issues that are available to all individual or institutional investors or in special public-debt obligations issued exclusively for purchase by the trust funds. The special debt obligations have fixed maturities based on the needs of the trust funds and bear interest equal to the average market yield at the end of the preceding month on all marketable interest-bearing obligations of the United States not due or callable for at least four years after that date. One great advantage of investing in special issues is that disturbances in the capital markets are avoided. However, the trust funds simultaneously hold both public and special issues, with the bulk of the funds invested in the special issues.

During fiscal 1973, the OASI and DI trust funds earned $2.3 billion, equivalent to an annual yield of 5.6 percent; the HI trust fund earned $196 million, or an annual rate of 6.4 percent; and the SMI trust fund earned 6.1 percent. Some observers argue that the trust funds should be allowed investments in other than government securities and guaranteed obligations, while others believe that the present investment policies are sound and should not be changed. Thus, it is important to analyze the major arguments for and against the present investment practices of the trust funds.[7]

Maintaining Present Investment Policies. Several arguments are advanced for maintaining present trust-fund policies limiting the investments to

[6]Robert J. Myers, "The Past and Future of Old-Age, Survivors, and Disability Insurance," in William G. Bowen, Frederick H. Harbison, Richard A. Lester, and Herman M. Somers, eds., *The Princeton Symposium on the American System of Social Insurance: Its Philosophy, Impact, and Future Development* (New York: McGraw-Hill, 1968), p. 103.

[7]Myers, *Social Insurance and Allied Government Programs,* p. 74.

securities issued or guaranteed by the federal government. First, since the OASDHI program is designed for all of society, the trust funds must be confined to safe investments and not to speculative ventures that might impair the solvency of the program; and U.S. government securities are the safest form of investment available.

Second, departing from the present investment policies would directly involve the trust funds in the operations of the private economy or the affairs of state and local government. The trust funds have huge sums available for investment, and if these were invested in bonds or stocks of private firms, the federal government could control a large part of the free enterprise economy, thus, in effect, letting in socialism through the back door. And investing in the securities of state and local governments would involve the federal government in affairs that are beyond the scope of the OASDHI program.

Third, in order for the trust funds to obtain an adequate rate of interest with reasonable safety, the federal government would have to establish a rating organization to evaluate the various securities. If the investments were indiscriminately made, there would be serious danger of the loss of capital and reduction of investment income. However, establishing some type of rating organization for private securities would again involve the federal government in the private economy.

Changing the Present Investment Policies.   Those who are interested in changing the investment policies of the trust funds say that the trust funds should be allowed to invest in securities that represent social goods, such as hospitals, highways, public housing, schools, dams, and similar projects that yield large and widespread benefits to society as a whole.

There is little doubt that such investments by the trust funds would have a beneficial impact on the economy—for example, in projects designed to reduce poverty, such as public housing, special schools for the disadvantaged, slum clearance projects, and so on. In addition, the trust funds could provide loans to business firms to locate in ghetto areas and provide employment opportunities to the hard-core unemployed poor. It must be recognized, however, that there are dangers involved in such an approach. Investing in securities representing social goods would involve public funds, and decisions would have to be made regarding the priority of investments. Such decisions in regard to public funds, many feel, should be made by Congress rather than by the OASDHI trust-fund managers, since investments in social goods affect the economic welfare of the nation, and the elected representatives of the people should be the ones to determine what is best for the country.

Another argument is that the trust funds should be allowed to invest in private securities in order to obtain higher yields than are currently provided by government securities. This argument is somewhat defective on several grounds. Interest earnings provide only a relatively small part of the total income of the OASDHI program. Thus, higher-yielding private securities would have only a minor effect on the total income of the program, given the present funding policy. In addition, higher-yielding private securities carry more of the risk associated with investments, whereas government securities are notable for their safety. Finally, the potentially higher return must be weighed against the disadvantage of having the federal government heavily involved in the private sector of the economy.

Erroneous Trust-Fund Views

The nature of the OASDHI trust funds is often misunderstood. For the sake of convenience, these erroneous views can be classified as follows: (1) double taxation, (2) fictitious trust funds, and (3) an increase in the national debt from trust-fund investments.

Double Taxation. Critics of the OASDHI program charge that fraud is being perpetrated upon the American people in that they are taxed twice in the financing of OASDHI benefits. First, covered employees, employers, and the self-employed are taxed to pay benefits to those currently eligible to receive them. Then, the excess of the taxes collected over the amount needed to pay current benefits and expenses is invested in interest-bearing obligations of the federal government, and the government must tax the general public a second time to pay the interest on these obligations and also to repay the principal.

The double-taxation argument is fallacious. It is true that the federal government must levy taxes to pay the interest on the obligations held by the trust funds and to redeem the bonds. However, these taxes are not levied for the specific purpose of paying OASDHI benefits; rather, they are levied to meet the general costs of the federal government. If the OASDHI trust funds did not exist, the funds needed for general government purposes would have to be borrowed from other sources, and taxes would still have to be raised to pay the interest and principal on these borrowed funds.

Fictitious Trust Funds. Some critics claim that the trust funds are fictitious, since the securities held by them are merely IOUs issued by the federal government to itself. This argument is also erroneous. When the trust funds invest in government obligations, the trust funds are the lenders, and the Treasury is the borrower. The trustees of the funds receive and hold, as evidence of these loans and as assets, federal government obligations. These securities are in turn liabilities (part of the national debt) of the U.S. government, which must pay interest on them and must repay the principal when they are redeemed or mature. Securities are sold or redeemed when the trust funds require cash for disbursement.

The marketable securities held by the trust funds are identical in every way to the federal bonds purchased and sold on the open market by other investors in federal securities. Both they and the special obligations issued directly to the trust funds are backed by the full faith and credit of the United States. Interest on the securities held by the trust funds and the proceeds from the sale or redemption of such securities are credited to and form a part of each fund. The various trust funds are completely separate from the general fund of the Treasury and have the same lender status as other investors in federal securities.[8] Thus, the argument that the OASDHI trust funds are fictitious is completely erroneous.

[8]*Financing Old-Age, Survivors, and Disability Insurance, A Report of the Advisory Council on Social Security* (Washington, D.C.: U.S. Government Printing Office, 1959), pp. 18-22.

Increase in National Debt. Another specious argument is that trust-fund investments in federal obligations, which represent the national debt of the federal government, increase that debt. However, the national debt increases only if the expenditures by the federal government during a given fiscal year are greater than the receipts from taxes levied to meet those expenditures during the same period. When a deficit occurs, the Treasury must borrow funds to meet the deficit through the sale of federal securities, which increases the size of the national debt. And the purchase of federal obligations by the trust funds does not increase the amount of money the Treasury must borrow. If the trust funds did not exist and were not available as a source from which to borrow, the Treasury would have to borrow the same amount from other investments; it is only that the purchaser of the government obligations is a public agency rather than a private investor. And if the trust funds purchase federal obligations during a period in which the Treasury has no deficit, the result is only a direct or indirect transfer of federal securities from other investors to the trust funds. The size of the national debt still remains unchanged.

ACTUARIAL SOUNDNESS OF THE OASDHI PROGRAM

The actuarial soundness of the OASDHI program refers to the ability of the plan to deliver the promised benefits. Some critics claim that the OASDHI program is actuarially unsound and on the verge of financial bankruptcy. Whether this is true depends, of course, on the definition of actuarial soundness that is adopted.[9]

Concepts of Actuarial Soundness

One definition, which normally applies only to private pensions, is that such a plan is actuarially sound if the existing fund is large enough to pay all benefits accrued to date. Under this definition, if an actuarially sound pension plan should terminate, the retired pensioners would be secure in their pensions, and the active workers would have an equity in the pension assets reasonably commensurate with their accruals based on their service from the plan's inception to the termination date. If this definition is used, the OASDHI program is *not* actuarially sound. An earlier study by Robert J. Myers, based on this definition indicated that the Social Security trust funds were short by $321 billion. This means that, if the OASDHI program were to have terminated, an additional $321 billion would have been needed to pay future benefits to people on the rolls, to currently active members and their survivors, and to the survivors of previously deceased members who had not reached the minimum eligibility age for survivor benefits.[10]

---

[9]The various definitions of actuarial soundness that can be applied to the OASDHI program can be found in Myers, *Social Insurance and Allied Government Programs,* pp. 62-71.

[10]*Ibid.,* p. 67.

Although the OASDHI program is not actuarially sound based on the definition above, it does not follow that the program is financially insolvent and that the benefit rights of covered individuals are in jeopardy. That stringent definition, which is normally used in private pensions, is clearly inappropriate for the OASDHI program, for several reasons. First, the error of noncomparable performance standards is committed. As we saw in Chapter 2, social insurance and private insurance differ in character, content, and objectives, and so it is improper in principle to apply identical performance standards to them. The unfunded accrued liabilities for the present group of covered workers is based on the incorrect comparison of the OASDHI program to a private insurer selling individual life insurance policies. The private company must stress a fully funded program in order to have sufficient funds on hand to fulfill the terms of the contracts for present policyholders and also to pay off policyholders if they should surrender their policies and demand their cash values.

Second, since it is assumed that the OASDHI program will operate indefinitely in the future, it is reasonable to consider both the benefits promised the future entrants and the contributions that will be paid by them and their employers, in determining whether the program can meet its financial obligations to covered individuals and families. Thus, a fully funded program is unnecessary, since the contributions of the workers of the future and their employers can be relied on.

Third, because the OASDHI program is compulsory, those entering the labor force in the future, and their employers, must pay the tax contributions whether or not they are willing to participate in the program. So it is again reasonable to consider the contributions of the new entrants and their employers in determining whether the OASDHI program is actuarially sound. In contrast, private companies, which cannot assume that new policyholders will always join the company, must emphasize full funding.

Finally, the definition above is based on a closed-group concept, whereby only present members are considered. This is clearly invalid, since it is assumed that new entrants will participate in the OASDHI program because it is compulsory and will operate indefinitely.

Most actuaries generally agree that the severe definition of actuarial soundness described earlier should not be applied to the OASDHI program.[11] Thus, the concept of the deficit for present members is only a theoretical exercise and is not of true significance to the OASDHI program in the long run.

A less severe definition can be used to determine if the OASDHI program is actuarially sound, by evaluating it in terms of pay-as-you-go financing. Pay-as-you-go financing in this context means that annual receipts and annual disbursements under the OASDHI program should be approximately equal. And the OASDHI program can be considered actuarially sound under this system if the future contribution schedule is seen to approximate closely the estimated future benefit disbursements year by year.[12]

[11]*Ibid.*

[12]*Ibid.*, p. 68.

Test of Actuarial Soundness

As we have seen, the concept of actuarial soundness in the OASDHI program differs from the concepts applied to private pensions or to private insurance, since having sufficient funds on hand to pay off all accrued liabilities in the event of termination is not necessary in a program that will operate indefinitely into the future. The test of actuarial soundness, therefore, is not whether there are sufficient funds available to pay off all accrued liabilities, but whether the expected future income from the tax contributions plus interest on the trust-fund investments will be sufficient for meeting all anticipated expenditures for benefits and administrative costs over the long-run period considered in the actuarial valuation. Thus, the concept of unfunded accrued liability does not apply to the OASDHI program as it would to a private pension plan. If the OASDHI program operates indefinitely, it is proper to consider both the tax contributions from the new workers and the benefits that must be paid to them during the period considered in the actuarial valuation.

Based on the assumption of an indefinite future operation, the OASDHI program is considered actuarially sound if it is in actuarial balance. *It is in actuarial balance if the estimated future income from contributions and from interest earnings on the accumulated contingency trust funds will, over the long-range period considered in the valuation, support all the system's expenditures.*[13] Although the future experience may deviate from the actuarial cost estimates, it is the intent of Congress that the OASDHI program should be self-supporting and actuarially sound. This is expressed in the law by a contribution schedule that, according to the actuarial cost estimates, results in a system that is in actuarial balance or reasonably close thereto.

LONG-RANGE ACTUARIAL BALANCE

To determine whether the OASDHI program is self-supporting and is in actuarial balance over the long run will necessitate an analysis of the actuarial operations of the Old-Age, Survivors, and Disability Insurance Program (OASDI), the Hospital Insurance (HI) portion of the Medicare program, and Supplementary Medical Insurance (SMI).

OASDI Program

The 1971 Advisory Council on Social Security recommended that the level-benefits-level-earnings methodology should be replaced by a new methodology based on dynamic assumptions. This was done in 1972. The older methodology was based on the static assumptions of fixed benefits and an unchanging level of

[13]Social Security Administration, *Actuarial Cost Estimates,* p. 3.

earnings. The new actuarial methodology, which is based on dynamic assumptions with respect to benefits, taxable earnings, and the taxable wage base, is such that, if all actuarial and economic assumptions are realized, the financing will provide sufficient income so that future benefits can increase as fast as the Consumer Price Index, and as earnings increase, the taxable wage base will also increase. More specifically, the 1974 long-range cost estimates are based on the following dynamic assumptions:

1. Benefits will automatically increase with the Consumer Price Index, and the taxable wage base will also be adjusted as covered earnings increase. It is also assumed that if Congress were to grant larger benefit-table increases or were to liberalize benefits in any respect or hold down the earnings base, additional financing would be provided.

2. The schedule of benefits will be adjusted after 1974 to reflect increases in the Consumer Price Index.

3. The OASDHI taxable wage base and the amount exempt under the earnings test are both adjusted after 1974 to reflect increases in average earnings.

4. The short-range cost estimates through 1980 are based on the assumptions developed under Alternative I. [See Tables 7-3 and 7-4].

5. After 1980, the Consumer Price Index will increase at an annual rate of 3 percent, and average earnings will increase at 5 percent.

6. Current-cost financing is used, and the long-range actuarial-valuation period covers a period of 75 years.[14]

Table 7-1 illustrates the current cost of the OASDI program as a percentage of taxable payroll for the next 75 years, based on dynamic actuarial assumptions. The annual cost of the program is projected to increase slowly throughout the remainder of the century, finally leveling off at about 17-18 percent of taxable payroll after 2025. In effect, the cost projections for the next 75 years can be broken down into three periods of 25 years each. The first period will involve a gradual increase in costs; in the second, the increase will be more rapid; and the final period will be characterized by even higher but level costs.

The projected rapid increase in costs in the second period and the high costs in the third period are largely due to the demographic effect of a larger aged population in the future as compared to the working population. In addition, part of the increase is due to anomalies in the automatic benefit-adjustment provision under present law. The present provisions are projected to result in a faster increase in future awarded benefits than in future annual earnings. This difference will be relatively modest during the remainder of this century, but it is expected to widen substantially after that time.[15]

---

[14]*1974 Annual Report of the Board of Trustees of the Federal Old-Age and Survivors Insurance and Disability Insurance Trust Funds,* pp. 18 and 34-35.

[15]*Ibid.,* p. 37.

TABLE 7-1   Estimated Current Cost [a] of Old-Age, Survivors, and Disability Insurance System as Percent of Taxable Payroll [b] under Dynamic Assumptions [c] for Selected Years, 1985-2045

Calendar Year	Old-Age and Survivors Insurance	Disability Insurance	Total
1985	9.00	1.44	10.44
1990	9.52	1.51	11.03
1995	9.64	1.61	11.25
2000	9.54	1.77	11.31
2005	9.72	1.97	11.69
2010	10.56	2.13	12.69
2015	11.82	2.22	14.14
2020	13.47	2.24	15.71
2025	14.78	2.19	16.97
2030	15.46	2.14	17.60
2035	15.49	2.19	17.68
2040	15.40	2.28	17.68
2045	15.53	2.33	17.86
Average cost [d]	11.97	1.92	13.89

[a]Represents the cost as percent of taxable payroll of all expenditures in the year, including amounts needed to maintain the funds at about 1 year's expenditures.

[b]Payroll is adjusted to take into account the lower contribution rate on self-employment income, on tips, and on multiple-employer "excess wages" as compared with the combined employer-employee rate.

[c]See text for a description of the assumptions.

[d]Represents the arithmetic average of the current cost for the 75-year period 1974-2048.

Source: 1974 Annual Report of the Board of Trustees of the Federal Old-Age and Survivors Insurance and Disability Insurance Trust Funds. H.D. No. 93-313, Committee on Ways and Means, 93d Cong., 2d sess., 1974 (Washington, D.C.: U.S. Government Printing Office, 1974), p. 37, Table 22.

Table 7-2 illustrates the long-range actuarial balance of the OASDI program. The average long-range cost under dynamic assumptions is compared with the average rate in the tax schedule under present law. Based on dynamic assumptions, the OASDI program is underfinanced over the long range, with a negative actuarial balance of about 3 percent of taxable payroll. Both the OASI and DI portions of the total program have a long-range actuarial deficit equal to about 21 percent of their costs.[16] The actuarial balance of —2.98 percent of taxable payroll substantially exceeds the acceptable limit of variation of 5 percent of the program's cost (.69 percent of taxable payroll).[17]

The long-range actuarial deficit is largely due to a change in assumptions concerning fertility rates and population size. The new population projections are based on an ultimate total fertility rate of 2.1 children per woman, which is close to the population-replacement rate, whereas previous projections were based on ultimate rates of 2.3 and 2.8 children per woman. The lower projected

[16]*Ibid.,* p. 35.

[17]*Ibid.,* p. 38.

TABLE 7-2 Estimated Actuarial Balance[a] of Old-Age, Survivors, and Disability Insurance System as Percent of Taxable Payroll,[b] Dynamic Assumptions[c]

Item	OASI	DI	Total
Average cost of system	11.97	1.92	13.89
Average rate in present tax schedule	9.39	1.52	10.91
Actuarial balance	—2.58	—.40	—2.98

[a]As measured over the 75-year period, 1974-2048.

[b]Payroll is adjusted to take into account the lower contribution rates on self-employment income, on tips, and on multiple-employer "excess wages" as compared with the combined employer-employee rate.

[c]See text for a description of the assumptions.

Source: 1974 Annual Report of the Board of Trustees of the Federal Old-Age and Survivors Insurance and Disability Insurance Trust Funds, H.D. No. 93-313, Committee on Ways and Means, 93rd Cong., 1st sess., 1974 (Washington, D.C., U.S. Government Printing Office, 1974), p. 35. Table 20.

fertility rate results in a higher projected ratio of the aged to the active workers, and thus in higher costs expressed as a percentage of payroll.[18]

Another important factor affecting the long-range cost is the recent increase in the number of disabled-worker benefit awards. The number of these awards has significantly increased since 1971, raising the costs of the DI portion of the program.

Although the long-range cost estimates indicate a serious underfinancing of the OASDI program, the board of trustees, in its 1974 report, did not recommend an increase in tax contribution rates. The board believes that the new population and fertility projections will have a major cost impact on the program after the turn of the century, but not in the short run. Based on short-run cost estimates, the board concludes that it is unnecessary to increase the combined income for the OASDI and HI programs for the next five to ten years, and that, since the newly appointed Advisory Council on Social Security is studying the long-range financing of the program, there is sufficient time to await the council's recommendations before making specific proposals.[19]

It is also worthwhile to examine the experience of the combined OASI and DI trust funds with respect to their past and future operations. Trust-fund income and disbursements will be affected in the future not only by economic conditions, which will affect the level of employment and taxable earnings, but also by legislative changes. In addition, the automatic provisions will directly affect benefit amounts, the taxable wage base, and exempt amounts under the retirement test.

Because of the uncertainty of future economic conditions and because of the high sensitivity of future benefit levels to changes in the Consumer Price Index, two alternative sets of projections, based on changing economic conditions, are used to estimate the future progress of the combined OASI and DI trust funds. Table 7-3 indicates the range of assumptions concerning the future

[18]*Ibid.,* p. 35.

[19]*Ibid.,* p. 38.

Consumer Price Index and future increases in average wages. The economic assumptions under Alternative I are used to estimate the short-range costs of the program through 1980.

TABLE 7-3 Alternative Assumptions Concerning Future Increases in the Consumer Price Index and Average Wages, 1974-80

	Alternative I		Alternative II	
	Increase in Wages	*Increase in CPI*	*Increase in Wages*	*Increase in CPI*
Calendar year:				
1974	7.9	9.1	8.3	9.7
1975	8.5	5.7	9.3	7.1
1976	8.0	4.5	8.6	5.5
1977	7.6	3.2	8.4	4.8
1978	5.5	3.0	7.5	4.3
1979	5.5	3.0	6.0	4.0
1980	5.5	3.0	6.0	4.0

Source: 1974 Annual Report of the Board of Trustees of the Federal Old-Age and Survivors Insurance and Disability Insurance Trust Funds, H.D. No. 93-313, Committee on Ways and Means, 93d. Cong., 2d sess., 1974 (Washington, D.C.: U.S. Government Printing Office, 1974), p. 18.

In addition, certain assumptions are made regarding the effect of the automatic provisions on benefit increases, contribution and benefit base, and exempted amounts under the retirement test. Table 7-4 illustrates two alternative sets of assumptions concerning these factors.

TABLE 7-4 Alternative Assumptions Concerning Benefit Increases under the Automatic-Adjustment Provisions, Contribution and Benefit Base, and Amounts Exempt under the Retirement Test, 1974-78

Year	*General Benefit Increase (percent)[a] under Alternative—*		*Contribution and Benefit Base[b] under Alternative—*		*Annual Exempt Amount under the Retirement Test[b] under Alternatives I and II*
	I	*II*	*I*	*II*	
1974	11.0	11.0	$ 13,200	$ 13,200	$ 2,400
1975	4.4	5.5	14,100	14,100	2,640
1976	5.0	6.0	15,300	15,300	2,880
1977	3.5	5.0	16,500	16,500	3,120
1978	3.1	4.5	17,700	18,000	3,360

[a]Effective with benefits for June of the stated year. The 11-percent benefit increase in 1974 is to be made effective in 2 steps—an interim increase of 7 percent effective for the 3 months March, April, and May 1974, followed by the full 11-percent increase effective for June 1974.

[b]Effective on Jan. 1 of the stated year.

Source: 1974 Annual Report of the Board of Trustees of the Federal Old-Age and Survivors Insurance and Disability Insurance Trust Funds, H.D. No. 93-313, Committee on Ways and Means, 93d Cong., 2d sess., 1974 (Washington, D.C.: U.S. Government Printing Office, 1974), p. 18.

Table 7-5 indicates the operations of the combined OASI and DI trust funds under past law, and also for the near-term future based on two alternative sets of assumptions. Based on Alternative I, the combined OASDI trust fund will increase from about $44 billion in 1973 to about $46 billion in 1978. However, if Alternative II assumptions are used, the combined trust fund will gradually increase until 1976 and then decline in 1977 and 1978.

Finally, although the trust-fund assets are estimated to increase each year under Alternative I and in each of the years 1974-76 under Alternative II, the ratio of assets to annual outlays during the year is expected to decline. In 1973, the ratio of assets at the beginning of the year to expenditures during the year for the combined OASDI trust fund was 0.80. By calendar year 1978, the estimated ratio under Alternative I will decline to 0.51, and under Alternative II, to 0.48.[20] Thus, the financing principle of maintaining trust-fund balances approximately equal to one year's expenditures will not be fulfilled in the near future, based on present cost estimates.

Hospital Insurance

The Hospital Insurance portion of the Medicare program is also based on current-cost financing; however, the valuation period covers only 25 years, rather than 75. The adequacy of financing of the HI program is expressed as an actuarial balance—the difference between (1) the average of the tax rates established under present law; and (2) the average of the current costs for the 25-year period, adjusted to increase the HI trust fund to the level of one year's expenditures. The current cost for any year is the ratio of the costs of benefits and administrative expenses, plus an amount required to maintain the trust fund at the level of the next year's expenditures, to the effective taxable payroll. In projecting taxable payroll into the future, it is assumed that the taxable wage will be periodically adjusted as wages increase.

Table 7-6 illustrates the estimated actuarial balance of the HI program for the period between 1974 and 1998. The difference between contributions and costs is +0.02 percent of taxable payroll, which indicates that the program is in approximate actuarial balance. Before the 1972 amendments, the HI rates were considered inadequate, and the trust fund would have been exhausted after a short period. However, the 1972 and 1973 legislation adequately financed the future benefits. The HI trust-fund balance at the beginning of 1973 was only 40 percent of the projected expenditures for that year; but future projections indicate that, under the present financing schedule, the HI trust fund will reach 100 percent of the year's expenditures by the beginning of 1977 and will exceed 130 percent of the year's expenditures by the beginning of 1980.

Supplementary Medical Insurance

The Supplementary Medical Insurance (SMI) program is intended to be self-supporting from the monthly premiums of those covered and matching

[20]*Ibid.*, p. 27.

TABLE 7-5   Operations of the Old-Age and Survivors Insurance and Disability Insurance Trust Funds Combined During Selected Calendar Years 1960-73, and Estimated Future Operations During Calendar Years 1974-78 Under 2 Alternative Sets of Assumptions (In millions)

Calendar Year	Total	Contributions, less Refunds	Noncontributory Credits for Military Service	Payments to Noninsured Persons Aged 72 and Over	Interest on Investments
Past experience:					
1960	12,445	11,876			569
1965	17,857	17,205			651
1966	23,381	22,585	94		702
1967	26,413	25,424	94		896
1968	28,493	27,034	188	226	1,045
1969	33,346	31,546	94	364	1,342
1970	36,993	34,737	94	371	1,791
1971	40,908	38,343	187	351	2,027
1972	45,622	42,888	189	337	2,208
1973	54,787	51,907	191	303	2,386
Estimated future experience:					
Alternative I					
1974	61,409	58,398	192	307	2,512
1975	68,879	65,826	212	283	2,558
1976	76,065	72,912	345	262	2,546
1977	83,569	80,445	354	231	2,539
1978	89,924	86,779	364	200	2,581
Alternative II:					
1974	61,471	58,457	192	307	2,515
1975	69,407	66,341	212	283	2,571
1976	76,970	73,776	379	262	2,556
1977	85,015	81,880	385	233	2,517
1978	92,979	89,873	394	205	2,507

TABLE 7-5(continued)

Transactions during Period

Disbursements

Total	Benefit Payments	Payments for Vocational Rehabilitation Services	Administrative Expenses	Transfers to Railroad Retirement Account	Net Increase in Funds	Funds at End of Period
11,798	11,245		240	314	647	22,613
19,187	18,311		418	459	—1,331	19,841
20,913	20,048	3	393	469	2,467	22,308
22,471	21,406	11	515	539	3,942	26,250
26,015	24,936	17	603	458	2,479	28,729
27,892	26,751	16	612	513	5,453	34,182
33,108	31,863	20	635	589	3,886	38,068
38,542	37,171	26	719	626	2,366	40,434
43,281	41,595	30	907	749	2,341	42,775
53,148	51,459	49	837	802	1,639	44,414
61,310	59,294	72	1,013	931	99	44,513
68,669	66,500	89	1,054	1,026	210	44,723
75,676	73,357	105	1,116	1,098	389	45,112
82,862	80,396	120	1,181	1,165	707	45,819
89,770	87,153	134	1,238	1,245	154	45,973
61,310	59,294	72	1,013	931	161	44,575
69,042	66,869	89	1,058	1,026	365	44,940
76,878	74,546	106	1,128	1,098	92	45,032
85,239	82,729	123	1,201	1,186	—224	44,808
93,696	91,005	138	1,267	1,286	—717	44,091

Source: 1974 Annual Report of the Board of Trustees of the Federal Old-Age and Survivors Insurance and Disability Insurance Trust Funds, H.D. No. 93-313. Committee on Ways and Means, 93d Cong., 2d sess., 1974 (Washington, D.C.: U.S. Government Printing Office, 1974), p. 26, Table 13.

TABLE 7-6 Actuarial Balance of the Hospital Insurance Program, as a Percent of Taxable Payroll*

Average contribution rate in present schedule	2.65%
Average current cost	2.63
Actuarial balance	+ 0.02

*For the 25-year period 1974-1998.

Source: 1974 Annual Report of the Board of Trustees of the Federal Hospital Insurance Trust Fund (Washington, D.C.: U.S. Government Printing Office, 1974).

general-revenue contributions by the federal government. The total of these is intended to equal the incurred benefit and administrative costs, with a margin for contingency purposes. The monthly premium is periodically determined in December of each year for the following fiscal year starting July 1. As of July 1, 1975, the monthly premium was $6.70.

The concept of actuarial soundness applied to the SMI program is similar to that applied to private group term insurance. The SMI program is similar to yearly renewable term insurance, and in determining the actuarial soundness of the program, it is considered inappropriate to look beyond the period for which the premium rate and matching general-revenue contributions are determined.

TABLE 7-7 Estimated Income and Disbursements Incurred under Supplementary Medical Insurance Program, Fiscal Years 1967-1975 (In millions)

Fiscal Year	Premiums from Participants	Govern- ment Contributions[a]	Benefit Payments	Administrative Expenses	Interest on Fund	Net of Operations in Year
			Past Experience			
1967	$ 647	$ 647	$ 1,179	$ 190[b]	$ 15	$ —60
1968	699	699	1,500	151	21	—232
1969	903	904	1,698	210	23	—78
1970	936	937	1,982	223	12	—320
1971	1,253	1,253	2,081	260	17	+ 182
1972	1,340	1,342	2,278	293	29	+ 140
1973	1,427	1,430	2,480	279	45	+ 143
			Projected			
1974	1,683	2,008	3,245	463	55	+ 38
1975	1,845	2,327	3,807	469	72	— 32

[a]Includes interest for any delay in transfer of government contributions.

[b]Includes administrative expenses incurred prior to the beginning of the program.

Source: 1974 Annual Report of the Board of Trustees of the Federal Supplementary Medical Insurance Trust Fund (Washington, D.C.: U.S. Government Printing Office, 1974).

Two tests of actuarial soundness are applied to the SMI program. The primary test relates to the adequacy of income for the fiscal year that is not yet completed, but for which the monthly premium rate and level of general-revenue contribution have been established. The monthly premiums and matching federal funds should be sufficient for meeting all incurred benefit and administrative costs, with a margin for contingency purposes, for the period under consideration.

The second test of actuarial soundness is that the trust-fund assets at the end of the period should be as large as the liabilities incurred during the period, especially for those services and administrative expenses that have been incurred but for which payment has not been made. This test is considered necessary because the present method of financing the SMI program could be changed, and any deficit would then be a burden on the new financing system. In addition, the SMI trust fund should be large enough so that it is never in serious danger of becoming exhausted. This requirement can be fulfilled even if the other two tests of actuarial soundness cannot be met, since the existence of the fund would temporarily permit the payment of benefits even though the premium rate is inadequate.

The SMI program did not meet the first test of actuarial soundness during the early years of its operations, but it has done so in later periods. Table 7-7 indicates the estimated income and incurred disbursements for fiscal years 1967-75. Between 1967 and 1970, the incurred disbursements exceeded the SMI income, but for fiscal 1971 through 1973, the income has more than covered the incurred disbursements. For fiscal 1974, the primary test of actuarial soundness is also expected to be met, but a minor deficiency is projected to occur in fiscal 1975.

The second test of actuarial soundness—trust-fund assets equal to liabilities—has not been fulfilled. Table 7-8 illustrates the deficit for fiscal years 1967-75 and the ratio of the assets to liabilities. The ratios represent the extent to which the available funds can pay the accumulated liabilities. The deficit indicates the financial burden that would be placed on the financing system in the future if the present system of financing the SMI program were changed. Improvements in financing the program have reduced the deficit in recent years, so although the second test of actuarial soundness is not completely met, the actuarial status and solvency of the SMI program have been substantially improved. The board of trustees believes that the trust-fund balance will be sufficient to pay future benefits for the financing period under consideration as they become due.

ZERO POPULATION GROWTH AND THE OASDHI PROGRAM

The present financing system of the OASDHI program depends heavily on the active workers supporting the nonproductive retired aged. Therefore, movement toward zero population growth (ZPG) will have prfound effects on the future financial burden of the program.

TABLE 7-8 Summary of Estimated Assets and Liabilities of the Supplementary Medical Insurance Program, at the End of Fiscal Years 1967-1975 (In millions)

| | Past Experience | | | | | | | Projected | |
| | As of June 30, | | | | | | | As of June 30, | |
	1967	1968	1969	1970	1971	1972	1973	1974	1975
Assets:									
Balance in trust fund	$ 486	$ 307	$ 378	$ 57	$ 290	$ 481	$ 746	$ 1,151	$ 1,327
Premiums due and uncollected	1	1	1	2	2	2	2	2	2
Government contributions due and unpaid	25	90	9	18	26	1	—2	1	3
Total assets	$ 512	$ 398	$ 388	$ 77	$ 318	$ 484	$ 746	$ 1,155	$ 1,332
Liabilities:									
Benefits incurred but unpaid	$ 515	$ 625	$ 679	$ 681	$ 727	$ 750	$ 839	$ 1,184	$ 1,368
Administrative cost thereon	55	63	75	82	95	98	128	154	178
Premiums collected in advance	1	1	2	2	2	2	2	2	2
Government contributions thereon	1	1	2	2	2	2	2	2	3
Total liabilities	$ 572	$ 690	$ 758	$ 767	$ 826	$ 852	$ 971	$ 1,342	$ 1,551
Net surplus (or deficit)	$ —60	—292	—370	—690	—508	—368	—225	—187	—219
Ratio of assets to liabilities	.90	.58	.51	.10	.38	.57	.77	.86	.86

Source: 1974 Annual Report of the Board of Trustees of the Federal Supplementary Medical Insurance Trust Fund (Washington, D.C.: U.S. Government Printing Office, 1974).

Meaning of ZPG

Zero population growth is defined as a year during which the total population does not increase. ZPG can be attained by replacement-level fertility, which is the level of fertility by which a population replaces itself exactly under projected mortality rates and in the absence of immigration. The Bureau of the Census estimates that replacement-level fertility can be achieved by an average of 2.11 births per woman. Assuming a gradual movement toward the cohort fertility rate of 2.11, the Series X population series without immigration produces a stationary population about 288 million around 2050.[21]

Replacement-level fertility is not a remote goal; but it has actually been attained. The Census Bureau has estimated that the total fertility rate during 1972 was about 2.1 births per woman for the first half-year, and about 2.04 for the first nine months. The corresponding total fertility rates for 1973 that are used in the new Series E and F population estimates are, respectively, 1.9 and 1.8 births per woman. Thus, the total fertility rate is currently at or below replacement levels.[22]

Shifts in Age Distribution of Population

If the total fertility rate continues, it will have a profound impact on the future age distribution of the population, which in turn will affect the distribution of the OASDHI financial burden. The proportion of retired aged will sharply increase, and the financial burden of their support will fall on a shrinking base of active workers. Under ZPG conditions, the proportion of the population aged 65 and older will increase from about 10 percent in 1970 to 16 percent by 2050. In addition, the critical ratio of the aged to the active workers (ages 20-64) will increase from .19 to .28 during the same period, an increase of about 50 percent. The median age of the population will also rise sharply, from 27.9 years in 1970 to 37.3 years in 2050.[23] Thus, although the active workers under age 65 already bear a heavy financial burden, this burden will be greater in the future under ZPG conditions.

Financial Impact on the OASDHI Program

Consideration of the financial impact of ZPG on the OASDHI program suggests strongly that the program should not be unduly expanded in the future. Three broad conclusions emerge when the future financial burden of the OASDHI program is analyzed. First, because of the dramatic increase in the

[21]U.S. Bureau of the Census, *Current Population Reports,* Series P-25, No. 480, "Illustrative Population Projections for the United States: The Demographic Effects of Alternative Paths to Zero Growth" (Washington, D.C.: U.S. Government Printing Office, 1972), pp. 1-2; p. 22, Table 7.

[22]U.S. Bureau of the Census, *Current Population Reports,* Series P-25, No. 493, "Projections of the Population of the United States, by Age and Sex: 1972 to 2020" (Washington, D.C.: U.S. Government Printing Office, 1972), pp. 5, 8, and 23.

[23]George E. Rejda and Richard J. Shepler, "The Impact of Zero Population Growth on the OASDHI Program," *The Journal of Risk and Insurance,* Vol. XL, No. 3 (September 1973), 316, Table 1.

ratio of the retired aged to the active workers under ZPG conditions, the active workers will be faced with a relatively heavier future financial burden. Movement toward the ZPG state will result in an increase in the proportion of retired workers and a decline in the proportion of active workers. Assuming that the present contributory payroll-tax method continues, the proportion of workers from whom the taxes are collected will decline relative to the proportion of retired people receiving the bulk of the benefits. In 1970, about 84 percent of the population aged 20 and over consisted of those of working age, under 65. By 2050, under ZPG conditions, this will decline to about 78 percent. And the financial burden will be even greater if 60 becomes the future normal retirement age.

The increased financial burden for the active workers may be borne more easily if the economy grows sufficiently and part of the gain from growth is used to fund OASDHI benefits. For example, the growing proportion of the aged can be paid benefits at present levels if real per capita personal income increases by at least 1.01 percent annually up to 2050. However, this figure does not allow for any increase in real per capita OASDHI benefits to the aged. If real per capita benefits to the aged are increased even 1 percent annually in the future, then real per capita personal income must increase by at least 2.01 percent annually just to avoid increasing the real financial burden on the active workers based on current benefit levels. Since annual growth rates in excess of 2.01 percent appear incapable of being sustained until 2050, the real financial burden of the OASDHI program will fall heavily on a shrinking base of active workers.[24]

Second, the ZPG state will result in a changing emphasis on OASDHI benefits. Because of the larger proportion of retired aged, OASDHI retirement and Medicare benefits will become relatively more important. The larger number of older workers near retirement may create strong political pressures for substantial increases in retirement benefits, intensifying even further the burden on the active workers. In addition, owing to the larger proportion of retired aged, the rapidly spiraling increase in medical costs, if not contained in the future, will have an adverse cost impact on the Medicare program.

Finally, general-revenue financing of at least part of the OASDHI program may become desirable under ZPG conditions. The heavier financial burden that will fall on a shrinking base of active workers can thus be financed more equitably as the economy moves toward ZPG.

GENERAL-REVENUE FINANCING OF THE OASDHI PROGRAM

One of the most controversial issues in the financing of the OASDHI program is whether the general revenues of the federal government should be used for all or part of the future costs. As stated earlier, general revenues are now being used to pay only the costs of noncontributory wage credits for military service, payments to noninsured persons aged 72 and over, the federal government's matching share of SMI premiums, and the costs of covering certain

---

[24]*Ibid.,* pp. 316-21.

uninsured persons under the HI portion of the Medicare program. With these exceptions, the OASDHI program is completely self-supporting.

The idea of general-revenue financing is not new. The Committee on Economic Security, established by President Roosevelt in 1934 to develop the Social Security Act, recommended that the old-age benefits program should be eventually financed by contributions from employees, employers, and the federal government. However, the committee said, the government contribution would not be needed for two decades, since sufficient funds for the payment of benefits and administrative costs would be available until then from the employer-employee contributions. The federal government would begin to make its contribution from general revenues when the size of the trust fund started to decrease, and the government's contribution would be large enough to maintain an exact balance between income and outgo. The Social Security Act, however, did not provide for financing with government contributions, but solely from the contributions of the employees, employers, and interest earnings on the trust funds.[25]

At the present time, many foreign countries—including Australia, Austria, Belgium, Brazil, Canada, Chile, Costa Rica, Denmark, the Federal German Republic, Iceland, Ireland, Israel, Italy, Japan, Mexico, the Netherlands, New Zealand, Norway, the Philippines, South Africa, Spain, Sweden, Switzerland, and the United Kingdom—use general revenues to help finance their social-security programs. In contrast, the United States and a few other countries, such as Argentina and France, depend heavily on employer-employee financing of their social insurance programs. Several arguments are advanced in both support and opposition to the use of general revenues of the federal government for financing part or all of the OASDHI program.

Arguments for General-Revenue Financing

The major arguments for general-revenue financing include the following: (1) need for more adequate benefits, (2) heavy payroll-tax burden, (3) payment of welfare element, (4) greater individual equity in the payments of benefits, (5) funding of accrued liabilities, and (6) economic considerations.[26]

More Adequate Benefits. Although monthly OASDHI benefits have increased by more than 100 percent in the past seven years, proponents of general-revenue financing argue that more adequate benefits must be paid to permit a higher standard of living after retirement. They say that general-revenue financing is the only feasible method of substantially increasing the OASDHI retirement and survivorship benefits, and that the benefits will never be adequate if payroll taxes are relied on exclusively to finance them. Thus, general revenues

[25]Robert J. Myers, "Financing Features of Social Security," *The Journal of the American Society of Chartered Life Underwriters,* Vol. XXII, No. 2 (April 1968), 40-41.

[26]A discussion of the major arguments for and against general-revenue financing can be found in Robert J. Myers, "Various Proposals to Change the Financing of Social Security," *The Journal of Risk and Insurance,* Vol. XXXVI, No. 4 (September 1969), 355-63; and Dorothy S. Projector, *BLS Staff Paper No. 1: Issues in Financing Old-Age and Survivors Insurance,* U.S. Department of Labor, Bureau of Labor Statistics (Washington, D.C.: U.S. Government Printing Office, 1968).

must be used to meet part of the higher costs of substantial and necessary improvements in the OASDHI program. One proposal is that the covered workers, employers, and federal government should each bear one-third of the total costs; if this three-party sharing of cost is used, future OASDHI benefits could be considerably higher.

Heavy Payroll-Tax Burden. Another argument for general-revenue financing is that the present payroll-taxing method results in an unusually heavy tax burden on taxpayers, especially middle- and low-income wage earners. It is said that present payroll-tax rates have reached confiscatory levels, and that the taxpayers are beginning to protest and may even revolt.

Although the average monthly benefit paid increased less than threefold between 1950 and 1971, the average tax paid per covered person rose over 7.5-fold during the same period.[27] In addition, the 1975 tax rate for covered employees and employers is 5.85 percent on taxable wages of $14,100. Thus, both the workers and employers will pay a maximum tax of $824.85, or a total of $1,649.70. Some observers are particularly disturbed that many middle- and low-income wage earners are paying more in OASDHI payroll taxes than in personal income taxes. And the future payroll-tax burden will be even heavier, since the rates are scheduled to increase in the future, and the taxable wage base will also increase in accordance with the automatic provisions. Therefore, general-revenue financing of at least part of the OASDHI costs would permit some necessary and desirable payroll-tax relief.

It is pointed out that the increasing future financial burden will not fall evenly on all groups. Assuming that the present payroll-taxing method continues, the real burden will fall heavily on both the low- and middle-income groups. The heaviest burden of all will fall on the working poor, even though this group is largely exempt from the payment of personal income taxes. Furthermore, a recent research study by John Brittain indicates that the combined OASDHI and personal income tax rate is regressive over a wide range of income, a fact that results in discrimination against middle-income families. For example, a four-member middle-income family with a single earner who earns $10,800 pays a higher combined income and payroll tax rate than does an individual with higher earnings (up to about $20,000 annually).[28] This inequity could be reduced by help from general-revenue financing, which is based on the ability-to-pay principle and the progressive income tax.

In addition, the payroll tax by itself, although it is proportional up to the maximum wage base and regressive thereafter, has an overall effect that is regressive. For example, the middle-income worker earning $14,100 in 1975 paid a payroll tax on 100 percent of his covered earnings, but an upper-income worker earning $141,000 during the same period paid a payroll tax on only 10 percent of his earnings (the first $14,100). General-revenue financing could correct for the regressive nature of the OASDHI tax.

General-revenue financing becomes even more desirable when, along with their regressivity, the incidence of payroll taxes is considered. Economic theory

[27]Cohen and Friedman, *Social Security,* p. 33.

[28]John A. Brittain, *The Payroll Tax for Social Security* (Washington, D.C.: The Brookings Institution, 1972), p. 261.

suggests that all payroll taxes, whether paid by employers or employees, are absorbed by labor in the long run, in the form of lower wage increases, higher prices, or both. Empirical research studies support the proposition that most or all of the employer's portion of the tax is shifted to labor in the long run in the form of lower wage increases. (See Chapter 19.) This conclusion is extremely important from the viewpoint of public policy and income distribution. Since labor may bear the entire burden of OASDHI taxes, the financial impact on the working poor may be greater than is commonly believed. As stated earlier, under the present system both the OASDHI tax rate and taxable wage base will increase in the future; the incidence of these higher taxes will fall heavily on the working poor, and this burden must not be underestimated. John Brittain found that the highest payroll-tax rate (including unemployment insurance contributions) in the United States is approaching 13 percent and is paid by people who earn less than $4,200, the unemployment-insurance ceiling in most states.[29] Although the working poor pay little or nothing in personal income taxes, their total combined effective payroll tax from all sources is extremely heavy. In contrast, the wealthy may pay an effective personal income tax rate of 50 to 60 percent, but their effective payroll-tax rate is minimal.

Finally, the financial burden of OASDHI payroll taxes on the working poor should not be dismissed on the grounds that the benefits are weighted heavily in favor of the low-income groups, so that, on balance, the OASDHI program is highly progressive in its operations. *This argument ignores the important point that OASDHI taxes are levied on one group, but the cash-income benefits are largely received by other groups.* The working poor receive little comfort in knowing that the actuarial value of their benefits substantially exceeds the actuarial value of their contributions, when they have a critical present need for higher incomes simply to survive. And in the future, an even larger proportion of their personal income will be taken away involuntarily to help finance the OASDHI program. This undesirable effect can be avoided by a rebate of all or part of the OASDHI taxes paid by the working poor, with general revenues making up the difference.[30]

Payment of Welfare Element. General revenues can also be used to fund the welfare element in the OASDHI program. As stated earlier, the OASDHI program consists of both welfare and insurance elements, with the welfare element loosely defined as that part of the benefits paid that has little or no relation to the covered person's earnings and the payroll-tax contributions he has paid on those earnings. The welfare element can be viewed primarily as unearned benefits; that is, the benefits received by certain people, such as the aged and low-income groups, have little or no actuarial relationship to the value of their OASDHI tax contributions. At the present time, only a small fraction of the actual costs of the OASDHI benefits paid to the retired is met by their past tax contributions and those of their employers. The remaining costs are paid out

---

[29]*Ibid.,* pp. 12-13.

[30]For a discussion of payroll tax relief for the working poor, see U.S. Department of Health, Education and Welfare, Social Security Administration, Office of Research and Statistics, *Reducing Social Security Contributions for Low-Income Workers: Issues and Analysis,* Staff Paper 16 (Washington, D.C.: U.S. Government Printing Office, 1975).

of the tax contributions of current and future workers and their employers. It is estimated that the cost of paying full benefits to older workers is now about one-third of the cost of the OASDHI program.[31] These unearned benefits can be roughly viewed as the welfare element in the program.

The welfare element will continue to increase in the future. Under the automatic cost-of-living provision now built into the program, retirement benefits will increase automatically without a corresponding tax contribution from the retired aged, thereby increasing the welfare element. When the benefits increase automatically, the taxable wage base will also increase, and the burden will fall heavily on the working poor and middle-income families.

The costs of this welfare element, however, should be spread over a more equitable base, since they are social costs that should be shared by all of society. General-revenue financing is a more equitable method for doing this, since most general revenues are raised through the progressive income tax, which is based on the ability to pay. In contrast, the present OASDHI payroll tax is a flat tax levied on all covered earnings up to some maximum limit and does not take into account family size or unusually high expenses, such as medical expenses. General-revenue financing could be used to fund the welfare element in the program, and the present system of employee-employer contributions could then be used to finance the insurance element.

Greater Individual Equity. Another argument for general-revenue financing is that it would permit greater individual equity in the OASDHI program. One of the most serious criticisms of the present program is that the younger worker will receive benefits that are less than the combined employer-employee contributions made by and for him. Although a younger worker generally receives benefits equal to the actuarial value of his own contributions, an estimated 80 to 85 percent of the employer's contribution is used to provide benefits to groups who are unable to pay the full actuarial cost for their protection,[32] leaving only a relatively small proportion for additional benefits to the covered worker on whose behalf the contribution is made. Critics argue that this is unfair and inequitable, and that greater individual equity should be introduced into the OASDHI program by having the entire combined employer-employee tax used to provide benefits on behalf of the individual worker; at the same time, the social-adequacy principle would be preserved, since general-revenue financing would be used to pay the costs of the benefits for groups unable to pay the full actuarial cost of their protection.

Funding of Accrued Liabilities. Another argument, closely related to the one above, is that general-revenue financing should be used to fund the accrued liabilities under the OASDHI program.

To make the OASDHI program effective during its early years, Congress provided for full benefits to be paid to workers who were near retirement when first covered by the program, which meant that only a small proportion of the actual cost of their benefits was paid for by their contributions and those of their

---

[31]*Reports of the 1971 Advisory Council on Social Security,* p. 751.

[32]Social Security Administration, "Analysis of Whether the Young Worker Receives His Money's Worth under Social Security," in *President's Proposals,* Part I, p. 332.

employers. For example, based only on employee contributions, a married male aged 65 who retired at the beginning of 1962 had paid only about 8 percent of the actuarial cost of the benefits provided him.[33] Now someone had to pay for these unearned benefits.

The excess of the actuarial value of the benefits over the actuarial value of the contributions in the early years of operation of the program must be financed from future contributions. This means that future generations of covered workers receive protection that is less than the combined employer-employee contribution, because part of these combined contributions is used to make up for the cost of paying full benefits in the early years. However, if general revenues were used to pay these accrued liabilities, the total combined employer-employee contributions could be used to provide benefits on behalf of the contributing workers when they retire. This would provide an element of progressivity in the financing of the OASDHI program.

Economic Arguments for General-Revenue Financing. Some of the arguments used to justify general-revenue financing of the OASDHI program are based on economics. First, since the OASDHI tax is part of the total wage bill, as that tax increases, some firms may attempt to hold down their labor costs by substituting labor-saving capital equipment for some workers, thereby increasing unemployment. However, technical problems, high absolute costs of the capital equipment, financing difficulties, and labor-union resistance could act as barriers to complete substitution.[34]

Second, it is argued that higher OASDHI taxes, because they will increase the production costs of American firms, can contribute to inflation if they are shifted forward to the public in the form of higher prices. It is also charged that higher OASDHI taxes will impair the ability of American firms to compete in the international markets. A case in point is the shift of a greater portion of social-security costs to the government in Italy, with a reduction in the employer's position, in order to make Italian firms more competitive in the Common Market.

Finally, it is argued that general-revenue financing would improve the income-redistribution effects of the OASDHI program and thereby reduce poverty, since general-revenue financing would distribute the OASDHI tax more nearly in accordance with the ability to pay. Under this approach, there would be separate financing for the redistribution aspects of the present weighted benefit formula. Payroll taxes would finance benefits under a uniform wage-related computation, whereas general revenues would be used to finance the relative larger benefits received by the lower-income groups.[35] The redistribution-of-income effect of the OASDHI program will be analyzed further in Chapter 19.

---

[33]Robert J. Myers and Bertram Oppal, *Actuarial Note Number 20, Studies on the Relationship of Contributions to Benefits in Old-Age Benefit Awards,* U.S. Department of Health, Education and Welfare, Social Security Administration, Division of the Actuary (June 1965), Table 3.

[34]Tax Foundation, Inc., *Economic Aspects of the Social Security Tax* (New York: Tax Foundation, 1966), p. 24.

[35]Bowen, Harbison, Lester, and Somers, eds., *The Princeton Symposium,* p. 16.

Arguments against General-Revenue Financing

Several powerful counterarguments are offered against the use of general revenues to finance the OASDHI program, including the following: [36] (1) weakening of cost controls, (2) unjustified benefit increases, (3) difficulty of making improvements, (4) no appropriation of funds, (5) possible introduction of a means test, and (6) overall soundness of the present system.

Weakening of Cost Controls. It is argued that the present payroll tax acts as an important cost constraint, because if additional benefits are desired, higher payroll taxes must be paid. At present, Congress must recognize fully that the costs of any benefit increases must be paid by the covered employees and employers. Under general-revenue financing, Congress might vote changes in the OASDHI program without adequate consideration of the costs, on the grounds that general revenues can finance them.

Unjustified Benefit Increases. Another argument, closely related to the one above, is that Congress might increase and liberalize the benefits in an unjustified manner. Opponents of general-revenue financing fear that the true costs of increasing benefits would be obscured by general-revenue financing, and that in response to workers' demands, Congress would increase the benefits without providing the necessary financing. The present system encourages fiscal restraint by reminding the workers that they must pay higher taxes if they desire higher benefits.

Difficulty of Making Improvements. Some opponents of general-revenue financing argue that it would put the OASDHI program in the position of competing with all other government programs for a share of the general revenues of government. Then, if Congress considered other programs to be of higher priority, relatively smaller amounts would be made available for substantial improvements in OASDHI. For example, if general revenues should increase because of a full-employment economy, the OASDHI program would be competing for these funds with other programs—those for reducing poverty, rebuilding the cities, air and water pollution, crime, manpower training, education, and space—and these programs might have a higher priority than improvements in the OASDHI system. It is argued that these improvements are easier to make under the present financing system, because the OASDHI program does not significantly compete with other government programs for general-revenue funds.

No Appropriation of Funds. Under general-revenue financing, it is charged, Congress might refuse to appropriate the needed amounts, for political or budgetary reasons. In the past, government contributions to the OASDHI program have been authorized by law, but were not actually made as provided under the law, or were delayed for long periods. In this category were government contributions for the cost of benefits from military-service wage credits, those for the costs of benefits provided noninsured workers under the

---

[36]The major arguments against general revenue financing can be found in Robert J. Myers, "Social Security Taxes: Regressivity and Subsidies," *Tax Foundation's Tax Review,* Vol. XXXIV, No. 12 (December, 1973), 45-48.

Hospital Insurance program, and matching contributions under the Supplementary Medical Insurance program.[37]

This argument has some merit. Congress might be in a cost-cutting mood, and somewhat reluctant to appropriate all or part of the funds from general revenues needed to finance increased OASDHI benefits. This would be especially possible during a period of rapid inflation and substantial budgetary deficits, and an increase in the size of the national debt.

Introduction of a Means Test. Another argument against general-revenue financing is that there might be pressures to introduce a means test into the program, in order to exclude people with substantial incomes from being paid benefits.[38] Congress might be unwilling to appropriate funds from the general treasury to finance OASDHI benefits for those who did not need them. Thus, the entire character of the OASDHI program would be changed, since a means test is not required at the present time for receipt of benefits.

Soundness of the Present System. Opponents of general-revenue financing claim that the present financing provisions are sound, so there is no need to change. The Advisory Council on Social Security Financing believes that the costs of the program should be directly borne by those who benefit from it. The council argues that, under a contributory system of financing, covered workers are paid benefits as a matter of right, without establishing need. In addition, the contributions required under the system make it clear that OASDHI is not strictly a program of government aid, but is instead a cooperative program in which government provides some protection against old age, death, and disability. The council also argues that the earmarked taxes promote financial responsibility, since the covered workers clearly see that increases in benefits will result in higher costs and increased contributions.[39]

Second, it is argued that the present system is not regressive when the benefits are considered. An element of progressivity is introduced into the OASDHI program when low-income people receive relatively higher benefits compared to their contributions than do those with higher earnings. The regressiveness of the OASDHI tax will be analyzed in greater detail in Chapter 19.

Finally, opponents of general-revenue financing argue that the present system provides important psychological, political, and practical advantages. Many who contribute earmarked taxes toward their future economic security receive considerable satisfaction in knowing that they are entitled to benefits based on right, rather than to a government handout based on charity.

FUTURE FINANCING OF THE OASDHI PROGRAM

Let us examine some of the financing alternatives that have been proposed for the future to finance the OASDHI program: (1) continuance of the present

[37]Myers, "Social Security Taxes," pp. 99-100.

[38]*Ibid.*, p. 100.

[39]*Financing Old-Age, Survivors, and Disability Insurance,* pp. 8-9.

system, (2) general-revenue contributions, (3) modification of the payroll tax, and (4) the two-tier system.[40]

Continuation of the Present System

One possible future course of action is to continue the present financing method, based on the self-supporting contributory principle and payroll taxes paid by the covered employees, employers, and the self-employed. For the reasons stated earlier, supporters of the present financing system believe that the future financing of the OASDHI program should not be changed.

General-Revenue Contributions

Under this approach, general revenues would be used to finance part of the future costs of the OASDHI program. Three broad approaches are suggested for integrating general-revenue financing with the present contributory system: (1) fixed-percentage contribution, (2) unearned service credits, and (3) payment of the welfare element.[41]

Fixed-Percentage Contribution. Under this approach, a fixed percentage of payroll-tax collections would be contributed from general revenues. The advantage of this proposal is that the contribution would be the equivalent of a matching grant. In addition, if used incrementally, an extra earmarked contribution from general revenues would be required for each new benefit increase.

On the other hand, the fixed-percentage approach has certain disadvantages. Since the OASDHI benefits are usually lumped into packages, the matching principle has little disciplinary effect; meaningful rules for requiring general-revenue contributions are not established; and the method does not provide guidelines for limiting the drain on general revenues.

Unearned Service Credits. Here, the contribution from general revenues would be equal to the higher cost of benefits for the initially covered group, or to the cost of benefits paid to groups that have been blanketed in after their working careers were completed. In addition, general revenues would be used to pay the costs of unearned benefits that arise when the benefits are increased retroactively, or coverage is extended to new groups (such as medical doctors who retire shortly after being covered). As stated earlier, the cost of paying full benefits to people who have not contributed at the full actuarial rates is estimated to be at least one-third of the total cost of the system into perpetuity.[42] Thus, it is suggested that employees, employers, and the federal government each contribute one-third of the total cost of the program. This tripartite division would be phased in over a period of several years, as the need for additional revenues over and above the level of employee-employer contributions increases.

[40]Tax Foundation, Inc., *Issues in Future Financing of Social Security* (New York: Tax Foundation, 1967), pp. 32-47.

[41]Bowen, Harbison, Lester, and Somers, eds., *The Princeton Symposium,* pp. 64-65. See also U.S. Congress, Senate, Committee on Finance, *Report of the Panel on Social Security Financing* to Committee on Finance, Pursuant to S. Res. 350, 93d Cong., 94th Cong., 1st sess. (Washington, D.C.: U.S. Government Printing Office, 1975).

[42]Bowen, Harbison, Lester, and Somers, ed., *The Princeton Symposium,* p. 15.

Welfare Element. General revenues would be used to fund the welfare element embodied in the OASDHI program—that is, to meet the costs of the income-redistribution aspects of the program. The actuarial costs of the various benefits would be computed, and the payroll-tax contributions paid by employers and employees would be used to provide benefits based on the individual-equity principle (insurance element), whereas general revenues would be used to provide socially adequate benefits to those groups unable to pay the full actuarial cost of their protection (welfare element).

The advantage of this approach is that the insurance and welfare components are broken down, and a strong insurance system is retained. On the other hand, this approach is criticized on the grounds that the present system is already far removed from a traditional insurance system whereby the benefits are closely related to premiums, since a large part of all benefits can be classified as being in the welfare category. For example, a portion of the benefits paid to some people below the kink in the weighted benefit formula, which includes much of the minimum benefit, can be viewed as welfare. Thus, it is argued that the welfare-benefits approach, if applied broadly, does not offer sufficient discipline on decision making and would detract from the acceptability of the OASDHI program.[43]

Modification of the Payroll Tax

Modification of the payroll tax has been suggested for changing the financing of the OASDHI program. One proposal that bears serious consideration is to refund most or all of the payroll taxes paid by workers with incomes below the poverty line. Since the payroll-tax burden is extremely heavy for low-income workers, especially when the incidence of the employer's portion of the tax is considered, a rebate of OASDHI taxes to the working poor would help those who have steady jobs but are paid substandard wages. Even though the benefit formula weights the benefits heavily in favor of low-income groups, it is difficult to justify a financing method that drives the poor deeper into poverty.

Another proposal would integrate the OASDHI payroll tax with the personal income tax. People would be allowed to credit all or part of their payroll taxes against their individual income taxes and tax refunds would be made to those whose payroll credit exceeds their income tax liabilities. Retention of the payroll tax would have the psychological advantage of earmarking a tax to finance the OASDHI program, while the credit would reduce or eliminate the regressivity of the tax.[44]

Finally, exemptions could be granted for payroll-tax purposes, similar to the exemptions now allowed under the personal income tax. The OASDHI payroll tax would allow for the number of dependents a worker has, resulting in some consideration of the ability to pay. Under this approach, general-revenue contributions would be made to the trust funds for the taxes lost to the system. This technique would not be difficult to implement, since most firms use either tables or computers to determine the income tax liabilities of the workers.

[43]*Ibid.,* p. 65.

[44]*Ibid.,* p. 72.

Two-Tier System

Another proposal for financing the OASDHI program in the future is a two-tier system.[45] Under the first tier, a uniform benefit would be provided to all those eligible, regardless of their incomes and ability to pay. This benefit would be paid on the basis of the social-adequacy principle and would be financed out of general revenues. The second tier would float on top of the first, and would provide additional benefits based on the combined employer-employee payroll taxes.

The two-tier system has the advantage of clearly separating the welfare element from the insurance element, and separate financing methods would be used for each tier. Although the social-adequacy principle would be stressed in tier-one benefits, tier-two benefits would preserve the contributory principle and the principle of wage-related benefits. Thus, both social adequacy and individual equity could be combined in a desirable and logical fashion.

The Canadian system is one example of a two-tier system. A flat universal old-age pension is paid to each eligible person, without a needs test, and in addition, a wage-related contributory program is used that closely relates the individual's contributions to his benefits.

SUGGESTIONS FOR ADDITIONAL READING

> *Actuarial Cost Estimates for the Old-Age, Survivors, Disability, and Hospital Insurance System as Modified by the Social Security Provisions of Public Law 92-336.* Social Security Administration, Office of the Actuary, September 1972.

> Board of Trustees, Federal Hospital Insurance Trust Fund, *1974 Annual Report of the Board of Trustees of the Federal Hospital Insurance Trust Fund.* Washington, D.C.: U.S. Government Printing Office, 1974.

> Board of Trustees, Federal Old-Age and Survivors Insurance and Disability Insurance Trust Funds, *1974 Annual Report of the Board of Trustees of the Federal Old-Age and Survivors Insurance and Disability Insurance Trust Funds,* H.D. 93-313. Committee on Ways and Means, 93d Cong., 2d sess., 1974. Washington, D.C.: U.S. Government Printing Office, 1974.

> Board of Trustees, Federal Supplementary Medical Insurance Trust Fund, *1974 Annual Report of the Board of Trustees of the Federal Supplementary Medical Insurance Trust Fund.* Washington, D.C.: U.S. Government Printing Office, 1974.

---

[45]For a summary on how such a system would work, see Margaret S. Gordon, "The Case for Earnings-Related Social Security Benefits Restated," *Old-Age Income Assurance Part VI: Abstracts of the Papers. A Compendium of Papers on Problems and Policy Issues in the Public and Private Pension System,* Subcommittee on Fiscal Policy of the Joint Economic Committee, 90th Cong., 1st sess., 1968 (Washington, D.C.: U.S. Government Printing Office, 1968), pp. 72-78.

Bowen, William G., Frederick H. Harbison, Richard A. Lester, and Herman M. Somers, eds., *The Princeton Symposium on the American System of Social Insurance: Its Philosophy, Impact, and Future Development.* New York: McGraw-Hill, 1968. See, in particular, Otto Eckstein, "Financing the System of Social Insurance," in this volume.

Myers, Robert J., *Social Insurance and Allied Government Programs,* Chap. 5. Homewood, Ill.: Richard D. Irwin, 1965.

_____, "Social Security Taxes: Regressivity and Subsidies," *Tax Foundation's Tax Review,* Vol. XXIV, No. 12 (December 1973).

_____, "Various Proposals to Change the Financing of Social Security," *The Journal of Risk and Insurance,* Vol. XXXVI, No. 4 (September 1969).

Pechman, Joseph A., Henry J. Aaron, and Michael K. Taussig, *Social Security: Perspectives for Reform,* Chap. VIII. Washington, D.C.: The Brookings Institution, 1968.

_____, and Benjamin A. Okner, *How Is the Tax Burden Shared?* Washington, D.C.: The Brookings Institution, 1974.

Projector, Dorothy S., *BLS Staff Paper No. 1: Issues in Financing Old-Age and Survivors Insurance.* Washington, D.C.: U.S. Government Printing Office, 1968.

Tax Foundation, Inc., *Issues in Future Financing of Social Security.* New York: Tax Foundation, Inc., 1967.

Turnbull, John G. C. Arthur Williams, Jr., and Earl F. Cheit, *Economic and Social Security,* 4th ed., Chap. 3. New York: Ronald Press, 1973.

U.S. Congress, Senate, Committee on Finance, *Report of the Panel on Social Security Financing* to Committee on Finance, Pursuant to S. Res. 350, 93d Cong., 94th Cong., 1st sess. Washington, D.C.: U.S. Government Printing Office, 1975.

U.S. Department of Health, Education and Welfare, Social Security Administration, Office of Research and Statistics, *Reducing Social Security Contributions for Low-Income Workers: Issues and Analysis,* Staff Paper 16. Washington, D.C.: U.S. Government Printing Office, 1975.

chapter 8

The Problem of Health Care

A critical health-care problem exists in the United States. Millions of Americans experience economic insecurity because of poor health, difficulties in the payment of large medical bills, and inadequate access to high-quality medical care. Consumers are confronted with the fact that the costs of doctor bills, hospitalization, nursing homes, and other medical services have soared in recent years. It has become extremely difficult for some Americans to pay their medical bills, and an expensive hospitalization can seriously deplete or wipe out a family's savings.

In addition, because of a shortage of primary-care physicians and a maldistribution of health-care personnel, millions of Americans find that access to high-quality medical care is often difficult or nonexistent. Although the overall quality of our medical care is high, many consumers receive medical care that is poor, inadequate, or incompetent. Laymen are seldom able to judge the accuracy of the diagnosis and the quality of treatment provided by medical personnel. Furthermore, the quality of medical care is often very uneven, ranging from superb to poor, depending on the doctor, the hospital, and the geographical location.

Finally, the health care of many must depend on an inefficient and inadequate health-services delivery system. The present system often results in waste, maldistribution of medical resources, and inequities in access to high-quality medical care.

In this chapter, we shall analyze the problem of health care in the United States in considerable detail. In particular, we shall examine the following parts of the problem: (1) poor health, (2) spiraling medical costs, (3) inadequate access to medical care, (4) poor quality of medical care, (5) inefficient health-services delivery system, (6) ineffective financing, and (7) consumer dissatisfaction.

POOR HEALTH

The quality of health and overall health levels in the United States have substantially improved over time because of rising incomes, advancements in medical science, and improvements in nutrition, housing, sanitation, and education. Death rates have declined; life expectancy has increased; certain diseases, such as polio and diphtheria, have almost disappeared; and the use of miracle drugs has greatly reduced the danger from pneumonia and other infectious diseases.

Some diseases, however, present serious health problems. Adult coronary heart disease is the leading cause of death in the United States. Death rates for lung cancer, cirrhosis of the liver, and chronic lung diseases such as emphysema have also increased. And certain diseases, such as hepatitis, food-borne infections, and streptococcal infections, have occurred more frequently. So despite the fact that the overall level of health has generally improved over time, problem areas remain.[1]

Poor Health of Minority Groups

Poverty-stricken and racial-minority groups are in poorer health than is the general population. The life expectancy of the poor is shorter than for other groups; they have more chronic and debilitating diseases; their infant and maternal mortality rates are higher; and they are also less protected against infectious disease.[2] The need for dental care among the poor is particularly acute. More than 20 percent of the families with incomes under $3,000 have never visited a dentist. The poor suffer four times as many heart conditions as those in the highest income category, six times as many mental and nervous conditions, and almost eight times as many visual impairments.[3]

Further, a significant difference in health status exists between whites and nonwhites. Maternal deaths for nonwhite poor Americans in the inner cities occur six or seven times as often as in other sections of the same cities. Nationally, three nonwhite mothers die in childbirth for every white mother, and the ratio of nonwhite to white babies who die in childbirth is more than two to one. The life expectancy of black males is about seven years less than that of white males, and male American Indians have a life expectancy at birth of only 42 years.

In short, the poor are sick more often, die earlier, and have less access to medical care than other groups in the population. Thus, part of the health-care problem includes the health defects of the poor.

[1]U.S. Department of Health, Education and Welfare, *Toward a Social Report* (Washington, D.C.: U.S. Government Printing Office, 1969), pp. 2-3.

[2]U.S. Department of Health, Education and Welfare, *Toward a Comprehensive Health Policy for the 1970's: A White Paper* (Washington, D.C.: U.S. Government Printing Office, 1971), pp. 1-3.

[3]U.S. Congress, Senate, Subcommittee on Health, *Health Care Crisis in America, 1971,* Hearings before the Subcommittee on Health of the Committee on Labor and Public Welfare, 92d Cong., 1st sess., 1971, Part 2, pp. 196-97.

Comparison with Foreign Nations

Health levels in the United States can often be considered relatively poor when compared with those in foreign nations. Although the United States spends relatively more on medical care than does any other nation, the payoff from these expenditures is often low. In fiscal 1974 alone, national expenditures on health were $104.2 billion, or 7.7 percent of the gross national product.[4] Yet the United States ranks only thirteenth in infant mortality among the nations; eighteenth in male life expectancy at birth; and eleventh in female life expectancy.[5] What is more, these figures appear to be worsening: In 1950, the United States ranked fifth in infant mortality, but dropped to twelfth by 1960. Finally, at least five foreign nations have better maternal mortality rates than the United States, and death rates from tuberculosis and pneumonia are still higher than desired.

The dismal showing by this nation can be partly explained by the inadequate medical care provided to our poor. For example, several low-income counties in Mississippi had infant mortality rates in 1967 as high as 50 per 1,000 births, compared to about 22 per 1,000 for the United States as a whole.[6] In addition, many foreign nations have superior health records because of national health insurance, or health-service plans that place emphasis on preventive care and mass education relating to good health.[7]

On the other hand, the health-services delivery system cannot be held entirely accountable for the relatively low ranking of the United States; other factors are more important. First, the high U.S. infant-mortality rates are more a reflection of social problems than of medical problems. Factors such as poverty, malnutrition, poor housing, poor education, and racial or ethnic differences affect our infant-mortality rates more than do defects in the present health-services delivery system. Second, personal health habits have a major impact on the overall health of the population. The life-style of Americans is generally not conducive to good health. Many Americans overeat, drink excessively, smoke heavily, do not exercise, and are heavily burdened by personal or business pressures. These factors probably do more to explain the poor health of many Americans than does an inadequate health-care system. Finally, environmental factors such as air and water pollution are also detrimental to health.

SPIRALING MEDICAL COSTS

Total health expenditures have soared in the United States in recent years. Between fiscal years 1950 and 1974, health expenditures increased from about

[4]Nancy L. Worthington, "National Health Expenditures, 1929-74," *Social Security Bulletin,* Vol. 38, No. 2 (February 1975), 3.

[5]U.S. Dept. of HEW, *Toward a Comprehensive Health Policy for the 1970's,* p. 10.

[6]Charles L. Schultze, Edward R. Fried, Alice M. Rivlin, and Nancy H. Teeters, *Setting National Priorities: The 1972 Budget* (Washington, D.C.: The Brookings Institution, 1971), p. 215.

[7]The Carnegie Commission on Higher Education, *Higher Education and the Nation's Health: Policies for Medical and Dental Education* (New York: McGraw-Hill, 1970), p. 15.

$12.0 billion, or 4.6 percent of the gross national product, to $104.2 billion, or 7.7 percent of the GNP. The sharp increase is explained by population growth, increased use of medical services, and general price inflation. During fiscal years 1950-71, population growth accounted for 17 percent of the increase in health expenditures; greater use of medical services such as open-heart surgery or kidney dialysis accounted for 36 percent; and the remaining 47 percent was due to inflation.[8]

The costs of medical care have also been increasing at a rapid rate in recent years. Figure 8-1 illustrates the rise in medical-care prices between 1968 and 1972. The cost of a semiprivate room has increased much more rapidly than the Consumer Price Index; physicians' fees have also risen faster than the general price level. In contrast, the costs of drugs and prescriptions have tended to lag behind increases in the Consumer Price Index.

TABLE 8-1 Average Annual Percentage Change in the Consumer Price Index and Selected Medical-Care Components, 1950-70

Calendar Year	Average Annual Percentage Increase					
	All Items	Medical-Care Total	Physi-cians' Fees	Den-tists' Fees	Semi-private Room	Drugs and Prescrip-tions
1950-60:	2.1	3.9	3.4	2.5	6.6	1.7
1950-55	2.2	3.8	3.4	2.7	6.9	1.4
1955-60	2.0	4.1	3.3	2.4	6.3	2.0
1960-70:	2.7	4.3	4.7	3.8	9.8	-.1
1960-65	1.3	2.5	2.8	2.3	5.8	-.8
1965-70	4.2	6.1	6.6	5.3	13.9	.7

Source: Consumer Price Index, Bureau of Labor Statistics.

The rapid increase in medical-care prices can be viewed in greater perspective by examining their long-run trend. Table 8-1 is a summary of the average annual percentage change in the Consumer Price Index and in selected medical-care components for the period between 1950 and 1970. Notice that between 1965 and 1970, the Consumer Price Index increased at an annual rate of 4.2 percent, and total costs of medical care at an annual rate of 6.1 percent. However, during this same period, the cost of a semiprivate room in a hospital rose at a rate of almost 14 percent, and physicians' fees at a rate of 6.6 percent. Thus, the problem of spiraling medical costs centers primarily around the two major items of hospital care and physicians' fees, so we shall examine these two cost items in greater detail.

[8]U.S. Department of Health, Education and Welfare, *Cost of National Medical Care: A Chart Book* (Washington, D.C.: U.S. Government Printing Office, n.d.), Chart 3.

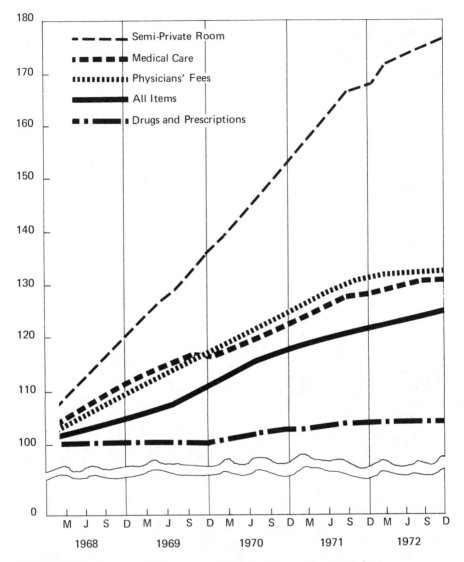

FIGURE 8-1   Quarterly Consumer Price Index and Medical-Care
Components, 1968-72 (1967 = 100)

Source: U.S. Department of Health, Education and Welfare, Social Security Administration,
Office of Research and Statistics, *Medical Care Price Changes under the Economic Stabilization
Program,* By Loucele A. Horowitz, Note No. 8 (May 15, 1973), p. 9, Chart 2.

Hospital Prices

Hospital services are the most expensive form of medical care. A patient in
a general short-term hospital receives a wide variety of services, including room
and board, laundry, laboratory tests, pharmaceuticals, access to highly special-

ized equipment, and the services of physicians, nurses, technicians, and other health personnel. These services are expensive. The total hospital expense per patient day in community hospitals averaged $114.56 in 1973, an increase of about 87 percent over 1968.[9]

There are many reasons for the sharp increase in hospital-care prices. The major factors are (1) an increased demand for hospital care, (2) the growth of health insurance, (3) higher wage costs, (4) higher nonlabor costs, (5) new technology, (6) the cost-reimbursement formula under Medicare, and (7) the changing style of consumers.

Increased Demand for Hospital Care. The increased demand for hospital care in recent years is due largely to population growth, rising per capita incomes, higher educational levels, and a greater awareness by consumers of health problems. In addition, the demand has increased because of health insurance, a complicating factor that will be analyzed next. The increased demand for hospital care has generally resulted in greater use of hospitals by consumers. However, the supply of health personnel necessary to meet that greater use has grown much more slowly, and the result has been an upward pressure on hospital prices.[10]

Research studies have shown that the demand for medical care is relatively inelastic with respect to price. The price elasticity of demand for medical care is estimated to be as low as .2, which means that the quantity of medical care demanded declines by only 2 percent when price increases by 10 percent.[11] Thus, if a hospital raises its daily room-and-board rates and prices of other services because of higher operating costs, consumers who require hospitalization are generally unresponsive to the price increase and will still demand the services provided by the hospital. And the relatively inelastic demand curve for medical care makes it possible for hospital administrators to shift the higher operating costs forward to the public through higher prices with little consumer resistance.

Growth of Health Insurance. Health insurance, both public and private, increases the demand for medical care, resulting in upward pressures on the price of hospital services.[12] More than 90 percent of the civilian population under age 65 is now covered for some type of private hospital insurance.

Insured people generally have higher hospitalization rates than uninsured persons, since they are more likely to be concerned about their health, to be better educated, and to have a greater awareness of the benefits from modern medicine. And, of course, they are less likely to be concerned about the rapid increases in hospital-care prices if they know that their health insurance will cover a large portion of their bills.

[9]Health Insurance Institute, *Source Book of Health Insurance Data, 1974-75* (New York: Health Insurance Institute, 1974), p. 5.

[10]See William F. Berry and James C. Daugherty, "A Closer Look at Rising Medical Costs," *Monthly Labor Review,* November 1968, pp. 1-8.

[11]Victor R. Fuchs, "The Basic Forces Influencing Costs of Medical Care," in U.S. Department of Health, Education and Welfare, *Report of the National Conference on Medical Costs* (Washington, D.C.: U.S. Government Printing Office, 1967), p. 19.

[12]*Ibid.,* pp. 20-21.

Further, doctors are more willing to hospitalize patients with health insurance. A doctor pressed for time may find it more convenient to place his patients in a hospital to conserve his time, and the presence of hospital insurance facilitates this process. Finally, some doctors place their patients in hospitals for diagnostic and other tests, which are covered only if the patient is hospitalized. The result is an overutilization of hospitals, and therefore of health-insurance benefits.

Higher Wage Costs. Wages and salaries are major cost items in providing hospital services, accounting for 58 percent of the total expense per patient day.[13] Hospital employees in the past were notoriously underpaid when compared with other groups in the economy. But the federal minimum wage law was extended to cover hospital employees in 1967, and because of higher wages and salaries paid to nurses, technicians, orderlies, and other hospital personnel, the operating costs of hospitals, and therefore their prices, have increased sharply.

Furthermore, hospital care is a labor-intensive industry. The continued advancement of medical science has resulted in an increased use of specialized and new technical equipment by hospitals, leading to a greater demand for skilled manpower. Hospitals have also hired an increasing number of unskilled and semiskilled employees to fill the positions of skilled workers who are in short supply. The overall result is that the number of employees per patient day has risen over time, and so total wage costs have increased.[14]

Higher Nonlabor Costs. Nonlabor costs have been increasing even more rapidly than labor costs in recent years. Hospitals must now pay more for food, drugs, and other commodities. They are better equipped with specialized facilities, such as intensive care units, rehabilitation units, pathology laboratories, and dental facilities, which are expensive to maintain and operate.

There is also a greater emphasis now on nonmedical comforts to the patients, such as private rooms, television sets, telephones, and air conditioning—items that increase not only the comfort of patients, but also the operating costs.

Finally, new hospital construction and plant expansion are more expensive. Higher construction costs, the increasing use of sophisticated and expensive technology, and hospital design also contribute to higher hospital costs.

New Technology. New medical technology and the use of highly specialized technical equipment also contribute to increased hospital operating costs. Open-heart surgery teams, kidney dialysis machines, and cobalt therapy are expensive to install and require considerable numbers of skilled employees to operate.

Patients who are hospitalized expect to be treated by the newest improvements in medical technology, and doctors demand that the hospitals provide the newest and best equipment to treat their patients. University medical centers and teaching hospitals are also expected to provide the most technologically

[13]U.S. Department of Health, Education and Welfare, Social Security Administration, Office of Research and Statistics, *Medical Care Costs and Prices: Background Book* (January 1972), p. 26.

[14]U.S. Department of Health, Education and Welfare, *A Report to the President on Medical Care Prices* (Washington, D.C.: U.S. Government Printing Office, 1967), pp. 28-29.

advanced equipment. And as a larger proportion of the population becomes able to pay for hospital care, these pressures on the hospitals become even greater. The overall effect is an increase in hospital operating expenses, which again must be reflected in higher prices.

Medicare Cost-Reimbursement Formula. Under the Medicare program, hospitals are reimbursed on the basis of their reasonable costs. But "reasonable costs" in most cases means actual costs. A formula that provides for reimbursement at cost provides no incentives for a hospital to become efficient and reduce its operating expenses. Prof. Herbert E. Klarman argues that reimbursement at cost under Medicare has caused a substantial increase in hospital unit costs, and that the volume of services reimbursed for increased by 75 percent or more after the Medicare program was enacted into law.[15] Since the hospitals were reimbursed on the basis of their costs, there was no incentive to hold down those costs. There was little reason for them to resist higher wage demands, since Medicare would pay for most or all of the raises; and they could purchase the best equipment and supplies, and Medicare would pay the bill.

Changing Style. Finally, changes in style and consumer tastes have also contributed to the substantial increase in hospital costs. Consumers are demanding the best and most sophisticated medical care available—care requiring more tests, more equipment, and more staff—which results in higher cost per patient day. Prof. Martin S. Feldstein believes that this factor alone largely explains the rapid increase in cost per patient day.[16]

Physicians' Fees

Physicians' fees have also risen more rapidly than the general price level. The major elements causing this increase are the following: (1) rapid increase in demand, (2) slower increase in supply, (3) Medicare cost-reimbursement formula, and (4) general price inflation.

Rapid Increase in Demand. The demand for the services of physicians has increased rapidly, resulting in an increase in medical fees. The increased demand is attributable to population growth, rising per capita disposable income, and a greater public faith in doctors.

In addition, changes in the characteristics of the population have also increased the demand for the services of physicians. Women see doctors more often than men do; older people more often than the general population; and urban dwellers more frequently than rural. Thus, those groups most utilizing the services of physicians are the ones whose numbers have increased more rapidly than those of other groups.

Furthermore, the expansion of health-insurance coverage has intensified the demand for physicians' services. Available data indicate that insured people utilize medical services more often than the uninsured; according to one study,

[15]Herbert E. Klarman, "Reimbursing the Hospital—Differences the Third Party Makes," *The Journal of Risk and Insurance,* Vol. XXXVI, No. 5 (December 1969), 563-66. See also Klarman, "Major Public Initiatives in Health Care," *The Public Interest,* No. 34 (Winter 1974), 110-12.

[16]Robert D. Eilers and Sue S. Moyerman, *National Health Insurance, Proceedings of the Conference on National Health Insurance* (Homewood, Ill.: Richard D. Irwin, 1971), pp. 202-3.

insured people were hospitalized for surgery 25 percent more than uninsured.[17] Feldstein has estimated that 31 percent of the increase in average fees between 1948 and 1966 was due to the higher level of insurance protection during that period.[18] Also, some physicians charge higher fees to patients with insurance than to those without.

Moreover, the demand for the services of physicians is relatively inelastic with respect to price, so they can increase their fees without losing patients. There are several reasons for this relative inelasticity. First, sick people who require emergency medical care have no choice whether to seek treatment. Second, patients often regard medical care as absolutely essential, even in non-emergency situations. Third, consumers usually either lack price information regarding a physician's fee or assume that more expensive care is better; they do not normally obtain price quotations from several physicians before entering the hospital for surgery. Finally, patients are often referred from one physician to another for treatment without a choice.

The increased demand for physicians' services is partly determined by the physician himself. He decides whether surgery is necessary, whether X rays and diagnostic tests should be given, whether a consultant must be called in, and whether a return visit is necessary.

Slower Increase in Supply. The demand for the services of physicians has grown more rapidly than the supply of physicians. For example, between 1950 and 1965, the demand for physicians' services rose by at least 41 percent, but the total number of doctors increased by only about 33 percent, and the number in private practice by only about 14 percent. Many were engaged in research or were employed as full-time staff in hospitals, full-time faculty members in medical schools, or full-time administrators. In addition, there was an actual decline in the total number of family physicians, such as pediatricians, internists, and general practitioners, because physicians tended to specialize in other branches of medicine. The more rapid increase in demand relative to supply has resulted, of course, in higher medical fees.

Medicare. After Medicare was enacted into law in 1965, physicians' fees rose rapidly. Between December 1965 and December 1966, they increased by 7.8 percent, compared to an average yearly increase of 2.8 percent for the period between 1959 and 1965.[19]

Medicare contributed to the increase in medical fees in at least two ways. First, it greatly expanded the demand by the aged for medical services. Medicare suddenly poured billions of dollars into a medical-care delivery system that was relatively fixed in supply, resulting in higher medical prices, including physicians' fees.

Second, and more important, the reimbursement formula for the payment of medical fees inadvertently provided incentives for many physicians to increase their fees. Under the earlier law, Medicare would pay 80 percent of the

[17]U.S. Dept. of HEW, *A Report to the President,* p. 21.

[18]Martin S. Feldstein, "The Rising Price of Physicians' Services," *The Review of Economics and Statistics,* Vol. LII, No. 2 (May 1970), 129.

[19]Theodore R. Marmor, "Why Medicare Helped Raise Doctors' Fees," *Trans-action,* September 1968, p. 14.

reasonable fee of a physician after the patient satisfied a $50 calendar-year deductible. A reasonable fee had to satisfy three requirements: (1) It had to be the customary charge for the service, rather than the fees charged to very wealthy or very poor patients; (2) the customary charge could not exceed the prevailing rate for the same type of service in the physicians' locality; and (3) the customary charge could not exceed the benefits that insurers would pay for similar medical treatment under their plans. Theodore R. Marmor claims that the Social Security Administration and private health insurers had no effective method of determining the customary fee of a physician, because a doctor might have a sliding scale of fees whereby poor patients were charged less than wealthy ones. In addition, health insurers generally lacked adequate data concerning the level of fees for individual doctors before the enactment of Medicare. Thus, Marmor concludes that doctors could upgrade their level of fees before or after Medicare went into effect without fear of being limited to some "customary" fee.[20]

Physicians may have had several reasons to increase their fees before or after the enactment of the Medicare program. First, some low-income aged patients could not afford to pay for medical care before enactment of Medicare, so they were charged a lower fee than those who were able to pay. The Medicare program made it possible for many aged low-income patients to pay higher fees.

Second, the Medicare program caused many physicians to reexamine their customary fee schedule, and to raise their fees in consequence. Third, the fees charged by some physicians may have been low compared to those charged by other doctors in the community, and they felt pressure to bring them into line. Finally, many physicians believed that, under the Medicare program, their "customary" fees would bind them for many years under government-sponsored insurance. There was some fear that the federal government might place a limit on what was considered reasonable; thus, medical fees were increased because of possible limitations in the future.

Inflation. Because of inflation, physicians today must pay more for the equipment, supplies, and health personnel necessary to practice medicine. Higher wages must be paid to office nurses and technicians; office equipment and supplies, such as stethoscopes and tongue depressors, have increased in price; higher office rents must be paid. In addition, physicians must also pay higher premiums for malpractice insurance, which can often cost many thousands of dollars annually. Therefore, because of higher operating expenses, physicians must periodically raise their fees to cover these expenses.

INADEQUATE ACCESS TO MEDICAL CARE

Millions of Americans find that access to high-quality medical care is often difficult; delays in seeing a physician and long periods of waiting for an appointment are common. The problem of inadequate access to medical care centers around the following areas: (1) shortage of physicians, (2) maldistribution of physicians, and (3) medical-school financial crises.

[20]*Ibid.*, pp. 14-19.

Shortage of Physicians

Although there are about 366,000 active and inactive physicians in the United States or about 171 physicians per 100,000 population, additional doctors are still necessary.[21] The Carnegie Commission on Higher Education has concluded that an acute shortage of health personnel exists, and that an additional 50,000 physicians are needed in the United States. The need is reflected in the uneven geographic distribution of physicians, the long waiting lines for medical care in hospital outpatient clinics, and the long workweek that physicians put in. Another indication of a shortage is the relatively large number of foreign medical graduates in the United States. About 15 percent of all physicians in the United States are graduates of foreign medical schools. In many cases, the quality of foreign medical education is considerably below that available in the United States.[22]

Maldistribution of Physicians

Although there is some disagreement concerning whether an absolute shortage of physicians exists, it is generally agreed that a serious maldistribution problem is present. The maldistribution, which aggravates the health-care problem, consists of two types: (1) geographic, and (2) by type of medical practice.

Geographic Maldistribution. Geographic maldistribution refers to the acute shortage of physicians in small towns, rural areas, and urban slums. In isolated semirural areas, there are only 81 physicians per 100,000 population. In isolated rural areas, the situation is even worse, with only 43 physicians per 100,000. In contrast, greater metropolitan areas have 171 physicians per 100,000 population.[23] Also, many smaller towns and communities often have no physicians at all. A study of 1,500 cities and towns in the upper Midwest revealed that there were no doctors in 1,000 of these communities.[24]

The health needs of the population are generally greater in rural areas, because rural family incomes are lower than those of the rest of the population. Furthermore, rural communities tend to have more older people and youths, and relatively few working-age adults, and the need for medical care is greater for the aged and children than for adults. Also, many rural residents must travel long distances to receive medical care.

In addition, farming is a hazardous occupation, and the problems of farm accidents and emergency medical treatment are especially important in rural areas. Many hospitals and communities cannot provide for emergency medical

[21] Health Insurance Institute, *1974-75 Source Book of Health Insurance* (New York: Health Insurance Institute, 1974), p. 58.

[22] The Carnegie Commission on Higher Education, *Higher Education and the Nation's Health,* p. 36.

[23] U.S. Department of Agriculture, Economic Research Service, *Rurality, Poverty, and Health,* Agricultural Economic Report No. 172 (Washington, D.C.: U.S. Government Printing Office, 1970), p. 6, Table 3.

[24] *Ibid.*

care because of inadequate ambulances and other mobile health services. Medical treatment and emergency care must be delayed, and long distances often must be traveled to receive help. The inadequate access to medical care in an emergency situation often results in death for an accident victim.

Finally, relatively few specialists practice medicine in rural areas. They tend to concentrate instead in the dense metropolitan areas, where the higher incomes and abundant population provide greater returns than they could get in sparsely populated, low-income rural areas. Therefore, general practitioners in rural areas have greater demands made upon them. They are usually elderly physicians who may be overworked and who may undertake more complicated surgery than the GPs in urban areas. Moreover, the bylaws of many rural hospitals tend to be less strict, encouraging such activities, which often result in medical care that is of low quality.

Another reason physicians generally prefer to practice in large cities is that many small rural communities have obsolete and inadequate medical facilities. Doctors prefer to practice near large medical centers or teaching hospitals, where sophisticated equipment and facilities are available for the practice of high-quality medicine. Also, many prefer to specialize and large, highly populated metropolitan areas permit them to utilize more fully their specialized skills. This is especially true in the case of surgeons, for whom adequate hospital facilities are an absolute necessity. And larger cities offer cultural advantages that the smaller rural communities lack; the existence of theaters, concerts, and good schools is an important consideration in determining where a physician will practice.

Residents in urban ghetto areas are also confronted with a serious shortage of physicians. In Los Angeles, there are 127 physicians per 100,000 population, but in the southeast district of Watts, a poverty area, there are only 39. In the impoverished Kenwood-Oakland area of Chicago, a total of five physicians serve a population of about 50,000; the physician-to-population ratio for this area is less than one-tenth that of the country as a whole. In Baltimore, 550,000 residents of slum areas have only 100 general practitioners to serve them, and most of these doctors are over 60 years old.[25]

Type of Medical Practice. The second form of maldistribution centers around the type of medical practice. Over the years, there has been a pronounced shift away from the general practice of medicine and toward specialization. Because of the rapid expansion of medical knowledge, most graduates of medical schools specialize. Less than 2 percent of them go into general practice, and internists and pediatricians are increasingly taking over the role of family physician.[26]

There has also been a relatively sharp decline in primary-care physicians, whereas certain types of medical practice have a surplus of practitioners.

[25]Citizens Board of Inquiry into Health Services for Americans, "Heal Yourself: Report of the Citizens Board of Inquiry into Health Services for Americans," in U.S. Congress, Senate, Subcommittee on Health, *Health Care Crisis in America, 1971,* Hearings before the Subcommittee on Health of the Committee on Labor and Public Welfare, 92d Cong., 1st sess., 1971, Part 2, p. 265.

[26]The National Advisory Commission on Health Manpower, *Report of the National Advisory Commission on Health Manpower,* Vol. I (Washington, D.C.: U.S. Government Printing Office, 1967), p. 14.

Primary-care physicians are general practitioners, pediatricians, and internists, who can treat most of the family's medical problems. Their average fees are generally lower than those of specialists, and they are usually concerned about the entire well-being of family members. Some evidence also suggests that hospitalization rates for patients treated by primary-care physicians are lower than for those treated by specialists. However, primary-care physicians constituted 75 percent of all physicians in 1931; by 1967, their number had declined to 39 percent of the total. On the other hand, certain medical specialities, including surgery, pathology, gynecology, urology, radiology, and ophthalmology, appear to have a surplus of physicians.[27]

The maldistribution problem must be solved to alleviate the health-care problem in the United States. Doubling the number of medical-school graduates will not alleviate the critical physician shortages in rural and ghetto areas if doctors cannot be persuaded to practice in these areas.

Medical-School Financial Crisis

Many medical schools are currently experiencing critical financial crises, which make it difficult to expand their enrollments to meet the problem of physician shortages. Some are being forced to dip heavily into their endowment funds; voluntary gifts are becoming increasingly difficult to obtain; federal funds and research grants have been reduced; and despite the high tuition charged by medical schools, the amount covers only a small fraction of the total cost of educating a physician. Yet, at the same time, the medical schools are being asked to expand their enrollments and play a more active role in solving the health-care problem in the United States.

POOR QUALITY OF MEDICAL CARE

The poor quality of medical care provided by some physicians, hospitals, and nursing homes is another part of the health-care problem. The quality of medical care varies widely, depending on the physician, hospital, and geographical location of treatment.[28]

Physicians

Competent observers have reported that some physicians do not keep up with scientific advancements in medicine and become rapidly obsolete after graduating from medical school. Some are either unwilling or unable to keep abreast of the rapidly changing scientific developments in medicine and the explosion of medical knowledge. Many work long hours, often more than 50 hours

[27]U.S. Dept. of HEW, *Toward a Comprehensive Health Policy for the 1970's*, p. 9.

[28]For an extensive discussion of the quality of medical care provided by physicians, see Robert S. McCleery, Louise T. Keelty, Russell E. Phillips, and Terrence M. Quirin, *One Life—One Physician: An Inquiry into the Medical Profession's Performance in Self-Regulation*, A Report to the Center for Study of Responsive Law (Washington, D.C.: Public Affairs Press, 1971).

weekly, and have little time to read medical journals, attend educational seminars, or otherwise keep up to date. As a result, the medical care provided by some physicians is of low quality and may even be incompetent, with considerable personal risk to the patient.[29]

Another aspect of the problem is that the average patient is totally unqualified to evaluate the quality of medical care that he receives. Many patients select their physicians on the recommendations of relatives or friends, or because of the doctor's warm personality, bedside manner, or distance from their homes. But these factors alone have no bearing on the quality of the physician's work; nor does the fact that he has a M.D. degree from an accredited medical school, and is licensed by the state, guarantee high-quality medical care.

Several studies have shown that the medical care provided by some physicians is inferior and of low quality. For example, many surgical operations are unnecessary. Over a million tonsil and adenoid operations are performed annually, especially on children, and an estimated 20 to 30 percent of the operations are considered unnecessary.[30] One study of hysterectomies indicated that two out of five had been unnecessary. Records of the Joint Commission on Accreditation also reveal unnecessary surgery by many physicians. One Michigan surgeon's diagnosis of menstrual pain in young girls as appendicitis led to the removal of normal appendixes in 80 percent of the cases. A surgeon in Indiana performed over 16,000 operations in a ten-year period, or an average of 5.2 daily for six days a week.[31] About 3,000 people die annually from blood transfusions, and many of the deaths are due solely to human error.

The increase in malpractice suits is another indication that some physicians provide low-quality or inferior medical care. In 1970, 6.5 medical malpractice claim files were opened for every 100 active practitioners, and the number has been steadily increasing. In 1970 alone, there was an increase of about 11 percent in new malpractice claims opened over cases closed.[32] Moreover, the commonly held viewpoint that most malpractice lawsuits are without merit is incorrect. The Commission on Medical Malpractice made a study of malpractice claims closed in 1970, and found that payments were made in 45 percent of the cases, whether a lawsuit was filed or not.[33]

The fear of medical malpractice lawsuits is forcing many physicians to practice "defensive medicine," which often results in unnecessary diagnostic tests or therapeutic procedures to prevent or defend against such suits. Or a physician may refuse to perform certain tests or procedures for fear of a lawsuit, even though the patient could benefit. Some physicians refuse to publish in professional journals for fear the material could be used against them in a lawsuit.

[29]See Selig Greenberg, *The Quality of Mercy: A Report on the Critical Condition of Hospital and Medical Care in America* (New York: Atheneum, 1971), Chap. 7.

[30]*Ibid.*, p. 188.

[31]Jeffrey O'Connell, "Rx for Medical Malpractice," *The Insurance Law Journal*, No. 569 (June 1970), 326-27.

[32]The Secretary's Commission on Medical Malpractice, *Medical Malpractice: Report of the Secretary's Commission on Medical Malpractice*, U.S. Department of Health, Education and Welfare (Washington, D.C.: U.S. Government Printing Office, 1973), p. 6.

[33]*Ibid.*, p. 10.

Hospitals

The quality of medical care in many hospitals is also questionable, according to many studies cited by the National Advisory Commission on Health Manpower. One study, of two community hospitals, indicated that 74 percent of the medical cases, 60 percent of all surgery cases, and 74 percent of all obstetrics and gynecology cases received only fair or poor medical treatment. Another study, of 98 different hospitals in New York City, revealed that only 57 percent of all patients and only 31 percent of the general medical cases received optimal medical care.[34] Further, many hospital deaths are unnecessary. More than 1,200 patients annually die of electrocution while receiving routine diagnostic tests or treatment.[35] These deaths are often recorded as from cardiac arrest or shock. More than 6,600 deaths occur annually in hospitals because of improper anesthesia. Because of a shortage of anesthetists, many nurses who are not sufficiently trained in the subject are nevertheless required to anesthetize patients.

Finally, many smaller hospitals have obsolete facilities and equipment and inadequate staff, and the quality of their medical care is often poor. More than one-third of our hospitals do not meet the minimum standards for accreditation by the Joint Commission on Accreditation of Hospitals, and many of these are smaller hospitals.[36]

Nursing Homes

The poor quality of many nursing homes for the aged is only now coming to public attention. More than 1 million Americans live in 20,000 nursing homes, most of which are proprietary homes run for profit. In many nursing homes, the numbers of qualified physicians and nurses are insufficient for providing high-quality medical care. In others, the aged may live in filthy rooms, be mistreated, have inadequate food, or be administered drugs improperly. One nursing-home study revealed the following:

1. Physician care in nursing homes is so scarce that it can be considered a national scandal.

2. Physician care when available is often minimal. In one midwestern city, three-fourths of the patients checked had not been visited by a doctor in six months. In one midwestern state, the average time spent by a physician per patient in 100 nursing homes was less than three minutes per week.

3. Many nursing homes are firetraps and unsafe. The National Fire Prevention Association considers nursing homes to be one of the most unsafe places in which to live.

4. The average daily cost per patient for food is less than $1 in many nursing homes.

5. One-seventh of the drug prescriptions to nursing-home patients are administered incorrectly. Also, drugs are commonly used to make patients easier to handle.[37]

[34]The National Advisory Commission on Health Manpower, *Report,* p. 39.

[35]O'Connell, "R for Medical Malpractice," p. 327.

[36]Greenberg, *Quality of Mercy,* pp. 189-90.

[37]See David H. Pryor, "Somewhere between Society and the Cemetary: Where we Put the Aged," *The New Republic* (April 25, 1970).

INEFFICIENT HEALTH-SERVICES DELIVERY SYSTEM

In order to understand the specific deficiencies in our health-services de-livery system, let us first examine briefly the major characteristics of the industry.

Nature of Health-Services Industry

The delivery of health care is organized around physicians, dentists, hospitals, and other health professionals and activities. There are about 366,000 physicians in the United States. Most of them are engaged in the solo practice of medicine, which is based on fee-for-service. The average physician is about 46 years old, works about 51 hours weekly, and sees about 127 patients each week. His income is well above average; the median annual income for self-employed physicians is about $41,000. And about one out of every six physicians in the United States was graduated from a foreign medical school.[38]

Most physicians rely on community hospitals for treating their patients. There are more than 7,100 hospitals in the United States. About 82 percent are community hospitals, with the remainder privately or federally owned. The average length of a hospital stay is about eight days.

The health-service industry is a major occupation in the United States. About 4 million people are employed in the health field, including registered nurses, licensed practical nurses, technicians, aides, orderlies, attendants, and other personnel.

Fragmentation and Lack of Coordination

The health-services industry is often described as a "cottage industry of small entrepreneurs," or as "pushcart vending in the age of supermarkets." The fact that the present system is fragmented and decentralized often results in great inefficiencies.[39] First, the solo practice of medicine is often an obstacle to the efficient organization of medical services. It works against the division and specialization of labor; against economies of scale in the use of equipment and personnel; and against professional intellectual stimulation and growth.

Second, the separation between hospitals and practitioners often leads to tensions and mismanagement of hospitals. The sharp separation of ambulatory-care, extended-care, acute bed-care, and home-care services frequently prevents individual patients from receiving rational and optimal medical treatment. Also, the ownership of pharmacy firms by some physicians raises serious questions of ethics and efficiency in the dispensation of drugs.

Finally, inadequate community and regional planning in the health-services industry often leads to a duplication of expensive facilities and misallocation of medical resources.

[38]American Medical Association, *Reference Data on the Profile of Medical Practice, 1971,* Center for Health Services Research and Development, 1971.

[39]Howard R. Bowen and James R. Jeffers, *The Economics of Health Services* (New York: General Learning Press, 1971), p. 7.

Inefficient Use of Health Manpower

Poor utilization of health manpower restricts the quantity of medical services available, the geographical extension of these services, and the ability to control medical costs.

Considerable evidence indicates that health manpower is often used improperly. The Joint Council of National Pediatric Societies has estimated that 75 percent of the pediatric tasks performed by a physician could be provided by properly trained child-health assistants, thereby freeing the pediatrician for more useful tasks. Many functions of obstetricians could be performed by nurse-midwives without any reduction in the quality of medical care. Experience with physician's-assistant programs indicates that former medical corpsmen or others with comparable training can, after additional training, perform a wide variety of tasks now performed by general practitioners. Many nurses in hospitals spend an inordinate amount of their time performing administrative tasks rather than caring for patients; one study showed that only 35 percent of their time was used in caring for patients; the remainder was used for administrative work.[40]

Inefficiencies in Hospitals

Hospitals also contribute to the waste and inefficiency and have inadequate incentives for reducing costs. Because of competition among hospitals and prestige factors, expensive equipment and facilities are often purchased, when they are demanded by medical staffs, even though the same equipment may be available in another hospital a short distance away. The purchase of cobalt radiation units or open-heart surgery equipment by several hospitals in the same area is an example of such duplication. Also, and perhaps as a result of such duplication, many hospitals maintain extensive facilities that are idle for long periods. A study revealed that 31 percent of the hospitals with open-heart surgery teams had not used them for a year.[41] Not only is this expensive, but highly skilled open-heart surgery teams that are used infrequently pose a risk to the patient because of possible deterioration in their quality.

Moreover, many hospital administrators lack the necessary technical skills for determining the need for technical equipment or for evaluating how much it should cost.[42] They may not be unduly concerned about the cost of the equipment, since, in the last analysis, the consumer or third-party insurer ultimately pays the bill, usually by reimbursing the hospitals on the basis of their actual costs in providing the service. For example, if a computer is purchased, the cost of providing one day of care is increased, resulting in a higher reimbursement rate by a third-party insurer.

Finally, many patients should be using less expensive facilities than hospitals. Many who are hospitalized for X rays and laboratory services could receive them from outpatient-care facilities. Others could receive excellent care

[40]U.S. Dept. of HEW, *Toward a Comprehensive Health Policy for the 1970's,* p. 11.

[41]*Ibid.*

[42]See R.D. Peterson and C.R. MacPhee, *Economic Organization in Medical Equipment and Supply* (Lexington, Mass.: D.C.: Heath, 1973).

in nursing homes or extended-care facilities. And some patients in hospitals stay longer than necessary; the reduction of one day in an average hospital stay could save about $2 billion annually in medical costs.

Geared to Sickness

Another inefficiency of the health-services delivery system is that it is geared to sickness and not health. There are few incentives to prevent illness or to diagnose it early, before it becomes critical. Physicians are reimbursed not on the basis of keeping their patients well, but on that of the services they provide after their patients become sick, so they have little financial incentive to avoid giving unnecessary care. Also, relatively few private health-insurance plans reimburse insureds for preventive care of physical checkups; they generally pay only for hospital and surgical services when he is ill.

Obstacles to Free Market

The medical profession has consistently advocated the free-market system in medicine. Doctors say that if patients are given the free choice of physicians with minimal interference from government, high-quality medical care will be provided based on free-market forces; that open competition for medical services and the profit motive in a free market will stimulate efficiency and provide a fair return; and that if the demand for medical services exceeds the supply, medical prices will rise, and the higher prices will then attract new suppliers to enter the market.

The market for medical services, however, is radically different from the free market depicted above, and numerous obstacles interfere with a free and open market for medical services. First, most hospitals do not operate on the basis of profit, and inadequate cost controls and reimbursement at cost by third-party insurers provide very few incentives to become efficient.

Second, there are many barriers to entry. Medical-school enrollments are limited, and the number of new physicians graduated each year is restricted. It is only recently that the American Medical Association has taken active steps to expand medical-school enrollments.

Third, a free market involves knowledge of prices by both buyers and sellers, but consumers have relatively little knowledge regarding medical prices. They generally do not know the fees charged by other physicians; there is no medical-care index of prices for a given geographical area; fees are seldom discussed; and many consumers often do not know the exact fee charged them by a doctor. Also, physicians do not compete on the basis of price, and most patients are incapable of determining the quality of the medical care they get.

Fourth, a free market involves choice. But in many cases, the patient has few options available to him. The physician decides if the patient should be hospitalized, requires an operation, or should be referred to a specialist. In addition, the concept of free choice of doctors by consumers is seldom valid. Many physicians are grossly overworked and refuse to take on new patients; the consumer must often settle for whatever physician is available rather than one of his choice.

Fifth, a free market generally involves alternatives. In medicine, acceptable alternatives are often not available to a patient. If a serious and expensive operation is necessary, there is little the patient can do about it.

Finally, the system is designed more for the convenience of physicians and other suppliers of medical care than for consumers of it, as when a physician places a patient in a hospital to conserve time, or refuses to make a house call.

In view of these facts, it is hardly correct to assume that the present system of medical care is based on free-market forces. The ignorance of consumers results in tremendous financial advantages to physicians. But the medical profession has consistently defended the present system and the protection of fees based on the fee-for-service principle, and opposed any innovations that depart sharply from the present system. As a case in point, until recently, the American Medical Association strongly opposed group prepaid medicine in favor of solo practice based on fee-for-service.

INEFFECTIVE FINANCING

The financing of health care also contributes significantly to the problem in the United States. Many of the problems analyzed earlier are either caused by or aggravated by health-care financing.

Based on Ability to Pay

The present financing of health care is based largely on the ability to pay, and not on the basis of health needs. The distribution of medical resources and access to medical care are determined by effective market demand rather than the medical needs of the people, and the inability to pay is a formidable financial barrier to medical care. The result is that many Americans with critical health problems do not receive treatment because they cannot pay for it.

The shocking need for more adequate dental care is an example. According to one study, 20 percent of the people in the United States between ages 45 and 54 had lost all their teeth, with the percentage increasing with advanced age. A National Health Survey study reported that nearly three-fifths of the population had not visited a dentist in the preceding year, and one-sixth of the population has *never* visited a dentist.[43] The inability to pay for dental care is a serious financial barrier for many Americans.

Distortion in Medical Care

Many of the maldistribution problems described earlier can be directly traced to the system of financing health care in the United States. Several examples can illustrate the problem:

1. Because specialists earn higher incomes and work shorter hours, most medical-school graduates enter specialty fields and abandon general practice.

2. Because consumers in the suburbs are better able to pay for specialists, physi-

[43]Carnegie Commission on Higher Education, *Higher Education and the Nation's Health*, p. 15.

cians move to the suburbs, thereby exacerbating the shortages of physicians in ghetto and rural areas.

3. Because of sizable financial gains, many physicians practice cosmetic surgery, which results in a neglect of the critically ill in favor of those with cosmetic needs.

4. Because hospitals cannot afford to treat patients without health insurance, private hospitals restrict their services to the affluent, which results in an overload of patients in public hospitals who are poor payment risks.

5. Because health insurance covers hospital charges, more persons are hospitalized than necessary.

6. Because private insurance is generally available only to those in good health, government must establish fragmented public programs for the unemployed, for the chronically ill, and for special groups afflicted with black lung disease, kidney disease, and other serious ailments.[44]

Inadequate Cost Controls

A final shortcoming of the health-care financing system is the inadequacy and ineffectiveness of the cost controls. For example, as stated earlier, the reimbursement of hospitals on the basis of costs provides no incentive for efficient operation. The cost-reimbursement formulas of private health insurers, Blue Cross, Medicare, and Medicaid make it relatively easy for hospital administrators to pass on higher costs to third parties. Relatively few reimbursement plans at present would base the income received by hospitals on their ability to operate efficiently and thereby control their costs. Because of inadequate cost controls, the present financing system also encourages the unnecessary utilization of high-cost facilities and services when less expensive alternative procedures could be used. Private health insurers generally do not make a determined effort to control medical costs, since that is not their basic function. And present cost-control measures, such as claim and utilization reviews, are often ineffective.

Defects in Private Health Insurance

Despite the remarkable growth of individual and group health insurance, expansion of coverage, liberalization of benefits, and the development of new contracts, critics argue that private voluntary health insurance is still inadequate and significantly contributes to the health-care problem in the United States.[45] They point out the following weaknesses.

First, serious gaps in coverage still exist. Although 182 million Americans, or about 87 percent of the civilian population, have some form of private health insurance, several groups with serious economic-insecurity problems—those most needing protection—have little or no coverage. Generally unprotected by private health insurance are two-thirds of the families with incomes

[44]Statement of Senator Edward M. Kennedy in U.S. Congress, Senate Committee on Finance, *National Health Insurance,* Hearings before the Committee on Finance, 92d Cong., 1st sess., on S.3, S.191, S.836, S.987, S.1376, S.1490, S.1598 and S.1623, 1971, pp. 25-29.

[45]For a critical evaluation of private health insurance, see Herbert S. Denenberg, "Those Health Insurance Booby Traps," *The Progressive,* September 1972, pp. 29-33.

under $3,000, children and mothers in low- and middle-income families, the unemployed and their dependents, migrant and seasonal workers, the working poor whose employers have no health plans, and the severely disabled.

Second, critics argue that private health-insurance benefits are inadequate. Even for those who are covered, the protection is less than complete, and gaps in coverage are common. About 24 percent of the civilian population lack coverage for hospitalization, about 25 percent for surgery, about 27 percent for X rays and laboratory tests, and about 67 percent for home and office visits. In addition, about 40 percent have no coverage for prescription drugs outside the hospital, and about 90 percent have no insurance protection for dental care. Coverage for care in nursing homes and extended-care facilities is limited— about 67 percent of the civilian population are without such coverage—and psychiatric care is covered only on a highly restricted basis. Finally, outpatient care and preventive services such as periodical physical examinations are often not covered.[46]

Further, despite the growth of major medical insurance, only about 40 percent of the population have this coverage, and even for those who do, the limits are often inadequate in a truly catastrophic illness. Open-heart surgery costs may exceed $50,000; kidney dialysis treatment or a kidney transplant may cost $25,000 or more; and an extended serious illness can cost over $100,000. Few major medical plans, individual or group, are adequate to cover such an illness.

Moreover, in the event of a serious illness, the effect of deductibles and co-insurance is often a large out-of-pocket outlay by the insured. For example, a $25,000 claim for open-heart surgery, in a plan with a $200 deductible and 20 percent coinsurance, means that the insured pays $5,160, or about 21 percent of the total bill, and such an expense can cause serious economic insecurity to a middle- or low-income family.

Knowledgeable health-insurance actuaries claim that the present system of coinsurance is faulty, since it is generally applied to all expenses in excess of the deductible, whereas it should be applied to only the first $500 or $1,000, where most expenses begin and end. For example, assume that a comprehensive major medical plan pays 100 percent of the first $1,000, then 80 percent of the excess up to a $15,000 maximum limit. But a superior approach would pay only 80 percent of the first $1,000, and 100 percent of the excess up to the maximum. Thus, if a $10,000 illness occurs, the insured would pay only $200, whereas he now pays $2,000 plus the deductible. *Such a plan would cost less and provide more comprehensive protection.*[47] Also, higher maximum limits could be provided at little additional cost, even up to $100,000 or more, by increasing the size of the deductible. A $200 deductible, $100,000 maximum-benefit plan would cost about the same as a $100 deductible, $10,000 maximum-limit plan,[48] and would provide far better protection.

[46]Marjorie Smith Mueller, "Private Health Insurance in 1973: A Review of Coverage, Enrollment and Financial Experience," *Social Security Bulletin,* Vol. 38, No. 2 (February 1975), 22, Table 1.

[47]E. Paul Barnhart, "Blames Govt., Insurers, Media for Nation's Health Care Woes," *The National Underwriter,* March 13, 1971, p. 11.

[48]*Ibid.*

Another weakness of private voluntary health insurance cited by critics is that it pays only a small fraction of the nation's total health bill, a fact that raises serious questions concerning the overall quality of the various coverages. For example, private health insurance paid only about 41 percent of total consumer expenditures for personal health care in 1973. The proportion of expenses paid for hospital care was much higher—private health insurance paid about 75 percent of that—but only about 49 percent of payment of physicians' bills and only about 7 percent of the costs of other types of medical care.[49]

It should be pointed out, however, that the preceding data are often used improperly by critics of private health insurance. For example, items such as drug sundries, sunglasses, nonprescription drugs, and similar expenses should not be insured even though they are included as part of the nation's total health bill. In addition, the medical expenses of people who do not carry private health insurance should not be included when analyzing the percentage of the total health bill paid by private insurers. Also, a distinction must be made between group health insurance and individual health insurance. When adjustments are made for these factors, private health insurers have a much better record. For example, a Health Insurance Institute study indicated that about half the claimants in group health insurance plans were reimbursed for 90 percent or more of their medical expenses, and about three-fourths for 70 percent or more.

It is also argued that private health insurance encourages the unnecessary utilization of expensive facilities. Many of the contracts call for payment only if the patient is hospitalized, so hospital beds are often used for routine diagnostic tests and examinations, which could be provided on a less expensive outpatient basis. In order to reduce unnecessary utilization of hospitals, it is suggested that coverage of outpatient ambulatory services should be expanded, thus also reducing hospital costs.

Another complaint is that health insurance pays only after you are sick, and that private plans are poorly equipped to provide preventive care. For example, relatively few cover vision care, yet periodic eye examinations could detect the early stages of glaucoma, which causes blindness in thousands of Americans each year. Coverage of mental disease is another example. Most health-insurance policies will cover the costs of a nervous breakdown in a hospital; but some nervous breakdowns might have been prevented by regular treatment from a qualified psychiatrist on an outpatient basis. With the exception of comprehensive group major medical insurance, most health insurance plans greatly restrict or exclude psychiatric care outside hospitals.

Finally, labor unions point out additional weaknesses of private health insurance. They say that private health insurers incur unduly high administrative expenses, especially for individual policies, whereby 47 percent of the total premiums written are used for operating expenses; that private health insurance fails to control costs or assure quality; and that it frequently directs medical treatment away from appropriate but uninsured low-cost medical care to high-cost but insured institutional care. The result is an overall increase in medical costs and health-insurance premiums.[50]

[49]Mueller, "Private Health Insurance," p. 37.

[50]Statement of Leonard Woodcock in Senate Committee on Finance, *National Health Insurance,* Hearings, pp. 114-15.

CONSUMER DISSATISFACTION

Consumers are becoming increasingly angry about the quality of medical care, the spiraling costs and limited insurance coverage, the difficulties in receiving medical care in emergency situations, and the often insensitive treatment provided by health professionals.

The Citizens Board of Inquiry into Health Services for Americans, which consisted of physicians, businessmen, politicians, welfare recipients, educators, and others, surveyed a cross section of consumers in the United States to determine their attitudes regarding the quality of the health care they get. The board found that some consumers were angry and frustrated at their lack of access to high-quality medical care.[51] This problem can be illustrated by the following statement:

> My doctor has a call hour between 7 and 8 in the evening. If anything happens to me or the kids after 8, I'm afraid to call him. They get mad because you didn't call during the hour. And if I take the kids to his office, I almost pray they're sick.[52]

The Citizens Board found that patients in every socioeconomic class are resentful of a medical-care system that requires payment or proof of ability to pay before a service is rendered. In particular, the poor are often refused medical services if they cannot pay in advance:

> A white farmer in Stone County, Arkansas, described driving his pregnant wife to Mountain View Hospital barely in time for their baby to be delivered. The nurse-supervisor greeted them with a demand for prepayment of $100. He told them he would return that afternoon with the money, which he could only raise by selling his cow and two pigs. "I had to run out the door and leave her or they wouldn't have taken her," he said.
>
> He returned with the money, and although he paid what he was told would be the total bill, the hospital sent him an additional bill the next month.
>
> "When word got around what had happened, the town all chipped in and bought the family a milk cow," one of his neighbors said.[53]

Many minority groups are reluctant to seek medical care because of cultural, psychological, or language barriers, and when they do, rebuffs may shake their confidence. The following statements are typical of these special problems:

> A Spanish-speaking mother recalled a visit with an injured child to the emergency room of a large city hospital. She was repeatedly put at the end of line while an interpreter was sought from another section of the hospital. By the end of the day, no interpreter had come, and she was told to take the child home and return the next day if she wished.
>
> Another woman described an equally futile trip to a hospital: "I thought I was expecting a baby once. I went into the hospital, and they had me undress in a little room. The nurse took my pressure and said she'd get a doctor. Then she left me. I

[51]Citizens Board, "Heal Yourself," pp. 243-60.

[52]*Ibid.*, p. 243.

[53]*Ibid.*, p. 259.

was there six hours. Finally, I just got up and left—no one was there—nobody noticed my leaving." [54]

The problems above clearly indicate that the health-services delivery system often works to the detriment of consumers, and that new, innovative approaches must be used to provide consumers with improved medical care and to overcome the health-care problems that now exist.

SUGGESTIONS FOR ADDITIONAL READING

Andreano, Ralph L., and Burton A. Weisbrod, *American Health Policy.* Chicago: Rand McNally College Publishing Company, 1974.

Baron, David, "A Study of Hospital Cost Inflation," *The Journal of Human Resources,* Vol. IX, No. 1 (Winter 1974), 33-49.

Bowen, Howard R., and James R. Jeffers, *The Economics of Health Services.* New York: General Learning Press, 1971.

Citizens Board of Inquiry into Health Services for Americans, "Heal Yourself: Report of the Citizens Board of Inquiry into Health Services for Americans," in *Health Care Crisis in America, 1971,* Hearings before the Subcommittee on Health of the Committee on Labor and Public Welfare, 92d Cong., 1st sess., 1971, Part 2, pp. 241-339.

Denenberg, Herbert S., "Those Health Insurance Booby Traps," *The Progressive,* September 1972, pp. 29-33.

Greenberg, Selig, *The Quality of Mercy: A Report on the Critical Condition of Hospital and Medical Care in America.* New York: Atheneum, 1971.

Klarman, Herbert E., "Major Public Initiatives in Health Care," *The Public Interest,* No. 34 (Winter 1974), 106-23.

McCleery, Robert S., Louise T. Keelty, Russell E. Phillips, and Terrance M. Quirin, *One Life-One Physician: An Inquiry into the Medical Profession's Performance in Self-Regulation,* A Report to the Center for Study of Responsive Law. Washington, D.C.: Public Affairs Press, 1971.

National Advisory Commission on Health Manpower, *Report of the National Advisory Commission on Health Manpower,* Vol. I. Washington, D.C.: U.S. Government Printing Office, 1967.

O'Connell, Jeffrey, "Proposed: No-Fault Insurance to Stem Malpractice Suits," *Prism,* July 1974, pp. 13-47.

Secretary's Commission on Medical Malpractice, *Medical Malpractice: Report of the Secretary's Commission on Medical Malpractice,* U.S. Department of Health, Education and Welfare. Washington, D.C.: U.S. Government Printing Office, 1973.

[54]*Ibid.,* p. 249.

Stevens, Rosemary A., "Critical Questions for Medicine's Future," *Prism,* February 1975, pp. 10-62.

Subcommittee on Health, Committee on Labor and Public Welfare, *Health Care Crisis in America, 1971,* Hearings before the Subcommittee on Health of the Committee on Labor and Public Welfare, 92d Cong., 1st sess., 1971, Parts 1-11. Washington, D.C.: U.S. Government Printing Office, 1971.

U.S. Department of Health, Education and Welfare, *Report of the National Conference on Medical Costs.* Washington, D.C.: U.S. Government Printing Office, 1967.

————, *A Report to the President on Medical Care Prices.* Washington, D.C.: U.S. Government Printing Office, 1967.

————, *Toward a Social Report,* Chap. I. Washington, D.C.: U.S. Government Printing Office, 1969.

chapter 9

Solutions to the
Health-Care Problem

Several techniques that are now used to meet the health-care problems in the United States, and several new approaches that have been proposed, are aimed at attacking the problem on all fronts. In this chapter, we shall examine some of the existing techniques and some of the new proposals—in particular, the following: (1) emphasis on loss prevention, (2) control of medical costs, (3) improvement of access to medical care, (4) expansion of health manpower, (5) improvement in the quality of medical care, (6) development of new health-care delivery systems, including prepaid group practice plans and health-maintenance organizations, and (7) improvement of private voluntary health insurance.

INCREASED EMPHASIS ON LOSS PREVENTION

Loss prevention is an ideal method for preventing premature death, poor health and disease, and injury. It can significantly contribute to the reduction of the health-care problem in the United States, by reducing human pain and suffering, promoting a positive sense of physical and mental well-being, and providing benefits that often substantially exceed the costs of medical treatment and rehabilitation.

Expanded Health Research

Expansion of health research is vitally necessary to prevent and control the leading causes of death and disease in the United States. It is particularly needed to reduce significantly the large number of deaths from heart disease and cancer. More than a million Americans die annually from heart ailments, and many of these deaths might be prevented through successful research into the causes of coronary artery disease. Past research sponsored by the American Heart Association has resulted in outstanding advances in preventing and controlling heart disease. Numerous deaths have been prevented because of the development of new drugs to control high blood pressure; of new techniques for diagnosing cardiovascular disease, such as X rays of blood vessels and catheterization; of synthetic artery grafts and artificial heart valves; and of new corrective surgery for congenital and acquired heart disease.

Research into the causes of cancer must also be expanded. More than 650,000 new cases of cancer are diagnosed annually, and more than 340,000 deaths from cancer occur each year. In the past, cancer-research expenditures have been relatively modest when compared to other programs; they are, for example, only about 4 percent of the sums spent on space research and technology. A major effort in biomedical research is absolutely necessary, particularly since new scientific discoveries in genetics, molecular biology, cell physiology, and virology now offer exciting opportunities for conquering cancer.

Furthermore, additional research is necessary to control the critical health problems of certain minority groups. For example it is estimated that one out of every 500 black Americans has sickle-cell anemia—a disease that results in general fatigue and periods of severe bone pain and organ dysfunction. Children with sickle-cell anemia perform poorly in school, and adults with the same disease have severe employment problems because of fatigue and absenteeism. Also, about 400,000 tenement children each year are poisoned by eating lead paint, resulting in moderate to severe brain damage for thousands of them.[1] Lead-paint poisoning is largely preventable through effective loss-prevention programs.

Health Education

Improvements in the health of Americans could be attained if adults were better informed about personal health habits, and made a determined effort to change their life-styles.[2] Poor nutrition, cigarette smoking, overindulgence in rich foods and alcohol, excessive use of drugs, inadequate exercise, and inadequate attention to certain symptoms take a heavy toll in death and disease.

Much health information is fragmented and uncoordinated, as in an isolated newspaper article, a public-service television announcement, or a short lecture by a physician. There is no national comprehensive health program for coordinating and stimulating efforts in health education. To overcome this defect, there has been proposed a National Health Education Foundation, which would be a nonprofit private foundation to promote and coordinate loss-prevention activities among private citizens.

Problem Areas in Loss Prevention

Certain problem areas in loss prevention must be recognized, and more intense efforts undertaken to reduce losses in these areas.

[1] U.S. Department of Health, Education and Welfare, *Toward a Comprehensive Health Policy for the 1970's: A White Paper* (Washington, D.C.: U.S. Government Printing Office, 1971), pp. 29-30.

[2] Charlotte K. Beyers, "Can Health Habits Really Be Changed?" *Prism,* May 1974, p. 67.

Automobile Deaths. In 1973, more than 55,000 persons were killed in automobile accidents. It is estimated that at least half these deaths involved motorists or pedestrians under the influence of alcohol. New and improved alcoholism programs are necessary to identify, control, and provide surveillance of druken drivers.

Pollution Control. Air pollution increases the incidence of respiratory disease and aggravates certain skin conditions and chronic diseases. The automobile is a major polluter of air. Pollution from automobiles can be reduced by developing new alternatives to the internal combustion engine and by reducing sulfur oxide emission from fossil fuels. The development of new fuels that reduce the level of air pollution would have substantial long-run effects on the health of Americans who are living in areas of smog and high pollution.

Control of Veneral Disease. Because of a looser and more promiscuous society, strongly oriented toward sex, veneral diseases have increased relatively over time, especially among teenagers. Gonorrhea has been increasing at 10 to 15 percent annually, and syphilis cases have also increased. About 3 million gonorrhea and 100,000 syphilis cases were reported in 1970, and it is suspected that there were many unreported.

Vaccinations for the Poor. Intensified efforts must be devoted to immunizations against certain communicable diseases in urban poverty areas. Vaccinations for young children in ghetto areas for diphtheria, tetanus, measles, and polio declined as much as 15 percent between 1969 and 1970.[3] As a result, new outbreaks pose continual health threats for the urban poor. These diseases are largely preventable.

CONTROLLING MEDICAL COSTS

Several new approaches have been proposed to meet the problem of spiraling medical costs. These proposals include the following: (1) reimbursement incentive plans, (2) more effective cost controls, (3) alternatives to hospitalization, and (4) comprehensive health planning.

Reimbursement Incentive Plans

Reimbursement incentive plans are designed to encourage cost reduction by rewarding hospitals with below-average costs and penalizing those whose costs are higher than average. Although reimbursement incentive plans are diverse and complex, they have two common objectives: to minimize the cost of hospitalization for given levels of medical care, and to minimize the cost of an illness episode.[4]

One basic approach is to establish a reimbursement price based on

[3]U.S. Dept. of HEW, *Toward a Comprehensive Health Policy.*

[4]Paul J. Feldstein, "An Analysis of Reimbursement Plans," *Reimbursement Incentives for Hospital and Medical Care: Objectives and Alternatives,* U.S. Department of Health, Education and Welfare, Social Security Administration, Office of Research and Statistics, Research Report No. 26 (Washington, D.C.: U.S. Government Printing Office, 1968), p. 17.

the mean average cost of all hospitals in the community, with hospitals operating below the mean rewarded, and those operating above the mean penalized. If hospitals in the community are operating on different portions of their long-run average cost curves under such formula, the low-cost hospitals may increase their provisions for medical care until their costs begin to increase. If high-cost hospitals are operating on the increasing portion of their long-run average cost curves, lower payments may cause them to cut back their services, which may then result in a decrease in unit costs. If high-cost hospitals are operating on the declining portion of their long-run average cost curves, they must either cease production of their services, change their services, or stop offering them at the established reimbursement price; and an increase in demand for their services may enable them to expand their output so that per-unit cost declines. In short, if the hospitals are rewarded when their operating costs are below the mean and penalized when their operating costs are above, the overall amount spent on hospital reimbursement will be less than if the total costs were reimbursed; and also, the more efficient hospitals will be encouraged to expand, while the less efficient will be forced to contract their services or become more efficient.[5]

Prospective reimbursement is another scheme with considerable potential in holding down medical costs. Blue Cross plans are gradually shifting from retrospective to prospective financing plans. Under the older, retrospective plan, hospitals participating in a Blue Cross plan determine the costs of providing medical services to Blue Cross subscribers, and the plan pays this amount. If costs increase, Blue Cross must bear the extra burden. Under the prospective reimbursement plan, however, Blue Cross and the hospitals agree on a rate schedule for the ensuing year whereby the hospitals will provide certain medical services for fixed fees. If the actual costs rise above the established fee schedule, the hospital must absorb the extra cost. On the other hand, the hospital has a strong financial incentive to reduce its costs, since it receives a windfall gain if the services can be provided for less than the established fee schedule. Several Blue Cross plans are currently experimenting with prospective reimbursement formulas, but it is still too early to evaluate the results of this financing method.[6]

In any reimbursement incentive plan, it is important to have controls to ensure that the quality of medical care is not diluted. These plans are based on the premise that the incentive payments depend on the hospital's ability to control its costs. Costs obviously can be reduced by lowering the quality of medical care or by limiting its scope, rather than by increasing the hospital's total operating efficiency. To avoid this danger, the quality of medical care must be periodically evaluated. One approach is to have a system of peer review, by competent teams of physicians, to determine if the hospital care is satisfactory or unsatisfactory by objective standards.

More Effective Cost Controls

More effective cost controls by third-party health insurers are also necessary to meet the problem of spiraling medical expenses. Effective cost-control procedures include claims review, utilization review, and recertification.

[5]*Ibid.,* p. 23-24.

[6]"Aid for Blue Cross in Nixon's Plan," *Business Week,* February 27, 1971, p. 96.

Claims-review controls, used by Blue Cross plans and other third-party insurers, involve careful screening and reviewing of claims. Eligibility for treatment is determined, and excessive charges are noted. Physicians are often consulted in claims review, and claims indicating unnecessary hospital admissions can be denied. In addition, an excessive charge for medical services is often adjusted downward after consultation with the physician setting the fee. Charges for excessive or inappropriate treatment may be only partially paid.[7]

Utilization review involves a committee of physicians who review the type and quality of medical care provided to hospitalized patients. Profiles of use classified by hospital, doctor, and diagnosis are determined based on statistical reports generated by data systems, and preexisting norms and standards are established. Those cases that deviate widely from normal or usual patterns can then be reviewed and investigated. Third-party health insurers find that utilization-review committees can be a powerful adjunct to claims review. Unresolved problem cases can be referred to the appropriate hospital or medical society committee for their assistance. The patient is thereby protected against economic exploitation, while the practicing physician is protected against arbitrary and capricious judgment.

Recertification programs require the attending physician to recertify the necessity for continued hospitalization of a patient after a definite period, such as 14 or 21 days. This cost-control procedure has been used successfully in Blue Cross plans and the Medicare program.

Alternatives to Hospitalization

Medical services provided by hospitals are a costly form of health care. In 1973, the average cost to hospitals per patient day was $114.56.[8] Many health-care experts estimate that a substantial proportion of hospital patients could be treated in outpatient clinics or extended-care facilities. At the present time, however, intermediate facilities between the physician's office and the hospital are in short supply. If more were available, physicians would be encouraged to use them for their patients rather than resorting to hospitalization.

In addition, research studies indicate that a significant percentage of hospital stays are unnecessary and wasteful. A study of a Teamsters' Union insurance plan in New York City concluded that one-fifth of the hospital admissions studied were unnecessary. In these cases, most patients were not considered seriously ill, and the various diagnostic procedures and tests could have been performed in the physician's office or in an outpatient facility.[9] Unnecessary hospital admissions obviously increase the costs of medical care, tie up needed hospital beds, and inconvenience the patients and their families.

---

[7]Walter J. McNerney, "List of Controls for Controlling Health Care Costs," in U.S. Congress, Senate, Committee on Finance, *National Health Insurance,* Hearings before the Committee on Finance, 92d Cong., 1st sess., 1971, pp. 180-81.

[8]*1974-75 Source Book of Health Insurance* (New York: Health Insurance Institute, 1974), p. 57.

[9]U.S. Congress, Senate, Subcommittee on Health, *Health Care Crisis in America, 1971,* Hearings before the Subcommittee on Health of the Committee on Labor and Public Welfare, 92d Cong., 1st sess., 1971, Part 3, p. 416.

In addition to treatment in an extended-care facility, other acceptable alternatives to hospitalization include outpatient care, organized home health-care services, and nursing-home care. Doctors should be encouraged to place their patients in the least costly appropriate facility. It is encouraging to note that many private health insurers and Blue Cross plans now cover outpatient care, extended care, and home health services rather than requiring hospitalization as a condition for coverage.

Comprehensive Health Planning

Inadequate planning at the state or local level often results in the uncoordinated development of health-care services and facilities, expensive duplication of equipment, underutilization of facilities, and serious gaps in the availability of health services. It is not uncommon for two nearby hospitals to duplicate expensive equipment or services, which are therefore often idle for extended periods. In addition, inadequate planning and lack of coordination often result in the construction of unnecessary hospitals or nursing homes in areas already adequately served, or in the continued operation of inefficient facilities, such as an obsolete hospital, where replacement with a modern health center would be more desirable.

To avoid construction of unnecessary facilities and expensive duplication of equipment, most states and large cities have established health planning councils, which plan for the coordination of comprehensive health services, health-manpower needs, and health facilities. To encourage more effective health planning, Congress has passed the Comprehensive Health Planning and Public Services Act, authorizing grants for state and areawide coordination of existing and planned health services, reduction of overhead costs by increasing utilization rates, prevention of construction of unnecessary hospital-bed capacity, and expansion of less costly health-care facilities. The act is also designed to encourage the development of needed health facilities and to upgrade the quality of medical care.

IMPROVING THE ACCESS TO MEDICAL CARE

Improving the access to medical care in the United States requires a wider distribution of physicians, as well as the elimination of all financial barriers to care. Several new proposals aim directly at (1) reduction of the maldistribution problem, and (2) removal of all financial barriers to care.

Reducing the Maldistribution Problem

As we saw in Chapter 8, physicians, dentists, nurses, and other health professionals are badly distributed throughout the economy. A relatively high proportion of physicians in private practice are concentrated in the large central cities and the suburbs, while relatively few are practicing in rural areas or in low-income neighborhoods. So those most in need of medical care are frequently the victims of inadequate access to it.

Several new approaches are designed to reduce the maldistribution problem. First, new models have been developed for delivering health services to rural areas and urban poverty neighborhoods that are short of physicians. One proposal is for area health-education centers, to be established nationally in areas with physician shortages. The centers would be satellites of existing medical and other health-science schools and would be developed around community hospitals, health-maintenance organizations, and clinics. They would provide for the teaching of health professionals on a rotation basis, would offer continuing education for local physicians and dentists, would assist community colleges in the training of allied health personnel, and would advise local health authorities on health problems. The Carnegie Commission recommends the development of 126 new health-education centers in these areas. It is estimated that if the proposed centers were developed, 95 percent of all Americans would have access to essential medical care and health service within one hour's driving time.[10]

Another new proposal is for the use of computerized communication systems in the organization and the delivery of health services in rural areas, including closed-circuit television, telephonic transmission of electrocardiogram tracings, electronic analysis of electrocardiograms, and computerized systems for the rapid recall of individual health records. Also proposed is the use of helicopters, small planes, and other forms of transportation for providing both emergency medical services and regular medical care to residents in outlaying rural areas. These models are aimed at using modern technology as a partial replacement for physicians and also to utilize more effectively the skills of those practicing in these scarcity areas.

Loan forgiveness is a method suggested for encouraging physicians to practice in scarcity areas. Physicians who agree to practice in rural areas or urban poverty neighborhoods for stipulated periods would have all or part of any loans cancelled that they had incurred for medical school. The Carnegie Commission recommends the cancellation of 25 percent of the maximum indebtedness that a student is eligible to incur if he agrees to practice medicine in a scarcity area. This means that the entire debt would be cancelled for physicians with only small amounts of indebtedness.[11]

Finally, the National Health Services Corps is another approach to the shortage of physicians in rural and low-income areas. The Corps consists largely of dedicated and public-spirited younger health professionals who agree to practice in areas now plagued by health-manpower shortages. The Corps places physicians, dentists, and nurses in rural or urban poverty areas and pays their salaries. The community involved then reimburses the Corps at a negotiated rate.

---

[10]The Carnegie Commission on Higher Education, *Higher Education and the Nation's Health: Policies for Medical and Dental Education* (New York: McGraw-Hill, 1970), pp. 7-9.

[11]*Ibid.*, p. 66.

Removal of Financial Barriers

Thousands of middle-income Americans, as well as the working and non-working poor, have inadequate access to medical care because of formidable financial barriers. These groups may lack the financial ability to pay for needed medical or dental care; they may have inadequate and limited health-insurance contracts; and they may be unable to pay for catastrophic medical expenses. These financial barriers to medical care must be removed if the access problem is to be solved.

The approaches to improving the financing of health care include cash subsidies to the poor, tax credits, substantial expansion of benefits and coverage for private voluntary health insurance, development of new catastrophe medical-expense policies, and reinsurance pools for high-risk groups. Since these proposals are closely related to national health-insurance plans, their treatment is postponed until Chapter 11, when the various national health-insurance proposals will be examined.

EXPANSION OF HEALTH MANPOWER

The number of health professionals in the United States must be sharply increased to reduce the shortages that now exist, to provide greater geographical access to medical care, and to ensure that high-quality medical care is available to everyone. Federal legislation, such as the Health Manpower Act of 1968 and the Allied Health Professions Personnel Training Act of 1966, has been helpful in expanding the number of qualified health professionals, but additional approaches are also necessary. Proposals include (1) an increased supply of physicians, (2) more efficient medical schools, (3) greater emphasis on the family practice of medicine, and (4) physicians' assistants.

Increased Supply of Physicians

The supply of physicians—in particular, the numbers of primary-care physicians, such as general practitioners, pediatricians, internists, and obstetricians—must be sharply increased to meet the future health needs of the nation. This can be done by expanding the enrollments in medical schools, by shortening the period of medical education, by providing greater financial assistance to medical students, and by increasing the educational opportunities for minority students in the various health professions.

Expanding Enrollment. The Carnegie Commission on Higher Education has recommended that the number of medical-school graduates should be increased from 10,800 in 1970-71 to 16,400 in 1978, or by 52 percent.[12] This expansion can be achieved in several ways.

First, existing medical schools could enroll additional students by plant expansion and by increases in the size of the average graduating class. Physical expansion of existing medical schools would permit the average class size to increase to at least 100 students, and in some schools, 200 or more. Moreover,

[12]*Ibid.,* p. 43.

available studies indicate that class size is unrelated to achievement by medical students on the National Board examinations, to attrition rates, to academic aptitudes, or to ultimate career choices.[13] Increasing the average class size to at least 100 students would save time for medical students, conserve teachers, and reduce initial investment and overhead expenses. Physical medical-school expansion, it is estimated, would increase the number of new medical students by at least 8 to 13 percent.[14]

Second, even though it would be expensive, the Carnegie Commission also recommends the formation of nine new medical schools. They would provide space for 900 to 1,350 more new students, another increase of 8 to 13 percent.

Finally, medical-school enrollments could be substantially expanded by shifting from a four-year to a three-year program. The shift would permit an additional 4,500 students to enter medical schools by 1976-77, an additional 31 percent increase from the 1973-74 period, without incurring increased construction costs. Since this recommendation could so quickly increase the number of new physicians, let us examine it in greater detail.

Shorter Period of Medical Education. A three-year program would enable the medical schools to increase the size of each graduating class by one-third without incurring large construction costs or sizable increases in their operating expenses.[15]

The period of formal training for the M.D. degree can be shortened in several ways without any reduction in the quality of medical education. The medical-school curriculum could be revised so that all required courses could be taken during the three-year period; two new classes could be admitted annually, thus making better use of the teaching faculty and laboratory facilities; courses could be offered during the summer, thereby eliminating one source of inefficiency now found in many medical schools; and students with extensive premedical or professional preparation could receive advanced standing. Some schools are now granting advanced standing to holders of the Ph.D. degree in the physical sciences, and the M.D.-Ph.D. combination is becoming more common. Finally, the internship year could be integrated with the period of residency, thereby shortening the time to become a practicing physician from eight years after receipt of the B.A. degree to six years.[16]

There are many advantages possible from a shift to a three-year program. Institutional cost per student would decline; the costs of new construction would be reduced; the loss of foregone income by medical students would also be reduced; and they would be able to start practicing medicine more quickly. However, since medical-school training would become more intensive, the additional faculty required would be an extra cost.[17]

[13]National Advisory Commission on Health Manpower, *Report of the National Advisory Commission on Health Manpower* (Washington, D.C.: U.S. Government Printing Office, 1967), Vol. I, p. 19.

[14]Carnegie Commission, *Higher Education,* p. 43.

[15]*Ibid.,* p. 48.

[16]*Ibid.,* p. 9.

[17]*Ibid.,* pp. 47-48.

Financial Assistance to Students. Increased financial assistance to medical students could also expand the number of primary-care physicians in the United States. In particular, student grants to disadvantaged minority groups would not only enable more minority students to enter the medical profession, but would provide greater educational opportunities for them and help to remove the financial barrier that prevents many qualified students from entering medical schools. In 1969, blacks accounted for less than 3 percent of all candidates for medical degrees. In part, this is due to the unwillingness of many minority students to go into debt to secure a medical degree; the thought of incurring indebtedness discourages many qualified disadvantaged students from seeking a higher education.[18] The Carnegie Commission recommends that federal grants, of up to $4,000 annually, be made available to low-income students.[19]

Student loans could also be made more widely available to all medical students, to reduce the financial barrier that now exists for many. Tuition rates are, in fact, often established at artificially low levels, with the remainder of the costs financed by private endowments, gifts, state appropriations, and federal and state research funds. However, even the reduced tuition, when combined with the delay in earning an income, prevents many low- or middle-income students from entering the medical profession. The result is that a disproportionate number of medical students come from upper-income families. Forty-five percent of medical students are from families in the top 10 percent income group.[20] Part of the reason, of course, is that the sons of doctors seem to receive preferential treatment from the admissions officers of medical schools.

More Efficient Medical Schools

To facilitate the expansion of health-care personnel, and to make health-care education more relevant and effective in view of the existing health-care problem, medical schools must become more efficient. Some major proposals for improving efficiency are development of new models for medical education, curriculum reforms, and financial incentives for increasing the numbers of health-care personnel.

New Models for Medical Education.[21] Since 1910, most medical schools in the United States have adopted the Flexner model as the basis of medical education. The Flexner model, or research model, stresses medical science as the foundation of medical education. The primary emphasis on science, however, may be inappropriate in view of the existing health-care problem in the United States. The Flexner model has two major defects. First, it ignores health-care delivery systems that are outside the medical school and teaching hospital. This is significant, since the present health-care delivery system has

[18]U.S. Dept. of HEW, *Toward a Comprehensive Health Policy,* p. 41.

[19]Carnegie Commission, *Higher Education,* p. 64.

[20]National Advisory Commission on Health Manpower, *Report,* p. 25.

[21]See Carnegie Commission, *Higher Education,* pp. 4-5.

been shown to be defective in providing comprehensive health services to all Americans. Second, the Flexner model isolates science in the medical school from science on the general campus, resulting in a serious duplication of effort and wasted resources. In addition, the fields of economics, sociology, and engineering are making important contributions to the field of health care and its delivery systems, but if medical schools were to have their own departments of economics, sociology, and engineering, expensive and wasteful duplication would again result.

Because of the defects in the Flexner model, modern medical schools are currently developing new models of medical education, which go far beyond the primary emphasis on science alone. The *health-care delivery model* emphasizes research in delivery systems, provides for advice to local hospitals and health authorities, coordinates the efforts of community colleges in the training of allied health professionals, and provides for continuing education for health-care personnel.

The *integrated science model* provides primarily for clinical education. The basic science courses and social-science courses would be taken by students on the main campus and not duplicated in the medical school. In this context, the medical school would be viewed primarily as a teaching hospital, which would stress clinical instruction in medicine and not courses in the basic sciences.

Curriculum Reforms. Medical schools are now in the process of critically examining and reforming their curricula in the light of the health-care problems now prevalent. Required courses in the basic sciences are being reevaluated with respect to their current relevance. For example, because laboratories now analyze most blood and urine tests, biochemistry courses are not as vital as they once were. Thus, in view of the knowledge explosion and trend toward specialization, certain premedical courses are considered unnecessary and are being deleted from the curricula.

In addition, many medical schools are integrating their curricula by tying together basic science courses with clinical instruction, areas that in the past have often been unrelated. The objective is to make the premedical-school courses and clinical instruction in the medical schools more relevant and useful.

Other curriculum reforms include student representation on admission and curriculum committees, greater freedom in the selection of elective courses, and greater emphasis on courses in comprehensive medicine rather than compartmentalized instruction.[22]

Financial Incentives. Financial incentives can also encourage medical schools to become more efficient and to expand the numbers of health-care personnel they turn out. One approach is to reward the schools on the basis of the number of students they graduate rather than the number enrolled. For example, a medical school could receive a capitation grant of $6,000 for each graduated medical student, thereby relieving the financial distress of many medical schools and also encouraging them to improve the efficiency of the entire educational process. The schools would have a strong financial incentive to shorten their curricula from four to three years, since, if graduating classes

[22]*Ibid.,* p. 52.

were one-third larger, schools would receive one-third more funds each year. In addition, the medical schools would have the financial incentive to fill the places vacated by students who drop out. Unfilled slots, currently estimated at 550-650 students, represent the output of five to seven medical schools, a costly loss to society in view of the critical health-manpower shortage.

Specialty in Family Practice

As we have seen, general practitioners, pediatricians, and internal-medicine specialists are in relatively short supply. A large proportion of medical-school graduates become specialists or go into research, teaching, industrial medicine, and public health; the majority do not become general practitioners. The result is a serious shortage of physicians with the necessary skills to meet the health needs of most families.

To meet the problem, medical schools have introduced a specialty in the family practice of medicine. It involves the training of medical students in the fields of family medicine, internal medicine, psychiatry, obstetrics, gynecology, surgery, pediatrics, and community medicine. The objective is to turn out doctors who can treat most of the health problems of a typical family.

Physicians' Assistants

It has been found that many routine medical functions now performed by physicians, but not requiring their level of knowledge and skill, could be delegated to assistants, who would be supervised by the physicians in their own offices. Such functions include record keeping, blood-pressure readings, drug injections, and elementary diagnosis. Physicians could thus expand their own potential productivity.

The armed services are a fertile source of potential physicians' assistants. Medical corpsmen have been effectively trained in the service to perform a wide variety of medical duties, and their valuable skills can be effectively used in civilian life to help meet the acute shortage of primary-care physicians. The MEDEX program at the University of Washington School of Medicine is one example of a successful program for utilizing these skills and experience. The ex-corpsman receives three months of academic training at the medical school and then serves a year of preceptorship in a doctor's office, during which the doctor continues to train the assistant to perform certain functions. It is estimated that about 3,000 ex-corpsmen could be recruited each year for MEDEX-type training programs.[23]

Although widespread training of physicians' assistants can increase the availability and accessibility of medical care, certain obstacles must be recognized. Legal barriers in the form of malpractice laws and state licensing codes may impede the delegation of responsibilites from highly trained physicians to less-trained physicians' assistants; the possibility of increased malpractice lawsuits may make it difficult for some physicians to obtain malpractice insurance; and some consumers may not accept the concept of physicians' assistants—

[23]Carnegie Commission, *Higher Education,* p. 39.

particularly the very rich and the very poor, who may feel they are receiving second-class and inferior medical care.

The problem, however, does not appear insurmountable. For example, few physicians'-assistant programs are in the field of anesthesiology, which is involved in a large proportion of malpractice claims; and a program of public education can go far to improve consumer acceptance of treatment by physicians' assistants.

IMPROVING THE QUALITY OF MEDICAL CARE

The quality of medical care provided by physicians has been proved highly uneven and variable, ranging from superb to poor. Numerous suggestions are offered to improve the quality of this care.

Improving State Licensing Boards

Before a physician can legally practice medicine, he must be licensed by the state. A state medical licensing board has two major functions: (1) to assess the quality of the physician's education by requiring him to pass an examination before a license is granted, and (2) to insure that physicians who are licensed remain qualified to practice medicine. It is argued that the state licensing boards have failed drastically in the second function.[24] This failure is partly due to inadequate state laws that make it difficult for state boards to withdraw a license from a medical offender. In addition, many state boards are reluctant to take disciplinary action against a physician by withdrawing his license even if he is unfit to practice medicine. Finally, many state boards are occupied primarily with the writing and grading of licensing examination and have insufficient time for disciplinary activities.

State licensing boards can be improved in several ways. First, legal loopholes in medical-practice laws should be closed so that the boards have clear authority to withdraw a license from an unqualified physician. Second, the state board should be primarily concerned with the discipline of medical offenders. It would have more time for the disciplinary function if the writing and grading of examinations were delegated to a national board; it is suggested that the state boards should delegate all testing to the National Board of Medical Examiners. Finally, state boards should be open to public review like any other judicial body.[25]

Continuous Education to Retain License

Another proposal is that a physician be required to engage in continuous formal education as a condition for retaining his license. Because of the explo-

[24]Robert S. McCleery, Louise T. Keelty, Russell E. Phillips, and Terrence M. Quirin, *One Life— One Physician: An Inquiry into the Medical Profession's Performance in Self-Regulation,* A Report to the Center for Study of Responsive Law (Washington, D.C.: Public Affairs Press, 1971), p. 67.

[25]Howard R. Lewis and Martha E. Lewis, *The Medical Offenders* (New York: Simon & Schuster, 1970), pp. 334-38.

sion in medical knowledge, many physicians become rapidly obsolete after they are graduated from medical school. Continuous education is necessary to maintain the physician's skills at high levels, but medical journals and standard reference texts are often inadequate for providing busy practitioners with the latest medical knowledge, so compulsory participation in organized formal programs has been suggested.

The National Advisory Commission on Health Manpower proposes that, as a condition for relicensing, medical doctors must demonstrate acceptable performance in programs of continuing medical education, or must successfully pass a challenge examination if they elect not to participate in a formal program. The educational programs and challenge examinations would be in the medical practitioner's area of specialty. The programs would not be punitive in nature, but would aim at making available the latest medical knowledge to the busy doctor.[26]

More Effective Peer Review

Some physicians may attempt procedures or recommend treatment beyond their professional competence, or may perform unnecessary surgery, prescribe unnecessary drugs, or recommend unnecessary hospitalization. These special problems can be controlled by more effective peer review.

Peer review now exists in various forms. County medical societies have committees for handling complaints; group-practice plans have extensive peer review of the medical care provided by doctor members; utilization-review and tissue-review committees are used to check on physicians' practices in hospitals; Blue Cross and Blue Shield plans also review the quality and appropriateness of medical care provided by physicians; and the Joint Commission on the Accreditation of Hospitals establishes standards for medical care in hospitals, which hospitals must meet at intervals of one to three years to retain their accreditation.

The problem is how to make peer review more effective and to extend its use to other areas of medical care. In particular, peer review is almost nonexistent with respect to the quality of medicine practiced by physicians in the privacy of their own offices.[27] Virtually nothing is known about the quality of medical care provided by physicians in private offices, clinics, emergency rooms, or outpatient departments; or about the complaints, problems, symptoms, or diseases that require such treatment. Many physicians are reluctant to have an evaluation made of that quality, and others fear that the privacy and confidentiality of the physician-patient relationship might be destroyed by peer review of medical care in offices. And lack of adequate records, poor handwriting by physicians, and lack of standard office records make review of office medicine difficult. But despite these obstacles, such peer review must be encouraged if the overall quality of medical care is to improve.

[26]National Advisory Commission on Health Manpower, *Report,* pp. 40-41.

[27]See McCleery et al., *One Life—One Physician,* pp. 146-47.

Foreign Medical Graduates

About one out of every six physicians practicing medicine in the United States is a graduate of a foreign medical school. Foreign medical graduates (FMGs) are permitted to assume major responsibilities for the medical care of patients even though they may be less educated and may achieve lower test scores than American medical-school graduates.

The National Advisory Commission on Health Manpower has found that FMGs have a lower level of professional competence than graduates of American medical schools. Although they must pass a standard examination, administered by the Educational Council on Foreign Medical Graduates, to be eligible for training in an approved hospital or to obtain a license by the state, the examination is considered less difficult than the National Board Examination, which American medical-school graduates must pass to be licensed. On examinations passed by 98 percent of American medical-school graduates, only 40 percent of the FMGs achieved a passing score. Moreover, the passing grades were clustered slightly above the passing mark rather than scattered over higher scores like those of the American school graduates. [28]

Another study, of FMG interns and residents in the same hospitals with American medical-school graduates, showed a lower level of professional competence in medicine by the FMGs. Thus, extensive periods of graduate training in the United States may not overcome the educational defects of the prior medical education of FMGs.

In order to upgrade the quality of medical care they provide, the National Advisory Commission recommends that foreign-trained physicians should pass tests that are equivalent to those required for the American-trained. The National Board of Medical Examiners would test the FMGs on the same basis as they do American medical-school graduates.

PREPAID GROUP-PRACTICE PLANS

Prepaid group-practice plans have considerable potential in reducing the health-care crisis in the United States. These plans represent a substantial departure from the traditional solo-practice, fee-for-service approach to the delivery of medical care. [29]

A prepaid group-practice plan is defined as a medical-care delivery system that has the responsibility of organizing, financing, and delivering health-care services to defined groups. Enrolled members pay a fixed annual fee and receive comprehensive health services based on the group practice of medicine. Examples of prepaid group plans include the Kaiser-Permanente Medical

---

[28]National Advisory Commission on Health Manpower, *Report,* pp. 42-46.

[29]An extensive discussion of group prepaid practice plans can be found in Merwyn R. Greenlick, "The Impact of Prepaid Group Practice on American Medical Care: A Critical Evaluation," *The Nation's Health: Some Issues, The Annals of the American Academy of Political and Social Science,* Vol. 399 (January 1972), 100-13; and Ira G. Greenberg and Michael L. Rodburg, "The Role of Prepaid Group Practice in Relieving the Medical Care Crisis," *Harvard Law Review,* Vol. 84, No. 4 (February 1971), 887-1001. The following section is drawn from these sources.

Group, the Health Insurance Plan of Greater New York (HIP), the Group Health Association Plan in Washington, D.C., the Community Health Association Plan in Detroit, and the Harvard Community Health Plan in Boston.

Basic Characteristics

Certain basic characteristics distinguish prepaid group-practice plans from private health insurance and Blue Cross-Blue Shield service plans. First, the plan has the responsibility for organization and delivery of health services to the group. The plan owns or leases medical facilities, enters into contracts with physicians to provide medical care on a group basis, hires ancillary personnel, and has general managerial control over the provision of services.

Second, prepayment is stressed. The member is charged an annual fee (usually paid monthly) and is offered a wide range of comprehensive health services. The subscriber may also be charged a nominal additional fee for certain services, such as physicians' visits. The payment of an annual fixed fee is an important advantage to the member, since it removes an important financial barrier to needed medical care and assures a wide range of health services.

Third, the group practice of medicine is stressed, whereby physicians are organized in multispecialty groups to provide a wide variety of services in meeting the health needs of the typical family.

Fourth, comprehensive health services are provided, including not only physicians' services in the office, hospital, or home, but also hospitalization, diagnostic services, laboratory services, X rays, and therapy. In addition, more and more plans are beginning to cover, at least partially, dental care, mental illness, drugs, nursing services, and vision care.

Fifth, the participating physicians are compensated otherwise than by fee-for-service. Although some plans pay the group physicians an annual salary, it is more common to use the capitation approach, under which the group partnership receives a fixed amount of money, based on a per capita sum for each subscriber, and then establishes partnership shares from the fund and determines the salaries for associates. The compensating arrangements also include bonuses for meritorious service, profit-sharing schemes, shares in the net earnings at the end of the year, and incentive pay to retain subscribers. Regardless of the arrangement, the relationship between the services rendered by a physician and the income he receives is altered, removing the financial incentive to perform unnecessary services and encouraging the most appropriate service.

Finally, dual choices are generally presented in the plan. This means that subscribers can select either the prepaid group-practice benefits or private health-insurance benefits, including Blue Cross and Blue Shield plans. The objective is to offer the subscribers an alternative to the prepaid plan in the event they become dissatisfied, thereby conforming to the traditional concept of freedom of choice. Subscribers enroll voluntarily in the group plan and are required to renew their choice every one to three years.

Advantages of Prepaid Group-Practice Plans

Prepaid group-practice plans have numerous advantages over the traditional approach to the delivery of health services.

Stress on Prevention. Prepaid group-practice plans place a heavy stress on preventive medicine, since they have strong financial incentives to do so. Under the traditional fee-for-service approach to medical care, physicians and hospitals are reimbursed on the basis of services provided; the more services they provide, the greater are their incomes, so there are no financial incentives to keep people healthy by stressing preventive care. In contrast, under prepaid group-practice plans, subscribers enter into fixed-price contracts for comprehensive medical care, so the group's net income will increase if the subscribers remain healthy.

Most plans provide a wide variety of preventive services, including multiphasic screenings, regular physical examinations, and access to medical specialists. Moreover, if the subscriber becomes ill, there is a strong incentive to treat the disease in its early stage in order to promote a prompt recovery and prevent a recurrence. Financial incentives also discourage utilization of high-cost facilities and unnecessary medical procedures. The goal is the patient's prompt recovery by means of the least costly facilities and service consistent with the medical care required. Under the traditional approach, if a hospital or medical facility is inefficient or performs unnecessary procedures, the higher costs are passed on to the patients or to private insurers; but if a prepaid group plan is wasteful and inefficient, these extra costs cannot be passed on, since the group's budget for the year is fixed in advance based on the number of subscribers. The group is penalized if its budget is exceeded, but rewarded for staying under it. Thus, prepaid group-practice plans encourage cost consciousness and the prevention of disease.

Lower Utilization Rates. Prepaid group-practice plans generally have lower utilization rates for both hospitalization and surgery. One study indicated a hospital-admission rate of 70 persons per 1,000 per year for group plans, compared to 88 per 1,000 under the traditional methods of providing medical care. Surgery rates are also lower; the same study showed 49 hospitalized surgical cases per 1,000 persons per year, compared to 69 under the traditional approaches.[30]

Several reasons account for these relatively lower hospital and surgical rates. First, unlike most private health-insurance plans, prepaid group-practice plans provide comprehensive medical services. Therefore, the subscribers have no incentive to be hospitalized for treatment, since their out-of-pocket costs are the same whether they are hospitalized or not. In contrast, many private plans cover certain services only when the patient is hospitalized, thereby providing some patients with a strong financial incentive to seek hospitalization. Also, a group physician has no financial incentive to hospitalize a patient, since his income is not increased by it, nor must he worry about alienating a patient by refusing to hospitalize him to take advantage of his insurance benefits.

Second, the financial incentives of hospitals and physicians are actually reversed, in a desirable way. Under the traditional, fee-for-service approach to medicine, hospitals must maintain a certain level of occupancy to remain financially solvent, so they may encourage the hospitalization of patients, and may even require staff physicians to guarantee a certain number of hospital inpatients at any given time. In contrast, in prepaid group-practice plans with hospital facilities, the same sums are available to the hospital regardless of the occupancy rates, and higher occupancy rates merely increase the costs without a

[30]U.S. Dept. of HEW, *Toward a Comprehensive Health Policy,* p. 33.

corresponding increase in income. Further, the financial incentive to perform unnecessary surgery is reduced, since the physician's income is not normally related to the number of services he provides. Indeed, surgery may require him to perform additional services. Thus, the physician has a strong incentive to keep his patients healthy. Also, prepaid group-practice plans eliminate the incentive to hospitalize patients for the convenience of the physician, since the same convenience—all patients in one central location, with all necessary diagnostic and therapeutic facilities and ancillary personnel—is available to him in a hospital-based group prepaid plan.

Third, prepaid group-practice plans can reduce utilization rates because of the greater control over the use of its facilities. If a subscriber becomes ill, since the goal is prompt recovery by using the most economical facility consistent with good medical care, the patient may be sent to an extended-care facility or provided with home-care services instead of being hospitalized, or minor surgery may be performed in the doctor's office. Thus, the unnecessary use of expensive hospital facilities is discouraged.

Finally, many group prepaid practice plans have a limited supply of hospital beds—for example, the Kaiser-Permanente Medical Group has fewer than 2 beds per 1,000 members, compared to about 4 per 1,000 nationally—and this limited supply may act as an important deterrent to hospital admissions.[31]

Lower Cost. There is some evidence that group plans are less expensive than the traditional modes of medical care. Some studies indicate that many groups' subscribers are receiving high-quality medical care at significantly lower costs. In some areas, costs are one-fourth to one-third lower than under the traditional methods of providing medical care.[32]

The major reason for the lower costs is that the prepaid group plans have effective control over the nature of the medical care provided and the place where the care is given—such as at an extended-care facility or at home, instead of a hospital. The National Commission on Health Manpower estimates that tremendous cost savings can result from better control over hospital utilization: A 25 percent annual reduction in hospital use could reduce the nation's medical bill by about $8 billion in 1975.

High-Quality Medical Care. Available studies indicate that the quality of medical care under prepaid group practice plans is as least as high as that provided under the fee-for-service approach to medical care. The test of any health-services delivery system is the health of the patients, and studies of infant-mortality rates, premature-birth rates, and mortality rates for the elderly show that group-plan subscribers often have lower rates than those receiving traditional medical care.

Several factors explain the generally high quality of medical care in prepaid group plans. First, because of the relatively small number of positions to be filled each year, and because inferior medical treatment can require expensive

[31]Milton I. Roemer, "Can Prepaid Care Succeed? A Vote of Confidence," *Prism,* April 1974, p. 57.

[32]U.S. Congress, House, Committee of the Whole House on the State of the Union, *Health: Message from the President of the United States Relative to Building a National Health Strategy,* Committee of the Whole House on the State of the Union, 92d Cong., 1st sess., H.D. No. 92-49, 1971 (Washington, D.C.: U.S. Government Printing Office, 1971), p. 6.

compensatory treatment later, the physicians who practice in the group are carefully selected. Most groups require the participating physicians to be certified by boards that attest to their competence in their fields of specialty. This creates a high degree of professionalism in group practice, so physicians with inferior credentials are undesirable.

Second, physician review and peer control also contribute to high-quality medical care. The care provided by participating physicians is reviewed by other physicians in the group. Some group plans also review their performance by means of audits from outside physicians.

Finally, certain institutional characteristics of prepaid group-practice plans contribute to high-quality medical care. The individual physician can consult other specialists in the group for a confirming opinion; the availability of a complete medical record in one location allows for a greater continuity in medical care; and the group physicians have more time to maintain their professional skills and competence, since a more regular work schedule allows them time to read current medical journals, attend medical conferences, and stay abreast of changing medical developments.

Other Advantages. Group plans provide considerable convenience to consumers. Since a full range of comprehensive services is available from one organization, often at a single location, the patient is not forced to visit numerous specialists in different locations, and he saves time. Also, most plans permit the subscribers a choice among the physicians in the plan, thereby preserving freedom of choice. Finally, the subscribers have access to medical care at night or over weekends as opposed to the situation under the solo-practice approach, where the family's physician is often unavailable during those times.

Group plans also offer great professional advantages to physicians. They may work more efficiently, since they are part of a highly specialized team; several physicians can use the same facilities, equipment, and ancillary personnel, thereby reducing the overhead costs of practicing medicine; and physicians benefit from the intellectual stimulation of a free and critical exchange of ideas with fellow professionals.

Disadvantages of Group Prepaid Practice Plans

Despite all these factors, critics have pointed out some defects of prepaid group-practice plans.[33] First, some subscribers feel that the medical care provided to them is too impersonal, and that a close physician-patient relationship is difficult to attain. It is argued that plan subscribers cannot select their own personal physicians, but must choose among those available in the group. In addition, it is claimed that the typical solo practitioner is more closely attuned to his patients' total needs and is more apt to view them as persons, not customers, than are his colleagues who practice in large group clinics. It should be noted, however, that although some consumers are dissatisfied, the overwhelming majority are pleased with the quality of medical care, the health-care facilities, and their relationship with physicians under group prepaid plans.

[33]See John H. Budd, "Can Prepaid Care Succeed? A Note of Caution," *Prism,* April 1974, pp. 15-17.

A second major criticism of these plans is that a subscriber must often wait a long time to receive an appointment; delays of two to three months are common. However, delays in obtaining an appointment under the traditional approach are also common, and group prepaid plans are not unique in this respect.

Third, it is also argued that the quality of medical care may not be as high as that provided by physicians engaged in solo practice—that the incentives for cost savings under group plans may result in a reduction of the quality or quantity or services delivered to subscribers. Critics point out that some members do not receive prompt hospitalization when necessary, that outpatient service is rushed, and that the appointment procedure is set up to discourage the use of the facilities.

Finally, critics also argue that economies of scale are not necessarily achieved in group-practice plans. Dr. Richard M. Bailey, in an empirical study of the group practice of medicine, concludes that the higher incomes of physicians in group practices are due largely to the sale of ancillary products (X rays, laboratory tests) and not from their increased productivity. He says that the economies of scale observed in other studies result largely from the inclusion of these ancillary services in gross measures of the output of physicians, rather than from greater physician productivity under the group practice of medicine.[34]

Health Maintenance Organization (HMO)

Health Maintenance Organizations (HMOs) are variations of the prepaid group-practice concept. An HMO can be defined as an organized system of health care, which provides comprehensive health services for enrolled members for a fixed prepaid annual fee. Regardless of how the HMO is organized, consumers are offered a variety of outpatient and hospital services through a single organization and through a single payment mechanism.

HMOs are not new; more than 7 million Americans receive comprehensive health services from HMO-type organizations. The Nixon administration in 1971 proposed a substantial expansion of HMOs nationally as a partial solution to the health-care problem in the United States. The advantages of HMOs include emphasis on the early detection and prevention of disease, incentives for holding down costs and increasing productivity of physicians, and opportunities for improving the quality and the geographical distribution of medical care.

In addition, studies indicate that hospitalization is significantly reduced by HMOs, owing largely to the emphasis on prevention, performing of minor surgery and other procedures in physicians' offices, and reduction of unnecessary medical procedures.

Finally, the quality of medical care under HMOs is generally high. One study indicated that birthrates, infant-mortality rates, and annual mortality

---

[34]See Richard M. Bailey, "Philosophy, Faith, Facts, and Fiction in the Production of Medical Services," *Inquiry.* March 1970, pp. 37-66.

rates for the aged were lower under HMOs than under the traditional methods of practicing medicine.[35]

On the other hand, HMOs, like prepaid group-practice plans, have some shortcomings. First, consumers must be informed and educated before HMOs are accepted nationally. One study indicated that knowledge about HMOs and the desire for such a system are greater among older people who are heads of large families—a group that would be expected to make the most sophisticated choices regarding medical care. This suggests, therefore, that consumers should be informed about the merits of HMOs before they are expanded nationally to all population groups.[36]

Second, many consumers have attitudinal barriers to the acceptance of medical care by HMOs. These perceptions are similar to those voiced by some who are dissatisfied with prepaid group-practice plans. Some consumers feel that the medical care provided by HMOs is impersonal, inconvenient, and requires a long waiting period for an appointment. Others feel a clinical or charitable atmosphere in their medical services. These attitudinal barriers may be formidable obstacles to the acceptance of HMOs by some consumers.

Barriers to Prepaid Group Plans

Several important barriers prevent the immediate implementation of prepaid group-practice plans. First, legal barriers may interfere with their establishment; many states have laws prohibiting the formation of consumer-proposed group plans and preventing physicians from delegating certain responsibilities to assistants. Second, the financial requirements are formidable barriers. It is estimated that to start a successful plan today requires 20,000 to 50,000 subscribers and capital requirements of $500,000 for startup costs before the opening day of operations. Finally, managerial barriers may also exist. There is insufficient managerial personnel with the necessary expertise to organize and manage prepaid group plans.

IMPROVEMENTS IN PRIVATE VOLUNTARY HEALTH INSURANCE

Private health insurance can also be improved to provide more meaningful economic security to Americans and to help reduce the health-care problem in the United States. Major health insurers, labor unions, purchasers of health insurance, physicians and hospital personnel, and public health officials generally agree on the need for (1) broadened benefits, (2) expansion of coverage, and (3) innovation.[37]

[35]U.S. Dept. of HEW, *Toward a Comprehensive Health Policy,* p. 35.

[36]*Ibid.*

[37]U.S. Department of Health, Education and Welfare, Social Security Administration, *Report on the National Conference on Private Health Insurance,* September 28-29, 1967. See also U.S. Department of Health, Education and Welfare, Social Security Administration, Office of Research and Statistics, *Private Health Insurance and Medical Care: Conference Papers* (Washington, D.C.: U.S. Government Printing Office, 1968).

Broadened Benefits

Private health insurance can be substantially improved through the broadening of benefits, especially those benefits that reduce the need for high-cost inpatient hospital care—in particular, expansion of ambulatory care, outpatient diagnostic services, and posthospital benefits in an extended-care facility. Coverage for nursing homes, convalescent hospitals, outpatient care, and organized home health services can also reduce the need for expensive hospitalization. Much of the care provided by hospitals could be given in less expensive outside facilities, lessening the need for hospitalization and thereby reducing the costs of medical care.

Expansion of Coverage

Private health insurance can also be improved by expanding coverage to those groups now without protection. The uninsured include the rural and urban poor, people not in the labor force, children and mothers in low-income and middle-income families, the long-term unemployed and their dependents, the low-income self-employed, marginal employees without group health-insurance plans, and migrant and seasonal workers. These groups are generally uninsured because they lack the financial ability to pay for private health insurance. Therefore, special provisions must be made to enable them to purchase the needed protection.

It is generally agreed that subsidies from public funds must be provided to the uninsured groups for complete protection of the population. Many proposed methods take the form of partial or complete reimbursement of premiums by the federal government to the poor for purchase of private health insurance. The proposals for subsidization of the poor are included in the various plans for national health insurance; these topics will be treated further in Chapter 11.

Encouragement of Innovation

As we saw in Chapter 8, the present health-services delivery system has numerous limitations. Private health insurers can actively participate in removing these limitations and can also encourage the development of new innovations in health care. They can play a greater role in community health planning, whereby medical resources can be utilized efficiently to avoid wasteful duplication of facilities; they can encourage the development of neighborhood health-care centers to make medical care available in ghetto areas; they can actively support less expensive alternatives to hospitalization, such as intermediate-care facilities and outpatient ambulatory programs; and they can actively support experimental programs to shorten the period of medical-school training, provide for the training of paramedical personnel such as physicians' assistants, and participate in the development of new rural medical-care delivery systems.

Private business can also employ more effective cost-control methods, including claims review, utilization review, and the recertification programs.

Finally, private health insurers can avoid practices that alienate consumers. Congressional hearings regarding the health-care problem have brought out numerous consumer complaints regarding industry practices, including the lack of clarity on policy coverage, misleading provisions, exclusions of high-risk groups, and the sudden cancellation of policies.

SUGGESTIONS FOR ADDITIONAL READING

American Academy of Political and Social Science, *The Nation's Health: The Annals of the American Adademy of Political and Social Science.* Philadelphia, Pa.: January 1972.

Campbell, Rita Ricardo, *Economics of Health and Public Policy.* Washington, D.C.: American Enterprise Institute for Public Policy Research, 1971.

Campion, Edward, "They Cut the Fat out of Our Curriculum," *Prism,* October 1974.

Carnegie Commission on Higher Education, *Higher Education and the Nation's Health: Policies for Medical and Dental Education.* New York: McGraw-Hill, 1970.

Ellwood, Jr., Paul, "Big Business Blows the Whistle on Medical Costs," *Prism,* December 1974.

Fein, Rashi, *The Doctor Shortage: An Economic Analysis.* Washington, D.C.: The Brookings Institution, 1967.

Greenburg, Ira G., and Michael L. Rodburg, "The Role of Prepaid Group Practice in Relieving the Medical Care Crisis," *Harvard Law Review,* Vol. 84, No. 4 (February 1971).

Hendrickson, Robert H., "Solo vs. Group Practice," *Prism,* November 1974.

Klarman, Herbert E., with the assistance of Helen H. Jaszi, *Empirical Studies in Health Economics.* Baltimore: Johns Hopkins Press, 1970.

National Advisory Commission on Health Manpower, *Report of the National Advisory Commission on Health Manpower,* Vol. I. Washington, D.C.: U.S. Government Printing Office, 1967.

Pettengil, Daniel W., "Writing the Prescription for Health Care," *Harvard Business Review,* November-December 1971.

Roemer, Milton I., "Can Prepaid Care Succeed? A Vote of Confidence," *Prism,* April 1974, pp. 13-67.

Rogatz, Peter, "Let's Get Rid of Those Surplus Hospital Beds," *Prism,* October 1974.

Social Security Administration, Office of Research and Statistics, *Reimbursement Incentives for Hospital and Medical Care: Objectives and Alternatives,* Research Report No. 26. Washington, D.C.: U.S. Government Printing Office, 1968.

Stewart, Charles T., Jr., and Corazon M. Siddayao, *Increasing the Supply of Medical Personnel: Needs and Alternatives.* Washington, D.C.: American Enterprise Institute for Public Policy Research, 1973.

U.S. Department of Health, Education and Welfare, *Toward a Comprehensive Health Policy for the 1970's: A White Paper.* Washington, D.C.: U.S. Government Printing Office, 1971.

chapter 10

Social Insurance and the Health-Care Problem

In addition to the methods discussed in Chapter 9, social insurance programs can also be used to help meet the health-care problems of certain groups in the United States. These programs provide some protection against the loss of income and crushing medical expenses from a serious disability or illness. The major social insurance programs that provide some health-care protection are the following: (1) OASDHI disability benefits, (2) Medicare, (3) temporary-disability insurance, and (4) workmen's compensation. Since workmen's compensation deals specifically with occupational injuries and disease, it merits special attention and will be analyzed later in Chapter 13.

OASDHI DISABILITY BENEFITS

Disability often occurs suddenly, and in many cases, the disabled worker loses several years of productive earnings. Relatively few workers have sufficient financial resources on which to draw during a period of long-term disability. In recognition of the possibility of such a crushing impact, disability benefits were first added to the OASDHI program (then called OASI) in 1954. The program has been broadened and liberalized several times since its inception, most recently as a result of the December 31, 1973, amendments.[1]

---

[1] A detailed discussion of the disability-income provisions in the OASDHI program can be found in Commerce Clearing House, *1974 Social Security and Medicare Explained—Including Medicaid* (Chicago: Commerce Clearing House, 1974). See also U.S. Department of Health, Education and Welfare, Social Security Administration, *If You Become Disabled* (Washington, D.C.: U.S. Government Printing Office, 1974).

Eligibility Requirements

A disabled worker generally must fulfill three major requirements to receive disability benefits. He must (1) have attained a disability-insured status, (2) satisfy the definition of disability stated in the law, and (3) fulfill a five-month waiting period.

Insured Status for Disability Benefits. A worker aged 31 or older must be fully insured and must have 20 quarters of coverage out of the last 40, ending with the quarter in which the disability occurs. The quarters need not be continuous.

Special rules apply to younger workers and to the blind. A person between 24 and 31 must have worked under Social Security for only half the time between age 21 and the time he became disabled. If he is under 24, he needs only six quarters of coverage out of the last twelve quarters, ending with the quarter when the disability began. These rules make it easier for younger employees to qualify for disability benefits.

Finally, as a result of the 1972 amendments, the blind are now exempt from the requirement of demonstrating a recent attachment to the labor force. They can qualify for benefits if they are only fully insured. They are not required to meet the substantial recent work test requirement that applies to other disability applicants. The required number of quarters depends on the worker's age when he first became blind. No less than six quarters nor more than 40 are ever required.

Definition of Disability. A strict definition of disability is used in the OASDHI program. A worker is considered disabled if he has a medically determinable physical or mental condition that (1) prevents him from engaging in any substantial gainful work, and (2) is expected to last (or has lasted) at least twelve months or is expected to result in death. The impairment must be so severe that he not only is unable to perform his previous work, but cannot, considering his age, education, and work experience, engage in any substantial gainful work that exists in the national economy. It is not necessary for the work to be full-time to be considered substantial; part-time work can be so considered. A job does not have to exist in the immediate area where the disabled worker resides, nor does a specific job vacancy have to be available for him. He does not have to be assured that he would be hired if he applies for the job. Jobs must exist in significant numbers, however, either in the region where the worker resides or in several regions of the country.

State agencies generally determine whether a worker is disabled, and the determination of disability in a particular case must be made from all the facts. The worker must provide medical evidence from physicians, hospitals, and other sources, indicating the severity of his condition and the extent to which the impairment prevents him from doing substantial gainful work. The worker's age, training, education, and previous work experience are also considered in determining whether he can work. If he cannot work at his regular job but can perform other substantial work, he is not considered disabled. The following conditions are generally considered sufficiently serious to qualify for disability benefits:

1. Loss of use of both arms, both legs, or an arm and a leg.
2. Total inability to speak.
3. Progressive cancer that is not controlled or cured.
4. Serious loss of kidney functions.
5. Progressive diseases that result in the loss of a leg or render it useless.
6. Severe arthritis that severely limits the use of the hands.
7. Diseases of the heart, lungs, or blood vessels that result in serious loss of heart or lung reserve, with breathlessness, fatigue, or pain.
8. Serious disease of the digestive system, resulting in weakness, anemia, and malnutrition.
9. Brain damage with severe loss of judgment, intellect, or memory.
10. Mental illness that results in an inability to get along with others, marked reduction of activities and interests, and deterioration in personal health.

The preceding definition of disability is subject to two major exceptions. First, special rules apply to the blind. Under the law, a person is blind if his vision is no better than 20/200 even with glasses, or if his vision field is 20 degrees or less. A disabled person between the ages of 55 and 65 satisfies the definition of disability if, by reason of blindness, he is unable to engage in substantial gainful activity in which he has previously engaged with some regularity over a substantial period of time. This means that the blind worker must only be unable to perform work that requires skills or abilities comparable to those required by the work he did regularly before he reached age 55 (or became blind, if later). However, benefits cannot be paid for any month during which he actually performs substantial work. Finally, if the blind worker is under 55, he can become entitled to cash benefits only if he is unable to engage in *any* substantial gainful work.

Second, a more stringent test of disability applies to disabled widows. A disabled widow (or dependent disabled widower) can receive reduced monthly disability-income benefits at age 50 that are based on the work earnings of the deceased spouse. A widow is considered disabled only if she is unable to engage in "any gainful activity" (rather than "substantial gainful activity," which applies to disabled workers)—that is, only if her impairment is so severe that she cannot work and the impairment is expected to last at least twelve months. Other factors, such as age, education, and previous work experience, cannot be considered in determining her disability as they would ordinarily be in disabled-worker cases.

In addition, the widow or widower must have become totally disabled before the spouse's death, or within seven years after the death. If a widow with children is receiving mother's benefits, she must become disabled before the payments end, or within seven years after termination. A disabled widower can receive benefits based on his wife's earnings only if she provided at least half his support at the time of her death.

Waiting Period. A disabled worker must fulfill a five-month waiting period to qualify for benefits. The 1972 amendments reduced the waiting period from six to five months. If the worker delays in filing an application for benefits, back payments are generally limited to the twelve months preceding the month he applies for benefits.

The shorter waiting period provides greater economic security to disabled workers. Under the old law, although a disabled worker became eligible for OASDHI disability-income benefits at the end of six months, the first check was paid after the seventh month of disability. And even though many workers are covered under employer- or union-sponsored short-term disability-income plans, the benefit periods are often less than seven months. Thus, a shorter waiting period reduces the financial hardship for those workers who have little or no other financial resources to draw on during the early months of a long-term disability.

Benefits

Four major disability benefits are available under the OASDHI program: (1) disability-income benefits, (2) disability freeze, (3) vocational rehabilitation services, and (4) Medicare benefits for the disabled.

Disability-Income Benefits. The monthly disability-income benefit payable to an eligible disabled worker is equal to the worker's primary insurance amount at the time of disability, except in those cases where an actuarial reduction applies.

The major groups who are eligible to receive OASDHI disability-income payments are the following:

1. *Disabled Worker.* A disabled worker under age 65 can receive a benefit equal to 100 percent of his primary insurance amount. He must be both fully insured and disability insured, meet the definition of disability and satisfy a five-month waiting period.

2. *Wife of a Disabled Worker.* The wife of a disabled worker at any age can receive benefits if she is caring for a child who is under age 18 or became disabled before age 22 and is receiving benefits based on the disabled worker's record. If the wife has no children in her care, she must be at least 62 to receive benefits.

3. *Unmarried Children.* Unmarried children under age 18, or under 22 if in school, are also eligible for benefits based on the disabled worker's earnings.

4. *Persons Disabled since Childhood.* A person who becomes disabled before age 22 can receive disability benefits if one of his parents is entitled to retirement or disability benefits or dies after being covered under the OASDHI program. The person disabled before age 22 does not need OASDHI work credits to receive benefits. The payments are based on the earnings of the parent and continue for as long as he remains disabled and the parent's eligibility continues. In addition, benefits can start again for an adult disabled in childhood who later recovers, but becomes disabled again within seven years after the previous disability ends. Also, the mother of a disabled son or daughter who is entitled to disability benefits is also eligible for benefits regardless of her age if she is caring for the son or daughter.

5. *Disabled Widow or Widower.* A disabled widow or dependent widower, or a surviving divorced wife under certain circumstances, can receive full benefits at age 65 and reduced actuarial benefits as early as age 50. A disabled widower can receive benefits based on his wife's earnings only if she was providing at least half

of his support at the time of her death. A surviving divorced wife who is disabled may receive benefits based on the earnings of her former husband only if their marriage lasted twenty or more years.

    6. *Dependent Husband.* A dependent husband age 62 or older may also be eligible for disability-income benefits under certain circumstances.

Several important points must be stressed when OASDHI disability-income benefits are analyzed. First, the monthly benefits are paid until the disabled person attains age 65, dies, or recovers from his disability. If his medical condition improves to the point where he is no longer considered disabled, benefits will continue for a three-month adjustment period—the month his condition improves plus two additional months—and will then terminate.

Benefits also continue during a nine-month trial rehabilitation period. If the recipient returns to work despite a severe health condition, his benefits may continue to be paid during a trial work period for up to nine months (not necessarily consecutive). The purpose of the trial period is to determine whether he is capable of working. If after nine months he is performing substantial gainful work, his benefits will continue for an additional three months. Thus, to encourage rehabilitation, the disability payments can be made for up to twelve months even though the work is considered substantial and gainful; However, if it is considered not to be substantial and gainful, the payments will continue on a regular basis. If his medical condition improves and is no longer considered disabling, the monthly payments will cease after a three-month adjustment period. A disabled widow, disabled dependent widower, or a disabled wife is not eligible for this trial work period. If she or he can perform substantial gainful work, benefits will terminate three months after the work begins.

Also, a new waiting period is not required if the worker becomes disabled a second time within five years after his benefits terminate because of recovery or return to work. These benefits begin with the first full month in which he is considered disabled. In the case of disabled widows or dependent widowers, the rule is the same, except that a seven-year period is used instead of five.

Finally, workmen's compensation benefits must also be considered in determining the monthly payment. Under the law, OASDHI disability-income payments must be reduced if the combined OASDHI and workmen's compensation benefit exceeds 80 percent of the worker's average monthly earnings before the disability. The average monthly earnings are determined by the highest of the following amounts: (1) average earnings based on the highest five consecutive years after 1950, including earnings in excess of the maximum taxable under Social Security, (2) average earnings used to compute disability-income benefits, or (3) highest single year of earnings in the last six years. The purpose of this provision is to encourage working and rehabilitation and discourage malingering.

Disability Freeze. A disability freeze means that certain quarters or years during which the worker is disabled are not counted in determining the number of quarters he needs to be fully or currently insured or insured for disability benefits. In addition, for purposes of computing the average monthly wage, any year during which the person is disabled can also be excluded. The purpose of the disability freeze is to prevent a worker from losing his insured status during a period of disability, or from having his future benefits reduced because of little or no earnings during the disability.

To qualify for the disability freeze, a worker age 31 and over must be both fully insured and have 20 quarters of coverage out of the last 40 quarters, including the quarter in which the disability occurs. As stated earlier, fewer quarters of coverage are required if the disabled worker is under age 31. In addition, if the worker is blind, the only requirement is that he be fully insured, and additional quarters of coverage are not required.

Vocational Rehabilitation and Special Employment Services. Disabled workers are eligible for vocational rehabilitation and special employment services. Vocational rehabilitation—counseling, training, and other services—is provided by state vocational rehabilitation agencies to a disabled worker to encourage him to return to work. In addition, employment counseling and special placement services are provided by the State Employment Service. If a disabled person who is entitled to benefits refuses counseling, training, and other services without good cause, he will lose his benefits.

Medicare for the Disabled. Medicare benefits are now available to disabled workers under age 65 who have been entitled to OASDHI cash disability benefits for at least 24 consecutive months.

Many disabled workers are either poor or unable to afford medical care while they are disabled. Available evidence indicates that more than two-fifths of those disabled seven months or longer are either poor or members of low-income groups,[2] and therefore experience considerable economic insecurity and poverty during periods of disability.

In addition, disabled people require more extensive medical care than the general population—about seven times as much hospital care, and about three times as much in physicians' services. And a substantial proportion of the long-term disabled—about 37 percent of those disabled seven months or more—lack private health-insurance protection.[3] Although group health-insurance plans generally permit conversion to an individual policy, many disabled workers cannot afford the higher premiums, or the policy may provide limited benefits with inadequate protection. Thus, in view of their limited incomes and inadequate health insurance, the long-term disabled have a clear need for Medicare benefits.

Financing

The OASDHI disability-income program is financed primarily by a payroll tax, which is paid by employees, employers, and the self-employed. The contribution rate for 1975 is 0.575 percent on the first $14,100 of earnings for both employers and employees; the self-employed pay 0.815 percent. These rates are scheduled to increase in the future. Also, the taxable wage base will increase under the automatic provisions. All tax contributions are appropriated

[2]Kathryn H. Allan and Mildred E. Cinsky, *General Characteristics of the Disabled Population,* Report No. 19, U.S. Department of Health, Education and Welfare, Social Security Administration, Office of Research and Statistics, July 1972, p. 46, Table 9.

[3]*Ibid.,* p. 44, Table 7.

to the Disability Insurance Trust Fund, which is then used to pay cash benefits and administrative expenses.

Rehabilitation services are generally financed by state and federal funds. In addition, subject to certain limitations, the law allows the Disability Insurance Trust Fund to reimburse the state vocational rehabilitation agencies for the costs of rehabilitating selected Social Security disability beneficiaries.

Administration

At the federal level, the Social Security Administration is responsible for payment of disability-income benefits. However, state agencies—usually state vocational agencies—perform the important administrative function of determining whether a worker's disability meets the definition established by law. The Social Security Administration reviews the decisions, to insure uniformity among the states and with national standards. Disability applicants are referred to the state agency for possible rehabilitation, and disability payments can be terminated for those who refuse such services without good cause.

Problems and Issues

The OASDHI disability program has improved substantially since its inception in 1954. The definition of disability has been liberalized; coverage has been expanded; the waiting period has been reduced; and Medicare benefits have been extended to the long-term disabled.

Despite these improvements, however, certain defects are still present.[4] The critical problems include (1) the small proportion of the disabled who receive benefits, (2) treatment of disabled widows, and (3) inadequate rehabilitation.

Relatively Few Receiving Benefits. An important social insurance objective is to provide a layer of income protection to the population with respect to certain well-defined risks, including the loss of income from long-term disability. It is doubtful that the OASDHI disability program is completely meeting that objective. In particular, *only about one in six of the severely disabled receive OASDHI disability benefits.*[5] The severely disabled are those disabled more than six months who are either unable to work altogether or unable to work regularly. It is true that many of these people, although they are ineligible for OASDHI disability benefits, may be eligible for early-retirement or survivorship benefits. But the proportion of the severely disabled who receive *any* OASDHI cash-income benefits is still discouraging. *Only one-third of the severely disabled receive any Social Security benefits.*[6]

[4]A complete discussion of major policy issues can be found in U.S. Congress, House, Committee on Ways and Means, *Committee Staff Report on the Disability Income Program* (Washington, D.C.: U.S. Government Printing Office, 1974).

[5]Philip Frohlich, *Denied Disability Insurance Applicants: A Comparison with Beneficiaries and Nonapplicants,* Report No. 11, U.S. Department of Health, Education and Welfare, Social Security Administration, Office of Research and Statistics, September 1970, p. 1.

[6]Allan and Cinsky, *Disabled Population,* p. 15.

Furthermore, *about four out of ten of the disabled who apply for OASDHI disability benefits fail to quality for them.* [7] Many fail to meet the severe definition of disability as established by law. Others are denied benefits because they are considered capable of working in some substantial gainful activity even though they are disabled. And many fail to qualify because of the waiting period.

The definition of disability imposes a severe hardship on older disabled workers. Handicapped younger workers have a greater potential for successful retraining and adjustment to a different line of work. However, this is not true for many older workers who withdraw from the labor force because of poor health. They may be considered incapable of working at their regular jobs, but not at some other job, since they are not totally disabled. As a practical matter, however, they are often unable to find another job—and yet they do not qualify for OASDHI disability benefits because they are considered capable of working in some substantial gainful activity.

A disabled person must also meet a recent-work requirement, which is designed to limit benefits to only those workers who have a recent attachment to the labor force. A person may satisfy the definition of disability but have his claim disallowed because of failure to meet this test. A worker aged 31 or older must be fully insured and have coverage for 20 out of the last 40 quarters to qualify for disability benefits. In this respect, a worker under age 24 is treated more favorably, since he needs only 1½ years of work in the three-year period ending when the disability begins. The current work requirement is clearly inequitable to older disabled people, who may have worked in covered employment over a longer period but still fail to qualify for benefits. Because of the progressive nature of their ailments, some workers are unable to work regularly enough to meet the recent-work test and maintain their insured status; but are still considered capable of working in a substantial gainful activity, and thus are not disabled according to law. And if the progressive disease later prevents the person from engaging in substantial gainful activity, the interruption of work caused by the disease may result in a loss of his insured status for disability benefits. There are workers who have paid into the OASDHI program for 20 or more years, yet fail to qualify for benefits because they cannot meet the recent-work test requirement. [8]

Finally, many severely disabled people do not receive disability benefits because they fail to apply—perhaps because they are not familiar with the program, or do not consider themselves sufficiently disabled to qualify for benefits.

The Advisory Council on Social Security has recommended numerous changes in the OASDHI disability program, two of which are especially worthy of consideration. First, workers should be allowed to qualify for disability benefits without having to meet a test of recent covered work, since this test is not required for other OASDHI benefits. The council believes that a valid test of

[7] U.S. Department of Health, Education and Welfare, Social Security Administration, Office of Research and Statistics, *Social Security Disability Applicant Statistics, 1968* (June 1972), p. 15, Table 1.

[8] Advisory Council on Social Security, *Reports of the 1971 Advisory Council on Social Security,* H.D. 92-80, Committee on Ways and Means, 92d Cong., 1st sess., 1971 (Washington, D.C.: U.S. Government Printing Office, 1971), p. 28.

disability determination could be made without having to resort to the recent-work requirement.

Second, workers aged 55 and over would be subject to a less severe test of disability—the one applied to blind persons, which is more liberal than the general disability definition. That is, an older worker should be considered disabled if he cannot engage in any substantial gainful activity that requires skills or abilities similar to those required in a job in which he has previously worked with some regularity over a substantial period of time.[9]

Treatment of Disabled Widows. Relatively few disabled widows are significantly helped by the OASDHI disability program, since they receive exacting treatment under the program with respect to reduced actuarial benefits, age requirements, and the definition of disability.

1. Reduced Actuarial Benefits. Disabled widows are eligible for monthly cash benefits if they can meet the strict definition of disability and can satisfy other requirements. The monthly benefits can start as early as age 50, but then are reduced in amount to 50 percent of the husband's primary insurance amount. As a result of the actuarial reduction, the benefits paid may be well below the poverty line; for instance, the average monthly benefit paid to a disabled widow aged 50 in 1972 was only about $94.[10]

To help improve the financial security of disabled widows (and disabled dependent widowers), the Advisory Council on Social Security recommends that the benefits paid them should not be actuarially reduced by reason of their beginning before age 65.[11]

2. Age Requirement. Disabled widows are required to be at least 50 years old to receive disability benefits, but there is little economic justification for denying them benefits until that age. A widow disabled earlier may be exposed to considerable economic insecurity, and her need for income may actually be greater than that of an older widow. Since the husband has died at an early age, she may have few accumulated assets on which to draw for present and future consumption needs. The Advisory Council on Social Security recommends that disability benefits to eligible disabled widows (and widowers) should be paid without regard to age,[12] thus greatly improving the economic-security position of younger impoverished widows who are disabled.

3. Harsher Definition of Disability. Disabled widows must satisfy a stricter definition of disability than is applied to the general working population. The disabled widow must be totally unable to work at any job. She must be so disabled that she is unable to engage in *any* gainful activity rather than in "substantial gainful activity."

It is difficult to justify a harsher definition of disability for disabled widows. The general definition, which applies to most disabled workers, is

[9]*Ibid.,* pp. 28-30.

[10]U.S. Department of Health, Education and Welfare, *Social Security Bulletin: Annual Statistical Supplement, 1972* (Washington, D.C.: U.S. Government Printing Office, 1974), p. 92, Table 67.

[11]Advisory Council, *Reports,* p. 32.

[12]*Ibid.,* p. 33. See also Paula A. Franklin, "The Disabled Widow," *Social Security Bulletin,* Vol. 38, No. 1 (January 1975), pp. 20-27.

difficult enough to meet, and a large proportion of applicants fail to qualify under the law. Disabled widows as a group are anything but affluent, and the more stringent definition only aggravates the poverty of this group.

Inadequate Rehabilitation Services. Research studies suggest that the rehabilitation of OASDHI disability beneficiaries is inadequate. *Rehabilitation services are provided to only about one-fifth of those who receive OASDHI disability benefits.*[13] It could be argued that because of the stringent definition of disability that is used to determine eligibility for these benefits, only a limited number of those receiving them are capable of being restored to productive work. But if this were so, any cost saving from rehabilitation would be limited; and this is clearly not the case, since a high rate of return is obtained from rehabilitation expenditures. *For each $1.00 of trust-fund money invested in rehabilitation services, a cost saving of $1.77 has been obtained,*[14] representing the value of present and future benefits that no longer have to be paid to disabled beneficiaries because of their rehabilitation and return to work.

Since 1966, the Disability Insurance Trust Fund has been authorized to reimburse the state agencies for the cost of vocational rehabilitation services provided to selected disabled people. Prior to the 1972 amendments, the amounts paid were limited to 1 percent of the disability benefits paid the preceding year. The 1972 amendments increased the limit to 1¼ percent for fiscal 1973 and 1½ percent for fiscal 1974 and beyond. This provision has the desirable effect of making rehabilitation services available to more of the severely disabled OASDHI recipients, who otherwise would receive low priority for rehabilitation by state agencies. In view of the substantial benefits from rehabilitation, the Advisory Council on Social Security recommends increasing the trust-fund expenditures for those services to 2 percent of the preceding year's disability payments.[15]

It must be recognized, however, that the present system for determining disability conflicts with the goal of successful rehabilitation. The probability of successful rehabilitation is increased if a potentially disabling disease can be identified and treated during its early stages; but the major objective of the OASDHI disability program is to provide benefits only to those who have progressed beyond the early stages of a disease and are now severely disabled. In this regard, the program is extremely effective in screening people who apply for benefits as to their degree of disability, and eliminating those not considered sufficiently disabled to qualify for benefits. Yet these are the people who would benefit most greatly from rehabilitation services, since the services would be provided during the early stages of disability.

This is the basic dilemma. If an applicant is denied disability benefits, the presumption is that he is *able to work.* But because of the denial, he may not seek rehabilitation services, and even if he does, the presumption of his being

---

[13]Ralph Treitel, "Rehabilitation of the Disabled," *Social Security Bulletin,* Vol. 34, No. 3 (March 1971), 22.

[14]Advisory Council, *Reports,* p. 31.

[15]*Ibid.*

able to work may reduce his chances of obtaining them, since the agency may feel he is not one of those most in need of rehabilitation. On the other hand, a person receiving disability benefits is considered severely disabled, and the presumption is that he is *unable to work* in substantial gainful activity. He may be unwilling to receive rehabilitation services because of his established status as a disabled person, and he may fear the loss of his benefits if the rehabilitation services are effective. Also, the rehabilitation agency may not wish to provide him services because he is presumed unable to work, and the likelihood of his successful rehabilitation is viewed as minimal. In any event, the probability of successful rehabilitation is less at this point than if it had begun earlier, when the person was less severely disabled.

Furthermore, the program's objective, of providing benefits only to those who have progressed beyond the early stages of disability to a more advanced stage, can also be questioned. An extensive and elaborate evaluation procedure is now used to determine disability for the purpose of paying benefits only to those unable to work in any substantial gainful activity. It is doubtful if this elaborate evaluation procedure can be justified, in view of such a narrow goal. In addition to the income-maintenance goal during disability, a broader objective should include the early identification, treatment, and rehabilitation of an applicant with a potentially disabling disease.[16]

Two proposals, made by capable researchers, are aimed at improving the effectiveness of the OASDHI disability program, especially from the viewpoint of early detection and treatment of disease and effective rehabilitation. First, all disability applicants, including those whose claims are denied, would be systematically recalled at intervals and reevaluated to determine changes in disability. Second, administrators would maintain contact with denied applicants in order to provide continuity between the evaluation of disability and vocational rehabilitation services.[17] If implemented, these proposals would do much to improve the effectiveness of the rehabilitation services under the OASDHI program.

MEDICARE

The Medicare program is designed to meet the problem of medical expenses of the aged. The 1965 amendments to the Social Security Act established a basic compulsory hospital-insurance plan for the aged and a related voluntary supplementary medical-insurance plan. Medicare benefits first began in July 1966, with the exception of posthospital care benefits in an extended-care facility, which were first covered in January 1967. The program has been changed numerous times since its inception, with the most recent changes occurring in

[16]See Richard T. Smith and Abraham M. Lilienfeld, *The Social Security Disability Program: An Evaluation Study,* Research Report No. 39, U.S. Department of Health, Education and Welfare, Social Security Administration, Office of Research and Statistics (Washington, D.C.: U.S. Government Printing Office, 1971), pp. 80-81 and 89-91.

[17]*Ibid.,* pp. 88-91.

1973 and 1974. The Medicare program currently consists of two related programs: (1) Hospital Insurance, and (2) Medical Insurance.[18]

Hospital Insurance

Hospital Insurance (Part A) of the Medicare program is a basic plan that covers major inpatient hospital services and related posthospital care for most of the aged. As a result of recent amendments, the program now covers other groups formerly ineligible and also provides for a broader range of health-care services.

Coverage. Five groups are currently eligible for Hospital Insurance benefits. First, Hospital Insurance covers everyone 65 and over who is entitled to monthly OASDHI retirement or survivorship benefits or to railroad retirement benefits as a qualified retirement beneficiary.

Second, a special transitional provision extended coverage to those aged who were ineligible for either monthly OASDHI or railroad retirement benefits, but attained aged 65 before 1968. However, those attaining age 65 after 1967 must have a certain number of quarters to qualify for benefits. Eighteen quarters of coverage are required for people who reached 65 in 1973, and 20 for those who reached 65 in 1974. The number of required quarters will eventually be the same as that required for a fully insured status.

Third, aged people who do not qualify under the provisions above can voluntarily enroll in the Hospital Insurance program and pay a monthly premium. The monthly premium is $40 in fiscal 1976 and will increase in the future at the rate of increase in the inpatient deductible. Also, to be eligible for Hospital Insurance, the person must enroll for Medical Insurance (Part B) and pay the monthly premium.

Fourth, as a result of the 1972 amendments, disabled people under 65 are also eligible for Hospital Insurance benefits, if they have been entitled to OASDHI or railroad reitrement cash disability benefits for at least 24 consecutive months.

Finally, in recognition of the crushing financial impact on the patient with a chronic kidney disease, the Medicare program now covers people under 65 who require hemodialysis treatment or a kidney transplant. Coverage begins with the fourth month after the patient first begins a course of hemodialysis. To qualify for coverage, the person must (1) have a medically determined chronic renal disease and require hemodialysis treatment or a kidney transplant, and (2) be either fully or currently insured, or else be entitled to monthly OASDHI benefits or be the spouse or dependent child of someone who is.

Benefits. The Hospital Insurance portion of the Medicare program provides three basic benefits: (1) inpatient hospital care, (2) posthospital extended care, and (3) posthospital home health services.

[18]An excellent discussion of the Medicare program can be found in Commerce Clearing House, *1974 Social Security,* Chap. 6, and U.S. Department of Health, Education and Welfare, Social Security Administration, *Your Medicare Handbook* (Washington, D.C.: U.S. Government Printing Office, 1974).

1. Inpatient Hospital Care. Inpatient hospital care is provided for up to 90 days for each benefit period. A benefit period, or spell of illness, begins when the aged person first receives inpatient hospital services and ends when he has been out of the hospital or skilled nursing facility for 60 consecutive days. As of 1975, the patient must pay an initial deductible of $92 for the first 60 days, plus a coinsurance payment of $23 daily from the 61st through the 90th day. If he exhausts the 90 days of benefits, he can draw on a lifetime reserve of 60 additional days, which is subject to a $46 daily charge. In addition, inpatient psychiatric hospital services have a lifetime limit of 190 hospital benefit days.

Hospital Insurance benefits typically include semiprivate accommodations, laboratory tests and X rays, dressings, operating room, nursing services, and drugs inside the hospital. However, there are certain exclusions. There is no coverage for the first three pints of blood, for private-duty nurses, for hospital services performed by physicians or other medical technicians employed by or working through a hospital, for extra charges for a private room (unless needed for medical reasons), or for personal comfort or convenience items, such as a telephone or television set furnished at the patient's request.

2. Posthospital Extended Care. A patient may not require continuous hospital care, but not be well enough to go home. If he needs full-time nursing care and other related health services that cannot be provided in his home, the physician may decide to transfer him to a skilled nursing facility that is equipped and staffed to furnish these services to the aged. The covered services, which include physical, occupational, and speech therapy, and medical social services, are paid in full for the first 20 days. For the next 80 days, the patient must pay a daily coinsurance charge of $11.50.

To qualify, the patient must have been hospitalized for at least three consecutive days and must be transferred to the skilled nursing facility within 14 days after discharge from the hospital. The 14-day limitation can be increased to 28 days if appropriate bed space is not available. In addition, the 14-day limitation can be modified for a patient whose medical condition is such that transfer to the facility within 14 days after hospital discharge is not medically appropriate—for example, a person with a fractured hip that will take some time to mend first. In such a case, the transfer can wait more than 14 days because the fracture is clearly related to the previous hospital stay.

The physician must certify that the patient requires admission to the skilled nursing facility because of a condition for which he was treated while in the hospital. Custodial care is not covered; the patient must require skilled care, and not merely assistance in eating, bathing, dressing, walking, or taking the right medicine. The skilled nursing home must also be approved for Medicare payments. It is possible for the physician to obtain advance approval of Medicare payment for posthospital extended-care services, to assure that payment will be made for a specified number of days in a skilled nursing facility for treatment of a specified medical condition.

3. Posthospital Home Health Services. An aged person may require certain services that can be given in his home by part-time visiting nurses, physical therapists, speech therapists, occupational therapists, and other health professionals. A maximum of 100 home health visits can be provided during a one-year period following a qualifying stay of at least three consecutive days in a hospital or extended-care facility and before the beginning of a new benefit period. The physician must establish a plan of home treatment within 14 days after discharge from the hospital or extended-care facility. In addition, the patient's condition must be one that requires skilled nursing care on an intermittent basis, or physical or speech therapy. The services must be furnished by a home health agency that participates in the Medicare program, and the home visits must be for the further treatment of a condition for which the aged patient was treated while in the hospital or extended-care facility.

Certain services and items are excluded, however, such as full-time nursing care, drugs and biologicals, personal comfort or convenience items, noncovered levels of care, and meals delivered to the aged person's home.

Financing. The Hospital Insurance plan is financed by a payroll tax paid by employers, employees, and the self-employed. In 1975, each of these groups paid a contribution rate of 0.90 percent on a maximum taxable wage base of $14,100. All contributions are deposited in a separate Hospital Insurance Trust Fund, which is similar to the OASI and DI trust funds. Hospital Insurance benefits for people who are not entitled to monthly OASDHI or railroad retirement cash benefits are financed out of the general revenues of the federal government. Finally, as stated earlier, those who voluntarily elect Hospital Insurance must pay a monthly premium, which is $40 in fiscal 1976.

The Medicare program provides for an annual review of hospital costs and for necessary increases in the initial deductible and coinsurance amounts. The initial inpatient deductible of $92 will be increased only in multiples of $4. Since the coinsurance amounts for inpatient hospital services (after 60 days) and post-hospital extended-care services (after 20 days) are one-quarter and one-eighth, respectively, of the initial deductible, they will also increase as the initial deductible increases.

Administration. The Social Security Administration has the primary responsibility of administering the Hospital Insurance program, but it also enters into agreements with state agencies and private insurers to help administer the program. Guidelines are established to determine whether hospitals, extended-care facilities, and home health agencies meet federal standards. These standards include the establishment of hospital utilization-review committees to determine the appropriateness and effectiveness of care, transfer arrangements between the hospitals and extended-care facilities, and appropriate fiscal records. State agencies, which are generally public health agencies, apply the standards and also give advice to the providers of medical care.

Each provider of medical services can deal directly with the federal government or elect an intermediary, such as a private insurer or Blue Cross plan, to process claims. The intermediary receives bills from the hospital, extended-care facility, or home health agency and determines the amount to be paid. The providers of medical services are reimbursed on the basis of reasonable cost, and the intermediary is reimbursed for reasonable administrative costs. The intermediary receives the funds from the federal government and is also responsible for the auditing of the records of the providers of service.

Medical Insurance

Medical Insurance (Part B) of the Medicare program is a voluntary program that covers physicians' bills and other related medical services. As a result of recent amendments, Part B has been considerably broadened.

Coverage. Except for the disabled, most people become eligible for Medical Insurance benefits when they first attain age 65. Under the old law, people were permitted to elect voluntarily the Medical Insurance benefits, but effective July 1973, those entitled to Hospital Insurance benefits are automatically enrolled for Medical Insurance benefits unless they voluntarily refuse the coverage. The automatic enrollment also applies to the disabled under age 65 who qualify for Hospital Insurance benefits. Eligible people who are not entitled to either monthly OASDHI or railroad retirement benefits can voluntarily enroll for Medical Insurance benefits without first being covered for Hospital Insurance benefits.

In addition, people receiving monthly public-assistance payments can be enrolled if the state agrees to "buy in" and pay the monthly premium; and aliens admitted for permanent residence can enroll if they have resided in the United States for at least five continuous years. About 95 percent of the eligible aged have elected to participate in the program.

As indicated earlier, an eligible individual is automatically enrolled for Medical Insurance when he first becomes eligible for Hospital Insurance unless he voluntarily declines the coverage. If a person declines to participate in Medical Insurance when he is first eligible, he can enroll during any general enrollment period, which is the period from January 1 through March 31 of each year. The monthly premium, however, will be 10 percent higher for each full year of delay for those who fail to enroll at their first opportunity or later withdraw from the program. A person can re-enroll in the program only once. The limitations on enrollment and reenrollment are designed to protect the program from adverse selection because of people who decide against enrolling when healthy but seek the protection when their health deteriorates.

Benefits. Medical insurance pays for physicians' services, outpatient hospital services, home health benefits, and other medical services and supplies. The plan pays 80 percent of the reasonable charges for covered services after a $60 calendar-year deductible. The patient pays the remaining 20 percent over the deductible. In addition, a carryover provision helps the person who would otherwise have to meet the $60 deductible twice within a short period. Eligible medical expenses in the last three months of the year can be applied to meet the deductible for the following year.

1. Physicians' and Surgeons' Services. The services of physicians and surgeons are covered whether performed in a hospital, office, extended-care facility, home, or group-practice plan. Services by dentists are covered only for surgery of the jaw or related structures, or setting of jaw fractures or facial bones. Certain services of podiatrists are also covered, as are certain limited services provided by chiropractors. Treatment by means of manual manipulation of the spine is covered, but only to treat a subluxation demonstrated by X ray to exist.

It should be noted that the $60 deductible and coinsurance charge of 20 percent do not apply to physicians' charges for X rays or for clinical laboratory services when the person is an inpatient in a qualified hospital. The full reasonable charge is paid, rather than 80 percent.

Certain services, however, are excluded. Medical Insurance does not cover routine physical examinations, eyeglasses and eye examinations, hearing aids, immunizations (unless directly related to an injury), and the services of certain practitioners, such as naturopaths and Christian Science healers.

2. Outpatient Hospital Benefits. Outpatient services of participating hospitals are also covered, including diagnostic tests, laboratory services, X-ray and radiology services, emergency-room services, and medical supplies such as splints and casts.

Outpatient physical-therapy services are covered if they are furnished under the direct supervision of a physician or are as part of covered home health services. A hospital or skilled nursing facility can also provide outpatient physical therapy under Medical Insurance to inpatients who do not have Hospital Insurance coverage or have exhausted their coverage. The services of a licensed physical therapist, whether provided in his office or the patient's home, are also covered.

3. Home Health Benefits. Home health visits ordered by a physician are covered, up to a maximum of 100 visits during a calendar year, without the requirement of prior hospitalization. This includes part-time nursing care, physical or speech therapy, occupational therapy, medical social services, and part-time services of home health aides. As a result of the 1972 amendments, 100 percent of the reasonable cost of covered home health care services is paid (after the annual deductible of $60), rather than 80 percent.

4. Other Medical Services and Supplies. Also covered are diagnostic laboratory tests; radiation therapy and X-ray services; surgical dressings, splints, and casts; rental or purchase of durable medical equipment, such as wheelchairs, crutches, or oxygen equipment; devices (other than dental) to replace all or part of an internal organ; and certain ambulance services. However, hearing aids, eyeglasses, false teeth, orthopedic shoes, and prescription drugs administered by the patient are excluded.

Financing. Each person enrolled for Medical Insurance must pay a monthly premium (in fiscal 1976, $6.70), which is then matched by an identical contribution from the federal government out of general revenues. In December of each year, the premium for a twelve-month period is established, to begin July 1 of the following year.

The monthly premiums and matching government amounts may be increased each year if medical costs continue to rise. However, they can be increased only if a general OASDHI benefit increase has occurred since the last premium increase, and the percentage increase in the premium cannot exceed the percentage of cash-benefit increase. Under present law, the federal government's share of Medical Insurance, which can never be less than 50 percent, will be used to pay the program costs not met through enrollee premiums. The purpose of this provision is to protect the real purchasing power of the aged, who otherwise would have to pay higher monthly premiums without a corresponding increase in monthly benefits.

Administration. The Social Security Administration has the responsibility for administering Medical Insurance. Contracts are entered into with private insurance carriers—including Blue Shield plans, private health insurers, and group prepaid practice plans—or state agencies to serve as administrative agents. The carriers determine the reasonable charges and allowable payments, and also disburse and account for Medical Insurance funds.

Two methods are available for the reimbursement of physicians' fees. First, under the *itemized bill* method, a beneficiary files an itemized bill with the Medicare carrier, and payment is made to him. The Medicare carrier determines the reasonable charges. The beneficiary receives direct payment for 80 percent of the reasonable charges above the $60 deductible. If the physician's actual fee exceeds the amount allowed as reasonable by the Medicare carrier, the patient must pay the excess.

Second, the physician can be paid under the *assignment* method, which can be used if only both parties agree to it. The physician accepts an assignment from the patient, and payment is made directly to the physician. Under this method, the physician agrees to accept the reasonable charge determined by the Medicare carrier as his total charge for the service. The Medicare carrier then pays the physician 80 percent of the reasonable charge, after subtracting any part of the $60 deductible that the patient may not have met. The physician can bill the patient only for the remaining 20 percent of the reasonable charge, any part of the $60 deductible not met, and for any services not covered.

In determining reasonable charges, the carrier will consider the customary and local prevailing charges in the community that are made by physicians and other suppliers of medical services. The federal government provides guidelines and statistical norms for establishing the customary and prevailing charges in a community.

Problems and Issues

Although the Medicare program has relieved more than 21 million senior citizens from the major part of their medical bills, certain problem areas remain: (1) incomplete coverage, (2) prescription drugs outside the hospital, (3) spiraling costs, (4) financing, (5) administrative defects, and (6) financial burden to the aged.

Incomplete Coverage. Although the Medicare program has been gradually broadened to include groups most in need of coverage—the long-term disabled under 65, people with serious kidney diseases, and the aged who are uninsured for OASDHI or railroad retirement benefits—there are still gaps in the coverage. First, the spouses of Medicare beneficiaries and other OASDHI beneficiaries between the ages of 60 and 64 are not covered, because under present law, Medicare benefits are generally limited to those 65 or over. (The long-term disabled and people under 65 with serious kidney diseases are major exceptions). However, people between 60 and 64 may find it difficult to obtain adequate private health insurance at reasonable rates. These groups include workers retiring early, and their spouses, widows, and parents. It has been proposed that Medicare benefits be made available at cost to people within these groups between the ages of 60 and 64.

Second, it is also proposed that Medicare be extended to cover the dependents of disability beneficiaries. Since many long-term disabled are either poor or members of low-income groups, their dependents may be unable to afford private health-insurance protection. The Advisory Council on Social Security does not, however, recommend covering them at the present time. Program costs would increase substantially; coverage of dependents is of lower priority than coverage of the long-term disabled; private health insurance is generally available to dependents who are not disabled; and coverage of dependents under Medicare would overlap with private health-insurance protection.[19]

Finally, some national health insurance proponents would gradually expand the Medicare program to cover the entire population. This important issue will be analyzed in Chapter 11, when the various national health insurance proposals are examined.

Prescription Drugs outside the Hospital. One major defect of the Medicare program is that the costs of prescription drugs outside a hospital or skilled nursing facility are not covered. These represent a large proportion of the total medical expenses of the aged, and moreover, are unevenly distributed among them. Aged people with chronic diseases, such as heart or respiratory ailments, arthritis, and rheumatism, are confronted with recurring drug expenses, and many drugs are absolutely essential to the survival of the chronically ill.

Prescription drugs account for about 20 percent of all private health-care expenditures of the aged, amounting to more than three times the drug expenses of the nonaged. Annual per capita drug expenses for the severely disabled are six times the expenditures for the general population. Moreover, most drug expenses incurred by the aged are not paid by private insurance; over 80 percent are paid directly by the aged, many of whom live in poverty. In view of these statistics, both the Task Force on Prescription Drugs and the Advisory Council on Social Security recommend coverage of prescription drugs.[20]

Such coverage, however, would present difficult problems of cost, administration, and claims reimbursement.[21] The Social Security Administration estimates that coverage of all drugs for the aged and disabled would cost about $3 billion annually, even with a $1 copayment charge.[22] The costs would be controlled by various methods, such as an annual deductible, reimbursement of all expenses with a percentage of the cost paid by the beneficiary (coinsurance), or reimbursement of all expenses with a fixed dollar amount to be paid by the beneficiary (copayment). The Advisory Council on Social Security believes that the problems of record keeping and administration can be reduced by copayment rather than by coinsurance or deductibles, and recommends a copayment charge of $2 for a new prescription and $1 for each refill prescription.

[19]Advisory Council, *Reports,* p. 51.

[20]*Ibid.,* p. 52.

[21]For an excellent discussion of this issue, see Robert J. Myers, *Coverage of Out-of-Hospital Prescription Drugs under Medicare* (Washington, D.C.: American Enterprise Institute for Public Policy Research, 1972).

[22]U.S. Congress, Senate, Committee on Finance, *Provisions Relating to Medicare—Medicaid and Maternal and Child Health,* Excerpt from S. Rept. 92-1230, Report of the Committee on Finance to Accompany H.R. 1, the Social Security Amendments of 1972, Senate Committee on Finance, 92d Cong., 2d sess., 1972 (Washington, D.C.: U.S. Government Printing Office, 1972), p. 269.

The administrative burden of covering *all* drugs would be enormous, since millions of small prescriptions would have to be paid. Effective utilization controls would be absolutely essential to insure that the reimbursed prescriptions are reasonable and necessary and are used only by Medicare beneficiaries. These controls, however, would be burdensome. To make the administrative problem manageable, it is proposed that only certain specified drugs necessary for the treatment of crippling or life-threatening common diseases should be covered. These diseases would include heart disease and high blood pressure, arthritis and rheumatism, genito-urinary conditions, diabetes, emphysema, and others to be specified.

Finally, claim-reimbursement procedures would also have to be established. The Advisory Council on Social Security recommends that payment should be made directly to the vendor. A reasonable charge would be established for each drug, to cover the vendor's cost in acquiring and dispensing it. A direct payment to the vendor would relieve the aged person of filing a claim; automatic data-processing equipment could be used; claims information would be readily available; and relating the reimbursement to cost could be done more efficiently.[23]

Spiraling Medicare Costs. Medicare costs are increasing at an alarming rate; earlier cost estimates of the program have been greatly exceeded. Based on recent cost estimates of the Hospital Insurance portion of the Medicare program, HI costs will exceed the cost estimates made in 1967 by some $240 billion over a 25-year period.[24] And the total monthly premium for Medical Insurance has had to be increased from $6 in July 1966 to $13.40 in July 1975, an increase of about 123 percent.

Two factors help explain the escalation in Medicare costs. First, the per-unit costs of physicians' visits, surgical procedures, and hospital days have risen enormously since the program's inception. Second, the number of services provided to Medicare beneficiaries has also increased, and many of these services may not be medically necessary. Thus, overutilization of plan benefits, combined with rising unit costs, are primarily responsible for the rapid increase in Medicare costs.[25]

Because of deep concern over Medicare costs, Congress added several important cost-control provisions to the program in 1972. First, there is a limitation on the coverage of Medicare costs. The secretary of Health, Education and Welfare is authorized to establish, on both the direct and indirect costs, limits that are considered reasonable prices for comparable facilities in the area. Maximum costs can also be established for groups of services, such as food or standby costs.

Cost limits are necessary because of the wide variation in costs from one institution to another, attributable to institutional size, patient mix, scope of services offered, and other, similar factors. But the unusually high costs of many institutions are due either to plush furnishings or to waste and inefficiency. If patients demand expensive services and plush surroundings, they

[23]Advisory Council, *Reports,* pp. 53-54.

[24]Senate Finance Committee, *Provisions,* p. 254.

[25]*Ibid.*

should not be denied them; but neither should the Medicare program be expected to pay for them. Likewise, if the health-care providers are guilty of inefficiency and waste, they should not be shielded from the economic consequences of them. Thus, cost controls can encourage greater efficiency and discourage wasteful, cost-increasing practices.

Congress also set limits on the amounts that are paid for physicians' charges. Medical Insurance pays only 80 percent of the reasonable charge in excess of the $60 calendar-year deductible. The "reasonable charge" for any service is either the "customary charge" of the provider of the service for the type of service rendered, or the "prevailing charge" of all providers of the same type in a geographical area, whichever is lower. The "customary charge" is the median rate charged for a particular type of service by a particular provider to enrollees during the calendar year prior to the fiscal year in which the claim is processed. The "prevailing charge" for any type of service is the 75th percentile of the distribution of customary charges for that service in an area. Payment is made on the basis of the *lowest of the customary, the prevailing, and the actual charges.* When payment is made on a reasonable-charge basis directly to individual suppliers (by assignment), the determination of reasonable charge by the carrier must be accepted as the full charge for the services, and the supplier cannot bill the patient for amounts in excess of that charge; otherwise, payment is made to the enrollee on the basis of an itemized bill.[26]

A third cost control has been the establishment of Professional Standards Review Organizations (PSRO), which require a number of physicians in a local area to review the quality of medical care and the necessity for Medicare services there. The PSRO has the responsibility for determining whether the medical care provided by institutions is medically necessary and is provided in accordance with professional standards. It also encourages attending physicians to utilize the less costly facilities and methods of treatment when they are medically appropriate. And it has the option of reviewing noninstitutonal care provided under the Medicare program. The PSROs were created because, in the past, the utilization-review procedures by physician staff committees and claims review by Medicare carriers and intermediaries were considered inadequate. Physicians are the only people competent to judge whether the services ordered by other physicians are medically necessary. Thus, the PSRO aims at reducing unnecessary or improper care through peer review at the local level.

Finally, the new law permits experiments to evaluate prospective reimbursement plans to improve the efficiency of Medicare. Prospective reimbursement plans, as discussed in Chapter 9, differ from the present arrangement of reimbursing institutions providing Medicare services on the basis of reasonable cost. In prospective reimbursement, a payment rate is established in advance of the period over which the rate is to apply, thus providing strong financial incentives to health-care providers to keep their actual costs at a level no higher than the agreed-upon rate. However, two potential disadvantages must be recognized.

First, there is no assurance that the costs to the federal government will be

---

[26] *1973 Annual Report of the Board of Trustees of the Federal Supplementary Medical Insurance Trust Fund,* H.D. No. 93-129, Committee on Ways and Means, 93d Cong., 1st sess., 1973 (Washington, D.C.: U.S. Government Printing Office, 1973), p. 30.

less under prospective reimbursement plans than under the present approach. Health-care providers may push for a rate high enough to cover all their costs, including research costs, bad debts, and a safety margin. The resulting reimbursement payment could actually be higher than the amounts paid now. And if the providers used their cost savings to expand services under the plan, the new expenditure level could result in higher prospective rates for future years.

Second, some health-care providers might attempt to cut back on the quality of medical services to reduce their actual costs and thereby maximize the difference between the reimbursement payment and the actual costs incurred. Thus, any prospective reimbursement plan must provide for adequate and widely accepted quality-control procedures to prevent a deterioration in the quality of medical services offered.

Financing Medicare. In the past, Hospital Insurance costs (Part A) have been consistently underestimated, causing serious concern to the Advisory Council on Social Security. Prior to the 1972 amendments, the contribution rates supporting the program were inadequate, and the Hospital Insurance Trust Fund would have been exhausted by 1973.[27] The 1972 amendments, however, provided for improved financing of the Medicare program, and the tax contributions are expected to be adequate to finance future benefits under the program.

The Advisory Council recommends, however, that the financing method for Medical Insurance (Part B) should be changed. Medical Insurance would be combined with Hospital Insurance in a single premium, and the separate monthly premium for Part B, which can be financially burdensome to many of the aged, would be eliminated. The monthly premium was originally $3, but by July 1975, it had increased to $6.70, or $13.40 for a couple. The annual premium of $160.80 that a retired couple would pay could absorb a high proportion of the relatively fixed incomes of many poor and low-income retirees. Combining Medical Insurance with Hospital Insurance in a single program would enable a person to pay for his medical-insurance protection during his working career, rather than after retirement when his income is reduced. Also, a single program would automatically cover all eligible aged beneficiaries and minimize the possibility that some might refuse the coverage because they could not afford the monthly premium.

Assistance from general revenues is a second important financing recommendation. The Advisory Council on Social Security recommends that they be used to finance one-third of the Medicare costs; employees and employers would each pay another third.

Four reasons are used to justify general-revenue financing for part of the Medicare costs. First, general revenues are necessary to pay part of the costs of protection for those already old when the Medicare program was first started, and to relieve the present and future generations of meeting these costs entirely by OASDHI contributions.

Second, general-revenue financing can provide for greater equity to individual workers. Although OASDHI cash benefits have some relationship to the covered earnings of worker and the tax contributions paid on those earnings,

[27]Advisory Council, *Reports,* p. 58.

under the Hospital Insurance portion of the Medicare Program, the protection is the same for all, regardless of the worker's earnings. A person who has only the minimum amount of coverage to be insured and makes only a minimum tax contribution has the same protection as the worker who has paid maximum taxes into the program throughout his entire working career. Thus, some groups pay tax contributions for Medicare benefits, which are considerably less than the actuarial value of their protection. In the absence of a general-revenue contribution, the regular worker and his employer, especially the highest paid worker, will be paying contributions exceeding the actuarial value of their protection in order to subsidize those workers who do not pay the full cost of the protection. It is argued, therefore, that general revenues should be used for this subsidization. Thus, the financial burden would fall partly on the nation as a whole rather than on the workers alone.

Third, general-revenue contributions are thought justified because of the savings to the taxpayers under the Medicare program. Without Medicare, the federal government would have the financial burden or providing necessary health care to the aged, and these increased costs would eventually have to be paid by all taxpayers. So since the nation as a whole benefits from Medicare, the saving in general revenues from such a program should be used partly to pay the costs of these persons whose contributions do not cover the full cost of their protection.

Finally, the Advisory Council on Social Security argues that the federal government now pays about one-fifth of the program costs (half the costs of Medical Insurance, plus the costs of Hospital Insurance for the uninsured aged covered under the transitional provision), and that moving to a one-third level is not unrealistic.[28]

Administrative Defects. As stated earlier, the Social Security Administration enters into contracts with fiscal intermediaries to help administer the Medicare program. However, a Senate Finance Committee report indicated that the performance of these intermediaries—private carriers, Blue Cross and Blue Shield, and state agencies—with respect to the administration of Medicare was often erratic, inefficient, costly, and inconsistent with congressional intent.[29] Private health insurers often allowed higher Medicare payments than their own plans paid; the quality of information submitted by the companies was often inadequate; cost controls were seldom rigidly enforced; and the Blue Shield plans initially refused to comply with a request to identify physicians who had been paid $25,000 or more under the Medicare program.

Prior to the 1972 amendments, the performance-evaluation reports on private health insurers, state agencies, and other fiscal intermediaries were considered confidential and not available to the general public. Some critics of the Medicare program said that the lack of public disclosure simply concealed the poor performance of many private carriers and intermediaries. There is a basic conflict, however, between the public's right to know and premature or errone-

[28]Advisory Council, *Reports,* pp. 70-72.

[29]U.S. Congress, Senate, Committee on Finance, *Medicare and Medicaid: Problems, Issues, and Alternatives,* 91st Cong., 1st sess., 1970 (Washington, D.C.: U.S. Government Printing Office, 1970), p. 20.

ous information that could seriously damage the contractor's reputation. The public should be made aware of the poor performance record of certain contractors, yet at the same time, the contractors should be allowed a reasonable time to review the reports before they are released, to avoid erroneous findings that could seriously damage their professional reputations.

In order to improve the administration of Medicare, the 1972 amendments provided for public disclosure of individual performance reports on private carriers, intermediaries, and state agencies; comparative evaluation reports of contractor performance; and program validation survey reports with the names of individuals omitted. But before the release date of a deficiency report, the concerned organization has the right to review the material to correct errors or issue a statement. However, only reports after January 1973 are available to the public; earlier reports are still considered confidential. The 1972 amendments also provided for public disclosure of deficiency reports regarding skilled nursing homes, home health agencies, and independent laboratories. The names of physicians and providers who have overcharged or have been convicted of submitting false statements will also be made public.

The secretary of Health, Education and Welfare is authorized to suspend or terminate Medicare payments to a provider who abuses the program; all Medicare providers must have a written overall plan that reflects an annual operating budget and capital-expenditure plan; there is a prohibition against reassignment of claims for benefits; payment can be cut off to patients and physicians for unnecessary hospitalization or admission to a skilled nursing facility; paramedical personnel must be tested for proficiency; and there are various penalties for fraudulent acts and false reporting. These recommendations should significantly improve the overall effectiveness of the Medicare program.

Financial Burden to the Aged. In 1973, about 18 percent of the family heads aged 65 and over, and about 49 percent of the unrelated individuals 65 or over, were either poor or members of low-income groups.[30] The high medical expenses that are not covered by Medicare can be a crushing financial burden for many of these poverty-stricken aged. They must deplete what savings they have accumulated, seek assistance from public programs, or receive help from relatives and friends.

It is clear that the Medicare program provides less than complete protection for medical expense incurred by the aged. In fiscal 1973, Medicare paid only 40 percent of their total medical expenses.[31] Several factors account for this relatively low percentage. First, there are many deductibles and coinsurance requirements in the program, primarily to control costs and reduce overutilization of benefits. It is argued, however, that they are ineffective for this purpose, since the physician is primarily responsible for utilization of the Medi-

[30]Anyone with an income below 125 percent of the poverty line is considered either poor or a member of a low-income group. See U.S. Bureau of the Census, *Current Population Reports,* P-60, No. 98, "Characteristics of the Low-Income Population: 1973," (Washington, D.C.: U.S. Government Printing Office, 1975), p. 145, Table 50, and p. 151, Table 51.

[31]U.S. Department of Health, Education and Welfare, Social Security Administration, Office of Research and Statistics, *Age Differences in Medical Care Spending, Fiscal Year 1973,* Note No. 8 (March 27, 1974), p. 1.

care program. It is he who decides whether the patient should be hospitalized or treated in a less costly outpatient facility; when to discharge the patient from the hospital and when to admit him to an extended-care facility; the number of office visits the patient requires; or whether surgery is necessary. Thus, the physician and not the patient is primarily responsible for utilization and control of costs.

Also, the deductibles under Hospital Insurance have steadily increased over time. The initial deductible for Hospital Insurance has risen from $40 originally to $92, the daily deductible for the 61st through 90th day from $10 originally to $23, and the daily deductible for the 21st through the 100th day for care in a skilled nursing facility from $5 to $11.50. Finally, the aged must meet a calendar-year deductible of $60 (up from $50) for the Part B portion of Medicare, plus a coinsurance requirement of 20 percent of the reasonable bill over a calendar-year deductible of $60. The combined impact of all deductibles can be financially burdensome for many low-income aged.

Medicare's numerous exclusions and limitations on coverages—and especially for prescription drugs outside hospitals—can present a severe financial burden to many low-income aged. Eyeglasses, hearing aids, dentures, and prosthetic devices, important medical expenditures for many aged persons, are also excluded. And when a transfusion is necessary, the patient must replace or pay for the first three pints of blood. Replacing it can be difficult for aged patients, since they and most of their friends are beyond the age for donating blood, and voluntary donors are often hard to find. Thus, many aged are forced to pay for the blood they need.[32] In addition, long-term care in a skilled nursing facility, and custodial care, are also excluded.

A third financial burden for some aged persons has been the periodic increases in the Part B monthly premium. However, this burden will be partially reduced in the future. The 1972 amendments provided that Medical Insurance premiums can be increased only if general OASDHI benefits have risen since the last premium increase, that the percentage of premium increase cannot exceed the percentage of cash-benefit increase, and that total beneficiary premiums cannot exceed half the total program costs.

Finally, Medicare is financially burdensome to the aged because of the assignment provision. As mentioned earlier, the physician can accept an assignment of benefits from the patient, whereby the physician agrees to accept the carrier's determination of a reasonable charge as his full fee. Except for the deductible and coinsurance requirements, aged patients pay nothing extra under this method. However, only about 55 percent of physicians accept an assignment of Medicare benefits,[33] and when they refuse it, the aged patients must pay the difference between what the doctor actually charges and what the fiscal intermediary says is a fair and reasonable fee. The excess amounts paid by elderly patients represent, in effect, a perverse form of reverse income redistribution—from the low-income aged to the upper-income physicians.

[32]U.S. Congress, Senate, Committee on Finance, *Social Security Amendments of 1971,* Hearings before the Committee on Finance, 92d Cong., 1st and 2d sess., on H.R.1, 1972, Part 4, p. 1806.

[33]U.S. Department of Health, Education and Welfare, Social Security Administration, Office of Research and Statistics, *Assignment Rates for Supplementary Medical Insurance Claims, Calendar Years 1970-72,* Health Insurance Note 46 (June 30, 1973), p. 2.

TEMPORARY-DISABILITY INSURANCE

Five states, as well as Puerto Rico and the railroad industry, have social insurance programs that provide partial replacement of wages lost because of a temporary disability. Rhode Island enacted the first temporary-disability insurance law in 1942, California in 1946, New Jersey in 1948, New York in 1949, Puerto Rico in 1968, and Hawaii in 1969. The cash benefits are designed to replace for a limited period part of the wages lost by insured workers who are unemployed because of sickness or injury.[34]

Although the programs are designed primarily to meet the problem of *nonoccupational illness or injury,* a few states may pay cash benefits for occupational disability under certain conditions. In California, Rhode Island, and Puerto Rico, the benefits are paid to temporarily disabled workers without regard to whether they are employed, unemployed, or in noncovered employment when their disability begins. Hawaii, New Jersey, and New York have two systems: (1) disability benefits for workers who become disabled while employed or shortly thereafter, and (2) disability benefits for people who become disabled while unemployed.

Coverage

The temporary-disability laws generally cover most commercial and industrial employees in private industry in the six jurisdictions. The major occupations usually excluded are government employees, interstate railroad workers, family workers, some employees of nonprofit organizations, and domestic workers except in New York and Hawaii. California, Hawaii, and Puerto Rico also cover agricultural workers in varying degrees, and Hawaii also covers state and local government employees. Self-employed people in California can elect to be covered on a voluntary basis. And in California and Rhode Island, individual workers can elect out of the program for religious reasons.

Methods for Providing Protection

In Rhode Island, a monopoly state fund provides benefits to all covered workers. In California, New Jersey, and Puerto Rico, the benefits can be provided either by a competitive state fund or by private insurers if an administrative agency approves the private plan. Hawaii and New York require firms to take positive action to provide temporary-disability insurance for their employees. In New York, the employees can self-insure, purchase the protection from private insurers, or obtain coverage from a competitive state fund. In Hawaii, the firms can either purchase the protection from private insurers or have an approved self-insurance plan; there is also a special state fund for unemployed workers, employees of bankrupt companies, and employees of noncomplying firms.

---

[34] A current description of temporary-disability insurance laws can be found in U.S. Department of Labor, Manpower Administration, *Comparison of State Unemployment Insurance Laws* (Washington, D.C.: U.S. Government Printing Office, 1972). This volume is periodically updated with supplements. The following section is based on the various laws as of January 1, 1975.

In those jurisdictions where private plans can be substituted for the state plan, certain statutory standards must be fulfilled. In California, the private plan must provide benefits at least equal in all respects to those provided by the state plan, and greater in at least one respect. In New Jersey, Hawaii, and Puerto Rico, the private-plan benefits must be at least as favorable as those provided by state plans. In New York, the private plan is not required to fulfill precisely all of the statutory benefits prescribed by law, but its benefits must be actuarially equivalent to the state formula, and certain minimum standards must be met. Cash benefits may be reduced if the private plan has a shorter waiting period, or extra benefits, such as hospital benefits.

Eligibility Requirements

Three major eligibility requirements are typically imposed before the claimant can receive benefits. (1) he must meet certain earnings or employment requirements; (2) he must be disabled as defined in the law, and (3) he must not have disqualifying income.

Earnings or Employment Requirements. The claimant must have a certain amount of past employment and/or qualifying wages to receive benefits. The purpose of this requirement is to limit benefits to only those who have demonstrated a substantial attachment to the labor force. New Jersey requires 17 weeks of employment, with weekly wages of at least $15. Hawaii requires 14 weeks of employment, for at least 20 hours in each week, and wages of $400 during the four completed calendar quarters preceding the first day of disability. Rhode Island requires 20 weeks of employment, with wages of at least $20 for each week, or $1,200 in wages in the base period. In California, the workers may qualify for benefits with $300 of earnings. New York covers the worker after four or more consecutive weeks of employment, and the protection continues for four weeks following termination of employment. Private plans, however, seldom use a base-period earnings or employment requirement to determine eligibility. The workers are either immediately insured or are required to serve a probationary period, such as one to three months.

Disability Requirements. The worker must be disabled as defined in the law. The intent of the laws is to cover the worker for a nonoccupational injury or illness. Disability is generally defined as the inability of the worker to perform his regular or customary work because of a physical or mental condition. New Jersey requires that the claimant be unable to perform any work for remuneration, and New York that he be unable to perform any work for which he is reasonably qualified by training and experience.

Certain types of disabilities are excluded. Four jurisdictions (California, New York, New Jersey, Puerto Rico) exclude or limit benefits for pregnancy. Disability caused by willfully self-inflicted injuries or by an illegal act is excluded in Hawaii, New Jersey, New York, and Puerto Rico. And California and Puerto Rico prohibit payments to drug addicts, dipsomaniacs, or sexual psychopaths who are confined in institutions.

Disqualifying Income. The claimant must not be receiving any disqualifying income. All states deny claims of people who are receiving unemployment insurance benefits, and they restrict temporary-disability benefits if workmen's compensation benefits are being paid. In California, a claimant who is eligible for workmen's compensation benefits cannot receive temporary-disability benefits unless the disability benefit is higher; in such a case, the worker is entitled to the difference from the disability fund. Hawaii pays no disability benefits if the worker is receiving workmen's compensation benefits, with the exception of those for permanent partial disability or total disability previously incurred. New Jersey excludes the payment of disability benefits for any week during which workmen's compensation is paid, other than for permanent partial or permanent total disability. New York excludes disabilities arising out of and in the course of employment, regardless of whether workmen's compensation is paid, and excludes benefits for any period during which workmen's compensation is paid, with the exception of permanent partial-disability benefits for a prior disability. In Rhode Island and Puerto Rico, a worker can receive disability benefits if there is doubt concerning his eligibility for workmen's compensation; the disability benefits must be repaid, however, if workmen's compensation benefits are received later. Finally, some jurisdictions have restrictions on temporary-disability benefits if the claimant is receiving regular wages even though he is not working, or is receiving income from an employer pension plan.

Benefits

A weekly disability-income benefit is the typical benefit paid in most jurisdictions. It is related to the claimant's previous earnings in covered employment and is normally intended to replace at least one-half his weekly wage for a limited period. All jurisdictions, however, have limits on the maximum and minimum amounts that can be paid. A waiting period of seven consecutive days of disability is generally required before the benefits begin. In California and Puerto Rico, the waiting period is waived if the worker is hospitalized. As of January 1975, the maximum weekly benefit was $119 in California, $104 in Hawaii, $85 in New Jersey ($90 for unemployed workers), $95 in New York, $72 in Rhode Island, and $90 in Puerto Rico ($30 for agricultural workers). The duration of benefit payments in all jurisdictions is generally limited to a maximum of 26 weeks.

In addition to weekly disability-income benefits, California also provides for a hospital and nursing-home benefit of $12 daily for 20 days in any one benefit period. No waiting period is required for hospital benefits.

Financing

Temporary-disability insurance benefits are financed by payroll taxes on covered wages. In all six jurisdictions, the covered employees must contribute to the programs, and in four of the six, the employers must also contribute.

In Rhode Island, the state plan is financed by an employee payroll tax of 1½ percent on the first $4,800 of annual wages. In California, workers covered under the state fund pay a 1 percent payroll tax on the first $9,000 of annual wages; the self-employed subscribers pay 1.25 percent on wages of $2,850 a quarter. In New Jersey, the state plan is financed by an employee payroll tax of 0.50 percent on the first $4,800 of annual covered wages, and employers pay a basic rate of 0.50 percent of covered payroll, which is subject to modification by experience rating. Employees insured under private plans in New Jersey, California, and Puerto Rico cannot pay more than they would pay to the state fund. In New York, the covered employees contribute 0.50 percent on the first $60 of weekly wages up to a maximum of 30 cents weekly; the employers must bear any additional costs of the plan. In Puerto Rico, both employees and employers contribute 0.5 percent of the worker's wages up to $9,000. In Hawaii, the employee contributions are limited to one-half the cost of providing benefits, with a maximum limit of 0.50 percent of weekly earnings up to the annual taxable wage base. The employers pay the balance of the costs.

Administration

In Rhode Island, New Jersey, California, and Puerto Rico, the temporary-disability insurance programs are administered by the same agency that administers the unemployment-insurance program. In New York, however, the plan is administered by the state workmen's compensation board, and in Hawaii, by the Department of Labor and Industrial Relations.

One advantage of having the unemployment-insurance agency administer the law is that the temporary-disability program can be closely coordinated with unemployment insurance. The administrative agency collects the payroll contributions, maintains wage records, determines eligibility, and pays benefits to the workers under the state-operated programs. The claimants file their claims by mail with the agency.

In contrast, in New York and Hawaii, claims are filed with the employers, the private insurers, or the labor union health and welfare fund that operates the private plan. The determination and payment of disability benefits are handled almost exclusively by these organizations. The state agency is limited to supervising the private plans, establishing performance standards, and settling disputed claims.

Employees insured by private plans in California, New Jersey, and Puerto Rico must also file claims with the private concerns, and the state unemployment agency is limited to only supervisory and adjudicative functions.

Problems and Issues

Among the problems associated with the temporary-disability insurance plans is the fact that the private-insurance market for temporary-disability benefits has been declining relative to the state funds. The proper balance between private insurers and state funds is a sensitive issue, and the arguments for and against state funds are similar to those regarding workmen's compensation insurance.

In California, coverage under private plans declined from 52 percent in 1951 to about 7 percent in 1973; in New Jersey, from about 65 percent in 1956 to about 37 percent in 1971. The reason for the sharp decline is that private insurers cannot effectively compete with the state funds under the current benefit and financing provisions.

Private insurers in California have found it difficult to compete with the state fund because of unfavorable legal requirements, which include periodic statutory liberalization of benefits. Also, regulations that were adopted in 1961 now prevent private insurers from covering only selected low-risks based on age, sex, and wage levels. These regulations, intended to reduce adverse selection against the state fund, have hindered the operations of private insurers in California, giving them such difficulty in competing with the state fund that they have gradually lost most of their market.

In New Jersey, the state fund has been able to provide temporary-disability benefits on more favorable terms to employers than the plans provided by private insurers. In the past, the state plan has paid out more in benefits than it has received in contributions, and has met the deficit by drawing on a cash reserve. Since the benefits paid were not matched by higher employer tax rates or wage levels, the state plan cost less for employers than did those of private insurers, which have to charge premiums that are commensurate with the benefits. The appearance of artificially low costs for the state plan was a formidable obstacle for the private companies to overcome, and they gradually lost part of their market to the state fund. In recent years, the deficits in the state fund were financed largely by transferring funds from the unemployment-insurance program, but in 1971, New Jersey increased both employer and employee contribution rates to generate additional revenues for the state plan, and the higher costs should improve the competitive position somewhat for the private insurers.

The adequacy of benefits is another important issue. Because of restrictions on coverage, exclusions of certain groups, waiting periods, and statutory limits on benefits, the programs fall short of providing substantial economic security to workers who have nonoccupational disabilities. Although more than four-fifths of the employees in private industry are covered in the six jurisdictions with temporary-disability insurance plans, other groups in need of protection—such as domestic workers, government employees, and employees of nonprofit organizations—are generally excluded. Thus, to the extent that these groups are excluded from coverage, the goal of universal short-term income protection for nonoccupational disabilities is not being attained.

Finally, temporary-disability insurance plans restore only a small fraction of the total wages lost during periods of nonoccupational disability. In 1970, the plans restored only about 29 percent of the total wages lost by workers in private industry who were covered by temporary-disability insurance laws.[35]

SUGGESTIONS FOR ADDITIONAL READING

Advisory Council on Social Security, *Reports of the 1971 Advisory Council on Social Security.* HD. No. 92-80, Committee on Ways and Means,

[35]*Social Security Bulletin,* January 1972, p. 27.

92d Cong., 1st sess., 1971. Washington, D.C.: U.S. Government Printing Office, 1971.

Commerce Clearing House, *1974 Social Security and Medicare Explained —Including Medicaid.* Chicago: Commerce Clearing House, Inc., 1974.

Feldstein, Martin S., "An Econometric Model of the Medicare System," *The Quarterly Journal of Economics,* Vol. LXXXV, No. 1 (February 1971).

Franklin, Paula A., "The Disabled Widow," *Social Security Bulletin,* Vol. 38, No. 1 (January 1975).

Myers, Robert J., *Medicare.* Homewood, Ill.: Richard D. Irwin, 1970.

Smith, Richard T., and Abraham M. Lilienfeld, *The Social Security Disability Program: An Evaluation Study,* Research Report No. 39, U.S. Department of Health, Education and Welfare, Social Security Administration, Office of Research and Statistics. Washington, D.C.: U.S. Government Printing Office, 1971.

Somers, Herman M., and Anne R. Somers, *Medicare and the Hospitals: Issues and Prospects.* Washington, D.C.: The Brookings Institution, 1967.

Turnbull, John G., C. Arthur Williams, Jr., and Earl F. Cheit, *Economic and Social Security,* 4th ed., Chaps. 11 and 12. New York: Ronald Press, 1973.

U.S. Congress, House, Committee on Ways and Means, *Committee Staff Report on the Disability Income Program.* Washington, D.C.: U.S. Government Printing Office, 1974.

U.S. Congress, Senate, Committee on Finance, *Medicare and Medicaid: Problems, Issues, and Alternatives,* Committee on Finance, 91st Cong., 1st sess., 1970. Washington, D.C.: U.S. Government Printing Office, 1970.

U.S. Department of Health, Education and Welfare, Social Security Administration, *Your Medicare Handbook.* Washington, D.C.: U.S. Government Printing Office, 1974.

chapter 11

National Health Insurance

The United States is one of the few advanced nations in the world that does not have some form of national health insurance covering its citizens. Such a plan has been proposed to solve our health-care crisis.

National health insurance is a delicate and sensitive issue, involving consumers, the medical profession, state and federal government, labor unions, and private health insurers. There has been considerable discussion and analysis of the various proposals, shedding much light on the desirability of such a plan in the United States.[1] In this chapter, we shall consider the following topics: (1) the rationale for a national health insurance plan, (2) the criteria for an effective plan, and (3) the major national health insurance legislative proposals.

RATIONALE FOR NATIONAL HEALTH INSURANCE

The justification for national health insurance can be reduced to four major arguments: (1) the basic right of all citizens to medical care, (2) reform of the present health-care delivery system, (3) the inferior medical care received by the poor, and (4) greater redistribution of income.

[1]For an excellent discussion of national health insurance issues, see Robert D. Eilers and Sue S. Moyerman, eds., *National Health Insurance: Proceedings of the Conference on National Health Insurance* (Homewood, Ill.: Richard D. Irwin, 1971). See also Tax Foundation, Inc. *Problems and Issues in National Health Insurance* (New York: Tax Foundation, Inc., 1974).

Basic Right to Medical Care

Proponents of national health insurance feel that all citizens have a basic right to medical care, and a national plan would ensure equitable treatment by providing access to high-quality care to all.

The right of every citizen to a basic education is often cited as a parallel to support a plan for national health insurance. Regardless of his ability to pay for it, each citizen is entitled to a public elementary and high school education. In contrast, it is said, medical care is generally available only to those who can afford it, and since many citizens cannot, they may not receive the medical care they require. Thus, according to the argument, medical care should be considered a social good, available to all citizens, and a national health insurance plan would ensure that availability.

The public-education analogy is a slippery concept, which must be carefully analyzed. The right to medical care and the right to public education involve subtle differences. First, public education involves compulsory school attendance until a stated age and the observance of state laws regarding education. In contrast, with few exceptions, a citizen cannot be forced by law to undergo medical treatment even if it is necessary to correct a serious health condition.[2]

Second, the government does not pay for other necessary goods and services for people who can afford them. For example, the government provides money for food, shelter, and clothing to the poor under public-assistance programs; but although these goods are absolutely essential, the government would be abusing its power if it made food, clothing, and shelter available to all citizens, regardless of their ability to pay. Consequently, it is argued that since most Americans can afford medical care, as evidenced by the widespread ownership of private health-insurance contracts, a federal subsidy to all citizens for medical care, regardless of their ability to pay, is unnecessary and unsound.

Despite these philosophical hangups, however, it is generally agreed that all citizens should have access to medical care, and that the lack of ability to pay for it should not be a barrier.

Reformation of Health-Services Delivery System

As indicated in Chapter 8, the present health-services delivery system is marred by numerous defects, including spiraling medical costs, inadequate access to medical care, waste and inefficiency, ineffective financing, and consumer dissatisfaction. The traditional fee-for-service approach to payment for medical care, the solo practice of medicine, and the inadequacies of private health insurance are also being severely criticized. Thus, it is argued that, to reform the present system, a new system of national health insurance under government sponsorship is necessary. Some proposals would simply build on the present system, while others, more drastic, would scrap it and replace it with an entirely new one. The various national health insurance proposals will be analyzed later in the chapter.

[2]Eilers and Moyerman, *National Health Insurance,* p. 263.

Inferior Medical Care to the Poor

National health insurance, it is proposed, is also needed to correct the critical problem of the inadequate medical care received by the poor. As we have seen, the low-income groups are in relatively poorer health than the general population; they have inadequate access to high-quality medical care because of their inability to pay and the unwillingness of many physicians to practice in ghetto areas.

Of course, proponents say, that any new system should not be limited to only the poor, since they may be stigmatized by the use of such services; instead, a new national health insurance system should be created to cover all citizens. This point can be illustrated by the experience of OEO Community Comprehensive Health Care Centers in black ghetto areas in Philadelphia. Although the quality of medical care they provided was often superior to that received by middle-income and upper-income suburban residents, the utilization of these centers was relatively low, since the blacks viewed this type of medical care as a form of "poor man's medicine," and they wanted instead what the affluent members of the community received.[3]

Greater Redistribution of Income

A less persuasive argument is that national health insurance would result in a greater distribution of income, since it would involve substantial subsidies from the middle- and upper-income groups to the poor.

However, there are better ways of redistributing income than by national health insurance. If a reduction in poverty and greater income equality are national goals, then it would be better to redistribute cash income, by means of a negative income tax plan or a modification of the tax system. Cash payments to the poor would enable them to spend their income according to their needs, rather than forcing them to spend the funds on medical care. In addition, cash payments to the poor are preferable from the viewpoint of political decision making, since the issue of income redistribution is made clear.[4]

CRITERIA FOR EFFECTIVE NATIONAL HEALTH INSURANCE

An effective national health insurance program should ideally aim at correcting each of the defects in the present health-care delivery system. Competent researchers who have studied the idea of national health insurance generally agree that the following requirements should be fulfilled: (1) universal coverage, (2) comprehensive benefits, (3) equitable financing, (4) effective cost controls, (5) consumer and provider acceptance, (6) efficient administration, (7) reorganization of health care, and (8) advance preparation.[5]

[3]Statement of Charles Hall in Eilers and Moyerman, *National Health Insurance*, p. 261.

[4]Statement of Mark V. Pauly in *Ibid.*, pp. 106-7.

[5]See Herman M. Somers and Anne R. Somers, "Major Issues in National Health Insurance," *Milbank Memorial Fund Quarterly*, Vol. I, No. 2, Part 1 (April 1972), 177-209; and Eilers and Moyerman, *National Health Insurance*. The following section is based on these sources.

Universal Coverage

Universal coverage of the population would be necessary for a national health insurance plan to be effective. No one who desires coverage should be excluded. The goal of economic security for the nation is more easily achieved when the entire population is protected against the risk of financial ruin from poor health and the inability to pay for medical care.

In addition, the goal of universal protection should not be defeated through the imposition of stringent eligibility requirements that limit entry into the plan. In other words, no one should be excluded because of age, geographical location, social class or income, race, religion, or political beliefs. And pre-existing conditions should not be used to limit entry into the plan.

Comprehensive Benefits

An effective national health insurance plan should provide comprehensive health benefits to consumers. It should offer inpatient hospital care, private-duty nursing, extended-facility and nursing-home care, dental care, personal preventive medicine, rehabilitation services, ambulatory drugs, prosthetic devices, eyeglasses and dentures, and transportation to health faciiities. it should also provide mental-health services and the establishment of mental-health facilities.

In addition, the plan should stress preventive care and health-maintenance programs, such as health education and the formation of good health habits with respect to smoking, drugs, obesity, and accident prevention. It should provide for the early detection, screening, and treatment of certain diseases that are best treated when diagnosed in their early stages—for instance, glaucoma, hypertension, breast and cervical cancer, diabetes, hormone deficiencies, amblyopia, and PKU.

Effective Financing

A sound national health insurance plan should establish an effective financing system for health care. The financing of costs should be done in a way that is fair to all, with the cost burden distributed equitably among the various segments of the population.

Methods of Financing. Various combinations of premiums, payroll taxes, general revenues, and tax credits can be used to finance the costs of national health insurance,[6] and deductibles and coinsurance can be used as cost-sharing devices.

1. Premiums. The participants in the plan could be charged a specific premium, as in private health insurance, thus offering the advantage of an identifiable cost to the consumer. The disadvantage of this approach is that a

---

[6]For a discussion of these approaches, see Charles L. Schultze, Edward R. Fried, Alice M. Rivlin, and Nancy H. Teeters, *Setting National Priorities: The 1972 Budget* (Washington, D.C.: The Brookings Institution, 1971). See also Robert D. Eilers, *Financing Health Care: Past and Prospects* (Minneapolis: Federal Reserve Bank of Minneapolis, 1974).

uniform premium for all participants could be burdensome to the poor. This could be overcome by grading the premium downward according to the amount of income, but such a method would introduce a form of needs test into the program. It would also tend to identify the poor and possibly result in two separate insurance programs, with a splintering of the insured population as a result.

2. Payroll Taxes. A specific payroll tax to finance national health insurance would have the advantages of ease of collection, restraint on costs, and an increasing source of revenue as the economy grows. However, relying exclusively on a payroll tax has certain disadvantages. Both employers and employees might protest the significant increase in payroll taxes necessary to fund a national health insurance plan. The combined employer-employee OASDHI tax for 1975 was 11.70 percent on a taxable wage base of $14,100, and additional increases might be vigorously resisted.

Such a tax would be especially burdensome for low-wage earners, because it is a flat percentage of earnings up to some maximum level, because it makes no allowances for family size, and because, in the long run, employees bear not only their portion of the total payroll tax but that of employers as well when it is shifted backward to them in the form of lower wage increases, or forward in the form of higher prices.[7]

3. General Revenues. To finance all or part of the cost of national health insurance, the federal government could make a contribution out of its general revenues for that purpose. Since the bulk of federal general-revenue funds is derived from the personal and corporate income tax, and these taxes are more progressive than a flat payroll tax, the result would be to shift more of the cost burden of a national health insurance plan to the middle- and upper-income groups.

4. Tax Credits. If tax credits were used to finance a national health insurance plan, taxpayers would be allowed to deduct the premiums paid to the plan from their income tax liability. In effect, the taxes that would have been paid to the federal government would be used to finance the plan.

The tax-credit plan has the advantage of a minimum of federal control. It has the disadvantage, however, of not being an effective solution to the payment of health-care expenses by the poor. Low-income families generally pay little or no personal income taxes, so tax credits would not provide the funds for their payment of the insurance premiums. A government subsidy, such as an outright grant for payment of the premiums, would still be necessary.

5. Deductibles and Coinsurance. Two major advantages are claimed for the use of deductibles and coinsurance as cost-sharing provisions in a national health insurance plan: (1) they would hold down costs, and (2) they would reduce overutilization of benefits. On the other hand, people who require medical care might be discouraged from seeking treatment because of the deductible or coinsurance requirements. This consideration is particularly important in the case of the poor.

The impact of coinsurance and deductibles on the utilization of benefits is

[7]See John A. Brittain, *The Payroll Tax for Social Security* (Washington, D.C.: The Brookings Institution, 1972), pp. 252-55.

not completely clear at the present time, but research studies strongly suggest that utilization of benefits declines when a substantial coinsurance requirement is introduced into a plan. A Blue Cross-Blue Shield study showed that the introduction in one plan of a coinsurance requirement of 25 percent on hospital stays resulted in a 10 percent decrease in hospital admissions and a slight decrease in the duration of hospitalization. When the coinsurance requirement was subsequently removed, both hospital admissions and length of stays increased.[8]

Another study, by Scitovsky and Snyder, indicated that coinsurance leads to a substantial reduction in the use of physicians' services. The introduction of a 25 percent coinsurance requirement in a comprehensive plan for prepaid medical care resulted in a sharp reduction of about 24 percent in per capita physicians' services and also a decline of about 24 percent in the per capita cost of these services.[9]

These findings raise two questions: (1) does coinsurance reduce overutilization, and (2) does it discourage members from seeking medical care? With respect to the first question, Scitovsky and Snyder concluded that, after the coinsurance provision was introduced, the members *reduced their demand for the care of minor illnesses considerably more than they did their demand for care of other conditions.*[10] Visits to physicians for colds, respiratory infections, hay fever, coughs, and other minor ailments declined about 23 percent after the coinsurance requirement was introduced. Thus, the study suggests, coinsurance can reduce utilization of benefits for minor ailments.

There is always the danger, of course, that the lack of treatment for a minor disease may lead to a more serious disease later; so consideration must be given to whether people are dissuaded from seeking needed medical care because of coinsurance. An annual physical examination is assumed to be essential for good health, and Scitovsky and Snyder found that the insertion of coinsurance in the group prepaid plan under study led to a decline of about 19 percent in the per capita number of annual physical examinations. This suggests that coinsurance does indeed discourage members from seeking needed medical care.

It would seem that coinsurance might be suitable for middle- and upper-income families, but might impose a substantial financial burden on low-income families. This could be avoided by eliminating coinsurance entirely from national health insurance, or by reducing downward the coinsurance percentage for low-income groups. In addition, an across-the-board coinsurance requirement of 20 or 25 percent could deprive both low- and middle-income families of

[8]Statement of Robert M. Ball in U.S. Congress, Senate, Subcommittee on Health of the Elderly, *Barriers to Health Care for Older Americans,* Hearings before the Subcommittee on Aging, 93d Cong., 1st sess., 1973, Part 1, p. 88.

[9]Anne A. Scitovsky and Nelda M. Snyder, "Effect of Coinsurance on Use of Physician Services," *Social Security Bulletin,* Vol. 35, No. 6 (June 1972), p. 7. See also Blue Cross Association, *The Effects of Deductibles, Coinsurance, and Copayment on Utilization of Health Care Services— Opinions and Impressions from Blue Cross and Blue Shield Plans* (September 28, 1971); Charles P. Hall, "Deductibles in Health Insurance: An Evaluation," *The Journal of Risk and Insurance,* June 1966; and R.G. Beck, "The Effect of Co-Payment on the Poor," *The Journal of Human Resources,* Vol. IX, No. 1 (Winter 1974), 129-42.

[10]Scitovsky and Snyder, "Effect of Coinsurance," p. 15.

financial protection against catastrophic medical expenses. For example, with 25 percent coinsurance, a serious illness that results in a total medical bill of $20,000 would require an out-of-pocket outlay of $5,000. This could seriously deplete the savings of many families. Thus, an efficient financing plan should have a maximum absolute dollar limit on expenses to which the coinsurance percentage is applied. All covered medical expenses in excess of that maximum would be paid in full.

Financing Criteria. A system for financing a national health insurance plan should be judged by the following objectives:[11]

1. Elimination of Financial Barriers. No one should be denied needed health care because of an inability to pay; and the financing system should not discourage or delay preventive care and treatment.

2. Avoidance of Financial Hardship. No family or individual should be forced to bear an unusual financial hardship because of catastrophic medical expenses from an unpredictable illness or accident. The financing of the plan should clearly provide for the funding of large medical expenses to avoid financial hardship.

3. Avoidance of Initial Substantial Tax Increase. The financing plan should avoid an initial substantial tax increase to fund the program. A sharp tax increase may distort the supply of work effort and cause economic resources to be used inefficiently. Thus, a national health insuranc plan that takes large amounts away from the public in the form of higher taxes and returns them in the form of health-insurance benefits has a large hidden cost in the form of lower national income. In addition, a substantial tax increase is undesirable because it could cause the taxpayers to revolt and reject the plan.

The magnitude of total health-care spending must be recognized when tax increases are contemplated. For example, during fiscal year 1968-69, consumers spent about $34 billion on personal health care. If this private spending were transferred to the public sector, individual income tax collections would have increased by more than 30 percent; if the OASDHI payroll tax had been used to finance these expenditures, the rate would have more than doubled.[12]

Effective Cost Controls

A sound national health insurance plan should provide effective cost controls in order to encourage the efficient use of resources and discourage price inflation in medical care. The plan should encourage the use of relatively lower-cost inpatient hospital care. It should provide effective cost controls for hospitals, to moderate the forces that increase their costs, such as unnecessary duplication of equipment, unnecessarily high salaries, and increased personnel. Physician cost controls should also be used, to prevent higher fees and the overcharging of patients because of insurance. Finally, the financing method should encourage and foster cost-consciousness among physicians, hospital administrations, and patients.

[11]Martin S. Feldstein, "A New Approach to National Health Insurance," *Public Interest,* Spring 1971, pp. 93-94.

[12]*Ibid.,* p. 94.

Acceptance by Consumers and Providers

An effective national health insurance plan must be acceptable to both consumers and providers of health care. A system consumers dislike may lead to political opposition and lack of plan acceptance; and lack of cooperation or hostility by physicians and hospitals could severely cripple the success of the plan.

The following factors are generally considered important in gaining consumer acceptance: (1) consumers must participate in policy-making decisions and plan design; (2) all consumers must be eligible for coverage; (3) comprehensive health services must be available; (4) consumers must have access to medical services no matter where they are located; (5) the costs of the plan must be acceptable and not present substantial financial barriers to needed medical care; (6) quality controls concerning the medical care provided must be strictly enforced; and (7) the plan must provide for continued research into, and development of, new health-care delivery models.[13]

For the plan to be politically acceptable to physicians and other suppliers of health care, certain other criteria are important: (1) federal control over the private practice of medicine must be kept to a minimum; (2) a pluralistic system is necessary, using both private health insurance and government agencies, rather than a single government monopoly for providing health care; (3) a variety of payment methods—fee-for-service, capitation, salary, and others—should be established; (4) consumer options and freedom in selection of physicians must be built into the plan; and (5) reorganization of health care and the introduction of new delivery models must be phased in gradually, without severely disrupting the present system.

It is obvious that the criteria above will not be completely fulfilled, since some conflict with others. For example, effective cost controls may be acceptable to consumers but unacceptable to physicians, if they feel that federal controls are seriously interfering with the private practice of medicine. In the last analysis, any national health insurance plan will reflect political compromises and trade-offs among consumers, physicians, and government.

Efficient Administration

Efficient administration is a major policy question that must be recognized when national health insurance proposals are being analyzed. Administrative procedures should not be unduly complex, costly, or inconvenient. Considerable attention is often devoted to the design of a new income-maintenance plan or economic-security program and the policy implications associated with it; but in far too many instances, inadequate attention is given to the administration of the plan, and the result is that the plan objectives are not fulfilled. The administrative procedures can be bureaucratic, slow, and cumbersome, and the program then becomes inordinately expensive to administer. The administrative framework must provide for flexibility and adaptability to changing circumstances, because of rapidly changing health-care technology.

---

[13]David A. Kindig and Victor W. Sidel, "Impact of National Health Insurance Plans on the Consumer," in Eilers and Moyerman, *National Health Insurance,* pp. 19-38.

Reorganization of Health Care

Any financing plan for national health insurance must consider and encourage the reorganization of health care and the development of new health-care delivery models. It must permit experimentation with prepaid group plans, health maintenance organizations, rural health-care delivery models, and others. It would be disastrous to pour billions of new dollars into the present system, marred as it is by fragmentation, waste, inefficiency, ineffective cost controls, and other defects. Any new health-insurance plan must permit the development of new models that are superior to the present system of health care.

Advance Preparation

Finally, the financing of national health insurance must allow for advance preparation—a gradual phasing in of the new plan, and a setting up of administration well in advance of the plan's effective date. In particular, the supply of new health-care personnel, including physicians, dentists, nurses, paraprofessionals, and other ancillary personnel, must be increased to the maximum extent possible before the plan becomes operative. It is particularly important to avoid repeating the same mistakes associated with the introduction of Medicare and Medicaid. The supply of new medical resources was not substantially increased before the implementation of those programs, and the result was a massive infusion of billions in new funds into an already-burdened health-care delivery system, causing severe price inflation in medical costs. This mistake must not be repeated when the new national health insurance plan becomes operational.

MAJOR NATIONAL HEALTH INSURANCE PROPOSALS

More than eighteen national health insurance proposals have been introduced into Congress.[14] For the sake of convenience and ease of understanding, these proposals can be grouped into five major categories: (1) monolithic federal program, (2) extension of Medicare, (3) mandatory employer purchase of private health insurance, (4) tax-incentive plans, and (5) catastrophe-illness insurance.

Monolithic Federal Program

This approach calls for establishing a monolithic federal program of

[14]A description of national health insurance proposals can be found in U.S. Congress, Senate, Committee on Finance, *National Health Insurance, Brief Outline of Pending Bills,* 93d Cong., 2d sess. (Washington, D.C.: U.S. Government Printing Office, 1974); Health Insurance Institute, *A Summary of Seven Nation Health Insurance Proposals—93rd Congress* (New York: Health Insurance Institute, 1974); Daniel W. Pettingil, "Writing the Prescription for Health Care," *Harvard Business Review,* November-December, 1971; and Somers and Somers, "Majors Issues," pp. 177-209.

national health insurance under the OASDHI program. The federal government would take over both the delivery and the financing of health care in the United States, and the role of private health insurers would be sharply curtailed.

The Comprehensive National Health Insurance Act of 1974, sponsored by Sen. Edward M. Kennedy and Cong. Wilbur D. Mills, is an example of a federal monolithic program. The major features of their proposal are summarized as follows:

1. *Basic Approach.* Comprehensive health benefits would be provided to the population under the Social Security Act. Medicare would be retained, but Medicaid would be eliminated. Private health insurers would be restricted to acting as fiscal intermediaries and writing limited supplementary coverages.

2. *Benefits.* Benefits would include inpatient hospital and physicians' services, medical and other health services, home health services, extended care, mental-health service, prescription drugs, dental services, preventive care, well-child care, and prenatal care.

3. *Financing.* Payroll taxes of 4 percent would be levied on annual earnings up to $20,000. The employer would pay 3 percent, and the employee would pay no more than 1 percent. The self-employed would pay 2.5 percent up to $20,000, and people with earnings under $20,000 would pay 2.5 percent on their unearned income. The cost of subsidizing deductibles and copayments for the poor would be derived from general revenues.

4. *Deductibles and Coinsurance.* No deductible would be imposed on preventive care. An annual per-person deductible of $150 would apply to other services, with a limit of two deductibles per family. A copayment charge of $1 would apply to each prescription, and 25 percent coinsurance would apply to other services. There would be a maximum limit of $1,000 per family on cost sharing, but a lower amount for low-income families. Deductibles and copayments for the poor would be subsidized.

5. *Administration.* The program would be administered by a separate Social Security agency through fiscal intermediaries. Private health insurers would serve as the intermediaries.

When measured against the criteria described earlier for an effective national health insurance plan, the Kennedy-Mills proposal contains several desirable features, but it is also defective in many respects. On the positive side, the proposal provides broad and comprehensive health services to the entire population (except those under Medicare), and the poor are not covered in a separate plan. Strong cost controls are built into the program. In addition, major financial barriers to comprehensive health care are eliminated. No family would pay more than $1,000 annually in out-of-pocket expenses, and low-income families would pay even less, while deductibles and coinsurance for the poor would be subsidized out of the general revenues of the federal government. Finally, the financing mechanism, which is based on Social Security principles, would reduce the administrative problem of determining eligibility.

Despite these advantages, the Kennedy-Mills plan violates several of the criteria and raises doubts concerning its efficiency and effectiveness. Three defects are immediately apparent. First, the establishment of a single monolithic federal program can itself be seriously questioned. The transferring of health care from the private to the federal sector could result in a bureaucratic and cumbersome administration, complex regulations, and centralized authority. Health care is a rapidly changing and explosive field, demanding administrative flexibility and decentralization of authority. Despite the merits of the reforms contained in the Kennedy-Mills proposal, it is doubtful that they could be implemented through a monolithic system.

Second, reducing the role of private health insurers would limit them to (1) acting as fiscal intermediaries in the administration of the program, and (2) selling supplementary coverages. Most companies would have only a minor role as fiscal intermediaries, and the market for supplementary coverage would be generally limited to covering the $150 deductible ($300 for a family), the $1 copayment charge for prescription drugs, and coinsurance payments up to $1,000. This curtailment could create some severe economic dislocations. It is estimated that more than 200,000 health-insurance employees would be displaced, and the states would lose over $300 million in premium taxes, compounding further the problem of inadequate sources of public revenues. Also, there may be serious defects in private health insurance, but it is doubtful whether a single federal program could avoid them any more efficiently. It could be a case of "throwing the baby out with the bath water." A pluralistic system of health care might prove more appropriate and effective in the last analysis.

Finally, the Kennedy-Mills proposal would result in large initial tax increases, thereby violating an important criterion. If their plan had been enacted in 1974, when it was proposed, maximum annual OASDHI tax contributions for the individual worker would have increased from $772 to $972, or about 26 percent. The maximum tax paid by the employer would have increased from $772 to $1,372, or about 78 percent.

Extension of Medicare

Another approach would involve the extension of the Medicare program to cover the entire population. The National Health Insurance and Health Improvements Act, sponsored by Sen. Jacob K. Javits, would establish a national health insurance plan based on the gradual expansion of Medicare to all citizens. Benefits would be broadened to include many services not covered under the present Medicare program. The major features of the proposal include the following:

1. *Basic Approach.* The Medicare program would be gradually extended to cover the entire population, with priority given to the poor and disabled. Private health insurers would be given the first opportunity to provide the coverage.

2. *Benefits.* Basic Medicare benefits (Parts A and B) would be provided to all. Annual physical examinations, prescription drugs, and dental care would be phased in at a later date. Catastrophe coverage would also be introduced later.

3. *Financing.* The program would be financed by a 3 percent payroll tax paid by employees, employers, and the self-employed, and by federal general-revenue contributions. The annual taxable wage base for workers would be $15,000; for employers, no annual taxable wage base would apply. The federal government would pay 50 percent of the total costs.

4. *Deductibles and Coinsurance.* These would be similar to the Medicare program. A $1 copayment charge would apply to prescription drugs.

5. *Administration.* The federal government and private fiscal intermediaries would administer the program, but the secretary of Health, Education and Welfare could enter into agreements with the states to administer the program.

The Medicare approach to national health insurance has several advantages. First, the plan and administrative machinery are already in existence, and Medicare has already been extended to certain groups under age 65.

Second, private health insurers would play an important role under this proposal. Their expertise could be utilized, and they would be given the first opportunity to provide the health-care services through contracts with the secretary of Health, Education and Welfare. If the private health insurers performed inadequately, then an autonomous U.S. corporation or corporations would be given the job.

Third, the program would provide for more effective cost controls. The patient would be specifically protected from the payment of disallowed services—those considered unnecessary, unreasonable, or inappropriate. In addition, Professional Standards Review Organizations (PSRO) would monitor the program to prevent unnecessary and wasteful care.

Finally, broadened benefits would be phased in gradually, to avoid overloading the system. Coverage for annual physical examinations, dental care, and prescription drugs would be introduced later.

The Medicare approach, however, has several defects: The plan does not significantly reform the present health-care delivery system. Catastrophe coverage would not be immediately available but would be introduced at a later date, so truly comprehensive protection would not be initially provided. And if present Medicare reimbursement practices are still followed, the typical family would continue to pay a large proportion of its medical bills. Medicare covers only about 40 percent of the medical expenses incurred by the aged.

Mandatory Employer Purchase of Private Health Insurance

Under this approach, employers would be required to purchase private health insurance for their employees and the employees' dependents. The Comprehensive Health Insurance Plan, introduced by Sen. Robert W. Packwood, is an example. The major features of his proposal are these:

1. *Basic Approach.* There are three parts to the program: (1) a mandatory Employee Health Insurance Plan, which the employer must provide, but which is voluntary for the employee; (2) an Assisted Health Insurance Plan for the poor, uninsurable, unemployed, and those who are not in covered groups; and (3) a Federal Health Care Benefits Program for people 65 and over. Medicare would be retained, but Medicaid would be eliminated except for certain services.

2. *Benefits.* Benefits include inpatient hospital care, physicians' services, home health care, posthospital extended care, preventive services for children, prescription drugs, mental-health services, other preventive services, and an HMO option.

3. *Financing.* Under the mandatory plan, the employer would pay 65 percent of the costs for the first three years and 75 percent thereafter. Federal subsidies

would be available to employers with unusually high increases in premium costs. Under the assisted plan, the poor would not pay premiums, and the premiums of low-income persons would be based on their ability to pay. General revenues would be used to subsidize these groups.

4. *Deductibles and Coinsurance.* Those covered by Employee Health Insurance would pay the first $150 in annual medical expenses. Outpatient drugs would be subject to a separate $50 deductible. There would be a maximum of three deductibles per family. After satisfying the deductible, each enrollee would have to pay 25 percent of the costs of any additional bills. No family, however, would have to pay more than $1,500 in out-of-pocket expenses for any one year.

Under Assisted Health Insurance, working families with incomes up to $5,000 would pay no premiums at all. Deductibles, coinsurance payments, and maximum liability would be related to income levels.

Under the modified Medicare program for the aged, people 65 and over would pay the first $100 in medical costs, the first $50 in outpatient drugs, and 20 percent of other costs up to a maximum of $750 a year. Premiums and cost sharing would be reduced for low-income persons, with general revenues making up the difference.

5. *Administration.* Private health insurers would administer the program, except for the Federal Health Care Benefits Program for the aged.

To summarize the proposal, it consists of three parts. In the first, the employers would be required to provide health-insurance coverage, from private health insurers, for all workers. The employers would pay 65 percent of the costs for the first three years and 75 percent thereafter, with the employees paying the difference. Participation by employees would be voluntary. A typical employer plan covering the entire family is expected to cost at least $600 annually, with the employee paying $210.

Second, a government-subsidized plan would be established for the poor, uninsurable, unemployed, and those not in a covered group. The poor would pay no premiums, and those with low incomes would pay premiums based on their income, with general revenues of the state and federal government subsidizing the plan.

The third part would be the existing Medicare program for the aged, but with expanded benefits. The aged would pay the first $100 in medical costs, the first $50 in outpatient drugs, and 20 percent of all remaining costs up to a maximum of $750 annually.

The Packwood proposal contains several desirable features. It provides for federal subsidy for firms that are faced with a substantial increase in payroll costs because of the health-insurance plan. If the required premiums increased the employer's payroll by more than 3 percent, the federal government would pay him a subsidy for part of the excess. The subsidy would be limited to 75 percent of the excess in the first year, and reduced by 15 percentage points for each subsequent year.

The plan also encourages the development of Health Maintenance Organizations (HMOs) and preventive health care. It retains the institution of private health insurance, thereby reducing the growth of the federal government into the private sector. To reduce unnecessary surgery and the maintenance of underutilized facilities, it calls for professional-standards review organizations, to monitor the quality of medical care and the performance of physicians. And to provide for a more balanced growth in physical plant, the states would have the responsibility to review building plans for hospitals, nursing homes, and other health facilities.

The Packwood proposal, however, falls far short of fulfilling the criteria for an effective national health insurance plan. First, operating three major plans covering different parts of the population could present some serious administrative problems. It might also have the unfortunate effect of singling out and identifying the poor, and perhaps, in the end, delivering inferior health care to them.

Second, the various deductibles and coinsurance provisions might cause serious financial hardship to many low-income and middle-income families. For example, a family earning only $2,500 a year could pay as much as 9 percent of its annual income for medical care because of these requirements, and a family earning only $5,000 annually could pay as much as 12 percent. Moreover, once a family reaches $10,000 of annual income, the overall financing mechanism is regressive. A worker earning that amount would pay 15 percent of his income on medical care before reaching the maximum liability of $1,500, when all deductibles and coinsurance requirements stop. In contrast, a family with yearly earnings of $30,000 would pay only 5 percent of its income to reach that maximum limit.

Third, although the proposal would make the plan mandatory for employers, it would be voluntary for employees. Some employees may choose not to participate because they cannot afford the coverage. Thus, the goal of universal health-insurance protection is weakened.

Finally, the proposal lacks effective cost controls and does little to reform the present health-care delivery system. Competition among private health insurers, rather than controls by the federal government, would be the major technique used to control costs. However, the health-insurance industry has not been able to restrain medical costs effectively in the past, and it is questionable whether competition alone can do it in the future.

Tax-Incentive Plans

Under this approach, income tax credits and liberal income tax deductions would be used to encourage the voluntary purchase of private health insurance. People would receive income tax credits equal to all or part of the premiums they paid toward a qualified plan. Employers would be encouraged to offer an acceptable plan to their employees through higher income tax deductions for the premiums paid toward a plan that provides minimum benefits.

Medicredit. The Medicredit plan, sponsored by the American Medical Association, calls for the government to provide income tax credits for the voluntary purchase of a qualified health-insurance plan. Medicredit would offer both ordinary and catastrophe protection. The federal government would purchase insurance for the poor. Medicare would be retained, but Medicaid would be partly absorbed into the new program. The major features of the Medicredit proposal are summarized as follows:

1. *Basic Approach.* A sliding scale of tax credits would be applied against

personal income taxes to encourage the voluntary purchase of private health-insurance plans that provide specified benefits. Tax credits would be available for employers providing qualified plans. The federal government would pay the premiums for the poor.

2. *Benefits.* Minimum benefits under a qualified policy would include 60 days of hospital care, skilled nursing-facility services, physicians' services, outpatient and home health services, laboratory and X-ray services, dental services for children, and catastrophe benefits.

3. *Financing.* Tax credits ranging from 10 to 100 percent of the cost of a qualified health-insurance policy would be applied against the personal income tax of the purchaser. The poor and near-poor would receive vouchers from the federal government, with which to pay the premiums. The federal government would pay the costs of catastrophe coverage for all.

4. *Deductibles and Coinsurance.* Under the basic coverage, the patient would pay the first $50 per stay in the hospital or skilled nursing facility, 20 percent of the first $500 of outpatient or emergency-care expenses and home health care, 20 percent of the first $500 of medical-care services, and 20 percent of the first $500 for dental services. Under catastrophe coverage, a deductible of 10 percent of taxable income would apply, which would be reduced by deductibles and copayments paid toward the basic benefits.

5. *Administration.* Private health insurers would underwrite qualified policies under the direction of a Health Insurance Advisory Board. The state insurance departments would certify the private carriers and policies according to federal standards. The Department of Health, Education and Welfare would issue voucher certificates to the poor and near-poor.

Individuals and families would be granted income tax credits against the actual cost of the health insurance purchased, but the amount of the tax credit would depend on the income tax liability. The credit would decrease as the amount of income taxes increased. For people with an income tax liability of $10 or less, the credit would equal 100 percent of the premiums paid, a $501 tax would produce a 49 percent credit, and a tax of $891 or more would result in only a 10 percent credit. The poor and near-poor would receive payment vouchers from the federal government for the purchase of a qualified health insurance plan. Private health insurers would then present the vouchers to the federal government for payment.

For those who place great value on personal rights, voluntary initiative, minimum federal interference, and the preservation of private health insurance, the Medicredit plan appears attractive. The proposal would allow every participant to select his own physician and private health insurer, and would permit physicians and patients to maintain a direct professional relationship with a minimum of federal interference.

When measured against the criteria for an effective national health insurance plan, however, Medicredit is deficient in several respects. First, it provides for two plans—one for the poor and one for the nonpoor. The use of vouchers, to be redeemed by private insurers, would identify and stigmatize the poor. Such a voucher system is analogous to the food-stamp program, which many poor families detest because of the stigma of charity it carries. Furthermore, the administrative burden of keeping track of vouchers for over 32 million poor and low-income Americans would be horrendous. Finally, a two-plan system with the danger of two different levels of care could isolate even more the millions of poor Americans from the general population, thereby intensifying fear, distrust, and suspicion on both sides.

Second, Medicredit would not significantly change the present health-care delivery system, which is marked by price inflation, waste, inefficiency and inadequate access. Hospitals would still be reimbursed on the basis of reasonable costs, and physicians on the basis of fee-for-service. Moreover, the plan is open-ended regarding costs, and contains no effective cost controls. Pumping billions of new dollars into an essentially unchanged system without effective cost controls guarantees continuous and severe price inflation in future medical costs.

Third, the plan does not provide universal coverage. Emphasis on voluntary tax incentives alone might not stimulate all Americans to purchase private health insurance, because of their ignorance, neglect, undue optimism, insufficient tax advantages, or other reasons.[15] There is the possibility that millions would remain uninsured under the Medicredit plan, and that a subsidy through tax credits might not produce the desired effect on insurance purchases.[16]

Health Care. The healthcare plan, sponsored by the Health Insurance Association of America, is another tax-incentive approach to the health-care problem, but is vastly superior to Medicredit. The major features of the proposal are summarized as follows:

1. *Basic Approach.* Private health insurers would participate in a three-part voluntary program: (1) employer-employee plans, (2) individual plans, and (3) plans for the poor, near-poor, and uninsurable under subsidized state insurance pools. Comprehensive benefits would be phased in gradually. Catastrophe protection would also be provided. Other provisions would aim at restraining health-care costs, expanding ambulatory-care centers and health planning, and correcting for the maldistribution and shortages of health professionals.

2. *Benefits.* Standard benefits would include hospital and skilled nursing care, home care, physician and dental care, diagnostic laboratory and X-ray services, surgery and radiation therapy, maternity and well-child care, mental-health services, health examinations and immunizations, rehabilitation services, prescription drugs, and eyeglasses. Coverage for catastrophic losses up to $250,000 would also be provided.

3. *Financing.* Premiums would be paid by employers and employees and would be fully tax-deductible if the plan met federal standards. If it did not, the allowable income tax deduction would be gradually reduced and finally eliminated over a specified period. Under individual plans, policyholders would pay all premiums. The poor would pay no premiums, but the near-poor and uninsurable would pay partial premiums depending on their incomes. The balance would be paid by the general revenues of the federal and state governments.

4. *Deductibles and Coinsurance.* Coinsurance would be required for institutional care and physicians' services. Coinsurance for other services would range

[15]Somers and Somers, "Major Issues," pp. 188-89.

[16]Mark V. Pauly, *National Health Insurance: An Analysis* (Washington, D.C.: American Enterprise Institute for Public Policy Research, 1971), p. 28.

from nothing for preventive services to 50 percent for treatment of mental conditions. Low-income families would not be subject to cost-sharing provisions. Other families would be required to share in the costs according to income.

5. *Administration.* Private health insurers would administer the qualified group and individual plans. State pools would be underwritten by private health insurers, but the Department of Health, Education and Welfare would establish the necessary regulations. A Council of Health Policy Advisors would be established to coordinate the federal programs.

Healthcare has several parts, each of which is designed to correct part of the health-care problem that now exists. The specific objectives of the proposal include the following:

1. Increase the supply and improve the productivity and distribution of health manpower.

2. Develop ambulatory health-care services to promote health maintenance and reduce costly hospital use.

3. Improve health-care planning to distribute current and future health resources more equitably and effectively.

4. More directly contain the escalation in health-care costs and upgrade the quality of health care.

5. Establish national goals and priorities to improve health care.

6. Improve the financing of health care, including the costs of a catastrophe illness, for everyone.

The Healthcare plan attempts to control medical costs, improve the organization and delivery of health care, and make available comprehensive health insurance to all citizens up to a maximum of $250,000. Employers and employees would be encouraged to purchase voluntarily private health-insurance contracts through various income tax incentives. The Medicare program for the aged would be retained, but the Medicaid program would gradually be phased out. Finally, a separate plan for the poor and physically handicapped, subsidized by the federal and state governments, would be established.

Federal minimum standards for health-insurance benefits would be established. Heavy emphasis would be placed on benefits for ambulatory and preventive care, to encourage the use of lower-cost, out-of-hospital facilities. A maximum benefit of $250,000 would be established for a catastrophic loss.

The benefits would be gradually phased in to avoid overloading the present health-care delivery system. Progressively expanding comprehensive coverage would include hospitalization, extended care, nursing-home treatment, surgery, diagnostic service, general and special physicians' services, preventive checkups, maternity and well-baby care, prescription drugs, rehabilitation, visual care, psychiatric care, and dental care for children under age 19.

Employers would be encouraged by federal income tax incentives to purchase private health-insurance contracts. If the employer's plan met minimum standards, 100 percent of the premium costs would be tax-deductible. If the plan did not qualify, only 50 percent of the premiums would be deductible (compared to 100 percent at present). The deduction would be reduced to 25 percent for the second year and completely eliminated after that time if the plan failed to meet minimum federal standards. Tax incentives would also be provided for people who could not participate in any group health-insurance plan.

A separate plan would be established for the poor, near-poor, and uninsurable. State pools of private health insurers would be established to provide their benefits, and their premiums would be subsidized by the federal and state governments. The poor would not pay premiums, while the near-poor would pay premiums scaled to their income. People who were recently unemployed would be eligible on a month-to-month basis, subject to income qualifications. Coinsurance would be used for those medical-care expenses that were considered overutilized according to the plan's experience. However, there would be a maximum aggregate limit that a family would pay, which would be related to family income.

The Healthcare plan has much to recommend it as a model for national health insurance. It aims at correcting each of the major defects in the present delivery system. In addition, after the plan was gradually phased in, the benefits would be comprehensive at both the basic and catastrophe levels. Coinsurance would not apply to expenses beyond a maximum level, which means that a truly catastrophic loss would not seriously cripple the financial position of a typical family. The initial cost of the proposal would be relatively low, so there would be no sudden substantial tax increase. Finally, a severe overload on the present system would be avoided, since benefits would be phased in gradually, with priority given to the poor and near-poor.

On the negative side, however, as with Medicredit, there is no assurance that income tax deductions would provide the desired incentives for purchasing private health insurance. The tax advantages to moderate-income taxpayers might be negligible. In addition, although the present Medicaid program for the poor would be phased out, its equivalent could result from the operation of the state pool for those who are poor or uninsurable. The poor again would be identified in a separate plan. Finally, although a gradual phasing in of benefits is desirable, Healthcare would expand the benefits over a six-year period, thereby postponing the alleviation of much of the health-care crisis in the United States.

Catastrophe-Illness Insurance

Under this approach to national health insurance, it is assumed that most health-care plans are adequate, but that the typical family needs additional protection for a catastrophic loss.

The Catastrophic Health Insurance and Medical Assistance Reform Act, introduced by Senators Long and Ribicoff, is an example. The major features of their proposal are summarized as follows:

1. *Basic Approach.* The major thrust of the proposal is coverage of catastrophic losses. The program consists of three parts: (1) everyone would be covered against catastrophic losses under Mandated Catastrophic Health Insurance; (2) the poor would be provided basic benefits under the Federal Medical Assistance Plan; and (3) those who are not poor would be encouraged but not required to purchase their own policies under the voluntary certification program for basic health-insurance benefits.

2. *Benefits.* The benefits are similar to those of Medicare. Under the Catastrophic plan, inpatient hospital care would be covered after 60 days of confinement, with an unlimited number of days of coverage thereafter. In addition, after a $2,000 deductible is satisfied, 80 percent of other medical expenses would be paid. The Medical Assistance Plan for the poor would cover hospital care for up to 60 days in a hospital or skilled nursing facility, home health services, medical services, and preventive care, diagnosis, and treatment. Copayments, would not apply to the poor except for a $3 copayment charge for each of the first 10 physician visits per family. Under the voluntary program, private insurers would have their policies certified by the Department of Health, Education and Welfare.

3. *Financing.* The Catastrophic plan would be financed by a payroll tax paid by employees, employers, and the self-employed. The Medical Assistance Plan would be financed by the general revenues of the federal and state governments. Under the certification plan, employers, employees, and others would pay the premiums.

4. *Deductibles and Coinsurance.* Under the Catastrophic plan, hospital benefits would be covered after 60 days' confinement. After a $2,000 deductible, medical expenses would be reimbursed at a rate of 80 percent. Copayments would be limited to a maximum of $1,000 per family. Copayments generally would not apply to the poor, who are covered under a basic plan.

5. *Administration.* Both the Catastrophic plan and the Medical Assistance Plan would be administered through the Medicare program of the Social Security Administration. Private health insurers would serve as fiscal intermediaries.

The program would consist of three parts. The first is catastrophe coverage, to begin after the insured was hospitalized for 60 days. Eighty percent of the other medical expenses would be reimbursed after a $2,000 deductible was satisfied, and copayment would stop after the family incurred $1,000 of medical bills.

Second, a separate plan for low-income families would be established, with the benefits financed out of the general revenues of the federal and state governments.

The third part would be a voluntary certification plan, under which the nonpoor would be encouraged but not required to purchase their own policies from qualified private health insurers, whose policies, if they met certain minimum standards, would be certified by the Department of Health, Education and Welfare.

The plan would be financed through the OASDHI program, with employers and employees each paying a tax of 0.3 percent, ultimately increasing to 0.4 percent, on the taxable wage base for catastrophe coverage. The special plan for the poor would be financed out of the general revenues of the federal and state governments, and under the voluntary certification plan, employers, employees, and others would pay the cost of the premiums.

The approach of stressing only the coverage of catastrophe illness can be seriously questioned.[17] It is certainly desirable to cover a catastrophic loss by the elimination of financial barriers to payment, but the definition of what constitutes a catastrophic loss is vague and subjective. A middle-income worker

---

[17]For a discussion of the advantages and disadvantages of catastrophe health insurance, see the different viewpoints by Melvin A. Glasser and Robert J. Myers in "Catastrophic Insurance; Pipedream or Panacea?" *Prism,* August 1974.

may find a $5,000 medical bill financially crushing, but such a loss hardly dents the savings account of a highly paid executive. Fewer than 2 out of 1,000 persons under age 65 have a $5,000 medical bill in any year, so if a bill that size is considered a catastrophe loss, then relatively few people would qualify for benefits under a national catastrophe-insurance plan. Most middle-income families would probably have trouble meeting a medical bill well under $5,000. There is such a thing, however, as insurance without protection.

A federal catastrophe plan with a high deductible would probably result eventually in public pressures to lower the deductible. Successive reductions in the deductible could result in a single monolithic program, with all the inefficiencies and defects described earlier. Moreover, if the deductible were graded by income size, a needs test would be introduced into the plan. Finally, a national health insurance plan covering only a catastrophic loss would eliminate, or require revising, all outstanding private major medical contracts, which currently provide catastrophe protection to more than 83 million Americans.

THE FUTURE OF NATIONAL HEALTH INSURANCE

It can be concluded from the preceding analysis that no national health insurance plan currently proposed meets all the ideal requirements for an effective plan. Although it is dangerous to speculate on the precise form that national health insurance will take, three major conclusions can be drawn from the debate to date.

First, the question of the desirability of national health insurance is no longer an issue. It is generally agreed that a new system of health care is needed. The real issue is the form that the new system should take.

Second, it is also safe to conclude that any national health insurance plan will represent a political compromise among private health insurers, consumers, labor, government, and the medical profession. No single proposal will be adopted in its present form, and the final plan will represent the compromise of a great many groups. The best features of each proposal will probably be drafted into law. The major problem, of course, is to draft a compromise plan that effectively meets the existing health-care problems, and that is both workable and acceptable to the major power groups in the health-care field.

Finally, the institution of private health insurance will probably plan a pivotal role in any new system. Under all the plans except the Kennedy-Mills proposal, private health insurers would play an important role. Congress will most likely proceed very cautiously and will reject any scheme that, in effect, would scrap a major existing institution in the United States. The private health-insurance industry is well represented politically in Washington, and the Senate Finance Committee contains several members who are decidedly sympathetic toward it. For these reasons, the scrapping of the private health system and its replacement by a single monolithic federal system appear remote.

SUGGESTIONS FOR ADDITIONAL READING

American Enterprise Institute for Public Policy Research, *Comprehensive National Medical Care: Should the Federal Government Pro-*

vide a Program of Comprehensive Medical Care for All U.S. Citizens? College Debate Series. Washington, D.C.: American Enterprise Institute for Public Policy Research, 1972.

————, *National Health Insurance Proposals.* Washington, D.C.: American Enterprise Institute for Public Policy Research, 1974.

American Medical Association, *Current National Health Insurance Proposals.* Chicago: American Medical Association, 1971.

Burns, Eveline M., "Health Insurance: Not If, or When, but What Kind," *American Journal of Public Health,* November 1971, pp. 2164-75.

Committee for Economic Development, *Building a National Health-Care System.* New York: Committee for Economic Development, 1973.

Eilers, Robert D., and Sue S. Moyerman, eds., *National Health Insurance: Proceedings of the Conference on National Health Insurance.* Homewood, Ill.: Richard D. Irwin, 1971.

Falk, I.S., "National Health Insurance: A Review of Policies and Proposals," *Symposium on Health Care: Part II, Law and Contemporary Problems,* Autumn 1970, pp. 669-96.

Feldstein, Martin S., "A New Approach to National Health Insurance," *Public Interest,* Spring 1971, pp. 93-105.

Health Insurance Institute, *A Summary of Seven National Health Insurance Proposals—93rd Congress.* New York: Health Insurance Institute, 1974.

Pauly, Mark V., *National Health Insurance: An Analysis.* Washington, D.C.: American Enterprise Institute for Public Policy Research, 1971.

Pettengill, Daniel W., "Writing the Prescription for Health Care," *Harvard Business Review,* November-December 1971, pp. 37-43.

Roth, Russell B., "National Health Insurance—How and Why?" *Cincinnati Journal of Medicine,* April 1971, pp. 107-10.

Somers, Herman M., and Anne R. Somers, "Major Issues in National Health Insurance," *Milbank Memorial Fund Quarterly,* Vol. I., No. 2, Part 1 (April 1972), 177-210.

Tax Foundation, Inc., *Problems and Issues in National Health Insurance.* New York: Tax Foundation, Inc., 1974.

Turnbull, John G., C. Arthur Williams, Jr., and Earl F. Cheit, *Economic and Social Security,* 4th ed., Chap. 12. New York: Ronald Press, 1973.

U.S. Congress, Senate, Committee on Finance, *National Health Insurance,* Hearings before the Committee on Finance, 92d Cong., 1st sess., on S.3, S.191, S.836, S.987, S.1376, S.1490, S.1598, and S.1623, 1971. Washington, D.C.: U.S. Government Printing Office, 1971.

chapter 12

The Problem
of Occupational Safety
and Health

Every year, thousands of workers in the United States die from industrial accidents because of unsafe working conditions or unsafe personal acts on the job. Millions more are disabled for one or more days each year because of job-related injuries. In addition to pain and suffering, disabled workers are confronted with the serious problems of loss of income, payment of medical expenses, partial or permanent loss of bodily functions or limbs, and job separation. If the injury is particularly severe, the disabled worker must often undergo a traumatic financial, physical, and emotional readjustment, which can be especially hard on the younger workers who have several dependents and are deeply in debt.

Industrial accidents, however, are only a part of the occupational health and safety problem. Occupational disease is a growing problem, because of new technology that often creates a dangerous industrial environment. Many workers are now being exposed to new chemical and physical hazards that did not previously exist. Safety engineers were formerly concerned with the problem of industrial accidents and accident prevention; but current emphasis is on the broader occupational health and safety problem, which includes the total working environment, plant safety, accident prevention, occupational disease, and all other factors that influence the worker's health.

In this chapter, we shall examine the important problem of occupational safety and health. In particular, we shall consider the following areas: (1) industrial accidents, (2) occupational disease, (3) the costs of industrial accidents and disease, and (4) solutions to the occupational health and safety problem.

PROBLEM OF INDUSTRIAL ACCIDENTS

Magnitude of the Problem

The annual toll of industrial accidents is staggering. More than 14,000 workers annually die from job-related injuries. Another 90,000 sustain perma-

274

nent injuries, and more than 2 million miss one or more days of work each year because of industrial accidents and job-related diseases. Ten million workers a year require medical care or experience restricted activity because of job-related injuries.[1] These data do not reflect the pain and suffering of the disabled workers, nor the anguish of their families. Occupational injuries also result in the loss of billions in wages each year and the diversion of scarce economic resources to the payment of workmen's compensation benefits.

The probability of a disabling injury is relatively high for a new worker entering the labor force. Unless work injuries are significantly reduced, out of every 100 workers entering the labor force at age 20, one will die as the result of a work injury, six will be permanently disabled, and 68 will suffer one or more disabling injuries. *Of the original 100 workers, only 25 can expect to reach retirement without a disabling work injury.*[2] These data underscore the importance of reducing industrial accidents and the need for greater industrial safety.

It is also worthwhile to examine the accident records of key industries. Although data gathered by the National Safety Council and the Bureau of Labor Statistics are fragmented and their accuracy uncertain, we know that some industries are more hazardous than others. Figure 12-1 provides information on job-related deaths for selected industries, based on injury frequency rates—the number of disabling work injuries per 1 million employee-hours worked.[3]

Coal mining and contract construction are relatively hazardous industries, while employment in the trade sector or the federal government is relatively safe. The manufacturing sector ranks somewhere in the middle; but within it, there are important differences among the types and sizes of companies. Those with higher-than-average injury frequency rates include companies making lumber and wood products; food and kindred products; stone, clay, and glass products; and fabricated metal products.

In addition smaller firms within the manufacturing sector, which employ the majority of workers in the labor force, have poorer accident records than have the larger firms. The ratio of the injury rate for firms with fewer than 100 employees to the average injury rate in their industry is 3.1.[4]

The poor safety record of smaller firms is attributable to several factors. First, some smaller firms are financially weak, and for competitive reasons, they cannot afford to spend substantial amounts on effective safety programs, on providing in-plant health services to their workers, or making them adequately aware of the potential physical hazards. Second, smaller firms are generally ineligible for experience rating in workmen's compensation insurance. Thus, the

---

[1]National Commission on Workmen's Compensation Laws, *The Report of the National Commission on State Workmen's Compensation Laws* (Washington, D.C.: U.S. Government Printing Office, 1972), p. 31.

[2]U.S. Department of Labor, *Manpower Report of the President* (Washington, D.C.: U.S. Government Printing Office, 1968), p. 42.

[3]A corresponding measure of accident severity has also been computed for the various industries. The severity rate is the total days charged for work injuries per 1 million employee-hours worked.

[4]National Commission on Workmen's Compensation Laws, *Report*, p. 92, Fig. 5.2.

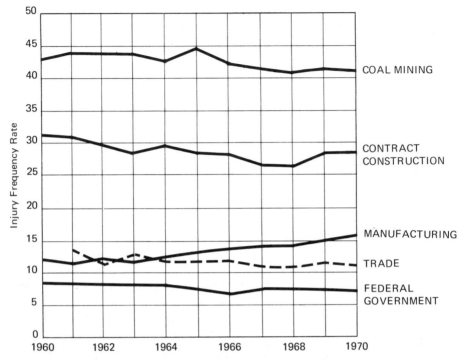

The injury frequency rate is the number of disabling work injuries per million employee-hours worked.

FIGURE 12-1
Work-Injury Frequency Rates for Selected Industries, 1960-1970.

Source: National Commission on Workmen's Compensation Laws, *The Report of the National Commission on State Workmen's Compensation Laws* (Washington, D.C.: U.S. Government Printing Office, 1972), p. 89, Fig. 5-1.

financial stimulus of potential premium savings is lacking. Third, workmen's compensation insurers, which can provide effective loss-prevention services, tend to concentrate their safety efforts on the larger firms. This is because the larger firms are more safety-conscious, and the substantial premiums they pay act as a powerful inducement for insurers to provide effective safety services so that the losses can be reduced. The expense loading in the premiums is also sufficiently large to generate the dollars necessary for effective loss-prevention services.[5] As a result, the larger firms generally have superior safety records.

The especially poor safety record of the coal-mining industry can be explained by unsafe working conditions, laxity in the observance of safety regulations by smaller and financially weaker mining companies, and inadequate enforcement of safety regulations by the Bureau of Mines, which has been

[5]C. Arthur Williams, Jr., *Insurance Arrangements under Workmen's Compensation,* U.S. Department of Labor, Wage and Labor Standards Administration, Bureau of Labor Standards, Bulletin No. 317 (Washington, D.C.: U.S. Government Printing Office, 1969), pp. 54-55.

hindered in the past by having an insufficient number of inspectors. Miners have charged that the companies often break or bend the law in their zeal for greater production, and that federal safety regulations are flagrantly violated by many companies. Because of these problems, Congress enacted the Federal Coal Mine Health and Safety Act in 1969. This act will be analyzed in greater detail later in the chapter.

Agriculture also has a relatively poor safety record. Substantial numbers of farmers and agricultural workers each year are killed in farm accidents. In 1973 there were 2,200 work deaths in agriculture, or a death rate of 61 per 100,000 workers. Tractor deaths are a particularly troublesome area, with an estimated 1,100 farm workers killed each year by tractor turnovers. Ralph Nader has said that tractor deaths could be largely eliminated by redesigning tractors to reduce instability and by installing roll bars to provide protection if the tractor overturns.[6]

Increase in Injury Frequency Rate

Another part of the problem is the increase in the injury frequency rate. Although the rate in the manufacturing sector steadily declined over the first several decades of this century, it has been rising since 1961, and was actually higher in 1970 than it had been since 1951:[7]

Year	Injury Frequency Rate
1930	23.1
1940	15.3
1950	14.7
1960	12.0
1970	15.2

In short, *the frequency of disabling work injuries has increased about 27 percent since 1960.* This represents a long step backward for a country that is deeply concerned with human safety and economic progress.

The reasons for the reversal in the long-term downward trend in injury frequency rates are not completely known. One explanation is that new technology—for example, modern technical processes and massive, high-speed machines—can create an entirely new working environment, with a substantial increase in physical hazards as a result. High-energy sources, such as laser beams, are now common in industry. Radioactive substances and mechanisms are also exposing greater numbers of workers to occupational disabilities.

Another explanation of the increase in the injury frequency rates is that during periods of economic expansion, business firms tend to hire a good many

[6]National Safety Council, *Accident Facts, 1974 Edition* (Chicago: National Safety Council, 1974), p. 85. See also the statement of Ralph Nader in U.S. Congress, Senate, Subcommittee on Labor, *Occupational Safety and Health Act, 1970,* Hearings before the Subcommittee on Labor of the Committee on Labor and Public Welfare, 91st Cong., 1st and 2d sess., on S.2193 and S.2788, 1969 and 1970, Part 1, p. 635.

[7]National Commission on Workmen's Compensation Laws, *Report,* p. 88.

marginal workers, who are generally inexperienced and lack adaptability, agility, and good work habits. During periods of strong aggregate demand, they are under heavy pressure to work faster and harder, and may also work overtime. The resulting fatigue and inexperience may combine to produce a higher injury frequency rate. Conversely, during periods of economic recession when aggregate demand is weak, marginal workers are laid off, and the more experienced and highly trained workers who remain on the job tend to improve the injury frequency rate.[8]

PROBLEM OF OCCUPATIONAL DISEASE

Occupational disease is becoming an increasingly prominent health problem. Respiratory disease is common among workers in the dusty trades; in other industries, workers are poisoned by lead and mercury; still others are being exposed to new toxic materials and chemicals. A study of 1,700 industrial plants in the United States revealed that 65 percent of the workers were exposed to harmful physical agents or to toxic chemicals, and only 25 percent were adequately protected. It is estimated that at least 390,000 new cases of occupational disease occur each year.[9] Thus, the problem of occupational disease as an important cause of economic insecurity warrants careful investigation.

New Technology

The United States is currently undergoing a technological revolution, with severe implications concerning the health of industrial workers. It is estimated that every twenty minutes, a new and potentially toxic chemical is introduced into industry. Carcinogenic chemicals, beryllium metal, epoxy resins, pesticides, and numerous other substances can threaten the worker's health. New technical processes and new sources of energy, such as atomic and ultrasonic, present enormous health hazards. Radioactive substances and radioactive machines expose workers to potential occupational diseases.

There is great need for intensive research in occupational health. Little is currently known about the effects of noise exposure and control measures, atmospheric contaminants, and latent diseases that result from new technology.

Continued Existence of Old Problems

Older occupational diseases continue to threaten the worker's health.

[8]For a further discussion, see American Enterprise Institute for Public Policy Research, *The Occupational Safety and Health Bill* (Washington, D.C.: American Enterprise Institute for Public Policy Research, 1968), pp. 8-13. See also Richard D. James, "Watch it There! Tired Young Workers Spur a Steady Increase in Industrial Accidents." *Wall Street Journal,* August 5, 1969, p. 1.

[9]U.S. Congress, Senate, Subcommittee on Labor, *Legislative History of the Occupational Safety and Health Act of 1970 (S. 2193, P.L. 91-596)*, prepared by the Subcommittee on Labor of the Committee on Labor and Public Welfare, 92d Cong., 1st sess., 1971 (Washington, D.C.: U.S. Government Printing Office, 1971), pp. 142-43.

Many workers are still disabled each year from lead and mercury. Workers in textile and cotton factories continue to contract pneumoconiosis, which appropriate engineering techniques do not completely control. Other occupational diseases are caused by the failure of firms to apply known loss-prevention techniques, through either apathy, ignorance, or false security. And little knowledge exists regarding the diseases that result from continuous exposure to industrial poisons.

Occupation Exposure and Chronic Diseases

Recent research indicates that certain chronic diseases are related to occupational exposures.[10] Cancer, heart disease, respiratory ailments, allergies, and other ailments can frequently be traced in part to conditions on the job. In other diseases, the relationship is clear and direct. For example, continuous exposure to asbestos, ionizing radiation, chromates, and certain dye intermediates can cause cancer. The highly toxic chemical betanaphthylamine, which has been used to produce textile dyes, has been shown to cause cancer of the bladder. Also, the distinction between occupational and nonoccupational illness is becoming increasingly difficult to determine—as in the case of heart disease, which can be traced to conditions of stress that exist both on and off the job.

Critical Problem Areas

Several problems in the field of occupational health are currently of such magnitude as to warrant special treatment. *Black lung disease,* caused by the inhalation of soft-coal mining dust, is progressive and crippling; afflicted coal miners experience severe difficulty in breathing and shortness of breath. Black lung disease has been recognized only recently as a specific occupational disease of the United States. Its incidence and severity are so widespread that special disability-income benefits are now payable to afflicted miners under the Federal Coal Mine Health and Safety Act of 1969.

Byssinosis is another crippling occupational disease, which affects thousands of textile workers. It is a lung disease that is caused by inhalation of cotton dust. The afflicted worker eventually becomes totally disabled because of continuous shortness of breath and chronic coughing. The textile industry until recently refused to recognize byssinosis as an official disease, despite the fact that thousands of British textile workers who had used American cotton had contracted it. The number of active and retired cotton textile workers who have the disease has been estimated as high as 100,000.[11]

Pesticides, herbicides, and fungicides in the agriculture industry can also result in serious occupational diseases. An estimated 800 workers a year are killed, and another 80,000 injured, because of the improper use of farm pesticides.[12] Many farm workers are migrant laborers who are least able to protect

[10]*Ibid.,* p. 142.

[11]*Ibid.,* p. 143.

[12]*Ibid.,* p. 144.

themselves against occupational disease. They generally live in poverty, have poor health and inadequate housing, and are hindered by language problems. Pesticide poisoning only aggravates their health and poverty problems.

Loud noise also creates a serious occupational health problem. Noise control in plants has been neglected, and substantial numbers of workers have suffered permanent hearing impairments. High-noise problems are particularly troublesome in earthmoving, lumbering, woodworking, and textile firms.

Occupational noise is now being recognized as a serious health problem. But noise-control measures are still inadequate in many plants. The loudest continuous noise that a worker can safely experience during an eight-hour day is 90 decibels, about the level that a motorcycle puts out. However, about 42 percent of business firms have noise levels that exceed 90 decibels, and this noise can result in a serious loss of hearing after steady exposure over a long period.[13] Also, excessive noise can result in poor safety experience, reduced morale, and a decrease in plant efficiency.

COSTS OF OCCUPATIONAL DISABILITY

The total physical, financial, psychological, and social costs of industrial accidents and occupational disease are gigantic. These costs fall heavily on disabled workers, business firms, and the economy.

Costs to Disabled Workers

Victims of industrial accidents and disease, and their families, bear heavy burdens in pain and suffering, loss of income, payment of medical expenses, economic insecurity of the surviving dependents, and rehabilitation costs.

The costs of pain and suffering are obviously incapable of being calculated. The worker who loses a limb, or whose spinal cord is severed, or whose body is burned, can never be adequately compensated in monetary terms alone. However, the pain and suffering of the more than 2 million workers who are disabled each year are indeed costs, which must be recognized even though they cannot be measured.

The loss of income is another high cost of occupational disability. Labor loses more than $1.5 billion in wages each year because of occupational disabilities, and state workmen's compensation benefits are generally inadequate for replacing these wages. In cases of temporary total disability, the average workmen's compensation payments replace less than half the worker's total wage losses.[14] The situation is also unsatisfactory for permanent total-disability

[13]Edward J. Kehoe, "Noise Control in the Industrial Environment," *The National Underwriter,* September 17, 1971, p. 45. See also U.S. Congress, House, Subcommittee on Public Health and Environment, *Noise Control,* Hearings before the Subcommittee on Public Health and Environment of the Committee on Interstate and Foreign Commerce, House of Representatives, 92d Cong., 1st sess., 1971, on H.R. 5275, H.R. 923, H.R. 3364, H.R. 6002, H.R. 6986 and H.R. 6988, Serial No. 92-30.

[14]Alfred M. Skolnik and Daniel N. Price, "Another Look at Workmen's Compensation," *Social Security Bulletin,* Vol. 33, No. 10 (October 1970), 15.

cases, when the worker loses his lifetime income. Berkowitz and Burton have attempted to estimate the percentage of economic loss that is replaced by workmen's compensation benefits in Pennsylvania and New Jersey when a worker there is totally disabled. They conclude that, in the case of a typical worker between the ages of 28 and 60, the benefits would replace only 38 to 54 percent of his lifetime economic loss in Pennsylvania, and 54 to 77 percent in New Jersey.[15] Based on these estimates, it is clear that totally disabled workers must themselves absorb a substantial percentage of the lifetime wages they lose because of an occupational disability.

The payment of medical expenses is another part of the cost to the worker. Although workmen's compensation insurance covers the medical expenses of most disabled workers, labor in the aggregate bears at least part of the costs. A worker may be disabled in an occupation that is not covered for workmen's compensation, or in one of the states that have time or amount limitations on the medical expenses that can be paid, or in one that provides less than full coverage for occupational disease. Thus, the occupationally disabled worker may be required to bear all or part of his medical expenses, depending on the state and the occupation in which he was injured.

The family also bears a heavy burden from occupational injuries. In addition to their anguish, they may suffer considerable uncertainty concerning the future continuation of their income. Relatively few states pay workmen's compensation benefits to the dependents of disabled workers, and death benefits to the survivors of deceased workers are often inadequate in terms of the family's need.

Finally, the disabled worker who requires rehabilitation services to be restored to his full working potential may have to absorb part of the rehabilitation costs himself. Most states have inadequate provisions in their workmen's compensation laws for the rehabilitation of disabled workers.

Costs to Business Firms

Business firms also incur heavy costs from industrial accidents and occupational disease. These costs can be classified into two major categories: insured and uninsured. *Insured costs* are the net premiums paid by the firm for workmen's compensation insurance, or, if the firm is self-insured, the actual sums paid to disabled workers and their dependents under the state workmen's compensation law, the amounts paid for medical care, and administrative costs.

The *uninsured costs* to a firm of occupational disabilities include the following:

1. Cost to repair damaged property, such as a machine
2. Wages paid for the time lost by workers who are not injured
3. Extra cost because of overtime
4. Cost of wages paid to supervisors for their time lost from the accident

[15]Monroe Berkowitz and John F. Burton, Jr., "The Income Maintenance Objective in Workmen's Compensation," *Industrial and Labor Relations Review*, Vol. 24, No. 1 (October 1970), 25 Table 4.

    5. Decreased output after the worker returns to work
    6. Cost of the learning period for a new worker hired
    7. Cost of a cancelled contract

The uninsured costs of an industrial accident are at least equal to the insured costs, and in many accidents, could substantially exceed them. Safety experts once applied the "four-to-one rule"; that is, for the industry as a whole, indirect (uninsured) costs of industrial accidents were about four times as great as the direct (insured) costs. This rule is no longer considered valid. The ratio of uninsured to insured costs varies by industry, by type of disability, by type of accident, and by individual firms. A more realistic ratio would probably be one-to-one.[16] Thus, when both the insured and uninsured costs are considered, firms have a strong financial incentive to prevent or reduce industrial accidents and disease.

Costs to the Economy

    The economy also bears a heavy burden from industrial accidents and occupational disease, because they lead to a substantial loss in the gross national product. Lost output cannot be stored up; the goods and services that the disabled workers could have produced in the absence of industrial injuries are lost forever. The costs of damaged equipment, medical care, and lost wages are additional economic costs that must be recognized. The National Center for Health Statistics estimates that the dollar amounts of lost production, damaged equipment, lost wages, medical treatment, and other costs as a result of job-related accidents totaled $9.3 billion in 1971.[17]

SOLUTIONS TO OCCUPATIONAL DISABILITY

    Effective programs and techniques must be undertaken to reduce the costs of job-related accidents and occupational disease. Three major approaches are (1) loss prevention, (2) federal legislation, and (3) workmen's compensation.

Loss Prevention

    Loss-prevention activities, to reduce both the frequency and the severity of industrial accidents and occupational disease, are the most effective solution to the problem of occupational safety and health. These programs attempt to determine the causes of occupational injuries and disease, and then undertake corrective action.
    There are two schools of thought among safety experts regarding the causes of work-related accidents.[18] The *engineering* approach stresses the im-

[16]Rollin H. Simonds and John V. Grimaldi, *Safety Management,* rev. ed. (Homewood, Ill.: Richard D. Irwin, 1963), pp. 85-91 and 103-32.

[17]National Commission on Workmen's Compensation Laws, *Report,* p. 31.

[18]*Ibid.,* pp. 90-91.

portance of environmental factors, and therefore calls for better design and construction of plants and equipment to prevent or reduce accidents. The *behavioral* approach, which is supported by educators and psychologists, places great emphasis on human factors, such as fatigue, boredom, sensory defects, alcoholism, and lack of motivation. The once-popular theory that certain workers are accident-prone is now questioned, since research has shown that it is the situation, not the worker, that is accident-prone. Both the engineering and the behavioral approach will continue to be used in preventing future work-related accidents.

Objectives of Loss Prevention. Loss-prevention techniques to prevent work-related accidents have two major objectives: humanitarian considerations and reduction of production costs.[19] Their primary purpose is to prevent personal suffering or death. Effective safety programs can reduce pain and suffering and prevent permanent physical impairments. The humanitarian objective also includes the prevention of the loss of income from a work-related accident, since workmen's compensation disability-income benefits are generally inadequate.

The objective of reducing production costs is also important, since, as we noted earlier, the uninsured costs of industrial accidents often equal or exceed the direct costs. By reducing both the insured and the uninsured costs, the firm may increase its profits, so it has a monetary incentive to make safety expenditures that reduce the frequency and severity of job-related accidents. From an economic viewpoint, a firm can profitably invest in safety programs until the last dollar spent on safety reduces the accident-premium portion of wages by a dollar, or reduces the firm's liability in lawsuits by a dollar. The accident-premium portion of the worker's wage refers to the extra wage that the firm must pay a worker to accept a job carrying the risk of accidents, instead of a job where accidents do not occur.[20]

Conflict between Maximum Profits and Optimal Safety. The firm's objectives of maximum profits and optimal safety can conflict with each other. Gordon, Akman, and Brooks point out clearly the nature of this conflict.[21] Industrial firms attempt to maximize their profits subject to various constraints or conflicting objectives, such as survival, growth rates, or individual goals. To be consistent with the objective of maximum profits, the optimal-safety objective must be expressed in terms of reduced costs or productivity gains. The firm's maximum-profit position, beyond which no additional profits can be realized from investment, production, or other courses of action, may conflict with the optimal-safety point—the point beyond which no positive changes in employee

[19]Simonds and Grimaldi, *Safety Management,* pp. 27-29.

[20]See John F. Burton, Jr., and Monroe Berkowitz, "Objectives Other Than Income Maintenance for Workmen's Compensation," *The Journal of Risk and Insurance,* Vol. XXXVIII, No. 3 (September 1971), 345-46.

[21]Jerome B. Gordon, Allan Akman, and Michael Brooks, "Systems Analysis and Worker Safety and Health Programs," in U.S. Congress, Senate, Subcommittee on Labor, *Occupational Safety and Health Act, 1970,* Hearings before the Subcommittee on Labor of the Committee on Labor and Public Welfare, 91st Cong., 1st and 2d sess., 1969 and 1970, on S. 2193 and S. 2788, Part 1, pp. 226-28.

safety can be accomplished by increased expenditures on safety programs. This conflict could arise when the gains in worker productivity from safety-program expenditures have *decreasing returns* for the firm even though additional improvements in worker safety are possible. This conflict can be illustrated by the following hypothetical schedule of safety expenditures, gains in worker productivity, and additional injuries that can be prevented:

Number of Safety Expenditures	Amount of Additional Safety Expenditure	Additional Increase in Worker Productivity	Additional Disabling Injuries Prevented
1	$ 50,000	$ 56,000	7
2	$ 50,000	$ 51,000	5
3	$ 50,000	$ 46,000	3

It is profitable for the firm to make the first safety expenditure of $50,000, since the gain in worker productivity, expressed as a dollar amount, exceeds the amount spent on safety. The second expenditure of $50,000 yields an additional increase of $51,000 in worker productivity and an additional decrease in the number of disabling injuries. The firm that wishes only to maximize profits should stop investing in safety programs at this point, even though the number of disabling injuries can be further reduced. If the third expenditure of $50,000 is made, an additional three disabling injuries can be prevented, but additional worker productivity declines to $46,000. The conflict between maximum profit and optimal safety becomes readily apparent. If the firm wants to reduce further the number of disabling injuries at this point, it must be willing to accept a lower total profit.

Another possible conflict could arise if the dollar difference between safety-program costs and productivity gains does not materialize; that is, if the productivity returns from safety programs are always less than the amounts invested in them. In this case, the safety programs may be subject to collective bargaining between the workers and the firm, or else reflected in federal and state legislation that would be a constraint on the firm's maximum-profit position.

Federal Legislation

In order to reduce the problem of job-related accidents and occupational disease, new federal legislation has recently been enacted, aimed at improving the occupational safety and health of workers and providing assistance to disabled coal miners.

Occupational Safety and Health Act of 1970. This act is one of the most important pieces of social legislation ever enacted into law. New legislation was considered necessary for several reasons. Research in industrial accidents and occupational disease at the state and national levels was not keeping pace with the exploding technology that was creating new physical hazards for American workers. Occupational safety and health standards in many states were narrow, with wide diversity among the states regarding the standards and the extent to which they were enforced. Enforcement in most states was weak, and competent occupational health and safety experts were in short supply; moreover, few states had modernized their occupational health and safety laws to protect today's workers. Existing state occupational-health programs had numerous defects, among which were lack of funds and personnel, low salary scales, lack of legislative support and concern regarding the health problems of workers, difficulties in filling staff vacancies, and lack of resources to identify statistically the nature of industrial health problems.[22] Because of these defects, Congress responded by enacting the Occupational Safety and Health Act of 1970.

The basic purpose of the act is to provide safe and healthful working conditions for every worker in the United States by reducing hazards at his place of employment.[23] To fulfill this purpose, the act provides for mandatory health and safety standards, research in occupational health and safety, information regarding the causes and prevention of industrial accidents and disease, education for employees and employers, the training of occupational health and safety specialists, and assistance and encouragement to the states to develop effective occupational safety and health programs.

1. Coverage. Coverage is very broad. The act applies to all firms engaging in business that affects commerce among the states. No minimum number of employees is required, nor must a firm be engaged in interstate commerce. Agricultural firms are also covered. State and federal employees are excluded, but federal agencies must establish health and safety programs in accord with the act's standards.

2. Federal Safety and Health Standards. One important provision gives the secretary of Labor the authority to establish interim, permanent, and emergency occupational safety and health standards. If a business firm violates a safety standard, the secretary can issue a citation and notify the firm of a proposed penalty. If the firm objects to either the citation or the proposed penalty, it can appeal to the Occupational Safety and Health Appeals Commission for a review of the case.

3. Inspections and Penalties. Federal inspectors are authorized to inspect any factory, plant, establishment, construction site, or other area where work is performed. The inspection must be made during regular working hours and in a reasonable manner.

An important provision permits an employee to request a special inspection if he believes that an imminent danger exists or that there is a violation of a safety standard that threatens his safety or health. Business firms are expressly forbidden from discharging or discriminating against any employee who exercises this right.

A penalty of $1,000 is assessed for each violation. For willful or repeated

---

[22]*Occupational Safety and Health Act,* Part 2, p. 1719.

[23]For a detailed explanation of the act, see Commerce Clearing House, *Occupational Safety and Health Act of 1970—Law and Explanation* (Chicago: Commerce Clearing House, 1971); and U.S. Department of Labor, *A Handy Reference Guide, The Williams-Steiger Occupational Safety and Health Act of 1970* (Washington, D.C.: U.S. Government Printing Office, 1973).

violations, the firm may be fined up to $10,000 for each violation. If an employer fails to correct a specified dangerous condition within a certain time period, he can be assessed an additional $1,000 for each day after expiration of the period. Also, if a willful violation results in the death of an employee, the employer is subject to a maximum fine of $10,000, imprisonment for up to six months, or both. A second conviction doubles the maximum penalties permitted under the law.

4. Record Keeping. Firms are required to maintain records and periodically issue reports relating to job-related deaths, injuries, and occupational disease. Also, the secretary of Labor can issue regulations regarding the development of information on the causes and prevention of industrial accidents and disease. Finally, firms must maintain employee-exposure records on employees who are exposed to toxic materials.

5. Evaluation. The Occupational Safety and Health Act of 1970 is a tough law that contains powerful provisions to reduce industrial accidents and disease.[24] The Department of Labor intends to concentrate on those highly hazardous industries that have the poorest safety records: construction, mining, meat-packing, air transport, transit, lumber, leather, wood products, iron and steel fabricating, clay and minerals, tobacco, foundries, pulp and paper manufacturing, printing and publishing, and nonferrous metals. To the extent that the act is adequately enforced, accident frequency and severity rates in dangerous industries can be expected to decline.

Another desirable feature is that business firms are being forced to make serious analyses of their safety programs. They must conform to federal safety and health standards or face substantial penalties, because the act has been strictly enforced since its inception. Since April 28, 1971, more than 86,000 inspections have been made, resulting in about 55,000 citations for 274,000 violations. Total fines and penalties of $7.3 million have been levied against noncomplying firms.[25]

In addition, the new act places great emphasis on occupational health and disease. Employers must not only keep accurate records about the exposure of employees to toxic materials; they must also comply with requirements of medical examinations or other health tests to protect the workers' health, and they must keep uniform records regarding the nature and occurrence of industrial accidents. Accurate national data on occupational disease are lacking, and questions are being raised regarding the validity of the National Safety Council and Bureau of Labor Statistics data on industrial accidents. A uniform record system will yield new and valuable information. Preliminary data gathered under the Occupational Safety and Health Act so far indicate that each year, one out of every eight workers in the private nonfarm economy is injured, killed, or stricken with an occupational disease. Contract construction has the worst record, with a rate of 22.5 cases for each 100 workers. Finance, insurance, and real estate are the safest industries to date, with only 2.8 cases for each 100 workers.[26]

[24]See "The Safety Act's Hidden Bite," *Business Week,* January 9, 1971, p. 20.

[25]Insurance Information Institute, *Insurance Educators' Letter,* Vol. 2, No. 7 (October 4, 1973).

[26]Insurance Information Institute, *Insurance Educators' Letter,* Vol. 2, No. 3 (March 7, 1973).

On the negative side, however, the tough safety regulations are having a profound impact on smaller firms, many of which find that the rules are complex, vague, and unnecessarily costing them more to do business. There is a good deal of anger, frustration, and confusion among small businessmen,[27] and some smaller firms have been forced out of business because of fines, penalties, and difficulties in complying. To the extent that firms must modify working conditions to comply with the act, the cost of business will be increased, and the result will be either lower profits or higher consumer prices, or both.

Black Lung Legislation. The Federal Coal Mine Health and Safety Act of 1969 was enacted to protect the safety and health of coal miners. The act established standards for permissible amounts of dust in coal mines, provided for the detection of black lung disease through periodic chest X rays, set up a cash-benefit program for miners who were totally disabled from black lung disease, and granted monthly cash payments to the widows of coal miners who died from the disease. If the recipient is receiving workmen's compensation benefits or disability benefits under a state program, the black lung benefit is reduced by the amount of the payment. After December 31, 1973, those states with workmen's compensation laws that provide black lung benefits based on standards established by the 1969 act will administer the black lung program.

Since the Coal Mine Act was passed into law, half of the nation's 2,800 coal mines have been shut down one or more times by the Bureau of Mines, and more than 33,000 citations for safety violations have been issued. But mining deaths have continued to increase because of violation of safety rules, and legal actions and court suits by the mining companies have made it difficult to collect the fines. In addition, the act has not been adequately enforced by the Bureau of Mines, because of an insufficient number of mine inspectors and, according to the bureau, because miners are not safety-conscious and coal mining technology is poorly developed.[28]

Another problem is the large number of coal miners and widows who are denied benefits under the act. As of December 1971, 322,582 claims had been processed and determinations made. *Of this number of claims, about 51 percent were denied.*[29] Most were denied because X rays did not disclose evidence of black lung disease. In addition, many claims were denied because the miners were not considered totally disabled; black lung benefits could be paid only if the miner was totally disabled because of pneumoconiosis—that is, incapable of engaging in substantial gainful activity—and only if the disease arose out of underground coal employment.

Because of the thousands of denied claims, many disabled miners com-

[27]Michael Jett, "An Asinine Situation, New Job-Safety Rules Perplex the Owners of Small Businesses; Needless Costs Cited," *Wall Street Journal,* February 20, 1973, p. 40. See also U.S. Congress, Senate, Subcommittee on Labor, *Implementation of the Occupational Safety and Health Act,* Hearings before the Subcommittee on Labor of the Committee on Labor and Public Welfare, 92d Cong., 2d sess., 1972.

[28]"Reform That Hasn't Stopped Disaster," *Business Week,* January 9, 1971, p. 20.

[29]U.S. Department of Health, Education and Welfare, Social Security Administration, Office of Research and Statistics, *The Black Lung Benefits Program: 2 Years of Experience,* by Philip R. Lerner, Note No. 21, December 7, 1972, p. 8, Table 2. See also "Black Lung Benefits: An Administrative Review," *Social Security Bulletin,* Vol. 34, No. 10 (October 1971), 11-21.

plained bitterly about the lack of fair and equitable treatment, and Congress made important changes in the program. Under the Black Lung Benefits Act of 1972, the definition of disability has been liberalized. A miner is now considered totally disabled if he cannot engage in gainful employment that requires skills and abilities comparable to those of the mining employment in which he was previously engaged with some regularity over a substantial period of time. The procedures for determining whether a claimant has black lung disease have also been liberalized. As a result of these changes, a higher proportion of disabled coal miners should be able to receive black lung benefits in the future.[30]

Workmen's Compensation

Workmen's compensation benefits are available to disabled workers for job-related accidents or occupational disease. Since workmen's compensation is a basic approach to occupational disability, it merits careful study, and we shall examine current programs in Chapter 13.

SUGGESTIONS FOR ADDITIONAL READING

Brinker, Paul A., *Economic Insecurity and Social Security*, Chap. 7. New York: Appleton-Century-Crofts, 1968.

Cheit, Earl F., and Margaret S. Gordon, eds., *Occupational Disability and Public Policy*. New York: John Wiley, 1963.

Commerce Clearing House, *Occupational Safety and Health Act of 1970—Law and Explanation*. Chicago: Commerce Clearing House, 1971.

Cummins, J. David, and Douglas G. Olson, "An Analysis of the Black Lung Compensation Program," *The Journal of Risk and Insurance,* Vol. XLI, No. 4 (December 1974).

National Commission on Workmen's Compensation Laws, *The Report of the National Commission on State Workmen's Compensation Laws,* Chap. 5. Washington, D.C.: U.S. Government Printing Office, 1972.

Simonds, Rollin H., and John V. Grimaldi, *Safety Management.* Homewood, Ill.: Richard D. Irwin, 1963.

Turnbull, John G., C. Arthur Williams, Jr. and Earl F. Cheit, *Economic and Social Security,* Chap. 8. New York: Ronald Press, 1973.

U.S. Congress, Senate, Subcommittee on Labor, *Implementation of the Occupational Safety and Health Act,* Hearings before the Subcom-

[30]An extensive analysis of the black lung program can be found in J. David Cummins and Douglas G. Olson, "An Analysis of the Black Lung Compensation Program," *The Journal of Risk and Insurance,* Vol. XLI, No. 4 (December 1974), 633-53.

mittee on Labor of the Committee on Labor and Public Welfare, 92d Cong., 2d sess., 1972.

U.S. Department of Labor, *A Handy Reference Guide, The Williams-Steiger Occupational Safety and Health Act of 1970.* Washington, D.C.: U.S. Government Printing Office, 1973.

chapter 13

Workmen's Compensation

Workmen's compensation laws provide cash benefits, medical care, and rehabilitation services to workers who are disabled from work-related accidents or occupational disease, and death benefits to the survivors of workers killed on the job. Workmen's compensation laws exist in 58 U.S. jurisdictions at the present time, differing widely with respect to coverage, adequacy of benefits, rehabilitation services, administration, and other provisions. Many of these laws contain defects that make it difficult for some workers to attain a reasonable standard of living while disabled.

In this chapter, we shall analyze the various state workmen's compensation laws, considering in particular the following areas: (1) development of state workmen's compensation laws, (2) objectives and theory underlying them, (3) statutory provisions, (4) defects in present workmen's compensation laws, and (5) recommendations for improvement.

DEVELOPMENT OF WORKMEN'S COMPENSATION

Workmen's compensation, now designed to provide benefits promptly to disabled workers without litigation or determining of fault, was the first form of social insurance to develop in the United States. Its development can be conveniently analyzed in three stages: (1) the common law of industrial accidents, (2) the enactment of employer-liability laws, and (3) the emergence of workmen's compensation legislation.

Common Law of Industrial Accidents

The common law of industrial accidents was the first stage in the development of workmen's compensation in the United States; its application dates back to 1837. Under the common law, a worker injured on the job had to sue his employer and prove negligence before he could collect damages. The employer was permitted to use three common-law defenses to block the worker's suit: Under the contributory-negligence doctrine, the injured worker could not collect if he had contributed in any way to his injury; under the fellow-servant doctrine, he could not collect if his injury had resulted from the negligence of a fellow worker; and under the assumption-of-risk doctrine, he could not recover if he had had advance knowledge of the dangers inherent in a particular occupation.

As a result of these defenses, relatively few disabled workers collected damages for their injuries. Lawsuits were expensive; the damage awards were small; legal fees had to be paid out of these small awards; and there was always considerable uncertainty regarding the outcome of the lawsuit. The disabled worker had two major problems to solve: the loss of income from the disabling accident, and the payment of medical expenses. Under the common law, these problems were largely unsolved, resulting in great economic insecurity and financial hardship to the disabled workers.

Enactment of Employer-Liability Laws

Because of the deficiencies in the common law, most states enacted employer-liability laws between 1885 and 1910.[1] These laws lessened the severity of the common-law defenses and improved the legal position of the injured workers. For example, three states substituted the less severe doctrine of comparative negligence for contributory negligence; the fellow-servant rule and assumption-of-risk doctrine were modified; employers and employees were denied the right to sign contracts that would relieve the employers of legal liability for industrial accidents; and surviving dependents were allowed to sue in death cases.

Despite some improvements, however, the fundamental problems experienced by disabled workers remained. The injured employee still had to sue his employer and prove negligence; he still had the problems of maintenance of income during disability and payment of medical expenses; and there were still long delays in securing court action, high costs of a lawsuit, and uncertainty of the legal outcome.

Emergence of Workmen's Compensation

The Industrial Revolution, which changed the United States from an agricultural to an industrial economy, also caused a great increase in the number of workers who were killed or disabled in job-related accidents. Because of limitations on both the common law and the employer-liability statutes, the states began to consider workmen's compensation legislation as a solution to the growing problem of work-related accidents.

---

[1]See C. Arthur Williams, Jr., *Insurance Arrangements under Workmen's Compensation,* U.S. Department of Labor, Wage and Labor Standards Administration, Bureau of Labor Standards, Bulletin No. 317 (Washington, D.C.: U.S. Government Printing Office, 1969), pp. 1-8.

Workmen's compensation laws existed in Europe in the 1880s, and by 1903, most European countries had enacted some type of legislation. But workmen's compensation was slower to develop in the United States. Maryland passed such a law in 1902, but it was limited in application and was subsequently declared unconstitutional. The stimulus for enactment of state workmen's compensation laws started in 1908, when the federal government passed a law covering certain federal employees, and by 1911, ten states had passed workmen's compensation laws. By 1920, all but six states had enacted such laws. Workmen's compensation programs exist in all states today.

Workmen's compensation is based on the fundamental principle of liability without fault. *The employer is held absolutely liable for the occupational injuries suffered by his workers, regardless of who was at fault.* The injured worker is compensated for his injuries according to a schedule of benefits established by law and normally does not have to sue his employer to collect benefits. The laws provide for the prompt payment of benefits to injured workers regardless of fault and with a minimum of legal formality.

OBJECTIVES OF WORKMEN'S COMPENSATION

Workmen's compensation programs have five basic objectives: (1) broad coverage of employees for occupational injury and disease, (2) substantial protection against the loss of income, (3) sufficient medical care and rehabilitation services, (4) encouragement of safety, and (5) an effective delivery system for benefits and services.[2]

Broad Coverage for Occupational Injury and Disease

A basic objective of modern workmen's compensation programs is to provide broad coverage of employees for occupational injury and disease. That is, the laws should cover most employees for all work-related injuries and occupational diseases.

Several reasons are often given to justify the exclusion of certain groups, but many of these arguments break down after careful analysis. First, it is argued that some firms should be excluded because they are small, or have poor safety records, or are reluctant to bear the costs of workmen's compensation benefits. However, many states have extended their workmen's compensation laws to cover most firms without undue financial distress. And if the cost of covering certain excluded groups is high, then the disabled workers and society in general are bearing the costs of occupational injuries to these groups, in the form of poverty or welfare payments. These costs should be charged to the firms and not to society.

Second, certain groups, such as household workers, are said to be excluded because they lack political influence. This, of course, is very poor justification for their exclusion from a modern workmen's compensation program. In

---

[2]National Commission on State Workmen's Compensation Laws, *The Report of the National Commission on State Workmen's Compensation Laws* (Washington, D.C.: U.S. Government Printing Office, 1972), pp. 35-40.

addition, certain groups were formerly excluded because of the constitutional requirement of due process, which required some states to enact elective laws. The question of due process, however, has limited relevance for modern workmen's compensation programs.

Third, some groups are excluded because of difficulties in administration. For example, certain employers, such as homeowners, who employ casual labor are excluded, as are small farmers, because of the substantial administrative burdens and difficulty in informing these groups about the law.

Finally, it is argued that, because of the principle of the freedom to bargain, employers and employees should negotiate to determine how much protection against work-related accidents is desired, and thus to what extent the workers should be covered under workmen's compensation. But many workers are not unionized and lack equal bargaining power with their employers, and few workers are in a position to determine accurately the probability of an occupational injury and the resulting economic loss. A mandatory workmen's compensation law can protect these workers from possible poverty and destitution.

Substantial Protection against Loss of Income

The second basic objective of workmen's compensation laws is that the benefits should replace a substantial proportion of the disabled worker's lost earnings. The measure of a worker's economic loss is the lifetime reduction in his remuneration because of the occupational injury or disease. Gross remuneration consists of basic wages and salaries, irregular wage payments, pay for leave time, and employer contributions for fringe benefits and OASDHI benefits. The measure of loss, however, is the difference in *net remuneration* before and after the work-related disability. Net remuneration reflects taxes, job-related expenses, fringe benefits that lapse, and uncompensated expenses that result from the disability. This concept can be illustrated by Figure 13-1, which indicates the elements of gross and net remuneration before and after the disability.

The view that workmen's compensation should restore a large proportion of the disabled worker's lost remuneration can be justified by two major considerations. First, workmen's compensation is social insurance, not public assistance. Public-assistance programs provide benefits based on a person's demonstrated need. Workmen's compensation benefits, however, should be closely related to the worker's loss of present and future income and so should be considerably higher than a subsistence level of income. Second, disabled workers normally give up their right to sue for economic damages and for pain and suffering, in exchange for the workmen's compensation benefits. Other social insurance programs, including OASDHI and unemployment insurance, do not require the surrender of a valuable right in exchange for benefits.

As a practical matter, however, both minimum and maximum weekly cash payments must be established. A minimum benefit is necessary to keep the disabled worker off welfare; a maximum amount must be set because highly paid workers are in a position to provide for their own disability-income insurance if the workmen's compensation benefits are inadequate. Some argue that setting a maximum limit on benefits is justified to reduce employer costs; but this argument unfairly calls upon disabled workers who were highly paid to bear a higher proportion of their own lost remuneration.[3]

BEFORE IMPAIRMENT		AFTER IMPAIRMENT	
+	Basic wages and salaries	+	Basic wages and salaries
+	Irregular wage payments	+	Irregular wage payments
+	Pay for leave time	+	Pay for leave time
+	Employer contributions for supplements	+	Employer contributions for supplements
=	Total remuneration	=	Total remuneration
—	Taxes	—	Taxes
—	Work-related expenses	—	Work-related expenses
		—	Expenses caused by injury or disease
=	Net remuneration	=	Net remuneration

Sufficient Medical Care and Rehabilitation Services

In keeping with the workmen's compensation objective of providing sufficient medical care and rehabilitation services to injured workers, the laws require the employer to pay their medical, hospital, and surgical expenses, as well as those for other health professionals, such as physical therapists.

Vocational counseling, guidance, retraining, and other rehabilitation services are also provided to restore the injured worker to gainful employment. Disabled workers who can be returned to productive jobs can experience a feeling of well-being and worth as a result; and adequate and prompt rehabilitation services can reduce workmen's compensation costs.

Encouragement of Safety

Workmen's compensation programs also aim at reducing work-related accidents and developing sound safety programs. Experience rating is used to encourage firms to be safety-conscious and to make a determined effort to reduce industrial accidents, since firms with superior accident records pay relatively lower workmen's compensation premiums. And the end result may be improvement in the competitive position of firms and industries with superior safety records. The laws allocate the costs of industrial accidents and occupational disease among those firms and industries responsible for them, so a firm or industry with a poor safety record may have to increase its prices, thereby losing some of its customers to others with lower rates of injury and disease. An individual firm with a poor safety record will generally have higher costs and lower profits, which weaken its competitive position.

[3]National Commission on State Workmen's Compensation Laws, *Report*, p. 37.

Effective Delivery System

Finally, workmen's compensation programs have the objective of providing an effective delivery system, by which the benefits and services are provided comprehensively and efficiently.

Comprehensive performance means that workmen's compensation personnel should exist in sufficient numbers and quality to carry out the objectives of the program. High-quality performance is expected of employers, physicians, state courts, and workmen's compensation insurers and agencies.

Efficient performance means that the services necessary to restore an injured worker are provided promptly, simply, and economically. Efficiency can be judged by comparing the workmen's compensation program with similar activities outside the system.

THEORIES OF WORKMEN'S COMPENSATION

Several legal and economic theories are used to justify the existence of workmen's compensation laws and the liability-without-fault principle on which the system is based.[4]

Occupational-Risk Theory

The occupational-risk theory is based on the premise that each industry should bear the costs of its own occupational disabilities as a cost of production, and that the costs of work-related injuries or disease should therefore be reflected in higher product prices.

The occupational-risk theory is defective in several respects. First, it suggests that the workers do not bear any of the costs of industrial accidents. This may not be entirely correct. Since a workmen's compensation insurance premium is based on the firm's payroll, its economic effects may be similar to those of a payroll tax; and current research studies suggest that, in the long-run, most payroll taxes are borne by labor.[5] To the extent that business firms view a workmen's compensation premium as part of the total wage bill, the costs of industrial accidents, as reflected in the premiums paid, may be shifted backward to the workers in the form of lower wage increases.

Second, the occupational-risk theory assumes that accident costs are shifted forward in the form of higher product prices. This might be difficult for a firm with a poor accident record if it is part of an industry where there is vigorous price competition, and the demand for the firm's product is elastic. Under these conditions, some accident costs may indeed be shifted backward to labor.

Finally, the typical worker bears a substantial proportion of the costs associated with his own injury because of a waiting period, restrictions on medical

[4]Herman Miles Somers and Anne Ramsay Somers, *Workmen's Compensation* (New York: John Wiley, 1954), pp. 28-29.

[5]See John A. Brittain, "The Incidence of Social Security Payroll Taxes," *The American Economic Review*, Vol. LXI, No. 1 (March 1971), 110-25.

payments in some states, inadequate disability-income benefits, incomplete restoration of the total economic loss, and inadequate rehabilitation services. These points will be developed more fully later in the chapter.

Least-Social-Cost Theory

The least-social-cost theory is based on the concept that workmen's compensation laws reduce economic losses from industrial accidents to a minimum. Firms have an incentive to reduce accidents because of the experience-rating provisions in the laws and because the uninsured costs often equal or exceed the insured costs of accidents.

Social-Compromise Theory

The social-compromise theory is that workmen's compensation represents a balanced set of sacrifices and gains for both employees and employers. The injured workers are willing to exchange the right to a jury trial in a lawsuit and a potentially larger award for a smaller but certain disability benefit. The firms are willing to pay some claims where liability may not exist, but can escape expensive litigation and the payment of a potentially higher judgment if the injured employee won the suit.

STATE WORKMEN'S COMPENSATION LAWS

Workmen's compensation provisions vary widely among the states. The variations are in the type of law, requirements for compliance, eligibility requirements, coverage of workers, types of occupational disease covered, benefit amounts, second-injury funds, and administration.[6]

Type of Law

Workmen's compensation laws are either compulsory or elective. Under a compulsory law, each employer within its scope must comply with the law by providing the specified benefits. The law is also compulsory for employees.

Five states have elective laws, whereby the employer can either elect or reject the state plan. If he rejects it, he loses his right to the three common-law defenses of contributory negligence, fellow-servant rule, and assumption of risk. Although most firms elect coverage, some do not, so some disabled employees are unable to collect benefits unless they sue for damages. Elective laws also permit the firms' employees to reject coverage, but they seldom do. Under most elective laws, it is presumed that both the employer and the employees elect coverage, unless a specific notice of rejection is filed prior to a loss.

[6]For a detailed description of current state workmen's compensation laws, see Chamber of Commerce of the United States, *Analysis of Workmen's Compensation Laws, 1975 Edition* (Washington, D.C.: Chamber of Commerce of the United States, 1975). See also National Commission on State Workmen's Compensation Laws, *Report,* pp. 31-114; and U.S. Department of Labor, Wage and Labor Standards Administration, Bureau of Labor Standards, *State Workmen's Compensation Legislation, Bulletin 161* (Washington, D.C.: U.S. Government Printing Office, 1969).

Complying with the Law

Under workmen's compensation laws, employers are generally exempt from damage suits by injured employees. If the employer complies with the law, the exclusive remedy available to the injured employee is to claim workmen's compensation benefits. He receives the benefits as established by law and does not sue his employer.

However, if the employer does not comply with the workmen's compensation law by purchasing insurance or by otherwise providing the required security, he is deprived of protection against lawsuits by his injured employees. If an employee elects to bring a suit for damages based on the employer's negligence, the employer is deprived of the three common-law defenses. In such a case, the injured worker has only to establish the employer's negligence to collect damages.[7]

Employers can comply with the law by purchasing a workmen's compensation policy, by self-insuring, or by obtaining protection from a monopoly or competitive state fund.

Most firms purchase a policy from a private insurer. The policy guarantees payment of the benefits that the employer is legally obligated to pay his disabled workers.

Self-insurance is permitted in 47 states. The laws require firms to meet certain requirements before they can self-insure: In most states, the firm must post a bond or deposit securities, and the workmen's compensation agency administering the law must approve the self-insurance plan.

In six states, employers must insure in an exclusive state fund. The reasoning behind monopoly state funds is that (1) workmen's compensation is social insurance, and private companies should not profit from the business; (2) exclusive state funds should have reduced expenses because of economies of scale and no sales effort; and (3) exclusive state funds have greater concern for the welfare of injured workers.

Twelve states permit employers to purchase insurance from either private insurers or competitive state funds. Competitive funds are established for the following reasons: (1) the fund provides a useful standard for measuring the performance of private insurers; (2) the states want to make certain that all employers can obtain the necessary protection; and (3) a competitive fund operates more efficiently if it faces competition from private insurers.[8]

Most states, if an employer does not meet the insurance requirements, enforce penalties of fines, imprisonment, or both. Also, some states enjoin the employer from doing business in the state until the insurance requirements are fulfilled.

Covered Occupations

State workmen's compensation laws do not cover all occupations. It is estimated that the state programs cover more than 62 million workers, or about

[7]James H. Donaldson, *Casualty Claim Practice*, rev. ed. (Homewood, Ill.: Richard D. Irwin, 1969), pp. 783-84.

[8]Williams, *Insurance Arrangements*, pp. 135-36, 151-52.

84 percent of all employed wage and salary workers. But eleven states cover less than 70 percent of their workers.[9]

In addition, there are numerous gaps in coverage among the states. Most states exclude agricultural, domestic, and casual employment, and only 17 states provide coverage for farmworkers on essentially the same basis as other employees. Some state laws have numerical exemptions, whereby small firms are not covered because they have few employees. And although all states have some coverage for public employees, there are marked variations in coverage. Some states have broad coverage; others limit coverage to employees of specified political subdivisions, or to workers employed in dangerous occupations; in still others, workmen's compensation coverage is optional with the state, city, or other political subdivision.

Eligibility Requirements

The covered worker must meet three tests before workmen's compensation benefits can be paid: (1) there must be an impairment—either temporary or permanent, either partial or total—or death; (2) the impairment or death must be caused by a covered injury or disease; and (3) the impairment or death must be work-related.[10]

Existence of an Impairment. An impairment is defined as a medical condition resulting from any anatomic or functional abnormality or loss. Thus, a worker whose hand is crushed in a machine has a medical impairment. An impairment is not the same thing as a disability, since a disability is not necessarily a purely medical condition. An employee is disabled when his ability to work in gainful activity is reduced from the impairment. The extent of the disability depends on the impairment and also on nonmedical factors, such as the worker's age and education.

Covered Injury or Disease. The impairment must be caused by a covered injury or disease. A traditional test of a covered injury is whether it is caused by an accident. An accident is generally defined as a sudden and unexpected event, which is determinable with respect to time and place—as in the case of a worker who is burned in a plant explosion. Most jurisdictions have defined an accident in a broad and liberal manner.

Certain injuries, however, may be excluded even though the accident occurs at work. State laws generally exclude injuries to a worker who willfully intended to injure himself or another person. Injuries due to employee intoxication, to willful failure to use safety devices or to observe safety rules, and to violations of law are also generally excluded.[11]

Early workmen's compensation laws did not make specific provisions for occupational disease. However, all states currently provide protection against occupational disease, although the coverage varies widely. Some states cover

[9]Alfred M. Skolnik and Daniel N. Price, "Workmen's Compensation under Scrutiny," *Social Security Bulletin,* Vol. 37, No. 10 (October 1974), pp. 5-8.

[10]National Commission on State Workmen's Compensation Laws, *Report,* pp. 49-51.

[11]Neil Carter, *Guide to Workmen's Compensation Claims* (New York: Roberts Publishing, 1965), p. 33.

only the occupational diseases that are listed in a schedule, while other states provide full coverage for all occupational diseases. Only 45 states provide full coverage.[12]

Work-Related Impairment. Finally, the injury or disease must arise out of and in the course of employment. The following situations generally fulfill the requirement of a work-related accident or disease:[13]

1. The employee is injured while performing specified duties at a specified location.

2. The employee is on the premises and is injured going to his work area.

3. The employee is injured going to and from work, where the firm furnishes transportation as part of the employment contract.

4. The employee is eating his lunch at a workbench and is injured by falling machinery.

5. A traveling employee is injured while staying overnight in a hotel that the employer designates.

6. Employees who travel are injured while engaging in activities that benefit the employer.

7. The employee eats food, furnished by the employer, that contains a harmful substance.

On the other hand, the following activities are generally not compensable:

1. The employee is injured on his way to work.

2. The employee is injured on a coffee break away from the premises, or after he leaves the premises.

3. The employee is traveling for the employer, but is furthering his own interests at the time of the accident.

4. The employee is injured at a hotel of his own choosing.

Types of Benefits

Workmen's compensation laws provide for several types of benefits. The major benefits are (1) medical care, (2) disability income, (3) death benefits, and (4) rehabilitation services.

Medical Care. All workmen's compensation laws provide medical care to injured employees. At the present time, 46 states provide unlimited medical care; others have either *time* or *amount* limitations on it.[14]

Disability Income. Disability-income benefits are paid to a disabled worker to compensate him for his lost wages. The injured worker must fulfill a

[12]American Mutual Insurance Alliance, "Workmen's Compensation: Update 1975," *Journal of American Insurance,* Winter 1974-75, p. 24, Chart 1.

[13]C. A. Kulp and John W. Hall, *Casualty Insurance,* 4th ed. (New York: Ronald Press, 1968), p. 213.

[14]For a discussion of these limitations, see National Commission on State Workmen's Compensation Laws, *Report,* p. 79.

waiting period, ranging from two to seven days. If he remains disabled for a certain number of days or weeks, however, the benefits are paid retroactively to the date of the injury. The waiting period is designed to eliminate short-term disabilities, to reduce administrative expenses, and to hold down workmen's compensation premiums.

The weekly benefit amount is based on a percentage of the worker's average weekly wage, such as 66⅔ percent, and the classification of his disability. Most states have minimum and maximum weekly benefits, and limits on the total number of weeks and the total dollar amount of the benefits. If the disability is permanent, however, a majority of the states pay lifetime benefits.

Four classifications of disability are used to determine the weekly benefit amount: (1) temporary total, (2) permanent total, (3) temporary partial, and (4) permanent partial.

1. Temporary Total. Most disability-income benefits are paid for temporary total disability. That is, a work-related injury or disease causes a temporary and total loss of earnings. The employee cannot work at all while he is recovering from the injury, but he is expected to recover fully—for example, when an employees breaks both legs at work. The disability ends when he recovers and returns to work.

As of January 1975, maximum weekly temporary-disability benefits paid by the states ranged from a high of $178 in Connecticut to a low of $80 in Oklahoma. Minimum payments ranged from $78 in Idaho to $7 in Kansas.[15]

2. Permanent Total. Permanent total disability means that the employee is permanently and totally disabled and is unable to work, or is unable to work regularly in any well-known branch of the labor market. For example, a worker's spinal cord may be severed in an industrial accident. Since he is presumed to be disabled for his remaining lifetime, he is classified as permanently and total disabled. In many states, losses also classified as permanent total disability include the loss of both eyes, or both arms, or both legs, and other types of disability specified in the law.

As of January 1975, maximum weekly permanent-total-disability benefits ranged from a high of $178 in Connecticut to a low of $50 in Oklahoma. Minimum payments ranged from $84 in Ohio to $7 in Kansas.[16]

3. Temporary Partial. Temporary partial disability means that the employee has sustained a temporary injury whereby he can perform only part of his duties, but he is not totally disabled and has no permanent impairment. For example, the employee has cut his hand and can work only part-time. The weekly benefit is a percentage of the weekly wages lost, subject to a maximum. The percentage is applied to the difference in his earned wages before and after the injury.

4. Permanent Partial. Permanent partial disability means that the employee has a permanent impairment, but he is not completely disabled. He may be able to work at his regular job or be retrained for other types of work. Two classes of permanent partial disability are used—scheduled and nonsched-

[15]Chamber of Commerce of the United States, *Analysis,* pp. 19-21, Chart V.

[16]*Ibid.*

uled. Scheduled injuries are listed in the law and include the loss of an arm, leg, hand, finger, or other member of the body. Nonscheduled injuries are of a more general nature, such as a head or back injury that disables the worker. In most jurisdictions, the amount paid for a scheduled injury is determined by multiplying a certain number of weeks by the weekly disability-income benefit, subject to some maximum limit. For example, a worker in Nebraska who loses his hand can receive maximum income benefits of $15,575. Also, in most states, the amount paid for a scheduled injury is in addition to the benefits paid during the healing period or while the worker is totally disabled.

The benefits paid for nonscheduled injuries are generally based on some proportion of the wage loss—the difference in wages earned before and after the injury—for a certain number of weeks. In most jurisdictions, there are limits on the maximum amounts or maximum number of weeks that the benefits can be paid.

Death Benefits. Survivors are paid death benefits if the worker is killed on the job. Two major death benefits are generally available: (1) cash-income payments to dependents, and (2) burial allowances. The cash-income payments vary widely among the states, and most jurisdictions have either time or amount limitations. Some states pay weekly or monthly income benefits to a widow for life, or until she remarries, or to children under age 18 with no limitation on amounts. Most states, however, limit the amounts that can be paid. The maximum amounts that can be paid to a widow with children, in those states with limits, range from a low of $15,000 in Mississippi to a high of $64,500 in Michigan.

Burial allowances are also subject to maximum amounts, ranging from $500 to $1,500. The burial allowances in most states pay only a fraction of the deceased worker's funeral expenses.

Rehabilitation Services. Rehabilitation services are available to severely disabled workers who are handicapped by their injuries. The goal of rehabilitation is the maximum restoration of a handicapped worker in every phase of his life, and this includes physical, mental, social, vocational, and economic considerations. Both medical and vocational services are necessary for complete rehabilitation. Medical rehabilitation aims at the maximum recovery of the worker's health and the maximum restoration of a bodily function. Vocational rehabilitation aims at enabling handicapped workers to reenter the labor force as productive citizens. This involves vocational training, job counseling, and selective job placement.

Second-Injury Funds

Second-injury funds exist in all but two states. If a worker with a permanent physical impairment is subsequently injured in a work-related accident, and the second injury along with the previous impairment causes the worker to be totally and permanently disabled, the amount of workmen's compensation benefits that must be paid is increased. For example, a worker with one eye may lose his second eye in a work-related accident, thereby becoming totally and permanently disabled. The employer pays only for the second injury, and the second-injury fund pays the remainder of the benefit award.

The purposes of the second-injury funds are (1) to encourage the hiring of physically handicapped workers, and (2) to allocate more equitably the costs of providing benefits to such employees. If a second-injury fund did not exist, employers would be reluctant to hire handicapped workers because of the higher benefits that might have to be paid if a second injury occurred. And the funds allocate the costs of industrial accidents more equitably because the current employer is held responsible for only the injury that occurred while the worker was in his employ, rather than for the total and permanent disability that resulted from the combined injuries.

Administration

Most states use a workmen's compensation board or commission to administer workmen's compensation claims. The law is administered either by an independent workmen's compensation agency or by the same agency that administers the state's labor laws.

Five states use the courts to administer the claims. The courts must either approve of the settlement or, if the parties disagree, resolve the dispute. In such cases, the court hears the case, determines the compensation payments, and issues judgments just as it would in any other case, except that it can order the payment of benefits beyond the date of the trial.[17] Court administration is generally considered poor. Workmen's compensation claims often present difficult administrative problems and require continuous supervision. The courts are not organized and equipped to provide the necessary services for efficient claims administration.

Claim Procedures.   The injured worker must file a claim for benefits with the appropriate workmen's compensation agency and give proper notice to the employer or insurer. Two methods are used to settle noncontested claims: (1) agreement, and (2) direct payment.

A majority of states use the agreement method, whereby the injured worker and the employer or insurer agree upon a settlement before the claim is paid. Some states require the workmen's compensation agency to approve the settlement before benefits are paid. One disadvantage of this approach is that the injured worker may agree to a settlement that is not in his best interest.

Some states use the direct-payment system, whereby the employer or insurer pay benefits immediately to the injured worker. He does not have to agree to a settlement or sign any papers before the payments start. If he fails to receive the proper benefits established by law, the workmen's compensation agency can intervene, investigate, and correct any errors.

If a case is contested, most state laws provide for a hearing by a hearing officer or referee. His decision can be appealed to a commission or appeals board, and then to the courts. If a state administrative agency administers the law, an appeal may also be taken to the courts.

---

[17]Donaldson, *Casualty Claim Practice,* p. 785.

DEFECTS OF WORKMEN'S COMPENSATION

Workmen's compensation has made remarkable progress since its inception. Benefits have been increased; coverage has been broadened to cover additional workers; emphasis on accident prevention and industrial safety programs has reduced injury frequency and severity rates. The quality of medical care for injured workers has significantly improved, and the concept has changed from the simple payment of monetary benefits to attempts at full restoration of injured workers from a medical, physical, vocational, and psychological point of view.

But despite these great improvements, several deficiencies still remain. The National Commission of State Workmen's Compensation Laws points out clearly the nature of these defects, which include (1) incomplete coverage, (2) inadequate benefits, (3) inadequate medical care and rehabilitation services, (4) administrative defects, (5) second-injury fund defects, and (6) experience rating and accident prevention.

Incomplete Coverage

Because of elective laws, numerical exemptions, and exclusions of certain occupations, such as agricultural, domestic, and casual work, millions of workers have no protection under workmen's compensation laws. An estimated 12 million civilian wage and salary workers, or about 16 percent of these workers, were not covered by state workmen's compensation laws in 1972. In eleven states, more than 30 percent of the labor force is not covered.[18] Since a fundamental principle of social insurance is to provide income protection to all workers, the gap in coverage represents a serious deficiency.

Five states still retain their elective laws. However, it is difficult to justify elective laws. Many states enacted them because they feared that the courts would declare a compulsory law unconstitutional; but since the constitutionality of workmen's compensation has been settled by the courts, this argument is no longer valid. Furthermore, even in those states with elective laws, most employers elect workmen's compensation benefits for their employees. If an employer fails to provide coverage, he loses the common-law defenses in an employee tort action, and he may have to pay very large damages. In effect, the threat of a lawsuit for damages makes the workmen's compensation law compulsory for most employers, even in states with elective laws.

In addition, numerical exemptions are seldom justified. Small firms generally have poor accident records, and many of them lack the financial resources to protect injured workers unless the law compels them to carry workmen's compensation insurance. Also, few uncovered workers can afford to initiate a successful damage suit against their employers for their injuries, so they may be exposed to serious economic insecurity if they are denied benefits because of numerical exemptions.

The exclusion of certain occupations represents another serious gap in coverage. Farm employment, for instance, which is one of the most hazardous

[18]Skolnik and Price, "Workmen's Compensation under Scrutiny," p. 5 and p. 7.

occupations, is excluded from coverage in most states; in only about one-third are these workers covered on the same basis as other employees. Deaths and disabling injuries from farm accidents have been increasing for more than a decade, and in 1969, farming was second to construction in the numbers of workers killed.[19] In addition to dangerous farm machinery, the workers are also exposed to the growing use of pesticides, herbicides, fungicides, and defoliants. The need for protection is even greater in view of the risk of occupational disease from these chemicals.

Inadequate Disability-Income Benefits

Although workmen's compensation disability-income benefits have been substantially increased in recent years, several states continue to pay benefits that are inadequate for meeting the disabled worker's actual need. The inadequacy of benefits is reflected in the following areas: (1) temporary total disability, (2) permanent total disability, (3) permanent partial disability, and (4) death benefits.

Temporary-Total-Disability Benefits. The laws in most states provide that temporarily and totally disabled workers should receive benefits equal to two-thirds of their average weekly wage. Many workers, however, do not receive benefits in that amount, since the maximum limits on weekly benefits set by some states are considerably below the two-thirds objective. In January 1975, *the maximum weekly benefits for temporary total disability in 18 states was less than two-thirds of the average weekly wage in the state.*[20] In addition, workmen's compensation benefit increases tend to lag behind increases in wage levels and the cost of living; there is a considerable lag between increases in wage levels and action by state legislatures in raising the statutory maximum; and a waiting period must be fulfilled before benefits are paid. For these reasons, many workers receive weekly benefits that restore less than two-thirds of their average weekly wage.

Furthermore, total-temporary-disability benefits are below the poverty line in many states. The 1974 national poverty level for a four-member nonfarm family was $96.92 weekly. But as of January 1, 1975, *the maximum weekly temporary-total-disability benefits in 22 states did not reach that poverty level.*[21] Thus, many workers experience considerable economic insecurity during periods of disability.

In analyzing the adequacy of temporary-total-disability benefits, the significance of the waiting periods and limits on the retroactive payment of benefits should not be underemphasized. A lengthy waiting period restricts the benefits paid for work-related injuries and forces the injured worker to bear much of the cost of an accident. Most states impose a seven-day waiting period and pay ret-

[19]U.S. Department of Labor, *Manpower Report of the President* (Washington, D.C.: U.S. Government Printing Office, 1971), p. 127.

[20]American Mutual Insurance Alliance, "Workmen's Compensation: Update 1975," p. 24, Chart 1.

[21]Chamber of Commerce of United States, *Analysis*, p. 21, Chart V.

roactive benefits only if the disability lasts more than 28 days. But the average period of temporary-disability cases in manufacturing industries is about 18 calendar days; so, in the absence of some employer fringe-benefit plan covering short-term occupational injuries, many temporary-total-disability cases are eliminated for disability-income benefits, and medical bills are the only benefits paid.

For example, although Nebraska provides for payment of 66⅔ percent of the worker's average weekly wage, its maximum weekly benefit for temporary total disability is $89. A factory worker who has an average weekly wage of $133.50 and is disabled for three weeks has a total wage loss of $400.50; because of the waiting period, he receives workmen's compensation benefits for only two weeks, or $178. Thus, instead of restoring two-thirds of his average wage, the workmen's compensation benefit replaces only about 44 percent of it. For highly paid workers, such as skilled craftsmen or machinists, the proportion of the lost wages replaced would be even lower.

The National Commission on Workmen's Compensation Laws recommends that, subject to the state's maximum weekly benefit, temporary-total-disability benefits should be at least 80 percent of the worker's *spendable weekly earnings,* and that until the state's maximum weekly benefit exceeds 100 percent of the state's average weekly wage, the maximum weekly benefit should be at least two-thirds of the worker's gross weekly wage. In addition, a waiting period of no more than three days' duration is also recommended, with payment of retroactive benefits after two weeks or less.[22]

Permanent-Total-Disability Benefits. Permanent-total-disability benefits, which are awarded to about 1,000 workers each year,[23] are also inadequate in many states. Only 30 states pay maximum weekly benefits for permanent total disability that are at least equal to two-thirds of the state's average weekly wage.[24]

Another defect is that some states have time and amount limits on permanent-total-disability benefits. These limits are illogical and often cause great economic insecurity to disabled workers. If a worker is permanently and totally disabled, he will probably remain in that condition for the rest of his life; yet many states terminate the benefits after maximum amounts are paid or after a certain time period has expired. In 12 states, a totally disabled worker is paid benefits for less than thirteen years. In 12 states, the maximum total benefit that a totally disabled worker can receive is less than $50,000, or less than seven years of full-time earnings for the average worker. Because of these limits, some totally disabled workers must apply for public-assistance benefits, or other community resources must be used to support them. The community must then absorb the costs that the employer should legitimately pay. Workmen's compensation laws are based on the principle of holding the employer responsible for the payment of work-related injuries or disease, and if the community is re-

[22]National Commission on Workmen's Compensation Laws, *Report,* pp. 59-60.

[23]*Ibid.,* p. 63.

[24]American Mutual Insurance Alliance, "Workmen's Compensation: Update 1975," p. 24, Chart 1.

quired to support some permanently and totally disabled workers after their benefits expire, this basic principle of employer responsibility is violated. If workmen's compensation is to provide adequate economic security, the various time and amount limitations for permanent and total disability cases must be eliminated. The additional cost would not be prohibitive, since these cases amount to less than one-tenth of 1 percent of all compensable cases.[25]

Permanent-Partial-Disability Benefits. One of the most pressing issues in workmen's compensation benefits is the payment of benefits for permanent partial disability. These benefits are the most expensive part of total workmen's compensation programs; cash benefits plus medical care account for more than 50 percent of all payments.

There are two principal problems in the payment of permanent-partial-disability benefits. First, there are wide variations from state to state. Most workmen's compensation laws contain schedules that indicate the amounts paid for specific impairments; but these schedules cover only a small proportion of medically identifiable impairments. The benefits for the specific impairments vary widely, depending on the state in which the injury occurred. The sampling below shows the maximum amounts that can be paid for certain listed impairments in selected states:

	Loss of Arm at Shoulder	Loss of One Foot	Loss of One Eye
Wisconsin	$26,500	$13,250	$14,475
Arkansas	13,300	8,312	6,650
Wyoming	6,800	4,300	5,000

Other illustrations are possible, but these should suffice. Although workmen's compensation benefits can never adequately compensate a worker for the loss of a limb, the injured worker should be entitled to a better schedule of benefits than exists at present.

A second problem area is that many states pay disproportionately larger benefits for minor disabilities than for the more serious cases of major permanent partial and permanent total disability. In 20 states, the cash benefits paid for minor permanent partial impairments accounted for 20 percent or more of the total outlays in compensation, and in four states, they accounted for more than 30 percent of the total.[26] In many states, relatively larger amounts are paid for minor permanent partial impairments than for the more serious permanent-total-disability cases.

Limitations on Death Benefits. Most states have time or amount limitations on the death benefits paid to survivors. Although the number of industrial deaths has declined over time, more than 14,000 workers are still killed on the job each year. The widows and children should be allowed to maintain them-

[25]Alfred M. Skolnik and Daniel N. Price, "Another Look at Workmen's Compensation," *Social Security Bulletin,* Vol. 33, No. 10 (October 1970), 10, Table 5.

[26]National Commission on State Workmen's Compensation Laws, *Report,* p. 67, Table 3.9.

selves at their former standard of living. At a minimum, the states should pay income benefits to widows for life or until they remarry, and to the surviving dependent children until they reach age 18 (or over 18, if disabled). Only 22 states provided this type of protection in 1975.[27]

Inadequate Medical Care and Rehabilitation Services

Some states still have limits on medical care and restrictions on occupational disease, and most provide inadequate rehabilitation services.

Limits on Medical Care. Most states provide unlimited medical care, but a few states place time or amount limits on the medical care provided to injured workers, creating a serious void in the system. The amount limitations are often unrealistically low. In January 1975, the maximum limit in Louisiana was $25,000; in Alabama, $35,000, and in New Mexico, $40,000.[28]

A few states also have time limitations, whereby an injured worker may be ineligible for further medical care if he has not received treatment within a certain time period. Thus, if any effects of a work-related accident are felt after the medical treatment is discontinued, the patient may be ineligible for further care.

In addition, many states provide inadequate supervision of medical care. The goal of workmen's compensation is to restore the worker's health as quickly as possible with a minimum of permanent disability. To attain this goal, the state workmen's compensation agency must supervise and control the medical care provided to injured workers. It should see that the worker's injury is accurately diagnosed at the outset, and supervise his care continuously until healing and recovery are complete. Unfortunately, only about half the states have a medical rehabilitation division to supervise the medical care provided to injured workers.[29]

Restrictions on Occupational Disease. Five states still restrict coverage of occupational diseases to only those listed in a schedule. Even if the schedules are broad and periodically revised, they tend to become obsolete because of rapid changes in technology that can cause occupational disease. The constant introduction of new chemical processes, new devices such as lasers, and new radioactive substances exposes thousands of workers to the risks of occupational disease. Thousands die or are disabled each year because of the effects of coal dust, cancer-causing chemicals, asbestos, beryllium, lead, cotton, and pesticides. Even when the state legislatures frequently revise their schedules of listed diseases, it is obvious that all types of occupational disease cannot be listed in a schedule. The worker has full protection against occupational disease only if all types are fully covered.

Inadequate Rehabilitation Services. Although rehabilitation of disabled

[27]American Mutual Insurance Alliance, "Workmen's Compensation: Update 1975," p. 24, Chart 1.

[28]Chamber of Commerce of the United States, *Analysis,* pp. 26-27, Chart VIII.

[29]National Commission on State Workmen's Compensation Laws, *Report,* p. 21.

workers is a major objective of workmen's compensation, most states fall short of providing effective rehabilitation services to injured workers.[30]

Several obstacles hinder the effective rehabilitation of disabled workers in many states. First, most states do not have a separate rehabilitation division within the workmen's compensation agency. The agency, as the first official authority to become aware of the worker's injury, is in a good position to promote his rehabilitation. Unless rehabilitation starts immediately after an injury, maximum physical restoration of the worker may be impossible. Lack of a rehabilitation division within the workmen's compensation agency can mean that some handicapped workers do not receive prompt medical, vocational, and rehabilitation services for full restoration.

Second, many states do not provide adequate maintenance benefits during rehabilitation. A severely disabled worker may find it financially impossible to undergo physical and vocational rehabilitation when additional funds are required. Even if full workmen's compensation benefits are paid during his rehabilitation, the additional costs of travel, tuition, equipment, and other expenses may discourage him from undertaking it. Maintenance benefits are essential for encouraging prompt rehabilitation.

Third, there is often a separation of functions between the workmen's compensation agency and the state vocational rehabilitation agency. Each state now participates in a joint federal-state program of vocational rehabilitation. But the program may be located in the state's department of labor or department of education, with no formal link or relationship to the workmen's compensation agency. Thus, there is often a lack of the necessary coordination between the two programs for effective rehabilitation.

Fourth, state rehabilitation agencies are often overburdened by nonoccupational disability cases—automobile accident victims, the congenitally disabled, and young disabled workers entering the labor force for the first time—handling the total number of both occupational and nonoccupational disabilities is beyond the capacity of most of these agencies. Also, the fact that agencies are expanding their services to the physically disabled and culturally disadvantaged means that some occupationally disabled workers may not be high-priority clients from the viewpoint of the agency.

Finally, existing workmen's compensation laws may dissuade some seriously disabled workers from rehabilitation. In a case where the degree of the injured worker's disability is in dispute, he may fear that his undergoing rehabilitation would show his disability to be less serious than he contends.[31]

Administrative Defects

Inadequate administration of state workmen's compensation laws is another deficiency. Many states are lax in the investigation and enforcement of

[30]John F. Burton, Jr., and Monroe Berkowitz, "Objectives Other Than Income Maintenance for Workmen's Compensation," *The Journal of Risk and Insurance,* Vol. XXXVIII, No. 3 (September 1971), 353-54.

[31]John G. Turnbull, C. Arthur Williams, Jr., and Earl F. Cheit, *Economic and Social Security,* 4th ed. (New York: Ronald Press, 1973), pp. 318-19.

coverage, supervision of claims and adjudication of contested claims, promotion of safety programs, and statistical analysis of the efficiency of workmen's compensation insurers and state agencies.

In addition, certain other problem areas deserve special comment. Labor unions charge that many states show little administrative concern for injured workers, by inadequately informing them about their compensation rights— young and unorganized workers often receive compensation advice only from company supervisors or claims representatives—and by permitting workmen's compensation insurers to perform most administrative functions relating to the law. The insurer receives the claim, accepts or denies it, controls the payments, and terminates the benefits, often without adequate supervision by the state workmen's compensation agency.

Claims supervision in many states is inadequate. In too many cases, an injured worker agrees to a lump-sum settlement or compromises his rights to full medical care under a compromise-and-release settlement, because the case is inadequately supervised by the state workmen's compensation agency. Attorneys favor lump-sum awards because they generally provide a larger fee with greater certainty; employers and insurers also tend to favor lump-sum settlements because they terminate liability and reduce claims for additional compensation for aggravation of the injury. But lump-sum settlements are inconsistent with the workmen's compensation objective of restoring lost wages on a systematic basis. Lump-sum settlements should be either forbidden or else confined to those special situations where they are in the best interest of the disabled worker, and then only after the workmen's compensation agency has carefully supervised and approved the settlement after consultation with the rehabilitation agency.

Another problem is the inadequate budgets and staff of many state workmen's compensation agencies. The quality of workmen's compensation insurers varies widely. Although most insurers pay claims promptly, some do not, and although most settle claims fairly, some will try to persuade injured workers to settle for less than the full amount they are entitled to. Because of inadequate budget and staff, many state workmen's compensation agencies cannot adequately police claim settlements.

Finally, the complexities of medical care, supervision of benefits, and rehabilitation make administration by a state agency more desirable than by the courts. Since the courts are not equipped to provide adequate supervision in these areas, court administration should be replaced by that of a state agency.

Second-Injury Fund Defects

A fundamental purpose of second-injury funds is to encourage employers to hire handicapped workers. However, many employers are unaware of the existence of second-injury funds, much less their functions and how they operate. Thus, they may be reluctant to hire severely handicapped workers because of the possible adverse effect on their workmen's compensation premiums.

In most states, the second-injury funds have too narrow a coverage of preexisting impairments and may thus be too limited to benefit very many handicapped workers. Many funds limit coverage to the loss of loss or use of a bodily member, such as a hand, eye, or leg. Also, some states have limitations that prevent an injured employee from collecting if the second injury merely aggravates the preexisting condition. The second-injury funds should be broadened to include all types of prior impairments, such as heart disease, arthritis, epilepsy, and polio. Such a change would increase the employment opportunities for workers with congenital diseases. Only 20 states now provide broad coverage of preexisting impairments under their second-injury funds.[32]

Finally, the inadequate financing of many second-injury funds makes it difficult to provide broad coverage for previous impairments. Some states finance their funds by assessments on employers for work-related deaths when the deceased worker has no surviving dependents, and others by general assessments against all employers, but the amounts collected are often insufficient for providing broad second-injury coverage.

Experience Rating and Accident Reduction

Another problem is the extent to which experience rating reduces work-related accidents and disease. It has been said that experience rating provides a strong financial stimulus for a firm to reduce injury frequency and severity rates, since workmen's compensation premiums are thereby reduced. Workmen's compensation insurers cite numerous examples in which safety representatives have used premium savings as a stimulus for firms to initiate effective safety programs. Firms that are experienced-rated and retrospectively rated have better safety records than those that are not eligible for experience rating.[33] And employers in highly hazardous industries must maintain safe working conditions to hold their costs down and remain competitive.

However, the overall effectiveness of experience rating in reducing accidents may in actuality be limited. Several factors cast doubt on its effectiveness.[34] First, since workmen's compensation premiums amount to only about 1 percent or less of payroll, the potential premium savings from accident-prevention activities are limited. Second, if, in establishing a safety program, a firm must hire safety engineers or hold safety classes in all departments and shifts, it incurs high fixed and indivisible costs, and the incentive effect from lower workmen's compensation costs may be reduced. Third, about 80 percent of all firms are ineligible for experience rating because of their small size. These firms are class-rated, and rate reductions are granted only if the experience of the entire class improves. If a single class-rated firm promotes effective safety programs, the resultant reduction in accidents that benefits the class as a whole is unlikely to have a measurable impact on the premiums of that firm. Fourth, even if the firms are experience-rated, the premiums paid may not accurately reflect the true economic losses. Segregation of loss experience into classes is somewhat arbitrary, and an individual firm may be classified with other firms that have

[32]National Commission on State Workmen's Compensation Laws, *Report,* p. 83, Table 4.7.

[33]Williams, *Insurance Arrangements,* p. 58.

[34]Burton and Berkowitz, "Objectives," pp. 349-52.

substantially different normal accident rates. Fifth, experience rating is normally based on the benefits paid to injured workers, not on the firm's safety record. Because of poor administration in some jurisdictions, employers there may prefer to reduce premiums by contesting claims rather than by initiating safety measures. Finally, because insurer safety programs and accident-prevention services are financed by a portion of the workmen's compensation premiums received, the amount allocated to a large firm may be significant, but the amount for a small firm may be inadequate for an effective safety program.

Prof. Monroe Berkowitz says that factors other then experience rating may have been more important in causing a reduction in accident rates over time. One key element is the incentive to reduce industrial accidents regardless of experience rating because the uninsured costs of an industrial accident, such as the lost production of employees not injured, or damaged parts and equipment, may equal or exceed the costs of the workmen's compensation benefits. Other incentive factors are public relations, employee morale, and labor-union pressure.[35]

IMPROVING WORKMEN'S COMPENSATION

The National Commission on State Workman's Compensation Laws concludes that workmen's compensation programs are generally inadequate and inequitable, and it urges the states to incorporate several important recommendations in their workmen's compensation laws. The essential recommendations are these:[36]

1. *Compulsory Coverage.* All elective laws should be abolished, and coverage should be compulsory for all employers.

2. *No Numerical or Occupational Exemptions.* Numerical exemptions should be abolished, and all employers of one or more workers should be covered. Also, as of July 1, 1975, farm workers should be covered on the same basis as all other employees. Household and casual workers should be covered under workmen's compensation at least to the extent that they are covered by Social Security. All government employees should also be covered. There should be no exemptions for any class of employees, including professional athletes and employees of charitable organizations.

3. *Full Coverage of Occupational Diseases.* Present restrictions on occupational disease should be eliminated, and all occupational diseases should be fully covered.

4. *Full Medical Care and Rehabilitation Services.* Medical care and physical-rehabilitation services should be provided without any limitations with respect to time or dollar amounts.

5. *Choice of Filing a Claim.* A worker may travel in several states. He should

[35]Monroe Berkowitz, *Workmen's Compensation: The New Jersey Experience* (New Brunswick, N.J.: Rutgers University Press, 1960), pp. 150-51. See also Burton and Berkowitz, "Objectives," p. 350.

[36]National Commission on State Workmen's Compensation Laws, *Report,* pp. 14-27 and pp. 125-30.

have the option of filing a claim in the state where he is injured, where he is hired, or where his employment is principally localized.

6. *Adequate Temporary Total Disability Benefits.* A worker who is temporarily and totally disabled should receive benefits at least equal to two-thirds of his gross weekly wage, subject to a maximum weekly benefit of at least 100 percent of the state's average weekly wage, by July 1, 1975. There should be no limitations with respect to time or total dollar amount during the period of disability.

7. *Adequate Permanent Total Disability Benefits.* A worker who is permanently and totally disabled should receive benefits at least equal to two-thirds of his gross weekly wage. By July 1, 1975, the maximum weekly benefit should be at least 100 percent of the state's average weekly wage. The benefits should be paid for life or for the duration of disability, without any limitations on time or total dollar amount. The definition of permanent total disability used by most states should be retained.

8. *Adequate Death Benefits.* Surviving dependents should receive at least two-thirds of the deceased worker's gross weekly wage. By July 1, 1975, the maximum weekly benefit should be at least 100 percent of the state's average weekly wage. The death benefits should be paid for life or until remarriage. In the event of re-marriage, two years' benefits should be paid in a lump sum. The death benefits for a dependent child should be paid until age 18, or until age 25 if he is a full-time student.

The commission rejected a proposal for a federal workmen's compensation plan, but urged the states to enact these essential recommendations without delay. The states were given until July 1, 1975, to comply with the recommendations. The programs are to be reevaluated at that time, and if sufficient progress has not been made, Congress will consider legislation to guarantee compliance. It is estimated that the recommendations could be met in 45 states by less than a 50 percent increase in workmen's compensation costs: In 21 states, the increase in costs would be between 30 and 49.9 percent; in 20, between 10 and 29.9 percent; and in four, less than 10 percent. These costs are considered to be within the economic capability of the states.

The commission also made several less essential recommendations for improving state workmen's compensation laws, including the following:

1. *Shorter Waiting Period.* To reduce the disabled worker's financial burden, all states should enact a waiting period of not more than three days, with retroactive benefits after two weeks or less of disability.

2. *Progressive Increase in Maximum Weekly Benefit.* The maximum weekly benefit should be progressively increased to at least 200 percent of the state's average weekly wage by 1981.

3. *New Basis for Calculating Benefits.* The weekly cash benefit should be equal to 80 percent of the worker's spendable weekly earnings. Spendable earnings are defined as gross earnings minus payroll taxes and job-related expenses, subject to a maximum weekly benefit. Under this approach, tax considerations or additional benefits for dependents would be unnecessary.

4. *Minimum Death Benefits.* Minimum weekly death benefits should be at least 50 percent of the state's average weekly wage.

5. *Coordination with Other Benefits.* Social Security benefits should continue to be reduced when workmen's compensation benefits are paid for permanent and

total disability. But in death cases, workmen's compensation benefits should be reduced if the surviving family receives Social Security payments.

6. *Protection against Erosion of Benefits.* People who are receiving permanent-total-disability benefits should have their benefits increased over time in the same proportion as increases in the state's average weekly wage.

7. *Free Choice of Physician.* A disabled worker should be allowed to select his own physician or choose from a panel of physicians approved by the workmen's compensation agency.

8. *Broad Coverage under Second-Injury Funds.* Second-injury funds should provide broad coverage for preexisting impairments, including epilepsy, polio, arthritis, and heart disease.

9. *Medical Rehabilitation Division.* Each state should establish a medical rehabilitation division within the workmen's compensation agency, to provide effective medical care and vocational rehabilitation services to disabled workers. Special cash maintenance benefits should be provided during the worker's rehabilitation.

10. *Time Limit for Filing Claims.* Time limits for filing claims should be liberalized. In the case of occupational disease, a substantial time period may elapse between exposure to a disease-causing substance and the worker's awareness of the disease.

11. *More Effective Administration.* Each state should have a workmen's compensation agency, which is staffed by full-time civil-service employees and financed by assessments against insurers and self-insurers.

12. *Limit on Lump-Sum Settlements.* Lump-sum settlements and compromise-and-release agreements, which terminate medical and rehabilitation benefits, should be used rarely, and only after the workmen's compensation agency approves of the settlement.

SUGGESTIONS FOR ADDITIONAL READING

American Mutual Insurance Alliance, "Workmen's Compensation: Update 1975," *Journal of American Insurance,* Winter 1974-75.

Berkowitz, Monroe, *Workmen's Compensation: The New Jersey Experience.* New Brunswick, N.J.: Rutgers University Press, 1960.

Brinker, Paul A., *Economic Insecurity and Social Security,* Chap. 8. New York: Appleton-Century-Crofts, 1968.

Chamber of Commerce of the United States, *Analysis of Workmen's Compensation Laws, 1975 Edition.* Washington, D.C.: Chamber of Commerce of the United States, 1975.

Cheit, Earl F., and Margaret S. Gordon, eds., *Occupational Disability and Public Policy.* New York: John Wiley, 1963.

National Commission on State Workmen's Compensation Laws, *A Compendium on Workmen's Compensation.* Washington, D.C.: U.S. Government Printing Office, 1972.

_____, *The Report of the National Commission on State Workmen's*

Compensation Laws. Washington, D.C.: U.S. Government Printing Office, 1972.

Rejda, George E., and Emil E. Meurer, Jr., "Crime Compensation Plans: An Extension of the No-Fault Principle," paper delivered at the annual meeting of the American Risk and Insurance Association, White Sulphur Springs, West Virginia, August 28, 1974.

Skolnik, Alfred M., and Daniel N. Price, "Workmen's Compensation under Scrutiny," *Social Security Bulletin,* Vol. 37, No. 10. October 1974.

Somers, Herman Miles, and Anne Ramsey Somers, *Workmen's Compensation.* New York: John Wiley, 1954.

Turnbull, John G., C. Arthur Williams, Jr., and Earl F. Cheit, *Economic and Social Security,* 4th ed., Chap. 9. New York: Ronald Press, 1973.

Williams, C.A., Jr., *Insurance Arrangements under Workmen's Compensation,* U.S. Department of Labor, Bureau of Labor Standards, Bulletin No. 317. Washington, D.C.: U.S. Government Printing Office, 1969.

APPENDIX
Extension of the Liability-Without-Fault Principle

Many states have now extended the liability-without-fault principle to include automobile-accident victims and to crime victims who suffer serious financial hardship because of violent crimes. Let us examine (1) no-fault automobile insurance, and (2) crime compensation plans.

No-Fault Automobile Insurance

Losses from motor-vehicle accidents are staggering. In a typical year, more than 50,000 people are killed on U.S. streets and highways, another 450,000 are seriously injured, and 4 million or more incur minor injuries. Automobile-accident victims and their families are confronted with the critical problems of payment of medical expenses, lost income, pain and suffering, grief over the death or disability of a loved one, or the loss of use of a bodily member.

There is much controversy about the method of compensating automobile-accident victims for their injuries. Numerous obstacles must be overcome before the victim can collect.[1] First, he must make a claim against the other driver's insurer, which owes him no loyalty. Second, under the tort liability system on

[1]Jeffrey O'Connell and Wallace H. Wilson, *Car Insurance and Consumer Desires* (Champaign-Urbana: University of Illinois Press, 1969), pp. 1-2. However, the student should note that if he has a medical-payments provision in his automobile insurance policy, medical expenses from an automobile accident are covered and paid by his own insurer even if he was at fault.

which present automobile liability insurance is based, he must show that the other driver is negligent, and this may be difficult if the cause of the accident cannot be accurately determined. Third, the amount that he can collect is not specified; it depends on such things as wage loss, pain and suffering, medical expenses, and many other factors. In addition, critics of the current reparations system say that automobile-accident claims are dominated by attitudes of distrust, confusion, and outright hostility.

Defects of the Fault System. Critics of the fault system, on which automobile liability insurance is based, cite among its defects the difficulty of determining fault, the limited scope of the reparations system, inequities in claim payments, cost inefficiencies, and delays in receiving benefits.[2]

1. Difficulty of Determining Fault. Automobile liability insurance does not automatically pay when a motorist or pedestrian is injured in an accident. The injured person must prove negligence by the person responsible for the accident in order to collect damages.

However, most accidents occur suddenly and unexpectedly, and details surrounding them can seldom be accurately determined. It is estimated that a driver averages 200 observations and 20 decisions per mile; a normally cautious driver could be held negligent because an incorrect decision in the last split second results in an accident. In addition, whether an injured motorist can collect anything often depends on court testimony several months or years later, and memory of the exact details of the accident may have faded. Also, since fault must be determined in order for damages to be paid, either party to the accident may be tempted to suppress or fabricate evidence to show that the other party is at fault.

2. Limited Scope of Reparations System. Another major shortcoming is that the coverage under the present auto-accident liability system is deficient in its scope of reparations. *The Department of Transportation found that only 45 percent of the seriously injured or the beneficiaries of those killed benefited in any way from the tort liability system. One out of every ten victims received no compensation from any source whatsoever.*

3. Inequities in Claim Payments. In the present system, smaller claims are overpaid, and serious losses are undercompensated. *For small claims with an economic loss of $500 or less, the average settlement is 4½ times the actual economic loss. For seriously or fatally injured victims with an economic loss of $25,000 or more, only about one-third is usually recovered.*

Small claims are overcompensated because the inflated settlements cost insurers less than taking the cases into court. In contrast, a large claim is likely to be vigorously resisted. Thus, despite the popular viewpoint that automobile personal-injury awards are large, the evidence indicates that substantial settle-

---

[2]A summary of the major defects of the tort liability system in automobile liability lawsuits can be found in U.S. Department of Transportation, *Motor Vehicle Crash Losses and Their Compensation in the United States, A Report to the Congress and the President* (Washington, D.C.: U.S. Government Printing Office, 1971), pp. 15-100. See also Robert E. Keeton and Jeffrey O'Connell, "Basic Protection Automobile Insurance," in Robert E. Keeton, Jeffrey O'Connell, and John H. McCord, eds., *Crisis in Car Insurance* (Urbana: University of Illinois Press, 1968), pp. 40-98.

ments are relatively rare when the entire population and total losses are considered.

4. High Cost and Inefficiency. The present system requires too much time and money spent in determining fault and not enough in paying automobile victims. *For every $1.00 in benefits paid to injured accident victims, expenses of $1.07 are incurred.*

A large percentage of each premium dollar is used to pay lawyers, claims investigators, and other costs of fixing blame. *For each $1.00 of liability-insurance premiums collected, 23 cents are used for the salaries and fees of defense attorneys, plaintiffs' attorneys, claims investigators, and other claim costs. Only 44 cents go to automobile-accident victims to compensate them for their losses.*

5. Delay in Payments. Significant numbers of claims are not promptly paid because of investigations, negotiations, and waiting for court dates. Only about half take an average of six months or less to settle. Moreover, the system is unduly slow in those cases where the need for prompt payment is the greatest. *Seriously injured persons or their survivors wait an average of 16 months for final payment from automobile liability insurance.*

No-Fault Insurance. Because of defects in the present tort liability system, many states have enacted no-fault insurance plans. Under the no-fault concept, the injured automobile-accident victim collects his financial losses from his own insurer and does not have to prove that the other driver is at fault. Twenty-three states have passed no-fault laws, which vary widely from state to state, and Puerto Rico has enacted a Social Protection Plan. Only the plans of Massachusetts and Puerto Rico will be described here.

In 1970, Massachusetts passed a modified no-fault law whereby bodily-injury claims under $2,000 are paid by the accident victim's own insurer, regardless of fault, if the victim has incurred less than $2,000 in expenses and lost wages (computed at 75 percent of his average weekly wage for the year preceding the accident). He does not have to sue the other party to the accident and prove negligence in order to collect. No benefits are paid for pain and suffering. However, the injured victim has the right to sue under certain conditions. He can sue for pain-and-suffering benefits if his medical expenses exceed $500, if there is a death or the loss of a bodily member, if there is a permanent and serious disfigurement, if there is loss of sight or hearing, or if there is a fracture. Thus, the plan is a combination of no-fault insurance for small claims and the tort liability system for the more serious cases.

In 1968, Puerto Rico enacted into law the Social Protection Plan, a first-party no-fault system, which is administered by the government. The tort liability system applies to losses above the plan benefits. The plan provides for unlimited medical benefits on a service rather than an indemnity basis. Disability-income benefits equal to 50 percent of weekly salary, with a $50 weekly maximum, are paid during the first year of disability. The benefit is reduced to $25 weekly during the second year. Dismemberment benefits up to $5,000 are also provided, and a funeral benefit of $500 can be paid to the survivors. The tort liability system is retained for pain-and-suffering losses over $1,000 and for economic loss over $2,000.

Evaluation. Critics of the present system feel that numerous advantages will result from the enactment of no-fault plans. Automobile liability-insurance premiums are expected to decline, although to what extent depends on the type of plan enacted and whether medical-expense benefits are considered primary. Elimination of the necessity to determine fault to collect benefits on minor claims is a great advantage, and the tort liability system is retained for the more serious cases in most state laws. A greater proportion of automobile-accident victims can be compensated for their injuries under no-fault insurance, and legal and administrative expenses can be reduced, with a larger proportion of the premium dollar available for benefits. Claims can be settled more promptly, since the need to prove negligence is reduced, and greater equity in claim payments is possible. Rehabilitation of accident victims is encouraged when the benefits are paid promptly by the first-party insurer, which is in a position to encourage rehabilitation. Court congestion should be reduced. Highway-safety programs and crash prevention should improve, since more adequate accident information should be generated.

One question that must be answered is whether the insured public is willing to accept a new program based on the no-fault concept. Available evidence suggests that, once its merits are explained to the public, the majority of Americans will prefer a no-fault system. A Department of Transportation study reported that 51 percent of those interviewed favored no-fault over the prevailing system; and consumer acceptance will undoubtedly increase if the no-fault system can be found to reduce insurance costs. The early experience of the Massachusetts plan indicates that large reductions in bodily-injury liability premiums are possible; they were reduced by more than 70 percent in a two-year period. In Puerto Rico, the Social Protection Plan has shown substantial reduction in administrative expenses. If other states can duplicate the experience of the Massachusetts and Puerto Rico plans, acceptance of no-fault insurance by the public should be forthcoming.

Crime Compensation

Crime compensation represents another extension of the liability-without-fault principle, whereby victims of violent crimes are compensated for their physical injuries, or their dependents are compensated if death occurs. Many states are becoming increasingly concerned about the victims of violent crimes who suffer serious physical injuries. Many innocent people are injured from muggings, beatings stabbings, shootings, and other violent acts. Others are killed in violent crimes, and the result is often financial hardship and destitution for their families. To collect damages from the perpetrators—if they are caught—is nearly impossible, since, even if they are not imprisoned, they seldom have any amount of assets.

As a result, several states have programs to compensate crime victims for their physical injuries. Crime compensation laws have now been enacted in twelve states: New York, California, Hawaii, Massachusetts, Maryland, Nevada, New Jersey, Rhode Island, Alaska, Florida, Illinois, and Washington.

Rationale of Crime Compensation. Crime compensation programs are based on two fundamental philosophies. The first is that, since the government has the primary responsibility for preventing crime, it should compensate crime victims for those offenses it fails to prevent. The second is an ethical argument, involving welfare considerations. It states that people in need are entitled to public aid by the state, especially those who are needy because of events beyond their control. Thus, crime victims or their survivors are entitled to assistance if they suffer serious financial hardship as a result of the crime. This second philosophy is particularly important for the poor, since many violent crimes occur in poverty areas, and the crime victims there are the least able to absorb the costs of serious physical injuries.

Basic Characteristics of Crime Compensation. Crime compensation programs have certain basic characteristics involving eligibility requirements, benefits, and financing.[3]

1. Eligibility Requirements. Several states—California, Maryland, New York, and Nevada—require that, to receive benefits, crime victims must demonstrate need. In New York, for example, the claimant must experience serious financial hardship as a result of out-of-pocket medical expenses and loss of earnings. California pays benefits only if there is need for such indemnification. Maryland requires serious financial hardship, and Nevada requires consideration of the victim's need for financial aid. Four states—Hawaii, Massachusetts, New Jersey, and Rhode Island—do not require a needs test, but follow instead the social insurance principle of providing benefits as a matter or right.

The crime victim must also experience certain types of losses to collect benefits; not all crime losses are covered. With few exceptions, the crime compensation laws pay benefits only for personal injury or death, and generally exclude property losses. Hawaii and California, however, cover property losses from crime under certain conditions—such as those occurring while the claimant was attempting to prevent a crime, assisting a law-enforcement officer, or apprehending a criminal.

The applicant must be an eligible claimant. Eligible claimants include the victim himself, his relatives, his family, and his dependents. The definition of dependent varies widely among the states. Hawaii and Nevada define it as a relative of a deceased crime victim who was totally or partly dependent on his income. Massachusetts restricts benefits only to certain dependents who are wholly or partially dependent on the victim for support, including the mother, father, spouse, spouse's mother, child, adopted child, illegitimate child, nephew, or niece. New York, Maryland, and California have a broader definition, which includes any financially dependent person who is hurt financially by the victim's death.

Certain people are ineligible for benefits, depending on state law. Some states exclude crime victims who refuse to cooperate with law-enforcement agencies. Others deny benefits to anyone who is an accomplice of the criminal or is criminally responsible for the crime. There are provisions in the laws for either reducing or denying the claim if the victim contributes to his own injury. And most states exclude the members of the criminal's family from benefits; for

---

[3]George E. Rejda and Emil E. Meurer, Jr., "Crime Compensation Plans: An Extension of the No-Fault Principle," paper presented at the annual meeting of the American Risk and Insurance Association, White Sulphur Springs, West Virginia, August 28, 1974. See also Herbert S. Denenberg, "Compensation for the Victims of Crime: Justice for the Victim as Well as the Criminal," *The Insurance Law Journal*, No. 574 (November 1970), 618-35.

example, a child who is the victim of a father's criminal act cannot collect benefits.

Deductibles are imposed in some states. New York, Maryland, and New Jersey require that the claimant incur out-of-pocket expenses of at least $100, or suffer a loss of earnings for at least two continuous weeks. Massachusetts requires the claimant to absorb the first $100 of any loss.

2. Benefits. Benefits are generally paid only for personal injury or death. They can be paid for medical expenses and loss of earnings, but limitations are usually imposed. New York has a maximum weekly limit of $100 for the loss of earnings, and a $15,000 aggregate limit. Alaska, Hawaii, Massachusetts, and New Jersey have limits of $10,000. Maryland imposes limits based on its workmen's compensation law. Rhode Island has a $25,000 limit.

In addition, the states have provisions to prevent double recovery. California, for example, provides for reduction of a claim if the victim receives indemnification from other sources. Maryland reduces the benefits if the claimant is receiving payments from the person who commits the crime or from other private or public sources. New York, Nevada, and Massachusetts have similar provisions to prevent double recovery.

3. Financing. The programs are financed primarily by general revenues appropriated by the state legislatures; some states provide for additional financing by imposing fines on convicted criminals. In California, anyone who is convicted for a crime of violence must pay a fine that goes into a special fund. Maryland also imposes a special fine when a person is convicted of a crime.

Evaluation. Crime compensation is very desirable as an income-maintenance program that provides cash-income payments and other benefits to crime victims and their families, alleviating their financial hardship. To the extent that the benefits are paid promptly to crime victims who otherwise would experience even greater financial hardship, the programs contribute to economic security. But present crime compensation programs have serious defects that interfere with their income-maintenance function.

First, relatively few crime victims in crime compensation states receive benefits for their injuries. In 1973, New York allowed only 718 claims, despite the substantial amount of crime in the state.[4] The small number aided can be explained by the financial-hardship test that must be satisfied in most states before the benefits can be paid, and by the fact that some crime victims are unaware that crime compensation programs exist.

Another defect is the relatively high administrative expenses of some programs. For example, during three fiscal years of operation, the Crime Compensation Board in New York spent about 40 percent of its appropriation for expenses other than claim payments.[5]

It is unfortunate that many states require a needs test before the benefits are paid. In effect, crime victims are treated as second-class citizens. If violent crime is considered a serious social problem, which few would dispute, then crime compensation programs should cover the masses to provide some

[4]Rejda and Meurer, "Crime Compensation Plans."

[5]Defense Research Institute, "Crime Victim Act—A Striking Analogy to No-Fault Insurance," *For the Defense,* Vol. 11, No. 7 (September 1970), 83.

protection against this important social risk. A needs test defeats this objective. Crime compensation programs should follow the social insurance principle of the payment of benefits based on right, rather than a needs test such as that found in public assistance.

Finally, considerable research is necessary to improve the programs. Accurate data must be made available regarding the number of victims made destitute by crimes, the proportion of claims denied, the financial experience of the programs, and the extent to which crime compensation benefits are reduced by payments from other sources.

chapter 14

The Problem
of Unemployment

Income maintenance is a critical element in the attainment of economic security. Most people depend on their work earnings as their major source of income. But widespread changes in business conditions, structural and technological changes, seasonal elements, and frictions in the labor market frequently interact to create unemployment for many groups; and the search for better jobs and geographical relocation are also causes of unemployment.

When earnings terminate from unemployment, the unemployed workers can be exposed to considerable economic insecurity in at least four ways. The first is obviously the termination of income. Unless the worker has replacement income from other sources (such as unemployment insurance) or past savings on which to draw, he will be economically insecure. Second, if, because of business conditions, the worker can work only part-time, his work earnings are reduced, and he may be unable to maintain a reasonable standard of living for himself and his family. Third, economic insecurity may result from the uncertainty of income. Because of seasonal elements, the worker may be unemployed for a certain period each year. A construction worker, for example, may experience psychological discomfort as the layoff season approaches, because of uncertainty regarding the continuation of his future income. Finally, some unemployed groups have great difficulty in finding new jobs. These groups include older workers, disadvantaged members of minority groups, and the hard-core unemployed. Workers beyond the age of 45 or 50 may have an extended duration of unemployment; the hard-core unemployed may be out of work for months or even years.

In this chapter, we shall analyze the nature of the unemployment problem in some detail, particularly in the following areas: (1) types of unemployment, (2) measurement of unemployment, (3) extent of unemployment in the United

States, (4) underemployment of human resources, (5) groups affected by unemployment, and (6) special employment problems of disadvantaged workers.

TYPES OF UNEMPLOYMENT

For purposes of prescribing appropriate public policy measures, some logical classification of unemployment is necessary. Although there is some disagreement on the meaning of full employment, it is most often defined as an unemployment rate that does not exceed 4 percent. A certain amount of unemployment is considered normal, since there are always some workers changing jobs and therefore temporarily unemployed, others whose jobs, although steady are seasonal, and the young workers entering the labor force for the first time, who may have some difficulty in finding initial employment. Thus, full employment does not mean that 100 percent of the labor force is employed.

Economists generally recognize the following types of unemployment: (1) unemployment due to deficiency of aggregate demand, (2) technological unemployment, (3) structural unemployment, (4) frictional unemployment, and (5) seasonal unemployment.[1]

Deficiency of Aggregate Demand

When total spending in the economy, or total aggregate demand for goods and services, is insufficient for generating an adequate number of jobs to provide full employment, unemployment—often called "demand-shortage unemployment"—is the result. This form of unemployment can be successfully attacked through appropriate monetary and fiscal policies—in particular, tax reductions—whereby total aggregate demand can be stimulated to generate additional jobs.

In addition, cyclical unemployment can be caused by a temporary decline in aggregate demand. There is nothing inherent in the American economy that ensures sufficiently strong aggregate demand at all times to generate full employment; since World War II, the United States has experienced recessions in 1948-49, 1953-54, 1957-58, 1960-61, 1969-70, and 1973-75. At other times, aggregate demand can be excessive, especially during wartime periods, straining the economy's potential and generating inflationary pressures.

Variations in the major components of total aggregate demand—consumer spending, investment spending by businesses, and government spending—often cause short-run fluctuations in the economy.[2] Consumer spending is usually relatively stable and is closely related to household income, but occasionally it can be an independent source of economic instability. Since consumption spending accounts for more than 60 percent of the gross national

[1]Council of Economic Advisers, *Economic Report of the President* (Washington, D.C.: U.S. Government Printing Office, 1964), pp. 166-68.

[2]For an extensive discussion of short-run instability in the economy, see Council of Economic Advisers, *Economic Report of the President* (Washington, D.C.: U.S. Government Printing Office, 1969), pp. 70-73.

product, small changes in consumer demand, especially in the areas of automobiles and other durable goods, can have a large impact on the economy.

The second component of aggregate demand—investment spending by business—can also cause economic instability. Businesses invest in new plant, machinery, and equipment to modernize and expand their productive capacity. The decision to invest is influenced by numerous variables, including anticipated increases in demand, rate of current capacity utilization, relative costs of capital and labor, corporate cash flow, interest rates, and borrowing costs. The responses by business to these variables are neither instantaneous, smooth, nor readily predictible; and because the production of capital goods generally requires long lead times, these responses must be spread out over long periods. The overall result of these investment decisions is often sharp fluctuations in investment spending, which cause considerable instability to the economy. That instability may be increased by residential construction, a vital component of investment spending. The amount of homebuilding depends on family formation, household income, and the availability of mortgage funds. When the economy expands rapidly, with inflationary pressures building up, credit conditions generally tighten; the reverse is true when growth slows down. Consequently, residential construction often moves opposite to the path of overall economic expansion, contracting when the rest of the economy is expanding.

Finally, sudden changes in federal spending can cause some economic instability in the economy—as, for example, the rapid increase in defense expenditures during the Korean War, the rapid decline in 1953-54, and the large outlays for the Vietnam War during the late 1960s.

Technological Unemployment

Technological unemployment results from the displacement of workers by labor-saving machinery, by new production techniques, or by new management methods.[3] Many displaced workers seeking employment have migrated to urban centers, only to find that technological change has reduced the number of unskilled and semiskilled manufacturing jobs for which they could qualify. Also, technological change may result in the closing of obsolete plants and facilities, thereby causing severe economic distress to many communities.

Technological change usually increases the productivity of labor; with higher productivity, less labor is needed to produce a given amount of output. One measure of labor productivity—output per man-hour—has increased in the private economy from 2 percent annually before the end of World War II to an average of 3 percent annually between 1950 and 1970.[4] Because of these trends, some economists believe that technological change is a major cause of unemployment, and they fear higher unemployment in the future because of automation that might eliminate all but a few jobs.

[3]National Commission on Technology, Automation, and Economic Progress, *Technology and the American Economy.* Report of the National Commission on Technology, Automation, and Economic Progress (Washington, D.C.: U.S. Government Printing Office, 1966), pp. xi-xiii.

[4]U.S. Department of Labor, *Manpower Report of the President* (Washington, D.C.: U.S. Government Printing Office, 1974), p. 16.

Impact on Unemployment. Although technological change can eliminate some jobs, it does not necessarily follow that total unemployment in the economy will increase.[5] Changes in the volume of unemployment depend on (1) output per man-hour, (2) growth of the labor force, (3) total aggregate demand for goods and services, and (4) average hours of work. The volume of total unemployment depends on the interaction of these four variables.

As productivity increases from technological change, less labor is needed for each dollar of national output; or, conversely, the same number of man-hours can produce more goods and services. Thus, if total aggregate demand does not grow fast enough to offset the increase in productivity, total employment must decline. However, if total demand increases more rapidly than productivity does (less any reduction in average hours worked), then total employment must increase.

The fact that the labor force is growing must also be considered. If total demand (as reflected in the gross national product, corrected for price changes) increases *less rapidly* than the *sum* of productivity increases and growth in the labor force (adjusted for hours of work), then unemployment must increase, because total demand will not generate a sufficient number of new jobs to offset both the decrease in the number of needed workers (due to greater productivity) and the increase in the labor force. However, if total aggregate demand expands *faster* than the labor-force growth plus the productivity increase (less the rate at which average hours of work decline), then unemployment will decline.

A simple example can make this clear. Assume that productivity increases by 2.8 percent annually from technological change, and that the labor force increases by 1.5 percent annually. (Average hours of work are quantitatively less significant and will be ignored.) Then, if total aggregate demand increases by 4.3 percent annually, total unemployment will remain steady. If total aggregate demand rises by over 4.3 percent annually, total unemployment will decline; conversely, if total aggregate demand increases by less than 4.3 percent annually, total unemployment will increase.

Thus, if total aggregate demand grows at the proper rate, an increase in total unemployment need not occur because of technological change. If the federal government increases aggregate demand too slowly, an increase in unemployment will occur. If aggregate demand expands too rapidly at full employment, inflation will result. There is nothing inherent in the economy that ensures that aggregate demand will always increase at the proper rate; but through appropriate monetary and fiscal policy, the federal government can compensate for deficiencies in aggregate demand or for too rapid an increase.

Automation and Unemployment. Some people are fearful that technological change and automation are destroying jobs at a rapid rate, and that unemployment will be permanently higher in the future. Automation means continuous automatic production, linking together several mechanized operations, in which the product being produced is automatically transferred from one operation to another.[6]

---

[5]National Commission on Technology, *Technology and the American Economy,* pp. 9-16.

[6]Gordon F. Bloom and Herbert R. Northrup, *Economics of Labor Relations,* 7th ed. (Homewood, Ill.: Richard D. Irwin, 1973), p. 460.

On the positive side, automation has a beneficial effect on employment. Menial jobs are eliminated, and leisure is increased. Goods can be produced at lower cost, thereby increasing the worker's real income. Although automation can eliminate jobs, it also creates new jobs in industries that manufacture automated equipment, and skilled workers are needed to maintain and repair the complex machines and controls.

On the negative side, however, automation and technological change can create serious unemployment problems, at least in the short run. Automation can cause entire plants to become obsolete and can substantially alter the job skills required in the labor market.[7] It can cause a massive displacement of workers in communities that are dependent on one industry for employment, as when an old plant that is inefficient and obsolete is shut down, and a new one built in another area.

So even though automation and technological change can eliminate jobs and displace workers in the short run, the long-run effects may be to expand employment and increase the standard of living. The National Commission on Technology, Automation, and Economic Progress concludes that there has been some increase in the pace of technological change, but that this acceleration should not increase more rapidly than the growth in aggregate demand during the next decade if appropriate public policy measures are taken.[8] That is, appropriate monetary and fiscal policies can expand employment opportunities, so that the displaced workers can be reabsorbed into the labor force. In addition, economic insecurity from technological unemployment can be reduced by retraining programs, relocation allowances and assistance in moving to new geographical areas, and greater cooperation by labor unions and management in the introduction of labor-saving machinery, as well as by severance pay and adequate unemployment-insurance benefits for the displaced workers.

Structural Unemployment

Structural unemployment can be defined as unemployment that affects primarily certain groups or individuals, and not the entire economy. This type of unemployment usually affects certain disadvantaged groups or certain depressed geographical areas. Although the expansion of aggregate demand can assist in reducing structural unemployment, other, more direct, measures are also necessary.

Much of the unemployment among the disadvantaged groups is structural in nature, such as that experienced by unskilled and uneducated workers, older workers, teenagers, and members of minority groups. In addition, considerable structural unemployment prevails in certain chronically depressed areas of Appalachia, the upper Great Lakes, northeastern New England, the Mississippi Delta region, parts of the Southwest, the Ozarks, and the Coastal Plains.

Several factors can cause structural unemployment. Many people are unemployed for extended periods because they are uneducated and unskilled. Changes in demand for a particular commodity, the relocation of an industry,

[7]*Ibid.*

[8]National Commission on Technology, *Technology and the American Economy,* p. 109.

or the exhaustion of a natural resource can cause chronic depression in a given geographical area. Workers who live in depressed areas may be unwilling or unable to relocate to new areas with superior employment opportunities. A declining industry, such as coal mining finds it necessary to lay off many workers. And many of the hard-core unemployed, because of poor education, poor work habits and motivation, lack of work skills, poor health, language problems, inadequate knowledge of job opportunities, and numerous other factors, are idle for long periods of time.

Frictional Unemployment

Frictional unemployment is generally related to the time lost in changing jobs rather than to job shortages resulting from insufficient aggregate demand.[9] When workers are changing jobs, they may experience a short period of unemployment between jobs. Because of imperfections in the labor market, they cannot find work immediately even if jobs are available. They may not know of other jobs, or if they do, they may lack the necessary labor mobility to relocate quickly.

The characteristics of available workers seeking jobs—such as those relating to skills, education, race, location, training, age, sex, and similar characteristics—may not completely match the characteristics that employers are seeking in filling the available jobs. The unemployment that results from this mismatching of workers and jobs can also be viewed as frictional.

Seasonal Unemployment

Finally, seasonal unemployment can result from fluctuations in business activity because of weather, customs, styles, and habits. Agriculture and construction are two important seasonal industries, with wide swings in employment throughout the year.

Seasonal variations in work lead to an inefficient use of manpower, since workers who are willing and able to work are thrown into unemployment. In particular, seasonality in construction causes a considerable waste of human resources. More than one-fourth of all wage and salaried workers in contract construction are unemployed sometime during the year, or roughly double the proportion in manufacturing and other nonagricultural industries.

Besides wasting manpower, seasonal variations also cause labor shortages during peak periods in certain occupations and geographical areas. Several studies indicate that the additional costs of employing workers during the winter months are small for many types of construction work and may be offset by the savings in unemployment-insurance benefits to construction workers.[10] In addition, the relatively high wages paid in the construction industry partly reflect the seasonal variations in the industry. Thus, greater stability of employment could temper the sharp upward trend in hourly wages for construction workers and improve their annual incomes at the same time.

[9]Bloom and Northrup, *Economics of Labor Relations,* p. 461.

[10]Council of Economic Advisers, *Economic Report of the President,* 1969, p. 103.

MEASUREMENT OF UNEMPLOYMENT

Before appropriate public policy solutions for solving unemployment can be prescribed, the extent of unemployment must be measured. This involves a consideration of basic labor-force concepts; in addition, criticisms of unemployment statistics should be examined.

Basic Labor-Force Concepts

The Bureau of the Census gathers monthly data on employment, unemployment, people outside the labor force, and other personal and occupational characteristics of the working population.[11] The information is collected from a national sample of about 47,000 households. The basic data are collected by the Census Bureau in its Current Population Survey, which is then turned over to the Bureau of Labor Statistics for analysis, interpretation, and publication. Explanations of terms used in these data follow.

Employed Persons. "Employed persons" include all civilians who worked at all during the survey week, as paid employees or in their own business, profession, or farm; or who worked at least 15 hours without pay in a family business. It also includes people who were not working that week but who have jobs or businesses from which they were temporarily absent because of illness, vacation, bad weather, a labor-management dispute, or personal reasons.

Unemployed Persons. "Unemployed persons" include all civilians who did not work during the survey week, but were available for work and made specific efforts to find employment during the preceding four weeks. Also counted as unemployed are people who did not work at all but were available for work and (1) were waiting to be called back to a job after they had been laid off, or (2) were waiting to report to a new wage or salary job scheduled to start within 30 days.

Civilian Labor Force. The "civilian labor force" is the total of all civilians classified as employed or unemployed according to the definitions above. The "total labor force" includes also all members of the armed forces stationed in the United States and abroad.

Unemployment Rate. The "unemployment rate" is the number of unemployed as a percentage of the civilian labor-force. Unemployment rates are also computed for different groups in the labor force, based on sex, age, race, marital status, occupation, and other characteristics.

Not in the Labor Force. People classified as "not in the labor force" are all civilians 16 years old and over who are not classified as either employed or unemployed. They are categorized according to the reasons why they are not in the labor force: those unable to work because of long-term mental or physical illness; those who are too old to work; those who believe that no jobs are avail-

[11]U.S. Department of Labor, Bureau of Labor Statistics, *How the Government Measures Unemployment,* Report 418, 1973.

able in the area, or at least no jobs for which they can qualify; those who are discouraged in their efforts to find work and drop out of the labor force; and those who are performing incidental family work for less than 15 hours weekly without pay.

Criticisms of Unemployment Statistics

Although the preceding concepts are extremely useful in identifying the major characteristics of the unemployed, unemployment statistics are subject to some criticism.[12] First, the total unemployment rate alone reveals little information and can be misleading. For example, in 1975, the economy was experiencing a severe recession. The national unemployment rate of 8.2 percent in January 1975 was at its highest level in 33 years, indicating that the economy was operating well below the full employment level. However, totals conceal as much as they reveal. The unemployment rate for some groups was even more serious than indicated by the national unemployment rate. During the same period, the unemployment rate was about 21 percent for teenagers; about 13 percent or blacks and other races; 15 percent for construction workers; and about 11 percent for blue-collar workers.[13] The point is that some groups have a greater incidence of unemployment than others, and the total unemployment rate is misleading by itself.

Second, unemployment data may understate the actual unemployment in the economy by failing to consider the "invisible unemployed."[14] The invisible unemployed, or hidden unemployment as it is sometimes called, refers to people who are not counted in the official unemployment statistics, such as workers who are discouraged by their efforts to find a job and drop out of the labor force. In addition, because of economic reasons, some workers who are working only part-time desire full-time employment. Although they are not working a full week (35 hours or more), they are counted as employed and not unemployed.[15] Also, many seasonal workers would like to work full-time the entire year; however, if they are neither working nor seeking jobs during the survey week, they are not counted as part of the labor force. Finally, many people with physical handicaps desire to work, but are unable to do so because of their disabilities.

Unemployment data are criticised also because they can exaggerate the true impact of unemployment on the economy. For example, the economic burden and financial hardship of unemployment fall primarily on married men who must work to support their families. However, in January, 1975, the unemployment rate for a married male worker with a wife present was only 4.5 per-

[12]See Bloom and Northrup, *Economics of Labor Relations*, pp. 429-31. See also Milton Friedman, "Unemployment Figures," *Newsweek*, October 10, 1969, p. 101.

[13]U.S. Department of Commerce, Bureau of Economic Analysis, *Business Statistics*, February 14, 1975, p. 3.

[14]See Joseph L. Gastwith, "Estimating the Number of 'Hidden Unemployed,' " *Monthly Labor Review*, March 1973, pp. 8-30.

[15]However, the Department of Labor computes separately an unemployment rate for part-time workers.

cent—a relatively low figure that suggests unemployment is not a major problem for this group.[16] In addition, it is argued that unemployment among women is not a critical problem, since most women in the labor force rely on the earnings of their husbands for support; that the relatively high unemployment rates among teenagers should not be viewed with alarm, because most youths depend on their parents for their financial support; that many people remain unemployed by deliberate choice; and that the duration of unemployment between jobs is relatively short.

UNEMPLOYMENT IN THE UNITED STATES

To determine the magnitude of the unemployment problem, let us examine the unemployment record in the United States and the economic and social costs of unemployment.

Extent of Unemployment

The volume of unemployment in the United States has fluctuated over time. Although many causal factors are associated with unemployment, the level of business activity is a critical element in determining its amount. During the Great Depression of the 1930s, when business activities were severely depressed, unemployment reached massive proportions. In 1933, about one in four workers in the civilian labor force was unemployed, often for considerable periods. However, unemployment rates have been far more moderate since that time, especially since World War II.

Table 14-1 shows the numbers of unemployed and the unemployment rates for selected years between 1947 and 1975. Based on the concept of no more than 4 percent unemployment as full employment, the United States has experienced few periods during which full employment has been attained. In particular, unemployment rates have sharply increased during the postwar recessions of 1948-49, 1953-54, 1957-58, 1960-61, 1969-70, and 1973-75.

Duration of Unemployment

Some unemployed workers find jobs quickly and do not even fulfill the one-week waiting period that is required for collecting unemployment-insurance benefits in most states. Others are unemployed for several months and eventually exhaust their unemployment benefits. Thus, the duration of unemployment must also be considered when evaluating the burden of unemployment.

In January, 1975, 7.5 million workers, or 8.2 percent of the labor force, were unemployed. Fortunately, the duration of unemployment was relatively short for most workers. About 44 percent of the unemployed workers were out of work for only five weeks or less.[17] The unemployment was essentially transi-

[16]*Business Statistics,* February 14, 1975, p. 3.

[17]U.S. Department of Labor, Bureau of Labor Statistics, *Employment and Earnings,* Vol. 21, No. 12, February 1975, p. 52, Table A-35.

TABLE 14-1   Unemployment in the United States, 1947-1975
(Numbers in thousands)

Year	Total Civilian Labor Force	Number Unemployed	Percent of Civilian Labor Force
1947	59,350	2,311	3.9
1948	60,621	2,276	3.8
1949	61,286	3,637	5.9
1950	62,208	3,288	5.3
1951	62,017	2,055	3.3
1952	62,138	1,883	3.0
1953	63,015	1,834	2.9
1954	63,643	3,532	5.5
1955	65,023	2,852	4.4
1956	66,552	2,750	4.1
1957	66,929	2,859	4.3
1958	67,639	4,602	6.8
1959	68,369	3,740	5.5
1960	69,628	3,852	5.5
1961	70,459	4,714	6.7
1962	70,614	3,911	5.5
1963	71,833	4,070	5.7
1964	73,091	3,786	5.2
1965	74,455	3,366	4.5
1966	75,770	2,875	3.8
1967	77,347	2,975	3.8
1968	78,737	2,817	3.6
1969	80,733	2,831	3.5
1970	82,715	4,088	4.9
1971	84,113	4,993	5.9
1972	86,542	4,840	5.6
1973	88,714	4,304	4.9
1974	91,011	5,076	5.6
1975 May	92,940	8,538	9.2

Source: U.S. Department of Labor, *Manpower Report of the President* (Washington, D.C.: U.S. Government Printing Office, 1975), p. 203, Table A-1. *Business Statistics,* June 13, 1975, p. 3.

tional and was due to job changes, seasonal factors, and delays in finding jobs upon entry or reentry into the labor force.

It is misleading and incorrect, however, to assume that the duration of unemployment is inconsequential for all workers. Many are out of work for extended periods.

In January, 1975, 1.5 million workers were unemployed for 15 weeks or more. Of this total, 620,000 workers had been looking for a job for 27 or more weeks, almost double a year earlier.[18] The economic insecurity for many of the long-term unemployed is severe. Many are excluded for unemployment-insur-

[18]*Ibid.,* p. 5.

ance benefits, and even if covered, they may exhaust their benefits, deplete their savings, incur heavy debts, and experience other financial hardships.

The duration of unemployment can also be viewed in terms of year-long experience; that is, how many workers experience some unemployment throughout the year? For example, about 2.8 million workers were unemployed during an average week in 1968, but this average-week figure does not indicate the actual number who were unemployed. Different workers may be unemployed throughout the year, and some more than once. About 2½ million workers were unemployed for 15 or more weeks during 1968; of this number, about three out of five were unemployed at least twice throughout the year. Consequently, it is estimated that about 11 million persons experienced some unemployment during 1968, roughly four times the number unemployed in the average week.[19]

Severity of Unemployment

Figures on the unemployment rate and the duration of unemployment can be combined to determine the severity of unemployment. Unemployment is more severe during recession periods because *more* people are unemployed, and because they remain unemployed for *longer* periods.

The severity of unemployment is determined by multiplying the unemployment rate by the average length of time the unemployed are seeking work. The result represents the average period of unemployment per person in the labor force, when the employed workers with a zero unemployment rate are included in the average. Table 14-2 is an index of the severity of unemployment between 1948 and May 1973, showing how it has increased during recession periods.

Industries and Unemployment

Certain industries experience relatively higher unemployment rates than others. Manufacturing employment is greatly affected by business cycles, and particularly manufacture of durable goods that have wide fluctuations in consumer demand, such as automobiles and appliances. Workers in the highly seasonal construction industry—both skilled craftsmen and laborers—experience high rates of unemployment, as do agricultural workers, especially farm laborers. Rural dwellers working in mines, forests, and fisheries experience irregular employment, poor working conditions, and low wages. In sharp contrast are workers in finance, insurance, real estate, services, and government who have relatively little unemployment.

Location of Unemployment

Unemployment is not evenly distributed throughout the country. Certain communities experience substantially higher unemployment rates than the

[19]U.S. Department of Labor, *Manpower Report of the President* (Washington, D.C.: U.S. Government Printing Office, 1969), pp. 42-43.

TABLE 14-2   Unemployment Rates, Duration of Unemployment, and an Index of Unemployment Severity, 1948-73

Year	Unem- ployment Rate (1)	Average Duration of Unemployment In Weeks (2)	In Days (3)	Index of Unemployment Severity: Days of Unemployment per Person in Labor Force (4)
1948 Recession	3.8	8.6	43.0	1.6 Recession
1949	5.9	10.0	50.0	3.0
1950	5.3	12.1	60.5	3.2
1951	3.3	9.7	48.5	1.6
1952	3.0	8.4	42.0	1.3
1953 Recession	2.9	8.0	40.0	1.2 Recession
1954	5.5	11.8	59.0	3.2
1955	4.4	13.0	65.0	2.9
1956	4.1	11.3	56.5	2.3
1957 Recession	4.3	10.5	52.5	2.3 Recession
1958	6.8	13.9	69.5	4.7
1959	5.5	14.4	72.0	4.0
1960 Recession	5.5	12.8	64.0	3.5 Recession
1961	6.7	15.6	78.0	5.2
1962	5.5	14.7	73.5	4.0
1963	5.7	14.0	70.0	4.0
1964	5.2	13.3	66.5	3.5
1965	4.5	11.8	59.0	2.7
1966	3.8	10.4	52.0	2.0
1967	3.8	8.8	44.0	1.7
1968	3.6	8.5	42.5	1.5
1969 Recession	3.5	8.0	40.0	1.4 Recession
1970	4.9	8.8	44.0	2.2
1971	5.9	11.4	57.0	3.4
1972	5.6	12.1	60.5	3.4
1973 (May)	5.0	10.0	50.0	2.5

Source: Geoffrey H. Moore, *How Full Is Full Employment? and Other Essays Interpreting the Unemployment Statistics* (Washington, D.C.: American Enterprise Institute for Public Policy Research, 1973), p. 19, Table 3.1.

national average. In November, 1974, some cities with unusually high unemployment rates included the following:[20]

[20]U.S. Department of Labor, Manpower Administration, Office of Planning and Evaluation, Division of Labor Market Information, *Labor Force Data for States and Major Labor Areas,* November 1974.

Lowell, Mass.	11.1%
New Bedford, Mass.	10.8
San Juan, Puerto Rico	10.4
San Diego, Calif.	9.8
Atlantic City, N.J.	9.7
Detroit, Mich.	9.3
Buffalo, N.Y.	8.8
Tacoma, Wash.	8.8
Bridgeport, Conn.	8.7
Jersey City, N.J.	8.6
U.S. Unemployment Rate	6.2

In addition, among the population of any individual city, unemployment varies greatly. The rates are highest in urban poverty areas and decline as one moves out to the suburbs. This can be illustrated by Table 14-3, which shows the unemployment rates for selected labor force groups in poverty and non-poverty areas. In 1974, the unemployment rate for both sexes, age 16 and over, in poverty areas in the United States was 7.2 percent, but only 5.2 percent for nonpoverty areas. Likewise, the unemployment rate for the same group in metropolitan poverty areas was 9.8 percent, but only 5.3 percent for nonpoverty areas.

Finally, there is a higher rate of unemployment in rural areas. In the rural South, for example, mechanization in cotton production and other techno-logical changes have displaced millions of farm workers. In Appalachia, which comprises 12 states and part of West Virginia, technological improvements in the coal industry have caused widespread unemployment and an out-migra-tion of people. The Mississippi Delta area has severe problems of underemploy-ment, widespread poverty, malnutrition, and hunger. Similar problems can be found in the Southwest, with considerable poverty, unemployment, and under-employment for blacks, American Indians, and Spanish-speaking Americans who reside there. Technological improvements in agriculture will continue to reduce the demand for farm workers in these areas, and workers must look to other industries for employment. Attraction of new industries into depressed rural areas has proved difficult so far; continued out-migration may be the only solution open to low-income farm workers who are experiencing prolonged un-employment and poverty.

Costs of Unemployment. Widespread unemployment is costly to the economy, to individuals and families directly affected, and to society. These costs are both economic and noneconomic.

1. Economic Costs. Unemployment has some direct and real costs to the economy. First, there is the loss of gross national product that could have been produced if all economic resources had been fully employed. Because of under-utilization of manpower resources and high unemployment rates, the economy is not able to attain its full production potential, and the gross national product suffers. The loss in GNP can be considerable; for example, it is estimated that between 1958 and 1965, the nation lost $260 billion of output because of wasted manpower, idle plant capacity, and high unemployment rates.[21]

[21]Council of Economic Advisers, *Economic Report of the President* (Washington, D.C.: U.S. Government Printing Office, 1967), p. 42.

TABLE 14-3 Unemployment Rates for Selected Labor Force Groups in Poverty and Nonpoverty Areas, by Sex, Age, and Color 1973-74

Sex, age, and color	Total United States				Metropolitan areas				Nonmetropolitan areas			
	Poverty areas		Nonpoverty areas		Poverty areas		Nonpoverty areas		Poverty areas		Nonpoverty areas	
	1973	1974	1973	1974	1973	1974	1973	1974	1973	1974	1973	1974
Total												
Both sexes, 16 years and over	6.5	7.2	4.6	5.2	9.0	9.8	4.7	5.3	4.7	5.4	4.3	5.0
Males, 20 years and over	4.4	5.0	3.0	3.6	6.8	7.7	3.0	3.7	2.9	3.2	2.9	3.3
Females, 20 years and over	6.3	6.8	4.6	5.2	7.9	8.2	4.7	5.2	5.1	5.7	4.3	5.3
Both sexes, 16-19 years	18.9	21.2	13.8	14.9	27.0	28.3	14.5	15.6	13.7	16.4	12.0	13.2
White												
Both sexes, 16 years and over	4.6	5.3	4.3	5.0	6.6	7.6	4.4	5.0	3.8	4.4	4.1	4.8
Males, 20 years and over	3.5	3.8	2.8	3.4	5.6	6.3	2.9	3.5	2.6	2.8	2.8	3.2
Females, 20 years and over	4.6	5.5	4.4	5.0	5.7	6.9	4.4	5.0	4.1	4.9	4.2	5.0
Both sexes, 16-19 years	12.0	14.2	13.0	13.9	16.6	18.1	13.5	14.4	10.2	12.5	11.6	12.7
Negro and other races												
Both sexes, 16 years and over	10.8	11.6	7.5	8.5	11.6	12.3	7.4	8.3	9.3	10.3	8.2	9.8
Males, 20 years and over	7.0	8.1	4.7	5.9	8.1	9.4	4.6	5.8	4.6	5.6	4.9	6.5
Females, 20 years and over	9.8	9.4	7.1	7.6	9.9	9.4	6.9	7.1	9.7	9.6	8.5	10.3
Both sexes, 16-19 years	33.4	36.1	27.1	29.5	36.7	38.8	28.0	30.7	27.8	31.8	22.6	23.9

Source: U.S. Department of Labor, Bureau of Labor Statistics, *Employment and Earnings,* Vol. 21, No. 7, January 1975, p. 164, Table 38.

Second, extended unemployment causes millions of man-years of labor to be lost forever. Labor is a perishable commodity, in the sense that it cannot be stored up. An hour of human labor, once lost because of unemployment, is lost forever. It has been said that 70 to 80 million man-years of labor were lost during the Great Depression of the 1930s as a result of massive and extended unemployment.[22]

Finally, extended unemployment retards economic growth. Vigorous economic growth is necessary for full employment and a higher standard of living. The economy does not attain its true growth potential if current manpower resources are unemployed or underutilized.

2. Noneconomic Costs. The noneconomic costs of unemployment fall heavily on individuals, families, and society. When people are unemployed for extended periods, skilled workers may experience some deterioration in their skills; others may lose self-respect and suffer depression in their morale and mental attitude.

The cost to families is also heavy—in particular, to nonwhite minority families in urban slum areas. The National Advisory Commission on Civil Disorders has found that high unemployment rates in urban slums often cause serious family tensions and contribute to family breakdown. During times of high unemployment, men living within these poverty areas are seeking employment but unable to find it; or the only jobs they can obtain are at the low end of the occupational structure and do not have the status to command the worker's self-respect or that of his family and friends. As a result, the nonwhite family head feels that his unemployment or underemployment is a continuous reminder that he is inferior, and this reinforces his feeling of inadequacy.

In addition, unemployment seems to contribute to divorce and separation among black families. Some evidence suggests a close correlation between the number of nonwhite married women who are separated from their husbands each year and the unemployment rate for nonwhite males 20 years old and over. In 1967, the percentage of married men who were either separated or divorced from their wives was more than twice as high among unemployed nonwhite men as among employed nonwhite men.[23]

Finally, unemployment also entails heavy costs to society and aggravates many important social problems. In particular, the relatively high unemployment rates in urban slums have fostered political discontent among the disadvantaged and were contributing factors to the riots and civil disorders that plagued many American cities in the 1960s.

UNDEREMPLOYMENT OF HUMAN RESOURCES

Unemployment is only one form of underutilization of human resources; underemployment must also be considered. Wasted manpower is evident in

[22]Chester A. Morgan, *Labor Economics* (Austin, Tex.: Business Publications, Inc., 1970), p. 223.

[23]The National Advisory Commission on Civil Disorders, *Report of the National Advisory Commission on Civil Disorders* (Washington, D.C.: U.S. Government Printing Office, 1968), pp. 128-31.

the large numbers of workers who are working in jobs that do not utilize their full skills, those who are outside the labor force but still desire to work, and those involuntarily employed in part-time positions. Thus, underemployment can be classified into three major categories: (1) workers employed below their actual or potential skill level, (2) people outside the labor force seeking work, and (3) involuntary part-time work.

Workers Employed below Their Skill Level

The employment of workers below their actual or potential skill level is impossible to measure adequately; strictly speaking, there are relatively few people who are not underemployed to some extent. This form of underemployment often results from racial discrimination, poor education, inadequate diet, and deficient medical care. It can be reduced by the elimination of racial discrimination and by the wider distribution of the education, housing, health, and nutritional benefits now enjoyed by most of the population.

People outside the Labor Force Seeking Work

Many people who are neither working nor actively seeking jobs would like to work. Many housewives with family responsibilities are prevented from working because of insufficient child-care facilities for their children. Illness and disability prevent some people from working in physically demanding jobs, and long-term disabilities dissuade some from even seeking work. Many are out of the labor force because of school attendance. And others do not look for work because they are discouraged and believe that it would be impossible to find it.

The Department of Labor has made several studies on the number of people outside the labor force and their reasons for not seeking work. In 1973, 57.2 million were not in the labor force. Of this number, about 4.5 million, or about 8 percent, wanted a job.[24] The reasons for not working included ill health, school attendance, family responsibilities, and the belief that no work was available. These barriers to employment could be greatly reduced by improved health care, arrangements for child care, referral to suitable jobs, and other services. Of particular concern is the large number of those who drop out of the labor force because they are discouraged in their efforts to find jobs. Of the 4.5 million outside the labor force who wanted jobs in 1973, 680,000 or about 15 percent, were in this category.

Involuntary Part-Time Work

Millions of workers who want to work full-time are working part-time because full-time jobs are unavailable, or because their regular workweek has been reduced below 35 hours for economic reasons (slack work, materials shortages, waiting to start a new job). In 1973, 13.4 million workers were on part-time schedules. Of this number, 2.5 million, or about 19 percent, were working part-time for the reasons given.[25]

[24]U.S. Department of Labor, *Manpower Report of the President,* 1974, p. 30, Table 4.

[25]*Ibid.,* p. 18.

WHO ARE THE UNEMPLOYED?

The groups most prone to the economic hardship of prolonged and wide-spread unemployment include the following: (1) teenagers, (2) older workers, (3) women, (4) uneducated and unskilled workers, and (5) seasonal workers. In addition, disadvantaged workers and the hard-core unemployed face special unemployment problems, and will be discussed separately.

Teenagers

Despite sustained economic growth during recent periods, the teenage unemployment rate is extremely high. In January 1975, the unemployment rate for youths between ages 16 and 19 was about 21 percent.[26] Although the unemployment rate for all workers has declined since 1961, the teenage rate has declined very little.

Several factors help explain the relatively high unemployment rates for teenagers.[27] First, the rate is raised by the many young people who remain in school to pursue a higher education and are frequently entering and leaving the labor force as a result. Second, the federal minimum wage of $2.10 an hour, because it may exceed the marginal-revenue product of teenagers, may dissuade many employers from hiring them. Third, state child-labor laws may restrict job opportunities for many young people. Finally, many teenagers are unemployed because they consider the available jobs to be low-paying and unattractive. Youngsters in positions that they view as dead-end, low-wage jobs do not hesitate to quit, since comparable jobs are easy to find, and unemployment is the result.[28]

Older Workers

Workers past the age of 45 or 50 may experience great difficulty in finding new jobs once they become unemployed. Seniority rights tend to protect the jobs of older workers, but once they lose their jobs, they are apt to remain unemployed for longer periods than are the younger workers. Although the unemployment *rate* for older workers is relatively low, the *duration* of unemployment is long. The average duration is about 50 percent greater for workers 45 and over than for those between 25 and 45.[29]

There are several reasons for this disparity.[30] An older worker who loses his job because of automation and technological change may have work skills that are obsolete and not readily transferable, making it very difficult for him to find a new job.

[26]*Business Statistics,* February 14, 1975, p. 3.

[27]Ewan Clague, *Unemployment: Past, Present, and Future* (Washington, D.C.: American Enterprise, Institute for Public Policy Research, 1969), pp. 13-18.

[28]Martin Feldstein, "The Economics of the New Unemployment," *The Public Interest,* No. 33 (Fall 1973), 11-12.

[29]U.S. Department of Labor, *Manpower Report of the President,* 1969, p. 112.

[30]Bloom and Northrup, *Economics of Labor Relations,* p. 440.

In addition, some older workers are relatively immobile and reluctant to relocate geographically. When employment opportunities are limited in the local community, many displaced older workers, who have established homes in the community and made lifetime friendships, find it extremely painful to relocate because of their homes and friends.

In many cases, older workers voluntarily retire instead of accepting unemployment or sporadic employment at low wages; some are discouraged in their attempts to find new jobs and voluntarily withdraw from the labor force; others are in poor health or are disabled, making it extremely difficult for them to maintain a full-time attachment to the work force.

Finally, as discussed in Chapter 4, age discrimination by employers and the reluctance of many firms to hire older workers are additional employment barriers.

Women Workers

The unemployment rate for adult women is considerably higher than for men. In January, 1975, the rate for women aged 20 and over was 8.1 percent, compared to 6 percent for men of the same ages.[31]

Most working women divide their time between homemaking and work outside the home, and the competition of homemaking responsibilities often causes them to be tardy or absent from work, or to stop working during periods of emergency in the home. Some, particularly married women, frequently enter, leave, and then reenter the labor force, but have difficulty in finding jobs immediately. The participation of some women in work outside the home may also be seasonal in character.

Finally, many women experience discrimination in employment based on sex. Some are denied jobs simply because they are females; or the only jobs they can get are in relatively low-paying categories.[32]

Unskilled and Uneducated Workers

Lack of skills is the cause of widespread unemployment among nonfarm laborers. In 1973, the unemployment rate for this group was 8.4 percent, in sharp contrast to a rate of 2.2 percent for professional and technical workers during the same period.[33] The labor market for unskilled laborers has tended to decline in recent years because of technological change and mechanized equipment that continue to displace them. Highly skilled professional workers, however, are in great demand, and the shortage of workers within this category has driven their unemployment rate down to relatively low levels.

Uneducated workers also have high unemployment rates. The rate among high school dropouts is especially high; for example, it was 26.7 percent in 1972, compared to 5.6 percent for the economy as a whole.[34] High school dropouts

[31]*Business Statistics,* February 14, 1975, p. 3.

[32]Clague, *Unemployment,* p. 13.

[33]U.S. Department of Labor, *Manpower Report of the President,* 1974, p. 275, Table A-17.

[34]*Ibid.,* p. 298, Table B-8.

are largely young workers who enter the labor force with relatively few skills and talents to offer employers. Consequently, they often work in low-paying service occupations, retail trades, or as laborers. They may also work in jobs that require little formal training but are highly sensitive to business fluctuations.

Seasonal Workers

About one-fifth of all unemployment in 1968 was attributed to seasonal swings in employment in agriculture, construction, and other industries.[35] Little change has occurred in the overall degree of seasonal variations in employment in the United States since World War II, and no significant action has been taken to reduce the degree of seasonal unemployment. In contrast, many highly industrialized foreign countries, especially countries with severe winters, have taken aggressive and positive steps to reduce seasonality in the construction industry.

SPECIAL EMPLOYMENT PROBLEMS OF DISADVANTAGED WORKERS

Disadvantaged workers are those who are unemployed or underemployed because of poverty, inadequate education, poor health, inadequate work skills, or poor motivation. In addition, numerous sociological, psychological, and institutional barriers prevent these workers from being easily absorbed into the labor force.

Blacks

Although black workers have made substantial economic gains over time, their unemployment rate is still about double that of white workers. The rate for blacks and other races in January, 1975, was 13.4 compared to 7.5 percent for white workers.[36]

A major reason for the high unemployment rates for blacks is that many blacks work in low-skilled and low-paying occupations—as unskilled laborers, in semiskilled production jobs, or in service work—where higher unemployment rates often prevail. Their employment in these occupations is due in turn to other factors: for example, racial discrimination and discriminatory hiring practices, which keep them out of better jobs. In addition, blacks have higher school-dropout rates and are therefore often inadequately educated. Ghetto schools tend to be overcrowded, have inadequate facilities, and are often staffed by less-qualified teachers. Studies indicate that, in the critical skills of verbal and reading ability, blacks fall further behind whites for each year of school completed. The result is that relatively more black students drop out of school. A study made in the metropolitan North and West showed that black students were more than three times as likely to drop out of school by age 16 or 17 as

[35]U.S. Department of Labor, *Manpower Report of the President,* 1969, p. 9.

[36]*Business Statistics,* February 14, 1975, p. 3.

white students were.[37]   Since high school dropouts generally lack the skills to enter the normal job market, they are forced into the lower-paying, low-status, unskilled occupations, where higher unemployment typically prevails.

Finally, the high aspirations of many black workers cause them to reject low-paying, low-status jobs that are available, because they feel that these occupations are below their dignity as human beings. These undesirable occupations—janitors, domestics, bus boys, dishwashers, unskilled laborers, menial factory work, and so on—are generally dead-end jobs that pay low wages and have no future.

Spanish-Speaking Americans

Workers with Spanish origin, including Puerto-Ricans and Mexican-Americans, also have unusually high unemployment rates. During the fourth quarter of 1974, the unemployment rate for workers with Spanish origin was 8.2 percent, representing 329,000 workers who were unemployed.[38]

The Spanish-speaking groups have high unemployment rates because of language barriers, inadequate education and work skills, and racial discrimination. Many are employed in low-status, low-paying jobs as laborers, service workers, or domestics, or in semiskilled operations.

The educational system in the United States is oriented toward the culture of middle-class white society, as opposed to the distinct culture of Spanish-speaking Americans. Their inferior education is due in part to language and reading problems. When Spanish is the only language spoken in his home, a student is handicapped in mastering the English language. Many students therefore perform poorly in school and drop out, resulting in considerable poverty, unemployment, and underemployment.

American Indians

American Indians are probably the most disadvantaged minority group in the nation. There are about 793,000 Indians in the United States, with nearly half living in urban areas and most of the others on reservations. Many Indians have serious health problems, receive inadequate education, and lack familiarity with the English language; as a result, they have few marketable skills, earn low incomes, are handicapped by their culture when seeking jobs, and experience extremely high unemployment and underemployment rates. Average annual income for reservation Indians is estimated to be $1,500. Their unemployment rates average 40 percent and go as high as 90 percent on some reservations during the winter months.[39]   The widespread unemployment results in a tragic waste of human resources.

[37]National Advisory Commission on Civil Disorders, *Report,* p. 237.

[38]U.S. Department of Labor, *Employment and Earnings,* Vol. 21, No. 7, January 1975, p. 62, Table A-56.

[39]U.S. Department of Labor, *Manpower Report of the President* (Washington, D.C.: U.S. Government Printing Office, 1973), p. 40.

Reducing Indian unemployment is a monumental task. Most Indians live in areas that are remote from industrial centers where jobs can easily be found; the traditional Indian culture is not intrinsically job-oriented, and does not provide common incentives to work for pay similar to those confronting other American workers; and the assistance provided Indians in the past has been inadequate for overcoming the serious obstacles they face.

Many Indians migrate from the reservations into the cities, only to face similar problems of poor housing, inadequate schools, lack of marketable work skills, and high unemployment and underemployment rates. Because of their culture, many Indians who migrate to the cities desire to maintain their communal and social separation from white society. Thus, the gap between the Indians and the mainstream of society is widened, and the alienation is more severe. Also, the nature of Indian life on the reservation often does not prepare them to be easily absorbed into city life. Consequently, high unemployment and underemployment rates, along with the grinding pressures of poverty, cause many Indians to become disillusioned with city life and subsequently return to their reservations.

Ex-Convicts

Ex-convicts suffer from multiple handicaps that present great obstacles to the attainment of good jobs. More than 100,000 convicts are released from federal and state prisons each year, but the rate of recidivism is high, with at least one-third returning to prison as repeat offenders.[40]

Convicts possess certain characteristics that hinder them severely in their efforts to find employment upon release.[41] Some felons are irrevocably committed to crime, and others adhere to society's conventional values; but the majority are aimless and uncommitted to any goals. The majority of convicts are between the ages of 16 and 30; many have mental problems and are disturbed and frustrated; others are alcoholics, drug addicts, or sex deviants. Many convicts are high school dropouts, and a substantial proportion is severely handicapped educationally. Furthermore, most have unstable work records and lack vocational skills. A sizable proportion of prison inmates are blacks, American Indians, and Spanish-speaking minorities who come from families with poverty backgrounds. Others come from broken homes. Many convicts are bitter against society and have failed in their relationships with families and friends. And very few have much self-esteem.

In view of these characteristics, ex-convicts' prospects for good jobs are often bleak. Their lack of adequate job skills and good work experience, their poor work attitudes, and their low educational level hurt them in an economy that places a premium on education and technical skills. Effective vocational and work training programs are often not available to people in prison; if they are, they may be unrealistic, since decent jobs may not be available upon the prisoners' release, or because the jobs for which the convicts have been

[40]The President's Commission on Law Enforcement and Administration of Justice, *The Challenge of Crime in a Free Society, A Report by the President's Commission on Law Enforcement and Administration of Justice* (Washington, D.C.: U.S. Government Printing Office, 1967), p. 45.

[41]*Ibid.*, p. 160.

trained—such as manufacturing license plates—are very scarce outside prison. A prison record can be a crippling obstacle to attaining a decent job: Some business firms refuse to hire people with prison records; licensing restrictions may deny them access to certain types of jobs; they may be ineligible for certain kinds of employment (some building-trade labor unions, for example, refuse to accept convicts as apprentices); and they may have difficulty obtaining bonds for certain types of employment, such as in banks. Mistrust of ex-convicts by many employers and the public often alienates them further from society and intensifies their bitterness. Finally, some long-term offenders find it extremely difficult to adjust to a life of work outside prison because of years of institutional life and brutal monotony.

Hard-Core Unemployed

The hard-core unemployed are people who have not worked during most of the past year, have no work record or an unstable work record during the past five years, and are school dropouts. The U.S. Department of Labor estimates that 500,000 people, mostly concentrated in the 50 largest cities, are members of this group and are unemployed for half or more of the year.[42]

The hard-core unemployed face serious problems that make it extremely difficult for them to hold full-time jobs. These problems include poor education, lack of work skills, poor work history, poor health, lack of transportation to work, inadequate child-care facilities, racial discrimination, and poor work attitudes. Some are alcoholics, drug addicts, or ex-convicts. Many are poorly motivated, are discouraged, and lack basic skills in reading and writing.[43] The following groups are those most represented among the hard-core unemployed:

1. *Young Blacks.* They live in urban centers in the North; they are angry, rebellious, and insecure. They are high school dropouts, lack marketable skills, and reject the present political and social system in solving their problems.

2. *Older Negro Men and Women.* These people are aged 45 or over and have lived in cities most of the adult lives. Many migrated to northern industrial centers to work at defense jobs during World War II, and when the jobs ended, although they had acquired industrial experience, they did not have the seniority or union support to make the transition to civilian jobs.

3. *New Rural Migrants.* These people migrated to northern cities in large numbers, mostly from rural backgrounds and from unproductive farms in Mississippi, Louisiana, Alabama, Arkansas, Virginia, and Georgia, where they were displaced by mechanization in agriculture. They are uneducated, lack industrial skills, and are unprepared to cope with urban life.

4. *Puerto Ricans.* These are concentrated primarily in the Northeast, and have educational and language problems. Money is a major goal, and many drop out of school as soon as it is legally possible. This group competes with blacks for the most menial jobs and experiences severe discrimination in employment.

[42]U.S. Department of Labor, *Manpower Report of the President,* 1969, p. 4.

[43]Lawrence A. Johnson, *Employing the Hard-Core Unemployed, AMA Research Study 98* (New York: American Management Association, Inc., 1969), pp. 34-35.

5. *Mexican-Americans.* They reside primarily in the Southwest and are largely immobile. They are poorly educated, lack industrial skills, and are restricted to mainly agricultural employment because of racial discrimination.

6. *American Indians.* These experience high unemployment rates on Indian reservations or in large industrial cities to which they migrate. They are handicapped in seeking jobs by poor education, bad health, and their culture.

The National Alliance of Businessmen has compiled a profile of the typical hard-core unemployed, based on interviews with them in urban ghetto areas. The typical hard-core unemployed person has the following characteristics:

Unemployed for at least 18 months.

Parents were unskilled.

Never provided with intensive skill training.

Has no more than sixth-grade education.

Lacks transportation to work.

Has seen a doctor only once during his lifetime.

Lives with 1½ families.

Has a police record and has spent at least 30 days in jail.

Is married, with three children.[44]

The hard-core unemployed must be provided with skill training, literacy training, and successful work experience to develop new motivation if they are to succeed as stable, productive employees in a competitive society. One program aimed directly at the hard-core unemployed is Job Opportunities in the Business Sector (JOBS), sponsored by the National Alliance of Businessmen. JOBS, an important program for attacking the difficult problems of the hard-core unemployed, will be analyzed later, in Chapter 15.

Handicapped Workers

Handicapped workers are another disadvantaged group with employment problems. They are not accepted by many employers and find the barriers to decent employment formidable. Many live in urban and rural slums, where their problems are aggravated by inadequate medical care, inadequate housing, and other environmental conditions. Estimates of the physically handicapped people in the United States include the following:[45]

1. *The Blind.* Of the 150,000 blind people of working age, only 50,000 are employed.

2. *Paraplegics.* Of the 60,000 paraplegics of working age, 10 percent are veterans; but only 39 percent of the veterans and 47 percent of the nonveterans are working.

3. *Epileptics.* Of the 2 million epileptics, 400,000 are of working age. The unemployment rate is extremely high; it is estimated to range from 15 to 25 percent.

[44]*Ibid.,* p. 33.

[45]U.S. Department of Labor, *Manpower Report of the President* (Washington, D.C.: U.S. Government Printing Office, 1967, p. 142.

4. *Cerebral Palsy.* An estimated 200,000 people with this disability are of working age, but relatively few are employed. The United Cerebral Palsy Association has a goal of 10 percent employment for handicapped workers.

Undoubtedly, many of the physically handicapped in these categories could become employable through vocational training programs and other services.

Employment Barriers to Hiring Disadvantaged Workers

In view of the unusually high unemployment rates experienced by disadvantaged groups, employment opportunities must be expanded. Certain employment barriers, however, make it extremely difficult for disadvantaged workers to be easily absorbed into the labor force. These barriers are (1) social-psychological, (2) access, and (3) institutional.[46]

Social-Psychological Barriers. Social-psychological barriers are poor work atttitudes, poor motivation, poor work aspirations, and lack of perseverance in working.[47] Although the view that work attitudes and motivation among the disadvantaged are major barriers to their regular employment is not supported and accepted completely by many researchers, there is evidence suggesting that is has some validity—such as reports by some employers, who have hired men in poverty areas only to have them quit.

It should be noted, however, that the available evidence does not conclusively indicate that the disadvantaged always are poorly motivated and have negative work attitudes. Many studies have found that relatively more people of higher socioeconomic status have positive work attitudes than lower socioeconomic groups, but this conclusion is far from uniform. For example, a survey of Job Corps trainees showed that the aspirations of the disadvantaged youths enrolled in the program did not differ substantially from those of youths in a high socioeconomic status.[48] Perhaps it is best to conclude that poor work attitudes and poor motivation may be substantial employment barriers for some, but certainly not all, of the disadvantaged.

Access Barriers. Access barriers are obstacles that stand between the disadvantaged and the job. One type of access barrier can be classified as personal. For example, many Puerto Ricans, Mexicans, and blacks are poorly educated and have difficult language problems; others lack marketable work skills; many are in poor health. A police or prison record, or a history of bad debts, is an employment barrier. In addition, some of the disadvantaged are considered "different" or "strange" because they do not look like regularly employed workers. They may dress differently, have different hair styles, or be poorly groomed, and since their appearance does not conform to certain socially acceptable norms, the disadvantaged workers are less likely to be employed.

A second type of access barrier is related to the job search. Many dis-

[46]U.S. Department of Labor, *Manpower Report of the President* (Washington, D.C.: U.S. Government Printing Office, 1968), pp. 86-94.

[47]*Ibid.*, p. 86.

[48]*Ibid.*, p. 87. See also Leonard Goodwin, *Do the Poor Want to Work? A Social-Psychological Study of Work Orientations* (Washington, D.C.: The Brookings Institution, 1972).

advantaged workers seeking jobs do not know how to find them effectively. Those living in slums are largely confined to their own neighborhoods, but the available jobs may be in the outlying areas beyond their reach. They may lack knowledge regarding the existence and location of jobs, or the lack of transportation may impede their job-seeking efforts.

Data indicate that many disadvantaged workers learn about available jobs from their friends and relatives. But this source of job information is limited in slum areas, since the friends and relatives may themselves have little knowledge of jobs outside the immediate area, and the jobs they do know about are often low-paying, low-status jobs at the bottom end of the occupational structure.

Social segregation and personal isolation also act as barriers in the job search. Although blacks have improved their socioeconomic status over time, segregation in housing still prevails to a large degree. The effect of this segregation is to confine the networks of informal communication to within the ethnic communities. But the lower the social and economic status of the community, the weaker the intercommunity network is likely to be. Also, unemployment contributes to social isolation. Thus, in ghetto areas, the disadvantaged person who is out of work for long periods suffers a double burden. He is relatively isolated within his own community, and he is also segregated from the larger community outside the ghetto. This relative isolation makes it difficult for many disadvantaged workers to acquire information about jobs.

A third type of access barrier is the lack of transportation to the jobs. Business firms and new jobs are moving to the suburbs, with relatively few opening up near center-city slums. The ghetto resident often does not have a car in which to commute to the suburbs, and public transportation may be inadequate and time-comsuming. In addition, it should be noted that teenagers in ghetto areas desperately need after-school jobs such as baby-sitting, grass cutting, snow shoveling, and the like; but these jobs exist largely in the middle- and upper-income areas, which may be inaccessible for slum teenagers because of transportation problems. Without part-time work, ghetto teenagers may drop out of school, a step that can lead to a lifetime of low-level employment or chronic unemployment.

Institutional Barriers. Institutional barriers are those set up by employers to block the hiring of many disadvantaged workers. Several types of institutional barriers exist. First is discrimination by employers with respect to race, age, or sex.

Second, employer hiring standards can present formidable obstacles to employment. In particular, the requirement of a high school diploma or its equivalent has a major impact on the employment of disadvantaged workers, many of whom are high school dropouts. This requirement had become almost a standard practice of employers until recent manpower programs focused attention on the disadvantaged workers and their need for jobs. Many unskilled workers can be profitably employed without their having earned high school diplomas; and possession of a diploma is no guarantee of good job performance.

Finally, pre-employment tests often present substantial employment barriers to workers who lack a good command of the English language. Those with serious reading and language problems are at a distinct disadvantage. Moreover, the tests may be culturally biased, by not recognizing the cultural differences between the disadvantaged and middle-class white society. Also, some disadvantaged workers may approach the test with fear and hostility. Thus, it is not surprising that many disadvantaged workers score poorly on standardized employment tests and are refused employment as a result.

SUGGESTIONS FOR ADDITIONAL READING

Bloom, Gordon F., and Herbert R. Northrup, *Economics of Labor Relations,* 7th ed., Chap. 14. Homewood, Ill.: Richard D. Irwin, 1973.

Brinker, Paul A., *Economic Insecurity and Social Security,* Chap. 12. New York: Appleton-Century-Crofts, 1968.

Clague, Ewan, *Unemployment: Past, Present, and Future.* Washington, D.C.: American Enterprise Institute for Public Policy Research, 1969.

Feldstein, Martin, "The Economics of the New Unemployment," *The Public Interest,* No. 33 (Fall 1973), 3-42.

Joint Economic Committee, *The 1974 Joint Economic Report.* Washington, D.C.: U.S. Government Printing Office, 1974.

Moore, Geoffrey H., *How Full Is Full Employment? and Other Essays on Interpreting the Unemployment Statistics.* Washington, D.C.: American Enterprise Institute on Public Policy Research, 1973.

Turnbull, John G., C. Arthur Williams, Jr., and Earl F. Cheit, *Economic and Social Security,* 4th ed., Chap. 5. New York: Ronald Press, 1973.

U.S. Department of Labor, *Manpower Report of the President.* Washington, D.C.: U.S. Government Printing Office, 1975. See also the reports for 1967-74.

————, Bureau of Labor Statistics, *How the Government Measures Unemployment,* Report 418, 1973.

chapter 15

Solutions
to Unemployment

As we have seen, the causes of unemployment and underemployment are complex, and numerous approaches and techniques are called for to reduce them.
Some approaches aim at preventing unemployment through appropriate monetary and fiscal policy by the federal government to stimulate aggregate demand;
others aim at the retraining and relocation of displaced workers through manpower development and training programs. Some techniques are directed specifically at certain groups, such as disadvantaged workers in urban poverty areas,
and others at geographical pockets of unemployment, such as in depressed rural
areas. Finally, various private techniques are in use by industry and labor
unions.

In this chapter, we shall analyze the attempts at solution of the unemployment problem. In particular, we shall consider the following areas: (1) strategies
for full employment, (2) manpower development and training, (3) manpower
programs for disadvantaged workers, (4) evaluation of existing manpower programs, and (5) private techniques for reducing unemployment.

FULL-EMPLOYMENT STRATEGIES

Under the Employment Act of 1946, the federal government must take
positive steps to promote maximum employment opportunities for people who
are willing and able to work. Some specific strategies for promoting full employment are (1) expansion of aggregate demand by appropriate monetary and fiscal
policy, (2) creation of new jobs by the federal government, and (3) improved
labor-market information.

Expansion of Aggregate Demand

The federal government is empowered to pursue expansionary monetary and fiscal policies in order to stimulate aggregate demand and increase economic growth so that full employment can be attained.

Expansion of aggregate demand is extremely important in reducing unemployment, for several reasons. First, high levels of demand are necessary for the success of manpower development and training programs. Most manpower programs involve the private sector, and if aggregate demand is weak, jobs may not be available at the end of training.

Second, an increase in the total unemployment rate affects a large number of workers who would otherwise be competing for the available jobs. A 1 percent increase in the national unemployment rate amounts to an additional 860,000 workers who are unemployed.[1] Those workers thrown out of work would be competing with the completors of manpower training programs for the available jobs. Thus, a deficiency of aggregate demand weakens the effectiveness of manpower programs.

In addition, an expansion of aggregate demand means tight labor markets, and these improve the employment opportunities of workers who are employed part-time for economic reasons, so underemployment is reduced. Tight labor markets also tend to increase the wages of the working poor, thereby making it possible for them to work their way out of poverty. Business firms are more willing to train poorly qualified workers for the higher-paying skilled jobs when prosperity reduces to low levels the unemployment rates for skilled workers. Finally, high levels of aggregate demand tend to reduce the income differentials between black and white workers, thereby making it possible for more disadvantaged workers to attain a higher degree of economic security.

Expansionary Monetary and Fiscal Policy. Monetary policy refers to changes in the money supply and in the cost and availability of credit to achieve certain economic goals. One important goal of monetary policy is to help the economy attain full employment with reasonable price stability. To achieve this goal, the Federal Reserve System utilizes certain quantitative and selective tools to conrol the money supply.

During recessions, the Federal Reserve would expand the money supply by following an easy-money policy. The legal-reserve ratio could be lowered; the discount rate could be reduced; and the Federal Reserve would buy bonds in the open market. Conversely, during inflationary periods, the objectives of monetary policy are to contract the money supply and the level of spending by increasing the cost of borrowing and reducing the availability of bank credit. Thus, a tight-money policy would be followed. The legal-reserve ratio could be raised; the discount rate could be increased; and the Federal Reserve would sell bonds in the open market.

Discretionary fiscal policy can also be followed to attain full employment, stable prices, economic growth, and economic stability. *Fiscal policy* refers to changes in the level of taxes and government spending. Thus, during recessions, the federal government would attempt to stimulate aggregate demand by

[1] U.S. Congress, Senate, Joint Economic Committee, *Reducing Unemployment to 2 Percent,* Hearings before the Joint Economic Committee, 92d Cong., 2d sess., 1972, p. 74.

reducing taxes, increasing government spending, or both. Conversely, during inflationary periods, appropriate fiscal policy may require an increase in income tax rates, reductions in government spending, or both.

Both monetary and fiscal policies are used simultaneously to stabilize the economy. During certain periods, the actual performance of the economy may fall substantially below its potential level, with high rates of unemployment as a result. The federal government should then pursue expansionary monetary and fiscal policies to expand aggregate demand so that unemployment is reduced to its minimum frictional level. This may require an easy-money policy, tax reduction, and increases in government spending. At other times, aggregate demand may be excessive; the actual demands made upon the economy may exceed its potential to produce at stable prices, and inflationary pressures may build up. Thus, during inflationary periods, the federal government should initiate restrictive monetary and fiscal policies that dampen demand to levels consistent with full employment and stable prices. This may require a tight-money policy, tax increases, and reductions in government spending.

An extremely difficult problem, however, arises when monetary and fiscal policy must be used simultaneously to promote both full employment and control inflation. This often involves a painful and difficult public policy decision of choosing between full employment and inflation.

Unemployment—Inflation Trade-off. Economists generally believe that it is difficult for a growing economy to achieve simultaneously both full employment and stable prices, and that the economy must make a choice between the two. It is argued that expansionary monetary and fiscal policies, when used to stimulate aggregate demand so that full employment is attained, will also result in inflation; on the other hand, restrictive monetary and fiscal policies can promote price-level stability, but only at the cost of increased unemployment. Thus, the economy is confronted with a choice, or a trade-off, between inflation and unemployment.

The nature of this trade-off dilemma can be portrayed by the Phillips Curve in Figure 15-1. The Phillips Curve indicates the relationship between unemployment rates and the price level. It suggests that full employment can be achieved only by inflation, and, conversely, that stable prices may mean excessive unemployment.

There is some evidence that the inflation-unemployment trade-off has worsened over time; that is, the Phillips Curve has shifted to the right. In Figure 15-1, at the 4.0 percent unemployment rate—the point of full employment—the annual rate of inflation in the mid-1950s was 2.8 percent. The annual rate of inflation currently at the full-employment level exceeds 4.5 percent, and the curve representing the trade-off between inflation and unemployment has shifted outward over time.[2]

Various solutions have been proposed to reduce the trade-off dilemma. These proposals include more effective public policy measures for reducing demand-pull, cost-push, and structural inflation; an effective incomes policy for limiting wage increases to increases in productivity; a freeze on wages and

[2]George L. Perry, "Inflation versus Unemployment: The Worsening Trade-Off," *Monthly Labor Review,* Vol. 94, No. 2 (February 1971), 70.

FIGURE 15-1   Phillips Curve: Trade-Off between
Inflation and Unemployment

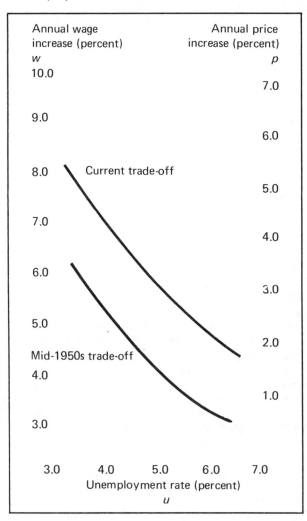

Source: George L. Perry, "Inflation versus Unemployment: The Worsening Trade Off," *Monthly Labor Review,* Vol. 94, No. 2 (February 1971), 71, Chart 1.

prices; measures for reducing the market power of labor unions and business firms; and greater emphasis on increasing the productivity of labor.[3] Space considerations preclude an analysis of these proposals, but it is safe to conclude

[3]For a discussion of proposed solutions to the trade-off dilemma, see U.S. Congress, Senate, Joint Economic Committee, *The 1974 Joint Economic Report,* 93d Cong., 2d sess. (Washington, D.C.: U.S. Government Printing Office, 1974). See also Council of Economic Advisers, *Economic Report of the President* (Washington, D.C.: U.S. Government Printing Office, 1974).

that an effective public policy solution to the unemployment and inflation trade-off dilemma does not exist at the present time.

Monetary Policy versus Fiscal Policy. The relative importance of monetary and fiscal policy as tools for stabilizing the economy and promoting full employment is a controversial subject.[4] Prof. Milton Friedman believes that monetary policy and changes in the money supply are the most important techniques that the federal government can employ to influence the level of economic activity.

Friedman believes the Federal Reserve should allow the money supply to grow automatically at a constant annual rate of somewhere between 3 and 5 percent, to correspond to the real growth rate in the American economy. He rejects fiscal policy as an effective stabilizing tool and believes that changes in the money supply are more important. He also believes that the Federal Reserve should not use discretionary monetary policy to stabilize the economy. Changes in monetary policy affect the economy only after a long and variable lag, and future economic conditions are difficult to forecast precisely. For these reasons, he believes a constant growth in the money supply would be more stabilizing to the economy than discretionary monetary policy.

On the other hand, the fiscalists argue that fiscal policy is the most important technique available to the federal government to stabilize the economy. The leading proponent of this position is Dr. Walter W. Heller, former chairman of the Council of Economic Advisers. Heller argues that effective fiscal policy was responsible for the sustained prosperity that prevailed in the United States in the 1960s—in particular, that the tax cut in 1964 unshackled the economy and allowed it to grow more rapidly, thereby providing for greater employment. He rejects Friedman's scheme for a constant increase in the money supply on the ground that a rigid and static rule is inappropriate in a dynamic, changing society.[5]

Limitations of Monetary and Fiscal Policy. Monetary and fiscal policy have limitations as stabilization tools for promoting full employment.[6] First, recent research studies based on econometric models suggest that the long-run employment rate cannot be significantly reduced below 4 percent by expansionary monetary and fiscal policies, even if a tight labor market reduced the unemployment rate for mature male workers to unusually low levels. For example, if substantial expansion of aggregate demand reduced the unemployment rate for men 25 or over to 1.5 percent, the unemployment rate for teenagers would still be over 10 percent, and the overall unemployment rate would be reduced to only 3.4 percent.[7]

Second, even though the unemployment rate can be reduced by an expan-

[4]See Milton Friedman and Walter W. Heller, *Monetary vs. Fiscal Policy* (New York: Norton, 1969).

[5]*Ibid.*, p. 29.

[6]See Committee for Economic Development, *Fiscal and Monetary Policies for Steady Economic Growth* (New York: Committee for Economic Development, 1969), pp. 54-56.

[7]Statement of Martin S. Feldstein in U.S. Congress, Senate, Joint Economic Committee, *Reducing Unemployment to 2 Percent*, p. 24.

sion of aggregate demand and economic growth, the disadvantaged workers who are structurally unemployed may receive relatively few benefits. Even at full employment, the unemployment rate for these workers may still be abnormally high. Therefore, additional measures, such as manpower development and training programs, are also necessary for reducing structural unemployment.

Third, monetary and fiscal policy are crude tools that cannot be applied with precision. The economic effects of proposed changes in policy cannot be accurately measured in advance, the need for discretionary policy is recognized only after a time lag, and the effects of a policy change are likely to occur only after long and variable lags.

Fourth, monetary and fiscal policy have often been destabilizing in the past. For example, some economists feel that the tight-money policy of the Federal Reserve during the first half of 1957 actually contributed to the subsequent 1957-58 recession.

In addition, many believe that monetary policy should not be relied on to offset inadequate fiscal policy. The time lags associated with each policy measure may be different and may lead to poorly synchronized results. Also, expansionary fiscal policy may result in budgetary deficits that require considerable financing by the government in the financial markets; and if monetary policy is too restrictive, chaotic conditions may develop in the financial markets in which the government borrows.

Finally, the effects of monetary and fiscal policy are often dissimilar. Monetary policy may affect certain sectors of the economy more than others. Restrictive monetary policy often leads to high interest rates in the mortgage markets, with an adverse effect on the housing industry. And state and local governments often face difficult financing problems when they attempt to borrow in tight money markets.

Automatic Stabilizers.   Automatic stabilizers are elements built into the fiscal system that tend to offset automatically any fluctuations in economic activity. The stabilizers tend to bolster the income flows of business firms and households during periods of business downswings, and conversely, to hold down the growth of income during periods of business upswings.

1. Personal and Corporate Income Tax.   The federal personal income tax is an important stabilizer that cushions the worker's take-home pay against fluctuations in his before-tax income. That is, when incomes decline during business downswings, income taxes decline proportionately more. Thus, personal income tax receipts of the federal government behave in a desirable countercyclical fashion, decreasing relatively more than income during recessions and increasing relatively more than income during prosperity. In addition, the corporate income tax tends to reduce fluctuations in the after-tax profits of business firms, thereby tending to reduce fluctuations in business investment outlays and dividend payments.

2. Unemployment Insurance.   Unemployment insurance also acts as an automatic stabilizer, since its benefits are sensitive to increased unemployment and react quickly during cycle downswings. During three of the four U.S. recessions between 1948 and 1961, approximately 24 to 28 percent of the decline in national income was offset by an increase in unemployment-insurance benefits.[8] On the other hand, unemployment benefits are less effective as a counter-cyclical stabilizer during business upswings. From the viewpoint of short-run fiscal policy, they should decline as national income increases; however, they tend to lag considerably at such times. That is, unemployment-benefit payments continue to increase for a period of time during business upswings, turning downward only some months after the turning point of the cycle has been reached. Thus, their stimulative impact during business downswings is prolonged and carried over into the expansion phase of the cycle, when economic activity is increasing. This lag can be explained by the slow decline in unemployment during the initial months of cyclical recovery, because the recovery of the manufacturing sector of the economy, where most cyclical fluctuations occur, is slower than that of other sectors.

    3. Other Stabilizers. Other public income-maintenance programs, such as public assistance, also function as automatic stabilizers. In particular, General Assistance benefits at the local level are sensitive to cycle downswings and tend to increase during periods of prolonged unemployment. Farm-aid programs also respond to economic cycles. If farm prices decline during recessions, farm price-support subsidies to agriculture will increase. Conversely, if farm prices rise during cyclical upswings, farm price subsidies tend to decline.

    Finally, personal and corporate savings also tend to reduce business fluctuations. During periods of short-term unemployment, an unemployed worker and his family may maintain their previous standard of living and consumption level by drawing upon their savings balances; and many corporations maintain their dividend payouts during recession periods even though sales and profits fall off.

    Since these automatic stabilizers reduce the size of secondary effects on consumer and business outlays, the severity in economic fluctuations is reduced. Under the present tax and unemployment-insurance systems, a decline in the gross national product automatically causes a reduction in government tax receipts and an increase in public transfer payments. The result is that a $1 reduction in GNP causes private income after taxes (disposable personal income and retained corporate profits) to fall by only 65 cents.[9]

    The evidence indicates that the automatic stabilizers have been effective tools during the postwar period. It has been estimated that during recent downswings, they have prevented an average of 36 to 52 percent of the decline in income that would have taken place if they had not been operative.[10]

    But despite the effectiveness of the automatic stabilizers in reducing the severity of recessions, they have several limitations as countercyclical tools.[11] First, they cannot prevent fluctuations in economic activity, but can only limit their severity. For example, although they moderate business downswings, they

[8]George E. Rejda, "Unemployment Insurance as an Automatic Stabilizer," *The Journal of Risk and Insurance,* Vol. XXXIII, No. 2 (June 1966), 195-208.

[9]Council of Economic Advisers, *Economic Report of the President* (Washington, D.C.: U.S. Government Printing Office, 1969), p. 72.

[10]Peter Eilbott, "The Effectiveness of Automatic Stabilizers," *The American Economic Review,* Vol. LVI, No. 3 (June 1966), 450-65.

[11]Council of Economic Advisers, *Economic Report of the President,* 1969, pp. 72-73.

cannot by themselves generate a recovery. If the downswing is caused by strong and persistent elements, the automatic stabilizers may not be powerful enough to stop a long and serious recession. Discretionary fiscal policy by Congress would still be necessary.

Second, if the economy falls substantially below the full-employment level of output, a return to that level is made more difficult by the dampening effects of the automatic stabilizers. In such a case, large doses of fiscal and monetary stimuli—such as increased government expenditures, reduced tax rates, and the easing of credit—may be necessary to expand aggregate demand so that the economy once again attains full employment.

Finally, the automatic stabilizers can cause a "fiscal drag" and hinder the long-run expansion of aggregate demand. As the economy grows and moves along its potential-output path with reasonably steady prices, federal tax revenues tend to increase by about 6 percent annually.[12] Unless the growth in tax revenues is offset by an increase in government expenditures or by a reduction in taxes, the revenues act as a "fiscal drag" by siphoning off income. The drag could be offset by the private sector if business firms would increase their investment expenditures faster than the growth in internal funds, or if households would reduce their rate of savings. Another possibility is federal revenue sharing with the states. However, under normal conditions, the automatic stabilizers impede the necessary expansion in aggregate demand.

Creation of New Jobs

The government can also create new jobs to reduce structural unemployment to more tolerable levels. It is estimated that a billion-dollar expenditure at the federal level can create an additional 89,000 jobs, and that the same expenditure at the state or local level would create 110,900 jobs.[13]

The federal government can subsidize jobs in the private or public sector on behalf of people who are having difficulties in finding employment. In addition, for those of the disadvantaged who cannot find jobs in the regular economy, some people believe that the federal government should act as an employer of last resort.

Public-Service Employment.   Because of the 6 percent unemployment in 1971, the Emergency Employment Act of 1971 established a new, temporary program of subsidized public-service jobs in state and local government. The Public Employment Program (PEP) is different from other manpower programs, since the federal government directly subsidizes the jobs at the state or local level, and training services are not part of the program. The jobs created are transitional; they are designed to provide work only until permanent employment is available in the public or private sector. During fiscal 1973, about

---

[12]Council of Economics Advisers, *Economic Report of the President,* 1969, p. 73.

[13]U.S. Congress, Senate, Subcommittee on Employment, Manpower, and Poverty, of the Committee on Labor and Public Welfare, *Work in America, Report of a Special Task Force to the Secretary of Health, Education and Welfare,* 93d Cong., 1st sess., 1973 (Washington, D.C.: U.S. Government Printing Office, 1973), p. 131.

180,000 people obtained jobs under PEP with state or local government units. Their average starting wage was $2.93 per hour.[14]

On the positive side, the PEP program can be quickly implemented without requiring the applicants to undergo previous training for a position; the states and local communities are generally able to provide additional public services without a large tax increase; and the majority of workers in public employment can be paid wages above the poverty threshold, thereby attaining more than a subsistence standard of living.

On the negative side, however, two problems are emerging: First, the poor, uneducated, and unskilled workers have obtained only 18 percent of the PEP jobs;[15] so the program is not reaching a sizable proportion of the disadvantaged workers. And second, many states and communities, because the jobs are only temporary, may lay off their PEP employees if federal funding dries up. Thus, the PEP program is not a permanent solution to the employment problems of disadvantaged workers.

Employer of Last Resort. The National Commission on Technology, Automation, and Economic Progress has recommended that the federal government should be an employer of last resort, by providing jobs for the hard-core unemployed in useful community enterprises. And the President's National Advisory Commission on Rural Poverty also recommends that the federal government provide jobs to every unemployed person willing and able to work.[16]

The Commission on Technology and Automation recognizes that expansionary monetary and fiscal policy, as well as manpower training programs, can create jobs, but these approaches may not provide jobs to all who are willing to work. The commission views the labor market as a "queue" or long line, with workers lined up according to their education, ability, and work skills. The more educated and highly skilled workers are near the front of the line, with the less skilled following in terms of their relative attractiveness to employers. The least attractive workers, at the end of the line, include the hard-core unemployed with few talents, skills, or education to offer employers. The commission argues that monetary and fiscal policy affects the front of the queue and works toward the rear; but the greatly disadvantaged workers near the end of the line may not be reached by monetary and fiscal policy unless very inflationary conditions are created. Consequently, the federal government must provide jobs to the disadvantaged as an employer of last resort. The commission claims that many productive public-service jobs can be created to satisfy public needs for better parks, roads, schools, hospitals, colleges, universities, libraries, rest homes, public buildings, reduction of water pollution, cleaning up the countryside, and the rehabilitation of slums.

[14]U.S. Department of Labor, *Manpower Report of the President* (Washington, D.C.: U.S. Government Printing Office, 1974), p. 155; p. 358, Table F-1.

[15]*Ibid.*, p. 154.

[16]National Commission on Technology, Automation, and Economic Progress, *Technology and the American Economy* (Washington, D.C.: U.S. Government Printing Office, 1966); and President's National Advisory Commission on Rural Poverty, *The People Left Behind* (Washington, D.C.: U.S. Government Printing Office, 1967).

Although this approach can reduce unemployment, it has some defects. First, the costs can be substantial. The President's Commission on Income Maintenance estimates that if government acts as an employer of last resort by offering jobs to all comers at the minimum wage, an estimated 9 million workers could be covered at a cost of $16 billion.[17] To reduce costs, some system of priority might have to be used. But then, only those workers falling within certain categories would have guaranteed jobs, and the program would be not universal but categorical in nature, with the same defects as any categorical income-maintenance plan that provides only income.

Second, the number of productive or effective jobs that are possible could limit the size of the program. Many new public-sector jobs can improve the quality of public services, but their number is not unlimited. And they would require expenditures for supervisory personnel, training, and administration. Consequently, to be most effective, the jobs should be carefully planned according to the need for public services, rather than to the development of public jobs on a massive scale.

Third, if the guaranteed public jobs pay the minimum wage, considerable economic adjustments may occur. Large numbers of workers who are currently employed in industry at wages below the minimum may transfer from private to public employment for the higher wages. Then, as wage-rate differentials and employment opportunities fluctuate over the business cycle, there may be repeated shifts from the private to the public sector, and vice versa.

Finally, some public-service jobs may be dead-end jobs with little future advancement. The psychologically destructive impact on the morale of workers from useless make-work jobs is well known. This possible effect must be offset against the potential improvement in work productivity and skills as a result of the work experience.

Tax Incentives. Tax incentives are also proposed as a technique for creating additional jobs. A special task force to the Secretary of Health, Education and Welfare has recommended tax incentives to employers, to encourage the hiring, training, and upgrading of disadvantaged workers; and special tax breaks to lower-income individuals and families, to encourage greater work effort and the spending of money in low-income areas, so that jobs would be created where they are needed. These tax breaks would include forgiveness of OASDHI taxes, greater deductions for child-care expenses, and lower marginal tax rates on earnings for people on welfare.[18]

Improved Labor-Market Information

Most job seekers have comparatively little knowledge of the available jobs within their community or state.[19] The low-income worker in need of a job may

[17]President's Commission on Income Maintenance Programs, *Poverty amid Plenty: The American Paradox* (Washington, D.C.: U.S. Government Printing Office, 1969), p. 143.

[18]U.S. Congress, Senate, Subcommittee on Employment, Manpower, and Poverty, *Work in America*, p. 129.

[19]See *Ibid.*, p. 34.

apply for and obtain one that he has heard about by chance, without knowing of the available alternatives; and because the job frequently turns out to be unsatisfactory, he will end up by rejoining the ranks of the unemployed. If more complete information on the job market were disseminated, unemployment could be reduced. A computer job bank is one approach to the problem of gathering and disseminating more meaningful job information. Computer job banks will be treated more fully later in the chapter.

MANPOWER DEVELOPMENT AND TRAINING

Although monetary and fiscal policy can expand aggregate demand and increase economic growth, all groups do not share equally in the benefits of that growth. Manpower development and training programs are necessary for reducing structural unemployment—and particularly, special programs for disadvantaged minority workers, who experience high unemployment rates and often have a marginal attachment to the labor force.

Manpower programs attempt to develop the worker's abilities by training, education, and retraining, and then to match his skills with job requirements. Also, a successful manpower policy involves job creation, so that the newly trained workers can find meaningful employment. Thus, an effective manpower policy has three fundamental goals: (1) development of workers' abilities, (2) matching of workers with jobs, and (3) creation of jobs to make the most of the workers' abilities. [20]

Development of Abilities

Development of workers' abilities to their true potential involves the establishment of occupational training programs, educational programs for the disadvantaged, and rehabilitation services to people with physical, mental, or cultural handicaps.

Of the many occupational training programs in existence, the Manpower Development and Training Act (MDTA) is one of the most important. MDTA programs provide training in areas where job shortages exist, or where there is a need for the retraining of workers who are displaced by technological change. They also offer training opportunities for groups with critical unemployment problems.

MDTA programs involve two types of training: institutional, and on-the-job. Institutional programs provide formal training in classrooms and are generally limited to occupations where there is a continuous demand—automobile mechanic, licensed practical nurse, welder, clerk typist, nurse's aid, and so on. In contrast, in on-the-job training (OJT), people are learning their jobs as they work at them. Their employers receive a subsidy for hiring workers taking this training.

OJT programs generally have several advantages over institutional train-

[20]U.S. Department of Labor, *Manpower Report of the President* (Washington, D.C.: U.S. Government Printing Office, 1969), p. 3.

ing. They have a lower unit cost to the federal government; they afford immediate job relevancy, with a high probability of a job upon completion of training—a particular boon to many disadvantaged workers who perform poorly in formal classroom situations; and the hourly wages tend to be higher for OJT completers. In fiscal 1972, OJT completers averaged $4.21 an hour, compared to only $2.76 for the institutional MDTA completers.[21]

Matching Workers with Jobs

After training, the workers and the available jobs must be brought together. Several approaches can be used.

First, the public employment service can be substantially improved to match up workers and jobs more effectively. The Employment Service (ES) is a federal-state operation with over 2,000 local offices, which vary widely in quality, orientation, and effectiveness. Traditionally, ES has been used as a passive labor exchange, merely referring qualified workers to employers with job openings. As a result, it has acquired a reputation for doing little for poor and unskilled workers. The President's Commission on Income Maintenance in its field investigation discovered that many of these workers viewed a trip to the employment office as a waste of time.[22] However, because of passage of the MDTA and Economic Opportunity Act of 1964 and development of the Human Resources Concept in 1965, the Employment Service has now taken positive steps to help disadvantaged workers find jobs.

Second, a national computerized job bank is another promising approach for matching workers and jobs. Most states and large cities have their own job banks; these cover areas containing 74 percent of the nation's population.[23] The Employment Service constantly programs the job-bank computers with data on the available jobs. An unemployed worker tells an employment counselor his education, training, and employment background, and also his job skills and career plans. This information is then matched with the various available jobs. Thus, the potential worker's talents and skills are better utilized, and his freedom of choice is expanded.

Third, expansion of adequate child-care facilities is also extremely important in the matching of workers and jobs. Many women need jobs but are prevented from working because of the lack of day-care facilities for their children. This is particularly important to mothers who are receiving benefits under the Aid to Families with Dependent Children program (AFDC).

Fourth, improvements in transportation are also necessary, especially for disadvantaged workers, since most new jobs are being created in the suburbs and outlying areas, not near the poverty neighborhoods in the central cities. Many poor ghetto workers lack automobiles to commute to the suburbs. Public transportation may not be available, or if it is, it may be costly and time-consuming. The income of most slum workers is low even when they are employed,

[21]U.S. Department of Labor, *Manpower Report of the President*, 1974, p. 53, Table 5.

[22]President's Commission on Income Maintenance Programs, *Poverty amid Plenty*, p. 100.

[23]U.S. Department of Labor, *Manpower Report of the President*, 1974, p. 62.

and transportation costs could reduce real income to the level where work incentives are dampened. Moreover, without transportation, slum residents may have little knowledge of the plants and new jobs that are opening up in the suburbs.

To meet this problem, special transportation demonstration projects have been established, in Baltimore, Los Angeles, Buffalo, St. Louis, and Nassau and Suffolk counties on Long Island, to provide bus lines from slum areas to suburban plants or large industrial areas. Special car pools sponsored by the Department of Housing and Urban Development transport workers living in the Watts area of Los Angeles to the plants where they are employed. Although transportation projects on a large scale are costly, they substantially improve the matching of workers and jobs.

Finally, financial assistance—transportation costs, costs of moving household goods, and an allowance to support the family until the first paycheck is received—has enabled workers to move to areas where new jobs are located. Only a small number of workers have received such relocation assistance, however, so this approach has not made a sizable dent in the poverty threshold or in greatly reducing high unemployment rates in an area. But where the assistance has been given, the moves have resulted in a substantial reduction in unemployment and an increase in earnings. Most relocated workers have remained in the new areas; less than 20 percent have returned to their original homes.

Creation of Jobs

The final step in an effective manpower policy is the creation of new jobs, so that the newly trained workers can find employment at the end of training. As we have seen, this can be done by pursuing an expansionary policy of full employment and rapid economic growth; by using federal subsidies and tax incentives to private firms, in order to encourage greater employment in the private sector; and by stressing manpower programs that actually create new jobs. Such programs include the Neighborhood Youth Corps, which provides jobs to disadvantaged youths during the school year and during the summer months, and the Public Employment Program, which provides public-service jobs in state and local government agencies.

MANPOWER PROGRAMS FOR DISADVANTAGED WORKERS

High unemployment and underemployment rates in urban slums and depressed rural areas make it very difficult for disadvantaged workers living in these areas to be absorbed into the labor force. Other groups suffer from serious language, cultural, physical, mental, or psychological handicaps that make meaningful employment difficult. It is worthwhile to examine in greater detail some solutions to the unemployment problems of special disadvantaged groups, including American Indians, Spanish-speaking minority groups, migrant farm workers, convicts in prison, and the hard-core unemployed.

American Indians

As indicated in Chapter 14, the unemployment rate on Indian reservations averages 40 percent. Among the special efforts being made to reduce this high rate are attempts to promote economic development on the reservations, such as through the location of manufacturing plants there. This program is relatively small, however, and only a fraction of the Indian labor force is participating.[24]

The Neighborhood Youth Corps (NYC) provides jobs for many of the Indian youths who are unemployed, giving them what is often their only source of income and employment.

Finally, there are special manpower programs for Indians, which are funded directly from Washington. In 1972, more than $3 million in MDTA funds were allocated for special training programs for Indians, including skill-training programs in the construction trades, health services, and clerical occupations.[25] Counseling services, remedial education, and job placement services are also provided. Manpower programs on the reservations, however, are often handicapped by the absence of jobs in the local communities.

Considering the high rates of unemployment that still exist on Indian reservations, the various programs can hardly be called a smashing success. Different cultures of the various tribes, geographical settings, and varying stages of economic development present serious obstacles to effective Indian training and employment programs. Also, Indians relocating off the reservation are often totally unprepared in terms of education and vocational training to find decent jobs in the cities. Many simply end up in the slums or on skid row; others become discouraged and return to the reservation with increased bitterness. Finally, the white man's historical record of injustice to the Indian has damaged Indian relations with the federal government and has caused the Indian to become suspicious of the real intent of the white man.[26]

Spanish-Speaking Groups

Mexican-Americans, Puerto Ricans, and other workers of Latin-American heritage have serious unemployment problems because of language barriers, limited education, and low skill levels. Special programs are necessary to reduce these employment obstacles.

Special efforts have been made to enroll Spanish-speaking Americans in the various manpower programs administered by the Department of Labor.[27] In fiscal 1972, nearly 250,000 Spanish-speaking Americans were enrolled in

[24]U.S. Department of Labor, *Manpower Report of the President*, 1969, p. 108.

[25]U.S. Department of Labor, *Manpower Report of the President* (Washington, D.C.: U.S. Government Printing Office, 1973), p. 41.

[26]Herbert E. Striner, "Toward a Fundamental Program for the Training, Employment, and Economic Equality of the American Indian," in U.S. Congress, Senate, Joint Economic Committee, *Federal Programs for the Development of Human Resources, A Compendium of Papers, Volume 1,* Subcommittee on Economic Progress of the Joint Economic Committee, 90th Cong., 2d sess., 1968 (Washington, D.C.: U.S. Government Printing Office, 1968), pp. 294-95.

[27]See U.S. Department of Labor, *Manpower Report of the President,* 1973, pp. 103-6.

these programs, accounting for 13 percent of the total enrollments, a proportion far above their representation in the population. In some programs, the proportion was close to 20 percent: These programs included the Work Incentive program for welfare recipients (WIN), Job Opportunities in the Business Sector (JOBS), and the Concentrated Employment Program (CEP), which aims at the hard-core unemployed in urban slums and rural poverty areas. In addition, the Job Corps has developed eight centers that are specifically oriented toward the young Spanish-speaking worker. Bilingual staff members administer the program, and special efforts are made to recruit young enrollees from the Spanish-speaking community.

However, greater efforts must be made to reduce the serious language problems of many Spanish-speaking workers. Racial discrimination, especially in the southwestern part of the United States, must be reduced. And white society must recognize that poverty, economic insecurity, and persistent unemployment among Spanish-speaking workers can no longer be tolerated. Greater involvement by whites in the Southwest is essential for improving the quality of life and economic security of Spanish-speaking minorities.

Convicts

Several promising approaches are now being used to train convicts for meaningful jobs while in prison. The most important is the work-release program in effect in many prisons. The work-release concept was first introduced in Wisconsin over 40 years ago for prisoners convicted of misdemeanors, and was extended on a larger scale in 1959 to those convicted of felonies in North Carolina. Favorable experience here led to the adoption of work-release programs in South Carolina, Maryland, Nebraska, and other states. Under these programs, trusted convicts hold full-time jobs outside the prison during the day and return to the prison or work-release centers at night. The prisoners usually pay for their transportation to work, work clothes, tools, and other incidental expenses, as well as union dues and income taxes. Some states require convicts to reimburse the state for room and board. Any remaining funds are sent to their families for support, are used to pay debts and fines, or are saved for future use after completion of their sentences.

The President's Commission on Law Enforcement and Administration of Justice recommends that work-release programs should be expanded,[28] on the grounds that they teach the convict good work habits and skills while in prison, and that a good job record in prison makes it easier for him to find meaningful employment after release; the money sent to the convict's family helps to hold down public-assistance costs; and making the convict feel that he is useful partially overcomes the stigma of prison life. On the negative side, however, it must be recognized that relatively few convicts are in work-release programs in most prisons. This partly reflects the basic distrust of convicts by prison officials, and the fear of the public furor that might arise if some convicts escaped while on a work-release job.

[28]President's Commission on Law Enforcement and Administration of Justice, *The Challenge of Crime in a Free Society* (Washington, D.C.: U.S. Government Printing Office, 1967), pp. 176-77.

Another approach is the halfway house, which is designed to make the transition from prison to society easier. Men recently released from prison spend a short time in the halfway house, under supervision. They receive room and board, and efforts are made to help them find jobs. Halfway houses have been established in many states and local jurisdictions. A famous one, Dismas House in St. Louis, Missouri, named after the Reverend Charles Dismas Clark, S.J., is a phenomenal success in terms of a low recidivism rate; only a small fraction of the ex-convicts who have passed through its program have returnd to prison.

Prerelease guidance, before a convict is released, can also be helpful. The objective is to impart certain knowledge to convicts to make their outside adjustment easier. For example, convicts in the Nebraska Penal Complex are exposed to a wide variety of subjects in prerelease counseling, including personal finance, credit, purchase of automobile insurance, availability of manpower training programs, sex instruction, drug abuse, legal rights under the law, and numerous other subjects.

Finally, many prisons have vocational and educational training programs for convicts, but all too often, inadequate funds limit their scope. Also, the programs are often of low quality, and well-paid jobs may not materialize when the convict is released.

Hard-Core Unemployed

Several worthwhile programs currently exist for the hard-core unemployed. Job Opportunities in the Business Sector (JOBS) aims directly at their employment problems.

The JOBS program is sponsored by the National Alliance of Businessmen, which works with government on reducing the problems of the hard-core unemployed. Business firms in large cities pledge to provide them a certain number of jobs and amount of training, in line with the program's goals of hiring, retaining, and retraining.

The JOBS program has several key characteristics. First, it involves a commitment by private firms to hire the people first and then train them afterward. Formal written entrance tests are normally not used; hiring standards are relaxed; and business firms deliberately seek out and recruit the hard-core unemployed.

Second, firms absorb the normal costs of training the workers, but the extra training costs are shared by the federal government and industry. These extra costs stem from the added training and other specialized services necessary to bring the hard-core unemployed up to a satisfactory productivity level and keep them on the job.

Third, the program makes available to private industry the services and financial support of the federal government that are needed to furnish the hardcore unemployed with the range and depth of services that can make them productive workers.

Fourth, to help foremen and supervisors understand the unique problems of the hard-core unemployed, "sensitivity" programs are used. In addition, the rank-and-file workers are trained as job coaches and counselors, in a form of the "buddy system" whereby "sensitized" workers are paired with the trainees to provide assistance in adjusting to the job.

Finally, the intensive training, counseling, and supportive services are designed to make the hard-core unemployed permanent members of the labor force. The skills and training offered are now opening doors to advancement for people who were formerly considered unemployable.

For the JOBS program to succeed, however, private employers must stress certain key points. The JOBS program cannot succeed unless management is totally committed. This involves special efforts to recruit the hard-core unemployed, since many of the disadvantaged do not actively seek employment. Some jobs may have to be restructured for the hard-core unemployed, to make them easier to master. The companies must teach basic skills in reading, writing, and arithmetic, and offer special counseling services to overcome the fear of failure, despair, lack of hope, and poor work habits. Management must be willing to tolerate high rates of absenteeism, tardiness, and turnover. And a good job with promotion possibilities must be open at the end of training; training the hardcore unemployed for dead-end jobs with no future is self-defeating.

Although the JOBS program offers numerous advantages to the hard-core unemployed, its success may be seriously jeopardized by industrial slowdowns or recessions. Layoffs can threaten the nationwide efforts to rehabilitate the unemployable. During the 1969-70 and 1973-75 recessions, many of these workers were laid off in the automobile and farm-equipment industries. Layoffs are usually on the basis of seniority, whereby the last hired are the first laid off; and since more of the disadvantaged workers will not have been employed for very long, they will be the first to lose their jobs during recession periods. The danger is that many will permanently drop out of the labor force and simply return to the streets. Firms should maintain contact with the hard-core workers while they are temporarily unemployed, to encourage them to remain in the labor force. And meanwhile, adequate unemployment-insurance benefits can cushion the blow of unemployment for them.

EVALUATION OF MANPOWER PROGRAMS

The effectiveness of manpower programs must be evaluated to determine whether the investment in human capital yields positive net benefits to the nation. The studies that have been made of the subject yield conflicting conclusions, which do not indicate such positive net benefits clearly and conclusively. Most studies evaluating the effectiveness of manpower programs can be criticized on one or more of the following grounds: (1) No control group was used in the experiment; (2) the participants under observation were seldom observed for more than one year; (3) there was disagreement concerning the program's goals and objectives; (4) the impact of training on the individual was seldom measured with accuracy; and (5) the definition and measurement of benefits and costs differed according to whether the program was being evaluated from the viewpoint of society, of the trainee, or of the taxpayer.

The Subcommittee on Fiscal Policy of the Joint Economic Committee has made an extensive evaluation of the effectiveness of manpower training programs and has also reviewed previous studies of their impact on the poor.[29] Five programs were analyzed and evaluated in some depth: the Manpower Development and Training Act (MDTA), the Neighborhood Youth Corps (NYC), the Job Corps, Job Opportunities in the Business Sector (JOBS), and the Work Incentive Program (WIN). The following broad conclusions emerge from the study:[30]

1. Although $6.8 billion has been poured into manpower programs and 6.1 million persons trained between 1963 and 1971, the programs have not reduced poverty to any considerable degree. Manpower programs are not an effective substitute for income-maintenance programs.

2. Although manpower training programs can increase the earnings of the poor and can reduce the poverty gap, continued income supplementation is likely to be necessary for the average trainee. The most optimistic studies estimate that average posttraining annual earning levels of the typical trainee are still well below the poverty line. For example, one study of MDTA trainees revealed that their average earnings were only $3,100, more than $800 below the poverty level.

3. The effectiveness of training depends greatly on economic conditions and the characteristics of the individual trainee. High levels of unemployment in the economy make it impossible for trainees to realize the full benefits of training. Moreover, high unemployment reduces potential earning increases; job placement is more difficult; and placement of trainees is likely to be at the expense of other displaced workers.

4. For some programs, the improvement in the economic condition of trainees is large enough to recover the costs incurred, which is sufficient to justify the program on economic grounds alone. However, some programs cannot be justified on the basis of posttraining earning increases, and there is no agreement concerning the extent to which this type of training should be subsidized.

5. Finally, despite substantial public expenditures on research and evaluation of the programs, there is little reliable information concerning the effectiveness and impact of training. Some large and important manpower programs have been subject to only crude and preliminary investigations and evaluation.

Although some manpower programs are reasonably successful in improving the earnings potential of disadvantaged workers, the programs overall have serious limitations in reducing total unemployment in the United States. First, the programs are expensive and slow. Complete and thorough training of unemployed workers takes a lot of money and time, and thus cannot sharply reduce total unemployment in a relatively short period. Second, based on the past experience, the impact of manpower programs on total unemployment is slight; it would take years to expand them to the level where unemployment is signifi-

[29]U.S. Congress, Senate, Subcommittee on Fiscal Policy of the Joint Economic Committee, *Studies in Public Welfare, Paper No. 3, The Effectiveness of Manpower Training Programs: A Review of Research on the Impact of the Poor,* a staff study prepared for the use of the Subcommittee on Fiscal Policy of the Joint Economic Committee, 92d Cong., 2d sess., 1972 (Washington, D.C.: U.S. Government Printing Office, 1972).

[30]*Ibid.,* pp. iii-iv and 1-14.

cantly reduced, even if increased funding were available. Third, training programs are often not geared to available jobs, so trainees often cannot find jobs at the end of their training. Fourth, under many programs, relatively few disadvantaged workers are enrolled, complete the training, and are placed in jobs. Finally, the various manpower programs overlap, are fragmented, and lack coordination. A comprehensive national manpower policy must be developed to replace the numerous, fragmented and piecemeal programs that now exist. This process will involve the consolidation of many existing programs for better coordination.

PRIVATE SOLUTIONS TO UNEMPLOYMENT

Various private techniques are also used to reduce or ease the financial pain of unemployment. These programs include supplementary unemployment benefits (SUB), employment and wage guarantees, severance pay, and employment stabilization techniques.

Supplementary Unemployment Benefits

Many laid-off workers receive state unemployment-insurance benefits, but the benefits are generally inadequate, since they restore only a small fraction of the unemployed worker's wage loss. To remedy this situation, many labor unions have supplementary unemployment benefits (SUB) plans, private plans of unemployment benefits whose eligibility and benefit requirements are linked directly with and designed to supplement state unemployment insurance, so that the unemployed worker has a larger fraction of his wage loss restored.[31]

The United Automobile Workers negotiated the first modern SUB plans with the major automobile companies in 1955. SUB plans have now spread to other industries, including steel, rubber, agricultural equipment, aluminum, can making, women's apparel, glass, and cement, many of which suffer problems of recurring unemployment.

Reasons for SUB Plans.[32] The primary reason for the existence of SUB plans is, as stated earlier, that most state unemployment-insurance benefits are inadequate. The SUB supplement added to them tends to restore a larger fraction of the wage loss, thereby easing the blow of unemployment to the worker. In particular, SUB plans are important in cyclical industries, such as automobiles and steel, where the threat of unemployment is great during depressed business conditions.

Many employers also like SUB plans. They help to reduce worker resistance to technological change that may displace some employees. SUB plans also enable employers to keep their labor force intact during temporary layoffs. Since the SUB benefits help the unemployed worker to maintain his standard of living while waiting to be recalled, he has less incentive to seek a new job.

[31]Joseph M. Becker, S. J., *Guaranteed Income for the Unemployed: The Story of SUB* (Baltimore: The Johns Hopkins Press, 1968), p. 6.

[32]*Ibid.*, pp. 50-71.

Finally, employers also desire SUB plans because they encourage the workers to accept layoffs rather than exercise their "bumping" rights under the seniority system. "Bumping" may reduce plant efficiency as workers displace each other in domino-like fashion, and employers prefer that the first worker accept the layoff rather than initiate the series of job changes.

Benefits. Although SUB plans take many forms, benefits are generally paid under two types of plans: (1) pooled funds, and (2) individual accounts.[33] The pooled-fund plan is the most common arrangement. It is, in effect, an insurance plan whereby unemployment losses are pooled on behalf of all eligible employees. The employer contributes on the basis of a certain number of cents per hour worked into a central fund, and the SUB benefits are paid out of this fund.

Under the pooled-fund approach, SUB plans pay benefits that, when added to state unemployment-insurance benefits, replace a large proportion of the worker's wage loss—in many cases, 60 to 95 percent. Dependents' allowances are also paid in most plans. For example, a Ford Motor Company employee receives a total weekly benefit (SUB plus unemployment insurance) equal to 95 percent of his net wages, less $7.50. The benefits can be paid for up to 52 weeks.

The individual-account plans do not pool unemployment losses, but instead establish a separate account for each eligible employee. The employee may draw on his account if he becomes unemployed. Any remaining sums are refunded to him if he becomes permanently unemployed. The individual-account plan is primarily a form of compulsory saving. If the employer did not contribute to it, the worker would probably receive a higher wage in lieu of the benefit. Also, in some plans, the worker has an individual choice; he can authorize the employer to deduct a certain amount from his pay, which the employer then matches. Finally, various profit-sharing plans may allow withdrawal of sums when the worker is unemployed.

Evaluation of SUB. Fr. Joseph Becker has analyzed extensively the effects of SUB plans on the economy, and has come to the following broad conclusions.[34] First, SUB payments have offset differences among the states with respect to the payment of unemployment benefits to covered workers. SUB benefits are higher in those states where unemployment benefits are lower. Thus, almost every union member receives the same benefit relative to his wage, regardless of the state in which he works.

During the early SUB negotiations, unemployment-insurance costs were expected to increase, because the workers' incentives to find other jobs would be weakened, and because some employees would choose layoffs rather than find other work, thereby increasing the number of unemployment-insurance recipients. Father Becker's second finding was that SUB payments may have increased the cost of unemployment insurance, but not to any measurable or significant extent.

Third, state unemployment-insurance benefits will probably not be

[33]*Ibid.*, p. 5.

[34]*Ibid.*, pp. 275-94.

increased in the future to the point where they equal the SUB payments. For this to happen, unemployment-insurance taxes would probably have to double; the number of improper payments would also increase; and labor mobility could be lessened. Thus, the probability is slight that unemployment benefits will be liberalized to the level of SUB payments.

Fourth, SUB plans have little effect on either the demand for labor or the supply of workers. Both SUB and shorter-workweek benefits may have caused some employers to stabilize their employment, with a tendency to work a smaller work force for longer hours. Also, SUB plans have helped employers to maintain their work force during temporary layoffs. In addition, some evidence suggests that some high-seniority workers prefer layoffs over work.

So on an overall basis, SUB plans appear to meet the principal objectives of all concerned parties. The plans have worked to meet the threat of unemployment for the workers. From the employer's viewpoint, they have lessened worker resistance to technological change, have helped to maintain the work force during slack periods, and have induced workers to accept layoffs rather than exercise their "bumping" rights. Thus, the plans have tended to exert beneficial effects on the economy since their initiation.

Employment and Wage Guarantees

Labor unions have attempted to negotiate employment or wage guarantees as an important goal of improved income maintenance to union members. Employment and wage guarantees assure those who are starting work, or are available for work, a minimum amount of employment or payment of straight-time weekly wages for a certain number of weeks.

Employment and wage guarantees are written into only a relatively small number of collective-bargaining agreements, and the number of covered workers is not large; the Department of Labor estimates that only about 600,000 workers are covered under the various plans. The wage guarantees generally range from one week to a year. They are concentrated primarily in the consumer-goods and service industries, and in firms with a stable employment history.

Severance Pay

Severance pay, often called dismissal wages, termination pay, or layoff allowances, is another technique to meet the financial distress of unemployment. Severance pay is paid to workers who lose their jobs permanently; the benefit amount is usually based on previous wages and length of employment. The worker does not have to remain unemployed to collect severance pay, nor are his benefits affected by the receipt of other income-maintenance benefits.

Severance pay performs two major functions.[35] First, from the employee's viewpoint, the benefits can be viewed as indemnification for loss of valuable property rights in the job. The worker's time and skills may be invested in a

[35]*Ibid.*, p. 4.

particular job for considerable periods, or even a lifetime. The permanent loss of the job, in effect, represents the loss of a valuable capital good.

Second, severance pay replaces part of the income lost during unemployment. This is particularly appropriate when the loss of the job is permanent. Since severance pay is paid independently of actual unemployment, the unemployed worker has no reason to delay seeking a new job. Most severance benefits are paid in a lump sum, although a few plans pay installment benefits, and thus roughly resemble SUB plans.

Employment Stabilization

Many private firms use stabilization techniques to smooth out fluctuations in employment, especially from seasonal variations in business.[36] Reducing fluctuations in seasonal unemployment not only makes it possible for more workers to be employed steadily throughout the year, but is more profitable for a business firm. It reduces unemployment-insurance tax rates, which are based on the unemployment experience of the firm. It helps maintain the employer's work force, thereby reducing his costs of hiring and training new, inexperienced workers. It spreads his costs, such as salaries and rents, over the entire year, thus cutting the cost of excess plant capacity. And it reduces the danger that frequent layoffs may affect employee morale and productivity, and that because of irregular and unstable employment, some workers may become dissatisfied and seek other jobs.

Management can use several techniques to reduce seasonal fluctuations in business. First, more efficient production activities can be undertaken. Products can be dovetailed so that the firm can produce the year round. For example, a firm manufacturing lawn furniture in the summer can produce snow shovels, sleds, and snow blowers during the winter. Also, a firm can make more determined efforts not to depend entirely on one product for its revenue. Many products have limited lifetimes, since new research and technology cause old products to become obsolete at an alarming rate. In fact, a firm can diversify into totally unrelated lines, so that fluctuations in one product do not hinder overall profits. Also, better scheduling practices can be adopted to provide for year-round employment.

Second, employers can initiate more efficient sales, pricing, and credit policies. During slack seasons, greater discounts can be given, prices can be reduced, and more liberal credit terms can be allowed. Salesmen can be encouraged to solicit business during the off-season. For example, air-conditioning manufacturers may have an aggressive sales drive in February to level out. seasonal variations in business.

Third, firms can also initiate improved inventory-control methods. Sales-forecasting methods can be improved, and greater attempts can be made to produce for inventory the year around. Also, firms can attempt to forecast more accurately the future course of the economy. It is widely recognized that most

---

[36]See Harold C. Taylor, *What the Individual Firm Can Do to Contribute to Business Stabilization* (Kalamazoo, Mich.: The W.E. Upjohn Institute for Employment Research, 1962).

firms expand their inventories too rapidly during booms, and cut back on their inventories too sharply during recessions.

Finally, some consideration must also be given to technological unemployment. The traumatic impact of technological change on older workers can often be lessened. Management and labor unions can cooperate closely so that labor-saving machinery is introduced gradually. And automation funds, severance pay, retraining, and adequate unemployment benefits can help cushion the blow of technological unemployment to displaced workers.

SUGGESTIONS FOR ADDITIONAL READING

Betcher, Dan M., "Wage Rates, Inflation, and Employment," *Monthly Review,* March 1974, pp. 13-19.

Bloom, Gordon F., and Herbert R. Northrup, *Economics of Labor Relations,* Chap. 15. Homewood, Ill.: Richard D. Irwin, 1973.

Brinker, Paul A., *Economic Insecurity and Social Security,* Chap. 13. New York: Appleton-Century-Crofts, 1968.

Committee for Economic Development, *Training and Jobs for the Urban Poor.* New York: Committee for Economic Development, 1970.

Joint Economic Committee, *The 1974 Joint Economic Report,* 93d Cong., 2d sess., 1974. Washington, D.C.: U.S. Government Printing Office, 1974.

Rosow, Jerome M., ed., *The Worker and the Job: Coping with Change.* Englewood Cliffs, N.J.: Prentice-Hall, 1974.

Sheppard, Harold L., and Neal Q. Herrick, *Where Have All the Robots Gone? Worker Dissatisfaction in the 1970's.* New York: Free Press, 1972.

Turnbull, John G., C. Arthur Williams, Jr., and Earl F. Cheit, *Economic and Social Security,* Chap. 5. New York: Ronald Press, 1973.

U.S. Congress, Senate, Joint Economic Committee, *The Inflation Process in the United States,* A study prepared for the use of the Joint Economic Committee, by Otto Eckstein and Roger Brinner, 92d Cong., 2d sess., 1972. Washington, D.C.: U.S. Government Printing Office, 1972.

_____, *Reducing Unemployment to 2 Percent,* Hearings before the Joint Economic Committee, 92d Cong., 2d sess., 1972. Washington, D.C.: U.S. Government Printing Office, 1972.

U.S. Congress, Senate, Subcommittee on Employment, Manpower, and Poverty, of the Committee on Labor and Public Welfare, *Comprehensive Manpower Reform, 1972,* Hearings before the Subcommittee on Employment, Manpower, and Poverty, of the Committee on Labor and Public Welfare, 92d Cong., 2d sess., 1972, Part 1. Washington, D.C.: U.S. Government Printing Office, 1972.

_____, *Work in America, Report of a Special Task Force to the Secretary of Health, Education and Welfare,* 93d Cong., 1st sess., 1973. Washington, D.C.: U.S. Government Printing Office, 1973.

U.S. Department of Labor, *Manpower Report of the President.* Washington, D.C.: U.S. Government Printing Office, 1975.

chapter 16

Unemployment Insurance

Unemployment insurance is a federal-state program that provides for partial income replacement during periods of short-term involuntary unemployment. All states pay benefits to temporarily unemployed workers in covered employment who have a current attachment to the labor force and fulfill certain eligibility requirements. The benefits are paid as a matter of right, with no demonstration of need. Thus, covered workers receive some income replacement, and the aggregate unemployment benefits maintain purchasing power in the economy, prevent a downward spiral of deflation, and cushion the economic impact in communities with large numbers of unemployed workers.

The unemployment-insurance system in the United States consists of several distinct programs: a federal - state unemployment insurance program in all states, as well as the District of Columbia, Puerto Rico, and the Virgin Islands; a federal-state program of permanent extended benefits, which pays additional benefits during periods of high unemployment; a permanent unemployment insurance program for ex-servicemen (UCX), established in 1958; a program for federal civilian employees (UCFE), as of 1955; and the Railroad Unemployment Insurance Act, for railway workers.

In this chapter, we shall be primarily concerned with the various state unemployment-insurance programs, including those for extending benefits during periods of high unemployment. The following areas will be covered: (1) development of unemployment insurance, (2) objectives of unemployment insurance, (3) state unemployment-insurance provisions, (4) financing and administration, (5) defects of unemployment insurance, and (6) recommendations for improvement.

DEVELOPMENT OF UNEMPLOYMENT INSURANCE

Prior to the enactment of the Social Security Act in 1935, only limited assistance was available to unemployed workers.[1] Some states had established work relief programs, which provided some assistance to the indigent; however, they were required to work or perform other public services in return for the aid. Private charities also gave some assistance, but their limited financial resources precluded payment of unemployment benefits for extended periods. Some labor unions also provided temporary assistance, but to relatively few recipients. A few firms had established private unemployment plans, but financing problems and massive unemployment during the depression of the 1930s made it difficult to provide extensive aid. Finally, a few states, including Wisconsin in 1932, considered or enacted unemployment-insurance legislation. The Wisconsin law later served as the basis of the unemployment-insurance provisions of the Social Security Act of 1935.

That act established a federal-state system of unemployment insurance, rather than one completely administered by the federal government, to meet the problem of national unemployment, because it was feared that a completely federal program would be unconstitutional. Also, because of disagreement concerning benefits, financing, administration, and other areas, it was believed that each state was best suited to develop its own unemployment-insurance program, and that state administration was more feasible than federal administration. Each state was free to develop its own program, subject to certain federal minimum standards.

The Social Security Act of 1935 encouraged the states to enact these programs through the use of a tax offset. A federal uniform tax was levied on the payrolls of covered employers—those that employed eight or more workers for 20 or more weeks in a calendar year. If the state had an acceptable unemployment-insurance program, 90 percent of the employers' tax could be deducted or offset and used by the state to meet its own unemployment problems, rather than going to the federal government. The remaining 10 percent of the tax was paid to the federal government for administrative expenses. Employers in states without unemployment-insurance laws would not have a competitive advantage over those in other states, because they would still have to pay the federal payroll tax, but their employees would be ineligible for unemployment-insurance benefits. Thus, the states had a strong financial incentive to enact acceptable unemployment-insurance laws, and by 1937, all states had done so.

In 1939, an amendment limited the payroll tax to 3 percent of the first $3,000 for each covered worker, against which 90 percent of the state contributions could be offset. The federal tax was increased to 3.1 percent in 1961 and to 3.2 percent in 1970; however, the total employer credit is still limited to 2.7 percent.

---

[1]The historical development of unemployment insurance in the United States can be found in Daniel Nelson, *Unemployment Insurance: The American Experience, 1915-1935* (Madison: University of Wisconsin Press, 1969). See also U.S. Department of Health, Education and Welfare, Social Security Administration, *Social Security Programs in the United States* (Washington, D.C.: U.S. Government Printing Office, 1973), pp. 55-72.

Each state must meet certain federal minimum requirements if the covered employers are to receive a tax offset against the federal tax and if the state is to continue receiving federal grants for administration. One requirement is that all unemployment taxes must be deposited in the unemployment trust fund of the U.S. Treasury. Although the fund is invested as a whole, each state has a separate account, which is credited with its unemployment contributions and its share of interest on investment. The state may withdraw funds from its account for unemployment benefits in the state.

Another federal requirement, designed to protect labor standards, is that the states cannot deny benefits to an otherwise eligible person who refuses to accept a new job under any of the following conditions: (1) if the position is vacant because of a strike, lockout, or other labor dispute; (2) if wages, hours, and working conditions are substantially less favorable than those of similar jobs in the community; and (3) if, as a condition of employment, the worker is required to join a company union, or resign from or refrain from joining any legitimate organization.

Federal law also requires the states to enact a system of experience rating to encourage employers to reduce unemployment, and to meet certain standards concerning the administration of the program.

Finally, under the Employment Security Amendments of 1970, the federal-state system of unemployment insurance was further broadened and liberalized. Coverage was extended to 5 million more workers; special extended benefits could be paid automatically by special triggering provisions during periods of high unemployment; the taxable wage base was increased from $3,000 to $4,200 for each covered worker; and the tax rate was increased from 3.1 to 3.2 percent.

OBJECTIVES OF UNEMPLOYMENT INSURANCE

Unemployment insurance has both primary and secondary objectives. The primary objectives involve assistance to individual workers during periods of involuntary unemployment. The secondary objectives stress the promotion of economic efficiency and stability.[2]

Primary Objectives

The most important objectives of unemployment insurance deal with helping the unemployed worker; all other goals are secondary. For most workers, the duration of unemployment is relatively short, and unemployment assistance can be confined to the payment of weekly benefits. But in some cases, unemployment may be prolonged and involve vocational training and other adjustments; unemployment benefits can help support these workers during their readjustment period.

[2]Committee on Unemployment Insurance Objectives, *Unemployment and Income Security: Goals for the 1970's, A Report of the Committee on Unemployment Insurance Objectives Sponsored by the Institute* (Kalamazoo, Mich.: The W.E. Upjohn Institute for Employment Research, 1969), pp. 14-22.

Provide Cash Payments during Involuntary Unemployment. One objective is to provide the individual worker with cash payments in a dignified manner during periods of involuntary unemployment. The benefits are paid as a matter of right, with no demonstration of need required. Short-term, temporary layoffs constitute the major unemployment risk for most workers, so unemployment benefits are normally paid only for short periods—generally 26 to 39 weeks, depending on the state. Long-term unemployment and hard-core unemployment are generally considered outside the scope of unemployment insurance; other measures are necessary for these, including manpower training programs, retraining of displaced workers, intensive counseling, and relocation.

Maintain the Worker's Standard of Living. Unemployment insurance also has the objective of maintaining to a substantial degree the unemployed worker's current standard of living. This can be achieved by providing benefits that are adequate in amount and duration.

In the United States, the worker's standard of living is generally determined by his wage level. Therefore, since it is assumed that the temporarily unemployed worker will soon be recalled to his regular job or reemployed in a new job at about the same wage level, his unemployment benefits should bear some reasonable relation to prior wages in order to maintain this standard of living as nearly as possible, rather than simply provide a minimum level of subsistence.

Unfortunately, low statutory maximums on weekly benefit amounts make this objective difficult to attain. Although the average weekly unemployment benefit today can purchase more than did the average benefit paid in 1939, the benefits are still inadequate in terms of maintaining the worker's current standard of living. This deficiency will be examined in greater detail later in the chapter.

Provide Time To Locate or Regain Employment. Another important goal of unemployment insurance is to provide adequate benefits to enable the temporarily unemployed worker to locate or regain employment consistent with his work skills and experience from previous employment, without requiring him to break or jeopardize his established job relationship. For example, a highly skilled machinist for an automobile manufacturer is not required to take a job as a day laborer during a temporary layoff caused by model changeover; the benefits make it possible for him to endure unemployment for a short period while waiting to be recalled to work. In addition, if the worker with marketable skills is permanently separated from his job, he should be allowed the time to shop around for a new job consistent with his previous work skills and experience. Unemployment benefits make this possible.

Help Unemployed Workers Find Jobs. Finally, unemployment insurance aims at helping unemployed workers find new jobs. They can be helped to locate job opportunities through close coordination with the appropriate manpower and employment service. If the worker is permanently displaced from his regular job, he should receive assistance in making a vocational readjustment or in overcoming other employment obstacles. If there is a communication problem, and the permanently displaced worker with marketable skills does not know how to find a new job, the agency administering the unemployment-insurance program can provide him with information about job opportunities. A promising approach is the use of a computerized job bank to match job openings with the vocational skills of unemployed workers.

Secondary Objectives

The secondary objectives of unemployment insurance, involving the promotion of economic efficiency and stability, can be achieved by strengthening the positive impact of unemployment insurance on the economy and minimizing its negative effects.

Desirable Countercyclical Effects. During business downswings, unemployment-insurance benefits quickly increase, thereby bolstering personal income and consumption spending. This effect takes place whether the unemployment is confined to a local area or is widespread during a national recession.

This desirable countercyclical effect on the economy can be increased by the payment of more adequate unemployment benefits, and by increasing the benefit amounts and duration of payments beyond their usual levels during periods of widespread unemployment.

Improved Allocation of Social Costs. Another objective is to better allocate the social costs of unemployment by distributing them among the employers in some relation to their layoff experience. If the firms with high unemployment experience are charged with the costs of unemployment, these costs can be included in the costs of production, which can then be reflected in higher product prices. Resource allocation is thereby improved, to the extent that the social costs of unemployment are charged to the production of the particular goods and services that give rise to them. Certain industries in particular, such as construction and apparel manufacturing, have relatively high unemployment rates; allocation of a larger share of the unemployment costs to such industries would reflect more accurately the true costs of their products in the marketplace.

Improving Manpower Utilization. Unemployment insurance can promote greater economic efficiency and stability by encouraging unemployed workers to find jobs promptly and, where necessary, helping them to improve their job skills.

Certain aspects of unemployment insurance indirectly promote better manpower utilization. To reduce malingering and preserve work incentives, the benefits are substantially below prevailing wage levels. Also, unemployment-insurance recipients must register for work at the employment office, thus making possible their quicker reentry into the labor force. Finally, the Employment Service in recent years has played a more active role in improved manpower utilization through the training, retraining, and counseling of workers, especially disadvantaged workers.

Encourage Employers To Stabilize Employment. By the use of experience rating, unemployment insurance can encourage some employers to stabilize their employment. Some firms can do little to stabilize their employment patterns; for others, the amount of potential tax savings may be insufficient to induce them to reduce their unemployment. But evidence indicates that significant unemployment-tax differentials exist among firms within an industry, reflecting differences in unemployment experience.[3] So apparently, many firms can reduce their unemployment taxes through more aggressive efforts to stabilize employment. In addition, for the many larger firms that pay substantial unemployment taxes, avoiding worker layoffs as much as possible often results in lower taxes. On the other hand, the experience-rating system should not be abused by firms seeking to reduce their costs by contesting legitimate claims.

Maintenance of Skilled Work Force. Unemployment insurance contributes to a more stable labor supply by enabling employers to maintain their skilled or experienced work force during temporary interruptions of production. Because the benefits provide income maintenance during such periods, the skilled workers are not forced to seek other jobs, and they are free to return when they are called back.

STATE UNEMPLOYMENT-INSURANCE PROVISIONS

Aside from having to meet broad federal requirements regarding financing and administration, each state is free to develop its own unemployment-insurance program. Each state determines coverage, eligibility requirements, benefit amounts, duration of payments, and disqualification provisions.[4]

Coverage

Coverage for unemployment insurance is generally limited to employment covered by the Federal Unemployment Tax Act (FUTA). The federal law now applies to private firms that employ one or more workers in each of 20 different weeks in a calendar year, or that pay wages of $1,500 or more in a calendar quarter during the current or preceding calendar year.

The federal law excludes agricultural workers, family workers, domestic workers, and the self-employed. Service workers for nonprofit organizations are not required to be covered under federal law, but under state law, they must be covered if the nonprofit organization employs four or more workers in 20 weeks in the current or preceding calendar year. In addition, the federal law requires the states to cover certain services performed in state hospitals and institutions of higher education, and it permits a political subdivision of a state to elect coverage of services performed in county and municipal hospitals and institutions of higher learning.

Most jurisdictions have extended unemployment-insurance coverage beyond the requirements of federal law. At least 42 jurisdictions cover state and local government employees under varying conditions. The District of

[3]Committee on Unemployment Insurance Objectives, *Unemployment and Income Security*, p. 21.

[4]The basic characteristics of state unemployment-insurance programs can be found in U.S. Department of Labor, Manpower Administration, *Comparison of State Unemployment Insurance Laws* (Washington, D.C.: U.S. Government Printing Office, 1972). This volume is periodically updated with supplements. The following section is based on the various laws as of January 6, 1975.

Columbia, Hawaii, Minnesota, and Puerto Rico have special coverage provisions for farm labor. Domestic workers in Arkansas, the District of Columbia, Hawaii, and New York are also covered under certain conditions. New York covers the services of a person who is employed by a son or daughter. California covers the self-employed under certain conditions.

Eligibility Requirements

All states require covered unemployed workers to fulfill the following eligibility requirements to receive benefits: They must (1) have earned qualifying wages or have been employed for a specified period, (2) be able to work and be available for work, (3) actively seek work, and (4) be free of any disqualifications.

Qualifying Wages or Employment. To qualify for unemployment benefits, the worker must have earned a specified amount of wages or must have worked for a certain period of time within his base period, or both. The base period is commonly a four-quarter or 52-week period preceding the claim for benefits. The purpose of this requirement is to limit unemployment benefits to workers with a current attachment to the labor force.

The amount of wages that must have been earned during the base period is stated in several ways. First, some states express their earnings requirements in terms of a specified multiple (commonly 30) of the weekly benefit amount, or (commonly 1½) of high-quarter wages. For example, if the weekly benefit is $25 the worker needs qualifying wages of $750; if high-quarter wages are used, the worker must have earned in the base period 1½ times the amount earned in the highest quarter of that period. In addition, most states using a multiple of the weekly benefit method have the additional requirement that the worker have earned wages in at least two quarters.

Second, the amount of base-period wages can also be stated in terms of a flat minimum amount of earnings, which can range from $150 to $1,200. Some states using this method also require wages in more than one quarter to qualify for benefits. For example, Nebraska requires wages of at least $200 in each of two quarters, with a total of $600 for the base period.

Finally, some states require the applicant to have worked a certain number of weeks with at least a specified weekly wage. For example, Hawaii requires 14 weeks of work, plus wages equal to 30 times the worker's weekly benefit amount.

The work-experience requirement eliminates a significant proportion of unemployed workers from benefits. Even though the worker may be in covered employment, protection is never guaranteed if the work requirements are not satisfied.

Able To Work and Available for Work. To collect benefits, the unemployed worker must be both able to work—that is, physically and mentally capable of working—and available for work. One evidence of his ability to work is his filing of claims and registration for work at a public employment office; all states require a claimant to do this. In addition, several states have a provision that a claimant who becomes sick or disabled after filing a claim and registering for work is still eligible for benefits, provided no offer of suitable work is refused.

His availability means that the claimant is ready, willing, and free to work. Once again, registration for work at a public employment office provides some evidence of availability. If the unemployed person refuses suitable work or places substantial restrictions on the type of work he will accept, he may be considered not available for work and may be refused benefits.

Actively Seeking Work.   Most states require claimants to seek work actively or make a reasonable effort to obtain it, in addition to registering for work at the local employment office.

Free of Disqualification.   The major causes of disqualification in most states are voluntary separation from work, discharge for misconduct, refusal of suitable work, and unemployment owing to a labor dispute. The disqualification may include one or more of the following: (1) postponement of benefits for a certain period, (2) cancellation of benefit rights, or (3) a reduction in benefits otherwise payable.

The disqualification period is usually the one-week waiting period required of all claimants plus a specified number of consecutive calendar weeks. The theory of denying benefits for a specified period is that, after a limited period, the worker's unemployment is attributable to labor-market conditions rather than to his disqualified act. Thus, he should not be punished further by the denial of benefits beyond that period.

1. Voluntarily Leaving Work.   In all states, if a worker voluntarily quits his job without good cause, he is ineligible for benefits. If he has a good cause for leaving, however, the benefits are not denied. In many states, the meaning of "good cause" is restricted to reasons associated with the job, attributable to the employer, or involving fault on the part of the employer. The theory is that if the employer creates conditions of work that no reasonable person can tolerate, the worker's separation is involuntary, and he should then be compensated. On the other hand, if the worker quits for other reasons, he causes his own unemployment and should not be eligible for benefits.

2. Discharge for Misconduct.   If a worker is discharged for misconduct, about half the states disqualify him for a variable number of weeks according to the seriousness of the misconduct. For example, a worker may be discharged for continuous absence from work without notice, violation of company safety rules, or failure to observe reasonable obligations toward supervisors and fellow employees. Such reasons would call for relatively light penalties.

On the other hand, the worker may be discharged because of gross misconduct, such as an assault, committing a felony in connection with work, or dishonest or criminal acts. Many states provide for heavier penalties in these cases, such as disqualification for the entire duration of unemployment, or cancellation of wage credits, entirely or partly.

3. Refusal of Suitable Work.   Since one objective of unemployment insurance is to preserve the worker's skills and allow him reasonable time to find employment comparable to the job he held earlier, most states have criteria to determine whether the claimant is refusing suitable work. These criteria include the degree of risk to his health, safety, and morals; his physical fitness and previous training, experience, and earnings; the length of his unemployment and the prospects for securing local work in his usual occupation; and the distance of available work from his home.

4. Labor Disputes. All states have restrictions on the payment of benefits to workers who are unemployed because of a labor dispute. Some states, however, exclude certain labor disputes from these restrictions. Some pay benefits if the workers are unemployed because of a lockout by the employer; several pay benefits if the strike results from the employer's failure to conform to the provisions of a labor union contract or to the labor laws of the state; and most pay benefits to workers who are unemployed because of a strike if they are not participating in the labor dispute, financing it, or directly interested in it.

Unempioyment during a labor dispute is generally disqualified for several reasons. First, strikes and lockouts are tactics of economic warfare in which the state should remain neutral. Payment of unemployment benefits to striking workers amounts in effect to a subsidy by the state and violates that neutral position. Second, the payment of benefits means that the employers are financing the strike, since the unemployment tax is paid entirely by them in most states. Finally, the denial of benefits is justified on the grounds that the workers are not involuntarily unemployed, but have elected to exercise their right to strike.

5. Other Causes. In certain states, special groups may be disqualified from receiving unemployment benefits. Students who are unavailable for work while attending school are generally disqualified in most states. Pregnant women are disqualified in 23 states, and 15 states still continue to exclude women who quit their jobs because of marital obligations.

All states except Iowa have special disqualification provisions covering fraudulent misrepresentation to obtain or increase the unemployment benefits. All states have provisions for recovering benefits paid to people who are not entitled to them. However, research studies by competent scholars indicate that the number of fraudulent claims and the amount of abuse of the system are relatively minor.[5]

Most states disqualify a person if he is receiving disqualifying income. This may consist of wages in lieu of notice, dismissal wages, workmen's compensation for temporary partial disability, benefits from an employer's pension plan, or primary insurance benefits under the OASDHI program. In many states, if the income is less than the weekly unemployment benefit, the claimant receives the difference.

Benefits

Federal law does not establish benefit standards in the federal-state

---

[5]See Joseph M. Becker, *The Problem of Abuse in Unemployment Benefits* (New York: Columbia University Press, 1953), pp. 303-38. See also Leonard P. Adams, *Public Attitudes toward Unemployment Insurance: A Historical Account with Special Reference to Alleged Abuses* (Kalamazoo, Mich.: The W.E. Upjohn Institute for Employment Research, 1971), p. 74.

system of unemployment insurance. The benefits vary widely among the states, and diverse and complex formulas are used to determine their amounts.

Waiting Period. All except eight states require a one-week waiting period of total unemployment before the benefits are payable. Some states waive the waiting period if the unemployment results directly from a disaster, and the governor discloses a state of emergency.

The waiting period is required because it eliminates short-term claims, thus reducing administrative expenses, cutting down the cost of the program, and making it possible to pay higher benefits to those workers who are unemployed for longer periods. Also, from an administrative viewpoint, the waiting period provides additional time to process claims.

Benefit Year. The benefit year is typically a one-year period, or 52 weeks, during which an unemployed worker can receive benefits. Most states use an "individual benefit year," whereby the benefit year for any individual claimant is related to the date of his unemployment and the filing of a claim. In most states using individual benefit years, the benefit year begins with the week in which the worker files a valid claim.

Weekly Benefit Amount. The weekly benefit amount is the amount paid for one week of total unemployment. It varies with the worker's past wages, in order to compensate him for a fraction of his weekly wage loss, within certain minimum and maximum dollar limits.

One of three methods is used to determine the weekly benefit amount. The first, used in most states, is to base benefits on a *fraction of the worker's high-quarter wages,* up to the maximum, since this calendar quarter represents most nearly his full-time work. This fraction is 1/26 in twelve states, which results in the payment of benefits equal to 50 percent of the full-time wage for workers with 13 full weeks of employment during their high quarter. For example, assume that a worker earns $150 weekly during his high quarter, totaling $1,950. Applying the fraction of 1/26 to this amount gives him a weekly benefit of $75, or 50 percent of the full-time weekly wage. However, some workers are unemployed during part of their high quarter; to compensate for this, many states use a fraction greater than 1/26 (such as 1/25 or 1/24). And some states use a weighted schedule to provide relatively higher benefits to low-paid workers.

Nine states compute the weekly benefit as a *percentage of the worker's average weekly wages* in his base period or in part of the base period. For example, the weekly benefit may be 50 to 67 percent of the worker's average weekly wage, up to some statutory maximum.

The third method, used in four states, is to compute the weekly benefit as a *percentage of annual wages.* For example, in New Hampshire, base-period wages of $6,600 result in a maximum weekly benefit of $80. If the base-period wages are only $600, the minimum weekly benefit is only $14. Most states employing this technique use a weighted schedule that provides relatively greater benefits to low-wage workers.

Minimum and Maximum Benefits. All states have minimum and maximum limitations on the weekly benefits. The minimum weekly benefit for an unemployed worker with no dependents ranges from $5 in Hawaii to $30 in Indiana.

Some states pay maximum benefits that are expressed as absolute dollar amounts, such as $90 weekly. More than half, however, have a *flexible maximum weekly benefit.* Under this arrangement, the maximum benefit is adjusted annually or semiannually in proportion to wage levels within the state. The maximum weekly benefit is generally expressed as 50 percent of the state's average weekly wage in covered employment. The advantage of this approach is that benefits will automatically increase as wage levels in the state rise. The maximum weekly benefit paid to a worker with no dependents ranges from $60 in Illinois, Indiana, and Mississippi to $127 in the District of Columbia.

Partial Unemployment. All states except Montana have provisions for the payment of unemployment benefits when underemployment reaches a certain level. In most states, a worker is considered partially unemployed during a week of part-time work if he earns less than his weekly benefit amount from his regular employer or from odd jobs. Some states consider a worker partially unemployed if he earns less than his weekly benefit plus an allowance either from odd jobs or from any source. The benefit paid for a week of partial unemployment is usually the weekly unemployment benefit less wages earned in the week, but with a specified amount of earnings disregarded in computing the benefit.

Dependents' Allowances. Eleven states provide additional unemployment allowances for certain types of dependents. Children under age 16 or 18 are included, as are stepchildren and grandchildren in most states. In addition, most states pay benefits on behalf of older children who are unable to work because of some mental or physical disability, and some states include under certain conditions a nonworking spouse or other dependents. The benefit paid is normally a fixed sum of $1 to $22 per dependent.

Duration of Benefits. The maximum potential duration of unemployment benefits varies from 20 to 36 weeks, but in most states, it is 26 weeks.

In many cases, the maximum potential duration of benefits is not available to the unemployed worker. Only a small number of states have a potential duration of benefits that is uniform for all claimants; in most, it is variable, depending on the individual worker's wage credits or weeks of employment. The various formulas generally limit the maximum total benefits to a multiple of the weekly benefit amount or to a fraction of the base period wages, whichever is less. Most states with variable durations have a maximum limit of 26 weeks.

Extended Unemployment Compensation. Many workers exhaust their unemployment benefits during periods of high unemployment. The 1970 amendments established a permanent federal-state program of extended unemployment compensation to meet this problem. The program provides for up to 13 additional weeks of benefits to workers who exhaust their regular state benefits during such periods. The overall limit on both regular and extended benefits is 39 weeks.

The program is funded equally by the federal government and the states and can be operational at either the national or state level. The national "on" indicator is triggered when the seasonally adjusted rate of insured unemployment for all states equals or exceeds 4.5 percent in each of the three most recent calendar months.[6] The national "off" indicator is triggered when the seasonally adjusted rate of insured unemployment falls below 4.5 percent in each of three consecutive months.[7]

The "on" indicator for any individual state is triggered when the rate of insured unemployment (not seasonally adjusted) is (1) 4 percent or more during a period of 13 consecutive weeks, and (2) equals or exceeds 120 percent of the average rate for the corresponding 13-week period in each of the two preceding calendar years.[8] The "off" indicator in the state is triggered when the rate of insured unemployment either (1) is less than 4 percent, or (2) falls below 120 percent of the average rate for the corresponding period in each of the two preceding calendar years.[9]

As of December, 1974, ten states were paying extended unemployment insurance benefits, including California, Massachusetts, Michigan, Nevada, New Jersey, New York, Oregon, Rhode Island, Vermont, and Washington.

Because of unusually high unemployment, some persons may still be unemployed after exhausting both regular and extended benefits. Under the Emergency Unemployment Compensation Act of 1974, an additional 13 weeks of unemployment benefits can be paid to those unemployed workers who have exhausted their regular and extended benefits. Thus, benefits can be paid up to one year to those workers experiencing an extended duration of unemployment. Unless extended by Congress, the emergency unemployment insurance program will expire December 31, 1976, but payments can continue through March 31, 1977.

Because of the severe recession in 1974, Congress also passed the companion Emergency Jobs and Unemployment Assistance Act of 1974. Under this program, special unemployment insurance benefits of up to 26 weeks can be paid to workers residing in areas of high unemployment who are not covered by state unemployment insurance programs. These groups include state and local government employees, farm workers, and domestic employees. The special benefits are funded entirely by the federal government. Unless extended by congress, the special program will expire March 31, 1976.

FINANCING UNEMPLOYMENT INSURANCE

Employer Contributions

In most states, unemployment-insurance programs are financed solely by employer contributions. The Federal Unemployment Tax Act levies a permanent tax on employers of 3.2 percent on the first $4,200 of annual wages paid to each covered worker. The employers can credit toward the federal tax any state

[6] For the period prior to December 31, 1976, the rate of insured unemployment is 4 percent.

[7] *Ibid.*

[8] The states have the option of waiving the 120 percent criterion until December 31, 1976.

[9] *Ibid.*

contributions paid under an approved unemployment-insurance program and any tax savings under an approved experience-rating plan. The total employer credit is limited to a maximum of 2.7 percent. The remaining 0.5 percent is paid to the federal government and used for federal and state administrative expenses, for financing the federal government's share of the extended-benefit program, and for interest-free loans to states whose benefit reserves are depleted.

Because of a desire to strengthen their unemployment reserves, nine states now provide for a standard contribution rate in excess of 2.7 percent; and five states provide for a taxable wage base in excess of $4,200, while one state (Hawaii) has an annual wage base equal to 90 percent of the state's annual wage. Alaska has the highest wage base, $10,000, explained by the relatively higher wages paid in Alaska and the desire to maintain fund solvency.

Employee Contributions

Except in Alabama, Alaska, and New Jersey, employee contributions are not used to finance unemployment-insurance programs. There are several reasons why most states do not require employee contributions: First, it is felt that employees should not contribute because they have no control over their unemployment; second, labor unions oppose employee contributions on the grounds that they further reduce take-home pay, and that employees already bear the tax burden as consumers in the form of higher prices; third, employers fear greater labor-union demands for higher wages if employees contribute; and fourth, as the use of experience rating for employers increases, it is considered undesirable to develop a similar system for employee rates.

Experience Rating

All states have some type of experience-rating system whereby individual employer contribution rates are based on their own experience. Experience rating is a highly controversial issue, and numerous arguments are advanced both for and against the concept.[10]

Arguments for Experience Rating. The arguments used to justify experience rating include the following: (1) stabilization of employment, (2) proper allocation of costs, and (3) greater employer interest and participation.

1. Stabilization of Employment. The argument that experience rating encourages firms to stabilize their employment is attributed to Prof. John R. Commons, who said that workmen's compensation tends to reduce industrial accidents, since employers are held responsible for the costs of industrial injuries, and, similarly, experience rating in unemployment insurance would cause some employers to reduce their unemployment if they were charged with its costs.

[10]See Joseph M. Becker, S.J., *Experience Rating in Unemployment Insurance: Virtue or Vice* (Kalamazoo, Mich.: The W.E. Upjohn Institute for Employment Research, 1972); and William Haber and Merrill G. Murray, *Unemployment Insurance in the American Economy* (Homewood, Ill.: Richard D. Irwin, 1966), pp. 330-57.

The viewpoint that experience rating causes firms to stabilize employment is subject to considerable debate. Empirical research studies are limited, and the results are generally inconclusive. Three studies are available: (1) a survey by Charles A. Myers of 247 Wisconsin employers in 1937-38, (2) a study by Taulman A. Miller of 238 Indiana employers during 1941-42, and (3) a survey of 3,500 employers by the Connecticut Employment Security Division in 1968. The results of these studies showed that the majority of firms are not at all influenced by experience-rating provisions; only about 25 percent of them indicated that experience rating strongly influenced them to stabilize their employment.[11] It appears safe to conclude that experience rating may encourage some but certainly not all employers to stabilize their employment, and that the extent to which it can reduce unemployment falls far short of expectations. Consequently, other arguments must be used to justify experience rating.

2. Proper Allocation of Unemployment Costs. It is said that experience rating results in the proper allocation of unemployment costs, since those firms more responsible for unemployment pay higher contribution rates, which are then reflected in higher product prices.

This argument is based on the assumption that unemployment costs are shifted to consumers in the form of higher prices. However, Prof. Richard A. Lester concludes that no more than one-third of the employers' contributions is shifted to consumers.[12] This conclusion is based on several factors. A firm may compete in many states, but the employer contributions vary considerably among the states because of different experience-rating formulas and benefit levels; consequently, the size of the tax that the firm may shift is uncertain. Then, employer contribution rates may fluctuate sharply from year to year, and the uncertainty of the size of the tax, as well as annual fluctuations in contribution rates, reduces the possibility of forward shifting. Furthermore, highly competitive industries—such as construction, apparel, and food products—are apt to pay higher employer contribution rates and also to have a wide dispersion of rates among the firms within the industry, as opposed to the relatively stable, lower-taxed industries such as public utilities and banks, which tend to be monopolistic. However, firms in highly competitive industries may be the least likely to shift the tax to consumers. Finally, Lester concludes that because the employer contribution rates are relatively small when compared to total payroll costs, the possibility of forward shifting is again reduced. For these reasons, Lester estimates that most employer contribution taxes are probably borne by the employers.

Another factor working against the cost-allocation argument is the maximum ceiling on employer contribution rates, which places an upper limit on the tax contributions that are paid by firms with very unstable employment experience. Although some firms with high unemployment rates pay the maximum contribution rates, these rates seldom fully reflect the true costs of the unemployment generated by these firms. The result is that many of them are subsidized by the firms with greater employment stability.

[11] Becker, *Experience Rating,* pp. 37-38.

[12] Richard A. Lester, *The Economics of Unemployment Compensation* (Princeton, N.J.: Princeton University, Industrial Relations Section, 1962), pp. 60-68.

3. Greater Employer Interest. Finally, it is argued that experience rating encourages greater employer interest and participation in unemployment-insurance programs. Experience rating may cause some firms to have a greater interest in benefit levels and pending unemployment-insurance legislation. Also, employers may have a greater interest in preventing the payment of dishonest claims, and in the efficient administration of the program.

Arguments against Experience Rating. The major arguments against experience rating include the following: (1) little control by firms over employment, (2) employer resistance to benefit increases, (3) penalizing of some employers, (4) inadequate trust-fund income, and (5) automatic destabilizer.

1. Little Control over Employment. It is argued that most unemployment is caused by a deficiency in aggregate demand, cyclical forces, and structural changes in the economy, factors over which firms have little control. In addition, firms in very stable industries pay lower contribution rates even though they make no determined efforts to stabilize their employment. Thus, it is said that the firm with little control over unemployment should not be penalized by the payment of high rates.

2. Employer Resistance to Benefit Increases. Another argument is that some business firms oppose the liberalization of unemployment benefits because of the higher contribution rates they will pay. Many firms evaluate proposed benefit increases in terms of their effect on experience rating and may lobby in the state legislatures to oppose these increases.

3. Penalizes Some Employers.[13] Firms that hire the hard-core unemployed under a national manpower program, such as JOBS, increase their risk of higher taxes under experience rating, since the hard-core unemployed are less likely to find jobs if they should be laid off. In addition, experience rating does not recognize those firms that help reduce unemployment by expanding their labor force—in fact, quite the contrary. In the reserve-ratio experience-rating formula, the payroll denominator is increased, so an expanding employer may actually end up in a higher tax bracket under experience rating. Consequently, experience rating has a perverse influence when the highest tax rewards are given to firms that do nothing to hire the hard-core disadvantaged, but those that take active steps in this regard are penalized.

4. Inadequate Income. Critics of present financing methods oppose experience rating on the grounds that lower contribution rates provide inadequate income to the system, and so unemployment reserves may be depleted to dangerously low levels during periods of extended unemployment. Critics point out that many state unemployment programs are inadequately financed. For example, during the recessions of 1958 and 1961, Congress was forced to pass temporary legislation to assist states that had drawn down their unemployment reserves to dangerously low levels. In addition, the average employer contribution rate declines during a period of prosperity, when the unemployment re-

[13]Richard A. Lester, "The Uses of Unemployment Insurance," in William G. Bowen, Frederick H. Harbison, Richard A. Lester, and Herman M. Somers, eds., *The Princeton Symposium on the American System of Social Insurance: Its Philosophy, Impact, and Future Development* (New York: McGraw-Hill, 1968), pp. 171-72.

serves should be building up rapidly. Thus, it is argued that experience rating causes the system to be underfinanced.

5. Automatic Destabilizer. Experience rating is said to be a destabilizer, because unemployment-tax rates increase during business downswings when the firms are least able to pay. Thus, the recession is aggravated because of the higher unemployment taxes that must be paid.

The empirical evidence, however, generally disproves the viewpoint that experience rating is a destabilizer. Table 16-1 is a summary of four major studies on the countercyclical impact of experience rating on the economy. A change is stabilizing (S) when it is in the same direction as the economy and is destabilizing (D) when it is in the opposite direction. These studies indicate that both absolute unemployment taxes and unemployment-tax rates tend to move in the proper countercyclical direction.

Several factors help explain why experience rating may not be an automatic destabilizer. First, there is a time lag between the increased unemployment experienced by a firm during a recession and the higher tax rates that must be paid under an experience-rating tax schedule. Most state laws provide for the computation of tax rates for all covered employers once each year, and the computed rate is usually effective for an entire 12-month rate year. In most states, the computation date for new tax rates is six months prior to the effective date of the tax. June 30 is the date most commonly used for computation of employer tax rates; the rate usually becomes effective on the following January 1.

For example, assume that a tax rate is computed for a firm on June 30, 1977, a period of prosperity, and that the rate is set at 2 percent. The tax rate that is computed on June 30, 1977, will not become effective until January 1, 1978, and will remain at 2 percent throughout 1978. Now assume that a downswing occurs in 1978, with a high rate of unemployment experienced by the firm. Although the firm has a higher level of unemployment in 1978 than in 1977, it will still continue to pay the tax rate of 2 percent throughout 1978.

On June 30, 1978, a new tax rate will be computed, and because of rising unemployment, assume that the rate is increased to 2.2 percent. However, that new tax rate will not become effective until January 1, 1979. Thus, despite the downswing that occurred in 1978 and the subsequent increase in unemployment experienced by the firm, the increased taxes established under the experience-rating tax schedule will not have to be remitted until 1979.

In view of the additional fact that unemployment taxes are paid quarterly, it is quite possible for the time lag to be as long as 21 months between the onset of recession and the time the increased taxes are paid. Most of our postwar recessions have been relatively short, averaging a year or less, so *the recession may be over before the higher taxes are paid.* As a result, they would be paid during the upswing of the cycle, a desirable situation from the viewpoint of countercyclical stability, and one of the reasons that experience rating is not necessarily destabilizing to the economy.

Second, absolute unemployment taxes also generally move in the proper countercyclical direction. A distinction must be made here between an unemployment tax rate (such as the average employer contribution rate) and absolute

TABLE 16-1 Summary of Four Studies[a] of the Stabilizing (S) and Destabilizing (D) Effects of Unemployment-Insurance Taxes

Calendar Year	Andrews and Miller — Effect	Raphaelson[b] — Effect	Rejda — Period of Upswing or Downswing	Rejda — Effect	Palomba — Business Cycle	Palomba — Effect
1946	S		1945-IV ⎫			
1947	S		⎬ upswing	S		
1948	D	S	1948-IV ⎭		1948-IV ⎫	
1949	D	D	1948-IV ⎫ 1949-IV ⎬ downswing	S	⎪	
1950	S	S	1949-IV ⎭		⎪	
1951	S	S	⎫		⎬ I	S
1952		S	⎬ upswing	S	⎪	
1953		S	1953-III ⎭		1953-II ⎭	
1954		S	1953-III ⎫ 1954-III ⎬ downswing	S	1953-II ⎫	
1955		D	1954-III ⎭		⎬ II	S
1956		S	⎬ upswing	S	⎭	
1957		D	1957-III ⎫		1957-III ⎫	
1958		D	1957-III ⎫ 1958-II ⎬ downswing	S	1957-III ⎬ III	S
1959		S	1958-II ⎭ ⎬ upswing	S	⎭	
1960		S	1960-II ⎭		1960-II ⎫	
1961		S	1960-II ⎫ 1961-I ⎬ downswing	S	1960-II ⎬ IV	S
1962			1961-I ⎫ ⎬ upswing	S	⎭	
1963			⎬ upswing	S	1964-IV ⎭	
1964			1964-I ⎭			
Percent stabilizing	66.7	71.4		100.0		100.0

[a]William H. Andrews and Taulman A. Miller, "Unemployment Benefits, Experience Rating, and Employment Stability," *National Tax Journal,* September 1954; Arnold H. Raphaelson, "Massachusetts Unemployment Compensation, 1948-1961, A Study in Countercyclical Finance," *Research Report No. 32 of Federal Reserve Bank of Boston,* 1966; George E. Rejda, "Unemployment Insurance as an Automatic Stabilizer," *The Journal of Risk and Insurance,* June 1966; and Neil Anthony Palomba, *A Measure of the Stabilizing Effect of the Unemployment Compensation Program—With Emphasis on the Experience Rating Controversy,* Ph.D. Dissertation, University of Minnesota, 1966.

[b]This study covers the state of Massachusetts only.

Source: Joseph M. Becker, S.J., *Experience Rating in Unemployment Insurance: Virtue or Vice* (Kalamazoo, Mich: The W.E. Upjohn Institute for Employment Research, 1972), p. 46, Table 4-1.

unemployment taxes. From the viewpoint of automatic stabilization, the critical item is the relation between the absolute amount of taxes that have to be paid and the national income during different stages of the business cycle.

Regarding the countercyclical effect, changes in the unemployment-tax rate are not as important as the absolute amount of taxes that have to be paid. During periods of downswing, workers are laid off, hours of work are reduced, and marginal firms may go out of existence. The result is that aggregate taxable payrolls for the entire economy may decline (or increase less rapidly).[14] Thus, the base to which the unemployment-tax rate is to be applied may decline during a downswing.

The significant point here is that, although the unemployment-tax rate may increase during a downswing (and the empirical evidence does not support this conclusion, by any means), the rate would be applied to a decreasing tax base, because of the decline in taxable payrolls. Thus, the absolute amount of unemployment taxes may decline with national income in a desirable counter-cyclical manner. Conversely, the unemployment-tax rate may decline during a period of upswing (again, the empirical evidence does not support completely this conclusion), but the tax base to which the rate is to be applied may increase, since aggregate taxable payrolls generally expand during prosperity because of rising employment.

Thus, it is quite possible for the absolute amount of unemployment taxes to increase during prosperity even though the unemployment-tax rate may decline. From a countercyclical viewpoint, this is desirable, because unemployment taxes would be increasing along with national income during a period of upswing.

Finally, any destabilizing features associated with experience rating are partly offset by the experience-rating provisions used by the states. Most states use three years of payroll experience in their formulas when determining the firm's unemployment-tax rate. The adverse financial impact of a year of high unemployment and lower payrolls, which would tend to increase the firm's tax rate, could be diluted by the favorable experience, if any, of the other two years.

Experience-Rating Provisions. The following section briefly describes the major features of experience-rating provisions.

1. Requirements for Experience Rating. Employers are required to meet certain federal and state requirements before they are eligible for experience rating. First, most states require new or newly covered employers to have one to three years of unemployment experience before experience rating is used. However, as a result of the 1970 amendments, the states can assign new employers a reduced tax rate (but not less than 1 percent) to lessen the initial tax burden. Second, many states require a minimum balance in the unemployment fund before any reduced rates are allowed. The purpose of this solvency requirement is to make certain that the fund is adequate to pay benefits. Finally, many states provide for a suspension of reduced rates or an increase in employer contribution rates when the fund falls below certain specified levels.

2. Types of Formulas. Five experience-rating formulas are used: the

---

[14]U.S. Department of Labor, Bureau of Employment Security, *Handbook of Unemployment Insurance Financial Data, 1946-1963* (1964), pp. 59-60.

reserve-ratio, benefit-ratio, benefit-wage ratio, compensable separations, and payroll-decline formulas. Although the formulas are complex and vary greatly, they have the common objective of establishing the relative experience of individual employers with respect to unemployment or benefit costs. Only the reserve-ratio method will be discussed, since it is used in 32 states and is the most popular method for determining individual employer contribution rates.

The reserve-ratio system is essentially cost accounting. Each employer has an individual record, in which are recorded payroll amounts, tax contributions, and unemployment benefits paid. The benefits paid are subtracted from the tax contributions, and the resulting balance is divided by the payroll to determine the reserve ratio. In most states, the payroll used is an average of those of the last three years. The employer's contribution rate depends on his reserve ratio, as well as the size of the state unemployment reserve fund. (A reduction in the overall reserve fund may require an alternate tax schedule involving higher rates.) The higher the reserve ratio, the lower the tax rate. However, the reserve-ratio method is designed to make certain that no employer receives a rate reduction unless he contributes more to the fund over the years than his workers receive in benefits. The following is an example of the reserve-ratio method:

If the reserve ratio is:	The contribution rate will be:
10.0% and above	0.1%
9.5% to but not including 10.0%	0.2%
9.0% to but not including 9.5%	0.3%
8.5% to but not including 9.0%	0.5%
8.0% to but not including 8.5%	1.0%
7.5% to but not including 8.0%	1.5%
7.0% to but not including 7.5%	2.0%
6.5% to but not including 7.0%	2.5%
Below 6.5%	2.7%

As a result of state experience-rating provisions, the taxes paid by covered employers are considerably below the 2.7 percent rate. In 1972, the estimated average employer contribution rate for all the states was 1.8 percent of taxable payroll.[15]

3. Other Features. Various methods are used in experience rating to determine which employer should be charged with the benefits that an unemployed worker collects. Seven states charge the *most recent employer,* on the theory that he has primary responsibility for the unemployment. Twelve states charge *base-period employers in inverse chronological order.* This method is based on the theory that responsibility for unemployment lessens with time. A maximum limit is placed on the amount charged to the most recent employer; when this limit is reached, the next most recent employer is charged, and so on. Most states, however, charge employers *in proportion to base-period wages,* because it is believed that unemployment results from general labor-market conditions rather than from the separations of any single employer.

[15]U.S. Department of Health, Education and Welfare, Social Security Administration, *Social Security Programs in the United States* (Washington, D.C.: U.S. Government Printing Office, 1973), p. 68.

Noncharging-of-benefit provisions are used in most states, whereby certain unemployment costs are not charged to employers, including benefits paid for appealed cases that are reversed, and benefits paid following a period of disqualification for a voluntary quit, misconduct, or refusal of suitable work.

In about half the states, employers can obtain lower rates by voluntary contributions. The voluntary contribution increases the balance in the employer's account (in reserve-ratio states), and a lower rate results by which the employer saves more than the amount of the voluntary contribution.

Finally, provisions in all states specify the conditions under which the employer's experience can be transferred to another employer acquiring the business.

Unemployment-Insurance Trust Fund

All unemployment-insurance tax contributions are deposited in the Federal Unemployment Trust Fund, which is administered by the secretary of the Treasury. The fund as a whole is invested, but each state has a separate account, which is credited with the unemployment-tax contributions collected by the state, plus the state's share of the interest on investments. The sums allocated to each state's account are generally used to pay unemployment benefits in that state, although, under certain conditions, a state can utilize the allocated sums to supplement federal administrative grants for buildings, supplies, and other administrative expenses. Thus, unemployment benefits are paid exclusively through a public fund, and no private unemployment plans can be substituted for the state plan.

Business downswings tend to hit some states harder than others. In particular, the highly industrialized states with cyclical industries (for instance, Michigan and Pennsylvania) tend to have relatively higher unemployment rates during business declines, and at times, individual state accounts have declined to dangerously low levels. If a state experiences rapidly depleting reserves because of high unemployment, it can borrow additional sums interest-free from the federal unemployment account to finance benefit payments.

The adequacy of state reserves to finance benefits during periods of prolonged unemployment is subject to some dispute. One commonly accepted measure, developed by the Bureau of Employment Security, is that a reserve is adequate if it is at least 1.5 times the highest twelve-month benefit-cost rate (ratio of benefits paid to payrolls) during the previous decade. At times, many states fail to meet this standard. For example, at the end of fiscal 1969, the national average was 1.78. Thirty-five states, as well as Puerto Rico and the District of Columbia, fulfilled the 1.5-times rule. But 14 states, accounting for over 41 percent of the covered workers, did not meet this requirement.[16] The reserves of these states must be strengthened to assure the payment of benefits during severe and prolonged recessions. One proposal is that the federal taxable wage base should be raised for this purpose. The size of the taxable wage base is a controversial issue that will be analyzed later in the chapter.

[16]U.S. Congress, Senate, Committee on Finance, *Unemployment Compensation,* Hearings before the Committee on Finance on H.R. 14705, 91st Cong., 2d sess., 1970, p. 151.

ADMINISTRATION

Each state administers its unemployment-insurance program by maintaining records, collecting taxes, determining eligibility, processing claims, and paying unemployment benefits. Each state is required to designate an employment security agency to perform these functions. Some states use an independent board or commission; some designate an independent department of state government, which reports directly to the governor; and some use the state department of labor or workmen's compensation agency as the employment security agency.

The agencies operate through more than 2,100 local employment offices, which process the claims and act as employment exchanges by providing job development and placement services. The unemployed worker normally registers for work at the public employment office and reports regularly (usually weekly). He usually files a weekly claim for benefits at the same office, but in some cases, the claims are filed by mail. Without good cause for late reporting, the worker must file for benefits within seven days after the week for which the claim is made. The employment security agency administering the program usually pays the benefits by check, but in some states, local offices also pay benefits.

The states must provide claimants who are denied benefits an opportunity for a fair hearing. The worker can appeal first to a referee or impartial tribunal and then to a board of review. If necessary, the board's decision can be appealed in the courts.

The employment security agency also administers the interstate agreements for workers who move to different states. These are special wage-combining agreements on behalf of workers who earn wages in two or more states.

All states except four have statewide advisory councils on unemployment insurance, which are generally made up of labor representatives, employer groups, and public representatives. The advisory council helps the employment security agency to formulate policy and to solve administrative problems.

Federal and state expenses for administering the unemployment insurance programs are financed out of the 0.5 percent residual federal unemployment tax.

DEFECTS OF UNEMPLOYMENT INSURANCE

Although the 1970 amendments corrected several deficiencies, many still remain in state unemployment-insurance programs. The major defects are (1) incomplete coverage, (2) inadequate benefits, (3) the small proportion of unemployed receiving benefits, (4) harsh disqualification standards, (5) exhaustion of benefits, and (6) inadequate taxable wage base.[17]

[17]A discussion of the basic issues in unemployment insurance can be found in James R. O'Brien, "Unemployment Insurance: The Urgency for Reform," *The American Federationist,* April 1974. See also Saul J. Blaustein, *Unemployment Insurance Objectives and Issues: An Agenda for Research and Evaluation* (Kalamazoo, Mich.: The W.E. Upjohn Institute for Employment Research, 1968); and Merrill G. Murray, *Income for the Unemployed: The Variety and Fragmentation of Programs* (Kalamazoo, Mich.: The W.E. Upjohn Institute for Employment Research, 1971).

Incomplete Coverage

In fiscal 1973, 67 million workers out of a total civilian labor force of about 89 million were covered for unemployment insurance.[18] However, that still left about 22 million workers, or about 25 percent of the civilian labor force, not covered. The noncovered jobs are primarily in four major classifications: (1) state and local government, (2) domestic service, (3) farm and agricultural processing, and (4) nonprofit organizations.[19] In addition, unemployment insurance does not generally cover young workers seeking their first job, and re-entrants into the labor force. And about 46 percent of the unemployed in 1973 were in these categories.

Many noncovered industries are excluded for political, administrative, financial, and technical reasons. For example, state and local government employees are excluded because a state cannot be taxed without its consent; however, as stated earlier, most states now cover certain government employees. Domestic service is excluded because of administrative problems, difficulty in collecting the unemployment tax from employers, potentially high costs, and large numbers of part-time workers. Nonprofit organizations are generally excluded on the grounds that they suffer little unemployment, that they have been traditionally free from taxation, and that since they depend on charitable contributions, they should not be required to share in the costs of providing benefits to workers in profit-making organizations. Farm employees are generally excluded because of inadequate actuarial data, potentially higher costs, record-keeping and administrative problems (as with migrant farm workers, traveling from state to state), and the inability of farmers to bear the high costs of the program. New entrants into the labor force are excluded because, with little or no employment experience, they cannot meet the eligibility requirements, and because they do not have a current attachment to the labor force.

Some critics of the present system argue that many of the reasons above are no longer valid, and they put forth several reasons for wider coverage of workers. First, the risk of unemployment for workers in noncovered occupations is just as great as it is for workers in covered industries. More than half of the noncovered workers are in state and local government, and are also exposed to the threat of unemployment; and farm workers and migrant workers are highly vulnerable to layoffs.

Second, many workers in excluded occupations have low-wage jobs that are vulnerable to layoffs because of seasonal and cyclical forces. These workers have inadequate savings on which to draw when they are unemployed, and they receive no severance pay when their employment is permanently terminated.

Third, critics point out that administrative problems and potentially high costs are no longer significant arguments for excluding some workers. For example, the OASDHI program has been extended to cover farm workers and

[18]U.S. Department of Labor, *Manpower Report of the President* (Washington, D.C.: U.S. Government Printing Office, 1974), p. 45, and p. 253, Table A-1.

[19]Note, however, that these groups were temporarily covered for special unemployment insurance benefits under the Emergency Jobs and Unemployment Assistance Act of 1974 if they resided in areas of high unemployment. Unless extended by Congress, this program will expire March 31, 1976.

domestic employees despite some administrative problems. In addition, studies indicate that coverage of farm workers would cost no more than that of workers in industries, such as construction.[20] Critics also argue that unemployment for farm workers is generally higher than for the national economy, a fact that points out the critical need for coverage, and that the substandard wages that are paid in agriculture necessitate coverage for unemployment benefits during layoff periods.

Finally, to the extent that unemployment insurance excludes large numbers of vulnerable groups, the social insurance objectives of covering the masses and providing a layer of economic security for all workers are not attained.

Inadequate Benefits

Unemployment-insurance benefits in many states are inadequate for maintaining the worker's previous standard of living. A commonly accepted principle of benefit adequacy is replacement of at least 50 percent of the worker's average weekly wage. However, in 1973, 15 states with about 50 percent of the nation's covered workers paid weekly unemployment benefits that were less than half the average weekly wage.[21] This situation is due largely to rising wages since World War II and the statutory limits on maximum benefits in most states, which, in effect, have turned the program into a flat-benefit system for most workers.

Another measure of the general inadequacy of benefit levels is a comparison of the average and maximum unemployment-insurance benefits with the poverty line. The 1974 national poverty level for a four-member nonfarm family was $96.92 weekly. But as of January, 1975, *all 50 states paid average weekly benefits for total unemployment that were below the poverty line, and 37 states paid maximum weekly unemployment benefits that were below the poverty line.*

In view of the inadequate benefits paid in many states, critics argue that federal benefit standards must be established. One proposed standard would require the states to pay maximum benefits that are at least two-thirds the *average wage of all covered workers* in the state. Labor unions go one step further and favor an amount equal to at least two-thirds of the unemployed worker's *full-time weekly wage.* Most states at present are not meeting either of these standards. In 1973, only five jurisdictions (Arkansas, Hawaii, South Carolina, Utah, and the District of Columbia) were paying maximum benefits of approximately two-thirds the average weekly pay of covered workers.[22] Thus, if these federal proposals were enacted, most states would be required to increase their benefits. The estimated national cost of the programs would increase by 15 percent, but the costs among the states would vary greatly.[23]

[20]U.S. Department of Labor, *Manpower Report of the President* (Washington, D.C.: U.S. Government Printing Office, 1971), p. 125.

[21]U.S. Department of Labor, *Manpower Report of the President,* 1974, p. 46, Chart 9.

[22]*Ibid.*

[23]American Enterprise Institute for Public Policy Research, "Publications Analyze Bills on Forestry and Welfare," *Memorandum,* Spring-Summer 1974, p. 7.

Proponents offer two major arguments for increasing benefit standards.[24] First, because unemployment benefits in most states replace only a small fraction of the wage loss from unemployment, they are simply too low to meet the nondeferable living expenses of the unemployed workers. The proportion of average weekly wages replaced by average unemployment benefits has been declining since 1945, when benefits replaced about 42 percent of national average weekly wages in covered employment. By the end of 1968, this proportion had declined to about 34 percent.[25] Thus, substantial improvements in benefits are necessary to restore a larger fraction of the wage loss.

Second, proponents say that since the wage-loss replacement ratio is lower in many states than the national norm, work incentives would not be reduced by the payment of higher benefits. The benefits paid would not exceed 50 to 67 percent of the worker's prior wage level, depending on the standard adopted, and so his work incentive could be preserved.

Proponents believe that federal standards are necessary to achieve these improvements because the individual states are slow to act and will not take the initiative to increase benefits to more adequate levels. Some states are reluctant to grant a substantial increase in benefits because of the additional costs to employers; state legislatures typically represent business interests more extensively than they do consumer and labor-union groups.

Small Proportion Receiving Benefits

Another serious problem of unemployment insurance is that only a small proportion of the total unemployed at any time receive unemployment benefits. Between 1962 and 1972, less than half the unemployed workers received benefits, and only about 38 percent received benefits in an average week in 1973.[26]

There are several reasons for this unfortunate situation. Many unemployed workers are new entrants or reentrants into the labor force and have not fulfilled the eligibility requirements; some are in noncovered industries; many are denied benefits because of the waiting period imposed in most states; others are disqualified for various other reasons; and many remain unemployed after they exhaust their benefits.

Social insurance programs ideally should cover the masses, but since only a relatively small number of the total unemployed receive benefits at any time, serious questions can be raised concerning the effectiveness of current programs of unemployment insurance as a primary defense against short-term unemployment.

[24]See American Enterprise Institute for Public Policy Research, *Legislative Analysis: The Pending Unemployment Compensation Amendments,* Analysis No. 19 (Washington, D.C.: American Enterprise Institute for Public Policy Research, 1969), pp. 27-31.

[25]*Ibid.*

[26]U.S. Department of Labor, *Manpower Report of the President,* 1974, p. 260, Table A-6, and p. 331, Table D-5.

Harsh Disqualifications

Another problem is the harsh disqualification provisions that still exist in many states. About 2 million workers are disqualified for unemployment benefits each year, most of them for the voluntary termination of employment without good cause, discharge for misconduct, refusal to accept suitable work, or pregnancy or marital obligations. Most states have tightened their disqualification provisions in recent years. In 1958, there were 14 disqualifications for each 1,000 claimant contacts; by 1969, the number of disqualifications had increased to about 27 for every 1,000 claimant contacts.[27]

Some labor-union leaders protest that the disqualification provisions in most states are too harsh and should be liberalized. They believe that payment of benefits should not be postponed for more than six weeks in situations involving voluntary quits, discharge for misconduct, and job refusals. It is argued that, although the worker initially causes his own unemployment by some disqualifying act, he should not be punished by the denial of benefits if he cannot find a job after a reasonable period. They say that six weeks is the longest period during which it is reasonable to presume that the original disqualifying act continues to be the main cause of unemployment; that if the worker remains unemployed after six weeks despite his efforts to find a job, that his unemployment is due more to a softening of the labor market than to the disqualifying act.

Some students of unemployment insurance, however, argue against this idea, claiming that such a provision would violate a basic unemployment-insurance principle by giving benefits to workers whose unemployment is voluntary. They think the states should tighten rather than liberalize disqualification provisions, because postponement of benefits for only up to six weeks may cause some workers to malinger in order to receive benefits, thereby increasing abuses under the program.

Exhaustion of Benefits

Another problem is the relatively large number of claimants who exhaust their benefits and are still unemployed. Most states provide for a potential maximum duration of 26 to 39 weeks, with 26 the most common. However, the maximum duration is not available to all claimants because the duration of benefits generally varies with the amount of past earnings or employment. In some states, the average unemployed worker can expect to receive 26 or more weeks of benefits, but in others, the average potential duration of benefits is only 18 or 19 weeks. Thus, the proportion of the claimants who exhaust their benefits and are still unemployed varies among the states from 5 to 35 percent.[28]

In view of this fact, a maximum uniform duration of 26 to 39 weeks has

[27]Adams, *Public Attitudes*, p. 73.

[28]U.S. Congress, Senate, Committee on Finance, *Unemployment Compensation*, p. 163.

been recommended for all states, for two major reasons.[29] First, a large proportion of claimants exhaust their benefits, even during periods of light unemployment, before they find jobs. For example, during 1969, when the unemployment rate was only 3.5 percent for all workers, about 20 percent of all unemployment-insurance beneficiaries used up all their benefits.[30] Such workers often have no further income protection, regardless of the length of time it takes them to find new jobs or to be recalled to their former ones. Second, many workers are thrown out of work because of technological change, shifts in demand, plant relocations, declining industries, and such factors; and a substantial proportion of these workers may exhaust their benefits before finding new jobs. So a uniform duration of benefits would provide greater economic security to unemployed workers.

Inadequate Taxable Wage Base

The $3,000 taxable wage base was increased to $4,200 by the 1970 amendments, because of a rapid increase in administrative expenses. However, the $4,200 wage base is now considered inadequate.

When the $3,000 wage base became effective in 1939, 93 percent of the total wages paid was taxable under the state laws and the Federal Unemployment Tax Act. However, by 1969, only 46 percent of wages in covered employment was subject to federal taxes under the $3,000 limit. After the wage base was raised to $4,200, about 53 percent of total wages in covered employment was taxable in 1972.[31] To restore the taxable wage base to its 1939 position would require a wage base equal to that of the OASDHI program. If this goal cannot be achieved, it is argued, the wage base should be increased to at least $6,000.

A higher taxable wage base is considered necessary for several reasons. First, it would reduce inequities among employers in the financing of benefits. Some high-wage employers pay unemployment taxes on only a small proportion of their total payrolls, whereas others may pay taxes on 90 percent or more of theirs. A higher taxable wage base would force the high-wage employers to pay a relatively larger share of total benefit costs.

Second, a higher taxable wage base would increase the capacity of the states to raise additional revenues for more adequate unemployment benefits and program improvements. It would also increase the adequacy of unemployment reserves and reduce the risk of insolvency in those states where a severe recession could deplete the reserves to dangerously low levels.

Finally, the present narrow wage base tends to limit the effectiveness of experience rating. A higher base would widen the range within which experience

[29]Haber and Murray, *Unemployment Insurance,* p. 205.

[30]Council of Economic Advisers, *Economic Report of the President* (Washington, D.C.: U.S. Government Printing Office, 1974), p. 279, Table C-26; and Merril G. Murray, *The Duration of Unemployment Benefits* (Kalamazoo, Mich.: The W.E. Upjohn Institute for Employment Research, 1974), p. 27, Table 8.

[31]U.S. Congress, Senate, Committee on Finance, *Unemployment Compensation,* pp. 80-81.

rating could operate, and thus make possible a more meaningful differentiation among employers.

IMPROVING UNEMPLOYMENT INSURANCE

The following section highlights the major areas where improvements are necessary to make unemployment insurance function more effectively as an income-maintenance program.

Extension of Coverage

Unemployment insurance should be extended to cover permanently the large numbers of workers who are now excluded for benefits in most states—including farm workers, state and local government employees, employees of nonprofit organizations, and domestic workers.[32] These workers frequently are employed at relatively low wages, have little job security, are highly vulnerable to layoffs, and seldom receive severance pay when laid off. To cushion the immediate impact of the extension of coverage, the employers of newly covered groups should be permitted to pay lower contribution rates until sufficient experience is gained to determine the appropriate rate. Such a measure, of course, would require that these employers be subsidized by the current tax-paying employers during the adjustment period.

More Adequate Benefits

Unemployment benefits must be increased to prevent a severe reduction in the worker's standard of living between jobs. Some proposals call for the benefits to replace at least 66⅔ percent of the unemployed worker's average weekly wage; others, at least 50 percent. In addition, the statutory ceiling on benefits in most states should be removed to permit the payment of more adequate benefits.

Uniform Duration of Benefits

The maximum duration of 26 weeks of regular benefits in most states is not available to all claimants, because the duration varies according to the amount of past earnings or employment. In particular, low-wage disadvantaged workers may receive benefits for shorter periods, but they are likely to remain unemployed for longer periods. This fact, plus the number of claimants exhausting their regular benefits even during periods of light unemployment, strongly suggest that a uniform duration standard of 26 weeks or more is necessary.

[32]These groups were temporarily covered for special unemployment insurance benefits under the Emergency Jobs and Unemployment Assistance Act of 1974 if they resided in areas of high unemployment. Unless extended by Congress, payments under this program will terminate March 31, 1976.

Qualification Requirements

Only a small fraction of the total unemployed now collect benefits. Social insurance programs should provide a layer of income protection to the masses, but stringent eligibility requirements defeat this objective. Something is tragically wrong with a system that pays benefits to, at best, only about two out of five unemployed workers during normal periods.

All states have eligibility requirements that restrict benefits to workers with a current attachment to the labor force. A common requirement is employment of 14 to 20 weeks. To permit additional workers to qualify for benefits, no more than 15 weeks of employment should be required as a condition, and no more than two quarters in the base year. Also, the measure of past employment in some states as a flat dollar amount discriminates against low-wage workers, since they must work longer periods to qualify for benefits. Such a dollar amount should not be the sole criterion for qualification.

Disqualifications

Stringent disqualification standards should be discouraged. Some disqualifications are completely justified, but many are unreasonable and have no relationship to the worker's ability to work or his availability for employment. In most cases, the maximum penalty for a disqualification should not exceed six weeks. Unemployment extending beyond six weeks may be attributed to a softening of the labor market rather than an indication of the worker's unwillingness to work. Thus, even if the disqualification is justified, the unemployed worker should not be unduly penalized for his mistakes.

Increase in Wage Base

The taxable wage base should be increased to at least $6,000, in order to strengthen the financing of unemployment to permit the payment of more adequate benefits, and to force high-wage employers to pay a relatively larger share of the costs, thus correcting a serious inequity that now exists.

SUGGESTIONS FOR ADDITIONAL READING

American Enterprise Institute for Public Policy Research, *Unemployment Compensation: Proposed Permanent Changes.* Washington, D.C.: American Enterprise Institute for Public Policy Research, 1974.

Becker, Joseph M., *Experience Rating in Unemployment Insurance: An Experiment in Competitive Socialism.* Baltimore and London: The John Hopkins Press, 1972.

Blaustein, Saul J., *Unemployment Insurance Objectives and Issues: An Agenda for Research and Evaluation.* Kalamazoo, Mich.: The W.E. Upjohn Institute for Employment Research, 1968.

Bowen, William G., Frederick H. Harbison, Richard A. Lester, and Herman M. Somers, eds., *The Princeton Symposium on the American System of Social Insurance: Its Philosophy, Impact, and Future Development.* New York: McGraw-Hill, 1968.

Committee on Unemployment Insurance Objectives, *Unemployment and Income Security: Goals for the 1970's, A Report of the Committee on Unemployment Insurance Objectives Sponsored by the Institute.* Kalamazoo, Mich.: The W.E. Upjohn Institute for Employment Research, 1969.

Edgell, David L. and Stephen A. Wandner, "Unemployment Insurance: Its Economic Performance," *Monthly Labor Review,* Vol. 97, No. 4 (April 1974).

Felstein, Martin S., "Unemployment Insurance: Time for Reform," *Harvard Business Review,* Vol. 53, No. 2 (March-April 1975).

Haber, William, and Merrill G. Murray, *Unemployment Insurance in the American Economy.* Homewood, Ill.: Richard D. Irwin, 1966.

Lester, Richard A., *The Economics of Unemployment Compensation.* Princeton N.J.: Princeton University, Industrial Relations Section, 1962.

Malisoff, Harry, *The Insurance Character of Unemployment Insurance.* Kalamazoo, Mich.: The W.E. Upjohn Institute for Employment Research, 1961.

Munts Raymond, and Irwin Garfinkel, *The Work Disincentive Effects of Unemployment Insurance.* Kalamazoo, Mich.: The W.E. Upjohn Institute for Employment Research, 1974.

Murray, Merrill G., *The Duration of Unemployment Benefits.* Kalamazoo, Mich.: The W.E. Upjohn Institute for Employment Research, 1974.

_____, *The Treatment of Seasonal Unemployment under Unemployment Insurance.* Kalamazoo, Mich.: The W.E. Upjohn Institute for Employment Research, 1972.

O'Brien, James R., "Unemployment Insurance: The Urgency for Reform," *The American Federationist* (April 1974).

Papier, William, "What's Wrong with Unemployment Insurance," *The Journal of Risk and Insurance,* Vol. XXXVII, No. 1 (March 1970).

Rejda, George E., "Unemployment Insurance as an Automatic Stabilizer," *The Journal of Risk and Insurance,* Vol. XXXIII, No. 2 (June 1966).

Roche, George S., *Entitlement to Unemployment Insurance Benefits.* Kalamazoo, Mich.: The W.E. Upjohn Institute for Employment Research, 1973.

Stevens, David W., *Assisted Job Search for the Insured Unemployed.* Kalamazoo, Mich.: The W.E. Upjohn Institute for Employment Research, 1974.

Turnbull, John G., C. Arthur Williams, Jr., and Earl F. Cheit, *Economic and Social Security,* 4th ed., Chap. 6. New York: Ronald Press, 1973.

U.S. Department of Labor, Manpower Administration, *Comparison of State Unemployment Insurance Laws.* Washington, D.C.: U.S. Government Printing Office, 1972. See also the periodic supplements to this volume.

chapter 17

Poverty
and Public Assistance

Although economic growth and expanding employment have reduced absolute poverty in the United States, millions of Americans still remain poor. Since they cannot attain a reasonable standard of living with respect to food, housing, clothing, and other necessities, they experience great economic insecurity.

It is important to reduce the remaining poverty in the United States for several reasons. First, poverty causes economic insecurity not only to the poor, but to the entire economy, since the undesirable by-products of poverty include disease, crime, delinquency, and immorality. Second, poverty impairs the quality of life for individual human beings; it deprives people of not only material goods but also human dignity. Finally, poverty results in lost production because of the waste of human resources.

Public-assistance programs are used to meet the problem of poverty in the United States. The benefits are paid only upon the demonstration of need and the fulfillment of strict eligibility requirements. Their basic function is to provide cash income, medical care, and other services to the needy aged, blind, disabled, families with dependent children, and other poor groups. In this chapter, we shall analyze the problem of poverty and the role of public-assistance programs in meeting it. In particular, we shall consider the following areas: (1) nature and causes of poverty, (2) nature and reasons for public assistance, and (3) basic characteristics of major public-assistance programs.

POVERTY

Nature of Poverty

Poverty can be defined as an insufficiency of material goods and services, whereby the basic needs of individuals or families exceed their means to satisfy

401

them. An individual and his family require food, clothing, medical care, housing, and other basic necessities. The family's basic needs depend on the number and ages of the family members, their place of residence, and their condition of health. The family's ability to meet its basic needs depends on current money income, past savings, property ownership, and access to credit. When the individual or family cannot satisfy certain minimum needs, they are living in poverty.

Absolute Poverty.   Poverty can be measured on an absolute basis. The Bureau of the Census has computed several poverty thresholds for different-sized families to determine the extent of absolute poverty in the United States. The poverty threshold is essentially defined as an amount about three times the cost of a nutritionally adequate diet. The various thresholds are adjusted for differences in family size, sex of the family head, number of children, and farm versus nonfarm residence; and they are also adjusted annually to reflect changes in the Consumer Price Index. Individuals and families whose money incomes are below the poverty thresholds are counted as poor. Based on the March, 1974 Current Population Survey by the Bureau of the Census, the poverty threshold for a four-member nonfarm family was $4,540; and for an unrelated individual, $2,247.[1]

Based on these poverty thresholds, about 23 million people were counted poor in 1973, or about 11 percent of the population. This represents a sharp decline in absolute poverty since 1959, as shown in the following illustration:[2]

Total poor in 1959	39.5 million (about 22 percent of the population)
Total poor in 1973	22.9 million (about 11 percent of the population)

The decline in absolute poverty was due largely to economic growth rather than to the effectiveness of the various antipoverty programs. Economic growth and full employment are important in reducing poverty for several reasons. A tight labor market increases the money wages of the working poor, allowing them to work their way out of poverty; economic growth provides better employment opportunities for the unemployed poor and for those with low-paying or part-time jobs; and full employment reduces the unemployment rates for skilled workers to relatively low levels, which makes firms more willing to train poorly qualified people for skilled jobs.

The Bureau of the Census has also established income levels for the near-poor—those who have incomes slightly above the poverty line, but are far from affluent—which are based on 125 percent of the poverty thresholds. In 1973, an additional 10 million were counted as near-poor. Thus, about 33 million people, or about 16 percent of the total population, were either poor or near poverty in

---

[1]See U.S. Department of Commerce, Bureau of the Census, "Characteristics of the Low-Income Population, 1973 (Advance Report)," *Current Population Reports,* P-60, No. 94 (Washington, D.C.: U.S. Government Printing Office, 1974), p. 10, Table 7.

[2]*Ibid.,* p. 1.

1973.[3] These data clearly indicate that a serious poverty problem is still present in the United States.

Relative Poverty. Poverty can also be measured on a relative basis—that is, relative to the goods and services that the nonpoor receive. Although their absolute money income may increase over time, some may consider themselves poor if the goods and services they can purchase are relatively fewer than those purchased by the more affluent groups.

One rough measure of relative poverty is to determine the percentage of the nation's aggregate income that is received by the lowest-income fifth of the families. The following table gives the percentage share of aggregate income before taxes that was received in 1947 and 1972 by each fifth of the income-ranked families:[4]

	1947	1972
Lowest fifth	5.1%	5.4%
Second fifth	11.8	11.9
Third fifth	16.7	17.5
Fourth fifth	23.2	23.9
Highest fifth	43.3	41.4
Top 5 percent	17.5	15.9

These data show that income inequality has not been significantly reduced over time, and that the relative position of low-income families has not improved between 1947 and 1972.[5] Thus, although absolute poverty has declined, this is not true of relative poverty.

Poverty-Stricken Groups. The principal poverty groups in the United States are the aged, blacks and other nonwhite races, the working poor, families headed by women, large families, and poor children.[6]

1. Aged Poor. Of the 20.6 million aged in the United States in 1973, about 3.3 million, or about 16 percent, were living in poverty.

2. Blacks and Other Nonwhite Races. Blacks and other racial minorities are poor because of racial discrimination, high unemployment and underemployment rates, cultural and language problems, and inferior educational facilities. Of the 23 million poor in 1973, about 7.8 million, or about 34 percent, were in this category.

3. The Working Poor. A persistent myth, that people are poor because they are lazy and refuse to work, is exploded once the empirical data are

[3]*Ibid.,* p. 12, Table 10.

[4]Council of Economic Advisers, *Economic Report of the President* (Washington, D.C.: U.S. Government Printing Office, 1974), p. 140, Table 34.

[5]For an excellent discussion of income inequality in the United States, see Lester C. Thurow and Robert E. B. Lucas, *The American Distribution of Income: A Structural Problem,* Joint Economic Committee Print (Washington, D.C.: U.S. Government Printing Office, 1972); and Peter Henle, "Exploring the Distribution of Earned Income," *Monthly Labor Review,* Vol. 95, No. 12 (December 1972), 16-27.

[6]Data concerning the number of poor within these categories are derived from Bureau of the Census, "Characteristics of the Low-Income Population, 1973 (Advance Report)."

examined. In 1972, about 12.7 million poor were in the working-age category between 14 and 64. Of this number, 47 percent worked sometime during the year, and about one-fourth worked full-time for the entire year.[7] The poor who did not work were generally ill or disabled, students in school, or women with family responsibilities that made it difficult for them to work.

4. Families Headed by Women. Many women are forced to support their families when their husbands are absent from the home because of death, desertion, divorce, or imprisonment. Of the 21.8 million people in families headed by females in 1972, about 8.2 million, or about 38 percent, were counted as poor.

Economic growth is less effective in reducing poverty for families headed by women, because women are less likely to be employed, and therefore less affected by economic growth; because many mothers with children find it difficult to work full-time when day-care centers for their children are inadequate; and because, even if they can work, their employment is less steady and they earn lower wages than men do.

5. Large Families. Large families with children under age 18 are another important poverty group. For those with five or more related children, the incidence of poverty was about 30 percent in 1973.

6. Poor Children. Of the 23 million poor in 1973, about 9.5 million, or about 41 percent, were poor related children under age 18.

Causes of Poverty

The precise causes of poverty are not completely known. Three theories, however, have gained some acceptance in the professional literature.[8]

The *random-events theory* states that individuals or families are poor because of events largely beyond their control. For example, a person may become disabled; a family head may die prematurely, resulting in poverty for the family; the family may break up from a divorce or desertion; there may be a decrease in demand for the services of people working in certain occupations or living in certain areas or regions; the family's business may end in bankruptcy. These and other events are generally beyond the control of the individual or his family and help explain the high incidence of poverty among aged widows, disabled persons, farmers, and the long-term unemployed.

The *social-barriers theory* states that society follows formal or informal policies that cause poverty and make it difficult for the poor to escape from poverty. In other words, certain institutions or practices existing in the United States tend to perpetuate poverty. For example, racial discrimination is a social barrier that helps to explain poverty among certain minority groups. Discrimination in housing, artificial employment barriers by craft labor unions, preem-

[7]U.S. Department of Commerce, Bureau of the Census, "Characteristics of the Low-Income Population, 1972," *Current Population Reports,* P-60, No. 91 (Washington, D.C.: U.S. Government Printing Office, 1973), p. 5.

[8]Robert J. Lampman, *Ends and Means of Reducing Income Poverty* (Chicago: Markham Publishing Company, 1971), pp. 36-37.

ployment hiring tests, and the requirement of a high school diploma are other institutional practices that perpetuate poverty, especially for the hard-core unemployed. Finally, the alienation and social isolation of the poor from the rest of the community often result in a distinct culture of poverty among them.

The *personal-differences theory* states that people are poor because of personal characteristics that make them different from the majority—for instance, inadequate education and work skills, low productivity, poor motivation and work habits, mental or physical disabilities, lack of salable skills, alcoholism, or drug addiction.

Attacking Poverty

The major approaches and proposals for reducing poverty in the United States include expansionary monetary and fiscal policies to promote rapid economic growth and full employment; area and regional redevelopment; manpower development and training programs for the disadvantaged; war-on-poverty programs under the Economic Opportunity Act of 1964; improvements in social insurance and a system of family allowances; housing and rent subsidies for the poor; food stamps; school lunch programs and public health services for children; and public-assistance programs, as well as numerous others.

It is beyond the scope of this text to analyze each of these programs and approaches in detail.[9] Instead, we shall devote our attention to public-assistance programs and the role they play in reducing poverty. Public-assistance programs are major economic programs aimed directly at the poor. These programs have distinct characteristics and differ markedly from social insurance.

NATURE OF PUBLIC ASSISTANCE

Public-assistance programs are joint federal-state programs that provide income, medical care, and other services to poor individuals and families to help meet their basic living needs, when age, illness, disability, family breakup, or other factors beyond their personal control interfere with individual initiative in providing for necessities.

Basic Characteristics

Public-assistance programs have several characteristics that distinguish them from social insurance.[10] First, various benefits are provided to poor individuals and families whose income, assets, and available sources of support fall

[9]For a discussion of the various public income-maintenance programs and other approaches for attacking poverty, see John G. Turnbull, C. Arthur Williams, Jr., and Earl F. Cheit, *Economic and Social Security*, 4th ed. (New York: Ronald Press, 1973), Chap. 16; Sar A. Levitan, *Programs in Aid of the Poor for the 1970's*, rev. ed. (Baltimore: The Johns Hopkins Press, 1973); and George F. Rohrlich, ed., *Social Economics for the 1970's* (New York: Dunellen, 1970).

[10]Turnbull et al., *Economic and Social Security*, pp. 10-11.

below some officially determined standard of need. The benefits consist of (1) cash payments, (2) medical-care vendor payments, and (3) social services, such as counseling on family problems, assistance in locating better housing, referral to community resources, and homemaker services.

Second, welfare applicants must demonstrate a need or meet the requirements of a means test. The benefits are never automatically paid on the basis of an earned right, and they are adjusted to the individual's or family's financial resources and needs.

Third, the benefits are generally financed out of the general revenues of government rather than from specific earmarked taxes. Federal grants-in-aid are available to the states to help finance the costs of the joint programs.

Fourth, with the exception of Supplemental Security Income, public-assistance programs at the operational level are generally administered by the states or local communities, or both. Determination of need, cost-of-living differences, and benefit amounts differ widely from state to state. Consequently, administration at the state or local level is necessary because public officials and welfare agencies must use discretion and judgment in determining benefit amounts and need.

Finally, because of the discretionary needs test and stringent eligibility requirements, public-assistance benefits are difficult to predict in advance. For these reasons and because of the stigma of charity attached to the receipt of benefits, most people do not consider the availability of public-assistance benefits in their economic-security plans.

Reasons for Public Assistance

Public-assistance programs are necessary for several reasons. First, they provide cash payments, medical care, and social services to poor persons and families who are not covered under social insurance or other public income-maintenance programs.

Second, public assistance is used to provide supplemental income to people whose benefits from social insurance or other public programs are inadequate, to those with small or nonexistent financial resources, and to those whose special needs require income supplements or services.

Third, some individuals and families are unable to attain a minimum standard of living because of physical, psychological, or emotional problems. In these cases, public-assistance benefits help compensate for these and other adverse economic forces that are beyond their control or understanding.

Fourth, public assistance is used because of society's philosophy toward the poor. Owing to personal factors and character defects, some people are unable or unwilling to work and contribute to society. Although they are unproductive, society does not necessarily cast these people aside as worthless. Society must always assist its less able members to become productive if possible, but the dignity and true worth of a human being are seldom measured only in monetary and economic terms. For this reason, society is unwilling to permit the poor to starve, and public assistance is used to provide a subsistence level of living to both the "deserving" and "undeserving" poor.

Finally, public assistance is designed to encourage some welfare recipients to become financially self-sufficient, through various social and rehabilitative services. The programs have safeguards so that dependence on welfare is neither encouraged nor prolonged.[11]

Eligibility Requirements

To collect public-assistance benefits, a person must fulfill certain eligibility requirements, involving (1) demonstration of need, (2) property limits, (3) relatives' responsibilities, and (4) age restrictions.

Demonstration of Need. Federal law requires public-assistance applicants to demonstrate need, but the standards used by the individual states to determine need vary greatly. Under the joint federal-state programs, each state determines its own standard, against which the individual's or family's resources are then measured. Various budgets for different classifications of poor individuals and families are established, which include allowances for food, clothing, shelter, utilities, and other necessities of life. Theoretically, the cash public-assistance benefit is the difference between the cost of total living requirements under the standard of need established by the state and the amount of the welfare applicant's income and other financial resources. From a practical viewpoint, however, the actual benefit paid is often below the state's standard of need, because of statutory and administrative maximum limits on payments, stringent eligibility requirements, and failure of many states to set their standards of need according to current costs. Finally, under the federal Supplemental Security Income program for the aged, blind, and disabled, the applicant's earned and unearned income and other financial resources must be within certain prescribed limits for him to be eligible for benefits.

To encourage welfare recipients to work, a certain amount of earned and unearned income can be disregarded in determining eligibility for public-assistance benefits. For example, on a quarterly basis, under the federal Supplemental Security Income program, the first $60 of earned or unearned income can be disregarded. The first $195 of earned income plus half the remainder can also be disregarded.

Under the Aid to Families with Dependent Children (AFDC) program, the state must disregard the earnings of students, and may also disregard, within certain prescribed limits, income set aside for the children's future needs. Also, the first $5 of monthly income from any source may be disregarded. Finally, in determining AFDC benefits, the state must disregard the first $30 of earned income, plus one-third of the remainder.

Property Limits. All states limit the ownership of real and personal property, but the limits vary widely among the states. Welfare recipients can own their own homes, but about one-third of the states disqualify an applicant if the value of the home exceeds a specified amount. In regard to personal property, single persons can have accumulated savings of $300 to $500, and in some states, $2,000, if this amount includes the cash value of private life

[11]Harry L. Lurie, ed., *Encyclopedia of Social Work,* 15th issue (New York: National Association of Social Workers, 1965), p. 596.

insurance. Most states permit the ownership of an automobile for employment purposes or because of other special circumstances or conditions.

Responsibility of Relatives.   In determining eligibility, many states also consider whether the poor person has close relatives who can help support him. Some states take active steps to secure this support.

The major purpose of requiring close relatives to contribute to the support of the poor is to reduce public-assistance costs and hold down taxes. However, several disadvantages result from this approach.[12]   First, the relatives themselves (such as adult children) may be poor and unable to contribute. Second, some needy people may refuse to apply for public assistance because they do not wish to burden their children or other close relatives. Third, requiring close relatives to support the needy may cause strained family relationships and invoke resentment toward the poor. Fourth, there is a changing social attitude toward the economic responsibility of relatives of the needy person. Aged parents or other relatives may become poor because of social or economic factors over which the children have little or no control; and it is argued that society rather than the children should support these people. Finally, it is often difficult and expensive for the states to enforce the requirement that fathers assume primary responsibility for the support of their families.

Age Restrictions.   Many public-assistance programs have age restrictions. Under the Supplemental Security Income program, the needy aged must be at least 65. Under Aid to Families with Dependent Children, most states require at least one child to be under age 21. The federal government participates in the payments made by the states to poor families until the youngest child is 18, or 21 if he is in school.

TYPES OF PUBLIC ASSISTANCE PROGRAMS

There are four major public-assistance programs in the United States: (1) Supplemental Security Income for the aged, blind, and disabled, (2) Aid to Families with Dependent Children, (3) Medicaid, and (4) General Assistance.[13]

Supplemental Security Income for the Aged, Blind, and Disabled

The 1972 amendments to the Social Security Act established a new Sup-

[12]Eveline M. Burns, "The Future Course of Public Welfare," in *Position Papers and Major Related Data for the Governor's Conference Commemorating the 100th Anniversary of the New York State Board of Social Welfare To Help Plan New Approaches to Public Welfare in the United States* (New York: The Governor's Conference on Public Welfare, 1967), p. 17-18.

[13]A description of the major characteristics of these programs can be found in U.S. Congress, Subcommittee on Fiscal Policy of the Joint Economic Committee, *Studies in Public Welfare, Paper No. 2, Handbook of Public Income Maintenance Programs,* 92d Cong., 2d sess., 1972 (Washington, D.C.: U.S. Government Printing Office, 1972); and U.S. Department of Health, Education and Welfare, Social Security Administration, *Social Security Programs in the United States* (Washington, D.C.: U.S. Government Printing Office, 1973). A current description of the Supplemental Security Income program can be found in James C. Callison, "Early Experience under the SSI Program," *Social Security Bulletin,* Vol. 37, No. 6 (June 1974), 3-11 and 30.

plemental Security Income (SSI) program for the aged, blind, and disabled, replacing the older, state-administered programs of Old-Age Assistance (OAA), Aid to the Blind (AB), and Aid to the Permanently and Totally Disabled (APTD). The new program became effective January 1, 1974. However, the joint federal-state program of Aid to Families with Dependent Children (AFDC) will still be continued.

Federal Minimum-Income Guarantee. Under the SSI program, all the poor aged, blind, and disabled are guaranteed a monthly income of at least $146 for an individual or $219 for a couple. As we have seen, on a quarterly basis, the law provides that the first $60 of earned or unearned income can be disregarded, so those who receive at least $20 of monthly income from the OASDHI program or from other sources (that are not need-related) are assured a total monthly income of at least $166 for an individual or $239 for a couple.

In addition, on a quarterly basis, the first $195 of earned income, plus half the remainder, can also be disregarded. The purpose of disregarding a certain amount of earned income is to encourage the aged, blind, and disabled to work, giving them a higher monthly income in addition to the SSI payments.

National Eligibility Standards. National uniform eligibility standards are established for the SSI program. An aged, blind, or disabled person is eligible for SSI payments if his financial resources are less than 1,500, or $2,250 for a couple. In determining the amount of resources, the value of a home, household goods, automobile, personal effects, and property needed for self-support can be excluded if their value is reasonable. Life insurance policies can also be excluded if the face amount of all policies totals less than $1,500; if it exceeds that amount, the cash surrender value must be counted as a resource. However, current welfare recipients who are covered under state programs with higher resource limits will still retain their eligibility.

In addition to the resource limitation, an aged person must be age 65 or over, and a blind or disabled person must fulfill the definition of blindness or disability. Formerly, each state prescribed its own definitions of blindness and disability to determine eligibility for benefits under the AB and APTD programs. But in the SSI program, the definition of disability employed in the OASDHI program is used, and blindness is defined as a central visual acuity of 20/200 or less in the better eye with the use of correcting lenses. Tunnel vision is also covered as a sight limitation. Also, a disabled drug addict or alcoholic is ineligible for benefits unless he is undergoing appropriate medical treatment. In such a case, the payments made on his behalf are paid only to protective third parties.

State Supplementation. Prior to the enactment of the SSI program, several states paid the aged, blind, and disabled public-assistance benefits that exceeded the federal minimum guarantee. Under SSI, these states must supplement the benefits for those beneficiaries who otherwise would have been adversely affected by the transition to the new program. For other beneficiaries, state supplementation is optional.

Whether the supplementation is mandatory or optional, the states can either administer the supplementary program themselves or arrange to have the benefits paid by the Social Security Administration. In the latter case, the administrative expenses are paid by the federal government, but the costs of the supplemental benefits are paid by the states.

Financing.   The federal SSI cash payments are financed entirely by the federal government out of its general revenues. In addition, the states can continue to provide to the aged, blind, and disabled the social services that were formerly provided under the OAA, AB, and APTD programs. In such cases, the federal government will pay 75 percent of the cost of the services (90 percent for family planning), subject to the overall limitations established by the State and Local Fiscal Assistance Act.

The federal government does not participate directly in the financing of state supplemental benefits. A "hold harmless" clause, however, is included in the new law, whereby the federal government assumes all of the state's cost of supplemental payments that exceeds its calendar-year 1972 share of the costs of assistance provided to the aged, blind, and disabled.

Administration.   The SSI program is administered by the federal government. The Social Security Administration is responsible for the determination of eligibility and benefit amounts, and the payment of the monthly SSI checks. And, as stated earlier, if the state desires, the Social Security Administration will also administer the supplemental-payments program and will assume all administrative costs.

Evaluation.   The new SSI program is a great improvement over previous public-assistance programs. At least five major advantages will result from it: First, a national minimum income of at least $146 monthly for an individual, or $219 for a couple, is now guaranteed to the aged, blind, and disabled.

Second, the new SSI program eliminates many undesirable welfare practices that existed under the OAA, AB, and APTD programs. Many poor older people refused to apply for OAA benefits because of lien laws whereby the state could sell their homes after their death, or because of relative-responsibility laws whereby their sons and daughters would be subject to an income test. Under the SSI program, lien laws and relative-responsibility laws are not used. Also, the stigma of charity is now reduced, since the Social Security Administration, rather than some state or local welfare agency, will administer the cash-payment portion of the program.

Third, national uniform eligibility standards will be applied in every state, overcoming the earlier defect of widely varying standards of need, income limitations, property limits, blindness and disability definitions, and other eligibility requirements.

Fourth, the separation of social services, which will continue to be provided by state welfare agencies, from the payment of cash benefits is highly desirable. The SSI recipient will receive a monthly check from the Social Security Administration and is not required to accept social welfare services as a condition of eligibility.

Finally, the new SSI program will provide needed financial relief to the financially burdened states, since the federal government pays the entire costs of monthly cash payments.

On the negative side, however, the new SSI program represents at best a piecemeal approach to meaningful welfare reform. Proposals for such reform will be analyzed in greater detail in Chapter 18.

Aid to Families with Dependent Children

One of the most controversial public-assistance programs is Aid to Families with Dependent Children (AFDC). The original Social Security Act of 1935 provided federal grants to the states to help poor children whose need was based on the death or incapacity of a parent, or on a parent's continued absence from the home. AFDC programs now provide benefits to poor children and one or two adults caring for the children because of the death of a parent, mental or physical incapacity of a parent, unemployment of the father, or continued absence of a parent from the home.

General Requirements. The states establish eligibility requirements for AFDC benefits within the framework of federal law. First, the child must be poor and living with a close relative; one exception is that payments may be made on behalf of a child living in an approved foster home if the child was eligible for or was receiving benefits prior to placement in the home. Second, the states may impose maximum age requirements. Most AFDC programs require the child to be under age 18; the 1965 amendments allow the states to continue payments until age 21 if the child is regularly attending school.

Work-Incentive Program. To restore as many AFDC families as possible to employment and financial independence, the 1967 amendments established a work-incentive program (WIN) for AFDC recipients. All recipients *must register* for work and training unless they are exempt from registration. The welfare agency administering the program must refer appropriate AFDC recipients to work and training programs administered by the U.S. Department of Labor. Prior to the 1971 amendments, such registration was optional, but it is now mandatory except for the following excluded groups: (1) children under 16 or full-time students enrolled in school or training programs, (2) ill or aged persons, (3) AFDC recipients who are living beyond reasonable commuting distance from a work project, (4) people who must care for ill or incapacitated members of the household, (5) mothers of children under age 6, and (6) the mother or other female caretaker of a child if the father or another adult male relative is in the home and has registered. The welfare agency must provide supportive social services, financial aid, medical assistance, and the necessary child-care facilities for all AFDC recipients who are referred to work and training programs. Those who refuse to accept work or training will lose their benefits.

The AFDC program contains three major incentives designed to encourage recipients to work, and to expand employment opportunities by the states and employers.[14] First, a certain amount of earned income of AFDC recipients—the first $30 of monthly earnings plus one-third of the remainder, and a limited amount for work-related expenses—can be disregarded in determining the amount of cash assistance.

Second, tax credits are available to employers who agree to hire WIN participants. The tax credit is equal to 20 percent of the wages paid to the participant in the first year of training. The workers must be retained in unsubsidized jobs for at least twelve months following the twelve months for which the tax

[14]U.S. Department of Labor, *Manpower Report of the President* (Washington, D.C.: U.S. Government Printing Office, 1973), pp. 37-38.

credit is claimed. The employer's annual tax credit is limited to a maximum of $25,000 plus half his remaining tax liability. The costs incurred by employers in training WIN employees on the job are also paid under the program.

Third, the states are encouraged to provide the necessary WIN social services, since the federal government now pays 90 percent of the costs of these services. In the past, the federal government paid only 80 percent of the cost of manpower activities and 75 percent for child care and supportive services. Thus, increased federal funding should encourage greater state activity in the placement of WIN enrollees.

Finally, a negative incentive is also used. The 1971 amendments provide for a reduction or termination of federal funds if the state welfare agency does not provide the necessary social services to at least 15 percent of all mandatory AFDC registrants.

AFDC-UF. The AFDC program also extends coverage, at the state's option, to children who are poor because of unemployment of the father (AFDC-UF). In addition to the needs test, the father must meet three additional tests to make his family eligible for AFDC-UF benefits: He must have a work history that demonstrates a recent and substantial attachment to the labor force; he must not be currently working more than 100 hours per month; and he must not be eligible to receive unemployment-insurance benefits concurrently. If these tests are fulfilled, the family is eligible to receive AFDC benefits. The AFDC-UF program is now a permanent part of the AFDC program; however, it is optional with the states, and only 25 jurisdictions have enacted AFDC-UF programs.

Financing. The AFDC program is financed jointly by the federal government and the states. Federal grants-in-aid are available to the states if they meet certain federal requirements, as follows: (1) The applicant must demonstrate need; (2) the state must consider the applicant's available income and resources in determining the amount of assistance; (3) the program must operate on a statewide basis; (4) the state must participate in the costs of the program; (5) the state must provide the federal government with a plan for administering the program; (6) a single state agency must administer the program; (7) an opportunity for a fair hearing must be provided to any person whose application for assistance is denied; and (8) the plan must not include any residence requirement barring a citizen of the United States otherwise eligible for aid. Within these limitations, however, the states have considerable latitude and freedom in determining the organization and administration of their programs, the eligibility requirements, and the amount of AFDC payments.

Formulas are used to determine the federal government's share of the costs of the AFDC program. The formulas are designed to provide a relatively higher federal matching of funds to the states with more limited financial resources. Sliding scales in the formulas provide for a variable matching of funds depending on the state's per capita income. The federal government pays five-sixths of the first $18 of average monthly payment, plus 50 to 65 percent of the next $14 (depending on the state's annual per capita income), with a monthly-average maximum of $32 per recipient.

The federal government and states each pay 50 percent of most administrative expenses and costs of services, but the federal government pays 90 percent of the cost of social services provided to WIN enrollees.

Other Provisions. Emergency assistance can be provided in crisis situations to poor families with children. The states can give up to 30 days of emergency assistance during a twelve-month period to families with children under age 21. The aid may be money payments, payments in kind, or vendor payments for a wide variety of needs, including food, rent, utilities, and other necessities.

The law also provides for the location of absent parents. If welfare agencies cannot locate an absent parent of AFDC children through all available sources, the Internal Revenue Service will make available any information it has concerning his or her whereabouts.

The AFDC programs are a storm center of controversy and have been under heavy attack. Their serious defects and numerous disincentives have led to proposals for bold and sweeping welfare reforms. These defects and reform proposals will be analyzed in Chapter 18.

Medicaid

The 1965 amendments to the Social Security Act created a new Medical Assistance program—commonly called Title XIX, or Medicaid—to cover the medical expenses of the poor. Medicaid is a joint federal-state program that provides medical assistance to poor families with dependent children, the aged, the blind, the permanently and totally disabled, and other poor groups. Medicaid has been changed several times since its inception in 1965, with the most recent changes occurring in 1972.[15]

Eligible Groups. Only certain groups are eligible for Medicaid benefits. First, the states *must* provide medical assistance to the *categorically needy.* These include the following groups: (1) recipients of categorical money payments who were formerly covered under the OAA, AB, and APTD programs, and those receiving money payments under the AFDC program; (2) persons who would be eligible for money payments except for an eligibility condition or requirement that is prohibited by Title XIX of the act, such as a lien imposed on the property of an individual prior to his death; and (3) children under age 21 who would otherwise be eligible for AFDC benefits except for an age or school-attendance requirement.

If a state wishes, it *may* include as "categorically needy" those persons who are receiving benefits under the Supplemental Security Income (SSI) program. Although a state is generally not *required* to include those who newly became eligible for SSI benefits when the program went into effect in January, 1974, or in months thereafter, it *must* cover as a categorically needy person any needy aged, blind, or disabled adult if it would have been required to furnish such assistance under its Medicaid plan that was in effect on January 1, 1972.

Second, the states have the *option* of extending Medicaid coverage to

---

[15]For an excellent discussion of the various state Medicaid plans, see Commerce Clearing House, *1974 Social Security and Medicare Explained—Including Medicaid* (Chicago: Commerce Clearing House, 1974), Chap. 7.

certain other categorically needy groups: (1) persons in a medical facility who are not receiving financial assistance but would be eligible if they left the facility; (2) persons eligible for, but not receiving, assistance under the categorical programs; (3) an essential spouse—that is, one essential to the well-being of a recipient; (4) children under age 21 in foster homes or institutions for whom public agencies are assuming financial responsibility; and (5) all financially eligible individuals under age 21.

Third, the states also have the *option* of extending coverage to the *medically needy.* The medically needy are people who meet the eligibility requirements of the categorically needy, except that their income and resources, although insufficient to pay their medical bills, exceed the levels for eligibility for financial assistance. If a state elects to cover the medically needy under its Medicaid program, all those in similar circumstances among the aged, the blind, the disabled, and families with dependent children must also be included if they meet the eligibility requirements.

Finally, in determining eligibility for Medicaid benefits, the states cannot impose an age requirement exceeding 65 years, a durational residence requirement excluding any person residing in the state, or a citizenship requirement excluding any U.S. citizen.

Income Limits. The income limits for the categorically needy are the same as those established by the state for the receipt of cash benefits under the category of assistance to which the applicant is characteristically related. However, for the medically needy, federal financial participation in the Medicaid program is not available for any member of the family with annual countable income that exceeds 133⅓ percent of the highest amount that would ordinarily be paid by the state under its AFDC program to a family of the same size without any income or resources. For a single individual, annual countable income cannot exceed 133⅓ percent of the highest amount that would ordinarily be paid to an AFDC family of two persons. Thus, a flexible income test is used that takes medical expenses into consideration, but does not impose rigid income standards that arbitrarily deny help to people with large medical bills.

In addition, Medicaid limits the financial responsibility of relatives for medical-care costs. The only responsibility of relatives is that one spouse can be made financially responsible for the other spouse, and parents can be held responsible for the medical costs of children under age 21 (or over 21 if blind or disabled). Thus, the states cannot require the children to pay the medical expenses of their parents aged 65 or over.

Finally, the Medicaid programs cannot impose any property liens, and the states are not allowed to recover the amounts paid for medical costs. One exception is that the state can recover the cost of benefits from the estate of a person who was 65 or older when he received such assistance, but only after the death of his surviving spouse, and only if there are no dependent disabled children or any surviving children under age 21.

Basic Services. The Medicaid program must provide the following basic services to the categorically needy:

1. Inpatient hospital services
2. Outpatient hospital services
3. Other X-ray and laboratory services
4. Skilled nursing-home services for people aged 21 or over
5. Physician services
6. Home health services for any eligible person entitled to skilled nursing-home services
7. Early and periodic screening and treatment of mental and physical defects for eligible children under age 21.

The states also have the option of providing other medical services, including private-duty nursing, clinic services, dental services, physical therapy, prescribed drugs, dentures, prosthetic devices, eyeglasses, intermediate-care-facility services, and others. And if the state elects to cover the medically needy under its Medicaid plan, either the basic services listed above or seven of the first 14 listed services must be provided under the plan. If skilled nursing-facility services or inpatient hospital care are included in the seven basic services, then the services of physicians must also be provided when the person is hospitalized or is in a skilled nursing facility.

The 1972 amendments resulted in several important changes with respect to the scope of Medicaid services. First, to control the rapid increase in Medicaid costs and provide some financial relief to the states with a financial crisis, Congress repealed the earlier provision that required the states to broaden the scope of their Medicaid services and cover all those unable to pay (such as the medically needy) by July 1, 1977. In addition, the maintenance-of-effort requirement, which prevented a state from reducing its aggregate Medicaid expenditures from one year to the next, was repealed. The states are now permitted to cut back Medicaid and are not required to move toward comprehensive programs.

Second, to improve the health of poor children, the Medicaid program must also provide early screening, diagnosis, and treatment services for children under age 21. If the state fails to provide these services, it will be penalized by a 1 percent reduction in AFDC matching funds from the federal government. All AFDC families must be informed of the child health-screening services, and corrective services must actually be provided. Finally, the Medicaid program must also provide family-planning services to eligible people desiring them.

Cost Sharing. In order to control Medicaid costs, recipients may be required to share in the costs. Prior to the 1972 amendments, deductibles and other cost-sharing provisions could be imposed on the medically needy, but not on the categorically needy. However, as a result of the 1972 amendments, only the basic Medicaid services are exempt from deductibles and cost sharing by categorically needy recipients. Cost-sharing provisions are permitted for the optional medical services, although they must be nominal in amount.

The medically needy, on the other hand, must share in the cost of Medicaid services. They must pay a monthly premium, which varies according to size of income. In addition, the states have the option of requiring the medically needy to pay a deductible, cost-sharing, or similar charge for the Medicaid benefits. These charges must also be nominal.

Financing. Medicaid plans are financed jointly by the federal government and the states. Various formulas are applied to determine the federal share of the total costs of vendor payments, services, training, and administration. A federal medical-assistance percentage, ranging from 50 to 83 percent, depending on the state's annual per capita income, is used to determine the federal share of payments to the suppliers of medical care. The federal government will not share in the expenditures for medically needy families whose income is more than 133⅓ percent of the income limit used in the state's AFDC program. However, different percentages are applied to administrative costs, training of staff personnel, and other services. The federal government will pay 100 percent of the cost of inspecting a skilled nursing facility or intermediate-care facility, 90 percent of administrative costs for family-planning services, 90 percent of the development and installation costs of mechanized claims-processing and information-retrieval systems, and 75 percent of the administrative costs of operating the systems.

General Assistance

General Assistance (GA) is a residual welfare program provided by states and local communities to poor persons and families who are ineligible for help under federally aided public-assistance programs. In a few states, GA is also used to help people who receive inadequate benefits from federally aided programs to meet their basic needs. GA is often the only welfare program available to temporarily or permanently unemployed people who are ineligible for unemployment-insurance benefits or whose benefits are inadequate or exhausted. About one-third of the states, however, refuse to help a family with an employable person in the household except in defined emergency situations.

The state and local GA programs are generally more limited in the amount and duration of assistance than are the federally aided assistance programs. In some states, GA programs provide only emergency or short-term aid; in others, assistance is limited to specific situations; a few states limit the length of time that the poor can receive help; and in many states, limitations on GA benefits and services are established from time to time because of insufficient funds.

General Assistance programs are financed either from state and local funds or from local funds alone. They are especially sensitive to the business cycle; the number of recipients aided tends to increase during recessions.

SUGGESTIONS FOR ADDITIONAL READING

Callison, James C., "Early Experience under the SSI Program," *Social Security Bulletin,* Vol. 37, No. 6 (June 1974), 3-11 and 30.

Council of Economic Advisers, "Chapter 5, Distribution of Income,"

Economic Report of the President. Washington, D.C.: U.S. Government Printing Office, 1974.

Harrington, Michael, *The Other America.* Baltimore: Penguin, 1962.

Marmor, Theodore, ed., *Poverty Policy.* Chicago: Aldine-Atherton, 1971.

The President's Commission on Income Maintenance Programs, *Poverty amid Plenty: The American Paradox,* Report of the President's Commission on Income Maintenance Programs. Washington, D.C.: U.S. Government Printing Office, 1969.

Rejda, George E., *Public Assistance and Other Income Maintenance Programs.* Bryn Mawr, Pa.: The American College of Life Underwriters, 1970.

Schiller, Bradley R., *The Economics of Poverty and Discrimination.* Englewood Cliffs, N.J.: Prentice-Hall, 1972.

Steiner, Gilbert Y., *The State of Welfare.* Washington, D.C.: The Brookings Institution, 1971.

Thurow, Lester C., and Robert E. B. Lucas, *The American Distribution of Income: A Structural Problem,* Joint Economic Committee Print. Washington, D.C.: U.S. Government Printing Office, 1972.

Turnbull, John G., C. Arthur Williams, Jr., and Earl F. Cheit, *Economic and Social Security,* 4th ed., Chaps. 15 and 16. New York: Ronald Press, 1973.

Wilcox, Clair, *Toward Social Welfare,* Chaps. 2 and 16. Homewood, Ill.: Richard D. Irwin, 1969.

chapter 18

Public Assistance:
Problems and Issues

Economists, legislators, and the tax-paying public are becoming increasingly concerned about the goals and effectiveness of public-assistance programs, and hostility and resentment toward the programs are growing. Economists criticize the programs for failure to meet the income needs of the poor, exclusion of large numbers of the poor, and numerous disincentive effects. Legislators are concerned because of the growing fiscal crisis in the states and the increasingly heavy financial burden from public-assistance programs. Public assistance itself is widely misunderstood and criticized by those taxpayers who believe that people should not receive income without working. The programs are also unpopular with many public-welfare officials and social workers who administer them. And the welfare recipients often accept the benefits with distaste and acute awareness of the stigma of charity attached to them. It is difficult to find another public income-maintenance program that rivals public assistance in its unpopularity, in its repugnance, and in its general unacceptance by many segments of the American public.

In this chapter, we shall analyze critically the problems and issues associated with present public-assistance programs, and some of the changes that have been suggested. Most of the criticisms center around the controversial Aid to Families with Dependent Children (AFDC) and Medicaid programs. In particular, we shall consider the following areas: (1) defects of public-assistance programs, (2) the growing AFDC welfare crisis, (3) Medicaid problems and issues, and (4) welfare reform proposals.

DEFECTS OF PUBLIC ASSISTANCE

Public-assistance programs have numerous defects that severely limit their effectiveness in meeting the poverty problem. Analysis of these defects clearly indicates that monumental and sweeping welfare reforms are necessary.

Exclusion of Large Numbers of the Poor

Public-assistance programs in the United States aim directly at the poor, yet millions of poor people are ineligible for benefits. Only about 38 percent of the poor families received income from public assistance in 1973.[1]

Several factors help explain the exclusion of large numbers of the poor from welfare benefits. First, public assistance is *categorical* in nature. The programs are generally confined to the aged, blind, permanently and totally disabled, and families with dependent children. Many poor people who might be able to become more productive and self-sufficient if given aid are in none of these categories. Some of the groups who are not helped significantly by any federally aided public-assistance programs are the following: the working poor under age 65, where the family head works either full-time or part-time throughout the year; most poor children living with both parents or someone other than a close relative; children who are poor because of unemployment of a parent; needy disabled people who are not both permanently and totally disabled; poor mothers who are employable but for whom no jobs are available; most of the poor under age 65 who are either unemployed or underemployed; and people who are losing their vision but are not sufficiently blind to qualify for benefits.[2]

Second, because of a serious financial crisis and erosion of the tax base on which to raise additional public revenues, many states are hard pressed to fund existing public-assistance programs and consequently do not participate in all programs provided under federal law. For example, not all states participate in the AFDC-UF program, which provides benefits to needy children because of unemployment of the father. Also, because of financial difficulties in raising revenues, many states impose limitations in their public-assistance programs that result in narrower provisions than those found in the federal law; or, to reduce public-assistance costs, they add restrictive provisions that are not expressly prohibited by federal law. The result is that public-assistance programs often exclude large numbers of individuals and families in great need.

Third, the standard of need used in many states is often extremely low, so that many truly needy people do not receive public-assistance benefits because their incomes are slightly above the state standard.

Finally, many poor individuals and families are effectively excluded from public-assistance benefits because of eligibility requirements unrelated to need. It is possible to be poor and yet be denied aid because of stringent requirements that have little relationship to one's poverty.

---

[1]U.S. Bureau of the Census, *Current Population Reports,* Series P-60, No. 98, "Characteristics of the Low-Income Population, 1973," (Washington, D.C.: U.S. Government Printing Office, 1975), p. 129, Table 42. See also Committee for Economic Development, *Improving the Public Welfare System* (New York: Committee for Economic Development, 1970), p. 10.

[2]The Advisory Council on Public Welfare, *Having the Power, We Have the Duty; Report of the Advisory Council on Public Welfare* (Washington, D.C.: U.S. Government Printing Office, 1966), p. 24.

Inadequate Benefits

Another serious limitation of public-assistance programs is that the benefits in most states provide an income below the poverty line. In September 1974, AFDC families received an average monthly payment of about $210; the amounts ranged from about $50 in Mississippi to about $310 in New York.[3]

Many states do not meet the standards of need that they themselves define. Because of the critical problem of insufficient funds, many states have statutory limits on the maximum benefits that can be paid, so welfare recipients are often paid benefits that are less than their full need. For example, in 1971, 46 percent of the AFDC families had some unmet need, with an average monthly amount of unmet need about $65.[4]

There is also wide variation among the states with respect to the benefits paid and the percentage of the state's population on welfare. In March, 1971, the maximum monthly benefit that could be paid to a four-member AFDC family ranged from a low of $60 in Mississippi to a high of $375 in Alaska; about 83 per 1,000 civilian population in California were receiving AFDC payments, and 70 per 1,000 in New York, but in New Hampshire, the rate was only 20 per 1,000.[5]

Receipt of Multiple Benefits

Although the monthly cash benefits are generally inadequate when considered alone, most welfare recipients are eligible for benefits from more than one program. The result is that some welfare recipients are better off financially than many families who work full-time and are not on welfare. Most public-assistance recipients, in addition to having a certain amount of earned income disregarded in determining need, are eligible for Medicaid benefits, food stamps, public housing, reduced-price or free school lunches, health services, and other benefits. The receipt of multiple benefits often results in administrative problems, waste and duplication, and a possible dampening of work incentives.

A study by the Joint Economic Committee of 1,758 households in six low-income areas clearly reveals the problem of multiple benefits. The study showed that 60 percent of the households received benefits from one or more programs; 40 percent received benefits from two or more, and 11 percent from five or more programs.[6] Table 18-1 gives examples of households receiving substantial total

[3]*Social Security Bulletin,* Vol. 38. No. 3 (March 1975), p. 44, Table M-33.

[4]U.S. Department of Health, Education and Welfare, Social and Rehabilitation Service, National Center for Social Statistics, *Findings of the 1971 AFDC STUDY: Part II, Financial Circumstances: Highlights,* NCSS Report AFDC-2 (71) (Supplement) (January 12, 1972), p. 7.

[5]U.S. Department of Health, Education and Welfare, Social and Rehabilitation Service, National Center for Social Statistics, *AFDC: Selected Statistical Data on Families Aided and Program Operations,* NCSS Report H-4 (71) (Washington, D.C.: U.S. Government Printing Office, 1971), Item 30.

[6]U.S. Congress, Subcommittee on Fiscal Policy of the Joint Economic Committee, *Studies in Public Welfare; Additional Material for Paper No. 6: How Public Welfare Benefits Are Distributed in Low-Income Areas,* 93d Cong., 1st sess., 1973 (Washington, D.C.: U.S. Government Printing Office, 1973), p. 95.

TABLE 18-1 Examples of Households Receiving Large Numbers of Welfare Benefits

A. A couple in eastern city supporting a young child and the wife's teen-aged brother, with 6 benefits:

Program	Amount per Month
AFDC	$ 21
General assistance	83
Food stamps	34
Medicaid	123
Public housing	106
Neighborhood Youth Corps	18
Benefits, total	$ 385
Earnings	429
Total income	$ 814

B. 17-year-old mother of 2 children in South Atlantic City, with 9 benefits:

Program	Amount per Month
AFDC	$ 176
Welfare grant for special needs	50
Food stamps	20
Medicaid	33
Public health services	21
Public housing	56
Housing relocation grant	2
Concentrated employment (CEP)	6
Neighborhood Youth Corps	178
Benefits, total	$ 542
Earnings	56
Total income	$ 598

C. A 3-generation family of 5 in southern city, with 11 benefits:

Program	Amount per Month
AFDC	$ 79
Old-Age Assistance	91
Social Security (Old-age benefits)	77
Social Security (disability benefits)	131
Veterans' pension	221
Free school lunches	8
Medicare	8
Medicaid payment for medical service	14
Medicaid payment of Medicaid premium	6
Rent supplements	55
Neighborhood service center	1
Benefits, total	$ 691

D. A mother of 10 children in midwestern city, with 5 benefits:

Program	Amount per Month
AFDC	$ 616
Food stamps	110
Free school lunches	11
Public health services	3
OEO emergency health services	53
Benefits, total	$ 793

E. Elderly husband and wife in rural counties, with 6 benefits:

Program	Amount per Month
Old-Age Assistance	$ 85
Social Security	70
Surplus commodities	22
Medicare	372
Medicaid payment for medical services	5
Medicaid payment of Medicare premium	6
Benefits, total	$ 560

Source: U.S. Congress, Subcommittee on Fiscal Policy of the Joint Economic Committee, *Studies in Public Welfare: Additional Material for Paper No. 6: How Public Welfare Benefits Are Distributed in Low-Income Areas,* 93d Cong., 1st sess., 1973 (Washington, D.C.: U.S. Government Printing Office, 1973), p. 95.

benefits from multiple programs. In many cases, the value of the total benefit package exceeds the median wages paid in the community, and the welfare benefits are not taxed. The result is that some welfare recipients have little incentive to go off the welfare rolls.

The student is cautioned against misinterpretation of the preceding data. Many welfare recipients do not have access to all possible benefits and do not participate in all the programs even when they are available. For example, public-housing programs are not available in many communities, and only 68 percent of the AFDC families participate in the food-stamp and food-distribution programs.[7] Also, the data are not derived from a nationally drawn sample, and any inferences must be confined to only the six low-income areas. However, despite the data limitations, the receipt of multiple welfare benefits raises serious public policy questions concerning the overall adequacy of benefits, administrative efficiency, and possible work disincentives.

Stringent Elibility Requirements

Another welfare defect is the imposition of eligibility requirements that are harsh and often unrelated to need, to hold down welfare costs. Wide variation exists among the states not only in need standards, but in the amounts of property that can be held, coverage of unemployed fathers, age and school requirements for children, waiting periods following the absence of the father, and denial of assistance if the family includes an employable member. Because of factors having nothing to do with need, many poor people are denied benefits.

Needs-Test Defects

The needs test is wasteful, confusing, and time-consuming, and restricts social caseworkers in their counseling activities. The test is often administered in a demeaning and degrading manner, inflicting a loss of individual privacy and a violation of personal rights. These defects have been partly overcome by an HEW directive that directs the states to determine need by the declaration system rather than by detailed personal investigation.

Financing Problems

Many cities and states are suffering critical financial crises that severely restrict their ability to improve substantially their public-assistance programs. Demands for more liberalized programs are increasing, but the cities and states are hard pressed to meet them because of a static or declining tax base, insufficient sources from which new public revenues can be derived, and growing demands for other public services, such as improved schools, highway construction, sanitation facilities, public-housing programs, and the elimination of

---

[7]U.S. Congress, Subcommittee on Fiscal Policy of the Joint Economic Committee, *Studies in Public Welfare; Paper No. 1, Public Income Transfer Programs: The Incidence of Multiple Benefits and the Issues Raised by Their Receipt,* 92d Cong., 2d sess., 1972 (Washington, D.C.: U.S. Government Printing Office, 1972), p. 25.

water and air pollution. The public-assistance programs must compete for the limited funds available for the many critical social and economic needs now prevailing.

The financial crisis in welfare is concentrated largely in the central cities, to which the poor and disadvantaged migrate in large numbers. New York, in particular, has been confronted with a "welfare boom" and a fiscal crisis in raising sufficient public revenues to meet higher public-assistance costs. The greatest financial burden falls on the states that provide relatively liberal welfare benefits—California, Illinois, New York, Pennsylvania, and New Jersey.

Administrative Defects

In a study of welfare administration, the Joint Economic Committee has concluded that public-assistance programs are "an administrative nightmare." [8] First, complicated eligibility and budget requirements are difficult to verify, evaluate, and determine in a routine and efficient fashion. Complex payment policies are confusing to both welfare recipients and social caseworkers; claimants often drop their applications for benefits out of sheer frustration, and busy caseworkers are buried in paperwork. Delays in the processing of applications are common.

Second, because of heavy case loads, complexities in the processing of applications, and excessive paperwork, caseworkers do not have adequate time to provide effective counseling services to the poor. Repeated changes in regulations continually force staff personnel to implement new policies. Litigation by welfare recipients and reorganization also disrupt normal routine functions. And because of heavy work loads, staff turnover is excessively high, resulting in inadequate training and supervision of new staff.

Finally, because the present system is understaffed, complex, and inconsistent, administrative errors in the payment of benefits occur often. A study by the Department of Health, Education and Welfare revealed that one out of every 20 welfare recipients was ineligible for benefits, and one in four was being paid either too little or too much. The researchers concluded that it was not that the welfare recipients were cheating the system, but rather that a chaotic administrative system was cheating the entire nation. [9]

Inadequate Social Services

Recent amendments have emphasized the rehabilitation of welfare recipients by providing them with more effective social services. But counseling and rehabilitative services for families, children, and the aged or disabled may still be quite inadequate. Recent studies concerning the efficiency of social ser-

[8]U.S. Congress, Subcommittee on Fiscal Policy of the Joint Economic Committee, *Studies in Public Welfare; Paper No. 5 (Part 1), Issues in Welfare Administration: Welfare—An Administrative Nightmare,* 92d Cong., 2d sess., 1972 (Washington, D.C.: U.S. Government Printing Office, 1972), pp. 1-2.

[9]Statement of John Veneman, Under Secretary of the Department of Health, Education and Welfare, in *Ibid.,* pp. 2 and 35.

vices have indicated that, even when the services were provided by highly trained professionals serving small case loads, there has been no significant reduction in the welfare rolls.[10]

In addition, even when intensive counseling services are provided, the welfare group receiving the services is often no better off than are other groups who are not receiving services. For example, of two groups of delinquent high school girls, one group received intensive therapy, while the other received no services. There were no significant differences between the two groups with respect to continued delinquent behavior or recidivism rates.[11]

Social services are also criticized on other grounds. The services are loosely defined; they are offered without consideration of the competence of the staff; little systematic research is done on ideal staffing patterns; many services serve only a bureaucratic function; accountability concerning the effectiveness of the services is low; and limited client participation often results in a self-defeating, paternalistic pattern in the delivery of services.

AFDC WELFARE CRISIS

Most criticisms of welfare are directed at the AFDC program. Analysis of these defects clearly indicates that the present AFDC program must be abolished or sharply modified.

Expanding Welfare Rolls

The AFDC program has been growing at an alarming rate and is now reaching catastrophic proportions. In the last decade, AFDC case loads have more than doubled, and costs have more than tripled. The proportion of children in the United States who are receiving AFDC benefits has increased from 3 percent in the mid-fifties to 9 percent today. In September 1974 about 11 million people were receiving AFDC cash payments.[12]

In addition, the function of the program is shifting from aid to widows and orphans to support of families with absent fathers. In 1971, families with absent fathers accounted for about 76 percent of the total AFDC families.[13] The fathers were absent because of desertion, divorce, legal separation, separation

[10]U.S. Congress, Subcommittee on Fiscal Policy of the Joint Economic Committee, *Studies in Public Welfare; Paper No. 5 (Part 2), Issues in Welfare Administration: Intergovernmental Relationships,* 93d Cong., 1st sess., 1973 (Washington, D.C.: U.S. Government Printing Office, 1973), pp. 116-19.

[11]*Ibid.,* pp. 118-19.

[12]U.S. Congress, Senate, Committee on Finance, *Social Security Amendments of 1972,* Report of the Committee on Finance to accompany H.R.1, 92d Cong., 2d sess., 1972 (Washington, D.C.: U.S. Government Printing Office, 1972), p. 409; and *Social Security Bulletin,* March 1975, p. 44, Table M-33.

[13]U.S. Congress, Senate, Committee on Finance, *Social Security Amendments of 1971,* Hearings before the Committee on Finance on H.R.1, 92d Cong., 1st sess., 1971, p. 478; and U.S. Dept. of HEW, *Findings of the 1971 AFDC Study,* p. 6.

without court decree, imprisonment, or not being married to the mother Indeed, the heart of the AFDC welfare crisis is family breakup, which then requires financial support for the dependent children. Unless this problem is reduced in the future, the AFDC rolls will probably continue to expand. Between 1970 and 1971 alone, the number of poor families headed by women increased by 15 percent, while the number of families with both the father and the mother present declined in absolute numbers during the same period.[14] The increasing proportion of families headed by women is a reflection of the problem of family breakup, as well as of the unwillingness of many fathers to marry the mothers of illegitimate children.

The relatively rapid increase in the AFDC welfare rolls is due to several factors.[15] First, eligibility requirements have been broadened since 1961, enabling the states to extend coverage to families with unemployed fathers, to a second adult in the family, and to older children if attending school. Second, several Supreme Court decisions have struck down certain provisions that had tended to restrict coverage, such as a state residency requirement. Third, the states have liberalized their budget standards and standards of need, making more poor people eligible for assistance. Fourth, there has been an increase in the proportion of poor families applying for welfare, owing in part to the organizing efforts of welfare rights groups and the various poverty programs that have reduced the stigma of charity and encouraged greater numbers of the poor to apply for aid. And the proportion of families who are accepted for welfare has also risen—perhaps because of the more liberal interpretation of eligibility requirements by social caseworkers—as has the proportion of poor families headed by women, a factor we have already noted. Finally, increasing urbanization of the population and the great migration from rural to urban areas since World War II have brought to the cities greater numbers of poor people who must rely on cash income for their survival.

Work Disincentives

The present AFDC program has several provisions that discourage working. One is the "30 and ⅓" rule, by which the states must disregard the first $30 of monthly earnings, plus one-third of the remainder, in determining AFDC benefits. The result is that the AFDC recipient who works may have a higher total income than a full-time worker not on welfare. A working mother whose income is higher than the state's need standard is ineligible for welfare; but one whose earnings are less than the state standard can receive AFDC supplementation beyond that level because of application of the "30 and ⅓" rule, and this may bring her a total income (work earnings plus welfare payments) that is higher than that of the woman who has only her work earnings. A disincentive to work is thereby created, since a working woman not on welfare may reduce her hours of work to qualify for state supplementation.

[14]U.S. Congress, Senate, Committee on Finance *Social Security Amendments of 1972,* p. 409.

[15]The President's Commission on Income Maintenance Programs, *Poverty amid Plenty: The American Paradox,* Report of the President's Commission on Income Maintenance Programs (Washington, D.C.: U.S. Government Printing Office, 1969), pp. 121-22.

Then, once the person succeeds in obtaining AFDC benefits, the application of the "30 and ⅓" rule and the additional amounts that must be paid for other welfare benefits can also dampen work incentives. For monthly earnings over $30, the welfare recipient loses $2 of benefits for each $3 of earnings. This amounts to an unusually high marginal tax rate of 67 percent, and the rate can be even higher when multiple welfare benefits are considered—food stamps, Medicaid, public housing, reduced-price or free school lunches, and so on. The recipient of multiple benefits may actually be worse off financially by working, since the value of the total welfare package is reduced. In some cases, the benefits from certain programs may be completely lost. For example, AFDC cash benefits are reduced by working; higher amounts must be paid for food stamps; higher rent must be paid for public housing; higher prices must be paid for school lunches; and if countable money income is high enough, Medicaid benefits may be lost. The net gain from one extra dollar of work earnings may be so small as to discourage working. One study of low-income urban households receiving five or more welfare benefits indicated that the financial gain from working was relatively small or even negative. For 70 percent of the households, $1 of additional work earnings would net them no more than 33 cents and as little as zero (or even a negative amount); 18 percent would net 33 to 49 cents on their extra dollar of earnings; and only 5 percent would gain between 75 cents and $1.[16]

Finally, full-time male workers are excluded from AFDC benefits in most states. However, they may be better off financially by going on welfare than by working, especially if the job is in a relatively low-paying occupation. For example, some observers estimate that a male head of a four-member household who earns less than $1.85 per hour in Illinois, or less than $2.16 per hour in New York, would receive more money by going on welfare than by working.[17] Thus, strong discentives not to work are built into the present program.

Family Breakup

Exclusion of the working poor also tends to encourage family breakup. If a male full-time worker does not earn as much as his wife, he may desert to make his family eligible for welfare. In cases where the male fathers an illegitimate child, the mother may receive welfare benefits if the man is not in the home, so the couple may refuse to marry because only in that way can the children receive welfare payments.

AFDC-UF Defects

The unemployed-father portion of the AFDC program has numerous

[16]U.S. Congress, Subcommittee on Fiscal Policy of the Joint Economic Committee, *Studies in Public Welfare; Additional Material for Paper No. 6*, p. 108. See also U.S. Congress, Subcommittee on Fiscal Policy of the Joint Economic Committee, *Studies in Public Welfare; Paper No. 4, Income Transfer Programs: How They Tax the Poor*, 93d Cong., 2d sess., 1974 (Washington, D.C.: U.S. Government Printing Office, 1974).

[17]Statement of Elliott L. Richardson, in U.S. Congress, Senate, Committee on Finance, *Family Assistance Act of 1970*, Hearings before the Committee on Finance, 91st Cong., 2d sess., 1970, Part 2, pp. 408-9.

defects. The program is voluntary, and only 25 states currently provide assistance to unemployed needy fathers. The number of poor families in this category receiving help is small: Out of a total AFDC case load of about 3 million families, only about 136,000 received assistance in December, 1971.[18] The program may discourage working, since the state supplement may be lost if the part-time worker works more than 100 hours monthly. The fact that people collecting unemployment-insurance benefits are ineligible for AFDC-UF payments precludes the states' supplementing the unemployment benefits if they are relatively low. Finally, unemployed fathers must demonstrate a recent attachment to the work force, a requirement that denies aid to many poor families whose fathers experience long-term unemployment.

Work Incentive Program

The Work Incentive program (WIN) was enacted by Congress in 1967 to encourage welfare recipients to work. But many states have inadequate work training programs, and the number of welfare recipients who benefit is relatively low; of the 110,200 WIN terminations in fiscal 1972, only 30 percent had completed training and had obtained jobs.[19] Other problem areas include almost no on-the-job training for WIN enrollees, lack of adequate child-care facilities to allow mothers to work, lack of transportation to training and to jobs, lack of medical supportive services to correct physical defects, lack of referrals from welfare agencies in some states, lack of jobs for trainees in tightening labor markets, and inadequate administration.[20]

Finally, many welfare recipients are trained for doubtful jobs, which would probably bring them less income than they could get by remaining on welfare. The U.S. Department of Labor has said that at least two-thirds of the AFDC mothers and one-third of the AFDC-UF fathers in the mid-1960s could not have held jobs that would have supported their families at the income levels they could attain while on welfare.[21]

These defects, however, may be corrected by recent changes in the WIN program. Incentives for employers to hire WIN enrollees have been increased through the use of tax credits. The states are required to provide more adequate child-care and transportation services. And increased funds are now available for on-the-job training and subsidized public-employer jobs. These changes are expected to strengthen the program considerably.

AFDC Welfare Myths

Much of the American public is bewildered and misinformed regarding

[18]U.S. Congress, Subcommittee on Fiscal Policy of the Joint Economic Committee, *Studies in Public Welfare; Paper No. 2, Handbook of Public Income Transfer Programs,* 92d Cong., 2d sess., 1972 (Washington, D.C.: U.S. Government Printing Office, 1972), pp. 152-54, Tables 3 and 4.

[19]U.S. Department of Labor, *Manpower Report of the President* (Washington, D.C.: U.S. Government Printing Office, 1973), p. 55.

[20]*Ibid.,* p. 39.

[21]U.S. Department of Labor, Manpower Administration, *The Potential for Work among Welfare Parents,* Research Monograph No. 12 (Washington, D.C.: U.S. Government Printing Office, 1969), p. 5.

the behavior of welfare recipients and the nature of public-assistance programs. These are some of the persistent myths surrounding the AFDC program.[22]

1. *Welfare is a way of life.* One myth is that welfare families remain on welfare for their entire lifetime. However, there is considerable turnover of the welfare rolls. The average AFDC family is on the rolls for only 23 months. Only about 7 percent of the families are on welfare for more than ten years, and these long-term cases usually involve some form of disability.

2. *Welfare recipients are cheaters.* Studies indicate that deliberate fraud by welfare recipients is relatively low, occurring in less than 1 percent of the cases. In cases of either overpayment or underpayment, administrative errors or misinterpretation of the welfare regulations are generally responsible, rather than deliberate cheating by welfare recipients.

3. *Most welfare children are illegitimate.* The evidence indicates that about 68 percent of the children in welfare families are legitimate and born in wedlock. Although the proportion of illegitimate children on welfare has tended to increase, the majority of benefits are still paid on behalf of legitimate children.

4. *Welfare rolls are full of loafers.* Less than 1 percent of welfare recipients are able-bodied unemployed males. The welfare rolls generally consist of people who are unable to work. Children account for 56 percent of the welfare recipients, and the aged, blind, and disabled for 25 percent. The remainder are mothers, most of whom are prevented from working because of family responsibilities and inadequate day-care centers for their children, but 14 percent of whom do work, either full-time or part-time.

5. *Welfare mothers keep having children for higher benefits.* One insidious myth is that many welfare mothers deliberately bear additional children to get higher welfare benefits. However, the typical welfare family consists of a mother and three children, and since 1967, there has been a trend toward smaller welfare families. The majority of children are conceived or born before the family applies for welfare. Moreover, the typical payment for an additional child is only $35 monthly, which does not cover the extra cost involved in raising the child. Finally, many states have maximum limits on AFDC payments, and families at the maximum level do not receive higher amounts if additional children are born.

6. *Most welfare families are black.* Whites are the largest racial group and account for 49 percent of the welfare families. Blacks account for only 46 percent of the total, while the remaining 5 percent consists of Spanish-speaking Americans, Indians, orientals, and other minority groups.

7. *Welfare mothers squander the funds.* It is argued that, if welfare mothers receive additional funds for their children, they will squander the funds on alcohol, big cars, and luxuries. However, surveys show that most funds are spent for the family's welfare and are not squandered. The welfare mothers indicated that any extra funds would be used for more food and clothing, and improved housing.

MEDICAID PROBLEMS AND ISSUES

Numerous problems and issues are associated with the various state-federal Medicaid programs. Several of them are in deep financial trouble.

[22]See U.S. Department of Health, Education and Welfare, Social and Rehabilitation Service, *Welfare Myths vs. Facts* (Washington, D.C.: U.S. Government Printing Office, 1971).

Medicaid costs are soaring; taxpayers are protesting because of the higher taxes necessary to support these and other public programs; several states are confronted with serious fiscal crises and find it financially difficult to raise new public revenues; the poor continue to demand adequate medical care and improved Medicaid programs; Congress is deeply concerned about the costs, waste, inefficiencies, and administrative defects associated with Medicaid programs; and recent legislative changes have resulted in sharp cutbacks in the scope of Medicaid services, greater restrictions on eligibility, and numerous cost-control and cost-sharing provisions.

Because of the serious defects associated with the various Medicaid pro grams, Congress enacted many amendments to Title XIX of the Social Security Act in 1972 that will have a profound impact on future Medicaid costs, scope of services offered, eligibility, and program administration. The new Medicaid amendments deal with the following areas: (1) escalation in costs, (2) cutbacks in programs, (3) cost-sharing provisions imposed on the poor, and (4) restrictions on eligibility.

Sharp Escalation in Medicaid Costs

In recent years, Medicaid costs have risen nationally from about $2.5 billion in 1967 to about $9.7 billion in 1973, an increase of 288 percent.[23]

There are several reasons for this rapid increase. First, it reflects the larger number of people who are receiving benefits under the various categorical public-assistance programs—in particular, the number of AFDC recipients— since Medicaid programs must cover the categorically needy, whose number has grown substantially. The law, since amended, required the states to cover also the medically needy by July 1, 1977, and many states did so long before the deadline date, further expanding the Medicaid rolls.

The former law also required the states to broaden the scope of medical care and services offered under their Medicaid programs, and moved in the direction of liberalizing the eligibility requirements. All states were required to have comprehensive Medicaid programs by July 1, 1977, and forbidden to reduce their aggregate expenditures for their share of Medicaid costs from one year to the next. The combined effects of the movement toward comprehensive Medicaid programs, the maintenance of financial effort, and the liberalization of Medicaid eligibility requirements have led to substantial increase in Medicaid costs.

The adverse impact of price inflation in health care, of course, has also contributed to the rise in Medicaid costs. For example, the cost of a semiprivate hospital room alone increased by over 82 percent between 1967 and 1973.[24]

The financial burden of Medicaid programs on the states has been especially heavy. Medicaid costs account for a substantial proportion of state spending on welfare programs. In Illinois, over two-fifths of the state's welfare expenditures are used to support Medicaid; in New York, about one-third. And

---

[23]*Social Security Bulletin,* August 1974, p. 66, Table M-29.

[24]*Ibid.,* p. 72, Table M-36.

because of a fiscal crisis, difficulties in raising new public revenues, erosion of the tax base, and taxpayer revolt against the payment of new and higher taxes, the states have found the burden of expanded Medicaid programs to be most severe.

Cutbacks in Medicaid Programs

Because of the heavy Medicaid burden, Congress reversed itself in 1972 and made many changes in the program that should provide some fiscal relief to the financially hard-pressed states, and also hold down federal spending. Numerous cost-reduction measures were also introduced. Some of these important changes are the following:

1. *Repeal of Comprehensive Medicaid Program Requirement.* The states are no longer required to move toward a comprehensive Medicaid program and liberalized eligibility by July 1, 1977.

2. *Repeal of Maintenance-of-Effort Requirement.* The requirement under which a state could not reduce its aggregate expenditures for its share of Medicaid costs from one year to the next has been repealed.

3. *Limits on Payments to Skilled Nursing Homes.* Federal financial participation in skilled nursing-facility-care and intermediate-care per diem costs is not available to the extent that these costs exceed 105 percent of the previous year's level. However, the federal government participates in costs above 105 percent if they result from increases in the federal minimum wage or additional required services or new federal laws.

4. *Reduction in Federal Sharing.* A one-third reduction in federal matching payments for long-term stays in hospitals, nursing homes, intermediate-care facilities, and mental institutions is authorized if the states fail to have effective utilization-review programs for controlling the utilization of institutional services. The reduction can be made also if the states fail to conduct independent professional audits of patients as required by law.

5. *Other Cost-Control Provisions.* Limits are imposed on federal payments for disapproved capital expenditures; limits on prevailing physician charges are similar to those in the Medicare program; more specific eligibility requirements are applied to skilled nursing and extended-care facilities; and the medically needy can be required to pay premiums, copayments, or deductibles for the benefits provided.

The cost savings under the new Medicaid amendments are estimated to total about $790 million for 1974.

Although the Medicaid changes have the desirable objectives of providing fiscal relief to the states, reduction of waste and inefficiency, and control of overutilization, certain provisions can be criticized. The repeal of the provisions that required the states to provide comprehensive Medicaid services by July 1, 1977, and maintain their Medicaid financial efforts strikes at the very heart of the Medicaid law. Congress originally intended that comprehensive health services should be made available to all who were unable to pay for them because of inadequate incomes, and that all indigent and medically needy persons would eventually be covered for comprehensive health care. However, the permitted cutbacks in the scope of the state Medicaid programs and restriction on coverage represent a serious departure from the earlier national commitment of improved health for all the poor and near-poor.

The limitation on the federal matching of funds for skilled nursing and intermediate-care facilities to 105 percent of those costs for the previous year may well have an adverse effect on the quality of care. In many states, the amounts allowed for care in skilled nursing homes are significantly below the full cost of care in these institutions, and substantial increases in rates are necessary to insure adequate care. Many nursing homes are unable to hire adequate staff because of the low wages paid, and the quality of care is often poor. The goal of substantially upgrading the quality of health care in nursing homes may be more difficult to achieve if the rates are limited to a 5 percent annual increase.

Cost-Sharing Imposed on the Poor

Cost-sharing provisions are emphasized under the new amendments. The medically needy are now required to pay a monthly premium, graduated by income, for Medicaid benefits. The states can also require them to pay a nominal deductible or copayment amount, which does not have to vary by income.

In addition, cash-assistance recipients can be required to pay a nominal deductible or copayment amount for the optional Medicaid services (but not for the mandatory services). This provision is undesirable in many respects. The poor are the least able to pay for their medical care, and some who need such care may be discouraged from seeking early treatment because they are unable to pay. This could result in higher costs at a later date that could have been prevented by earlier treatment. Deductibles and copayment are used as restraints against the overutilization of services, for which poor patients are generally not responsible. The providers of health care are the ones primarily responsible for costs, and more effective cost-control measures can probably do more to reduce the problem of overutilization of benefits than the imposition of premiums, deductibles, and copayments on the poor.

Finally, the share of the cost that the poor are asked to assume is inordinately large. Of the estimated $790 million reduction in Medicaid costs as a result of the 1972 amendments, the cost-sharing provisions imposed on Medicaid recipients come to $89 million, or about 11 percent of the total.[25] It is difficult to justify economically the imposition of such a heavy financial burden on the poor, who are least able to pay for their medical care.

Restrictions on Eligibility

The 1972 amendments have resulted in a general tightening of eligibility requirements for Medicaid benefits. As of January 1, 1974, no state is required

[25]*Social Security Bulletin, loc. cit.*

to furnish medical assistance to any aged, blind, or disabled person who would not have been eligible for aid under the state's plan as of January 1, 1972. If a state desires to provide Medicaid benefits based on the 1972 standard, it must incorporate a "spend-down" provision in the plan, whereby a person is entitled to Medicaid benefits only if his income (after deducting incurred medical expenses) does not exceed the state's standard for medical assistance in effect as of January 1, 1972. This means that states are not required to provide Medicaid benefits to newly eligible recipients who qualify for cash assistance after January 1, 1974, under the new Supplemental Security Income program for the aged, blind, and disabled.

It should be noted, however, that the 1972 amendments did make some desirable changes regarding eligibility. First, the Medicaid "notch" effect is reduced by the new law. The "notch" is an income cutoff point beyond which the individual or family becomes ineligible for Medicaid benefits. It can cause a strong disincentive to work, since a Medicaid recipient may reduce his work efforts as his earnings approach the level where all Medicaid benefits are lost. Under the new law, there is protection against the complete loss of Medicaid benefits because of increased earnings; a family that becomes ineligible for Medicaid because of increased employment earnings can continue to receive the benefits for four additional months.

Second, all states must cover the medical care of an otherwise qualified person for the three months prior to his application for Medicaid. (This provision was formerly optional.) Some people may not apply for medical assistance until after they start receiving treatment—perhaps because they are unaware that they are eligible for Medicaid, or because their illness prevents them from applying sooner. Now, after such a person applies, his medical expenses for the preceding three months are covered.

WELFARE REFORMS

Many critical observers believe that monumental welfare reforms are necessary to overcome the limitations of public assistance. In the late 1960's, several groups studied the welfare crisis and made some worthwhile recommendations. These groups included the Advisory Council on Public Welfare, the National Advisory Commission on Civil Disorders, and the Arden House Conference on Public Welfare. Their general recommendations for improving public-assistance programs included national standards for minimum payments, greater federal financing, eligibility and administrative reforms, expansion of employment and work incentives, expansion of child day-care centers, a systems approach to poverty, and a national system of income supplements. Many of these recommendations have been implemented, but it is still widely believed that the old system of public assistance must be scrapped and replaced by an entirely new program. Present welfare reform proposals center around three basic approaches: (1) a negative income tax, (2) guaranteed employment and wage subsidies, and (3) universal demogrant plans.

Negative Income Tax

Many economists propose the enactment of some negative income tax plan (NIT) as a measure to help solve the poverty problem.

Basic Concepts.   NIT plans could take many forms, and it is beyond the scope of this text to analyze all possible variations.[26] All plans proposed, however, have three common features: (1) The NIT payment would be based on family income, size, and composition; (2) the major eligibility test would be a comparison of the family's income with the *breakeven* level of income determined for that type of family; (3) and the family's income would be taxable, but the tax rate would be substantially less than 100 percent. Thus, three variables are present: the basic allowance (*A*), the breakeven level of income (*B*), and the tax rate (*t*). It is impossible to change one variable without changing the other two, since they are interrelated. The basic allowance is equal to the product of the tax rate and the breakeven level of income. Thus, $A = t(B)$. For example, if the breakeven level of income is set at $4,400 for a family of four, a tax rate of 50 percent yields a basic allowance of $2,200.

The following table illustrates how an NIT plan would work for a four-member family living in an urban city. If the family has no income, it receives a basic NIT benefit of $2,200, assuming a 50 percent marginal tax rate and a breakeven level of $4,400. If the family has an annual income of $3,000, the NIT benefit is reduced to $700, making the total family income $3,700. And when the family's income reaches $4,400—the breakeven level—no NIT benefits are paid.

Earned Income	NIT Payment	Total Income
None	$ 2,200	$ 2,200
$ 1,000	1,700	2,700
2,000	1,200	3,200
3,000	700	3,700
4,000	200	4,200
4,400	0	4,400

Arguments for the Negative Income Tax.   The arguments offered in support of a NIT plan are based on the implicit assumption that it can overcome many inherent defects now found in public assistance and other public income-maintenance programs.

1. Ineffectiveness of Present Programs.   It is charged that present public income-maintenance programs do not reach many of the hard-core poor. Because of the categorical nature of the programs, millions of poor people receive

[26]For a complete discussion of the various plans, technical problems, and other details, see Christopher Green, *Negative Income Taxes and the Poverty Problem* (Washington, D.C.: The Brookings Institution, 1967); James C. Vadakin, "A Critique of the Guaranteed Annual Income," *The Public Interest,* No. 11 (Spring 1968), 53-66; and James Tobin, Joseph A. Pechman, and Peter M. Mieszkowski, "Is a Negative Income Tax Practical?" in *Income Maintenance Programs, Vol. 1: The Proceedings,* Hearings before the Subcommittee on Fiscal Policy of the Joint Economic Committee, 90th Cong., 2d sess., 1968, pp. 247-73.

little or no financial assistance from major social insurance programs. The working poor, in particular, who generally receive few benefits from existing programs, would benefit much more from an NIT plan.

2. More Efficiency in Reducing Poverty. NIT supporters argue that this technique is more efficient than are present programs in reducing poverty, since it would do something that present programs do inefficiently: *It would place cash immediately in the hands of the hard-core poor.*

3. Inadequacy of Public-Assistance Benefits. As we have seen, public-assistance benefit amounts are below the poverty line in most states, so many welfare recipients find it extremely difficult to attain even a minimum level of economic security. An NIT plan is considered necessary either to replace or supplement public-assistance benefits.

4. Loss of Jobs by Cybernetics and Automation. Supporters of an NIT plan or guaranteed minimum income plan argue that millions of jobs are being destroyed by cybernetics and automation, and that consequently, every person should be guaranteed enough income to live in decency and dignity. The guaranteed annual income would be an absolute and unconditional constitutional right.[27]

5. Less Cost to Taxpayers. Under some proposals, an NIT plan would replace many existing welfare programs, including public assistance, farm price-support programs, unemployment insurance, veterans' benefits, and others. Proponents of NIT argue that having one program replace the present "hodge-podge" of programs would place income in the hands of the poor more cheaply than at present, since many public welfare programs overlap and duplicate each other. Also, the NIT plan could be easily and more cheaply administered, since the NIT tax mechanism could be part of the income tax machinery of the federal government.

6. Correction of Tax Inequities. Although the poor pay little income tax because their incomes are below taxable levels, at the same time they receive few benefits from reductions in income tax rates or from increases in personal exemptions and allowable deductions. And they bear a relatively heavy tax burden from such regressive taxes as the sales tax and, in the case of the working poor, the OASDHI tax contributions on their limited earnings. The NIT plan would help counteract the regressiveness of the present tax system at low income levels and would improve its equity aspects.

7. Avoidance of Stigma of Charity. Most NIT plans now proposed call for an objective needs test based on only income and family size. Other eligibility requirements now imposed under public-assistance programs, such as ability to work, relatives' responsibility, previous taxes paid, age, retirement status, employment record, and similar factors would not be considered. All poor families with incomes below the poverty line, not just certain categories of families, would receive allowances.

The stigma of receiving welfare could be reduced in an NIT plan through

---

[27]See Robert Theobald, *Free Men and Free Markets; Proposed: A Guaranteed Income* (Garden City, N.Y.: Doubleday, Anchor Books, 1965). See also Robert Theobald, ed., *The Guaranteed Income: Next Step in Economic Evolution?* (Garden City, N.Y.: Doubleday, 1966).

the present personal income tax system. The beneficiary could file income tax forms at the beginning and end of a stated accounting period, and NIT allowances based on this information could be paid in a dignified and confidential fashion.

Arguments against the Negative Income Tax. Those who are critical of the NIT approach to poverty reduction offer the following counterarguments.

1. Reduction of Work Incentives. The principal objection to the NIT is that if benefits are paid to poor individuals or families to bring them up to the poverty line, many recipients will prefer the subsidy to work. However, the three-year negative income tax experiment in New Jersey and Pennsylvania does not bear out this theory.

More than 1,350 randomly selected families were observed over a three-year period, during which an experimental group received negative income tax benefits ranging from 50 to 125 percent of the poverty line and a control group received no transfer payments. The major conclusions from the study are as follows:

1. Observed changes in the labor supply in response to the experimental benefits were generally quite small. The various measures of labor supply indicate reductions relative to the control group of less than 10 percent. Many of the differentials were considerably smaller and often were not statistically significant from zero.

2. Statistically significant reductions in the labor supply among black families were seldom found. Indeed, in many cases, a statistically significant increase in work efforts was observed.

3. However, wives showed a large percentage reduction in the labor supply, and these responses were generally confined to nonblacks. But these responses were quite small in absolute terms. They were large only relative to the initially small amounts of labor supplied by wives. The reduction in the labor supply of wives had only a small effect on total family labor supply and earnings.

4. There were no significant reductions in the labor-force participation rates and employment rates for either white or black husbands. White husbands, however, reduced slightly the number of hours worked each week. About 95 percent of all husbands, in both the experimental and control groups, were in the labor force during any survey week throughout the experiment.

5. The receipt of cash benefits did not appear to have any systematic effect on the recipients' health, self-esteem, social integration, and perceived quality of life. Nor did the benefits adversely affect family composition, martial stability, and fertility rates.[28]

Based on these findings, several important public policy conclusions can be drawn from the New Jersey experiment.[29] First, a negative income tax plan with a basic benefit as high as the poverty line will not trigger a large-scale reduction in work effort among male family heads. Second, negative income tax benefits may result in a substantial reduction in the labor supply among the 15 to 20 percent of the low-income wives who are employed. Whether this is desir-

[28]U.S. Department of Health, Education and Welfare, Office of Economic Opportunity, *Summary Report: New Jersey Graduated Work Incentive Program,* December 1973, pp. ii-v.

[29]*Ibid.,* p. vi-vii.

able is a matter of individual value judgments. Finally, the small increase in unemployment rates for some male heads studied in the experiment is not necessarily undesirable. The benefits may allow the unemployed workers, especially younger workers, a longer period to search for new jobs, which may then result in better jobs at higher wage rates.

2. Neglect of the Fundamental Causes of Poverty.   Another counterargument is that an NIT plan would treat the symptoms of low earning capacity, but not its causes, which include inadequate education, lack of marketable skills, physical and mental disabilities, low productivity, poor motivation, and large families. Emphasis on manpower and vocational training programs, these critics say, is a superior although slower alternative to NIT. It should be pointed out, however, that manpower and training programs offer few benefits to some poverty-stricken groups, such as the aged poor.

3. Problems of Cost and Administration.   The NIT approach may be an expensive substitute for existing public income-maintenance programs, since, under some plans, NIT benefits would be paid to families above the poverty line to expand work incentives. If the guaranteed benefit is set at some poverty line, and if the percentage of earnings by which benefits are reduced is sufficiently low to preserve work incentives, large amounts of benefits may go to nonpoor, middle-income families.

The Council of Economic Advisers points out this problem in a simple example. Assume that a four-member family is guaranteed a NIT benefit of $3,300, reduced by 50 cents for every dollar earned—probably the maximum deduction necessary to preserve work incentives. Thus, a family earning $5,000 annually would have its NIT benefits reduced 50 percent, or $2,500, which would still leave the family with an $800 NIT benefit. Under this plan, all four-member families with incomes under $6,600 would receive benefits; the total cost would be $20 billion, with about half this sum going to nonpoor families.[30]

This example illustrates the trade-off problem that must be solved under the NIT approach. Three basic considerations must be treated: (1) the size of the NIT guarantee to meet the problem of income inadequacy; (2) the possible dampening of work incentives; and (3) the costs of the plan. These objectives conflict with each other. A high NIT guarantee reduces poverty, but costs are high and work incentives may be dampened. Setting the NIT guarantee well below the poverty line reduces costs and preserves work incentives, but does not eliminate poverty.

The problem of administration is another argument against an NIT plan. Critics argue that the alleged simplicity and low administrative costs of the various plans are deceiving. Reports would have to be filed, and payments would have to be based on some time period. Monthly payments would increase administrative costs, and lump-sum annual payments would be impractical, since the poor might be unable to budget properly to cover their expenses in the ensuing year. In addition, if eligibility were determined on the basis of past reports or estimates of future income, problems of overpayment and underpayment would occur. Circumstances between payment periods may change

[30]Council of Economic Advisers, *Economic Report of the President* (Washington, D.C.: U.S. Government Printing Office, 1969), p. 172.

because of unemployment or sickness, and some provision would have to be made regarding overpayments and underpayments. Finally, critics argue that an NIT plan would add to the proliferation of existing welfare programs and would further compound the government bureaucracy that now exists.

4. Nonreplacement of Present Welfare Programs. Another argument is that an NIT plan might not be able to replace existing welfare programs, as proponents now claim it would. To preserve incentives, most NIT plans provide for payments that fill only some fraction of the poverty gap, so some families might still be poor after receiving payments. In particular, NIT benefits to the aged and to AFDC families might be inadequate because of the need to preserve incentives for other groups, such as the working poor. Thus, critics say, poverty would still exist despite the adoption of an NIT plan, and public-assistance programs would still be needed.

Moreover, the counseling services now provided by the various public-assistance agencies would still be necessary. It should be pointed out, however, that effective counseling services might be more readily available to the poor under NIT, since the social workers would be relieved of the current time-consuming job of investigation of a recipient's income and assets.

5. Adverse Effect on Wages. A final counterargument is that, because guaranteed income payments would be supplements to the wages earned by low-income groups and would in effect subsidize the working poor, the question arises as to whether the payments would also subsidize marginal employers. These employers could remain in business by paying the low wages made possible by the guaranteed income payments made to the lower-income groups. Of course, this effect might be offset by the possible advantage of subsidizing employers who provide jobs for unskilled or low-skilled workers.

Integration of Negative Income Tax with OASDHI

If a negative income tax plan were enacted into law, the thorny problem of determining the role, if any, that the OASDHI progam would play must be resolved. One approach is to abolish the OASDHI program and replace it with an NIT plan. Given the facts, however, that the OASDHI program is widely accepted by the masses, does not require a needs test, and is used (and misused) as a political football, its abolishment appears politically unfeasible.

In addition, the OASDHI program is aimed at providing a layer of income protection for the masses, most of whom are not poor, and not solely at aiding the disadvantaged. An NIT plan, however, is public charity, albeit of a less onerous form, and, therefore, the bulk of the nonpoor population will not take kindly to a proposal that would replace the present OASDHI program with a relatively new and untried NIT plan.

And if the OASDHI program were abolished, there would be the additional problem of disposing of the OASDHI trust funds to which employees, employers, and the self-employed contribute. Serious legal, economic, and ethical questions would be raised regarding the disposition of these funds.

So, all things considered, it is unlikely that an NIT plan would replace the currently accepted OASDHI program; it would probably be used to supplement the present system of income-maintenance programs, including OASDHI. The knotty problem then would be to determine the manner of integration of the NIT plan with OASDHI.

One scheme for integration that bears serious consideration is the proposal of Pechman, Aaron, and Taussig in their analysis of needed reforms in the present OASDHI program.[31] They recommend two separate systems. One would be a reformed OASDHI program that is strictly wage-related. OASDHI benefits would be computed at the same percentage of earnings at all levels (which should silence the critics who argue for greater individual equity in the OASDHI program). The second system would be an NIT plan (or, alternatively, a reformed public-assistance program) for people who would not benefit from the OASDHI program. Under their proposal, NIT or public-assistance allowances would be paid to all households with incomes below some specified level, with the minimum allowance at least equal to a minimum subsistence standard of living for families of all sizes.

The aged would elect *either* an OASDHI retirement benefit based on their past earnings *or* an NIT allowance based on total money income, whichever provides the larger benefit. If the earnings-related OASDHI benefit were selected, the beneficiary would pay positive income tax rates on all his income, including the benefit. If the NIT allowance were selected, however, the beneficiary would waive the OASDHI benefit and would be subject to the NIT tax rate on all his income (except the basic NIT allowance).

The following example illustrates their proposal. Assume that an aged couple can receive an earnings-related OASDHI benefit equal to 50 percent of their past average family earnings. In addition, assume that the basic NIT allowance is $1,800 for a married couple, and that all additional income received by those electing the NIT allowance is taxed at 50 percent. If the couple has no other income, they will elect the NIT allowance when past average earnings are less than $3,666, the point at which the earnings-related OASDHI benefit is identical to the NIT allowance. That is, the OASDHI retirement benefit based on average earnings of $3,666 is $1,833, but the positive tax for a married couple with no dependents is $33. This leaves a net OASDHI benefit of $1,800.

On the other hand, if the couple has $1,000 of other income, they will elect the OASDHI earnings-related benefit if their past average earnings are over $2,828, an amount that results in an OASDHI retirement benefit of $1,414. The total income of $2,414 carries a positive income tax of $114, leaving an after-tax income of $2,300. If the couple elects the basic NIT allowance of $1,800, the tax on their other income of $1,000 is $500, which results in the identical after-tax income of $2,300.

Pechman, Aaron, and Taussig claim that this approach is advantageous because as total income including OASDHI retirement benefits increases, the NIT allowance is reduced and ultimately disappears. One defect, however, is that their plan is extremely expensive, since it involves closing the poverty gap for people in all age groups. Moreover, closing completely the poverty gap raises the serious question of possible dampening of work incentives for those with

[31]Joseph A. Pechman, Henry J. Aaron, and Michael K. Taussig, *Social Security: Perspectives for Reform* (Washington, D.C.: The Brookings Institution, 1968), pp. 197-201.

incomes slightly below the poverty line. A final criticism of the Pechman approach is that it would make OASDHI benefits taxable, something that Congress has considered in the past and rejected.

Family Assistance Plan. The Family Assistance Plan (FAP), proposed by the Nixon administration in August 1969, is one example of a welfare reform proposal based on the negative income tax concept. As originally proposed, the plan would guarantee an annual income of $1,600 to a four-member family. To encourage working, the first $720 earned, plus half the remainder, would be disregarded in determining the FAP benefits. Thus, a four-member family could earn $3,920 annually before the FAP benefits would terminate. The plan was later revised to provide an annual guarantee of $2,400 for a four-member family.

Congress later abandoned the FAP proposal as a viable solution to the welfare crisis. Both liberals and conservatives were opposed to the plan. Liberals opposed it on the grounds that the benefits were inadequate; the financial position of most poor people would have actually worsened rather than improved; strong disincentives not to work were built into the plan; it was unduly complex and would have created some serious administrative problems; and an onerous and compulsory work requirement was built into the plan as a condition of eligibility.[32] Conservative members of Congress opposed the FAP proposal because of the substantial increase in welfare costs that would result, particularly since it would have more than doubled the welfare rolls by including the working poor.

Since the welfare crisis would have worsened under the Family Assistance Plan, Congress did not enact it into law.[33] Instead, it began to consider welfare reform proposals that would require welfare recipients to work, a concept we shall take up next.

Guaranteed Employment and Wage Subsidies

Guaranteed employment in the public and private sectors and wage subsidies are also proposed as solutions to the welfare crisis.[34] Under this approach, employable welfare recipients are expected to work in public or private employment, and the concept of *workfare* is substituted for that of welfare. If the welfare recipients cannot find jobs in the private sector, the federal government will guarantee public-employment jobs. If the jobs in the

---

[32]For an extensive analysis of the argument that the financial position of the poor would have worsened under the FAP proposal, see George E. Rejda, "The Family Assistance Plan as a Solution to the Welfare Crisis," *The Journal of Risk and Insurance,* Vol. XXXVIII, No. 2 (June 1971), 169-79.

[33]The political implications and background of the FAP can be found in Daniel P. Moynihan, *The Politics of a Guaranteed Income: The Nixon Administration and the Family Assistance Plan* (New York: Random House, 1973).

[34]For an excellent discussion of a system of guaranteed public employment for the working poor, see Arnold H. Packer, "Categorical Public Employment Guarantees: A Proposed Solution.to the Poverty Problem," in U.S. Congress, Subcommittee on Fiscal Policy of the Joint Economic Committee, *Studies in Public Welfare; Paper No. 9 (Part 1), Concepts in Welfare Program Design,* 93d Cong., 1st sess., 1973 (Washington, D.C.: U.S. Government Printing Office, 1973), pp. 68-127.

private sector pay relatively low wages, federal wage subsidies will be paid to supplement them. Child-care facilities, transportation assistance, and supportive social services would also be provided, to encourage greater employment of able-bodied welfare recipients.

Basic Concepts of Workfare. The workfare approach to welfare reform is based on several basic concepts. First, work is viewed as the key element in ending dependence on welfare. It is charged that the payment of cash benefits based on need, which is the essence of the public assistance, has not worked, but has actually encouraged greater dependence on welfare.

Second, it is argued that the present system of cash payments has not improved the dignity, status, and quality of life for the poor, and that dependence on welfare only aggravates and compounds their misery. The payment of welfare benefits isolates the poor from the rest of society, and the stigma of charity associated with the benefits only humiliates and further degrades the recipients. On the other hand, work is considered rewarding, and income would be received in a dignified way in accordance with the national work ethic.

Finally, it is said that because social values have changed since the first AFDC programs were established by the Social Security Act of 1935, the payment of cash benefits to AFDC mothers to enable them to remain at home to care for their children is no longer valid. The labor force currently consists of a high proportion of working mothers, many of whom must now help support their families. One-third of all mothers with children under age 6 are working, and more than half the mothers with school-age children are in the labor force. In those families where the fathers are absent, two-thirds of the mothers with school-age children are in the labor force.[35] Thus, it is considered unfair and inequitable to pay welfare mothers to stay home and take care of their children; employable welfare mothers should be expected to work just as do the mothers who are not on welfare.

One example of the workfare approach to welfare reform is the proposal of Senator Russell B. Long.[36] The plan would encourage welfare recipients to work through guaranteed jobs and child care, with wage subsidies for people employed at low wages. Women with children under age 6 would be eligible for regular AFDC payments, but for other groups, no welfare assistance would be provided to employable welfare recipients who refuse to work. Three major types of employment assistance would be provided: (1) regular jobs in the private sector or in public or nonprofit agencies, with no wage subsidies; (2) partially subsidized public or private employment; and (3) newly developed jobs, with the federal government paying the full cost of wages and salaries. Three basic benefits would be available:

1. A guaranteed job opportunity with a newly established Work Administration, which pays $1.50 per hour for 32 hours, for a maximum weekly wage of $48.

[35]U.S. Congress, Senate, Committee on Finance, *Social Security Amendments of 1972*, p. 411.

[36]See U.S. Congress, Senate, Committee on Finance, *Welfare Reform, Guaranteed Job Opportunity, Explanation of Committee Decision*, 92d Cong., 2d sess., 1972 (Washington, D.C.: U.S. Government Printing Office, 1972). See also Alan A. Townsend, "Introduction: An Overview of Issues in the Coordination of Public Welfare Programs," in U.S. Congress, Subcommittee on Fiscal Policy of the Joint Economic Committee, *Studies in Public Welfare; Paper No. 7, Issues in the Coordination of Public Welfare Programs*, 93d Cong., 1st sess., 1973 (Washington, D.C.: U.S. Government Printing Office, 1973), pp. 1-13.

2. A wage supplement for a worker employed at less than $2 per hour (but at least $1.50 per hour), equal to three-fourths of the difference between the actual wage paid and $2 per hour.

3. A work bonus equal to 10 percent of the wages covered under the OASDHI program up to a maximum bonus of $400, with a reduction in the bonus as the husband's and wife's covered earnings increase above $4,000.

The Long proposal was not enacted into law. Instead, a stringent compulsory work requirement was built into the WIN program, by which employable AFDC recipients must register for work or training under the WIN program or lose their welfare benefits.

Compulsory-Work Issue. One legal and moral issue that must be resolved under the workfare approach is whether welfare mothers should be forced to work against their will. Many welfare mothers now voluntarily elect to work full-time, while others prefer to remain at home. In many cases, the jobs available to welfare recipients pay relatively low wages, and the family is seldom better off financially even when the mother works full-time. The AFDC grant is reduced as work earnings increase; higher amounts must be paid for food stamps, and higher rent for public housing; Medicaid benefits may be lost if the family's income reaches the maximum allowable. Moreover, child day-care facilities are in short supply, and even if free day care is available, many welfare mothers are not interested in working, especially if young children are in the home.[37] Indeed, the basic dilemma is not that the welfare benefits are so high as to encourage dependency on welfare, but that the wages paid from the available jobs are so low that reasonable alternatives to welfare are often not available. As a result, many welfare mothers have no strong personal inducement to enter the labor force.

The Special Task Force to the Department of Health, Education and Welfare, which was created to study the role of work in America, has concluded that welfare mothers should not be required to work against their will—that society must recognize that work in the home can be valid, productive, and socially useful, and that forcing mothers into the labor force is not the proper solution to welfare reform. The Task Force also recognizes, however, that continued dependency on cash welfare benefits is not the proper solution either; instead, it believes, the federal government should provide guaranteed employment at living wages to the central provider. Because family breakup is a critical factor in the AFDC welfare crisis, providing attractive work opportunities to lower-class men would encourage family stability, since a woman could anticipate marriage to a steadily employed and self-respecting man. Thus, the Task Force believes that the key element in welfare reform is the opportunity for the central provider to work full-time at a living wage.[38] Although it offers no detailed recommendations on how guaranteed and rewarding work at living wages

[37]Jack Ditmore and W.R. Prosser, *A Study of Day Care's Effect on the Labor Force Participation of Low-Income Mothers,* Evaluation Division, Office of Planning, Research and Evaluation, Office of Economic Opportunity, June 1973, p. 43.

[38]U.S. Congress, Senate, Subcommittee on Employment, Manpower, and Poverty, of the Committee on Labor and Public Welfare, *Work in America; Report of a Special Task Force to the Secretary of Health, Education and Welfare,* 93d Cong., 1st sess., 1973 (Washington, D.C.: U.S. Government Printing Office, 1973), pp. xiii and 140-48.

can be provided, the concept is an appealing approach to welfare reform that merits further analysis.

Universal Demogrant Plan

A universal demogrant plan, accompanied by substantial changes in the federal income tax, has also been proposed. A demogrant (from *demo-*, meaning "people," + *grant*) is a flat benefit paid to all those who are eligible, regardless of the sources or amounts of their other income, as a matter of right with no demonstration of need required. These flat benefits would be a substitute for public-assistance benefits and for personal deductions and exemptions under the federal income tax.

One version of a demogrant plan is the proposal by Earl R. Rolph, under which a proportionate tax would be levied on almost all income, except for the flat demogrant benefit. If the benefits were established at $800 for adults and $400 for children, a four-member family with no income would receive $2,400 annually. If a proportionate federal income tax rate were established at 33 percent, then a family with annual earnings of $7,200 would pay no federal income taxes and receive no demogrant benefits on a net basis, since its tax liabilities (33 percent of $7,200) would be offset by its grant of $2,400.[39]

A universal demogrant plan would be a powerful antipoverty tool, since it would result in a massive redistribution of income. A study of several demogrant proposals by Benjamin A. Okner indicates the extent to which they would reduce poverty.[40] The most expensive plan, providing an annual benefit of $1,500 to each adult and $300 to each child under age 18, would reduce the number of families in poverty by 80 percent, with a redistribution of about $47 billion of total income. The least expensive demogrant plan would reduce the number of families in poverty by 71 percent, with a redistribution of about $34 billion of total income. And since the benefits would be based on right and not need, the reduction of poverty could be accomplished in a dignified manner, without the stigma of charity now associated with public-assistance benefits.

On the negative side, however, demogrants are expensive, and their political implications must be carefully considered. Because of the massive sums involved, most demogrant proposals require the broadening of the individual income tax base. The study by Okner indicated that the annual gross outlays would range from a low of about $158 billion to a high of $215 billion. The substantial increases in federal income tax rates necessary to fund these programs raise questions concerning their political feasibility. And the massive redistribution of income they would generate, by which some families would on balance become "gainers" while other families became net "losers," gives rise to some concern about whether the American public would be willing to accept them—particularly, whether the potential "loser" families would accept the personal income tax increases required to support the benefits received by the "gainers."

[39]Earl R. Rolph, "The Case for a Negative Income Tax Device," *Industrial Relations,* Vol. 6, No. 2 (February 1967), 155-65.

[40]See Benjamin A. Okner, "The Role of Demogrants as an Income Maintenance Alternative," in U.S. Congress, Subcommittee on Fiscal Policy, *Studies in Public Welfare; Paper No. 9,* 1973, pp. 1-32.

SUGGESTIONS FOR ADDITIONAL READING

Aaron, Henry J., *Why Is Welfare So Hard To Reform?* Washington, D.C.: The Brookings Institution, 1972.

Barth, Michael C., George J. Carcagno, and John L. Palmer, *Toward an Effective Income Support System: Problems, Prospects and Choices, with an Overview Paper by Irwin Garfinkel.* Madison: University of Wisconsin, The Institute for Research on Poverty, 1974.

Committee for Economic Development, *Improving the Public Welfare System.* New York: Committee for Economic Development, 1970.

Goodwin, Leonard, *Do the Poor Want To Work? A Social-Psychological Study of Work Orientations.* Washington, D.C.: The Brookings Institution, 1972.

Green, Christopher, *Negative Income Taxes and the Poverty Problem.* Washington, D.C.: The Brookings Institution, 1967.

Lampman, Robert J., *Ends and Means of Reducing Income Poverty,* Chicago: Markham, 1971.

Moynihan, Daniel P., *The Politics of a Guaranteed Income: The Nixon Administration and the Family Assistance Plan.* New York: Random House, 1973.

Rejda, George E., "Family Allowances as a Program for Reducing Poverty," *The Journal of Risk and Insurance,* Vol. XXXVII, No. 4 (December 1970), 539-54.

_____, "The Family Assistance Plan as a Solution to the Welfare Crisis," *The Journal of Risk and Insurance,* Vol. XXXVIII, No. 2 (June 1971), 169-79.

Tobin, James, and W. Allen Wallis, *Welfare Programs: An Economic Appraisal.* Washington, D.C.: American Enterprise Institute for Public Policy Research, 1968.

U.S. Congress, Senate, Subcommittee on Employment, Manpower, and Poverty, of the Committee on Labor and Public Welfare, *Work in America; Report of a Special Task Force to the Secretary of Health, Education and Welfare.* Washington, D.C.: U.S. Government Printing Office, 1973.

U.S. Congress, Subcommittee on Fiscal Policy of the Joint Economic Committee, *Studies in Public Welfare,* Papers 1-15. Washington, D.C.: U.S. Government Printing Office, 1972, 1973, and 1974.

_____, *Income Security for Americans: Recommendations of the Public Welfare Study.* Washington, D.C.: U.S. Government Printing Office, December 5, 1974.

U.S. Department of Health, Education and Welfare, Office of Economic Opportunity, *Summary Report: New Jersey Graduated Work Incentive Program.* Washington, D.C.: Office of Economic Opportunity, 1973.

_____, Social and Rehabilitation Service, *Welfare Myths vs. Fact.* Washington, D.C.: U.S. Government Printing Office, 1971.

chapter 19

Economics
of Social Insurance Programs

From the viewpoint of individual economic security, both the OASDHI and the unemployment-insurance programs are extremely important in providing the worker with some protection against certain social risks. These programs, however, also have an important macroeconomic impact on the economy. They affect economic stability and growth, influence the redistribution of income, and help in maintaining consumption and aggregate demand. In addition, the incidence and burden of OASDHI payroll taxes have an economic impact that must also be considered.

In this chapter, we shall examine some economic effects of the OASDHI and unemployment-insurance programs. In particular, we shall consider the following areas: (1) the fiscal impact of the OASDHI trust funds; (2) the effects of the OASDHI program on economic stability and growth, redistribution of income, and consumption and saving; (3) the incidence and burden of OASDHI taxes; and (4) the economic impact of unemployment insurance.

ECONOMIC IMPACT OF THE OASDHI PROGRAM

Both OASDHI tax contributions and benefits are extremely important in the total federal budget. The contributions are the second most important source of revenue to the federal government, next only to individual income taxes. In fiscal 1975, social insurance taxes and contributions are estimated to total $85.6 billion, or about 29 percent of total federal receipts.[1] Likewise, next to national defense, OASDHI benefits paid are the second most important

[1]Council of Economic Advisers, *Economic Report of the President* (Washington, D.C.: U.S. Government Printing Office, 1974), p. 326, Table C-65.

federal expenditure. And since the OASDHI tax contributions and premiums are deposited in the four OASDHI trust funds and all benefit expenditures are made out of these funds, it is important to examine the fiscal impact of the trust funds on the economy.

Trust Funds in the Unified Budget

Before fiscal 1969, the federal budget presented annually to Congress excluded the receipts and expenditures of the OASDHI trust funds. Since that date, however, a unified budget is issued, which encompasses all programs of the federal government and its agencies, including the trust fund operations. The primary objective of the new unified budget is to measure more accurately the fiscal and economic impact of the federal government on the economy; so the fiscal impact of the OASDHI program on the total federal budget can be better measured and viewed through inclusion.

Table 19-1 shows the relationship of the OASDHI tax receipts and expenditures to the total federal budget for fiscal years 1971-75. It should be noted

TABLE 19-1 Social Security Program in the Unified Budget, Fiscal Years 1971-75 (in billions of dollars)

Receipts and Expenditures	Actual			Projected	
	1971	*1972*	*1973*	*1974*	*1975*
Total budget receipts	188.4	208.6	232.2	270.0	295.0
Individual income taxes	86.2	94.7	163.3	118.0	129.0
Corporation income taxes	26.8	32.2	36.1	43.0	48.0
OASDHI payroll taxes	40.6	45.1	53.7	66.3	73.6
SMI premiums	1.3	1.3	1.4	1.7	1.8
All other	33.5	35.3	37.7	41.0	42.6
Total budget outlays	211.4	231.9	246.5	274.7	304.4
National defense	77.7	78.3	76.0	80.6	87.7
OASDHI and SMI	43.1	48.2	57.8	67.4	78.2
All other	90.6	105.4	112.7	126.7	138.5
Total budget surplus or deficit	−23.0	−23.4	14.3	− 4.7	− 9.4
OASDHI budget surplus or deficit	− 1.2	− 1.8	− 2.7	0.6	− 2.8
Total excluding OASDHI	−21.8	−21.6	17.0	− 5.3	− 6.6

Source: U.S. Department of Health, Education and Welfare, Social Security Administration, Office of Research and Statistics, *The Fiscal and Budgetary Impact of the Social Security Program, 1970-75,* by Robert O. Brunner, Note No. 19 (June 27, 1974), p. 5, Table 2.

that an OASDHI surplus or deficit has an important effect on the overall budgetary surplus or deficit. For example, the projected OASDHI budget deficit of $2.8 billion in fiscal 1975 will increase the overall projected budget deficit from

$6.6 to $9.4 billion. So an imbalance between OASDHI receipts from the public (taxes and SMI premiums) and expenditures to the public (benefit payments and administrative expenses) has an important effect on the total unified budget. A deficit in the budget is fiscally expansionary, whereas a budgetary surplus is deflationary. Thus, public policy decisions concerning the OASDHI program must consider the impact of proposed changes on both the program itself and the economy.

Economists are concerned about the potential fiscal effects of the OASDHI program, while budget analysts are concerned with its financial solvency. Therefore, many economists and budget analysts believe the trust funds must meet two basic objectives: (1) the OASDHI program should be fiscally neutral, and (2) the trust funds should be maintained at a level equal to one year's benefit payments. [2]

Fiscal neutrality, or budget neutrality, occurs when the OASDHI payments to the public equal collections from the public. The first goal is achieved when OASDHI payments and collections are in balance, resulting in a neutral effect on the total unified budget.

The second goal is achieved when the trust funds have surpluses that are approximately equal to the annual growth in cash benefit payments. This goal of steady increases in the OASDHI trust funds can be achieved even if the program is fiscally neutral, because intragovernmental transactions, which on balance usually produce a surplus, and the interest earnings on the trust-fund assets are netted out in the unified budget. Thus, if the system is in fiscal balance, the trust funds will automatically increase. A fiscal balance in the OASDHI program produces a trust-fund surplus, and a fiscal surplus in the OASDHI program increases the trust-fund surplus. However, a fiscal deficit in the program does not necessarily result in a net reduction of the trust funds.

The available evidence indicates that the OASDHI program has seldom been fiscally neutral between 1959 and 1973. There has been a pattern of fiscal surpluses and deficits, irregular both in size and in direction. [3] A fiscally neutral program is considered highly desirable, for several reasons. First, the OASDHI payroll tax by itself is a regressive tax; it constitutes a relatively higher burden for low-income than for upper-income people. If a reduction of regressivity is desirable, then the relative importance of OASDHI payroll taxes in the total tax structure should be reduced. This could be accomplished by preventing the emergence of a surplus that results primarily from this source of revenue. A fiscal surplus in the OASDHI program can be viewed as a contribution from OASDHI payroll-tax revenues to the general government. This is exactly the reverse of a general-revenue contribution, which has been proposed as a partial solution to the regressive nature of the OASDHI tax.

Second, the OASDHI program may not be the most appropriate vehicle

[2]See U.S. Department of Health, Education and Welfare, Social Security Administration, Office of Research and Statistics, *Trust Fund Surpluses and Fiscal Neutrality in the Social Security Program,* by Robert O. Brunner, Note No. 8 (June 19, 1970); and *The Fiscal and Bugetary Impact of the Social Security Program in 1969,* by Robert O. Brunner, Note No. 24 (December 11, 1970).

[3]U.S. Department of Health, Education and Welfare, Social Security Administration, Office of Research and Statistics, *The Trust Fund and Budget Position of the Social Security Program,* by Robert O. Brunner, Note No. 11 (October 8, 1971), p. 2.

for discretionary countercyclical fiscal policy. Monetary and fiscal policies of the federal government are more appropriate techniques for stabilizing the economy. This is not to say, however, that the OASDHI program does not contribute to economic stability; it does tend to function as automatic stabilizer. But this is a secondary function and should not supersede its primary function of income maintenance. The countercyclical effects of the OASDHI program as an automatic stabilizer will be treated later in the chapter.

Finally, future OASDHI benefit increases, liberalization of the program, and the raising of revenues should aim at maintaining the program in a fiscally neutral position, with a margin for forecasting errors. Future benefit increases and financing proposals that would produce large surpluses or deficits in the OASDHI program are undesirable, since they would tend to destabilize the total unified budget. And just as the OASDHI program should not be destabilized by the total budget, the total budget should not be deliberately destabilized by the OASDHI program.

Economic Stability

Since the OASDHI trust funds are often not fiscally neutral, it is important to determine whether the program as a whole contributes to economic stability.[4] This involves consideration of the relationship of OASDHI tax collections to benefit payments, legislative changes in the benefit and tax schedules, and trust-fund deficits and surpluses.

OASDHI Taxes. For an ideal countercyclical effect, OASDHI tax collections should automatically decline during recessions, thereby making available relatively more funds for consumption and investment purposes. Likewise, during expansionary periods, OASDHI tax collections should automatically increase, thereby siphoning off funds that would otherwise be used for private consumption and investment.

Based on this analysis, the OASDHI payroll tax is a poor automatic stabilizer. Although it does not exert perverse effects on the economy by increasing automatically during recessions, nevertheless it does not respond in a sensitive way to changes in business activity. That is, in contrast to the federal income tax, actual OASDHI tax collections provide no evidence of increasing automatically during expansions and decreasing during recessions.

In addition, the contribution of OASDHI tax collections to economic stability is often hindered by poorly timed payroll-tax increases. Because of legislative tax schedules that extend many years into the future, the tax rates may increase automatically during recessions. For example, in 1937, a 2 percent tax on payrolls became effective five months before the beginning of a severe business recession. Tax-rate increases also went into effect during the 1953-54 recession, shortly before the beginning of the 1957 and 1960 recessions, and during the slowdown in economic growth in 1967. Thus, it can be concluded

---

[4]For an extensive analysis of the impact of the OASDHI program on economic stability, see Joseph A. Pechman, Henry J. Aaron, and Michael K. Taussig, *Social Security: Perspectives for Reform* (Washington, D.C.: The Brookings Institution, 1968), pp. 173-212; and Tax Foundation, Inc., *Economic Aspects of the Social Security Tax* (New York: Tax Foundation, Inc., 1966), pp. 51-54.

that the OASDHI payroll tax is a relatively poor automatic stabilizer, owing to its lack of sensitivity to changes in business activity.[5]

OASDHI Benefits. OASDHI benefits do tend to contribute to economic stability during business recessions, for two reasons. First, some older unemployed workers may retire early during recessions, since good jobs are not available, and the OASDHI benefits they receive help cushion the loss of work earnings. Second, OASDHI benefits generally increase after higher tax rates become effective, so the initial deflationary effect of the tax rate increase is somewhat offset. And in addition, greater attention is now being given to the timing of tax-rate and benefit increases from the viewpoint of appropriate fiscal policy.[6]

On the other hand, the effectiveness of OASDHI benefits as an automatic stabilizer is reduced during inflationary periods, because Congress will generally increase benefits then to offset the loss of purchasing power and real income. Also, under the automatic-adjustment provision, the benefits will rise automatically during periods of rapid inflation—and this is the wrong time, in terms of desirable countercyclical policy. Such an increase is justified, however, when the major function of the OASDHI program is considered. Its primary function is the maintenance of income to the aged and other beneficiaries; the automatic-stabilizer function is secondary.

OASDHI Trust Funds. Because the trust funds are seldom fiscally neutral, it is important to examine their actual behavior to determine their contribution, if any, to economic stability. Trust-fund surpluses and deficits can contribute to or detract from economic stability, depending on when they occur. Between 1937 and 1941, the trust-fund accumulations were considered undesirable in view of the relatively high unemployment rates that prevailed. The period between 1942 and 1956 was generally characterized by inflation and relatively high employment (except for the 1948-49 and 1953-54 recessions), and on balance, the trust-fund surplus accumulated during this period contributed to economic stability. Between 1957 and 1965, the trust funds showed both small deficits and surpluses. During 1966 and 1967, as inflationary pressures increased and fiscal and monetary policy became more restrictive, the trust funds showed a surplus, which tended to reinforce general fiscal policy.[7] And between 1968 and 1970, the trust funds also accumulated a surplus, which tended to reinforce the anti-inflationary policies that President Nixon had enacted. However, the substantial trust-fund surplus that occurred in 1969 was an important factor that contributed to the economic slowdown during that period. The combined OASDHI trust fund also accumulated a surplus in 1973 and 1974, thereby intensifying the recession that began in November 1973.

Total System. Payroll taxes, benefits, and trust-fund surpluses and deficits are not independent entities; the entire OASDHI program must be examined to determine its countercyclical impact on the economy. Peter Eilbott studied critically the effectiveness of the automatic stabilizers as a countercyclical

[5]Pechman et al., *Social Security*, pp. 183-84.

[6]*Ibid.*

[7]*Ibid.*, p. 209.

tool for three recessions and expansions from 1948 to 1960. He concluded that all built-in stabilizers during three postwar recessions prevented an average of 36 to 52 percent of the decline in national income that would have occurred in their absence. During expansionary periods, potential increases in national income were reduced by as much as 25 to 42 percent by the automatic stabilizers.

However, when the effects of the OASDHI program are excluded from the calculations, the total effectiveness of the automatic stabilizers is reduced during recessionary periods and enhanced during expansionary upswings. This is due to the steady increases in OASDHI benefits that occured throughout the postwar period. Therefore, after both benefits and taxes are considered, Eilbott concludes that *the OASDHI program has been stabilizing during recessions and destabilizing during expansionary periods.* [8] On balance, it would seem that the OASDHI program contributes to economic stability.

A more recent study, by Pechman, Aaron, and Taussig, comes to the same conclusion, despite the regressiveness of the payroll tax and the inappropriate timing of tax-rate increases during certain periods. However, this study says the contribution of the program to economic stability would have been greater if an elastic source of revenue (such as personal income tax) had been substituted for the payroll tax. [9]

Using the OASDHI Program as a Countercyclical Tool. Although policy makers cannot ignore the long-run fiscal impact of the OASDHI program, it is questionable whether tax rates, benefits, and the earnings base should be frequently changed because of short-run countercyclical considerations. Some social insurance scholars seriously question the desirability of using the program as a countercyclical tool. [10] They feel that, first, the financing of the program may be jeopardized. A sound social insurance program must have a definite plan for the financing of benefits, and arbitrary changes in tax rates for fiscal-policy purposes could seriously weaken its financial soundness. For example, if a severe recession required the reduction of OASDHI payroll taxes over an extended period, there would arise the danger of generating insufficient revenues for maintaining the financial solvency of the program. Moreover, frequent manipulation of payroll tax rates upward and downward might be psychologically disturbing to the insured population, and would surely make it difficult for businessmen to make rational business decisions.

Second, taxes are difficult to adjust upward and downward with great speed. Congress is slow to enact tax increases, and even tax reductions may take a considerable amount of time to accomplish. Thus, adjustment of OASDHI tax rates to business-cycle conditions might be difficult to achieve in time for it to do any good.

Finally, use of the OASDHI program for this purpose implies also adjustments in the benefit level. And a downward adjustment of benefits because of

[8]Peter Eilbott, "The Effectiveness of Automatic Stabilizers," *The American Economic Review,* Vol. LVI, No. 3 (June 1966), 458, Table 2; and 462-63.

[9]Pechman et al., *Social Security,* pp. 183-84.

[10]Robert J. Myers, "The Past and Future of Old-Age, Survivors, and Disability Insurance," in William G. Bowen, Frederick H. Harbison, Richard A. Lester, and Herman M. Somers, eds., *The Princeton Symposium on the American System of Social Insurance: Its Philosophy, Impact, and Future Development* (New York: McGraw-Hill, 1968), p. 101.

countercyclical considerations would be undesirable from the standpoint of sound social insurance policy. In particular, such an adjustment would reduce to poverty many of the aged who are now kept above that level only by the amount of their OASDHI benefits. Thus, it may be undesirable to use the OASDHI program as a short-run countercyclical tool.

Economic Growth

Most economists agree that economic growth can increase faster if the rate of investment increases. Assuming that full employment can be maintained, the federal government contributes to investment by accumulating a budgetary surplus, which adds to national saving and provides the necessary resources by which private investment can take place. National saving is defined as the difference between the nation's output and the consumption expenditures of consumers and government. Investment, however, is also equal to that portion of the nation's output that is not consumed. Thus, national saving is equal to private investment. It follows, therefore, that an increase in national saving can speed up economic growth by facilitating private investment. And a trust-fund surplus adds to national saving, whereas a trust-fund deficit subtracts from national saving.

Based on this analysis, the OASDHI program has probably had only a modest impact on the rate of economic growth.[11] The OASDHI trust funds can have a favorable effect on economic growth if they add to national saving in the long run. But the trust funds have historically generated only a relatively small surplus. Between fiscal 1959 and 1966, they had an average annual deficit of $12 million; between fiscal 1967 and 1971, their surplus averaged only about $4.3 billion annually; during fiscal 1973, the projected surplus had increased to $9.8 billion.[12] However, the relative contribution of this surplus to total national saving, and therefore the impact of the OASDHI program on economic growth, was small.

Redistribution of Income

The OASDHI program is a system of public transfer payments that leads to a redistribution of income, since the relative share of benefits received by some groups differs from their relative share in the financing of benefits. In particular, the lower-income groups receive proportionately larger benefits compared to their contributions, since the benefit formula weights the benefits heavily in their favor; large families receive relatively higher survivorship and retirement benefits than do single persons; the currently retired aged are receiving benefits whose actuarial value substantially exceeds the actuarial value of their contributions; and, subsequent benefit increases to retired OASDHI recipients also results in the receipt of large amounts of unearned income. The combined effect of these factors is a redistribution of income.

[11]Pechman et al., *Social Security*, p. 211.

[12]U.S. Department of Health, Education and Welfare, *Trust Fund and Budget Position*, p. 4, Table 1.

Types of Redistribution. Two major forms of income redistribution prevail in the OASDHI program.[13] The first is *interbracket income transfers,* whereby income is transferred from higher to lower income groups; the lower-income groups' benefits come to a higher proportion of their average taxable incomes than those of workers with higher incomes. Second, *intergeneration transfers* transfer income from one age group to another; in particular, from the younger workers in the labor force to the aged who have retired and are receiving benefits of higher actuarial value than that of their contributions.

Several researchers have attempted to measure the magnitude of both forms of income redistribution.[14] Elizabeth Deran, in measuring interbracket income transfers, concludes that redistribution has gradually increased over time, especially with respect to the OASDHI recipients who are receiving minimum benefits. This is because minimum benefit levels have been gradually increased, but the level of qualifying wages has remained constant.

To measure these transfers, Deran compares the basic monthly benefits received with average taxable wages (called a B/W ratio) for the different income groups. This value is a rough indicator of how much an OASDHI recipient receives in benefits compared to the taxes that he pays. Of two recipients, the one with the higher B/W ratio is considered better off, since he receives more for each tax dollar paid into the system. Income is redistributed over time from a low B/W beneficiary to a higher B/W beneficiary, who receives a relatively greater bargain for his contributions. For 1965, Deran computes a B/W ratio of .31 for a worker earning maximum taxable wages; for the low-income worker who barely qualifies for the minimum benefit, she obtains a B/W value of 2.6, indicating clearly that the lower-income person receives relatively higher benefits compared to the taxes paid than does the upper-income person.[15] Although the B/W values have increased for all income groups over time, the lower-income groups have made relatively greater gains, so it would seem that greater amounts of income have been redistributed from the higher to the lower income groups over time.

Deran has also studied the intergeneration redistribution of income. Present OASDHI recipients are enjoying windfall gains, since they have paid in taxes only a small fraction of the true actuarial cost of their benefits. For example, based on the 1965 law as amended, a married male worker who retired in 1970 would have paid taxes with a cumulative value of $4,567 at 3.5 percent compound interest, but the value of his benefits (discounted at 3.5 percent) would be $28,270. Thus, the value of the tax payments is 16.2 percent of the value of benefits.[16] Someone, however, must pay for this windfall bargain, and

[13]Elizabeth Deran, "Some Economic Effects of High Taxes for Social Insurance," in U.S. Congress, Subcommittee on Fiscal Policy of the Joint Economic Committee, *Old Age Income Assurance, A Compendium of Papers on Problems and Policy Issues in the Public and Private Pension System; Part III, Public Programs,* 90th Cong., 1st sess., (Washington, D.C.: U.S. Government Printing Office, 1967), pp. 196-97. See also Tax Foundation, Inc., *Economic Aspects,* pp. 48-49.

[14]See Henry Aaron, "Benefits under the American Social Security System," in Otto Eckstein, ed., *Studies in the Economics of Income Maintenance* (Washington, D.C.: The Brookings Institution, 1967), pp. 49-71; and Elizabeth Deran, "Income Redistribution under the Social Security System," *National Tax Journal,* Vol. 29, No. 3 (September 1966), 276-85.

[15]Deran, "Some Economic Effects of Higher Taxes for Social Insurance," p. 198, Table 7.

[16]*Ibid.,* p. 197, Table 6.

it is primarily the younger working generation, whose tax contributions are used to finance the benefits of the older generation. It is estimated that the cost of paying full benefits to today's retired workers is about one-third of the total cost of the OASDHI program.[17] These unearned benefits paid to the retired age can be viewed as an intergeneration transfer of income.

Arguments for Greater Redistribution. Some people believe that a greater redistribution of income should be achieved under the OASDHI program, for several reasons. First, it is argued that greater income redistribution would help to close the poverty gap. However, as we saw in Chapter 6, the OASDHI program is inefficient for this purpose, since most benefit increases aimed at closing the poverty gap would go largely to the nonpoor.[18] In addition, relatively large amounts must be spent to close a small fraction of the gap. Substantial benefit increases are necessary to reduce the poverty of the aged, but the same benefit increases would have only a minor impact on the poverty of the nonaged poor. And since the OASDHI program is primarily for the aged, but the majority of poor people are under age 65, the program is inefficient in redistributing income to them.

Second, it is said that greater amounts of income should be redistributed under the OASDHI program to reach a stated target. One target is to replace all or part of the income loss from certain well-defined social risks. For example, about half the OASDHI recipients have no other source of income, and benefit increases can replace a larger portion of the loss of income because of retirement, thereby providing greater economic security to the aged.

Finally, the OASDHI program can be used to reduce income inequality in the United States. Recent research studies indicate that the OASDHI program is extremely effective in this respect. The Council of Economic Advisers has estimated the extent to which the program reduces income inequality, using the technique known as the "variance in the natural logarithm of income." If perfect equality of income existed, this measure would have value of zero. A reduction in this value means that income inequality is reduced. For example, if a particular public income-maintenance program reduces the value of this measure from 0.7 to 0.6, a decline in income inquality is indicated.[19]

The following data based on this technique indicate the extent to which the OASDHI program reduced income inequality in the United States for 1970:[20]

All income	.74
All income, excluding Social Security	1.16
All income, excluding all transfer income	1.57

[17]U.S. Congress, House, *Reports of the 1971 Advisory Council on Social Security*, H. Doc. No. 92-80, 92d Cong., 1st sess., 1971 (Washington, D.C.: U.S. Government Printing Office, 1971), p. 75.

[18]See George E. Rejda, "Social Security and the Paradox of the Welfare State," *The Journal of Risk and Insurance*, Vol. XXXVII, No. 1 (March 1970), 17-39.

[19]Council of Economic Advisers, *Economic Report of the President*, 1974, pp. 179-80.

[20]*Ibid.*, p. 178, Table 49; and p. 179.

The value of the variance in the natural logarithm for all income, .74, indicates that income inequality existed in the United States. If OASDHI benefits are excluded, however, this measure sharply increases to 1.16, showing that income inequality would be even greater without the OASDHI program. And if *all* transfer payments are excluded (OASDHI, unemployment insurance, workmen's compensation, public assistance, government employee pensions, and veterans' benefits), the measure of income inequality increases even more. Thus, the Council of Economic Advisers concludes that the OASDHI program (along with public assistance) has dramatically decreased income inequality in the United States.

Arguments against Greater Redistribution. Those who are against a greater redistribution of income under the OASDHI program argue, first, that it would further weaken the social insurance principle of relating OASDHI benefits to average monthly earnings. The lower-income groups would be receiving benefits that have little or no relation to their average earnings and the tax contributions paid on these earnings.

Second, a greater redistribution of income under OASDHI would increase the welfare element in the program and dilute even more the insurance element. And if the welfare element is substantially increased, then the present system of payroll financing is objectionable; it should be financed more equitably by general revenues, since payroll taxes are not based on the ability to pay.

Third, a greater redistribution of income under the OASDHI program could reduce work incentives, especialy by increasing the minimum benefit. Not all those receiving the minimum benefit are low-income persons; many are, for instance, retired federal-government employees who have worked in the private sector just long enough to qualify for OASDHI benefits, or people who have deliberately worked only the minimum amount of time to qualify. The case is cited of a woman who was considering retirement from an administrative job that was not covered at that time under the program. She persuaded her brother who owned a department store, to hire her part-time, so she could earn $50 quarterly and accumulate a sufficient number of quarters to qualify for minimum benefits. Although she did not need the income, she reasoned that it was silly to pass up the benefits for which she could easily qualify.[21]

Finally, it is argued that there are superior methods of redistributing income to low-income people. In particular, personal and corporate income taxes are considered much more efective in reducing income inequality and redistributing income than is the OASDHI program.

Consumption and Saving

The OASDHI program also has important macroeconomic effects on consumption, saving, and the level of aggregate demand in the economy.

Consumption and Aggregate Demand. According to economic theory, the initial short-run impact of a new social insurance program financed by payroll taxes is deflationary, since disposable income, and hence consumption

[21]Deran, "Some Economic Effects of High Taxes for Social Insurance," p. 199.

spending, is reduced by the amount of the taxes. However, after a time lag, most tax contributions are paid out as benefits, and if the group receiving the transfer payments has a *higher marginal propensity* to consume than has the group on which the taxes are levied, the overall impact is expansionary. For example, assume that the working population under age 65 has a marginal propensity to consume of .75. Assume also that disposable income for this group is reduced by $100 because of a social insurance payroll tax, with this sum transferred to the aged and other low-income groups with a marginal propensity to consume of .90. The working population under age 65 reduces its consumption expenditures by $75 as a result of the $100 reduction in its disposable income. But the low-income groups gain $100, and their consumption increases by $90. Thus, the net gain in consumption spending is $15.

Based on this example, one is tempted to conclude that a greater redistribution of income under OASDH is desirable in order to shift the consumption function upward. Economists generally believe, however, that a redistribution of income from the upper to the lower income groups will not appreciably affect consumption spending, since recent empirical research on the consumption function indicates that differences in both the short-run and long-run marginal propensity to consume for the various income groups under $10,000 are not great. (This income level is used because the bulk of the OASDHI tax contributions are derived from the income groups under $10,000.) Table 19-2 illustrates this point. The marginal propensity to consume for the various income groups under $10,000 is roughly the same, suggesting that any interbracket income transfers from high to low income groups under the OASDHI program may result in only a modest expansion of aggregate demand.

TABLE 19-2 Short-Run and Long-Run Marginal Propensity to Consume for Various Income Groups

Income Bracket	Short-Run MPC	Long-Run MPC
$ 0 - 1,000	.33	.84
1,000 - 2,000	.32	.83
2,000 - 3,000	.32	.81
3,000 - 4,000	.31	.79
4,000 - 5,000	.30	.77
5,000 - 6,000	.29	.75
6,000 - 7,500	.29	.73
7,500 - 10,000	.27	.70
10,000 - 15,000	.25	.64
over 15,000	.18	.45

Source: Ralph D. Husby, "A Nonlinear Consumption Function Estimated from Time-Series and Cross-Section Data," *The Review of Economics and Statistics,* Vol. LII, No. 1 (February 1971), 78, Table 1.

On the other hand, it should be noted that the influence of the marginal propensity to consume, and any resulting multiplier effects, on consumption and spending is limited to only the *initial change* in disposable income for both the upper and lower income groups. If both OASDHI payroll taxes and benefits are increased, a permanent redistribution of income occurs in the direction of greater equality. Once this happens, the *average propensity to consume,* rather than the marginal propensity, will govern.[22] Since the average propensity to consume is higher for the lower income groups, the OASDHI program could be considered expansionary.

Other factors also suggest that, on balance, the OASDHI program is probably expansionary. Some business firms and industries with monopoly pricing powers may shift all or part of their portion of the OASDHI payroll tax forward to the public in the form of higher prices. Also, since the excess of tax contributions over benefits paid is invested by the OASDHI trust funds in government bonds, and the Treasury spends the sums it receives from the trust funds, the effects are expansionary, especially when a sizable proportion of government expenditures are used to finance war goods, as in recent years. Finally, labor unions may press for higher money wages because of the higher OASDHI taxes, which reduce real wages. The combined effects of these factors probably make the OASDHI program expansionary in the long run.

This analysis, however, must be carefully qualified. Social insurance programs can be deflationary at times when aggregate demand is depressed. Recent empirical studies, such as one by Wayne Vroman, on the macroeconomic effects of social insurance on aggregate demand show that the same program can be expansionary or deflationary during different time periods. Vroman found that the 1965 amendments to the Social Security Act increased the real gross national product by $2.7 billion for that year, but lowered it by $3.6 billion in 1966 (largely because of the Medicare program, which required an increase in OASDHI tax contributions). Vroman also concludes that social insurance programs, especially unemployment insurance, lend considerable stability to aggregate demand in the economy. The presence of social insurance reduces the impact multiplier of government expenditures on the real gross national product from 2.50 to 2.02. As a stabilizer of aggregate demand, social insurance is about seven-tenths as strong as the federal personal income tax.[23]

In summary, recent empirical studies regarding the effects of social insurance programs on the level and stability of aggregate demand come to the following conclusions: First, changes in social insurance provisions have measurable although modest effects on the level of aggregate demand. This is true even though changes in tax contributions and benefit payments are identical, because the multiplier effect from changes in social insurance transfer payments is greater than the multiplier effect resulting from changes in the tax contributions paid by employers, employees, and the self-employed. Second, equal increases in social insurance transfer payments and tax contributions affect not only the level but also the composition of aggregate demand, with consumer demand shifting away from durable goods toward nondurable goods and services. Finally, as social insurance programs grow in importance over

---

[22]Wallace C. Peterson, *Income, Employment, and Economic Growth,* 3rd ed. (New York: Norton, 1974), p. 166.

[23]Wayne G. Vroman, *Macroeconomic Effects of Social Insurance on Aggregate Demand,* U.S. Department of Health, Education and Welfare, Social Security Administration, Office of Research and Statistics, Staff Paper No. 2, July 1969, pp. 63-64.

time, their macroeconomic effects must be recognized by policy makers if prices and demand are to be effectively stabilized.[24]

Personal Saving. In regard to the impact of the OASDHI program on personal saving, one hypothesis is that the program reduces private saving, since the need to save for retirement purposes is reduced. But a second hypothesis states that the OASDHI program may provide an incentive to save more, since it reduces the major threats to the worker's economic insecurity, allowing him to seek additional savings goals.

The available evidence is inconclusive. One study by Prof. George Katona suggests that people who are covered by private and government pensions tend to save more in the long run than do those who are not covered. This can be explained, at least partly by the *goal gradient hypothesis,* which states that individual effort is more intensified the closer one is to his goal. Katona suggests that when the problem of saving for old age does not appear insurmountable, the closer a person is to the goal of adequate income for his old age, the harder he is willing to work to attain that goal. Thus, Katona concludes, collective retirement plans tend to promote greater individual savings.[25] Based on the preceding analysis, the OASDHI program promotes rather than retards individual saving in the long run.

On the other hand, a recent study by Alicia Munnell casts doubt on the proposition that the OASDHI program promotes private saving in the long run. She says that, although the OASDHI program appears to have a neutral influence on the savings rate, this apparent neutrality is really the net result of two strong but opposing forces. First, using time series and cross section data to support her position, she says that the OASDHI program depresses the savings rate since the guaranteed benefits reduce the need to save for old-age. Second, the OASDHI program indirectly stimulates the saving rate through its impact on retirement; a lengthening of the retirement period forces an individual to save more during his working years, and since the OASDHI program encourages retirement, it therefore stimulates saving. The net result is that the OASDHI program appears to have a neutral influence on the savings rate. She says, however, that this neutrality may not exist in the future. Although these two forces may have offset each other in the past, it is unlikely that this balance will continue in the future. Thus, with all other factors held constant, she believes that the net effect of the OASDHI program in the future will be a serious decline in the savings rate.[26]

Burden of OASDHI Taxes

In view of the fact that the OASDHI payroll tax is the second most im-

[24]*Ibid.*

[25]George Katona, *Private Pensions and Individual Saving,* Monograph No. 40 (Ann Arbor, Mich.: Survey Research Center, Institute for Social Research, 1965), pp. 1-6. See also Phillip Cagan, *The Effect of Pension Plans on Aggregate Demand: Evidence from a Sample Survey,* National Bureau of Economic Research, Occasional Paper 95 (New York: Columbia University Press, 1965).

[26]Alicia Haydock Munnell, *The Effect of Social Security on Personal Saving* (Cambridge, Mass.: Ballinger Publishing Co., 1974). See also "The Effect of Social Security on Personal Saving," *Social Security Bulletin,* Vol. 37, No. 11 (November 1974), pp. 29-30.

portant source of federal revenues, ranking only behind the personal income tax, it is important to analyze its economic burden. Our analysis will cover the incidence of OASDHI payroll taxes, their regressiveness, and the economic effects of seasonality in tax collections.

Incidence of OASDHI taxes. Tax incidence refers to the final resting place of the tax. Since the OASDHI tax is levied on the payrolls of most occupations and industries, the employee's portion of the total tax is borne entirely by the worker. He generally cannot escape paying it by changing occupations or by shifting it to someone else.

Business firms, on the other hand, do attempt to shift their portion of the OASDHI tax, so most or all employer payroll taxes are ultimately borne by labor in the long run. The firms may shift it backward to the workers in the form of lower wage increases, forward to the public in the form of higher prices, or both; or they may substitute labor-saving machinery for human labor as social insurance taxes increase. So it would seem that in the long run, labor pays the employer's portion of the tax.

Research studies generally support the hypothesis that all payroll taxes, whether paid out by employers or employees, are absorbed by labor in the form of lower wages.[27] Firms generally take the view that the OASDHI tax is part of the total compensation paid to labor, and that a payroll tax increase does not make labor more productive, but only increases the employer's cost. So a firm may attempt to reduce employment at the given wage, which includes the payroll tax. If the total labor supply is inelastic with respect to small wage changes, as is generally asumed, the same number of workers can remain employed only if their wages fall by the amount of the tax. In a cross-section analysis of countries with relatively high employer taxes, John Brittain found that the imposition of a payroll tax does tend to reduce wages by roughly the amount of the tax. [28] What usually happens in practice is that money wages do not actually fall, but the firm recoups the higher OASDHI tax by granting lower wage increases than it would without the tax, thus shifting the employer's portion of the tax to labor.

The conclusion that labor may bear the entire burden of payroll taxes has several important implications.[29] First, if payroll taxes have no net cost impact on business firms, the incentive to substitute capital for labor is reduced. The conclusion that the entire tax falls on labor then weakens the commonly held argument that higher payroll taxes tend to promote automation and the displacement of workers, with higher unemployment as a result.

Second, the view that labor bears the full burden of the tax is important for collective-bargaining purposes. If both employers and labor unions recognize that employer payroll taxes are clearly part of the total cost of hiring labor, along with fringe benefits and actual money wages paid, this recognition may lead to a trade-off between fringe benefits and wage increases on one hand and employer contributions on the other.

[27]See John A. Brittain, *The Payroll Tax for Social Security* (Washington, D.C.: The Brookings Institution, 1972), Chaps. II and III; and Joseph A. Pechman, *Federal Tax Policy,* rev. ed. (New York: Norton, 1971), pp. 176-78.

[28]John A. Brittain, "The Incidence of Social Security Payroll Taxes," *The American Economic Review,* Vol. LXI, No. 1 (March 1971), 110-25.

[29]*Ibid.*

Third, the ultimate incidence of the tax is important from the view-point of income distribution. Since labor may bear the entire burden of payroll taxes, the impact and burden of these taxes on the lower-income groups may be greater than is commonly believed. The fact that the OASDHI tax by itself is regressive would suggest that payroll taxes as a form of taxation should be reduced or even eliminated. The lower-income groups could be exempt from all or part of the OASDHI tax, or the income tax could be substituted for all or part of the payroll tax.

Finally, the view that labor bears the entire burden of payroll taxes is also important in evaluating the OASDHI program. Although the Social Security Administration concedes that the entire payroll tax is borne largely by labor in the aggregate, the employers' portion is ignored when the tax paid by individuals is calculated, on the grounds that is is impossible to impute the employers' tax to individuals when comparing lifetime taxes and benefits under the OASDHI program. But if OASDHI taxes are paid by labor as a group, they must also be paid by workers as individuals. Thus, it may be better to make imperfect imputations that are roughly right than to settle for being precisely wrong. Imputation of employer payroll taxes to individuals would mean that wage and salary earners would be credited with paying the entire tax for unemployment insurance, and under the OASDHI program, twice as much as the amount that is actually being deducted from their covered earnings. And if individual taxpayers become aware of the true burden of OASDHI taxes, there might be decreased reliance on this regressive form of taxation.

Regressive or Progressive. It is commonly believed that, based on wages alone, the OASDHI tax is proportional up to the taxable wage base, and regressive thereafter. However, the taxes are paid out in benefits largely to lower-income groups who have little or no other income. Since the benefit formula weights the benefits heavily in favor of these groups, it is argued that, on balance, the OASDHI program is highly progressive in its operations.

But the preceding viewpoint is misleading when one major characteristic of the program is considered. *The OASDHI tax is levied on one group in the economy, but the benefits are largely received by other groups.* Thus, if the taxes paid and benefits received are aggregated by income classes, distortion of the real burden of the OASDHI tax may result. At any given time, the tax is either proportional or regressive with respect to the incomes of covered workers who must pay it. But the benefits are paid largely to people with little other income. Thus, a more accurate analysis of the regressivity or progressivity of OASDHI taxes and benefits can be obtained if the two groups are analyzed separately—the taxpayers and the beneficiaries.

When the tax side is considered alone, an assumption must be made concerning the incidence of the employer tax. If it is assumed that the employer shifts the tax forward to the public, the OASDHI tax is as regressive as any other consumption tax. If the tax is assumed to be shifted backward, it is slightly progressive up to $7,000 or $8,000 of money income, and regressive thereafter.[30]

When the group receiving the benefits is analyzed, the OASDHI program is considered highly progressive.[31] The benefits account for two-thirds or more of

[30]Pechman et al., *Social Security*, p. 179.

[31]*Ibid.*

the total family income for those families with money incomes of less than $2,000, but only 2 percent or less of the total money income of families in the upper-income groups. This effect comes about largely because of the weighted benefit formula and the lack of large amounts of other money income by low-income OASDHI beneficiaries.

Seasonality. The collection of OASDHI taxes is characterized by a strong seasonal element. People who earn high enough incomes pay the maximum tax before the end of the year, and then have an increased disposable income for the remainder of the year before resuming payment of OASDHI taxes the following January. This seasonality in OASDHI tax collections creates an unevenness in disposable income in the economy.

Joseph M. Bonin has analyzed the economic effects of seasonality in OASDHI collections and arrives at several major conclusions.[32] First, between 1952 and 1964, seasonality in Social Security tax collections had considerable influence on personal consumption expenditures. The impact was strong enough to alter the variation in purchase of consumer durable goods, about 24 to 65 percent of which was explained by the seasonality in OASDHI tax collections.

Second, payment of the maximum tax before the end of the year results in a temporary "windfall" increase for people with higher-than-average incomes. Thus, an inverse relationship exists between the distribution of seasonality and the burden of the tax. In addition, termination of the tax has an expansionary effect on the economy that occurs at the same time as the normal peak buying period of the year—the Christmas-shopping season—thus intensifying the peak-load problem in the economy.

Finally, seasonality in Social Security tax collections has increased over time, owing primarily to the failure to increase the maximum taxable wage base concurrently with rising wage levels. Also, extensions of coverage and higher tax rates have increased the absolute magnitude and the economic impact of the seasonal fluctuations. It is estimated that a taxable wage base of about $15,000 annually will remove most of the seasonality now present in OASDHI tax collections.

ECONOMIC IMPACT OF UNEMPLOYMENT INSURANCE

Analysis of the economic impact of unemployment insurance requires a consideration of both its primary and secondary objectives. As explained in Chapter 16, the primary objective is to assist the worker during short-term involuntary unemployment by the payment of weekly cash benefits whereby his purchasing power can be maintained, and the secondary objective is to promote economic stability. Thus, two major areas of unemployment insurance must be analyzed: (1) its effectiveness in maintaining purchasing power, and (2) its effectiveness in promoting economic stability.

[32]Joseph M. Bonin, *Some Economic Effects of Seasonality in OASDHI Tax Payments,* U.S. Department of Health, Education and Welfare, Social Security Administration, Office of Research and Statistics, Research Report No. 20 (Washington, D.C.: U.S. Government Printing Office, 1967), pp. 43-44.

Maintenance of Purchasing Power

Students of unemployment insurance generally agree that, in order to maintain the unemployed worker's purchasing power so that his standard of living is not unduly reduced, the weekly unemployment benefit should be at least equal to 50 percent of the worker's average weekly wage. Some proposals would require weekly benefits at least equal to two-thirds of the state's average weekly wage. In addition, some experts recommend the payment of dependents, benefits. It is generally agreed that most occupations should be covered, and that a benefit duration of at least 26 weeks should be provided.

From the viewpoint of individual economic security, unemployment-insurance programs are generally deficient for maintaining the purchasing power of unemployed workers. Studies made some years ago found this to be true,[33] and the current situation is not much better. Only 26 states paid maximum unemployment benefits in 1972 that restored 50 percent of the covered worker's average weekly wage.[34] In addition, the more realistic standard of paying a maximum benefit equal to two-thirds of the state's average weekly wage is met in only a few states. Thus, most states must make substantial improvements in the level of unemployment benefits to enable unemployed workers to maintain their previous purchasing power.

Finally, only a fraction of those unemployed at any given time receive unemployment insurance benefits. *At best, the various state programs maintain purchasing power for only about one-third of the unemployed during periods of high employment and not much more than 50 percent during recession periods.*[35] This is due primarily to coverage limitations, restrictive eligibility requirements, exhaustion of benefits, disqualification provisions, and the initial waiting period.

Economic Stability

For a desirable countercyclical effect, unemployment benefits should increase sharply during business downswings and decline markedly during upswings; and unemployment-tax rates should not increase during recession periods. Thus, a correct evaluation of unemployment insurance as an automatic stabilizer requires an analysis of both benefits and taxes during upswings and downswings.

Unemployment Benefits. Unemployment benefits do respond in a sensitive way to cyclical declines. A study of four postwar business cycles between 1948 and 1964 indicated that, during three of the four downswings, approximately 24 to 28 percent of the decline in national income was offset by an in-

[33]See Joseph M. Becker, *The Adequacy of the Benefit Amount in Unemployment Insurance* (Kalamazoo, Mich.: The W.E. Upjohn Institute for Employment Research, 1961); and Richard A. Lester, *The Economics of Unemployment Compensation* (Princeton, N.J.: Princeton University, Industrial Relations Section, 1962).

[34]U.S. Department of Labor, *Manpower Report of the President* (Washington, D.C.: U.S. Government Printing Office, 1972), p. 73.

[35]Merrill G. Murray, *Income for the Unemployed, The Variety and Fragmentation of Programs* (Kalamazoo, Mich.: The W.E. Upjohn Institute for Employment Research, 1971), p. 11.

crease in unemployment benefits.[36] This suggests that the performance of unemployment insurance as an automatic stabilizer could be improved by increasing benefit levels.

But despite their quick response to cyclical downswings, the benefits are relatively ineffective as an automatic stabilizer during upswings. From the viewpoint of desirable short-run fiscal policy, the unemployment benefits should decline sharply as national income increases. However, the evidence indicates that they tend to lag considerably during periods of economic upswing. As we saw in Chapter 15, they seem to increase during the initial states of recovery, turning downward only some months after the lowest point of the cycle has been reached, and carrying their stimulative impact into the expansion phase of the next cycle.

Finally, it should be noted that the unemployment benefits can be destabilizing at times, when the entire business cycle is considered. Prof. Neil A. Palomba, in a variance analysis study of unemployment insurance, found that during first and fourth of the four postwar cycles under study, the benefits were stabilizing over the entire cycles, but during the second and third, they were destabilizing.[37]

It must be remembered, however, that the primary objective of unemployment insurance is to maintain the purchasing power and income of the unemployed worker; the goal of economic stability is secondary.

Unemployment Taxes. The behavior of unemployment-insurance tax collections and tax rates must also be examined when the countercyclical effects of unemployment insurance are analyzed. A common belief is that the experience-rating provisions in state unemployment-insurance laws aggravate cyclical downswings by increasing taxes at the wrong time. An increase in unemployment results in an increase in unemployment benefits, which decreases the size of the state's account in the unemployment-insurance trust fund. Thus, employer contribution rates must go up, and the increased tax burden aggravates the business-cycle downswing.

Current research studies suggest that this view of experience rating is incorrect, and that unemployment taxes have actually been stabilizing rather than destabilizing during postwar business cycles. One study of the cyclical behavior of absolute unemployment taxes, the collection ratio, and the average employer contribution rate during four postwar cycles shows that absolute unemployment taxes have tended to move in a desirable countercyclical manner—declining (or increasing less rapidly) during cycle downswings and increasing during cycle upswings.[38] In addition, the empirical evidence indicates no clear-cut cyclical tendency for the collection ratio and average employer contribution rate to increase significantly during downswings.

Palomba also concludes that unemployment-tax collections and experience rating are stabilizing. In his study of four postwar cycles, he found

---

[36]George E. Rejda, "Unemployment Insurance as an Automatic Stabilizer," *The Journal of Risk and Insurance,* Vol. XXXIII, No. 2 (June 1966), 195-208.

[37]Neil A. Palomba, "Unemployment Compensation Program: Stabilizing or Destabilizing?" *Journal of Political Economy,* Vol. 76 (January-February 1968), 91-100.

[38]Rejda, "Unemployment Insurance," pp. 195-208.

that unemployment collections behaved in a stabilizing rather than destabilizing fashion during all four periods, even though the degree of stability they imparted was small (the variance in GNP was reduced less than 3 percent). In addition, Palomba concludes that the various state experience-rating formulas reveal no real differences from a stabilizing point of view, and that a flat 2.7 percent tax rate would have been almost as stabilizing as the actual collections under each state experience-rating formula.[39]

Finally, in an econometric study of the macroeconomic effects of social insurance programs on aggregate demand, Wayne G. Vroman also concluded that unemployment contributions under present state unemployment-insurance programs impart considerable stability to the economy.[40]

Experience Rating and Economic Stability. In Chapter 16, we examined the reasons why experience rating may not be destabilizing. These reasons bear repeating.

First, experience rating may not be destabilizing during recession periods because of the time lag between an increase in unemployment in the firm and higher employer contribution rates. Owing to the time lag and the relative shortness of our postwar recessions, the recession may be over before the higher tax rates have to be paid. Thus, employer contribution rates do not immediately increase for firms during periods of recession.

Second, during periods of high unemployment, workers are laid off, so taxable payrolls tend to decline, and the absolute unemployment taxes paid by the firms on behalf of the laid-off workers are eliminated. The result is that absolute unemployment taxes tend to decline during recessionary periods (or else increase less rapidly) in a desirable countercyclical manner.

Finally, employer contribution rates have only a minor influence in reducing the stabilizing effect of unemployment benefits. The benefits tend to stimulate aggregate demand in the economy, but their stimulative effects are reduced somewhat by the dampening effects of employer contribution rates. Higher employer contributions after a period of unemployment (after a lag of one to two years) increase a firm's unit costs. If the firm increases its prices to offset these higher unit costs, real disposable income is reduced, thus partially offsetting the stabilizing effect of unemployment benefits. But the magnitude of this effect is minor; in the long run, employer contributions rates reduce by only about one-fourth the effectiveness of state unemployment benefits as an automatic stabilizer.[41]

So the empirical evidence supports strongly the conclusion that experience rating was not a destabilizer during the postwar recessions we have had. However, we must not conclude that experience rating is therefore not a destabilizer. It may be that experience rating was not destabilizing during these recessions largely because of the relative briefness of the downswings. There is no assurance that this desirable situation will prevail in the future. If future recessions should be prolonged and severe, there is no doubt that experience rating would be highly undesirable from a countercyclical viewpoint.

[39]Palomba, "Unemployment Compensation Program," pp. 95-96.

[40]Vroman, *Macroeconomic Effects,* pp. 72-73.

[41]*Ibid.*

SUGGESTIONS FOR ADDITIONAL READING

Brittain, John A., "The Incidence of Social Security Payroll Taxes," *The American Economic Review*, Vol. LXI, No. 1 (March 1971), 110-25.

———, *The Payroll Tax for Social Security*. Washington, D.C.: The Brookings Institution, 1972.

Brunner, Robert O., *The Fiscal and Budgetary Impact of the Social Security Program, 1970-75*. U.S. Department of Health, Education and Welfare, Social Security Administration, Office of Research and Statistics, Research and Statistics Note 19, June 27, 1974.

Eckstein, Otto, ed., *Studies in the Economics of Income Maintenance*. Washington, D.C.: The Brookings Institution, 1967.

Gorden, Margaret S., *The Economics of Welfare Policies*. New York: Columbia University Press, 1963.

Lester, Richard A., *The Economics of Unemployment Compensation*. Princeton, N.J.: Princeton University, Industrial Relations Section, 1962.

Munnell, Alicia Haydock, *The Effect of Social Security on Personal Saving*. Cambridge, Mass.: Ballinger Publishing Co., 1974.

Palomba, Neil A., "Unemployment Compensation Program: Stabilizing or Destabilizing?" *Journal of Political Economy*, Vol. 76 (January-February 1968), 91-100.

Pechman, Joseph A., Henry J. Aaron, and Michael K. Taussig, *Social Security: Perspectives for Reform*. Washington, D.C.: The Brookings Institution, 1968.

Rejda, George E., "Unemployment Insurance as an Automatic Stabilizer," *The Journal of Risk and Insurance*, Vol. XXXIII, No. 2 (June 1966), 195-208.

Tax Foundation, Inc., *Economic Aspects of the Social Security Tax*. New York: Tax Foundation, Inc., 1966.

Vroman, Wayne G., *Macroeconomic Effects of Social Insurance on Aggregate Demand*. U.S. Department of Health, Education and Welfare, Social Security Administration, Office of Research and Statistics, Staff Paper No. 2, July 1969.

chapter 20

Income-Maintenance Programs for Special Groups

The preceding chapters have focused primarily on the OASDHI program, unemployment insurance, and workmen's compensation as the major public income-maintenance programs for providing economic security to workers and their families. There are, however, for special groups, separate income-maintenance programs that can be classified as both social insurance and government retirement and insurance programs. In this chapter, we shall analyze the major income-maintenance programs for the following special groups: (1) veterans, (2) railroad workers, (3) federal civilian employees, and (4) state and local government employees. [1]

VETERANS

Congress has always been generous to people who have served in the armed forces during both wartime and peacetime periods. Ex-servicemen are currently eligible for a wide variety of programs and benefits designed to help them readjust to civilian life, to reward them for the patriotic defense of their country, to provide cash income to disabled veterans, and to provide compensation payments to their survivors. The various programs include cash-income payments for service disabilities, pensions for non-service-connected disabilities, educa-

---

[1] For a detailed explanation of the basic characteristics of these programs, see U.S. Congress, Subcommittee on Fiscal Policy of the Joint Economic Committee, *Studies in Public Welfare; Paper No. 2, Handbook of Public Income Transfer Programs*, 92d Cong., 2d sess., 1972 (Washington, D.C.: U.S. Government Printing Office, 1972); and U.S. Department of Health, Education and Welfare, Social Security Administration, *Social Security Programs in the United States* (Washington, D.C.: U.S. Government Printing Office, 1973).

tional and training allowances, dependents' benefits to the survivors of deceased veterans, hospital and nursing care in military hospitals, domiciliary and restorative care, prosthetic appliances, and outpatient medical and dental care. Other benefits are unemployment insurance for ex-servicemen, burial allowances, loans for the purchase of homes, farms, and businesses, job-placement preference, vocational rehabilitation, and numerous others.

Many programs have the major objective of assisting the veteran's readjustment to civilian life. Since most recently discharged veterans have served during the Vietnam War, it is worthwhile to examine some problems that can cause economic insecurity for Vietnam-era veterans.

Unemployment Problems

The unemployment rate for Vietnam veterans between the ages of 20 and 24 was 8.9 percent in 1973, compared to 4.9 percent for the economy as a whole; and the 1973 unemployment rate for black and other minority veterans was 8.4 percent, or about double the rate for white veterans.[2] Many younger Vietnam-era veterans had little civilian work experience, and they often lacked high-priority job skills. Both factors hindered them in their job search.

The unemployment problem was aggravated further by two additional problems: the unpopularity of the Vietnam War, and drug addiction. The Vietnam War and the presence of U.S. forces in Southeast Asia caused bitter and violent demonstrations, student revolts, polarization of groups who opposed and those who supported the war, and an overall tearing apart of the social fabric in this nation. Unlike those of previous wars, the Vietnam veterans heard few expressions of gratitude from the American public for their participation. And their failure to find jobs convinced many veterans that because they had served in an unpopular war, few Americans really cared about their unemployment problems.

In addition, some Vietnam veterans had a serious drug-addiction problem. One estimate is that 100,000 to 150,000 servicemen became addicted to heroin between December 1969 and the end of the war—a number that represented 10 to 15 percent of the men who served in Vietnam during that period.[3] Servicemen who are addicted to drugs generally receive medical and psychiatric treatment in military hospitals before they are discharged; however, despite the treatment, the drug problem for many veterans still remains with them in civilian life.

Reducing Unemployment for Veterans

The federal government recognized the serious unemployment problem of veterans by launching the Jobs for Veterans Program. The program is a cooperative effort, involving government, business, labor, and community organizations. Its majors features are the following:

[2]U.S. Department of Labor, *Manpower Report of the President* (Washington, D.C.: U.S. Government Printing Office, 1974), p. 57.

[3]"Returning Heroes Get the Cold Shoulder," *Business Week,* July 31, 1971, pp. 46-48.

1. National coverage of the unemployment problem by television, press, and radio.

2. A mail campaign to more than 900,000 employers asking that veterans be given assistance and priority in jobs

3. Heavy advertising and publicity in industrial and labor journals

4. A government steering committee to coordinate the efforts of federal agencies

5. Letters to governors, mayors, and labor-union leaders to develop active support and participation in solving the unemployment problem for veterans

6. Manpower services, counseling, testing, referrals, and job-placement services by the public employment service on a priority basis.[4]

The program has been quite successful. The original objective, to provide job assistance to over 1 million Vietnam-era veterans, was exceeded by the placement of 1.3 million veterans in various jobs and training programs in fiscal 1972.[5]

The Transition Program of the Department of Defense is another important program, which prepares military personnel for civilian jobs six months prior to their release. The servicemen are given intensive skill training, education, counseling, and employment assistance before they are discharged.

The Employment Service provides special manpower services to veterans and is responsible for seeing that veterans receive preference in job referrals and manpower training programs. The special manpower services include visits by employment personnel to military bases to provide job information, counseling, and placement assistance to veterans about to be discharged.

The Office of Veterans' Reemployment Rights in the Department of Labor administers a program by which veterans are assisted in exercising their legal rights to the jobs they held before they entered the service. These rights include higher wage rates, fringe benefits, and seniority that they would have received if they were not in the military.

Finally, the Unemployment Compensation for Ex-Servicemen (UCX) program is also important in reducing the financial hardships and economic insecurity of unemployed Vietnam veterans. Eligibility for benefits is based on the unemployment-insurance law of the state in which the veteran files a claim for benefits after discharge. To qualify for UCX benefits, he must have served 90 or more continuous days of active military service, unless he was separated from the service because of a service-connected disability. He must also have been discharged under conditions other than dishonorable; he must not have received a bad conduct discharge, or if an officer, he must not have resigned for the good of the service.

Although the various programs, along with economic growth, have reduced the unemployment rates for Vietnam-era veterans, some groups of them still experience serious unemployment problems. The unemployment rate for disabled veterans was estimated to be 14 percent in fiscal 1972, and the rate for

[4]U.S. Department of Labor, *Manpower Report of the President* (Washington, D.C.: U.S. Government Printing Office, 1971), p. 62.

[5]U.S. Department of Labor, *Manpower Report of the President* (Washington, D.C.: U.S. Government Printing Office, 1973), p. 35.

minority veterans was abnormally high, 13 percent, during the same period.[6] These groups will continue to have significant unemployment problems in the future.

Inadequate Educational and Vocational Skills

Because many discharged Vietnam veterans are young and have little work experience, they find themselves at a competitive disadvantage in an economy that places a premium on education and training. Since they cannot find good jobs, an increasing number are returning to school to take advantage of the educational opportunities provided under the GI bill.

The Vietnam Era Veterans' Readjustment Assistance Act provides educational allowances and vocational rehabilitation benefits for veterans and their dependents. A veteran attending school full-time in an approved educational institution can receive $270 monthly—or $321 if he has one dependent, and $366 if he has two. The benefits can be paid for up to 36 months. If the veteran is attending school on a part-time basis, the benefits are scaled downward. Subsistence allowances can also be paid to veterans with service-connected disabilities who are participating in vocational rehabilitation training, and training allowances to those who are receiving training on the job.[7]

Disabled Veterans

Two major income-maintenance programs are available for disabled veterans: (1) compensation for service-connected disabilities, and (2) pensions for non-service-connected disabilities. Veterans disabled from an injury or disease that occurs on active duty are eligible for monthly cash payments. The benefits are based on the degree of disability and range from $32 for a 10 percent disability to $584 for a 100 percent disability. In addition, monthly benefits of more than $1,400 can be paid to severely disabled veterans, such as those with multiple amputations. Dependents' allowances can also be paid if the disability has a rating of at least 50 percent.

A monthly pension can be paid for a non-service-connected disability if the veteran is totally and permanently disabled. The pension is based on financial need, and an income test is used to determine eligibility. The annual income limits are from $3,000 for a single veteran to $4,200 for a veteran with dependents. The monthly payments vary between $5 and $305, depending on income, number of dependents, requirements for the regular aid and attendance of another person, and periods during which some veterans receive care in a VA facility.

Pensions can also be paid to eligible unmarried widows and children of veterans who have died from non-service-connected disabilities. An income test is also required here; the maximum annual income limits are $3,000 for the widow and $4,200 if she has one or more children. The monthly benefits range

[6]U.S. Department of Labor, *Manpower Report of the President,* 1973, p. 36.

[7]For a discussion of recent veterans' legislation, see Veterans Administration, *Benefits for Veterans and Service Personnel with Service since January 31, 1955, and Their Dependents,* VA Pamphlet 20-67-1, Revised, January 1975.

from $5 to $108 for a widow alone and from $49 to $128 for a widow with one child, plus $20 for each additional child.

Dependency and Indemnity Compensation

Dependency and indemnity compensation (DIC) benefits can be paid to widows, children, and dependent parents of veterans who died while in service or as the result of a service-connected disability. The monthly DIC payments to widows are based on the rank of the deceased serviceman and range from $215 to $549. Additional monthly benefits are paid on behalf of orphaned children. No income test is used to determine eligibility for DIC payments, except for benefits to the dependent parents. Monthly payments to parents range from $4 to $123, depending upon income and martial status. Benefits cannot be paid to a parent living alone with an income in excess of $3,000 annually or, if living with a spouse, a combined income in excess of $4,200.

RAILROAD WORKERS

Separate social insurance programs are established for railroad workers and their families. Protection is provided for retirement, disability, death, unemployment, and sickness. Railroad workers are currently covered for social insurance benefits under two important programs: (1) the Railroad Retirement Act, and (2) the Railroad Unemployment Insurance Act. In addition, occupational disabilities are covered under the Federal Employer's Liability Act.

Railroad Retirement Act

The Railroad Retirement Act evolved out of the early pension plans established by the railroads, some of which dated back to the nineteenth century. Before the enactment of the Social Security Act, a majority of railroad employees were covered by these pension plans. Because of the severe depression of the 1930s, however, many plans experienced critical financial problems, and federal assistance was sought. Congress responded by enacting the Railroad Retirement Act in 1934, but the act was subsequently declared unconstitutional. A second attempt in 1935 resulted in only limited protection for railroad workers, largely because the tax provisions were declared unconstitutional by a lower court. Finally, the 1937 amendments resulted in a compromise that was acceptable to both employers and employees. The act has been amended several times since its inception, with important changes made by the amendments passed in 1971, 1972, and 1973.

Types of Benefits. The Railroad Retirement Act provides for numerous benefits, including retirement and disability annuities, death and survivorship benefits, and Medicare benefits. Also, a special supplementary annuity and residual payment are also available.

1. Retirement Benefits. A regular retirement annuity can be paid at age 65 if the worker has at least ten years of railroad service. A reduced annuity is payable between ages 62 and 64. A full annuity can be paid at age 60, however, with no actuarial reduction for early retirement, if it starts July 1, 1974 or later, and the annuitant is a male with 30 years of railroad service. The maximum monthly retirement annuity payable to an employee who is not awarded a supplemental annuity ranges from $137 to $576, depending on earnings and years of service.

A special guaranty provision provides that the total monthly benefits paid to the worker and his family will be at least 10 percent higher than the amounts he would have received if his railroad earnings had been covered by the Social Security Act.

A supplemental annuity can also be paid under certain conditions. The retired railroad worker must be at least 65, have 25 years or more of credited service, and have a current connection with the railroad industry.[8] Also, since 1973, the worker must retire at age 65 to receive the supplemental annuity. The supplemental annuity is equal to $45 monthly, plus $5 for each year of service, up to a maximum of $70.

2. Survivorship Benefits. Monthly and lump-sum benefits can be paid to the survivors of a deceased railroad employee. Benefits can be paid to a widow aged 60 or more, or to a widow at any age if she is caring for a child who is entitled to benefits. Benefits can also be paid to unmarried children under age 18, or under 22 if in school. In addition, a totally disabled widow can receive benefits as early as age 50. Also, benefits can be paid to a surviving disabled child at any age if the disability began before age 22. Dependent parents 60 or over can also receive benefits if there is no eligible widow, widower, or child. If no immediate family member is eligible for an annuity when the railroad worker dies, a lump-sum benefit can be paid to the widow or, if no eligible widow is present, to the person responsible for burial expenses. At present, the average lump-sum benefit is about $800. Finally, a dependent widower aged 60 or more, or as early as age 50 if totally disabled, can also receive monthly survivorship benefits.

The family's eligibility for survivorship benefits depends on whether the railroad worker is "insured" at death. This requirement is generall fulfilled if the worker had at least ten years of railroad employment and had a current connection with the railroad industry at the time of death.

3. Disability Benefits. Disability benefits can be paid to a railroad worker of any age who is permanently disabled for *all regular employment* and has at least ten years of railroad service. A disabled worker who is unable to work at his *regular railroad occupation,* with ten years of railroad service and a current connection with the railroad industry, can receive benefits at age 60, or at any age with 20 years of service. And in contrast to the OASDHI program, a waiting period is not required.

4. Residual Payment. A residual payment, which does not require an

---

[8]To meet this requirement, the employee must have at least 12 months of railroad service in the 2½ years before retirement or death. If he does not qualify on this basis, but has 12 months in some other 2½ year period, he may still fulfill the current connection requirement. This alternative applies only if the worker did not have a regular job in Social Security employment after the 2½ year period in which he did have such 12 months of railroad service. Self-employment does not break a current connection.

insured status, may also be available. The residual payment guarantees that the railroad worker and his family will receive retirement and survivorship benefits that are at least equal to the railroad retirement taxes paid by the worker. The residual payment is not made, however, if there are other benefits that will ever be payable, and it is paid only if the total benefits are less than the taxes paid by the worker. The worker may elect anyone to receive the residual payment.

5. Medicare Benefits. Railroad workers aged 65 or older are eligible for Medicare benefits on the same basis as other aged persons now covered by the OASDHI program. Aged railroad employees are eligible for both Hospital Insurance for the Aged and Supplementary Medical Insurance.

Financing. The Railroad Retirement Act is financed by employer and employee contributions, investment income on the trust funds, and transfers from the OASDHI trust funds under the financial interchange provision.

Regular retirement and survivorship benefits are financed by a payroll tax that is paid by both employees and the railroads. The tax receipts are credited to the Railroad Retirement Account, and any amounts not needed for current benefits and expenses are invested in government securities. The investment income from government securities is an important source of income to the program.

The Railroad Retirement Act provides that the taxable wage base for railroad benefits shall be one-twelfth of the annual maximum wage base that applies to the OASDHI program. Since the OASDHI tax base in 1975 was $14,100, the taxable wage base for railroad retirement benefits was $1,175 of monthly earnings. The employee's contribution rate is 5.85 percent on covered monthly earnings, and the corresponding rate for the railroad employer is 15.35 percent on covered earnings. Thus, the total contribution rate is 21.2 percent on annual covered earnings of $14,100.

Supplemental-annuity benefits are financed by a special tax paid entirely by the railroads. The tax rate is determined each quarter by the Railroad Retirement Board, and the funds for this program are segregated in a separate account. The employees do not contribute to the financing of supplemental annuities.

Financial Interchange. A financial interchange is used to coordinate the railroad retirement program with OASDHI. The provision is designed to place the Social Security trust funds in the same position they would have been in if railroad employment had been covered by the Social Security Act. Under the terms of the financial interchange, the railroad retirement program is credited with the additional benefits and administrative expenses that the OASDHI program would have had to pay on the basis of railroad earnings. The OASDHI trust funds are then credited with the payroll taxes that would have been accrued on the basis of covered railroad earnings. The net gain to the railroad retirement system from the financial interchange exceeded $6.5 billion for the period between 1937 and 1970.[9]

1972 and 1973 Amendments. Important changes were made in the Rail-

---

[9]Railroad Retirement Board, *Railroad Retirement Board Annual Report, 1970* (Washington, D.C.: U.S. Government Printing Office, 1970), p. 64.

road Retirement Act by the 1972 and 1973 amendments.[10] In 1972, Congress overrode President Nixon's veto and granted a temporary 20 percent increase in benefits. This was the third such temporary increase; there had been one of 15 percent in 1970, and of 10 percent in 1971. These temporary increases were extended by new legislation.

In 1973, three railroad retirement bills were signed into law. The following is a summary of the major changes:

1. The three temporary benefit increases in 1970, 1971, and 1972, which were scheduled to expire June 30, 1974, were extended to December 31, 1974.

2. A "pass-through" provision allowed railroad annuitants to receive the same dollar amount of any Social Security benefit increases in 1973 or 1974 to the extent that their benefits would have increased if their railroad employment had been covered under the OASDHI program. Also, a cost-of-living benefit increase, similar to the increase under the OASDHI program, was payable in July 1974.

3. Male railroad workers with 30 years of service could retire at age 60 with no actuarial reduction in benefits. This provision applies to beneficiaries receiving annuities after July 1, 1974.

4. All employee railroad retirement tax rates in excess of OASDHI tax rates were shifted to the railroad carriers, which in turn can shift the higher taxes to the freight shippers. The 1974 scheduled tax rate was 10.6 percent on covered wages for both the employer and the employee. The employee's part of the total tax was reduced to 5.85 percent for employment after September 1973. The 4.75 percent reduction in the employee's tax was added to the carrier's share, increasing it to 15.35 percent. The carrier could then shift this higher tax directly to the freight shippers by interim freight-rate and fare increases.

5. A railway labor-management committee was authorized to recommend a restructuring of the railroad retirement system to ensure actuarial soundness.

6. The railroad retirement provisions were brought into conformity with the 1972 OASDHI amendments.

Financing Problems.   The Railroad Retirement Account is in deep financial trouble and is on the verge of bankruptcy. The Commission on Railroad Retirement concludes that a serious actuarial deficiency is present in the financing of benefits, and unless the financing is improved, the system will be bankrupt by 1988.[11] The size of the reserve has declined relative to the rate of expenditures in recent years. It is estimated that the net annual cash-flow deficit from the Railroad Retirement Account, which began in fiscal 1971, will be $578 million by 1985. The reserve of about $5.4 billion in 1972 will decline to zero by 1988, and

[10]See Railroad Retirement Board, *Railroad Retirement Board Annual Report, 1972* (Washington, D.C.: U.S. Government Printing Office, 1973), pp. 29-38; and U.S. Department of Health, Education and Welfare, Social Security Administration, Office of Research and Statistics, *Railroad Retirement Legislation in 1973,* Note No. 15 (August 22, 1973).

[11]For an excellent discussion of the financial problems, see Commission on Railroad Retirement, *The Railroad Retirement System: Its Coming Crisis,* H. Doc. No. 92-350, 92d Cong., 2d sess., June 30, 1972; Railroad Retirement Board, *Annual Report, 1972,* pp. 32-38; and U.S. Congress, House, Committee on Interstate and Foreign Commerce, *H.R. 7200, Relating to Railroad Retirement, Background Information,* Committee Print No. 4, 93d Cong., 1st sess., 1973 (Washington, D.C.: U.S. Government Printing Office, 1973), pp. 41-43. See also A.M. Niessen, "Twelfth Valuation of the Railroad Retirement System: A Summary View," *Social Security Bulletin,* Vol. 36, No. 12 (December 1973), 13-19.

the projected cash deficit will continue to rise, to nearly $12 billion by the year 2000.

Three major trends explain why the railroad retirement system is rapidly approaching bankruptcy. First, railroad employment has sharply declined in the last 30 years, so there are less tax revenues available to fund the program.

Second, although the number of railroad workers paying taxes is declining, a greater number are eligible for benefits. In 1940, about seven active workers supported each beneficiary family; by 1972, there was less than one active worker for each beneficiary family on the rolls.

Finally, the benefit amounts have increased substantially and rapidly over time. Between fiscal years 1950 and 1971, benefit outlays increased more than sixfold. Gross benefit outlays will continue to rise up to 1995, but future tax contributions will fall far short of the amounts needed to fund the program. Interest earnings will no longer be available in the late 1980s, because the reserve in the Railroad Retirement Account will be exhausted at that time.

The Commission on Railroad Retirement has made several important recommendations to meet the coming financial crisis so that present workers and beneficiaries will not lose any benefits and vested rights. These recommendations include the following:

1. The railroad retirement system should be restructured into two separate tiers of benefits. Tier one should provide regular Social Security benefits, financed and paid for under the Social Security laws. A separate Social Security check would be paid. With respect to tier one, the Railroad Retirement Board would function as a claims agent for claims taking, adjudication, and certification of these benefits. Tier two would be a completely separate supplementary retirement plan, which would be administered by the Railroad Retirement Board. Tier two would augment the Social Security benefits and would float on top of tier one.

2. Legally vested rights of railroad workers and railroad beneficiaries to benefits based on Social Security-covered nonrailroad service should be guaranteed, but future accrual of these dual benefits should be stopped.

3. A firm financial plan should be adopted to finance the second tier of supplementary benefits through the Railroad Retirement Account on an assured, fully self-supporting basis by contributions from the railroad community through the crisis period of the next 20 to 30 years and then beyond.

4. The benefit formulas and provisions of the system should be restructured and revised to assure that the overall benefits in the future continue to bear a reasonable relationship to wages in a dynamic economy and to make benefits more equitable among the various groups of beneficiaries.

These recommendations would drastically change the present character of the Railroad Retirement Act. Tier one would provide regular OASDHI benefits, while tier-two benefits would be similar to private-pension benefits negotiated by labor and management. Entitlement to both OASDHI and railroad retirement benefits would not be permitted. The dual benefits are based on OASDHI coverage for only part of the worker's career, which involves a windfall element and excessive costs to the Railroad Retirement Account. Future accrual of dual benefits would automatically cease when railroad employment is fully covered by the OASDHI program.

Finally, the Commission recommends immediate sizable tax increases that will be sufficient to cover the projected future cash-flow deficits. It is recommended that the Railroad Retirement Account should not be permitted to fall below its present level of $5.5 billion. As tier-two benefit outlays increase in the future, the reserve should be at least equal to five times the annual rate of such expenditures.

Railroad Unemployment Insurance Act

Railroad workers were originally covered for unemployment benefits under the state unemployment-insurance programs. Coverage under state laws later proved impractical, largely because of the problem of providing equitable benefits to the employees who worked in several states, and also because of the reports that had to be filed in each state in which business was conducted. As a result, a separate program of unemployment insurance was established for railroad employees in 1938. In 1946, the program was extended to provide cash payments for sickness and special maternity benefits.

Unemployment and Sickness Benefits. Unemployment benefits can be paid to a qualified worker who fulfills certain eligibility requirements. Sickness benefits are payable to a railroad worker who is disabled from illness or injury. Benefits can also be paid to female employees who cannot work because of pregnancy, childbirth, or miscarriage.

To qualify for unemployment benefits, the worker must be unemployed, must register for work, and must be able, ready, and willing to work. In addition, he must have earned qualifying wages. A new benefit year is established each July 1 for unemployment and sickness benefits, and the worker must have earned at least $1,000 in railroad employment during the preceding calendar year (base year). No more than $400 of earnings can be counted for any one month. If the worker has no railroad service prior to the base year, he must have worked at least seven months for a railroad during the base year. Finally, an unemployed worker is disqualified for various periods if he refuses suitable work, fails to follow instructions to apply for work or to report to an employment office, leaves work voluntarily without good cause, makes a false or fraudulent statement to obtain benefits, or participates in a strike in violation of the Railway Labor Act.

Benefit Amount. The benefit amount depends on the worker's daily wage rate and earnings in the base year and on the length of unemployment or sickness. The daily benefit is based on a schedule in the law, or on 60 percent of his daily wage, but not to exceed $12.70. Unemployment benefits can be paid for up to ten days during each two-week claim period. Sickness benefits can be paid for up to seven days during the worker's first claim period in each benefit year, and for up to ten days in later claim periods.

The benefits can be paid for a maximum of 26 weeks for unemployment or sickness, but the total benefits paid cannot exceed the worker's creditable earnings in the base year. In addition, extended benefits can be paid under certain conditions if the worker exhausts his normal benefits. To qualify for extended benefits, he must have ten or more years of railroad service, must not have quit work voluntarily without good cause, must not have voluntarily retired, and, if sick, must be under age 65. Extended benefits can be paid for an additional 13 to 26 weeks, depending on the length of employment.

Financing. Unemployment and sickness benefits are financed by a payroll tax paid by railroad employers. The employees are not required to contribute. The payroll-tax rate is currently 4 percent of the first $400 of the worker's earnings for each month.

Occupational Disability

Railroad workers are not covered for workmen's compensation, but instead are covered under the Federal Employers' Liability Act (FELA), enacted in 1908. FELA benefits are not based on the liability-without-fault principle that is used in workmen's compensation; the disabled railroad worker must prove negligence to collect for his injuries. Proof of negligence, however, has been made easier, because the employer common-law defenses have been either abolished or modified. The railroad cannot use the assumption-of-risk doctrine or the fellow-servant rule to defeat the injured worker's claim for damages, and contributory negligence does not defeat the worker's claim, but merely reduces it.[12]

The awards under FELA can be substantially higher if the disabled worker suffers a serious injury and can meet certain stringent requirements. Earl F. Cheit concludes that some disabled workers may be in a better financial position under FELA than under workmen's compensation if they meet certain rigid conditions. They must prove that the railroad is negligent; they must have sustained serious occupational injuries; they must be represented by competent legal counsel; and they must win an appeal if the original claim is contested. Thus, Cheit concludes, in the upper-income ranges, the seriously disabled railroad worker may fare better under FELA than under workmen's compensation.[13] For example, a 54-year-old railroad brakeman in Texas had his leg amputated because of the employer's negligence. He sued the railroad and won $85,000. Under workmen's compensation, he would have collected maximum benefits of only $35 weekly for 200 weeks, or $7,000, plus the medical expenses after the accident.[14]

On the other hand, Cheit says, if any of the conditions given above are not met, the disabled railroad worker may receive nothing under FELA. He may lack proof of negligence; he may be dissuaded from filing a claim; he may have poor legal counsel; he may be unwilling or unable to wait a long period for a legal verdict; or he may lose the appeal if the claim is contested. For such a worker, FELA may produce only bitterness and frustration.[15]

[12]Herman Miles Somers and Anne Ramsey Somers, *Workmen's Compensation* (New York: John Wiley, 1954), p. 318.

[13]Earl F. Cheit and Margaret S. Gordon, eds., *Occupational Disability and Public Policy* (New York: John Wiley, 1963), p. 59.

[14]Statement of Ralph Nader in U.S. Congress, Senate, Subcommittee on Labor, *Occupational Safety and Health Act, 1970,* Hearings before the Subcommittee on Labor of the Committee on Labor and Public Welfare, on S.2193 and S. 2788, 91st Cong., 1st and 2d sess., 1969 and 1970, p. 628.

[15]Cheit and Gordon, *Occupational Disability,* p. 59.

FEDERAL CIVILIAN EMPLOYEES

Federal civilian employees are covered by numerous income-maintenance programs, which provide them with a high degree of economic security. Eligible employees can receive benefits from retirement annuities, group life and health insurance, unemployment insurance, workmen's compensation, sick leave, and severance pay.

Civil Service Retirement System

The Civil Service Retirement System is the major retirement program for federal civilian employees. The program was enacted in 1920 on behalf of federal employees who were forced to retire because of old age or disability, and it has been liberalized many times since its inception.

Benefits. Retirement annuities can be paid to eligible federal employees when they retire or become disabled. Benefits can also be paid to the widows and minor children of employees who die, and to the survivors of annuitants under certain conditions.

Federal employees have considerable flexibility in the choice of retirement age. They can retire at 62 with five years of government service, at 60 with 20 years, or as early as 55 with 30 years. If they retire because of disability, the benefits can be paid at any age as long as the disabled employee has a minimum of five years' service. The worker must retire at age 70 if he has 15 years of service.

If the worker terminates his employment or dies before completion of five years of service, his contributions are refunded. After five years of service, the terminating employee has the option of leaving his contributions in the plan or of withdrawing them. If the contributions remain in the plan, he can then receive an annuity at age 62.

The retirement benefit depends on the employee's past earnings and length of service. Benefits for new retirees average about $4,000 annually, far above the level of typical OASDHI benefits. The average retirement benefit for an employee with 30 or more years of service exceeds $6,600 annually.[16]

The program also contains a highly desirable automatic cost-of-living feature, which provides for an automatic adjustment of benefits whenever the Consumer Price Index increases by more than 3 percent annually. Thus, protection is provided against the loss of real income.

Financing. The civil-service program is financed by employee-employer contributions and by government appropriations. Covered federal employees contribute 7 percent of their basic salary, congressional employees contribute 7½ percent, and members of Congress contribute 8 percent. The federal government makes a matching contribution to help finance part of the costs. The contributions are deposited in the Civil Service Retirement and Disability Fund, and the amounts not needed for benefits and expenses are invested in government securities.

[16]U.S. Civil Service Commission, *The Civil Service Commission and Its Publics, Annual Report, 1970* (Washington, D.C.: U.S. Government Printing Office, 1970), p. 8.

The Civil Service Retirement System is currently experiencing a deficiency in the funding of benefits. The deficiency originally arose when the fund was first established, and employees were given credit for their prior service, but the federal government made no contributions to liquidate the past-service credits. The deficiency has increased over time, largely because of liberalization of benefits and inadequate contributions, and is now in excess of $50 million, or about 9 percent of payroll.[17] However, the deficiency is expected to be liquidated in the future by government appropriations, so that the programs can be soundly maintained.

Unemployment Insurance

When federal employees are laid off or have their appointments terminated, they are eligible for unemployment benefits similar to those provided workers in private industry. They are covered under the various state unemployment-insurance programs, with the weekly benefit and duration of benefits determined by the provisions of the states in which they work. The costs of unemployment benefits, however, are paid by the federal government.

Workmen's Compensation

Federal civilian employees are covered for workmen's compensation benefits under the Federal Employee's Compensation Act. The benefits, which include disability income, medical care, and death benefits to survivors, are substantially more liberal than those in many state programs. The benefit amounts are significantly higher; there are no limits on the duration of benefits; full medical expenses are paid; and generous death benefits are paid to the survivors of deceased employees.

Group Life and Health Insurance

Low-cost term life insurance and accidental death and dismemberment benefits are available to federal employees, normally in an amount that is at least $2,000 more than the employee's base pay. The minimum amount of each type of protection is $10,000. The insurance is made available through the Federal Employees Group Life Insurance program, whereby the federal government pays one-third of the cost, and the employee the remainder. The employee may take another $10,000 of insurance protection at his option, but he must pay the entire cost.

The federal government also sponsors a number of health-insurance programs for its employees, including basic health protection and major medical coverages. The government pays a portion of the premium, and the employee pays the remainder through payroll deduction. Since January 1975, the government's contribution has been increased to 60 percent of the average premium

[17]U.S. Civil Service Commission, *46th and 47th Annual Reports of the Board of Actuaries, Civil Service Retirement System, Fiscal Years Ended June 30, 1966 and 1967* (Washington, D.C.: U.S. Government Printing Office, 1970), pp. 38-39.

charged for the high-option coverage offered by the six largest insurance plans.[18]

In addition, federal employees are now eligible to participate in two new comprehensive prepaid group-practice plans—the Harvard Community Health Plan of Boston, Massachusetts, and the Columbia Medical Plan of Columbia, Maryland. The plans are open to eligible employees who reside in these geographical areas.

STATE AND LOCAL GOVERNMENT EMPLOYEES

The number of state and local retirement plans has increased sharply in recent years. About 2,200 now exist, covering more than 7 million employees and ranging in size from a few giant plans with more than 200,000 members to small plans with fewer than 100 members. State-administered plans are the most important and account for four-fifths of the total members. Pension plans for school employees constitute another important group. At the local level, there are plans exclusively for firemen and policemen.[19]

The explosive growth of state and local retirement plans is due largely to the increase in government employment and to the growing emphasis on employee benefit plans. Liberalization of public retirement plans will also accelerate in the future as labor unions continue to organize public employees. Thus, because of their substantial growth, public retirement plans are extremely important in the economy. Nearly all of us are affected, either as plan participants or as taxpayers who must support the programs, and the sizable pension-fund assets and investment practices have a significant impact on the capital markets.

Benefits

Public retirement plans provide numerous benefits to covered workers. They vary widely, but retirement, disability (whether or not it is job-incurred), and survivorship benefits are typically provided. Other, auxiliary benefits, such as vesting and cost-of-living adjustments, may also be available. The latter are becoming more common in public retirement plans. A few plans call for automatic changes geared to the Consumer Price Index; a small number use the variable-annuity approach to protect the purchasing power of the benefits; and many state legislatures periodically grant across-the-board increases in retirement benefits to compensate retired employees for the loss of real income.

Financing

Public retirement programs are financed from employee contributions,

[18]U.S. Department of Health, Education and Welfare, Social Security Administration, Office of Research and Statistics, *Changes in Federal Employees' Health Benefits Program,* Note No. 7 (March 26, 1974).

[19]Tax Foundation, Inc., *State and Local Employee Pension System, A Summary* (New York: Tax Foundation, Inc., 1969), p. 1.

government appropriations, and investment income. The proportion of total receipts from government appropriations accounts for about half the amounts needed to finance the program, investment earnings for about 17 to 24 percent, and the remainder of the funds are paid by the eligible government employees.[20]

Most plans require the employee to contribute, and the contribution rate is usually based on some percentage of the employee's salary. A study of 214 large state and local retirement plans showed that the contribution rate may be based on (1) a single percentage, (2) two percentages, or (3) a variable percentage of salary. About one-third of the plans use a single rate, of between 4 and 5.9 percent of the employee's entire salary.[21]

Government contributions for retirement benefits are an important and costly government outlay. Although the level varies widely across the nation, spending for retirement programs represents about 3 percent of the direct expenditures of state and local government; and in some states, such as New York, the government contribution equals 15 percent of payroll.[22]

Financing Problems and Issues

Public retirement programs present several important financing problems and issues, centering around the following areas: (1) higher pension costs, (2) inadequate funding, (3) vesting, and (4) investment of pension funds.

Higher Pension Costs. State and local public retirement systems paid benefits in 1973 totaling about $5.5 billion, which represented a substantial increase over earlier periods.[23] Most state and local government units are having difficulty raising additional public revenues to fund these higher costs, which are expected to rise even more in the future.

These upward cost pressures will arise from several sources. Increases in government employment will swell pension costs; higher wage and salary levels of government employees will also add to costs; the proportion of public employees who will be covered is expected to increase; pressures from labor unions could lead to liberalizations in the base upon which the benefits are computed, or to reductions in service requirements. The effect would be to increase the liabilities under the plan, while putting pressure on government to absorb a higher proportion of the additional costs. And the critical problem of the loss of purchasing power from inflation will undoubtedly lead to the addition of cost-of-living benefits to many plans. The result of these factors may be increased legislative appropriations, increases in employer contributions, or the drawing down of reserve funds—and the depletion of pension reserves could aggravate the underfunding problem that currently exists in many plans.

Inadequate Funding. Although many public retirement plans operate on

---

[20]*Ibid.*

[21]*Ibid.*, p. 2.

[22]*Ibid.*

[23]U.S. Department of Health, Education and Welfare, Social Security Administration, Office of Research and Statistics, *Benefits and Beneficiaries under Public Employee Retirement Systems, Calendar Year 1973,* Note No. 21 (July 23, 1974), p. 5, Table 1.

a sound financial basis, the degree of funding is inadequate in many others. Some disagreement exists among actuaries regarding the appropriate definition of actuarial soundness to be used to measure the financial condition of the plans.

Another controversial area is the definition of a *fully funded* plan. Under one definition, a public retirement plan is considered fully funded if the employee and employer contributions, plus investment income and other earnings, are sufficient to finance the plan over the long run without recourse to other public funds. An actuary must estimate both the normal and past-service costs of the plan to determine the proper level of funding. Normal cost is the cost of the benefits that are currently accruing to participants in the plan; past-service costs are the costs for service rendered before the plan was initiated and also for benefit improvements after the plan has been in operation. The past-service costs are generally not financed in a lump sum, but are amortized over a period of years. Thus, although contribution rates may be actuarially determined, the plan may not qualify as fully funded until several years have elapsed.

A study of the funding practices of 160 large public retirement plans showed that most plans used actuarially determined contribution rates. But few plans—only 23—could claim a fully funded status, even after many years of operation.[24] As stated earlier, public pension costs are expected to increase substantially in the future. If government fails to fund more adequately the expected higher costs of these plans in the future, the economic security of the covered worker and his family will be seriously threatened.

Vesting. Vesting is another controversial problem in the financing of public retirement plans. Vesting refers to the right that an employee has to the contributions made by the employer on his behalf, regardless of his employment status at retirement. Three types of vesting are normally found in public-retirement systems. One liberal provision gives the employee the immediate right to accrued retirement benefits at the time of employment. Deferred full vesting requires the employee to meet certain qualifications, such as a certain number of years of employment or some specified age, before the benefits vest. And deferred graded vesting entitles the employee to a percentage of his accrued benefits; the percentage increases as he fulfills additional requirements, until he is eventually entitled to full benefits. About two-thirds of the larger state and local plans, representing four-fifths of the total membership in the plans, provide for vesting. The most common vesting requirement is the fulfillment of a certain period of service, which can range from one to 27 years.[25]

From the viewpoint of the individual employee, liberal vesting provisions are highly attractive. However, they create two problems for government units. First, the upward cost pressures referred to earlier are intensified, since liberal vesting provisions add considerably to the pension costs. Second, since vesting is a technique to retain valuable employees, early vesting could lead to an expensive increase in labor turnover.

Investment of Pension Funds. Another issue involves the accumulation and investment of pension funds. Public pension plan assets are sizable: In

---

[24]Tax Foundation, Inc., *State and Local Employee Pension System,* p. 4.

[25]*Ibid.,* p. 3.

1970, total assets were about $55 billion; this amount is expected to increase to $100 billion by 1979.

In recent years, the pension-fund managers have invested relatively more of their funds in corporate bonds and stocks, with government securities receiving less emphasis. Furthermore, when the cash and security holdings of public pension plans are broken down by size, there is a concentration of assets in the hands of a relatively few large groups. Four pension plans out of a total of 2,165 under study held nearly $8 billion, or about one-fifth of the total assets of all plans; 17 plans accounted for about half the total financial assets.[26]

These factors are important in at least three respects. First, public pension funds can be expected to become an increasingly important source of private capital in the future. During the 1960s, public state and local retirement funds have provided about 4 to 5 percent of savings funds. Although this amount is relatively small compared to the funds of commercial banks, savings and loan institutions, and life insurance companies, it exceeds those from many other sources. Consequently, public retirement plans are expected to play an increasingly important role in the capital markets.

Second, the pronounced trend toward relatively greater investments in corporate bonds and stocks means that there may be greater government influence on the private investment markets in the future. And the relatively heavy concentration of pension assets in a comparatively small number of systems could lead to the dangerous situation of excessive government influence on the activities of private corporations.

Finally, the investments of public pension funds in the past have often produced inadequate yields. The current concentration of financial assets and the trend toward larger systems will require a higher level of investment management and supervisory skills on the part of the plan managers, especially since the investment objective of maximum return is the goal of the fund. The need for competent professional managers of pension-plan assets will create many challenges for state and local administrators in the future.

SUGGESTIONS FOR ADDITIONAL READING

Bleakney, Thomas P., *Retirement Systems for Public Employees.* Homewood, Ill.: Richard D. Irwin, 1972.

Commission on Railroad Retirement, *The Railroad Retirement System: Its Coming Crisis,* House Document No. 92-350, 92d Cong., 2d sess., June 30, 1972.

Committee on Veterans' Affairs, *A Study of the Problems Facing Vietnam Era Veterans on Their Readjustment to Civilian Life,* Senate Committee Print No. 7, 92d Cong., 2d sess., 1972. Washington, D.C.: U.S. Government Printing Office, 1972.

————, *Veterans' Benefits,* Senate Committee Print No. 1, 93d Cong., 1st sess., 1973. Washington, D.C.: U.S. Government Printing Office, 1973.

[26]*Ibid.,* p. 5.

House Committee on Interstate and Foreign Commerce and the Senate Committee on Labor and Public Welfare, *The Railroad Retirement System, Analysis of Actuarial and Financial Status and of Options Relating to Restructuring of the System,* Joint Committee Print, 92d Cong., 2d sess., 1972, Volume I and Volume III. Washington, D.C.: U.S. Government Printing Office, 1972.

Loughridge, Harry J., "The Elusive Nature of Veterans' Survivor Benefits," *The Journal of the American Society of Chartered Life Underwriters,* Vol. XVI, No. 1 (January 1972), 9-16.

Metz, Joseph G., "Public Employee Pensions: Prospects for the Future," *Tax Foundation's Tax Review,* Vol. XXXV, No. 7 (July 1974), 27-30.

Niessen, A.M., "Twelfth Valuation of the Railroad Retirement System: A Summary View," *Social Security Bulletin,* Vol. 36, No. 12 (December 1973), 13-19.

Railroad Retirement Board, *Railroad Retirement Board Annual Report, 1972.* Washington, D.C.: U.S. Government Printing Office, 1973.

Tax Foundation, Inc., *State and Local Employee Pension Systems, A Summary.* New York: Tax Foundation, Inc., 1969.

Turnbull, John G., C. Arthur Williams, Jr., and Earl F. Cheit, *Economic and Social Security,* 4th ed., Chap. 14. New York: Ronald Press, 1973.

U.S. Civil Service Commission, Bureau of Retirement, Insurance, and Occupational Health, *1971 Report.* Washington, D.C.: U.S. Government Printing Office, 1972.

U.S. Congress, Subcommittee on Fiscal Policy of the Joint Economic Committee, *Studies in Public Welfare; Paper No. 2, Handbook of Public Income Transfer Programs,* Joint Committee Print, 92d Cong., 2d sess., 1972. Washington, D.C.: U.S. Government Printing Office, 1972.

Index of Authors

Index of Subjects